T0227976

# Handbook
## of
# COMMUNICATIONS
# SYSTEMS
# MANAGEMENT

## 1999

Gilbert Held
*Editor*

**CRC Press**
Taylor & Francis Group
Boca Raton  London  New York

CRC Press is an imprint of the
Taylor & Francis Group, an  informa  business

First published 1999 by CRC Press
Taylor & Francis Group
6000 Broken Sound Parkway NW, Suite 300
Boca Raton, FL 33487-2742

Reissued 2018 by CRC Press

© 1999 by CRC Press, LLC
CRC Press is an imprint of Taylor & Francis Group, an Informa business

No claim to original U.S. Government works

**Library of Congress Cataloging-in-Publication Data**

Catalogue information available from the Library of Congress.

Publisher's Note
The publisher has gone to great lengths to ensure the quality of this reprint but points out that some imperfections in the original copies may be apparent.

Disclaimer
The publisher has made every effort to trace copyright holders and welcomes correspondence from those they have been unable to contact.

ISBN 13: 978-1-315-89336-5 (hbk)
ISBN 13: 978-1-351-07246-5 (ebk)

Visit the Taylor & Francis Web site at http://www.taylorandfrancis.com and the
CRC Press Web site at http://www.crcpress.com

# About the Editor

Gilbert Held is an award winning internationally recognized author and lecturer. He is the author of more than 40 technical books and 250 articles. Gil is the only person to twice win the highly competitive Karp Award. In addition, he has received an award from the American Publishing Institute, was selected to represent the United States at technical conferences in Moscow and Jerusalem, and was named as one of the top 100 persons in government, industry, and academia by *Federal Computer Week* for making a difference in the acquisition and utilization of computers. Some of Gil's recent titles include *Working with Network Based Images*, *Enhancing LAN Performance: Issues and Answers*, second edition, *Ethernet Networks*, third edition, and *Data and Image Compression*, fourth edition, all published by John Wiley & Sons of New York City and Chichester, U.K. Gil can be reached via email at 235-8068@mcimail.com.

# Contributors

C. WARREN AXELROD, *Senior Vice President, Corporate Information Systems, Carroll McEntee & McGinley Inc., Great Neck, NY*

LEE BENJAMIN, *Managing Consultant, New Technology Partners, Bedford, NH*

AL BERG, *Director of Strategic Technologies, NETLAN Inc., New York, NY*

CHARLES BREAKFIELD, *Senior Network Architect, Andersen Consulting, Dallas, TX*

DAVID BRIANT, *Vice President of Operations, MBI Communications Ltd., Guelph, ON, Canada*

ROXANNE BURKEY, *Independent Consultant, Dallas, TX*

BILL CAMARDA, *Consultant, Ramsey, NJ*

GARY CANNON, *Senior Consultant, GE Information Service, New York, NY*

DALE COHEN, *Electronic Messaging Team Project Manager, R. R. Donnelley & Sons Co., Chicago, IL*

SALLY CRAWFORD, *President and Chief Executive Officer, Crawford & Associates, Inc., Rosemont, IL*

DAVE CULLINANE, *Security Consultant, Digital Equipment Corp., Littleton, MA*

DAVID CURLEY, *Vice President, Worldwide Marketing, Mitel Corp., Kanata, ON, Canada*

VISHAL DESAI, *President, Salvi Group, Silver Spring, MD*

LAWRENCE D. DIETZ, *Vice President of Knowledge Centers, Giga Information Group, Santa Clara, CA*

ERNEST ENG, *Product Architect, Infonet Software Solutions Inc., Burnaby, British Columbia, Canada*

EDWARD H. FREEMAN, *Attorney, West Hartford, CT*

LOUIS FRIED, *Vice President, Information Technology Consulting, SRI International, Menlo Park, CA*

LEORA FROCHT, *Vice President, Fixed-Income Capital Market Systems, Smith-Barney, New York, NY*

ED FRYMOYER, *emf Associates, Mountain View, CA*

MONICA J. GARFIELD, *doctoral student, Department of Management, Terry College of Business, University of Georgia, Athens, GA*

BRUCE GREENBLATT, *Directory Architect, Novell, Inc., San Jose, CA*

STEVE GREER, *Product Marketing Manager, Telecommunications Techniques Corp., Germantown, MD*

*Contributors*

Amitava Haldar, *Senior Systems Analyst, AIC Consulting, Chapel Hill, NC*

Barbara J. Haley, *doctoral student, Management Information Systems Department, University of Georgia, Athens, GA*

Gilbert Held, *Director, 4-Degree Consulting, Macon, GA*

Kelly Hilmer, *doctoral student, Management Information Systems Department, University of Georgia, Athens, GA*

Frank Horwitz, *Founder and CEO, SecureNet Technologies Inc., Lynnwood, WA*

Sami Jajeh, *Director, Market Development, ExcelleNet Inc., Atlanta, GA*

Keith A. Jones, *Senior Data Services Consultant, Dun & Bradstreet, Palm Harbor, FL*

Diana Jovin, *Corporate Marketing Manager, NetDynamics Inc., Menlo Park, CA*

Gary C. Kessler, *Senior Member, Technical Staff and Chief Information Officer, Hill Associates, Colchester, VT*

Keith G. Knightson, *Associate Director, Telecom Architect Program, Canadian Government Telecommunications Agency, Kanata, ON, Canada*

Bill Koerner, *Senior Industry Consultant, Visual Communications Division, Hewlett-Packard Co., Fort Collins, CO*

Daniel A. Kosek, *Principal, Fountain Rock Technologies Inc., Walkersville, MD*

Robin D. Langdon, *Senior Product Manager for Broadband Technology, Larscom Inc., Santa Clara, CA*

Amin Leiman, *Manager, Computer Risk Management, Arthur Andersen & Co., Los Angeles, CA*

Chang-Yang Lin, *Professor of Computer Information Systems, Department of Information Systems, College of Business, Eastern Kentucky University, Richmond, KY*

David Litwack, *President, dml Associates, Fairfax, VA*

Andres Llana, Jr., *Consultant, Vermont Studies Group, King of Prussia, PA*

Peter Luff, *Marketing Manager, Telecommunications Techniques Corp., Germantown, MD*

Jack T. Marchewka, *Assistant Professor, Management Information Systems, Northern Illinois University, Dekalb, IL*

Patrick McKeown, *Professor of Management, Terry College of Business, University of Georgia, Athens, GA*

Colin Mick, *Consultant, Palo Alto, CA*

C. Kenneth Miller, *Founder and Chairman/Chief Technology Officer, StarBurst Communications, Concord, MA*

Martin Miller, *Manager, Computer Assurance Services, Deloitte & Touche, Seattle, WA*

Nathan J. Muller, *Consultant, The Oxford Group, Huntsville, AL*

William Hugh Murray, *Executive Consultant, Information Systems Security, Deloitte & Touche, New Canaan, CT*

Gordon L. Preston, *Consulting Manager, Bell Atlantic Network Integration, Frazer, PA*

T.M. Rajkumar, *Associate Professor of Management Information Systems, Miami University, Oxford, OH*

Marcus J. Ranum, *Chief Scientist, V-One Corp., Germantown, MD*

E. Eugene Schultz, *Program Manager, SRI International, Menlo Park, CA*

Greg Scileppi, *Executive Director, RHI Consulting, Menlo Park, CA*

Roshan L. Sharma, *Principal, Telecom Network Science, Dallas, TX*

John P. Slone, *Senior Systems Architect, Lockheed Martin Corp., Orlando, FL*

Ralph R. Stahl, Jr., *Chief Global Information Security Officer, Architecture Design and Engineering, Worldwide Information Systems, AT&T, Dayton, OH*

Martin Taylor, *Vice President of Network Architecture, Madge Networks, San Jose, CA*

Dan Thomsen, *Senior Research Scientist, Secure Computing Corporation, Roseville, MN*

Walker, Richer & Quinn, Inc., *Seattle, WA*

Trenton Waterhouse, *Marketing Manager for LAN Switching Systems, Cabletron Systems, Rochester, NH*

Doug D. Whittle, *Manager, Client Services Department, Pioneer Hi-Bred International, Inc., Des Moines, IA*

Leo A. Wrobel, *President and Chief Executive Officer, Premiere Network Services Inc., Dallas, TX*

Sean Yarborough, *Product Marketing Engineer, Telecommunications Techniques Corp., Germantown, MD*

# Contents

*Contents*

*Contents*

*Contents*

# Introduction

The field of data communications represents one of the most important areas of technology development in the last 25 years. As virtually all forms of electronic communications have become digital, data communications becomes almost redundant, but as there is no universal nomenclature to replace it, it remains data communications. Without data communications, today's global financial markets would be hard pressed to operate. Transportation companies would have an extremely difficult time providing the reservation service travelers take for granted and logistics to get them to their destinations without data communications. In fact, our quality of life would be greatly reduced.

The importance of data communications requires us to keep abreast of the many aspects of communications technology, ranging from LANs to WANs and intelligent agents, to the use of the Internet. To facilitate our desire to keep abreast of this important and rapidly changing field, this new edition of the *Handbook of Communications Systems Management* contains approximately 80 articles that were selected to provide you with detailed information covering the different facets of communications.

This handbook is subdivided into a series of ten sections, with articles grouped into each section to facilitate your ability to obtain information concerning a particular area of communications. The first section in this handbook, **Planning for Communications Systems**, includes articles which cover a range of planning topics, from Windows NT through disaster recovery.

In the second section in this handbook, **Business Management Issues**, we turn our attention to a series of articles focused upon such topics as electronic commerce, multimedia, and cost allocation. Recognizing the role of changing technology and our need to follow such changes, the third section, **Networking Technology**, consists of a series of articles that provide us with information on evolving technologies ranging in scope from voice and video on LANs to multicast networking, frame relay testing, and the potential use of hybrid/fiber/coaxial networks.

The glue that holds communications together and facilitates interoperability are standards. In the fourth section, **Interoperability and Standards Issues**, we turn our attention to this important topic. In the fifth section in this handbook, **Organizational Communications Services**, we examine the role of virtual private networks, popular email systems, and the 1996 Tele-communications Act.

Over the past few years the role of the Internet has had a profound effect upon both individuals and organizations. In section six, **The Internet and Internetworking**, we examine the Internet in detail, focusing attention upon topics ranging from the hidden cost of free TCP/IP protocol stacks to Web servers and security. In section seven, **Mobile Communications Systems**, we recognize the necessity to support the corporate traveler as well as understand the role of wireless communications in supporting access to LANs from building atriums as well as other locations from where it may be difficult, if not impossible, to string conventional cables.

The old adage "been there, done that," is recognized by the articles included in section eight. In this section, **Implementation and Case Studies**, we turn our attention to a series of articles which illustrate the efforts of communications personnel in implementing such projects as electronic messaging, voice on a LAN, the use of Ethernet switches, and a corporate intranet. Since experience is a most valuable learning tool, the cast studies presented in section eight can provide a considerable amount of food for thought that can assist us in our implementations.

Another area of concern for network professionals is the operation and management of modern networks. In the ninth section in this handbook, **Network Operations and Management**, we turn our attention to this important topic. Concluding this handbook, section ten is oriented towards the future. In this section, **Directions in Communications Systems**, a series of articles prepares us to take advantage of such emerging technologies as intelligent agents, cable modems, and voice recognition systems. From the planning aspects presented in the first section through information covering future directions in the tenth section, this handbook provides you with detailed information covering the operation and utilization of different communications technologies and the business and management practices required to successfully implement and operate different types of communications systems. As a yearly publication, the selection of articles for inclusion in this handbook becomes a repetitive process which can be facilitated by reader feedback. Thus, if there are topics you would like to see addressed in future editions of this handbook, please address your comments to me, either through the publisher by mail:

Auerbach
Handbook of Data Communications Management
535 Fifth Ave., Suite 806
New York, NY 10017
or via electronic mail to tshreve@crcpress.com

**Gilbert Held**
*Macon, GA*

# Acknowledgments

The preparation of an extensive handbook covering the many aspects of communications systems represents a considerable effort on the part of many persons. Those persons include the authors of the articles included in this handbook who took the time and effort to share their expertise with us, the previous editor of this handbook, Mr. Jim Conard, whose work in structuring this new edition is gratefully acknowledged, and Mr. Theron Shreve for coordinating this project. Last but not least, I would again like to thank Mrs. Linda Hayes for her typing and coordination efforts which produced the manuscript that evolved into this handbook.

# Section I
# Planning for Communication Systems

It is most appropriate to begin the initial section in this handbook with a series of chapters related to the communication systems planning process. Planning represents the first and perhaps most important stage in the life cycle of a communications project. If you can plan correctly, literally "cover all bases," and examine alternative courses of action, you will obtain a foundation of information which enables projects to be focused and to be implemented in a timely and economical manner. Thus, the old Boy Scout adage "proper planning prevents poor performance," commonly referred to as the "5 Ps," is most applicable to communication systems.

In this section we will turn our attention to a variety of planning topics. The first chapter in this section, "Improving Communication Between End Users and System Developers," introduces us to techniques we can use to enhance a user/developer relationship that can alleviate project controversies, reduce finger-pointing, and facilitate fixing problems in a cooperative manner.

Due to the growth in the use of Windows NT in the corporate environment, this operating system is rapidly becoming an integral part of communication systems. Recognizing the necessity to appropriately plan for the deployment of Windows NT, the second chapter in this section, "Windows NT Project Planning," covers this topic. This chapter will assist you in identifying resources to facilitate a migration to NT as well as indicate methods to use in selecting vendors to assist your organization in the computer transition process.

The third and fourth chapters contained in this section cover strategic planning and Internet security planning, respectively. In the chapter "Inventing the Future: Strategic Planning," we will examine a six-step procedure that can be used to facilitate the strategic planning process. In the chapter "Framework for Internet Security Planning," we will obtain an appreciation for the issues involved in Internet security, and how we can assess available security options.

In a networking environment, it is important to be able to determine the utilization of existing network equipment and transmission facilities as a mechanism to access the impact of day-to-day changes in transmission activity. The process by which this occurs is referred to as baselining and is covered in the chapter "Network Baselining as a Planning Tool," the fifth chapter included in this section. That chapter is followed by the inclusion of a topic which is rapidly gaining interest as corporations, government agencies, and academia apply Internet technology to their internal networks to develop intranets. Thus, the sixth chapter in this section, "Developing Corporate Intranets," provides us with information on how the Web paradigm differs from conventional client-server operations and the overall impact of an intranet on a company's bottom line.

Although we live in a technology-driven world, many times technological advances occur so rapidly we are hard-pressed to obtain their benefits. Fortunately for many persons involved in communications, the rapid evolution of cable modems has not translated into widespread product offerings as cable operators must first upgrade their infrastructure to accommodate the technology. This provides us with the ability to prepare for the use of cable modems, the focus and title of the seventh chapter in this section.

In concluding this section we will turn our attention to a topic which goes to the heart of the planning process, for if omitted the results can be catastrophic. That chapter, "Network Disaster Recovery Planning," provides us with detailed information covering different methods that can be employed to protect both equipment and transmission facilities from acts of God and acts of man. Thus, it is fitting that we conclude this section by examining how we can prepare for the unthinkable, for doing so provides us with the ability to have well-thought-out alternate courses of action to enable our organization to overcome problems that could conceivably put us out of business.

# Chapter 1
# Improving Communication between End Users and System Developers

*Jack T. Marchewka*

The traditional approach to information systems development (ISD) assumes that the process is both rational and systematic. Developers are expected to analyze a set of well- defined organizational problems and then develop and implement an information system (IS). This, however, is not always the case.

The full extent of IS problems and failures may not be known, as most organizations are less than willing to report these problems for competitive reasons. However, a report by the Index Group indicates that 25 out of 30 strategic system implementations studied were deemed failures, with only five systems meeting their intended objectives. Moreover, it has been suggested that at least half of all IS projects do not meet their original objectives.

A lack of cooperation and ineffective communication between end users and system developers are underlying reasons for these IS problems and failures. Typically, the user — an expert in some area of the organization — is inexperienced in ISD, while the developer, who is generally a skilled technician, is unacquainted with the rules and policies of the business. In addition, these individuals have different backgrounds, attitudes, perceptions, values, and knowledge bases. These differences may be so fundamental that each party perceives the other as speaking a foreign language. Consequently, users and developers experience a communication gap, which is a

0-8493-9965-3/99/$0.00+$.50
© 1999 by CRC Press LLC

major reason why information requirements are not properly defined and implemented in the information system.

Furthermore, differences in goals contribute to a breakdown of cooperation between the two groups. For example, the user is more interested in how information technology can solve a particular business problem, whereas the system developer is more interested in the technical elegance of the application system.

On the other hand, users attempt to increase application system functionality by asking for changes to the system or for additional features that were not defined in the original requirements specifications. However, the developer may be under pressure to limit such functionality to minimize development costs or to ensure that the project remains on schedule.

Subsequently, users and developers perceive each other as being uncooperative, and ISD becomes an "us vs. them" situation. This leads to communication problems that inhibit the user from learning about the potential uses and benefits of the technology from the developer. The developer, on the other hand, may be limited in learning about the user's functional and task requirements. As a result, a system is built that does not fit the user's needs, which, in turn, increases the potential for problems or failure. Participation in the ISD process requires a major investment of the users' time that diverts them from their normal organizational activities and responsibilities. An ineffective use of this time is a waste of an organizational resource that increases the cost of THE application system.

The next section examines the conventional wisdom of user involvement. It appears that empirical evidence to support the traditional notion that user involvement leads to IS success is not clear cut. Subsequently, this section suggests that it is not a question of whether to involve the user but rather a question of how or why the user should be involved in the ISD process. In the next section, a framework for improving cooperation, communication, and mutual understanding is described.

## USER INVOLVEMENT AND COMMON WISDOM

The idea that user involvement is critical to the successful development of an information system is almost an axiom in practice; however, some attempts to validate this idea scientifically have reported findings to the contrary. Given the potential for communication problems and differences in goals between users and developers, it is not surprising, for example, that a survey of senior systems analysts reported that they did not perceive user involvement as being critical to information systems development.

Moreover, a few studies report very limited effects of user involvement on system success and suggest that the usual relationship between system developers and users could be described as one in which the IS professionals are in charge and users play a more passive role.

There are several reasons why involving the user does not necessarily guarantee the success of an information system. These include:

- If users are given a chance to participate in information systems development, they sometimes try to change the original design in ways that favor their political interests over the political interests of other managers, users, or system developers. Thus, the potential for conflict and communication problems increases.
- Users feel their involvement lacks any true potential to affect the development of the information system. Consequently, individuals resist change because they feel that they are excluded from the decision-making process.

Despite equivocal results, it is difficult to conceive how an organization could develop a successful information system without any user involvement. It therefore may not be a question whether to involve the user, but how or why the user should be involved. More specifically, there are three basic reasons for involving users in the design process:

1. To provide a means to get them to "buy in" and subsequently reduce resistance to change.
2. To develop more realistic expectations concerning the information technology's capabilities and limitations.
3. To incorporate user knowledge and expertise into the system. Users most likely know their jobs better than anyone else and therefore provide the obvious expertise or knowledge needed for improved system quality.

While the more traditional ISD methods view users as passive sources of information, the user should be viewed as a central actor who participates actively and effectively in system development. Users must learn how the technology can be used to support them, whereas the system developer must learn about the business processes in order to develop a system that meets user needs. To learn from each other, users and developers must communicate effectively and develop a mutual understanding. This leads to improved definition of system requirements and increased acceptance, as the user and developer co-determine the use and impact of the technology.

## COOPERATION, COMMUNICATION, AND MUTUAL UNDERSTANDING

Effective communication can improve the ISD process and is an important element in the development of mutual understanding between users and system developers. Mutual understanding provides a sense of purpose to the ISD process. This requires that users and developers perceive themselves as working toward the same goal and able to understand the intentions and actions of the other.

To improve communication and mutual understanding requires increased cooperation between users and developers. As a result, many of the inherent differences between these individuals are mitigated and the communications gap bridged; however, the balance of influence and their goals affects how they communicate and cooperate when developing information systems.

## The Balance of Influence

In systems development, an individual possesses a certain degree of influence over others by having a particular knowledge or expertise. This knowledge or expertise provides the potential to influence those who have lesser knowledge. For example, a system developer uses his or her technical knowledge to influence the design of the information system. If the user has little or no knowledge of the technology, the system developer, by possessing the technical knowledge needed to build the application system, has a high degree of influence over the user. On the other hand, the user has a high degree of influence over the system developer if the user possesses knowledge of the domain needed to build the application system. By carefully employing their knowledge or expertise, the user and the developer cultivate a dependency relationship. Subsequently, the balance of influence between the user and developer determines how these individuals communicate with each other and how each individual tries to influence the other.

## Reconciling the Goals between the User and Developer

Even though users and developers may work for the same organization, they do not always share the same goals. More specifically, the nature of the development process creates situations in which the user and developer have different goals and objectives. For example, the developer may be more interested in making sure that the IS project is completed on time and within budget. Very often the developer has several projects to complete, and cost/schedule overruns on one project may divert precious, finite resources from other projects.

Users, on the other hand, are more interested in the functionality of the system. After all, they must live with it. A competitive situation arises if increasing the system's functionality forces the system to go over schedule or over budget or if staying on schedule or within budget limits the system's functionality.

In 1949, Morton Deutsch presented a theory of cooperation that suggests cooperation arises when individuals have goals linked in a way that everyone sinks or swims together. On the other hand, a competitive situation arises when one individual swims while the other sinks.

This idea has been applied to the area of information systems development to provide insight as to how goals might affect the relationship between users and developers.

Cooperation arises when individuals perceive the attainment of their goals as being positively related (i.e., reaching one's goals assists other people in attaining their goals). Cooperation, however, does not necessarily mean that individuals share the same goals, only that each individual will (or will not) attain their goals together. Here the individuals either sink or swim together.

The opposite holds true for competition. In competition, individuals perceive their goals as being negatively related (i.e., attainment of one's goals inhibits other people from reaching their goals). In this case, some must sink if another swims.

Cooperation can lead to greater productivity by allowing for more substitutability (i.e., permitting someone's actions to be substituted for one's own), thus allowing for more division of labor, specialization of roles, and efficient use of personnel and resources. Cooperative participants use their individual talents and skills collectively when solving a problem becomes a collaborative effort. Conflicts can be positive when disagreements are limited to a specific scope, and influence tends to be more persuasive in nature.

Cooperation also facilitates more trust and open communication. In addition, individuals are more easily influenced in a cooperative situation than in a competitive one. Communication difficulties are reduced when persuasion rather than coercion is used to settle differences of viewpoints. Honest and open communication of important information exemplifies a cooperative situation. Competition, on the other hand, is characterized by a lack of communication or misleading communication.

The competitive process also encourages one party to enhance its power while attempting to reduce the legitimacy of the other party's interests. Conflict is negative when discussions include a general scope of issues that tend to increase each party's motivation and emotional involvement in the situation. Defeat for either party may be less desirable or more humiliating than both parties losing. In addition, influence tends to be more coercive in nature. Competitive individuals tend to be more suspicious, hostile, and ready to exploit or reject the other party's needs and requests. The cooperative process supports trust, congenial relations, and willingness to help the other party's needs and requests. In general, the

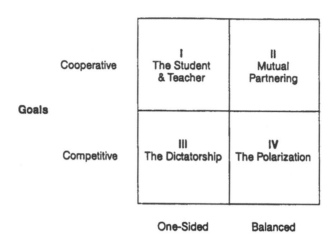

Exhibit 1. Classification of User/Developer Relationships.

---

cooperative process encourages a convergence of similar values and beliefs. The competitive process has just the opposite effect.

## A CLASSIFICATION OF USER AND DEVELOPER RELATIONS

Exhibit 1 provides a classification scheme for viewing potential user/developer relationships based on the interdependency of goals and their balance of influence. Classification of relationships clarifies the social process of user involvement (i.e., how the user currently is involved or how the user should be involved) in ISD.

### Quadrant I: The Student and Teacher

In this quadrant, the balance of influence is one sided; however, the goals between the user and the developer are positively related. Subsequently, this relationship resembles a teacher/student relationship for two reasons.

First, because the balance of power is one sided, the more experienced or knowledgeable individual most likely leads the ISD process. Because they both perceive their goals as being positively related, the less-experienced individual most likely follows the advice of the more influential individual.

The second reason has to do with a one-way model of learning. If the more influential individual leads the ISD process, he or she has more to offer in terms of being able to share his or her knowledge or expertise than the less-experienced individual. As a result, learning generally takes place in one direction as in a typical teacher/student relationship.

An example of this type of relationship is an experienced developer teamed with a novice user. The users' limited knowledge or experience may make it difficult to specify their requirements. The developer may then attempt to control or lead the ISD process, in which users contribute to the best of their knowledge or expertise.

Since these individuals perceive their goals as being positively related, the potential for resistance may be low. The user may view the development process as an opportunity to learn about the technology from the developer and may be easily influenced by the developer. An information system may be developed and viewed as successful; however, as the user becomes more experienced and familiar with the system, he or she may begin to request changes. Subsequently, these requests may result in higher maintenance costs later on.

## Quadrant II: Mutual Partnering

In this quadrant the user and developer share the same degree of influence and have positively related goals. Here users play a more active role in the ISD process than a novice, as their knowledge and level of expertise is greater. Because the developer also is experienced and knowledgeable in ISD, the potential for a two-way model of learning exists.

Users, for example, learn how the technology supports their needs, whereas the developer learns about the business processes. Because the goals of these individuals are positively related, the potential for resistance is low. Subsequently, a two-way model of learning suggests a higher degree of mutual learning and understanding where a system is being built successfully with lower maintenance costs later on.

## Quadrant III: The Dictatorship

In the third quadrant the individuals exhibit more of a dictatorial relationship, in which the individual with the greater potential to influence leads the ISD process. Resistance is high, because the goals of these individuals are negatively related. If the developer has the greater potential to influence the user, for example, he or she may view the user as a passive source of information. Users may perceive themselves as lacking any real chance to participate and then subsequently offer a high degree of resistance. The developer may build a system that fits the developer's perception of user needs or wants to attain his or her goals. As a result, a system is developed that does not meet the initial requirements of the user and ultimately exhibits high maintenance costs. The system might be characterized as a technical success but an organizational failure. On the other hand, if the user has the greater potential to influence the developer, the user tries to increase, for example, the functionality of the system to attain his or her goals. As a result, the developer offers passive resistance when asked to comply with the user's requests to minimize what the developer perceives as a losing situation. Conflicts may be settled through coercion with limited learning occurring between these individuals.

### Quadrant IV: The Polarization

The fourth quadrant suggests a situation in which both the user and developer have an equal balance of influence but negatively related goals. Mutual learning is limited or exists only to the degree needed by an individual to attain his or her goals. Settlement of conflicts is achieved through political means, and a high degree of resistance results if one side perceives themselves as being on the losing side. Conflicts increase each individual's motivation and emotional involvement in the situation, making defeat less desirable or more humiliating than both parties losing. These individuals may become more suspicious, hostile, and ready to exploit or reject the other party's needs or requests. Subsequently, this type of relationship may potentially be the most destructive and could lead to the abandonment of the IT project if neither side is willing to capitulate.

### STRUCTURING THE USER-DEVELOPER RELATIONSHIP

The framework presented in the previous section may be used to assess and structure the relationship between users and developers. A three-step process is now presented to assess, structure, and then monitor the social relationship between these individuals.

### Assessment

Assessment of the user/developer relationship is useful for choosing project participants as well as for gaining insight during the project if problems begin to arise. Using the framework presented in the previous section, a manager may begin by determining the potential balances of influence. Examples of such factors that affect the balance of influence for both developers and users include:

- The level of technical knowledge.
- The level of domain knowledge (i.e., knowledge of the business processes or functions that are the core of the IS project).
- The years of experience in the company or industry.
- The prior involvement in system development projects.
- The rank or position within the organization.
- The reputation (i.e., how the individual's level of competency is perceived by others in the organization).

Other factors relevant to the project or organization can and should be used to assess the balance of influence among individuals. Subsequently, the manager should begin to get a clearer picture as to whether the balance of influence will be one sided or balanced. The next step is to assess individuals' goals. An easy way to make this assessment is to ask each individual to list or identify factors that are important to him or her. Examples include:

- What do you have to gain should the project succeed?
- What do you have to lose should the project fail?
- How would you determine whether the project is a success or failure?

After having both users and developers list what is important to them, a manager can compare these items to determine whether the individuals have potentially conflicting goals. End users and developers need not have exactly the same items of interest; these items need only not cause a win/lose situation. Asking the individuals to list how they would determine whether the project is a success or failure may uncover other potentially conflicting goals. For example, a manager may discover that users value functionality over cost, whereas the developer is concerned with ensuring that the project is developed by a specific date.

**Structuring**

A manager has several alternatives that can alter the balances of influence. The first alternative — choosing project participants — has the greatest impact. In an ideal situation, a manager can choose from a pool of personnel that includes both users and developers with varying degrees of skill, expertise, and knowledge. Unfortunately, if the pool is small, the number of possible combinations is reduced. As a result, training may prove to be a valuable tool for users becoming more knowledgeable about technology and developers becoming more knowledgeable about the business processes and functions.

As suggested in the framework presented, the goals of these individuals may be the most important factor in improving the social process of system development. For example, involving novice or less experienced individuals on a project is desirable when the project participants perceive their goals as positively related; however, serious communication problems arise if these same participants have negatively related goals.

To increase cooperation, the goals of the development team should be structured so that the individuals' goals are positively related. This may be accomplished in a number of ways.

**Make Project Team Members Equally and Jointly Accountable.** This may be in terms of a bonus or merit system under which each of the project team members is equally and jointly accountable for the success or failure of the information system. In other words, both the users and developers should be concerned with such issues as the functionality of the system and with cost/schedule overruns.

**Goals Should Be Made Explicit.** Each individual involved in the development of the information system should have a clear, consistent perception that his or her goals are related in such a way that all sink or swim together. It is important not only that users and developers be held accountable using the same reward or merit system, but also that they are aware that each is held accountable in the same way.

**Management's Actions Must Reinforce Project Team Goals.** It is important that management not allow project team members the opportunity to point fingers or assign blame. Subsequently, the actions of management must be consistent with the goals of the project team members. This is the most difficult challenge of all, because a change in values, attitudes, and possibly culture is required. For example, if goals are to be positively related, there can be no "us versus them" ideology. Instead, both users and developers should see themselves as part of the same team.

### Monitoring

The goals and perceptions of the individuals may change over the course of the project. Just as the allocation of time and resources must be monitored during a project, the social process between the project participants should be monitored as well. Monitoring should be continual during the project to identify any problems or negative conflict before they adversely affect the project. Similar to assessment, a manager may want to look for warning signs. Examples of warning signs include:

**Finger Pointing When Problems Arise.** Project team members should fix the problem, not the blame.

**Negative Conflict.** Individuals focus on petty issues that do not move them closer to their goals but only serve one party at the expense of the other. However, users and developers should agree to disagree. Conflict can be positive, especially when developing innovative approaches or refining new ideas.

**Lack of Participation or Interest.** All members of the project should be involved actively. However, even when all members perceive themselves as having a cooperative relationship, some individuals may become less involved. This may occur when the balance of influence is one sided. Too often systems developers take control of the IS project and attempt to act in the best interest of the users. Although the developers may mean well, they may attempt to develop a system that the user never asked for and does not want.

Assessment, structuring, and monitoring should be a cycle. If specific problems are identified, a manager should assess the balance of influence and goals of the project team members. Changes can be made to alter or fine-tune the balances of influence or goals among the members. By managing this social process between users and developers, a manager increases the likelihood that systems that meet the objectives originally envisioned are developed on time and within budget.

## SUMMARY

This chapter suggests that even though users and developers may work for the same organization, they do not always share the same goals. Subsequently, problems in ISD arise, especially when the user is more interested in functionality and the developer is more interested in maintaining cost/time schedules.

Cooperation facilitates improved communication and leads to greater productivity, because individuals perceive their goals as being positively related. In addition, the goals of the individuals provide some insight as to how each party uses its influence in the development of an information system. This idea was presented through a classification of user and developer relationships that considered their interdependency of goals and their balance of influence. Using this framework, a manager can assess, structure, and monitor the social relationship between users and developers. Managing this social relationship may result in more systems being developed within budget and on schedule and that meet the needs of the user.

# Chapter 2
# Windows NT Project Planning
*Bill Camarda*

This chapter is intended to serve as a reference for the many organizations planning a migration to Windows NT. It describes how to identify resources to assist in the migration process, evaluate the installed base, choose vendors to assist in the transition, and planning a test run — all of the steps necessary to prepare for a full-scale rollout.

## INTRODUCTION

This chapter, intended for organizations that are planning a migration to Windows NT, covers:

- Identifying the organization's goals for deploying NT
- Identifying resources that can assist in the migration process
- Evaluating the organization's installed base
- Choosing vendor partners to assist in the migration
- Planning a pilot rollout
- Running a full-scale rollout

## ESTABLISHING BUSINESS AND TECHNICAL GOALS FOR NT DEPLOYMENT

Before beginning a migration to Windows NT, it is important to understand what the business and technical goals are.

### Business Goals for NT Deployment

Exhibit 1 lists some possible business goals for an NT project, along with the deployment issues that will need to be addressed to reach those goals.

### Technical Goals for NT Deployment

Exhibit 2 lists some possible technical goals for an NT project, along with deployment issues related to each of these goals.

0-8493-9965-3/99/$0.00+$.50
© 1999 by CRC Press LLC

**Exhibit 1. Business Goals and Deployment Issues**

| Goal | Deployment Issues |
|---|---|
| Improve internal communication to shorten product delivery cycles | Using Internet Information Server (IIS) to deploy an intranet; choosing the appropriate strategy for directory services (Windows NT Directory Services, Distributed File System, planning for Active Desktop, or integrating Novell Directory Services) |
| Improve communication with suppliers and customers to enhance organizational responsiveness | Using firewalls, Windows NT name resolution tools, and PPTP tunneling to build extranets that encompass business partners |
| More effectively leverage the corporation's data for decision-making | Architecting the NT network to support database mirroring and query-intensive OLAP network traffic |
| Reduce costs | Standardized hardware and software configurations, Zero Administration for Windows, NetPCs, support, training, and Help Desk issues |

**Exhibit 2. Technical Goals and Deployment Issues**

| Goal | Deployment Issues |
|---|---|
| Providing a standard user environment that simplifies maintenance and training | Zero Administration Windows; system profiles; standard hardware configurations |
| Centralizing security while giving users a single log-on to all network resources | Domain planning; user account planning; Distributed File System |
| Making all users accessible through a single enterprisewide network directory | Choosing between Windows NT Directory Services and the long-term Microsoft Active Directory strategic direction; or Novell's robust NetWare Directory Services (NDS). |
| Preparing for growth by maximizing scalability | Choosing multiprocessor hardware and considering new clustering options, such as Microsoft Cluster Server (formerly known as Wolfpack) |
| Reducing the risks of server and network failure | Choosing NTFS file systems, RAID disk solutions and server mirroring, and architecting your network with adequate backup domain controllers (BDCs) |

## Building the Migration Team

Once the goals have been established, the next step in planning a smooth migration to NT Workstation and/or NT Server is to divide the responsibilities. Most large organizations identify several teams, each with a leader and a specific role in planning and deploying Windows NT. These teams may include:

- A planning and coordination team that includes the project leader and representatives of each other team.
- An executive team that includes the IT organization's leader (or project manager responsible for the NT deployment); others with authority over relevant IT procedures; finance management; and executives from lines of business that will be impacted by the NT deployment.
- An installation team consisting of technicians who will actually install NT, as well as technical experts who can evaluate and test configurations for performance and compatibility.
- Training and/or support team(s) that may include help desk representatives, internal trainers, those responsible for hiring external trainers, and decision-makers responsible for providing adequate resources to frontline support staff.

In organizing these teams, it is all too common to disregard the central role of users: the people who will ultimately have to be productive with NT on a day-to-day basis. Bringing user representatives into the process early improves the likelihood of achieving wholehearted buy-in, and substantially improves a company's chances for success.

### IT Qualifications Needed for the Deployment Team

One way to identify the right internal and external resources for the NT deployment team is to work with Microsoft Certified Professionals (MCPs). In addition to hiring certified professionals, an organization may decide that certifying more of its existing IT staff as NT experts should be an important element of the deployment process. A company might consider providing training for installers, system administrators, support staff, and anyone else with day-to-day responsibilities for Windows NT systems.

There are currently four MCP certifications, and it is important to understand the differences among them:

- Microsoft Certified Systems Engineers (MCSEs) have passed four operating system exams; at least two of them related to Windows NT. There are currently two tracks: one for Windows NT 3.51 and another for Windows NT 4.0. The NT 4.0 core requirements contain deeper coverage of NT 4.0 Server deployment issues.
- Microsoft Certified Solutions Developers (MCSDs) have passed two core exams covering Windows 32-bit architecture, OLE, user interface design, and Windows Open Services Architecture components, along with two elective exams covering Microsoft development tools and/or SQL Server.

**Exhibit 3. Selected Resources Available on Microsoft's Web Site**

| Resource | Web address |
|---|---|
| Windows NT Deployment Guide | www.microsoft.com/ntworkstation/aantdeplguide.htm |
| Windows NT Migration Planning Template (Microsoft Project format) | www.microsoft.com/ntworkstation/aantprojtemp.htm |
| Guide to Automating Windows NT Setup | www.microsoft.com/ntworkstation/Deployment-guide.htm |
| Windows NT Workstation 4.0 Deployment Strategy and Details | www.microsoft.com/organizations/corpeval/1322.htm |
| Windows NT Server Enterprise Planning Guide | www.microsoft.com/ntserver/info/entplan.htm |
| Windows NT Server Domain Planning Guide | www.microsoft.com/ntserver/info/domainplanwp.htm |
| Windows NT Server Interoperability Planning Guide | www.microsoft.com/ntserver/info/ntsnwkinterop.htm |
| Windows NT Server TCP/IP Implementation Guide | www.microsoft.com/ntserver/info/tcpimplement.htm |

- Microsoft Certified Product Specialists (MCPSs) have passed one detailed operating system exam: either Windows NT Workstation, Windows NT Server, or 16-bit Windows.
- Microsoft Certified Trainers (MCTs) teach (or intend to teach) at Microsoft Authorized Technical Education Centers; Microsoft certifies both their subject matter expertise and exposure to some basic training techniques.

### Gathering Information Resources

It is helpful to gather as many deployment resources as possible early in the planning process. Not surprisingly, Microsoft is a prime source of free and low-cost information on deploying Windows NT. In addition to the Windows NT Workstation 4.0 Resource Kit and Windows NT Server 4.0 Resource Kit, Exhibit 3 lists many of the free resources available on Microsoft's Web site.

### EVALUATING THE INSTALLED BASE

Now that the teams are in place, it is important to thoroughly understand the computing environment into which Windows NT is being deployed. Consider these elements:

- Desktop PCs and servers that may be upgraded to, replaced with, or served by Windows NT systems
- Other equipment, especially mainframes, minicomputers, UNIX servers and workstations, and NetWare servers that Windows NT will need to coexist with

It is extremely helpful if a company has a detailed inventory of the desktop and server systems in use throughout the organization. If there is no detailed inventory, the company will need one before initiating a full-scale rollout. For the moment, however, the IS department can identify a representative sample of systems in order to begin creating standard configurations, testing them, and making "upgrade vs. replace" decisions.

### Planning for New Workstations

If the organization is purchasing new workstations, IS should seriously consider standardizing on one brand of PC throughout the organization. This has several benefits, including:

- A single point of contact for technical support (both hardware and Windows NT), troubleshooting, upgrades, and accountability.
- A single approach to manageability. While the new NetPC and Intel's proposed "Managed PC" may standardize hardware management, each leading vendor currently has its own approach — not necessarily compatible with anyone else's.
- Pricing leverage associated with quantity purchasing.

If at all possible, test proposed new workstation configurations on both Windows NT 4.0 and the betas of Windows NT 5.0 that will become increasingly available throughout late 1997 and early 1998. While early betas will not fully reflect the performance of the final product, preliminary NT 5.0 benchmarks can help an organization ensure that its systems will be useful well past the year 2000.

At this writing, a reasonable, minimum new system for NT Workstation 4.0 is a 200-MHz Pentium. Although better performance can be expected from higher-speed Pentium IIs, these microprocessors are only now being paired with chipsets that enable them to take full advantage of their inherent speed.

### Upgrade Planning for Existing Workstations

The installed base and normal upgrade schedule will play an important role in determining which existing systems are worth upgrading. Within this context, IS should start by determining the lowest-performance PC worth upgrading to NT Workstation. While NT Workstation can theoretically run on a low-end 486, most companies restrict upgrades to systems with substantially more power.

For example, where processing requirements are modest, a company might use Pentium 75 or Pentium 90 systems as a preliminary cutoff point. Systems slower than this would rarely be considered for upgrades to Windows NT. Starting from this baseline, the IS department would then test borderline systems to determine whether they will deliver adequate performance.

In most cases, these systems will require memory upgrades — probably to at least 32 MB. To determine whether these systems are in fact worth upgrading, IS will need to price the time and cost of these upgrades, and consider the remaining useful life of the hardware.

Where processing requirements are more substantial, IS might want to start with Pentium 133, 150, or 166 systems as a cutoff point — effectively ruling out all systems more than 18 to 24 months old. Again, it is important to take memory upgrades into account, although it is possible that some of your Pentium 133-166 systems are already configured with adequate memory to run Windows NT Workstation.

Whatever level is selected, it is helpful to check whether the organization's representative systems appear on Microsoft's Windows NT Hardware Compatibility List. Many major vendor systems intended for business use do appear on the list, although not all. While many systems that have not been certified by Microsoft will run Windows NT successfully, Microsoft will not support these configurations. If a company owns systems that do not appear on the Hardware Compatibility List, IS will have to decide whether to take full responsibility for supporting these workstations running NT. If these systems cannot be replaced, the organization may wish to identify third-party or vendor resources that can assist in maintaining them.

Before beginning testing, make sure the version of Windows NT selected reflects the latest Service Packs introduced by Microsoft. To check for the latest Service Pack — and to download it — visit: www.microsoft.com/NTServerSupport/Content/ServicePacks/Default.htm.

It is not enough to test Windows NT on stand-alone systems. IS needs to set up a test network that is as representative of the planned network as is practical.

## Evaluating and Testing Software

An organization does not need to test software carefully before deploying it widely on Windows NT systems. The following sections describe some of the issues to take into account.

## Win16 (Windows 3.x) Applications

Older 16-bit Windows applications will run in the new Windows 4.0 16-bit subsystem, a Windows 3.x emulator sometimes called "Windows on Windows" or WOWEXEC. IS will need to test both the reliability and the performance of applications running on this emulator. IS may also have to determine whether to run these applications in their own memory space (the default setting) or in a shared memory space with other Win16 applications (potentially faster, but one failed Win16 application can crash all Win16 applications running at the same time).

## DOS Applications

Many people have discovered that DOS programs will not run in Windows NT because they must address hardware directly. Many other DOS applications will work via Windows NT Workstation's DOS emulator. If the company still depends on DOS applications, they should be tested carefully. IS may also have to experiment with settings in each DOS application's Properties dialog box to maximize performance — especially settings in the Memory tab that control the amount of conventional, expanded, extended, and MS-DOS protected mode memory available to an application.

## Windows 95 Applications

Even if all the applications are 32-bit Windows applications that utilize the Win32 API, there are a few "gotchas," including:

- APIs specific to Windows 95 that are not available in Windows NT Workstation 4.0, such as Direct3D, Independent Color Matching, Plug-and-Play, "Flat Thunks," and the Pen API, as well as these Windows 95 OSR 2-specific APIs: FAT32 File System, DirectX 2, ActiveMovie, and Windows Internet Extensions API.
- APIs that are common to both operating systems but may work differently, including Unicode and some security attributes.

## Upgrading Custom Applications

Many companies depend on custom applications originally written for 16-bit Windows 3.x environments. For performance and compatibility reasons, organizations will usually want to port these applications to the Win32 API rather than running them in the "Windows on Windows" emulator.

This is, as programmers say, a nontrivial task. There are significant differences between Win16 and Win32 applications. In the Visual Basic environment, these include differences in naming, treatment of integers, and string routines; deserialized input; changes due to preemptive multitasking; and changes to DLLs. The bottom line: if the company wants to roll out revised Win32 custom applications when it rolls out Windows NT, IS should start updating those programs now.

### Identifying, Evaluating and Testing Peripherals

In addition to the PC hardware itself, IS will need to systematically identify all the peripherals and other devices the organization expects to use with NT Workstation or NT Server. Once this is done, IS should review Microsoft's Hardware Compatibility Web Page for Windows NT (http://www.microsoft.com/ntworkstation/hwtest.htm) to determine whether these devices have NT 4.0 compatible drivers. If in doubt, visit the vendor's Web site. IS should consider each of the following:

- Video cards
- Video capture cards
- Audio cards
- SCSI host adapters and devices, including CD-ROM drives, tape drives, removable media and scanners
- Other (non-SCSI) CD-ROM drives and tape drives
- Network interface cards (Ethernet, Fast Ethernet, ATM)
- ISDN adapters
- Modems and multiport serial adapters
- Printers
- PCMCIA (PC Card) devices
- Uninterruptible Power Supplies
- Mice and other pointing devices

If IS is deploying NT throughout the entire organization, then the availability of final-release (not beta) NT drivers should be considered as a prerequisite for future purchases. NT drivers should be tested carefully — especially video drivers that now run in the Windows NT kernel, where they can potentially impact Windows NT's stability.

### Integrating Macintosh Desktops

If an organization has an installed base of Macintoshes that it does not intend to replace with Wintel systems, its testing needs to encompass Windows NT Server Services for Macintosh. Services for Macintosh, a standard component of Windows NT Server, makes it possible to:

- Create Macintosh volumes on an NT Server system
- Support AppleShare, allowing NT disks and folders to appear on Macintosh client desktops
- Support AppleTalk networks, including AppleTalk Internet Routers — eliminating the need to purchase additional routers to support Macintoshes
- Provide file sharing and print services to Macintosh clients

Microsoft even provides a Web administration tool (available at www.microsoft.com/ntserver/webadmin/webadmindl.htm) that makes it possible to administer an NT Server system from a Macintosh (or any other) client, using a Web browser front-end.

There are some limitations to Windows NT Server's Macintosh support. Macintoshes cannot access other Windows clients, and neither the server nor other Windows clients can access files stored locally on a Macintosh. If these limitations will be a problem in an organization's environment, then IS might consider third-party products such as Dave (Thursby Software Systems, Inc., www.thursby.com, 1-817-478-5070) or MacLAN Connect (Miramar Systems, www.miramarsys.com, 1-800-862-2526).

### UNIX Servers and Workstations

Windows NT is increasingly being introduced into UNIX environments. Windows NT can integrate with UNIX workstations and servers, but users will probably have to rely on third-party products to accomplish their goals. Most companies need one or more of the following elements of UNIX/NT interoperability:

- Network File System (NFS) file and printer sharing
- X terminal access from Windows NT workstations to run X applications hosted on UNIX systems
- X terminal access from UNIX hosts to Windows NT, so UNIX systems can display Windows applications

As part of the project planning and testing, IS will need to identify the company's needs for UNIX interoperability and compare the products available to provide it. Of course, this means that project teams will need individuals with significant UNIX experience.

### Mainframes/Hosts

Some organizations may be planning to use Windows NT as a client/server platform that supplements mainframe-based legacy systems, or helps to migrate away from them. If so, IS should consider SNA gateways and associated hardware designed to:

- Improve desktop workstation response time
- Support query-intensive and communications-intensive applications
- Add redundancy and load balancing
- Support advanced groupware and intranet solutions cost effectively

As traditional dumb terminals have been replaced by PCs running terminal emulation software, traditional cluster controllers are also being replaced by SNA gateway software and hardware. These solutions, such as Microsoft's SNA Server and IBM's Comm Server, are typically much less expensive to purchase, install, and support than controllers were. They typically offer better performance as well.

SNA Server offloads network traffic from mainframes and IBM AS/400 midrange systems, freeing up host resources for line-of-business applications. It serves as a TCP/IP-to-SNA gateway, helping companies migrate to TCP/IP while retaining the reliability and securities advantages of SNA.

SNA Server also extends NT Server's existing domain-based unified sign-on capabilities to mainframe and AS/400 systems, so users who have been authenticated by a Windows NT domain controller can gain access to files, printers, databases, messaging systems, and other applications running on hosts — consistent with security restrictions that IS establishes.

To take full advantage of SNA Server or products like it, an organization will need robust server hardware. It may be necessary to integrate third-party mainframe channel adapters as well. For example, companies such as General Signal (888-GSN-DATA, www.gsnetworks.com) and Polaris Communications (1-800-353-1533, www.polariscomm.com) deliver PCI-based boards that support IBM's Enterprise System Connection (ESCON) high-speed connectivity.

Before deploying SNA Server, IS should check with its Microsoft account representative to understand Microsoft's strategic direction for this product. It has been rumored that Microsoft may eventually fold SNA Server functions into NT Server and SQL Server.

### Planning Issues to Handle Concurrently with Evaluation and Testing

As IS evaluates its installed base of hardware and software, the NT deployment teams can concurrently consider several other important issues. For example, they can:

- Create budgets and timetables for the deployment and rollout
- Determine which NT capabilities to deploy; which to disable; and which to deploy only on selected workstations
- Decide whether to deploy NT using Microsoft System Management Server (SMS) or third-party software delivery tools
- Plan for training installers, Help Desk personnel, and trainers

## CHOOSING AND MANAGING VENDORS

Among the most critical decisions IS will make is the choice of vendors to partner in the deployment of Windows NT. Many companies want the business; this is not surprising because services tend to deliver much higher margins than commodity hardware sales.

Given the rapid growth of Windows NT in the enterprise, many companies are focusing on delivering Windows NT services. These include major consultancies and system integrators such as EDS and Entex, as well as the services organizations of traditional hardware suppliers such as Digital and IBM. If NT is being deployed in a smaller company, that organization might choose a local or regional systems integrator or client/server developer to assist.

## Vendors with Strategic Microsoft Relationships

Microsoft maintains especially close relationships with some suppliers of PC and server hardware. These relationships certainly do not preclude users from choosing other suppliers, but they may be worth considering when making vendor decisions. At minimum, IS may want to question Microsoft's strategic partners on how they are delivering the benefits their alliances are supposed to provide — and question competitors on how they can deliver comparable benefits.

On the server side, Microsoft has announced especially close partnerships with Digital (DEC) and Hewlett-Packard. To varying degrees, these relationships have led these vendors to deliver more fully integrated solutions for NT deployment. For example, Digital already has 1400 engineers with NT certification from Microsoft. Digital's service offerings for NT include:

- Legacy NOS Migration to Windows NT services, including methodologies for migrating user files, access privileges, print services, and other features of legacy NOS environments, including NetWare, Banyan VINES, DEC PATHWORKS, IBM LAN Server.
- Building NT Applications for the Enterprise, services to plan, design, and implement client/server computing built on Windows NT.
- Software Support for Windows NT, services to provide support for Windows NT environments, with a selection of response times and problem-resolution capabilities.
- Installation and Startup for Windows NT and Windows NT Clusters, services to rapidly install, configure and implement NT servers and clusters.

Hewlett-Packard's recent partnership with Microsoft has thus far led to improvements in scalability on Intel-based servers, as well as a new family of Business Recovery Services intended to help companies prevent and recover from failures associated with NT servers.

It is important to note that while Microsoft's NT partnerships with Digital and Hewlett-Packard have been the most prominent to date, other leading vendors now offer extensive support for Windows NT. To cite just two examples, Unisys recently established the Enterprise NT Services organization, intended to offer a full suite of services for deploying mission-critical applications on NT systems; NCR also offers substantial Windows NT consulting services.

On the workstation side, Microsoft and Intel lead the NetPC effort intended to lower the cost of administration; partners in this effort include Compaq, Dell, Digital, Gateway 2000, Hewlett-Packard, Packard Bell NEC, and Texas Instruments.

As already mentioned, standardizing on a single provider of PCs, a single provider of servers, and a single provider of network interface cards can simplify management tasks for years to come. Whether preparing a formal RFP, or requesting proposals on a less formal basis, above all it is important to be explicit about what is expected from the vendor. In addition to cost, the following items should be considered when making choices:

- A track record with your company or companies like yours
- Availability of a trustworthy single point of contact
- Ability to deliver an end-to-end solution
- Support commitments, both for hardware and for Windows NT
- Availability of specific technical resources where and when you need them
- Product delivery dates and a vendor's track record in meeting them — especially if notebook PCs are involved
- Contract flexibility (e.g., the ability to substitute more advanced technologies for those covered in the contract)

### Testing Standard Configurations

Once IS has established standard configurations of both existing and new equipment, they should run detailed tests of:

- The NT installation process and automated batch scripts
- Network connectivity
- Applications software
- The uninstall process (restoring previous operating systems on upgraded computers)
- Disk space variables (both for installation and swap files)
- Local and server-based administration tools

IS may find that it needs to make adjustments to the standard client configuration to improve performance, compatibility, stability, or user convenience.

## PLANNING AND MANAGING A PILOT ROLLOUT

In most organizations, the next step is to perform a pilot rollout in a small department or division. Ideally, choose an organization that is open to new technology and not stressed by a major project deadline or recent down-sizing. (Obviously, some organizations may not have this luxury.) A typical pilot rollout may include the following steps:

- Prepare a detailed logistical plan for the pilot rollout, including tested scripts for automated installation from distribution servers.
- Prepare and implement a support plan, so users have immediate access to assistance when they need it.
- Plan a schedule (e.g., how many systems can be upgraded per day, and how long the pilot rollout will take).
- Notify users well in advance of the installation.
- Develop training materials that reflect both the performance of standard NT tasks and concerns unique to your company (e.g., logons, file locations, custom applications, etc.).
- Schedule training.
- Perform a verified backup, a virus-check, and disk defragmentation on all pilot machines that will be upgraded to Windows NT.
- Virus check all pilot machines prior to installation.
- If necessary, upgrade BIOSes, memory, or other hardware prior to installation.
- Make sure NT driver software is available for installation wherever needed.
- Run the installation at a time least likely to interfere with deadlines.

Once the pilot installation has taken place, IS should:

- Follow up to ensure all systems are working properly.
- Stay in close contact with all members of the pilot group to identify problems, questions, and other issues.
- Respond to user concerns and carefully track the changes that users request or require.
- Assign technicians to check real-world performance against expectations, so adjustments can be made, if needed, before a full-scale roll-out.
- Compare schedules and costs against expectations, so budgets and timeframes can be adjusted for the full-scale rollout later.

## PREPARING FOR FULL-SCALE DEPLOYMENT

Now that the pilot rollout has been conducted, IS can begin to prepare for the organizationwide rollout by:

- Creating budgets and schedules that reflect the actual experience.
- Revising the company's IT procedures to reflect the changes that NT will require, and notifying users where necessary.

- Performing a complete systems inventory and storing the information in a centralized database that can be updated to reflect changes to individual systems.
- Hiring or reassigning any additional staff needed for the full-fledged rollout.
- Rolling out Windows NT using the procedures used in the pilot rollout — adapted, of course, to reflect any necessary changes.

## CONCLUSION

This chapter has discussed many of the issues involved in successfully rolling out Windows NT Workstation. But Windows NT is inherently a networked operating system, designed for use in highly distributed environments. It is important to review the critical networking issues associated with planning an NT deployment — including what is needed to architect Windows NT domains that will serve your company well for years to come.

# Chapter 3
# Inventing the Future: Strategic Planning
*Doug D. Whittle*

The total strategic planning process allows departments to target their services and energies on high-payback and business-directed activities. Managers must decide whether to continue to lead their departments down the path of least resistance (i.e., providing general training and support services to users) — or move to the next stage of growth, which includes identifying strategic uses of technology to meet future corporate business needs. This chapter provides managers and their departments with a six-step procedure designed to help them to begin that journey and reap its rewards.

## LOOKING FORWARD

In every corporation and business, people are inventing the future. Those individuals are making conscious decisions that will affect a corporation's mission, what individuals do in their jobs, and even how they do their jobs. Because someone is responsible for inventing the future, who is that someone going to be — managers or someone else? If it is agreed that managers and their departments must take the lead in deciding their futures, where do they start? The answer is strategic planning.

## TOO BUSY

A frequently heard complaint from managers and staff is that they are too busy doing their jobs to participate in strategic planning. In today's corporate climate, it is no longer valid for groups to claim they are victims of too much work, not enough resources, and lack of senior management support.

Companies are quickly realizing that long-term success and survival is only achieved by planning for the future. Strategic planning, however, is not something that must occur only at a senior management or corporate level. If a department views itself as a business, formal planning efforts incorporating short-term objectives and long-term visions must take place at the department level. The following sections detail the steps that can be taken to achieve these goals.

## STEP ONE: ANALYZING THE CURRENT SITUATION

The first step in strategic planning is to conduct an objective analysis of the organization's current situation. If a written department mission statement exists, that would be the logical starting point. If not, one will be needed, so the following questions are still valid — they just enter the picture at a later time.

Managers can begin by taking a critical look at every word in the mission statement. What does it say about the department? According to the mission statement, what is the department? What does it do? What does it not do? What added value does it contribute to the organization or company? What are its standards of quality and service?

In other words, is the department doing what its mission statement says it does? Managers should then locate the corporate or company mission statement. Also, they can see to it their division or business unit has such a statement. The department's statement should be compared with these. Is the department's statement harmonious with the larger entities, or is there no apparent relationship between end-user computing and the division or company?

For now, it is enough to review the mission statement and identify areas that need further clarification, discussion, direction, or change. Managers should not attempt to create or rewrite the actual statement yet. If a formal mission statement does not exist, managers should move on to step two; they will still have a chance at writing one later!

## STEP TWO: DETERMINING THE DEPARTMENT'S IDENTITY

Step two requires broad shoulders and a strong dose of objectivity. Managers must look at their departments and their relationships with the overall business of their companies to identify the following areas: strengths, weaknesses, opportunities, and threats.

Managers should gather the members of their departments for at least a half day of soul searching. They should reassure everyone that outside-the-box thinking is expected, that all discussions will be kept within the room, and most important, that total honesty is necessary. In other words, nobody can get defensive or be offended if something in their area or department is identified as a weakness. The objective of this session: to obtain an honest snapshot of what the department really is.

Key resources within an operating unit and company should also be asked to provide input to these four areas as they see them related to the department. The objective remains the same — to gain a snapshot of the department, but this time, from an outside (i.e., client and manger) perspective.

Through guided exercise or discussion, participants should be asked to list the major strengths and weaknesses of the department. This list provides excellent self-feedback as well as obvious motivation for the staff. Strengths are areas of excellence; the functions and qualities that give the department a distinct advantage — its most outstanding resources and skills. A department may list top-notch product specialist as one of its strengths. A spreadsheet support person, for example, is truly an expert in a particular package.

Weaknesses are functions and qualities currently endemic in the department; the limitations in resources, skills, and capabilities. For instance, although managers may see product experts and specialists as a strength, a perceived weakness may be that the department is too specialized — that its support staff only knows their own world of specialties, and are currently unable to provide adequate support across product lines.

Weaknesses should not be perceived as failures; they are simply the areas in which the department has less strength. It may be entirely appropriate that it remains weak in some areas to provide more resources in the higher priority areas.

Opportunities are areas of potential and possibilities. What are the major favorable situations the department might optimize within the current and future environments? Perhaps an opportunity is a new company ideology that encourages reallocation and sharing of resources. The opportunities portion allows some futuristic, visionary, what-if type thinking.

Threats are potential unfavorable situations that get in the way of achieving success. They may result in negative effects if ignored. A threat would be zero-growth budgets for the upcoming fiscal year.

After the lists have been gathered, managers can compare and contrast the ideas from their staff with those of clients and management. How close or far apart are the two groups in their perceptions of the current environment? More important, managers should lead a discussion on what they discovered about the department. The challenge and the purpose of this exercise is to identify those opportunities that present the greatest potential for the company and in which the department can play a major role. What strengths will help the department move toward those opportunities? What are the greatest obstacles facing the department (i.e., threats and weaknesses)? To overcome those obstacles, upon what strengths will the department draw?

In short, this is an important first step in taking responsibility for the department's destiny. It is the elimination of excuses and the beginning of a commitment to identify what is right, what needs fixing, and what must change. It is the foundation upon which the entire strategic objective will be built.

## STEP THREE: DETERMINING THE DEPARTMENT'S FUTURE

After looking at what the department is today, managers must look at what the department should become tomorrow. What the department *should* become...not what it *wants* to become. They may be the same, but all too frequently, a staff may simply want to continue to do what they already do better (i.e., training and support), and avoid the tough task of pursuing a new or different path (e.g., consulting). After all, if an individual has spent the past eight years as a trainer, and he or she is an effective trainer and knows their products well, they could find all this visionary talk threatening, particularly if someone suggests that perhaps training is no longer the most important service the department can provide for the company!

True strategic planning, however, involves objectivity and honesty. It means identifying and meeting the most critical business needs, which most likely means significant changes, not only in how daily jobs are performed, but in what those daily jobs even are.

### Strategic Planning — The Long and Short of It

Strategic planning consists of two components: long range (three to five years) and short range (one year). Long-range planning includes educated guesses at where the department will be and what it will need to offer the company. But it should be based as much as possible on what managers should review strategic planning documents from both the corporate and business unit levels. Where are they headed? How might the department help them get there? What is it that the department can do to add the most value to the company?

The answer, managers may discover, could mean they will have to drop some of what they are currently doing to allocate some resources (e.g., people, time, or budget) to support high-priority business needs. The one-year plan will actually be put into a written document. Before beginning that document, managers should take another look at the area of mission statements.

## STEP FOUR: BACK TO THE MISSION STATEMENT

Once they have performed self-analysis and identified potential high-payback areas, managers must rewrite (or write for the first time) their new, all-improved, better-than-ever, future-bound mission statement. They should review the same set of questions provided earlier in this chapter, based on the information they have collected. Chances are managers will find their mission has changed. They may need to emphasize one area over another; they may drop some functions.

Whatever decision, managers should keep in mind the following guidelines for writing a mission statement. It should be brief, clear and simple, easy to remember, specific, realistic, and achievable. The ultimate test of an effective mission statement lies not in the appropriateness of the words chosen, but in how well it communicates the real purpose of the department — to internal staff and clients.

An effective starting point is for managers to review other mission statements, good and bad. Then, they should start putting down the words and phrases that say what the department is and what it does. Once a consensus has been reached on the mission statement, it should be made visible. It should be more than pretty words on a piece of paper. It is the birth certificate that justifies the department's very existence.

## STEP FIVE: THE PLANNING DOCUMENT

At this point, managers have identified where the department is and what it is. They have listed the high-payback opportunities and projects. Now it is time to make a commitment in writing to the department's continual development plans.

In most books on strategic planning, several different words are used to define the same functions. Managers can call them whatever they want; but be sure to include the following elements in their strategic planning: key result areas, goals, and objectives.

### Key Result Areas

Key result areas (KRAs) are the major, broad categories that must be addressed in the upcoming years. They are the critical few areas where priorities should be directed. Typically, well-chosen KRAs serve as umbrellas that cover any functions managers must address. Because they are broad, the chance are that they will also remain the same for more than one year. KRAs are usually one- or two-word descriptive labels.

For its first two years, one department worked with the KRAs of education, support, consulting, and documentation. The following year, it worked with the same KRAs as the information management division to which it reported: planning and budgeting; research and development; productivity; and personnel. It could still cover many of the traditional areas of the mission (e.g., support and education), but under the new, more encompassing KRAs of the division. Some other examples of KRAs might be: office automation, information delivery, customer service, client relationships, technical architecture, cost efficiencies, communication (internal and external), and general administration.

When identifying KRAs, managers should keep the following points in mind:

- Keep the total number of KRAs to between three and five.
- The collected KRAs encompass everything the department does. Managers should think of KRA as their primary file names under which they will nest several more specific file folders. In other words, they are broad enough (umbrellas) to cover the variety of goals they will now begin identifying.

### Goals

Goals are statements of future position. They make broad, visionary statements of where the department will be positioned two to four years down the road. Each KRA may have several related goals. Because they are futuristic visions, most goals remain the same for more than one year. An annual review of each goal is necessary because changes in technology and the business may necessitate a new goal direction.

A goal under the research and development KRAs could be: Clients will be using the most efficient platform for office automation. This is a broad statement of life as it can be several years from now. It is general and somewhat fuzzy statement of positive position. That goal will involve several measurable steps between now and then. Those steps are called objectives.

### Objectives

Objectives are the specific and measurable steps that will be accomplished within the planning year to move toward realization of the long-term goal. Any goal may have one or more objectives related to it in any given planning year. Objectives should be stated in measurable terms, much like a behavioral objective for training. Managers should state somewhere in the objective what is to be accomplished, when it will be completed, by whom it will be completed, and most important, how accomplishment of the objective will be measured to ensure success.

An objective related to the previous goal on the most efficient platform might read: Conduct research to identify and compare costs associated with word processing in mini and micro platforms (WHAT). Recommendations should be made on which client departments should be using which platform (HOW MEASURED). The research and resulting recommendations are due in written form no later than the end of the second quarter (HOW MEASURED and WHEN). The research team will consist of one member from the technical services department and one from the department (WHO).

The final planning document, then, will consist of a few KRAs, with each KRA having several goals. Beneath each goal will be one or more objectives. The following year, if planning has been pretty much on target (and barring any radical changes within the company), the KRA will probably remain the same. Most goals will remain for at least two years, perhaps more. Down the road some goals will be added. Objectives will change every year. They are the stepping stones that lead the department down a goal pathway.

## STEP SIX: DOING IT!

Once managers have a basic document that identifies their KRAs, goals, and objectives, they should share it with appropriate management. Do they agree this is the direction the department should be heading? Once managers have clarified their overall strategic direction, they should start working on objectives. Managers may want to limit participation to certain grade levels or positions, or they may want to involve everyone.

### The Value of Strategic Planning

The overall strategic planning process provides a department with opportunities to target its services and energies on high-payback and business-directed activities. Using a strategic plan builds the professional image, credibility, and visibility of the department. It provides opportunities and challenges for the staff that might otherwise be missed. The written documents provide the department with vehicles that help market its efforts and successes, which in turn enhances the department's image and perceived value throughout the company.

Departments must make a decision whether to continue down the path of least resistance (i.e., providing traditional training and support services to computer clients), or whether they will move to the next stage of growth, which includes identifying strategic uses of technology to meet corporate business needs.

Although training and support are critical for the successful implementation of technology, is it possible to outsource, for example, the basic office automation training? If so, managers should use the talents and skills of former trainers as consultants who will work more closely with individuals and groups of clients in the company to help them maximize the capabilities and potential of end-user products.

If, for instance, end users are still using end-user tools as standalone, independent products rather than as an integrated office automation suite, managers may not be returning the highest value that could be offered by their department to the company. If, in the words of consultant Naomi Karten, the services currently provided only help departments to "do nothing faster than ever before," departments may be left with a suite of services for which there are few customers, and that offer little value to the company.

It is easy to have a vague vision of what managers should or would like to be doing for their end users two to three years down the road. Unfortunately, it is also too easy to pass off that vision as something they simply do not have the time to do, because they are too busy putting out fires on a daily basis.

Strategic planning is the critical first step in taking accountability for the future. If managers fail to move from the positions of reactive fire fighters to those of proactive partners in corporate strategic planning, someone else within management may very well make those plans for them — plans that may or may not include them.

This next stage of growth promises challenges and opportunities. The larger world of information management and information services is already meeting the challenge of realigning itself to be more in step with overall business strategies. Departments that are willing to take those first steps into true strategic planning will find the rewards well worth the efforts.

## ACTION CHECKLIST

Before embarking down the road of strategic planning, managers must keep several points in mind, including the following:

- **Expect some rough spots the first time through.** If they have never been through the planning process, managers may find their first year somewhat cumbersome. But that pain usually goes away once they meet their first objective.
- **Combine realism with challenge.** Typically, the first time through a planning process, managers will be tempted to leap tall buildings in a single bound. They will probably take on more objectives than they can realistically complete in one year, and they will more than likely underestimate the time needed to complete some objectives. On the other hand, managers should not set objectives that are too simple. Well-chosen objectives should encourage stretching beyond the immediate comfort zone.
- **Do not expect to meet all objectives and goals.** Perhaps managers have taken on too many. Perhaps the business needs change suddenly. Objectives are targets that sometimes move. Managers do their best to achieve them. But when they miss the target, they should not give

up. Instead, they should analyze why they missed, then readjust and move on. The better-to-have-loved-and-lost-than-never-to-have-loved-at-all cliche certainly applies to strategic planning. If only a few words are changed, the same principle applies.

- **Look at the strategic plan as a living, breathing document, one that can and should change as the business needs change.** Goals and objectives are managers' general predictions of where they are headed. But they should expect the unexpected during the year. They should be prepared to make adjustments to their visions and then continue on.

# Chapter 4

# Framework for Internet Security Planning

*Monica J. Garfield and Patrick G. McKeown*

Internet security is a holistic process that is only as strong as its weakest link. Using an analogy to home design, this chapter presents a framework for understanding the issues involved in Internet security and assessing available security options.

## INTRODUCTION

As an easy-to-use interface that supports sound, video, and graphical displays, the World Wide Web is being increasingly employed by organizations of all sizes for electronic marketing and advertising, customer service, and ordering centers. This growing commercial use introduces new opportunities as well as new security risks. Many security concerns stem from flexible design techniques used to build the Internet, some of which make it difficult to identify exactly where data and requests are coming from or where outgoing data will travel.

Hackers are breaking into computers daily to sabotage or explore mission-critical data. Formulating a plan to thwart these curious onlookers and potential computer villains is no easy task, because there are many ways unwanted intruders can attempt to gain access to a corporate computer These are a range of measures available to help secure that environment.

Given the loosely controlled Internet infrastructure, the best way an organization can protect its Web environment is to provide security at the front door. Before an organization can do so, managers must first ask two questions:

- What is the organization trying to secure?
- What price is the organization willing to pay for this level of security?

0-8493-9965-3/99/$0.00+$.50
© 1999 by CRC Press LLC

**Exhibit 1. Internet Access Options**

| Type of Connection | Enterprise Network Connectivity | |
| --- | --- | --- |
| | Yes | No |
| Direct | Full Direct Connection | Standalone Direct Connection |
| Indirect (through third party) | Full Buffered Connection | Standalone Buffered Connection |

The answers to these questions provide the basis on which to formulate a security policy. This paper presents a framework that helps managers assess the broad range of issues involved in the creation of an Internet security plan. It does not provide the technical details needed to deploy security measures but rather a road map of the options that should be considered.

## CONNECTING TO THE WORLD WIDE WEB

The method an organization chooses to connect to the Web plays a major role in the level of functionality it obtains and the level of risk it faces. Exhibit 1 depicts the most common ways companies gain access to the Web, each of which is associated with different degrees of flexibility, costs, and security risk.

### Full Direct Connection

A full direct connection means that an organization has its own Web server directly connected to the Internet and to its enterprise network. This connection method has the greatest flexibility, the highest security risks, and potentially the highest start-up costs. It gives employees full access to the Web and the enterprise direct control over the Web site.

The actual hardware and software costs to set up a simple Web server are not high — all that is needed is a machine that can run as a server, which can be a Windows-based PC, a Macintosh workstation, or a minicomputer, plus server software. This software is typically easy to use and understand. The higher costs associated with a full direct connection result from the organization's need to protect the internal network from intruders. Securing a Web server from potential hackers requires a fairly high level of technical knowledge, because hackers are constantly improving their techniques.

### Full Buffered Connection

A full buffered connection means that an organization has a Web server connected to the Internet through a third party and directly connected to the enterprise network. This type of connection is comparable to the full connection in terms of security risks but, depending on how the third-party

**Exhibit 2. Degree of Flexibility, Costs, and Security Risk of Internet Connection Options**

|  | Degree | | |
| --- | --- | --- | --- |
| **Option** | **Flexibility** | **Costs** | **Security Risk** |
| Full Direct Connection | High | High | High |
| Full Buffered Connection | Medium | Medium | High |
| Standalone Direct Connections | Medium | High | Low |
| Standalone Buffered Connections | Medium | Medium | Low |

vendor designs the Internet connection, may provide less flexibility. Although the third-party vendor may also set up most of the necessary security components, many companies believe that further security is necessary. Under this configuration, the organization must still purchase and maintain the server hardware and software.

## Standalone Connections

Standalone direct connections and standalone buffered connections differ from full direct connections and full buffered connections because the Internet connection is not directly tied to the enterprise network. Would-be hackers therefore cannot gain access to the company's network. Likewise, employees may not have a direct Internet connection. This option is the most secure but usually the least flexible.

Many companies are implementing standalone buffered connections, in which Internet access not linked to the enterprise network is provided by a third-party, through outsourcing. When a company outsources its Web needs, it subcontracts with another company that specializes in creating and maintaining commercial Web pages. The costs associated with this popular option vary significantly. Organizations must weigh the benefit of increased security against the disadvantages of not having direct access to the Internet. Exhibit 2 summarizes the degrees of flexibility, costs, and security risk associated with each of the four connection options.

## SECURING THE NETWORK ENVIRONMENT

Securing a corporate network environment is similar to building a house. No amount of amenities can make up for the lack of a well thought-out design plan and a solid foundation. Without these, the house will always be flawed.

Security policies must also begin with a solid foundation in the form of virus protection and password integrity established before an Internet connection is obtained. Once the foundation has been laid, security managers can build strong and secure protection for a corporate network by moving through five levels of security:

- Patching and prevention of security holes.
- Encryption and authentication.
- Firewalls.
- Secure interfaces.
- Legal issues.

The following sections review these levels and the options available within each.

### Patching and Preventing Security Holes

If virus protection and password integrity form the foundation of a secure environment, the patching of known security holes marks the beginning of a supporting frame. Many of these holes result from the fact that the Internet, and many of the protocols associated with it, were not designed to provide a high level of security.

One known security hole results from the UNIX operating system which was designed by computer engineers to make their work easier to manage. The UNIX OS lets an approved user log in from anywhere at any time to administer the system. By gaining access to the root, system administrators can manipulate all files that reside on the UNIX workstation and from there enter a corporate network. Unfortunately, unauthorized users who know how to exploit these features can do the same thing. Fortunately, much of the server software and many of the operating systems can be altered to greatly improve security.

Although a knowledgeable systems administrator can patch many of the holes in the security armor of a company's server or network, others are not so easily fixed and still others are as yet unknown. As a result, one of the best ways to protect mission-critical information is to move it onto other servers or networks that are not connected to the Internet.

Yet some critical information usually needs to be available on the portion of the corporate network accessible to the Internet. Several steps can be taken to improve the security of this information.

### Identifying Security Holes

One way to begin to detect holes in the corporate server or network is to run a program designed to identify potential security risks. Many of these programs are controversial because they are also used by hackers. Yet it is precisely for this reason that organizations must use the programs, two of which are SATAN and Internet Scanner.

Other steps a network administrator may take include turning off unneeded UNIX functions that provide security holes and changing the default passwords. Web servers can also be set up in unprivileged mode, and the root directory should not be accessible. Sending NFS files outside the internal network should be prohibited, and send mail and mail aliases should be restricted. If FTP services are necessary, then the network administrator should restrict writable access to FTP's home directory. Files in the anonymous FTP should also not be writable or ownable. Restricting logins and hiding domain name services also helps secure the corporate environment.

## Monitoring Hacker Activity

Once known holes are patched, network administrators need to stay on top of who may be trying to break into their computers as well as at other Internet sites. Several mailing lists, such as those run by the CERT provide updates of security violations. The alert mailing list, for example, can be subscribed to with an E-mail message to request-alert@iss.net that contains the message subscribe alert. Such information is also available from Web sites.

Because only about 5% of all intrusions are detected and only 5% of these are reported, staying on top of who is trying to break into a corporate computer also requires that server logs be monitored for unusual activities. For instance, one of the new ways for hackers to break into Web sites is to put rogue code onto a Web server by overrunning a software buffer. This gives an intruder unauthorized access to the account under which the HTTP process was running. When oversights such as this are found in the software, the Web server needs to be quickly patched. Copycat hackers are only too ready to exploit the system flaws found and advertised by other hackers.

## Encryption Software and Authentication

Once security holes are identified and patched, managers should consider encryption software and authentication. Encryption programs let users encrypt their communications so that they cannot be as easily read by unauthorized parties. Using such software can be likened to locking the doors to a house or sealing an envelope. Encryption programs apply cryptographic algorithms to break down ordinary communication messages (i.e., E-mail) into unique codes that can be unlocked only by individuals who possess the unencryption key.

## Encryption

**Public-Key Encryption.** Public-key encryption is the most popular form of encryption, largely because of the program PGP. PGP, which was created by Philip Zimmermann and uses Rivest-Shamir-Adelman algorithms to encrypt messages, and is freely available on various Internet sites.

The basic premise of public-key encryption is that each user creates two unique keys, one that the user keeps and a public key that the user gives to others. The user then obtains the public keys of the desired recipients of a message and uses them to encrypt a file that only the receivers can unencrypt. Most users also sign their files with a unique signature (i.e., a block of characters) that receivers can verify by applying the sender's public key to the message.

**Private-Key Encryption.** Private-key encryption is less popular but considered to be robust. The main advantage of this form of encryption is that it lets users exchange their keys more securely than can public-key techniques. The most popular private-key encryption software is MIT's Kerberos.

**Hardware-Embedded Techniques.** Some companies are moving toward encryption techniques embedded in hardware. PCMCIA cards can be manufactured with the capability to provide secrecy and authentication for the user. This technology is still in its early stages, so its usability and acceptance are uncertain.

## Authentication

Various techniques, some of which have no cost and others that are encryption-based, are available to verify the identity of a sender and the authenticity of a message. Authentication becomes increasingly important for ensuring that individuals ordering products over the Web are who they claim to be. Some authentication methods include:

- Stipulating that a sender sign a message by citing something only the receiver and the sender would know (e.g., a discussion the sender and the recipient had the day before, a pet name, a favorite color). Obviously, this method works only when the sender and the receiver know one another.
- Using a three-way hand shake (i.e., sending a first message, having the receiver send a reply, and finally sending the actual communication).
- Using a program that creates a unique digital signature for the user. Many encryption techniques have the capability to create such signatures.
- Embedding a time stamp into an E-mail document. This method is used primarily to verify when a document was mailed for legal suits and contract issues.

## FIREWALLS

Firewalls are the dominant technology used to protect corporate networks from hackers. A firewall is a piece of software that lies between a company's internal network and the Internet and forms a barrier to prevent hackers from gaining access. Drawing from the analogy of home design, the designer needs to decide where to put windows and reinforced doors in the walls of a house. If a company creates a firewall without any windows, people inside the company cannot see out into the Internet and use many of its services. Thus firewall planning involves a tradeoff between user flexibility and the level of security provided for the internal network. Although no firewall is perfect in this attempt, many come close.

Once a corporation decides to put in a firewall, security personnel need to program the firewall to support the organization's security needs. A firewall can be restrictive or flexible depending on the company's goals. For instance, specific services, such as FTP, which is one of the most common ways for a hacker to break into a server, can be limited to reduce the probability of break-ins.

The primary purpose of a firewall is to look at every piece of information that is sent either into or out of the internal network. Firewalls act on a message on the basis of user identification, point of origin, file, or other codes or actions. There are four basic actions a firewall can take when it looks at a piece of information:

- The packet of information can be dropped entirely.
- An alert can be issued to the network administrator.
- A message can be returned to the sender after a failed attempt to send the packet through.
- The action can just be logged.

Several different types of firewalls protect the internal network at different network layers. The two most common types of firewalls are router-based IP level firewalls and host-based application-level firewalls.

### Router-Based IP-Level Firewalls

The router-based firewall focuses on packets — the basic unit of communications within the TCP/IP, the most commonly used protocol for Internet communications. Router-based firewalls control traffic at the IP level going into or coming out of the internal network, blocking or passing along data packets depending on the packet's header. They examine the network application service requested (e.g., FTP, Telnet protocol type [e.g., TCP, UDP, ICMP]), and the source and destination address of each packet that arrives at the firewall. The network administrator configures the packet-filtering firewalls to accept or reject packets according to a list of acceptable hosts, routes, or services.

Unfortunately, when a firewall is reading these packets, network performance may slow down by as much as 20%. Other drawbacks of router-based firewalls include:

- The firewalls do not allow for granular control of the packets.
- They are cumbersome to code and when set up incorrectly may offer a false sense of security.
- They usually do not log the actions that take place at the firewall, so the network administrator cannot monitor how hackers are attempting to break into the system.

### Host-Based Application-Level Firewalls

Host-based application-level firewalls are considered more flexible and more secure than router-based IP-level firewalls. They reside on a host computer, typically a dedicated UNIX machine, PC, or Macintosh and can be configured to support elaborate network access control policies with fine granularity. Application-level firewalls control network application connections (e.g., Telnet, FTP, SMTP) down to the individual or group level by type of action and time of action permissible. The ability to limit the time when certain functions run is particularly useful, because many renegade hackers, dubbed midnight hackers, work late at night and network administrators need to be able to restrict many of the potentially unsecured Internet functions during those hours.

One of the essential features of the application-level firewall is that it allows the network administrator to monitor a log of activities that take place at the firewall. This log can be used to identify potential breaches of security and to monitor resource usage.

A recent rash of network break-ins has been accomplished by IP-spoofing. IP-spoofing takes advantage of the UNIX OS, which erroneously presumes that anyone who logs in to a server using a previously approved TCP/IP address must be an authorized user. By altering the source IP, someone can spoof the firewall into believing a packet is coming from a trusted source. To combat this problem, many firewalls reject all packets originating from the external network and carrying an internal source IP.

### SECURE INTERFACES

The secure interfaces level of security is rather sophisticated, somewhat akin to installing a new form of support beams in a house. Secure interfaces are software programs that allow for additional security checks in the network interface. Several companies offer these interfaces, most of which work with the various Web browsers as well as with Web server software. The most common secure interfaces are Netscape Communications Corp.'s SSL and S-HTTP.

### SSL

SSL sits between TCP/IP and HTTP or other protocols such as SNMP or FTP. It provides privacy, authentication, and data integrity. MCI is one of the largest SSL users, employing the interface in InternetMCI. Other users include First Data Card Services (the world's largest credit-card authorization firm), First Interstate, Old Kent, Bank of America, Norwest Card Services, as well as MasterCard International.

## S-HTTP

S-HTTP extends HTTP to allow both the client and the server to negotiate various levels of security based on public-key encryption and provides encryption, authentication, and digital-signature features. It can also distinguish the origin of a particular document on any server. It was created by Terisa Systems, a joint venture between RSA Data Security and Enterprise Integration Technologies. S-HTTP's strengths include its availability and flexibility.

Both the SSL and S-HTTP have been competing to become the standard secure interface for commercial sites on the Web. To head off the competition, Terisa Systems released a developers' tool kit supporting both standards. Many other secure interfaces also exist, each with its own set of features.

## LEGAL ISSUES

Many companies overlook the potential legal issues associated with connecting to the World Wide Web. The press has focused attention on many of these issues, including the availability of child pornography, boot-legged software, and ease of infringement of copyright laws. Managers should be aware of these potential dangers and take measures to protect employees and enterprises from lawsuits and loss of valuable copyrighted data.

This layer of security is comparable to household plumbing, which allows for unwanted items to be flushed away. For example, if FTP access to the server is allowed, network administrators should consider either prohibiting external users from placing files on the server or frequently purging files off the server. This guards against unwanted guests using the server as a clearing house for pirated software.

One well-publicized case of such an incident occurred at Florida State University, where unknown individuals employed a seldom-used computer as a storage facility for pirated software. It is not implausible that the owners of the server may be found liable for what resided on the computer, regardless of whether they had knowledge about it, and be brought to court on copyright infringement charges.

To curb access to sexually explicit materials, many companies are restricting access to a variety of UseNet groups. Although this practice may cut off the source of some illicit materials, users have other ways of gaining access to such materials. Companies cannot monitor the actions of all employees, but they may be able to reduce the likelihood of access to inappropriate sites by educating employees on what type of behavior will not be tolerated and aggressively enforcing such stances.

Employees also need to be educated on copyright laws. Although it is fairly well known that copying commercial, nonshareware, computer programs is illegal, other forms of copyright infringement are less obvious. Downloading a copy of a favorite song or distributing an article found on the network without permission may violate copyright laws.

Companies need to be concerned not only with what employees obtain but also with what they post outside the company. Employees may unwittingly release strategic information over the Internet, thereby jeopardizing data or potential profits. The only way to guard against such situations is through employee education that also encourages people to contact their manager, in-house counsel, or network administrator when they have questions.

## CONCLUSION

The field of security and the threats to a corporate network will always be changing. The first step managers can take to secure a corporate network is to understand the range of security issues associated with Internet and Web access. The desired level of security must then be determined and security measures implemented.

Security needs to be viewed as a holistic process, because it is only as strong as its weakest link. Remaining aware of new developments in the field and continually adjusting security measures is one way of meeting the changing risks inherent on the Internet.

Some of the more recent yet still uncommon developments include HERF guns and EMPT bombs. Both of these threats can wipe out an entire data center, and the only way to be protected from them is to put corporate servers and data sources underground and secured in heavy paneling.

By monitoring server logs, staying alert to new security hazards, and altering the security system as needed, companies may be able to deter unwanted guests from visiting the corporate network. Organizations must also have adequate back-up plans that speed up recovery from the potentially devastating damages resulting from a successful security breach.

# Chapter 5
# Network Baselining as a Planning Tool

*Gilbert Held*

"Baselining" allows network administrators to determine the utilization of network equipment and transmission facilities. Although baselining has its origins in telephone company switch-capacity planning, it is also very applicable for communications network planning. Applying the baseline examination concept to a network provides communications managers with information that can be extremely valuable in their network optimization efforts.

## INTRODUCTION

Baselining provides a mechanism for determining the level of utilization of a network, including its computational and transmission facilities. As such, it plays a central role in a network manager's capacity planning effort because the baseline shows whether or not there is currently sufficient capacity available, as well as providing a foundation for future network measurements that can be compared to the baseline to indicate the direction of network utilization. Thus, the network baselining effort represents the first major step in the capacity planning effort.

In addition, baselining enables network managers and administrators to identify and respond to network capacity requirements before they become an issue, in effect providing a mechanism to head off network-related problems.

## BASELINING TOOLS AND TECHNIQUES

There are a variety of network baseline tools and techniques that can be used to facilitate an organization's capacity planning effort. The actual techniques employed are commonly based on the type of tool used. This chapter focuses on a number of commercially available network baselining tools and discusses appropriate techniques concerning their use.

0-8493-9965-3/99/$0.00+$.50
© 1999 by CRC Press LLC

## SimpleView

SimpleView is an easy to use and relatively inexpensive Simple Network Management Protocol (SNMP) management platform from Triticom, Inc. of Eden Prairie, MN. Through the use of SimpleView, users can retrieve statistical information maintained by Remote Monitoring (RMON) network probes. SimpleView supports a Management Information Base (MIB) walk capability shown in the MIB Walk window that lets a user click on a MIB group, select the group starting point, or double-click on the group to explode its elements, enabling a specific element from the group to be selected for retrieval.

## NEWT

NetManage of Cupertino, CA, well known for its Chameleon suite of Internet applications, also markets a program called NEWT that can be used to monitor the use of desktop applications as well as to provide statistics on network activity associated with individual users. Exhibit 1 illustrates the use of NEWTMonitor on the author's computer to monitor the number of simultaneous FTP sessions occurring over a period of time. Doing so can be extremely important, especially when used in conjunction with normal RMON traffic statistics that do not look beyond the data link layer. NEWT-Monitor enables the use of specific types of TCP/IP applications. In comparison, if the network probes and network management system support RMONv2, or can be upgraded to this new version of RMON, it can be used to obtain a distribution of traffic through the application layer.

Exhibit 2 illustrates the use of NEWTGraph to display different TCP/IP statistics by node. In the example shown in Exhibit 2, the author displayed Interface Errors for his node.

## EtherVision

When checking the activity associated with an individual network, users can choose from a variety of network monitoring programs. One such program is EtherVision, also from Triticom, Inc. of Eden Prairie, MN.

Exhibit 3 illustrates the statistics summary display based on the monitoring of frames using their source address for constructing a statistical baseline. EtherVision supports monitoring by either Source or Destination address, enabling users to build two baselines. In examining Exhibit 3, note that the statistics summary presented indicates the frame count over the monitored period of time, current network utilization in the form of a horizontal bar graph, and a summary of "average," "now" or current, and "peak" utilization displayed as a percentage, as well as the time peak utilization occurred. The latter can be extremely handy, as it allows a user to

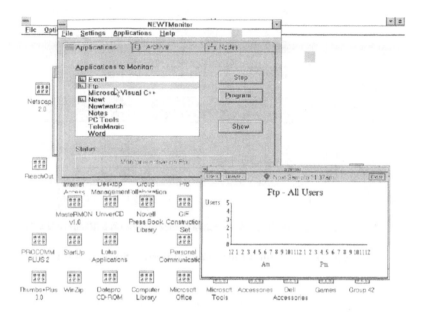

**Exhibit 1. The NetManage NEWMonitor Program.**

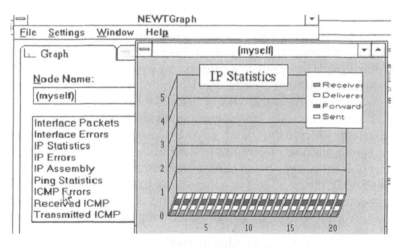

**Exhibit 2. The NetManage NEWTGraph Program.**

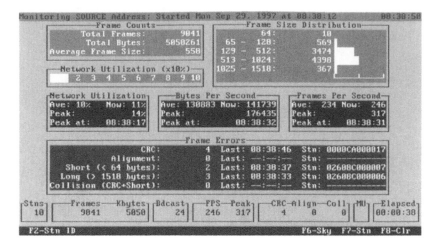

**Exhibit 3. The Triticom EtherVision Statistics Summary Display.**

run the program on a workstation connected to an Ethernet LAN and return at the end of the day to determine the peak percentage of network use as well as when the peak occurred.

Although not shown in Exhibit 3, an EtherVision user can also set the program to generate a report that will log each period of activity over a certain percentage of network activity. Then, using the logged report, a network manager or LAN administrator can easily determine the distribution of network utilization throughout the monitoring period.

In the upper right corner of Exhibit 3, note that EtherVision maintains a distribution of frames transmitted on the network based on their size or length, falling into five predefined intervals. By examining the distribution of frames based on their length, users can determine the general type of traffic flowing on a network. This is possible because interactive query-response applications are generally transported in relatively short frames. In comparison, file transfers, such as Web-browser pages containing one or more images, commonly fill frames to their full length. In examining the distribution of frame sizes shown in Exhibit 3, note that there are a relatively few full-sized Ethernet frames in comparison to the total number of frames encountered during the period of monitoring. This indicates a low level of file transfer and Web browser activity occurring on the monitored network.

Although EtherVision provides numeric information concerning network utilization, many users prefer to work with charts that note trends at a glance. To accommodate such users, EtherVision includes a number of built-in displays such as the one shown in Exhibit 4, which plots network

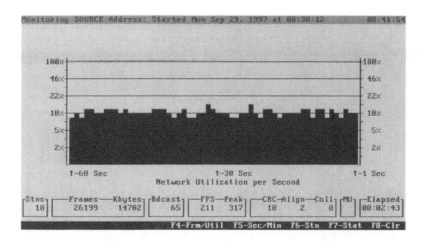

**Exhibit 4. EtherVision Displays Network Utilization Over a Period of Time.**

utilization over a period of time. By examining a visual display, users can immediately note any potential capacity-related problems. In the example shown in Exhibit 4, the maximum level of network utilization is slightly above 46%. However, based on the monitored period, network traffic rose from 22 to 46% numerous times during the monitoring period. Since an Ethernet LAN gets congested at utilization levels above 50% due to its CSMA/CD access protocol, and the effect of the delay associated with the use of a random exponential backoff algorithm after a collision occurs, Exhibit 4 indicates a baseline of network utilization that justifies careful attention and a scheduled remonitoring effort to ensure traffic on the network does not turn into a bottleneck.

### Foundation Manager

Foundation Manager, a product of Network General Corp., is a sophisticated SNMP Network Management System (NMS) platform that operates on Intel-based computers using different versions of Microsoft's Windows operating system.

Foundation Manager was recently upgraded to support the emerging RMONv2 standard. When used to gather statistics from an RMONv2-compatible probe, it can provide a summary of statistics through the application layer, allowing it to replace the use of multiple products to obtain equivalent information.

Exhibit 5 illustrates the use of Foundation Manager to monitor a local Token Ring network. In the example shown in Exhibit 5, two buttons under the Local Token Ring Monitoring bar were pressed to initiate two displays

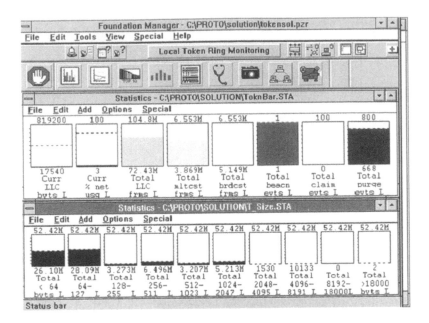

**Exhibit 5. Network General's Foundation Manager.**

of information from the Token Ring Statistics Group that an RMON probe on the local network accumulates. The first button clicked on is the bar chart icon to the right of the icon with the upraised hand in the form of a stop sign. Clicking on the bar chart icon results in the display of the top row of eight bar charts that indicate the total number of different types of frames and level of network utilization.

For example, the second bar chart located on the left side of the top display indicates that network utilization is at 3% on a 100% basis. Other bar charts on the top row indicate the current number of logical link control (LLC) bytes and frames, multicast frames, broadcast frames, beaconing frames, purge events, and claim events. The second row of bar charts in Exhibit 5 resulted from clicking on the third icon to the right of the raised hand icon. This sequence of ten bar charts indicates the distribution of Token Ring frames in a manner similar to the method that EtherVision used to summarize Ethernet frame sizes. Foundation Manager follows the RMON standard and provides a more detailed breakdown of the distribution of Token Ring frames by their length.

Similarly, when using Foundation Manager to monitor Ethernet networks, the program retrieves RMON probe-kept frame distribution information that is more detailed than that kept by EtherVision. However, it is

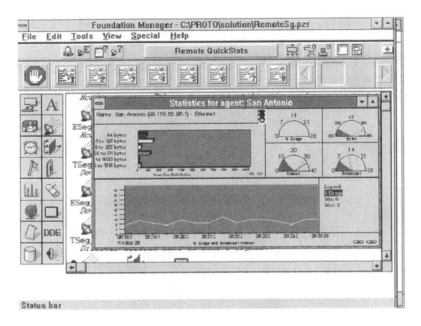

**Exhibit 6. Foundation Manager QuickStats Display.**

important to note that the retail price of EtherVision is under $500 and it can operate by itself. In comparison, the retail price of Foundation Manager is approximately $5000 and a single probe can cost approximately $1000, requiring an investment of an additional $5500 to obtain an enhanced level of frame size distributions as well as some additional features.

Two of the more interesting features of Foundation Manager are its Quick Stats and discovery and baselining capabilities. Exhibit 6 illustrates the use of the Foundation Manager Quick Stats feature to display a quick set of statistics for a remotely monitored network. In the example shown in Exhibit 6, statistics for an RMON probe connected to a network located in San Diego are displayed.

Foundation Manager is capable of displaying up to eight Quick Stats graphical reports at one time, with each report generated by clicking on an appropriate icon to the right of the icon with the raised hand in the form of a stop sign.

Each Quick Stats display presents summary information about a monitored network in a similar manner. In examining the statistics display for the network located in San Diego that is shown in Exhibit 6, the upper left display presents a distribution of frame length for the monitored LAN as a horizontal bar chart. The upper right portion of the display contains four

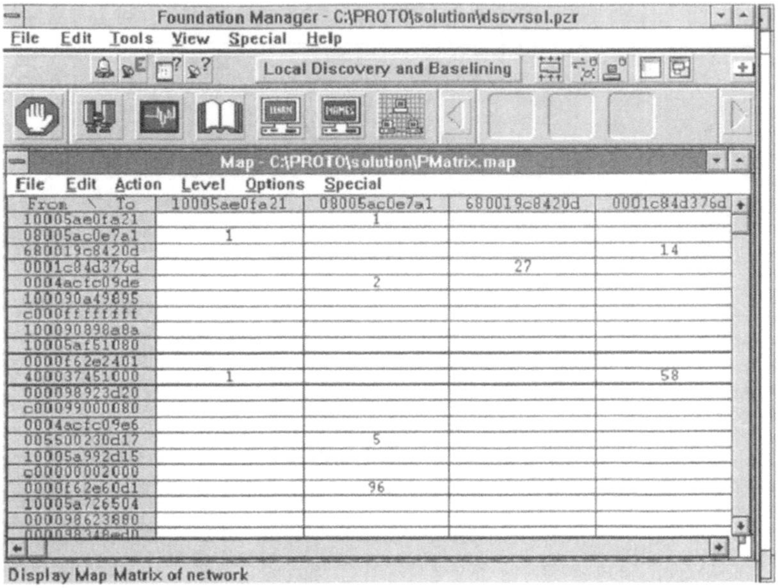

**Exhibit 7. The Local Discovery and Baselining Capability of Foundation Manager.**

gauges that provide a real-time view of network utilization, bytes transmitted, broadcast traffic, and frame rate. The lower half of the display shows a real-time plot over a period of predefined length for any two of the gauge values. Thus, the use of the Foundation Monitor Quick Stats display provides users with the ability to visually note important network baseline parameters both in real-time and over a period of time.

A second interesting feature built into Foundation Manager is its discovery and baselining capability. This capability is available for both local and remotely located networks being monitored, and provides the ability to gather pattern flow information that can be extremely valuable when attempting to determine if the cause of a high level of network utilization results from the activity of one or a few stations on the network.

Exhibit 7 illustrates the Foundation Manager local discovery and baselining display as a matrix map of network activity. The first portion of the title of the display, "discovery," results from the fact that the probe examines each frame flowing on the monitored network and discovers its source and destination by examining the source and destination addresses contained in the frame. The second portion of the title of the display, "baselining," results from the fact that Foundation Manager extracts information from a matrix table maintained by the probe that denotes the number of frames transmitted from one address to another. Thus, in examining Exhibit 7, such numerics as 1, 2, 27, 14, 58, 5, and 96 represent the number of frames transmitted from the address located in the row in the table to the address in the column portion of the table.

When baselining a network, matrix information should be considered as a mechanism to identify the cause of high network utilization. If Quick Stats or a similar display denotes a low level of network utilization, there is no need to use the matrix capability of Foundation Manager or a similar product to identify the actual flow of data between network stations. This is because even if the user can locate a station using too much bandwidth, a modification of the operation of the station will, at best, have a negligible effect upon improving network performance if the network already has a low level of utilization.

## CONCLUSION

Baselining is an important process that enables the communications manager and LAN administrator to quantify the status and activities of a network. In doing so, it provides a base of information that enables network trends to be identified, which can allow changes to be made to a network infrastructure prior to network capacity becoming an issue. Thus, network managers and administrators should consider using the tools and techniques described in this chapter as a mechanism to baseline their network infrastructure.

# Chapter 6
# Developing Corporate Intranets
*Diana Jovin*

Intranets are revolutionizing how internal organizations manage business processes. However, development of intranets is no trivial task. This chapter discusses the applications being built today, how the Web paradigm differs from client/server and the benefits it delivers, technical and operational issues, and the overall impact an intranet can have on a company's bottom line.

## MOVE OVER, LANS

The Web is revolutionizing business practices. It provides a path to increased revenue and new customers while significantly lowering the cost of technology and the cost of doing business. Although much of the Internet hype has focused on what is visible — that is, what companies are doing on their external sites — the biggest impact is taking place behind the scenes, through intranets that are replacing paper and LAN applications as the vehicle for company and group communications.

Intranets play a key role in reducing costs and increasing effectiveness and efficiency of internal information management. Intranet applications serve as productivity, sales, service, and training tools that can be disseminated through the organization at much lower cost than traditional paper, client/server, or mainframe implementations. In addition, intranets enhance the capabilities of traditional applications by extending portions of the application to a wider audience within the organization.

## THE INTRANET IMPACT — WHAT CAN AN INTRANET DO?

Applications made available on an intranet tend to fall into one of two categories — Web self-service and intranet reengineering. Web self-service applications make the process of information delivery more efficient by eliminating cost and redundancy from the information delivery cycle. Intranet reengineering applications, through the use of real-time information

0-8493-9965-3/99/$0.00+$.50
© 1999 by CRC Press LLC

delivery, change existing business processes. These applications enable companies to offer new products and services and increase the effectiveness of the business decision-making cycle.

### Web Self-Service

Web self-service applications allow users to access information more efficiently by eliminating an intermediary process or middleman whose sole function is facilitation of information access. These applications make information more readily available, accurate, and reliable. Examples include:

- **Employee directories.** Directories provide basic personnel information, including phone numbers, extension, addresses, and job descriptions that allow employees to update information such as address changes themselves, without going through the process of filling out an information change request form.
- **Human resources benefits.** Human resources applications allow employees to review their status on vacation and medical benefits, look up current status of 401(k) contributions, and change allocation of contributions to 401(k) funds.
- **Technical support.** Technical support applications enable employees and business partners to look up answers to technical issues directly from a technical support database and extend service capabilities beyond working hours.

### Intranet Reengineering

Intranet reengineering applications not only provide real-time information delivery, they also impact existing business processes and how decision making feeds into them. The following sections describe sample applications.

### Sales Force Automation

Web-based sales force systems provide the sales staff with immediate access to customer account status and activity. Whether in retail banking, brokerage, or other industries, viewing real-time status is a tool that the sales force can use to provide new products and better service. In some financial institutions, portfolio applications that make customer information immediately accessible to the sales force are replacing the practice of distributing customer account information in the form of monthly, paper-based reports.

### Manufacturing and Inventory

Inventory systems that interface between manufacturer and distributors can significantly improve processes such as inventory location and price protection. An example application that manufacturers are providing to distributors is inventory tracking, which provides information on availability, price, and location. In industries with price volatility, Web applications allow manufacturers to respond more quickly to price protection issues by enabling distributors to enter sales and order information that is processed immediately rather than in batch mode.

## Purchasing and Financial

Purchasing applications let employees submit purchasing requests directly from the Web. International companies can benefit from applications that provide the purchasing department with information on foreign exchange exposure and recommended cash position prior to purchase.

In these examples, real-time delivery of information can have significant impact on a company's product and service offering or its ability to respond more quickly to the customer. In some industries, the Web is redefining the competitive landscape. For example, banks, which have been losing share in back-office activities to software vendors such as Intuit, are using the Web to reclaim this space with applications that allow customers to enter request-for-quote or payment initiation directly over the Web with an easy-to-use interface.

## The Web as an Application Platform

The Web is compelling as an application platform because it provides both strategic and tactical benefits. Companies can harness the Web as a way to attract new customers and deliver new products and services. At the same time, companies can significantly reduce the costs of technology and doing business. These benefits combined make the Web an attractive platform over alternative implementations such as client/server or mainframe. Benefits include:

- **Global availability.** Web applications can be made available on a global basis, providing companies with a mechanism to go after a new set of customers or to integrate remote offices or business partners without building expensive proprietary networks.
- **Instant application distribution.** Applications can be deployed instantaneously worldwide, eliminating the need for installation of client-side software or for printing, reproduction, and distribution of paper-based information.
- Platform and version independence. Applications are server-based and can interact with any Web browser on any Internet-capable client. Applications are no longer tied to the client hardware platform and can easily be distributed across heterogeneous computing environments. Applications can be updated instantaneously, eliminating the hassle of version maintenance and support.

- **Reduced training costs.** Web applications have a common look and feel, which lowers training costs of applications traditionally presented in different types of GUI environments.
- **Increased data reliability.** Web applications can eliminate redundant data entry from paper forms. Reliability and availability of data is increased when the information holder can enter and update information directly.

With benefits that contribute to both increased revenue and decreased cost, the potential impact on a company's bottom line can be huge.

## NEW MODEL FOR DISTRIBUTED COMPUTING

The Web's benefits derive from its architecture. A Web application is not merely a client/server application with a Web browser interface. "Web-native" applications take full advantage of this architecture. "Web-enabled" applications typically miss the full set of benefits because they are tied to an existing client/server-based architecture. Four key areas in which the Web architectural model differs significantly from that of client/server include: network infrastructure, client-side requirements, server-side requirements, and management of database login.

### WAN vs. LAN

Web applications are deployed over a wide area network (WAN), in contrast to client/server applications, which are deployed over proprietary local area networks (LANs). There are two immediate implications in this difference: reach and cost.

In the WAN environment, companies can communicate with anyone connected to the WAN, including customers and business partners worldwide. LANs typically have a smaller reach and are also often expensive to install and maintain. WAN applications provide a means for a company to communicate with business partners or employees worldwide without building a global private network.

### Application Publishing — Server vs. Client

Web applications, in contrast to client/server applications, are primarily server-based, with a "thin client" front end. This thin client may do some business logic processing, such as data validation, but the bulk of the business logic is processed on the server side rather than on the client.

Client/server applications, in contrast, typically support "fat clients," in which the application is a sizeable executable running on the client. Although this model takes advantage of client CPU power for application processing, the client/server model does not provide the Web's primary benefit — instant application distribution. Web tools that provide client-side plug-ins typically call themselves "Web-enabled" as opposed to "Web-native" because they are not taking full advantage of the Web's architecture in instant distribution.

### N-Tier vs. 2- or 3-Tier

Web applications require a multi-tier, or n-tier, server architecture. Scalability takes a quantum leap on the Web, with a much larger application audience and greater uncertainty in the number of users who might choose to access the application at any given time.

Client/server applications hit the wall with a 2-tier architecture. To solve this problem, some client/server implementations have moved to a 3-tier architecture. Given the greater number of users who can access a Web application, even 3-tier models are not enough to sustain some of the heavy-duty applications being deployed today.

In addition, the Web provides the capability to move intranet applications, such as customer portfolio management, directly to the customer over the Internet. These applications can only migrate to the Internet environment if they have been designed to scale.

### Shared Database Connection vs. Individual Login

Web applications incur heavy CPU processing requirements as a result of the number of users accessing the application. As a result, well-designed systems provide users with persistent shared database connections. In this model, the user only ties up a database connection when he or she has pressed an action button, hyperlink, or image that requests data from the database. Once the data is returned, the database connection is free for another user, without requiring the database connection to be shut down and reopened for the new user.

In the client/server model, the user maintains an individual persistent database connection from the time he or she logs on to the time the application is exited. In this model, the database connection is inefficient because the user is logged onto the database regardless of whether a database action is taking place or whether the user is merely looking through the results that have been returned.

### Technical Considerations

Although a Web architecture delivers significant benefits, it also introduces new technical challenges, particularly with respect to scalability, state and session, and security. When developing applications and selecting development tools, it is critical to understand these challenges and how they are being solved by different vendors in the industry today.

### Scalability and Performance

Web-native applications (i.e., the application is server-based rather than a client-side browser plug-in) that provide the highest degree of scalability are deployed through an n-tier application server. Application servers first appeared in the market in December 1995 and have rapidly gained acceptance as a model that overcomes the limitations of the common gateway interface (CGI) in execution of scalable applications.

In the early stages of Web development, applications were executed through CGI. In this model, the Web server receives a request for data, opens a CGI process, executes the application code, opens the database, receives the data, closes the database, then closes the CGI process, and returns the dynamic page. This sequence takes place for each user request and ties up CPU time in system housekeeping because of the starting and stopping of processes. System housekeeping involved in executing the application increases proportionally to the size of the application executable.

Application servers, in contrast, stay resident as an interface between the Web server and database server. In this model, the Web server passes the request to the application server through a very small CGI relay or the Web server APIs. The application server manages the application processing and maintains persistent connections to the database. Enterprise-level application servers multiplex users across persistent database connections, can be distributed across multiple CPUs, and provide automatic load balancing and monitoring.

### State and Session Management

The Web is a stateless environment, meaning that information about the user and the user's actions are not automatically maintained as the user moves from page to page in the application. This presents obstacles to providing LAN-like interaction in the Web environment.

Some technology vendors have solved this problem by building session and state managers into the application server, which allows developers to build applications with persistent memory across pages. An early approach that also persists is to write "cookies" or files containing state information to the client browser. These files are read on each page access. This is a manual process that is less secure than server-based session and state memory.

### SECURITY

Security is a key to implementing business critical applications in the Web environment. The good news is that it is becoming easier to manage security on the Web.

**Exhibit 1. Possible Components of an Intranet Environment**

| Technology Component | Contribution to Security |
|---|---|
| Web server | User authorization and data encryption |
| Application server | Page navigation flow control |
| Database server | Database login |
| Firewall | Internal network access control |
| DCE infrastructure | Centralized security login and rules |

In building a secure environment, it is important to understand first, the intranet or intranet application's security requirements, and second, which technology component of the intranet solution is going to provide it. Exhibit 1 shows some of the components that might exist in an intranet environment and how they might contribute to different aspects of a secure solution.

Fine-grained security control appeared in the marketplace in mid-1996. Examples are control over navigation flow through the pages in the application and fine-grained user access control. For example, Acme Company may wish to grant Joe Smith access to a limited set of application pages only between 9:00 a.m. and 5:00 p.m. It may wish to grant Joe CEO, however, full access 24 hours a day. Acme Company will require both users to enter the application at a specific page and step through in a predetermined sequence. Breaking the flow of the application exits the user from the application.

## WHAT ABOUT JAVA?

Java is rapidly gaining momentum as the ideal programming language for the Internet, and one that can enhance client-side processing and GUI capabilities in a secure environment while maintaining Web advantages of platform independence and instant application publishing. Among its advantages are:

- **Web-secure publishing.** Java is designed from the ground up to run in a restricted environment, such as a Web browser. Java provides developers with the ability to distribute client-side applets that contain programming logic while ensuring the security of the local PC's environment.
- **Platform independence.** The platform independence of Java code means that developers can easily move applications from platform to platform without recompiling code or mixing development and deployment platforms.
- **Simple, high-level, object-oriented language.** Java is a true object-oriented language with syntax that is very similar to C++. Unlike C++, Java is simpler and provides a higher level of functionality. For example,

Java has no pointers to memory and provides automatic garbage collection. So all memory leaks and pointer manipulation problems that accompany C++ programs are eliminated with Java. Java also contains libraries providing built-in services such as thread support, string manipulation, I/O, networking, and graphical user interface, allowing developers to focus on solving business problems rather than code manipulation.

- **Fast development cycle.** Java provides run-time linking. Thus, when a new class is written, only that class needs to be recompiled. This provides for a very fast compile link test development cycle, especially when compared with C or C++, where the entire project must be relinked before the program can be tested.
- **Application partitioning.** Java is the only language that can run on both a Web client and Web server. Thus, if both the client and server code are implemented using Java, the developer has the flexibility to push the application partitioning decision to run-time. Application logic can be run on either the client or server, depending on which location will optimize system performance.

Some concerns exist about the practicality of Java when there are so many developers versed in existing languages, such as C++. However, the growing number of Java developers and support being given to Java by all major players in the Internet space suggest that Java is on its way to becoming the standard language for the Internet and other networking environments. Evaluation of intranet tools and technologies should include consideration of how they leverage Java.

## OPERATIONAL CONSIDERATIONS

In addition to sound tools and technology, a successful intranet also requires a solid operational plan. These plans differ significantly from company to company, but issues that will need to be considered and addressed are:

- Should the organization build in-house expertise or outsource Intranet development?
- Should purchases of tools and technology be centralized through one technology evaluation group, or dispersed throughout the company and individual business units?
- How should the company address training and education of the intranet?
- How can the company generate excitement and buy-in?

One common theme across companies, however, is to start with some simple but effective applications, such as employee directories. Successful operations plans use these applications to gain interest and excitement, and intranet champions within the organization take it from there.

Intranets can play a tremendous role in influencing or reflecting organizational culture, evident in the names being given to corporate intranets today. Examples of corporate intranets include:

- AT&T — Unified Global Network.
- Booz Allen & Hamilton — Knowledge On Line (KOL).
- J. C. Penney — jWeb.
- Florida Power — Power Web.
- Silicon Graphics (SGI) — Silicon Junction.

## CONCLUSION

The impact of intranets on corporate profits and productivity can be tremendous. The move to an intranet architecture requires rethinking some of the traditional assumptions of client/server architecture, but the benefits that can be reaped from the Web are enormous. Intranets are redefining the landscape of corporate America and can be a key to achieving or keeping competitive advantage.

# Chapter 7
# Preparing for Cable Modems

*Gilbert Held*

As the Internet gains in popular usage within corporate America, organizations are trying to establish ways to connect to the Information Superhighway at speeds that make economic sense. This chapter describes the operation of cable modems, a device that provides high-speed connectivity and enables the organization to take advantage of transmission rates of up to tens of millions of bits per second. Cabling infrastructure — the cabling within buildings — is another key component defined and discussed, to introduce the data center operations manager to a rapidly evolving new technology that can help keep the organization competitive.

## PROBLEMS ADDRESSED

During 1995, the use of the Internet expanded considerably, with tens of thousands of corporations, universities, government agencies, and individuals creating home pages on servers, while tens of millions of users surfed the World Wide Web. As corporations began to recognize the value of the Internet for building software applications, promoting products and services, and locating as well as disseminating information, the addition of graphics to World Wide Web home pages literally slowed Web surfing operations to a crawl, adversely affecting user productivity. Whereas the replacement of 14.4K bps modems by state-of-the-art 28.8K bps devices has assisted many users in speeding up their Internet search operations, even at that operating rate the display of a typical Web page containing one or two graphic images can result in a delay of 10 seconds to 15 seconds as the picture is "painted" on a monitor.

Recognizing the operating limitations associated with transmissions via the public switched telephone network, as well as looking for an additional source of revenue, several cable television (CATV) companies initiated broadband access trials to the Internet during 1995. Each of these trials involves the use of cable modems, which enables a personal computer (PC) to access the Internet via a common CATV coaxial cable at operating rates up to tens of millions of bits per second. Although cable modems are in their infancy, both independent market research organizations and many cable operators predict that the installed base of this new type of communications device will rapidly grow to over 10 million modems within a few years.

Due to the advantages associated with obtaining high-speed Internet access, as well as the potential economics associated with the use of cable modems to obtain such access, data center managers should consider preparing their facility for the infrastructure required to use cable modems.

This chapter discusses the nature of cable modems and describes their operation. The scope of the discussion also includes the cabling infrastructure being developed to provide a megabit transmission facility to residences and businesses. The chapter outlines the cabling requirements for installation within buildings, and the requirements that are necessary to access this new high speed information highway via the use of cable modems. The data center manager should have a background of knowledge concerning a rapidly evolving new technology and be able to support its use when corporate policy begins to include Internet issues.

## MODEM FUNDAMENTALS

The ability to appreciate why cable modems are able to provide a transmission capability that is an order of magnitude or more than conventional modems, used for transmission on the switched telephone network, requires knowledge of certain transmission concepts, including the Nyquist theorem. This section concentrates on the operation of conventional analog modems that are used on the switched telephone network. This can provide the data center manager with an understanding of why analog modems' operating rate is limited and how they may be able to overcome that operating rate limitation.

A conventional analog modem commonly used to transmit information over the switched telephone network is limited to a maximum operating rate of between 28.8K bps and 33.6K bps, with the rate achievable dependent upon the quality of the connection and according to the modulation technique employed. In theory, the maximum operating rate of an analog modem that has been designed for use on the switched telephone network is limited by the 4K Hz bandwidth provided by the communications carrier for a switched telephone channel.

In 1924 Nyquist proved, in what is now referred to as the Nyquist theorem, that the maximum signaling rate of a device is limited to twice the available bandwidth; beyond that rate, inter-symbol interference starts to occur and adversely affects the transmission. As an example, for the 4K Hz telephone channel, this means the maximum signaling rate of a modem used to transmit on that medium is limited to 8,000 baud. Baud is a term used to indicate signal changes per second.

## THE QUADRATURE AMPLITUDE MODULATION TECHNIQUE

The most commonly used modem modulation technique, quadrature amplitude modulation (QAM), uses a combination of phase and amplitude to convey the settings of a group of bits in one signal change, enabling four bits to be represented by one baud change. This in turn enables an 8,000 baud signaling rate to transport data at a rate of 32K bps when QAM is used for modulation.

Due to the 4K Hz telephone channel limitation, however, data transmission rates are limited to approximately 32K bps, with a slightly higher rate of 33.6K bps recently achieved by a few modem vendors using a modified QAM technique. Although the incorporation of data compression into modems provides a potential doubling to quadrupling of modem throughput, to between 67.2K bps and 134.4K bps, the ability of a modem to compress data depends upon the susceptibility of data to the compression algorithm being used. Because that susceptibility varies considerably as a modem user performs different operations, the end result is a variable compression rate; even though it is not noticeable during file transfer operations, that variable rate becomes extremely noticeable during interactive operations. In addition, even with the ability to compress data at a high rate, the resulting information transfer rate of 134.4K bps pales by comparison to the operating rate obtainable through the use of cable modems. It is clear that advances in modem and cabling technology are limited with respect to increasing the performance of modems used to communicate via the switched telephone network, however.

## CABLE MODEMS

The key difference between an analog modem designed for use on the public switched telephone network and a cable modem is in the bandwidth of the channels they are designed to use. Cable TV uses RG-11 cable for the main CATV trunk and RG-59 cable from trunk distribution points into and through residences and offices. Both types of coaxial cable have 75 ohms impedance and support broadband transmission, which means that two or more channels separated by frequency can be simultaneously transported on the cable.

### From Unidirectional to Bidirectional Systems

A cable-TV broadcasting infrastructure uses 6M Hz channels within the bandwidth of RG-11 and RG-59 cable to transmit a TV channel. Most CATV systems are currently unidirectional, which means that TV signals are broadcast from the CATV system operator without any provision for receiving a return signal. This transmission limitation is gradually being overcome as CATV operators begin to add bidirectional amplifiers to their networks that, when they are installed, will support transmission from subscribers in the reverse direction to conventional TV signal broadcasts. This will enable CATV systems to support the standardized transmit frequency range of 5M Hz to 42M Hz, and receive a frequency range of 54M Hz to 550M Hz, with 6M Hz cable TV channels.

By using one or more 6M Hz cable TV channels, a cable modem obtains the use of a bandwidth that is 1,500 times greater (6M Hz/4K Hz) than that provided by a voice channel on the switched telephone network. This means that the modem can support a signaling rate of twice the bandwidth, or 12M baud, on one TV channel, based upon the Nyquist theorem, before the occurrence of inter-symbol interference.

The primary difference between cable modems currently being used in field trials are in their use of one or more 6M Hz TV channels within the band of channels carried by a coaxial cable, and their methods of attachment to the CATV network. One cable modem manufactured by Zenith Network Systems, a subsidiary of Zenith Electronics, of Glenview IL, operates on 6M Hz channels at 4 M bps to the subscriber, using a special filtering technique to prevent data channels from interfering with adjacent information, which can be in the form of either data or video, that would co-exist with the data transmission provided by the cable modem. The uplink or return data rate occurs at 500K bps. Modem modulation is biphase shift key (BPSK), which means that two bits (bi) are encoded in each phase change, and the modem's phase changes are shifted in phase from one to another. This modem is also frequency-agile, which means it can be set to operate on any standardized channel on a broadband CATV system.

The Zenith cable modem is actually one portion of a series of components required for a PC to use the modem. A complete transmission system requires the use of a Zenith cable modem, Ethernet 10BASE-T adapter card with a 15-conductor pin connector, and a 15-conductor shielded cable to connect the cable modem to the adapter. Exhibit 1 illustrates the cabling required to connect a PC to a CATV network via the use of a Zenith Network Systems cable modem.

When the adapter card is installed in the PC, it in effect turns the computer into a client workstation. Because the adapter is an Ethernet 10BASE-T card, this means that the channel being used by the cable modem operates as one long CSMA/CD LAN, with each PC user competing with other PC users for access to the channel. This means that the CATV operator should segment its cable distribution system to limit the number of cable modems attached to any segment, similar to the manner in which conventional

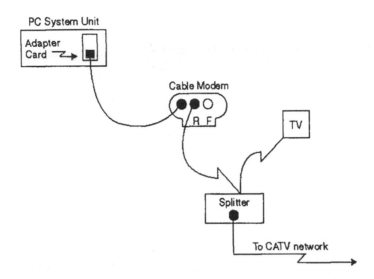

**Exhibit 1. Cabling for a Zenith Network Cable Modem System.**

LANs are limited with respect to the maximum number of workstations that can be connected to the LAN.

The connector labeled R on the rear of the cable modem is a reverse cable connector designed for networks that use a single coaxial cable. The second connector, labeled F, represents a forward cable connector that would be used if the modem were connected to a cable system that uses two cables. In such a system, one cable is dedicated to conventional CATV broadcasting through one-way amplifiers, which precludes reverse transmission on the same cable. This type of system also requires the use of a second cable to obtain a transmission capability in the reverse direction.

### A High-Speed Cable Modem Architecture

In addition to the previously described cable modem based upon the exclusive use of RF technology and biphase shift key modulation, Zenith Electronics Corporation announced a high-speed cable modem architecture. This architecture is based on the use of 16-VSB (vestigial sideband), a technique developed by Zenith as part of the organization's high-definition research, as well as the 256 quadrature amplitude modulation technology. Through the use of more complex modulation techniques for which more data bits can be represented by one signal change, the Zenith modem architecture can support data rates up to 40M bps on a 6M Hz cable channel.

Recognizing the fact that many cable TV systems will be limited to one-way transmission for the foreseeable future because of the time and cost associated with upgrading the CATV infrastructure, Zenith plans to support a range of options and speeds for upstream data transmission. According to Zenith, both telephone (analog modulation) and RF return path transmission capabilities will be incorporated into different versions of this new family of cable modems. For many cable modem applications, such as Internet operations, the use of the switched network for a return path should provide an acceptable level of performance. The rationale for this is best noted by examining the communications interaction between a potential cable modem user and the cable network as a user searches out and accesses various points on the World Wide Web.

**On the Web**

When users access a Web page, they transmit a universal resource locator (URL) address that represents the document they wish to view. This address is transported using the HTTP within a packet. The HTTP consists of an address that totals fewer than 100 characters, which are used to frame the address the message is being transported to, as well as the address of the originator of the request. The destination Web server uses the document address to locate the requested page on the server, retrieves it from disk, and forms a packet using the source address from the incoming packet as the destination address for the outgoing packets. If the requested document contains a full screen of text, the packet contain close to 2,000 characters, because a full screen of text consists of 80 columns by 24 rows of data (i.e., 1,920 characters). However, because a typical Web page contains one or more graphics, the total amount of data transmitted from the server to the user will be in actuality substantially more than 2,000 characters. For example, it is assumed that the Web page in question includes a 3 × 3-inch photograph, drawing, or schematic diagram that has been scanned using a resolution of 300 dots per inch. Regardless of the color of the image, each square inch of the image requires 11,250 bytes of storage. If the image was scanned using a 256-color resolution, each pixel requires a byte to represent its color, resulting in 90,000 bytes of storage per square inch. Thus, a 3 × 3-inch color image requires 270,000 bytes of storage.

Because HTTP breaks large files into small packets for transmission, the image might be carried by a sequence of approximately 100 packets, each roughly 2,700 bytes in length, to include packet overhead. Thus, the short, 100-character transmission from a user can result in a response of 280,000 bytes. Because a user connected to the Web typically clicks on hotlinks that represent document addresses to view other documents, most Web operations represent asymmetrical transmission, that is, more transmissions return to the user than the user actually originates. Thus, a high speed cable channel with a low speed reverse path occurring over the switch telephone network may actually be sufficient for most data transmission applications.

The previously described asymmetrical transmission operation of users was also recognized by Intel Corporation, which took it into consideration when designing its CablePort cable modem system. That cable modem is designed to provide an average downstream data rate of 27M bps and a 96K bps upstream rate. One interesting difference between Zenith and Intel concerning their cable modem systems is in the type of adapter card required to be used in the PC. Because Intel provides a higher downstream operating rate than what is usable by a 10BASE-T adapter card, the user must install a Fast Ethernet (100M bps) adapter card in the PC to be able to use the Intel cable modem. Although no commercial costs were provided by Zenith or Intel for field trial operations, it is worth noting that a Fast Ethernet adapter has a retail cost of approximately $250, whereas a 10BASE-T adapter can be obtained for less than $50.

A second difference between the Zenith and Intel modems concerns their upstream capability. Although Zenith's new architecture permits support of the switched telephone network for locations where CATV operators cannot provide reverse direction transmission, the Intel system did not offer this capability when this chapter was researched.

**RECOMMENDED COURSE OF ACTION**

Although the technology of cable modems is in its infancy, the data center manager can still plan for their use. Whereas the type of cable modem offered will depend upon the CATV operators' cable infrastructure (i.e., either unidirectional or bidirectional), as well as the cable modem vendor the data center manager selects, each cable modem requires the use of RG-11 coaxial cable. Thus, if the manager has previously installed such cabling as part of a legacy terminal to mainframe or legacy LAN wiring system and are considering its removal, he or she may wish to leave the cabling in place. If RG-11 cabling has not been installed, the data center manager may wish to consider contacting the local CATV operator to determine when cable modems will be supported and the type the operator intends to use. If it intends to use bidirectional transmission via RF modulation, the data center manager can develop a wiring plan that requires only the use of RG-11 cable. If the CATV operator says it intends to provide reverse transmission via the public switched telephone network, the wiring plan must be modified to ensure that each cable modem user will have an available telephone jack. By understanding how cable modems operate and planning the organization's wiring infrastructure to use this evolving technology, the data center manager will be prepared for its future use.

# Chapter 8
# Network Disaster Recovery Planning
*Nathan J. Muller*

Because there are many more links than host computers, there are more opportunities for failure on the network than in the hosts themselves. Consequently, a disaster recovery plan that takes into account such backup methods as the use of hot sites or cold sites without giving due consideration to link-restoration methods ignores a significant area of potential problems.

Fortunately, corporations can use several methods to protect their data networks against downtime and data loss. These methods differ mostly in cost and efficiency.

## NETWORK RELIABILITY

A reliable network continues operations despite the failure of a critical element. The critical elements are different for each network topology.

### Star Topology

With respect to link failures, the star topology is highly reliable. Although the loss of a link prevents communications between the hub and the affected node, all other nodes continue to operate as before unless the hub suffers a malfunction.

The hub is the weak link in the star topology; the reliability of the network depends on the reliability of the central hub. To ensure a high degree of reliability, the hub has redundant subsystems at critical points: the control logic, backplane, and power supply. The hub's management system can enhance the fault tolerance of these redundant subsystems by monitoring their operation and reporting anomalies. Monitoring the power supply, for example, may include hotspot detection and fan operation to identify trouble before it disrupts hub operation. Upon the failure of the main power supply, the redundant unit switches over automatically or manually under the network manager's control without disrupting the network.

0-8493-9965-3/99/$0.00+$.50
© 1999 by CRC Press LLC

The flexibility of the hub architecture lends itself to variable degrees of fault tolerance, depending on the criticality of the applications. For example, workstations running noncritical applications may share a link to the same local area network (LAN) module at the hub. Although this configuration might seem economical, it is disadvantageous in that a failure in the LAN module puts all the workstations on that link out of commission.

A slightly higher degree of fault tolerance may be achieved by distributing the workstations among two LAN modules and links. That way, the failure of one module would affect only half the number of workstations. A one-to-one correspondence of workstations to modules offers an even greater level of fault tolerance, because the failure of one module affects only the workstation connected to it; however, this configuration is also a more expensive solution.

A critical application may demand the highest level of fault tolerance. This can be achieved by connecting the workstation to two LAN modules at the hub with separate links. The ultimate in fault tolerance can be achieved by connecting one of those links to a different hub. In this arrangement, a transceiver is used to split the links from the application's host computer, enabling each link to connect with a different module in the hub or to a different hub. All of these levels of fault tolerance are summarized in Exhibit 1.

### Ring Topology

In its pure form, the ring topology offers poor reliability to both node and link failures. The ring uses link segments to connect adjacent nodes. Each node is actively involved in the transmissions of other nodes through token passing. The token is received by each node and passed on to the adjacent node. The loss of a link not only results in the loss of a node but brings down the entire network as well. Improvement of the reliability of the ring topology requires adding redundant links between nodes as well as bypass circuitry. Adding such components, however, makes the ring topology less cost-effective.

### Bus Topology

The bus topology also provides poor reliability. If the link fails, that entire segment of the network is rendered useless. If a node fails, on the other hand, the rest of the network continues to operate. A redundant link for each segment increases the reliability of the bus topology but at extra cost.

### NETWORK AVAILABILITY

Availability is a measure of performance dealing with the LAN's ability to support all users who wish to access it. A network that is highly available

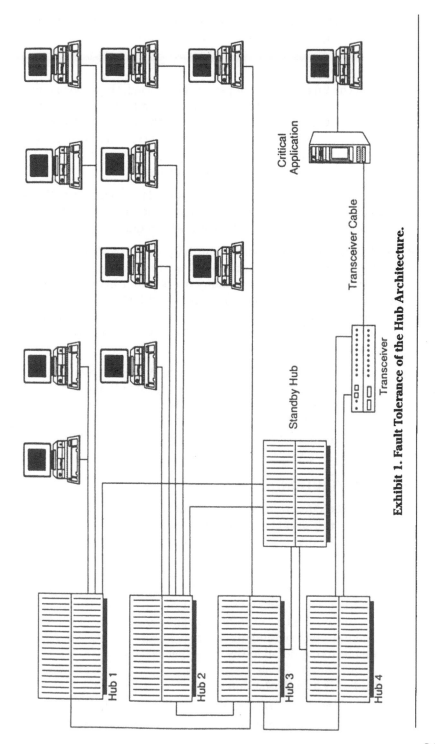

**Exhibit 1. Fault Tolerance of the Hub Architecture.**

provides services immediately to users, whereas a network that suffers from low availability typically forces users to wait for access.

## Component Availability

Availability on the bus topology depends on the load, the access control protocol used, and length of the bus. With a light load, availability is virtually ensured for any user who wishes to access the network. As the load increases, however, so does the chance of collisions. When a collision occurs, the transmitting nodes back off and try again after a short interval. The chance of collisions also increases with bus length.

With its multiple paths, a mesh topology, which is a variation of the bus topology, provides the highest degree of interconnectivity, which implies that the network is always available to users who require access.

A network based on a star topology can only support what the central hub can handle. In any case, the hub's LAN module can handle only one request at a time, which can shut out many users under heavy load conditions. Hubs equipped with multiple processors and LAN modules can alleviate this situation somewhat, but even with multiple processors, there is not usually a one-to-one correspondence between users and processors. Such a system would be cost-prohibitive.

The ring topology does not provide the same degree of availability as does a mesh topology but still represents an improvement over the star topology. The ring has a lower measure of availability than the mesh topology because each node on the ring must wait for the token before transmitting data. As the number of nodes on the ring increases, the time interval allotted for transmission decreases.

## METHODS OF PROTECTION

In today's distributed computing environments, with so much information traversing public and private networks, network managers must be acquainted with the available protection methods to ensure uninterrupted data flow and guard against data loss. On a wide area network (WAN), the choices include carrier-provided redundancy and protection services, customer-controlled reconfiguration, bandwidth on demand using ISDN, and dial backup. On the LAN, the choices include various recovery and reconfiguration procedures, the use of fault-tolerant servers and wiring hubs, and the implementation of redundant arrays of inexpensive disks. All these methods are discussed in detail in the following sections.

## Tariffed Redundancy and Protection

Among the traditional methods for protecting WAN facilities are the tariffed redundancy and protection services offered by such interexchange carriers as AT&T, MCI Communications Corp., and US Sprint Communications Co.

A reliable method for minimizing downtime on the WAN is to have redundant lines ready and waiting. When a link goes down, the standby facility can be activated until the source of the failure is determined and appropriate action taken to restore service. Having duplicate facilities is a prohibitively expensive option for most businesses because monthly charges accrue whether or not the facilities are used.

To minimize the effects of failed facilities on the same route, AT&T, for example, offers two special routing methods in conjunction with its digital and analog service offerings: diversity and avoidance.

**Diversity.** Diversity is available for ACCUNET T1.5, ACCUNET Spectrum of Digital Services (ASDS), 56k-bps Dataphone Digital Service (DDS), and voicegrade private lines. With diversity routing, designated groups of interoffice channels (i.e., AT&T's portion of the circuit) are furnished over physically separate routes. Each route entails installation and routing charges. A custom option for diversity furnishes the interoffice channels partially or entirely over physically separated routes when separate facilities are available. In this case, AT&T applies a special routing charge to each channel.

**Avoidance.** The avoidance option allows the customer to have a channel avoid a specified geographical area. The customer minimizes potential impairments, such as delay, that might be exacerbated by long, circuitous routes. It also enables the customer to avoid potential points of congestion in high-use corridors, which can block traffic. This option also gives customers the means to avoid high-risk environments that can be prone to damage from floods, earthquakes, and hurricanes.

### Further Protective Capabilities

Although special routing can minimize the damage resulting from failed facilities by allowing some channels to remain available to handle priority traffic, special routing makes no provision for restoring failed facilities. AT&T has attempted to address this issue with its automatic protection capability and network protection capability.

**Automatic Protection Capability.** Automatic protection capability is an office function that protects against failure for a local channel or other access for the ACCUNET T1.5 and ACCUNET T45 services. Protection of interoffice channels is provided on a one-to-one basis through the use of a switching arrangement that automatically switches to the spare channel when the working channel fails. To implement this capability, a separate local access channel must be ordered to serve as the spare, and compatible automatic switching equipment must be provided by the customer at its premises.

**Network Protection Capability.** Whereas AT&T's automatic protection capability guards against the failure of a local access channel, its network protection capability is designed to guard against the failure of an interoffice channel. Protection is furnished through the use of a switching arrangement that automatically switches the customer's channel to a separately routed fiber-optic channel on failure of the primary channel.

For both ACCUNET T1.5 and ACCUNET T45, an installation charge is incurred for the network protection capability. For the amount of protection promised, however, it may not be worth the cost, because most, if not all, of AT&T's interoffice channels are automatically protected, whether or not they use the network protection capability. When AT&T circuits go down, traffic is automatically switched to alternative routes.

### Dial Backup

Over the years, dial backup units have come into widespread use for rerouting modem and digital data set transmissions around failed facilities. Dial backup units are certainly more economical than leasing redundant facilities or opting for reserved service or satellite-sharing arrangements.

This method entails installing a standalone device or an optional modem card that allows data communication to be temporarily transferred to the public switched network. When the primary line fails, operation over the dial backup network can be manually or automatically initiated. At the remote site, the calls are answered automatically by the dial backup unit. When the handshake and security sequence are completed and the dial backup connection is established, the flow of data resumes. On recovery of the failed line, dial backup is terminated in one of two ways: a central site attendant manually releases the backup switch on the dial backup unit, or, when in the automatic mode, the dial backup unit reestablishes the leased line connection and disconnects the dial network call upon detection of acceptable signal quality.

### Rerouting on T1 Lines

To support applications requiring a full T1, dial backup over the public switched network is available with AT&T's ACCUNET T1.5 reserved service. With this service, a dedicated T1 facility is brought online after the customer requests it with a phone call. An hour or more may elapse before the reserved line is finally cut over by AT&T. This option may be acceptable under certain conditions, however, as a possible alternative to the loss of network availability for an indeterminate period. This is an effective alternative for the customer who has resubscribed to the ACCUNET T1.5

reserved service. If the customer has not resubscribed, this service is not a suitable alternative for routing traffic around failed facilities, if only because the local access facilities must already be in place at each end of the circuit.

### Customer-Controlled Reconfiguration

Management capabilities, such as customer-controlled reconfiguration (CCR) available using AT&T's Digital Access and Crossconnect System (DACS), can be a means to route around failed facilities. Briefly, the DACS is a routing device; it is not a switch that can be used for setting up calls (i.e., a PBX switch) or for performing alternate routing (i.e., a multiplexer switch). The DACS was originally designed to automate the process of circuit provisioning. With customer-controlled reconfiguration, circuit provisioning is under user control from an on-premises management terminal.

With customer-controlled reconfiguration, however, a failed facility may take a half-hour or more to recover, depending on the complexity of the reconfiguration. This relatively long period is necessary because the carrier needs time to establish the paths specified by the subscriber through use of a dial-up connection.

A recovery time of 30 minutes may seem tolerable for voice traffic, in which the public switched network itself is a backup vehicle, but data subscribers may need to implement alternate routing more quickly. Therefore, AT&T's DACS and customer-controlled reconfiguration service, and the similar offerings of other carriers, are typically used to remedy a long-term failure rather than to rapidly restore service on failed lines.

### ISDN Facilities

T1 multiplexers offer many more functions than does DACS with customer-controlled reconfiguration. In fact, the instantaneous restoration of high-capacity facilities on today's global networks calls for a T1 networking multiplexer with an advanced transport management system.

An ISDN-equipped T1 networking multiplexer offers yet another efficient and economical means to back up T1 and fractional T1 facilities. With ISDN, the typical time required for call setup is from 3 to 10 seconds. An appropriately equipped T1 multiplexer permits traffic to be rerouted from a failing T1 line to an ISDN facility in a matter of seconds rather than hours or days, as is required by other recovery methods.

Using ISDN facilities is more economical than other methods, including ACCUNET T1.5 reserved service. With the reserved service, the user pays a flat fee for a dedicated interoffice circuit over a certain length of time, including the time when the circuit remains unused. With ISDN, the user pays for the primary rate local access channels and pays for the interoffice channels only when used because these charges are time and distance dependent — just like ordinary phone calls.

With AT&T's high-capacity HO (384K bps) and H11 (i.544M bps) ISDN channels, users can avail themselves of the ISDN for backing up fractional or full T1 lines rather than pay for idle lines that may only be used occasionally during recovery. This is accomplished through a T1 multiplexer's capability to implement intelligent automatic rerouting, which ensures the connectivity of critical applications in an information-intensive business environment.

When confronted with congestion or impending circuit failure, the intelligent automatic rerouting system calculates rerouting on the basis of each likely failure. During a failure, the system automatically recalculates optimal routing, based on current network conditions. After restoration, the system again automatically calculates the most effective rerouting, should a second failure occur on the network. In this way, the system is always ready to handle the next emergency.

Because applications require different grades of service to continue operating efficiently during line failures, circuits must be routed to the best path for each application, not just switched to available bandwidth. This ensures that the network continues to support all applications with the best response times.

To avoid service denial during rerouting, voice transmissions can be automatically compressed to use less bandwidth. This can free up enough bandwidth to support all applications, both voice and data.

### DDS Dial Backup

Despite carrier claims of 99.5% availability on digital data services (DDS), this seemingly impressive figure still leaves room for 44 hours of annual downtime. This amount of downtime can be very costly, especially to financial institutions, whose daily operations depend heavily on the proper operation of their networks. A large financial services firm, for example, can lose as much as $200 million if its network becomes inoperative for only an hour.

An organization that cannot afford the 44 hours of annual downtime might consider a digital data set with the ability to "heal" interruptions in transmission. Should the primary facility fail, communication can be quickly reestablished over the public switched network by the data set's built-in modem and integral single-call dial back unit.

Sensing loss of energy on the line, the dial-backup unit automatically dials the remote unit, which sets up a connection through the public switched network. Data is then rerouted from the leased facility to the dial-up circuit. If the normal DDS operating rate is 19.2K bps, dial restoration entails a fallback to 9.6K bps. For all other DDS rates — 2.4K, 4.8K, and 9.6K bps — the transmission speed remains the same in the dial-backup mode. Downspeeding is not necessary.

While in the dial backup mode, the unit continues to monitor the failed facility for the return of energy, which indicates an active line. Sensing that service has been restored, the unit reestablishes communication over it. The dial-up connection is then dropped.

## RECOVERY OPTIONS FOR LANS

The LAN is a data-intensive environment requiring special precautions to safeguard one of the organization's most valuable assets — information.

The procedural aspect of minimizing data loss entails the implementation of manual or automated methods for backing up all data on the LAN to avoid the tedious and costly process of recreating vast amounts of information. The equipment aspect of minimizing data loss entails the use of redundant circuitry as well as components and subsystems that are activated automatically upon the failure of various LAN devices to prevent data loss and maintain network availability.

### Recovery and Reconfiguration

In addition to the ability to respond to errors in transmissions by detection and correction, other important aspects of LAN operation are recovery and reconfiguration. Recovery deals with bringing the LAN back to a stable condition after an error, and reconfiguration is the mechanism by which the network is restored to its previous condition after a failure.

LAN reconfigurations involve mechanisms to restore service upon loss of a link or network interface unit. To recover or reconfigure the network after failures or faults requires that the network possess mechanisms to detect that an error or fault has occurred and to determine how to minimize the effect on the system's performance. Generally, these mechanisms provide:

- Performance monitoring.
- Fault location.
- Network management.
- System availability management.
- Configuration management.

These mechanisms work in concert to detect and isolate errors, determine errors' effects on the system, and remedy these errors to bring the network to a stable state with minimal impact on network availability.

**Reconfiguration.** Reconfiguration is an error-management scheme used to bypass major failures of network components. This process entails detection that an error condition has occurred that cannot be corrected by the usual means. Once it is determined that an error has occurred, its impact on the network is assessed so an appropriate reconfiguration can be formulated and implemented. In this way, normal operations can continue under a new configuration.

**Error Detection.** Error detection is augmented by logging systems that keep track of failures over a period of time. This information is examined to determine whether trends may adversely affect network performance. This information, for example, might reveal that a particular component is continually causing errors to be inserted onto the network, or the monitoring system might detect that a component on the network has failed.

**Configuration Assessment Component.** This component uses information about the current system configuration, including connectivity, component placement, paths, flows, and maps information onto the failed component. This information is analyzed to indicate how that particular failure is affecting the system and to isolate the cause of the failure. Once this assessment has been performed, a solution can be worked out and implemented.

The solution may consist of reconfiguring most of the operational processes to avoid the source of the error. The solution determination component examines the configuration and the affected hardware or software components, determines how to move resources around to bring the network back to an operational state or indicates what must be eliminated because of the failure, and identifies network components that must be serviced.

**Function Criticality.** The determination of the most effective course of action is based on the criticality of keeping certain functions of the network operating and maintaining the resources available to do this. In some environments, nothing can be done to restore service because of device limitations (e.g., lack of redundant subsystems) or the lack of spare bandwidth. In such cases, about all that can be done is to indicate to the servicing agent what must be corrected and keep users informed of the situation.

Once an alternate configuration has been determined, the reconfiguration system implements it. In most cases, this means rerouting transmissions, moving and restarting processes from failed devices, and reinitializing software that has failed because of some intermittent error condition. In some cases, however, nothing may need to be done except notify affected users that the failure is not severe enough to warrant system reconfiguration.

For WANs, connections among LANs may be accomplished over leased lines with a variety of devices, typically bridges and routers. An advantage of using routers for this purpose is that they permit the building of large mesh networks. With mesh networks, the routers can steer traffic around points of congestion or failure and balance the traffic load across the remaining links.

### restoration Capabilities of LAN Servers

Sharing resources distributed over the LAN can better protect users against the loss of information and unnecessary downtime than a network with all of its resources centralized at a single location. The vehicle for resource sharing is the server, which constitutes the heart of the LAN. The server gives the LAN its features, including those for security and data protection, as well as those for network management and resource accounting.

**Types of Servers.** The server determines the friendliness of the user interface and governs the number of users that share the network at one time. It resides in one or more networking cards that are typically added to microcomputers or workstations and may vary in processing power and memory capacity. However, servers are programs that provide services more than they are specific pieces of hardware. In addition, various types of servers are designed to share limited LAN resources — for example, laser printers, hard disks, and the RAM mass memory. More impressive than the actual shared hardware are the functions provided by servers. Aside from file servers and communications servers, there are image and fax servers, electronic mail servers, printer servers, SQL servers, and a variety of other specialized servers, including those for videoconferencing over the LAN.

The addition of multiple special-purpose servers provides the capability, connectivity, and processing power not provided by the network operating system and file server alone. A single multiprocessor server combined with a network operating system designed to exploit its capabilities, such as UNIX, provides enough throughput to support 5 to 10 times the number of users and applications as a microcomputer that is used as a server. New bus and cache designs make it possible for the server to make full use of several processors at once, without the usual performance bottlenecks that slow application speed.

**Server Characteristics.** Distributing resources in this way minimizes the disruption to productivity that would result if all the resources were centralized and a failure was to occur. Moreover, the use of such specialized devices as servers permits the integration of diagnostic and maintenance capabilities not found in general-purpose microcomputers. Among these capabilities are error detection and correction, soft-controlled error detection and correction, and automatic shutdown in case of catastrophic error. Some servers include integral management functions (e.g., remote console management). The multiprocessing capabilities of specialized servers provide the power necessary to support the system overhead that all these sophisticated capabilities require.

Aside from physical faults on the network, there are various causes for lost or erroneous data. A software failure on the host, for example, can cause write errors to the user or server disk. Application software errors may generate inaccurate values, or faults, on the disk itself. Power surges can corrupt data and application programs, and power outages can shut down sessions, wiping out data that has not yet been written to disk. Viruses and worms that are brought into the LAN from external bulletin boards, shareware, and careless user uploads are another concern. User mistakes can also introduce errors into data or eliminate text. Entire adherence to security procedures are usually sufficient to minimize most of these problems, but they do not eliminate the need for backup and archival storage.

**Backup Procedures.** Many organizations follow traditional file backup procedures that can be implemented across the LAN. Some of these procedures include performing file backups at night — full backups if possible, incremental backups otherwise. Archival backups of all disk drives are typically done at least monthly; multiple daily saves of critical databases may be warranted in some cases. The more data users already have stored on their hard disks, the longer it takes to save. For this reason, LAN managers encourage users to offload unneeded files and consolidate file fragments with utility software to conserve disk space, as well as to improve overall system performance during backups. Some LAN managers have installed automatic archiving facilities that move files from users' hard disks to a backup database if they have not been opened in the past 90 days.

Retrieving files from archival storage is typically not an easy matter; users forget file names, the date the file was backed up, or in which directory the file was originally stored. In the future, users can expect to see intelligent file backup servers that permit files to be identified by textual content. Graphics files, too, are retrieved without having the name, backup date, or location of the file. In this case, the intelligent file backup system compares the files with bit patterns from a sample graphic with the bit patterns of archived files to locate the right file for retrieval.

As the amount of stored information increases, there is the need for LAN backup systems that address such strategic concerns as tape administration, disaster recovery, and the automatic movement of files up and down a hierarchy of network storage devices. Such capabilities are currently available and are referred to as system storage management or hierarchical storage management.

### Levels of Fault Tolerance

Protecting data at the server has become a critical concern for most network managers; after all, a failure at the server can result in lost or destroyed data. Considering that some servers are capable of holding vast quantities of data in the gigabyte range, loss or damage can have disastrous consequences for an information-intensive organization.

Depending on the level of fault tolerance desired and the price the organization is willing to pay, the server may be configured in several ways: unmirrored, mirrored, or duplexed.

**Unmirrored Servers.** An unmirrored server configuration entails the use of one disk drive and one disk channel, which includes the controller, a power supply, and interface cabling, as shown in Exhibit 2. This is the basic configuration of most servers. The advantage is chiefly one of cost: the user pays only for one disk and disk channel. The disadvantage of this configuration is that a failure in either the drive or anywhere on the disk channel could cause temporary or permanent loss of the stored data.

**Mirrored Servers.** The mirrored server configuration entails the use of two hard disks of similar size. There is also a single disk channel over which the two disks can be mirrored together, as shown in Exhibit 3. In this configuration, all data written to one disk is then automatically copied onto the other disk. If one of the disks fails, the other takes over, thus protecting the data and ensuring all users have access to the data. The server's operation system issues an alarm notifying the network manager that one of the mirrored disks is in need of replacement.

The disadvantage of this configuration is that both disks use the same channel and controller. If a failure occurs on the channel or controller, both disks become inoperative. Because the same disk channel and controller are shared, the writes to the disks must be performed sequentially — that is, after the write is made to one disk, a write is made to the other disk. This can degrade overall server performance under heavy loads.

**Disk Duplexing.** In disk duplexing, multiple disk drives are installed with separate disk channels for each set of drives, as shown in Exhibit 4, malfunction occurs anywhere along a disk channel, normal operation continues on the remaining channel and drives. Because each disk uses a separate disk channel, write operations are performed simultaneously, offering a performance advantage over servers using disk mirroring.

Disk duplexing also offers a performance advantage in read operations. Read requests are given to both drives. The drive that is closest to the

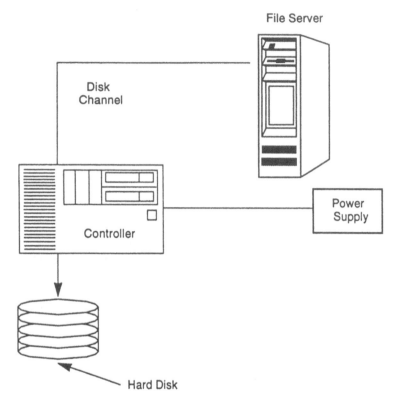

**Exhibit 2. Unmirrored Disk Drive Configuration.**

---

information responds and answers the request. The second request given to the other drive is canceled. In addition, the duplexed disks share multiple read requests for concurrent access.

The disadvantage of disk duplexing is the extra cost for multiple disk drives, also required for disk mirroring, as well as for the additional disk channels and controller hardware. However, the added cost for these components must be weighed against the replacement cost of lost information plus costs that accrue from the interruption of critical operations and lost business opportunities. Faced with these consequences, an organization might discover that the investment of a few hundred or even a few thousand dollars to safeguard valuable data is negligible.

## REDUNDANT ARRAYS OF INEXPENSIVE DISKS

One method of data protection is growing in popularity: redundant arrays of inexpensive disks (RAID). Instead of risking all of its data on one high-capacity

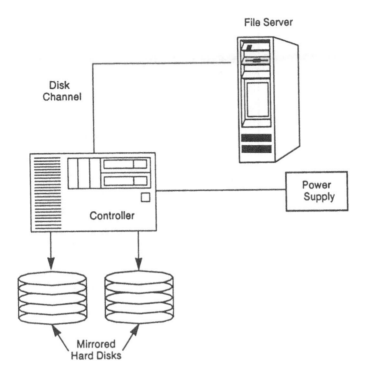

File Server

Disk
Channel

Power
Supply

Controller

Mirrored
Hard Disks

**Exhibit 3. Configuration for Disk Mirroring.**

disk, the organization distributes the data across multiple smaller disks, offering protection from a crash that could wipe out all data on a single, shared disk. Exhibit 5 illustrates redundant arrays of inexpensive disks. Other benefits of RAID include:

- Increased storage capacity per logical disk volume.
- High data transfer or input/output rates that improve information throughput.
- Lower cost per megabyte of storage.
- Improved use of data center floor space.

RAID products can be grouped into the categories described in the following sections.

### RAID Level 0

Technically, these products are not RAID products at all, because they do not offer parity or error- correction data to provide redundancy in the event of system failure. Although data striping is performed, it is accomplished without fault tolerance. Data is simply striped block-by-block

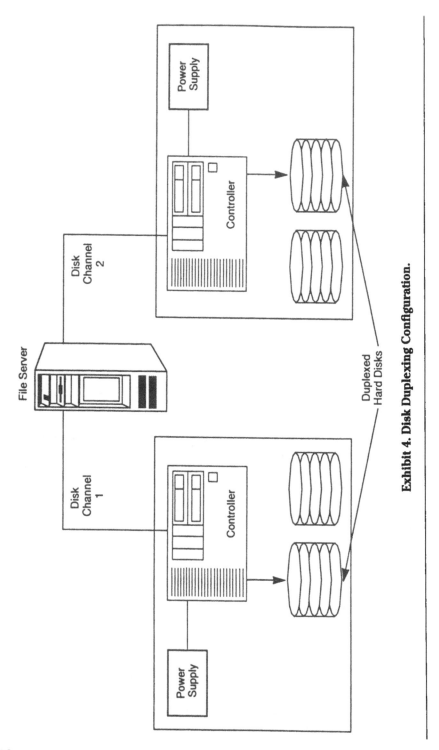

**Exhibit 4. Disk Duplexing Configuration.**

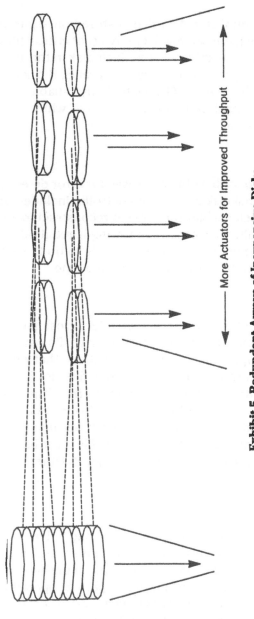

**Exhibit 5. Redundant Arrays of Inexpensive Disks.**

across all the drives in the array. There is no way to reconstruct data if one of the drives fails.

### RAID Level 1

These products duplicate data that is stored on separate disk drives. Also called mirroring, this approach ensures that critical files are available in case of individual disk drive failures. Each disk in the array has a corresponding mirror disk, and the pairs run in parallel. Blocks of data are sent to both disks simultaneously. Although highly reliable, Level 1 is costly because each drive requires its own mirror drive, which doubles the hardware cost of the system.

### RAID Level 2

These products distribute the code used for error detection and correction across additional disk drives. The controller includes an error-correction algorithm, which enables the array to reconstruct lost data if a single disk fails. As a result, no expensive mirroring is required. The code, however, requires that multiple disks be set aside to do the error-correction function. Data is sent to the array one disk at a time.

### RAID Level 3

These products store user data in parallel across multiple disks. The entire array functions as one large, logical drive. Its parallel operation is ideally suited to supporting imaging applications that require high data-transfer rates when reading and writing large files. RAID Level 3 is configured with one parity (i.e., error-correction) drive. The controller determines which disk has failed by using additional check information recorded at the end of each sector. However, because the drives do not operate independently, every time an image file must be retrieved, all the drives in the array are used to fulfill that request. Other users are put into a queue.

### RAID Level 4

These products store and retrieve data using independent writes and reads to several drives. Error-correction data is stored on a dedicated parity drive. In RAID Level 4, data striping is accomplished in sectors rather than bytes or blocks. Sector-striping offers parallel operation in that reads can be performed simultaneously on independent drives, which allows multiple users to retrieve image files at the same time. Although multiple reads are possible, multiple writes are not because the parity drive must be read and written to for each write operation.

## RAID Level 5

These products interleave user data and parity data, which are then distributed across several disks. Because data and parity codes are striped across all the drives, there is no need for a dedicated parity drive. This configuration is suited for applications that require a high number of input/output operations per second, such as transaction processing tasks that involve writing and reading large numbers of small data blocks at random disk locations. Multiple writes to each disk group are possible because write operations do not have to access a single common parity drive.

## RAID Level 6

These products improve reliability by implementing drive mirroring at the block level so data is mirrored on two drives instead of one. Up to two drives in the five-drive disk array can fail without loss of data. If a drive in the array fails with RAID Level 5, for instance, data must be rebuilt from the parity information spanned across the drives. With RAID Level 6, however, the data is simply read from the mirrored copy of the blocks found on the various striped drives. No rebuilding is required. Although this results in a slight performance advantage, it requires at least 50% more disk capacity to implement.

Vendors continually tout the effectiveness of various RAID solutions. In truth, the choice among RAID solutions involves tradeoffs between cost, performance, and reliability. Rarely can all of these requirements be satisfied simultaneously, especially when trying to address high-availability, large-scale storage needs.

## OTHER CONSIDERATIONS

As more businesses interconnect their computers at remote locations and run critical applications over WANs, they are discovering that financial and operational losses can mount quickly in the event of internetwork downtime. Businesses of all types and sizes are recognizing that disaster recovery plans are essential, regardless of the particular computing environment. The disaster recovery plan should be a formal document that has been signed off by senior management, IS management, and all department heads. The following items should be addressed in any disaster recovery plan.

### Uninterruptible Power Supplies (UPSs)

UPSs are designed to provide temporary power so attached computer systems and servers can be shut down properly to prevent data loss. UPSs are especially important in WANs. Because of the distance among links, sometimes reaching thousands of miles, WANs are more susceptible to power problems than LAN segments. Therefore, using battery backups to protect against fluctuations and outages should always be the first line of defense.

Although most central sites have UPSs, many remote sites typically do not, usually as a cost-savings measure. However, battery backup can be very inexpensive, costing only a few hundred dollars, which is cheap compared to the cost of indeterminate network downtime. Moreover, some UPSs have simple network management protocol (SNMP) capabilities, which lets network managers monitor battery backup from the central management console. For instance, every UPS can be instructed using SNMP to test itself once a week and report back if the test fails. The network manager can even be notified if the temperature levels in wiring closets rise above established thresholds.

### Generators

To keep computers operating during a prolonged loss of power, a generator is required. A generator is capable of supplying much more power for longer periods of time. Using a fuel source, such as oil, a generator can supply power indefinitely to keep data centers cool and computers running. Because generators can cost tens of thousands of dollars, many companies unwisely decide to skip this important component of the disaster recovery plan.

Unless an organization has experienced a lengthy outage that has disrupted daily business operations, this level of protection is often hard to justify. However, many office buildings already have generators to power lighting and elevators during electrical outages. For a fee, tenants can patch into the generator to keep data centers and networks operating.

### Off-Site Storage

Mission-critical data should be backed up daily or weekly and stored off site. There are numerous services that provide offsite storage, often in combination with hierarchical storage management techniques. In the IBM environment, for example, this might entail storing frequently used data on a direct access storage device (DASD) for immediate usage, whereas data used only occasionally might go to optical drives, and data that has not been used in several months would be archived to a tape library.

Carriers, computer vendors, and third-party firms offer vault storage for secure, offsite data storage of critical applications. Small companies need not employ such elaborate methods. They can back up their own data and have it delivered by overnight courier for storage at another company location or bring it to a bank safety deposit box. The typical bank vault can survive even a direct hit by a tornado.

In addition to backing up critical data, it is advisable to register all applications software with the manufacturer and keep the original program disks in a safe place at a different location. This minimizes the possibility of both copies being destroyed in the same catastrophe. Software licenses, manuals, and supplementary documentation should also be protected.

### Surge Suppressors

In storm-prone areas like the Southeast, frequent electrical storms can put sudden bursts of electricity, called spikes or surges, on telephone lines. These bursts can destroy router links and cause adapters and modems to fail. To protect equipment attached to telephone lines, surge-suppression devices can be installed between the telephone line and the communications device. Surge suppressors condition the power lines to ensure a constant voltage level. Many modems and other network devices have surge suppressors built in. The disaster recovery plan should specify the use of surge suppressors whenever possible, and equipment should be checked periodically to ensure proper operation.

### Spare Parts Pooling

Most companies can afford to stockpile spare cables and cards but not spare multiplexer and router components that are typically too expensive to inventory. Pooling these items with another area business that uses the same equipment can be an economical form of protection should disaster strike. Such businesses can be identified through user group and association meetings. The equipment vendor is another source for this information.

After each party becomes familiar with the disaster recovery needs of the other, an agreement can be drawn up to pledge mutual assistance. Each party stocks half the necessary spare parts. The pool is drawn from as needed and restocked after the faulty parts come back from the vendors' repair facilities.

### Switched Digital Services

Carriers offer an economical form of disaster protection with their networks of digital switches. When one link goes down, voice and data calls are automatically rerouted or switched to other links on the carrier's network. Examples of switched digital services are switched 56K bps, ISDN, and frame relay. Many routers now offer interfaces for switched digital services, allowing data to take any available path on the network. The same level of protection is available on private networks, but it requires spare lines, which is often a very expensive solution.

## Multiple WAN Ports

A well-planned internetworking system avoids single points of failure. This entails equipping nodes with redundant subsystems, such as power, control logic, network cards, and WAN ports. Routers, for instance, need multiple WAN ports so if a primary line goes down, the router automatically can use the backup line on another port.

Even branch sites with remote-access routers should have multiple WAN ports. If the first line goes down, the remote router is programmed to auto-dial into a second line on another port, which remains inactive until needed. The second port can dial up a switched 56K line that is paid for on a usage basis.

## Links to Remote Sites

WANs of three or more sites often link the remote locations to the primary site but not to each other. Though this strategy saves linkage costs, it risks leaving remote workers stranded should the main office's services go down. To keep branches up and running, inexpensive links should be established among them. The links' bandwidth should be adequate to keep critical systems communicating.

As long as backup circuits are available, routers can run a routing protocol that understands link states and can reroute around points of network failure. The routing information protocol (RIP), often used in smaller WANs, does not support link states, but the open shortest path first (OSPF) protocol does. OSPF runs on TPC/IP networks and is the protocol of choice for larger internetworks.

## Periodic Testing

It is advisable to test the disaster recovery plan periodically to check assumptions and to find out whether the plan really works. After giving users advance notice, the network manager can come in after business hours, unplug one of the communication links, and see what happens. If something unexpected occurs, it is necessary to fine tune the disaster recovery plan and test again.

With certain types of network equipment, such as multiplexers and switches, several disaster-simulation scenarios can be programmed in advance and stored for emergency implementation. With the integral network modeling capability of some T1 multiplexers, network planners can simulate various disaster scenarios on an aggregate or node level anywhere in the network. This off line simulation allows planners to test and monitor changing conditions and determine their precise impact on network operations.

Any outage should be treated as an unannounced test of the disaster recovery plan. Network managers should determine if the response was adequate and if the response can be improved.

## Worst-Case Scenarios

Planning how to provide communications connectivity based on the assumption that the entire network is inoperable is a sound business practice, especially for organizations in areas of the country that can suffer widespread damage from hurricanes, tornadoes, floods, and earthquakes. Whole nodes may have to be replaced to get the network back into proper operation, requiring advance arrangements with suppliers so the necessary equipment can be obtained on very short notice instead of when it comes off a production run.

Many vendors of switches, hubs, routers, and multiplexers offer network recovery services at a reasonable cost and guarantee equipment delivery within 24 hours of the request. Even carriers offer disaster recovery services. AT&T Global Information Solutions, for example, offers crisis management services designed to allow customers to occupy a regional AT&T crisis center within two to four hours after a disaster. The customer gets fully restored voice and data communications and computer-ready floor space.

Some companies specialize in disaster recovery services. SunGard Recovery Services Inc., for instance, offers customers a hotsite backup center for mainframe computers. The company also addresses the needs of PC-based environments and offers PC software that helps identify which services are critical to operations. Its overnight assistance program rushes equipment — PCs, servers, and modems, as well as bridges, multiplexers, and routers — to any customer site. As part of its mobile recovery program, SunGard maintains a fleet of trailers that are ready for dispatch to customer sites for use as temporary workspace.

## Training

Often overlooked in the disaster recovery plan are provisions for training, essential because in an emergency reactions to impending disaster must be automatic. End users must save data and shut down applications at the first sign of trouble. Network managers must be able to assess quickly the criticality of numerous alarms and respond appropriately. Help desk operators must be able to determine the nature and magnitude of the problem to address end user concerns. LAN administrators must be able to determine the impact of the problem on local networks.

## Insurance

The disaster recovery plan should provide for the periodic review of the organization's insurance policy. Of particular concern is to what extent information systems, network components, and applications software are covered in the event of a disaster. The policy should be very specific about what the insurance company does and does not cover. Ambiguities must be resolved before a disaster occurs, not after.

Reviews also provide an opportunity to add provisions for system or network upgrades and expansions that occurred in the time since the policy was initially written. Though this may add to the policy's cost, it is still much less compared to the wholesale replacement of equipment that falls outside of the insurance contract.

## Risk Assessment

The disaster recovery plan should include a review of the physical layout of data centers, wiring closets, floor and overhead conduits, and individual offices that contain computers and data communications equipment. All equipment and cabling should be kept in a relatively safe place and not exposed to objects that are likely to fall and cause damage should disaster strike. Desks, tables, shelves, and cabinets should be solid enough to safely fasten equipment to them, to survive minor earthquakes. Whenever possible, equipment should not be positioned under water sprinklers. These and other precautions can even lower insurance costs.

## SUMMARY

The methods mentioned in this chapter are only a few of the many network restoration and data protection options available from carriers, equipment vendors, and third-party firms. As more businesses become aware of the strategic value of their networks, these capabilities are significantly important to organizations. A variety of link-restoration and data-protection methods can provide effective ways to meet the diverse requirements of today's information-intensive corporations that are both efficient and economical. Choosing wisely from among the available alternatives ensures that companies are not forced into making cost/benefit tradeoffs that jeopardize their information networks and, ultimately, their competitive positions.

# Section II
# Business Management Issues

Communication networks are both business tools as well as a business that requires the application of sound business management practices. Recognizing these facts, this section was established to provide readers with detailed information covering business management issues with respect to internal and external organizational business practices. With respect to internal business practices, chapters in this section cover such topics as methods to integrate Web and enterprise computing and the allocation of network costs to your end-user community. Chapters that are oriented towards external business topics will provide you with information ranging in scope from establishing an infrastructure for electronic commerce to obtaining an appreciation for the telecommunications policy process which provides information on the rate-making process.

The first chapter in this section, "Developing a Trusted Infrastructure for Electronic Commerce Services," introduces us to the necessity to use certificates that vouch for the legitimacy of persons conducting or attempting to conduct electronic commerce. This chapter discusses the use of commercial exchange services, secure electronic mail, and secure Web transactions, providing a foundation for understanding the importance of a public key certificate infrastructure and its value for electronic commerce.

In the second chapter in this section we turn our attention to the regulatory process. As noted at the beginning of the chapter titled "An Overview of the Telecommunications Policy Process," a company cannot create a new communications network without understanding regulation and the new levels of competition ushered in by the Telecommunications Reform Act of 1996. Recognizing this truism, this chapter provides us with a brief overview of the evolution of regulatory milestones to include the important Telecommunications Reform Act of 1996. Using the evolution of reform milestones as a base, this chapter proceeds to introduce us to the players that influence rate-making and how we can negotiate with both public utility commissioners as well as communication carriers. For those of us accustomed to paying retail, this chapter provides information which can be used to enhance our organization's bottom line.

The third chapter in this section also is very relevant to today's networking environment as it is focused upon multimedia networking, a technology exhibiting a phenomenal increase as organizations add multimedia support to both client and server computer systems. In the chapter "Business Aspects of Multimedia Networking," we will become acquainted with the business and technical issues associated in the design of multimedia networks. Thus, this chapter will provide us with information required to appropriately plan for the delivery of multimedia applications over the corporate network in a manner that is both technically and financially feasible.

The fourth chapter in this section also is focused upon a very popular topic. In the chapter "Integrating the Web and Enterprise Business Systems," issues related to enterprise business applications in the context of the World Wide Web are examined. The capabilities and limitations of the Web to include security, performance, backup and user management are discussed in this chapter in the context of integrating the Web and corporate applications. A list of key questions are both asked and answered to provide you with suggested methods to construct a Web presence that can be used for both supporting external and internal customers.

The last chapter in this section, "Cost Allocation for Communications Networks," covers a topic some of us may recall associated with the term chargeback. Regardless of the term used, allocating the cost of a network to those who use it is an important topic which organizations are increasingly exploring. Although most organizations centrally fund the cost of network operations, doing so can be viewed as similar to providing users with a communications buffet. That is, regardless of how much they use, the price remains the same. While most users may not take a disproportionate advantage of this type of billing situation, it does not allocate cost in a fair and equitable manner. Thus, as more organizations seek to allocate or chargeback networking cost in a more equitable manner, the last chapter in this section will gain in its importance on your reading list.

# Chapter 9
# Pricing Methods Across Linked Networks

*Keith A. Jones*

Designing and developing an effective network cost allocation system so it is compatible with the host chargeback system is no easy task. However, data center managers must implement a strategy to recover costs across linked networks and to demonstrate to senior-level management that the data center is more than a service bureau — it is a profit center, as well.

## PROBLEMS ADDRESSED

Data centers, when under efficient management, provide services to a business enterprise that are recovered by a cost allocation system that distributes these costs to customer business units. Operational expenses can be allocated across data communications network infrastructures along the lines of chargeback systems established for the host processing environments.

Most data center managers are already very much aware of all the host system resources that must be charged back to their users. This includes the most common direct system use charge categories (e.g., host CPU, system printer, DASD storage, and tape drive units) as well as indirect resource costs that must be billed (e.g., space, utilities, and technical support services).

Many data center managers may not be as well aware of the resources that must be charged to recover costs across host-linked enterprisewide information networks — or the impact that such networks can have on their host resource costs. Use of these networks can result in new categories of host data center costs that must be recovered through more complex pricing methods. Although data center managers can readily accommodate any of the more conventional unexpected changes in data center operating expense (e.g., a rise in utility or paper costs) by using an industry-standard strategy that adjusts availability of host access to match available capacity, they are often uncomfortable at the prospect of charge-out across their host network links. This is primarily because they are not as aware of their options for recovering unexpected changes in costs of supporting an enterprisewide data network.

## CHARGEABLE RESOURCES

At first, it is easier for a data center manager to focus on effects to support chargeback of direct network costs on services involving equipment with very short paybacks and high plug-compatibility. The ideal initial resources are modems, terminals, printers, and if already in place, a central help desk telephone line to contact vendors.

The ideal arrangement is to leverage the volume-purchasing power of the central-site data center to obtain the lowest possible direct cost for the business client users. In addition to increasing economies of scale in purchase of hardware, software, and supplies, the data center can offer a central focal point for vendor contacts, negotiations, and coordination of maintenance services — at lower pass-through costs than can be obtained by independent arrangements.

Data center managers should begin viewing their function as more than just a service bureau for data processing services. The network-linked host data center provides expanded opportunities to offer an enterprisewide range of business information management support services (e.g., computer systems hardware and software purchasing, inventory control, financial analysis, and physical plant engineering).

Especially if existing departments within the organization already offer such basic services, the data center does not have to provide these services directly. Instead, data center management should increasingly position and present its overall operation as a ready and effective conduit to help enable each business enterprise client to tap into — and leverage — existing packets of expertise within the organization. Data center managers are in a unique position to identify common areas of operational business needs and present both internal and external sources as options to help pool costs.

Regardless of the source of the resources that make up the information enterprise network and host system costs that are to be allocated across the client service base, the primary consideration of the data center manager must be that of defining the categories of use that are to be charged. The chargeable resource categories must be easily understood by the customers who are to be billed and must be measurable by use statistics that can be readily accumulated for the review of customers in their billing statement. This is true regardless of whether the costs are to be allocated according to direct line item unit measure charges or indirect fee assignments.

As with the host chargeback system, it is first of all necessary to be able to identify — and track — all possible network services and resources. Once there is a reasonable assurance that a system of resource accounting procedures has been established that does not allow any network cost or any contingent host system cost to escape unaccounted for, data center managers can consolidate individual categories of network services and resource costs into network cost pools suitable for use in pricing out network chargeback billings.

The definition of these cost pools must be sufficiently detailed to support future strategy for directing patterns of desirable network use in a manner that is predictable and compatible to host cost-efficiency and cost-containment procedures. In other words, categories of resource that are identified to network customers for cost allocation purposes must serve to increase customer awareness of the types of expenses involved in managing the network, regardless of how much is to be billed to recover costs of each resource type.

## NETWORK RESOURCE CATEGORIES

The chargeable resources for enterprisewide network cost allocation can absorb some of the data center resources (e.g., printing, database use, data media, and data center operational services) as well as the resources required for the network. The most important network resource categories are discussed in the following sections.

### Cable

The costs of cabling to connect enterprisewide network devices can easily be the largest and most complicated category of all network management expenses. Among the available options are:

- **Coaxial cable.** An example is the cable used in IBM 3270 terminals. It is expensive but extremely reliable and compatible with most of the existing network methods. It is often kept in stock by data centers.
- **Unshielded twisted-pair cable.** Also known as telephone wire, this is inexpensive but subject to interference; it often causes host-linkage error.
- **Shielded twisted-pair cable.** Although similar to the unshielded telephone wire, this is wrapped like coaxial cable. It is moderately expensive and moderately dependable.
- **Fiber-optic cable.** This has the widest possible range of applications, and it is the most reliable cable option.

- **Wireless networks.** These are increasingly feasible options, especially when rapid installation is desired and the physical layout of the business enterprise facility is suitable.

## Linkages

In network terms, these are interconnectors, or plug-compatible interfaces, between networks and host lines. Linkage components include:

- **Plugs.** These include cable connectors and data switches, splitters and sharing devices, wire ribbons, and all other interface linkage hardware. This is typically the most overhead-intensive cost category in network management because it requires inventory control and planning to have every possible plug-type on hand.
- **Modems.** Modems and all other dial-up line management devices as well as communications line multiplexing hardware are most critical to line-speed costs.
- **Wire boxes.** These involve all the business enterprise physical plant or facility-determined access hardware and management.

## Workstations

This category includes microcomputer configurations that are connected at each local network node or station. The components are:

- **Terminals.** These can include intelligent workstations through gateway servers.
- **Storage.** Storage elements can include the fixed hard disk (if available at the workstation node), diskettes, and any dedicated tape or CD-ROM storage devices.
- **Personal printer.** This is included if a dedicated printer is attached.

## Servers

This category always comprises an intelligent workstation with the minimum CPU and storage required by the particular network control methods used. It includes:

- **File-server hardware.** This includes the file-server workstation and all network boards that it controls, including LAN boards and host gateway link boards as well as LAN boards and other specialized hardware.
- **File-server software.** This includes the network file management control software and shared applications.

## Storage

High-volume mass storage is frequently needed for backup and archival purposes, which may involve technical support and specialized hardware or software well beyond the usual range of support for LAN administrators. This may include optical memory, imaging, CD-ROM jukeboxes, or other advanced technology with many gigabytes of storage capacity. The need for this technology is increasingly likely if the client network involves graphics, engineering, or any other application requiring intensive backup cycles and complicated version control. The use of high-volume mass storage is usually controlled from a dedicated server that automatically manages files and application software. The client-server may be a minicomputer that functions as a front-end processor to manage enterprise network message requests for real-time access to host programming functions or a back-end processor to manage online access to a host database.

## Communications

This is by far the most cost-intensive network resource. Telecommunications can make or break the network chargeback system, and unfortunately it is an area in which a data center may have limited options. Much can be learned about network billing from a local telecommunications company, often at great expense.

## LAN Administration Support

This can include the salaries of the local LAN administrator and the LAN help desk personnel, the costs of training, and the costs of host-based support of LAN inventory, purchasing, billing or any other service provided by the data center. It can also involve both short-term and long-term leasing of network hardware or software, diagnostics, or user training. This category can be large or small, depending on the client. In some cases, clients may prefer to provide some of the LAN technical support; in others, a data center may provide it all.

**Internet Gateway Access.** Whether the data center network is SNA or TCP/IP dictates whether it is an option to establish the enterprise's own Internet Gateway, which can cost as much as 10 intelligent workstations. That gateway, however, can be cost justified if the enterprise organization does any kind of business on the Internet.

Typically, business on the Internet takes one or more of three forms: E-mail, user news groups, or a home page on the World Wide Web (WWW, or just the Web). A dedicated gateway requires substantial UNIX-related technical expertise to establish and maintain. A more viable option is a dedicated line to an online service account, which normally costs no more than a single workstation, and internal enterprise customers can still be supported in the three major functional business support areas.

Both a dedicated gateway and a dedicated line can usually be financed using long-term methods. If Internet access is a legitimate enterprise business need, it can be more than easily justified. If not, until the demand (and real need) for Internet access can be precisely predicted, it is often feasible to simply pass through direct charge billing of departmental accounts on online services with Internet access, such as Compuserve, Prodigy, or America Online.

## EXPENSE CATEGORIES

The next step in developing an enterprisewide network cost-allocation system is to assign all expenses into a manageable number of nonoverlapping categories. Most data center managers can develop a matrix of network resource categories that has a direct correspondence to their host data center resource assignment matrix. If there is no existing host data center expense matrix to use as a model for defining the network cost allocation expense matrix, the data center manager can begin by grouping the basic categories of network expenses. Exhibit 1 shows a basic network expense assignment matrix.

There are two important considerations. First, each of the categories in the expense matrix must correspond to budget line items that will be forecasted and tracked by a business enterprise financial controller or accountants assigned to audit network costs. Second, expense line items must be defined so they are clearly separated from all other items and there is limited opportunity to assign expenses to the wrong category or, even worse, duplicate direct and indirect costs.

Although the data center manager should consult with the financial controllers who audit the network before preparing the network cost assignment matrix, the data center manager must usually define how the resource allocation procedures are to be administered, which include assumptions about the methods for measurement and assignment of enterprisewide network resource use and billing obligations. The proposed network resource cost allocation matrix should also be reviewed with the prospective network customers. In addition, the anticipated categories of host-lined data network expenses should be reviewed by the business enterprise organizational management before any pricing strategy or rate structure is determined for the enterprisewide network cost chargeout.

## RATE DETERMINATION

To expand enterprisewide business information services and allocate host system costs across interconnected distributed networks, data center managers must change their fundamental view from a centralized focus to a

**Exhibit 1. Basic Network Expense Assignment Matrix**

| | Resources | | | | |
|---|---|---|---|---|---|
| **Expenses** | **Stations** | **Servers** | **Linkages** | **Storage** | **Telecom** |
| **Fixed Costs** Equipment Facilities Insurance Interest Maintenance Salary | | | | | |
| **Variable Costs** Consultants Database Support Help Desk LAN Support Paper Supplies Telecom Support Vendors | | | | | |
| **Surcharges** Diagnostics Disaster Recovery Documentation Planning Prevention Tuning Training | | | | | |
| **Total Costs** | | | | | |

decentralized one. This change in focus must include a reorientation to accommodate market-driven as well as demand-driven operations planning.

Data center managers are increasingly in a position of competition with alternative outside vendor sources for every product and service that has traditionally been a vital part of their exclusive business organizational domain. It is therefore necessary for data centers to begin defining their pricing structure on not only what chargeable resources there are but how each of the resources is charged to help achieve strategic market advantage over the competition.

Data centers can no longer simply apply a straight distribution formula to recover costs but must also factor in potential future costs associated with the risk that new technology will be available at lower cost and that business enterprise users may bypass the data center. Unless the data center manager is also an expert in both financial management and risk management, this usually means an increasing emphasis on leasing or subcontracting most new services and resources at short-term premium rates, until a sufficient economy of scale can be achieved by bundling enterprisewide data network resource demands to reduce risks as well as costs.

In some cases, host-linked network domains may be large enough to achieve the break-even economies of scale quickly, especially if sufficiently large proprietary data stores are involved. In most cases, however, the process will be more like a traditional tactical penetration to achieve a dominant share of mature, nongrowth market segments, also known as buyer's markets. The management of the central site host data center must go the business enterprise customer rather than the other way around.

If a data center cannot package centralized services as superior to the competition, not all costs may be recovered. Furthermore, the ultimate determination of what constitutes a chargeable resource is not simply a data center expense that must be recovered but is now also an information network service or resource that a business enterprise customer must want to buy.

The manner of rate determination is directly determined by the network resource allocation strategy and chargeback system cost-control objectives. The most basic consideration determining the rate structure is whether data center management has decided to fully recover network costs on the basis of actual use or to distribute indirect costs of a network resource pool evenly among all of its users. This consideration applies to each network resource category as well as to each category of network customer.

As a basic rule of thumb, the decision of whether to recover costs on the basis of actual use or to distribute costs evenly among business enterprise users is largely determined by the extent to which a resource is equally available for shared, concurrent use or is reserved exclusively for use by an individual network user. If the resource is shared, the rate structure is based on forecasted patterns of use, with sufficient margin to absorb potential error in the forecasted demand as well as the potential probability of drop-off in demand for network services. On the other hand, rate structures can be based on underwriting network capital equipment or financing service–level agreements, which provide greater security for full recovery of all costs from an individual business enterprise customer on the basis of annualized use charges, with provisions for additional setup fees and disconnection fees to recover unforeseen and marginal costs.

As a matter of practical reality, the decision on which of the two methods of rate determination to use must also take into account the availability of dependable enterprisewide network use measurements to support direct line charges. It is also critical to first determine whether the costs that must be recovered will vary depending on the level of use (e.g., the pass-through costs of data transmission over a public telecommunications carrier line) or will be fairly well fixed regardless of whether they are fully used at all times when they are available (e.g., the on-call network technical support cost of labor). It is also important to attempt to define all assumptions on which each resource cost recovery strategy is based; this identifies all the conditions that would necessitate a change in the rate structure and exactly how each cost will be recovered in the event of major changes in enterprise information network use or underlying rate strategy assumptions.

The degree to which the enterprisewide network chargeback pricing can be easily understood by the customer largely determines how effectively all costs are recovered. It is also critical that business enterprise clients be aware of the goals of each rate decision. Depending on how responsibly they use the network, each individual enterprise network customer can help or hurt overall efficiency of the LAN as well as all interconnected LANs and the host.

## RECOMMENDED COURSE OF ACTION

Opportunities exist to broaden the data center's customer base through identifying and establishing chargeback methods for host-linked enterprisewide information networks. These new categories, however, require more complicated pricing methods. Increasing economies of scale make network chargeout a valuable strategy for the data center manager and staff. Data center operations managers should:

- Initially focus on services based on equipment with short paybacks and high compatibility, such as modems, terminals, printers, and a help desk phone line to vendors.
- Begin viewing their function as more than service bureau for data processing. Instead, the data center manager should position the data center as a resource for where expertise can be found in the organization.
- Identify and track all network services and resources, including cable, linkages, workstations, servers, storage, communications, and LAN administration support.
- Establish, if possible, the organization's own Internet Gateway.
- Develop a matrix for defining network cost allocation expenses, to assign all expenses into nonoverlapping categories.

Chapter 10

# Developing a Trusted Infrastructure for Electronic Commerce Services

*David Litwack*

For businesses to embrace open systems such as the Internet as a means of conducting commercial transactions, methods of ensuring security must be more fully developed. This chapter proposes ways of confirming sender and recipient identities, protecting confidentiality, and date and time stamping in an effort to develop a trusted network infrastructure for electronic commerce.

## INTRODUCTION

The use of internetworking applications for electronic commerce has been limited by issues of security and trust and by the lack of universality of products and services supporting robust and trustworthy electronic commerce services. Specific service attributes must be addressed to overcome the hesitation of users and business owners to exploit open systems — such as the Internet — for commercial exchanges. These service attributes include:

- **Confirmation of identity (non-repudiation).** This indicates proof that only intended participants (i.e., creators and recipients) are party to communications.
- **Confidentiality and content security.** Documents can be neither read nor modified by an uninvited third party.
- **Time certainty.** Proof of date and time of communication is provided through time stamps and return receipts.
- **Legal protection.** Electronic documents should be legally binding and protected by tort law and fraud statutes.

## SERVICE ATTRIBUTE AUTHORITY

To support these service attributes, an organization or entity would need to provide:

- Certificate authority services, including the registration and issuance of certificates for public keys as well as the distribution of certificate revocation and compromised key lists to participating individuals and organizations.
- A repository for public key certificates that can provide such keys and certificates to authorized requesters on demand.
- Electronic postmarking for date and time stamps, and for providing the digital signature of the issuer for added assurance.
- Return receipts that provide service confirmation.
- Storage and retrieval services, including a transaction archive log and an archive of bonded documents.

These service attributes could be offered singly or in various combinations. The service attribute provider would have to be recognized as a certificate and postmark authority. The following sections describe how a service attribute provider should work.

### Certificate Authority

Although public key encryption technology provides confidentiality and confirmation of identity, a true trusted infrastructure requires that a trusted authority certify a person or organization as the owner of the key pair. Certificates are special data structures used to register and protectively encapsulate the public key users and prevent their forgery. A certificate contains the name of a user and its public key. An electronic certificate binds the identity of the person or organization to the key pair.

Certificates also contain the name of the issuer — a certificate authority (CA) — that vouches that the public key in a certificate belongs to the named user. This data, along with a time interval specifying the certificate's validity, is cryptography signed by the issuer using the issuer's private key. The subject and issuer names in certificates are distinguished names (DNs), as defined in the International Telecommunications Union-Telecommunications Standards Sector (ITU-TSS) recommendation X.500 directory services. Such certificates are also called X.509 certificates after the ITU-TSS recommendation in which they were defined.

The key certificate acts like a kind of electronic identity card. When a recipient uses a sender's public key to authenticate the sender's signature (or when the originator uses the recipient's PKS to encrypt a message or document), the recipient wants to be sure that the sender is who he or she claims to be. The certificate provides that assurance.

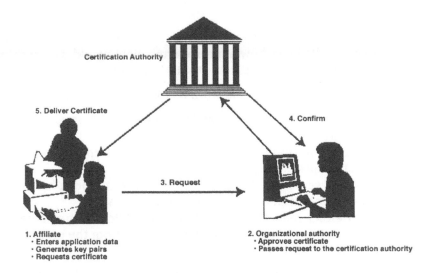

**Exhibit 1. The Registration Process.**

A certificate could be tied to one individual or represent an organizational authority that in turn represents the entire organization. Also, certificates could represent various levels of assurance — from those dispensed by a machine to those registered with a personally signed application. Additional assurance could be provided by the personal presentation of a signed application along with proof of identity or by the verification of a biometric test (e.g.,fingerprint or retina scan) for each use of the private key.

Exhibit 1 shows a possible scenario for obtaining a certificate. The registration process might work as follows:

- The affiliate (i.e., candidate for certificate) fills out the application, generates private-public key pairs, and sends for the certificate, enclosing his or her public key.
- The organizational authority approves the application.
- The organizational authority passes the certificate application to the certification authority.
- The certification authority sends back a message confirming receipt of the application.
- After proper proofing, the certification authority sends the certificate to the applicant-affiliate.
- The applicant-affiliate then loads the certificate to his or her workstation, verifies the certificate authority's digital signature, and saves a copy of the certificate.

## Digital Signatures

Exhibit 2 illustrates how a digital signature ensures the identity of the message originator. It shows how a message recipient would use an originator's digital signature to authenticate that originator.

On the Web, authentication could work as follows:

- The originator creates a message and the software performs a hash on the document.
- The originator's software then signs the message by encrypting it with the originator's private key.
- The originator sends the message to the server attaching his or her public key and certificate to the message, if necessary.
- The server either requests the originator's public key from a certificate/key repository or extracts the certification from the originator's message.

With this service, the authentication authority could either attach an authentication message verifying the digital signature's authenticity to the originator's message or provide that authentication to the recipient via a publicly accessible database. Upon receipt, the recipient would either acknowledge the originator's authenticity via the attached authentication message or access the public key and certificate from the publicly accessible database to read the signature.

To provide such levels of assurance, the certification authority must establish proofing stations where individuals and organizations can present themselves with appropriate identification and apply for certificates. The authority must also maintain or be part of a legal framework of protection and be in a position to mount an enforcement process to protect customers against fraud.

## Certificate Repository

The certificate authority also provides the vehicle for the distribution of public keys. Thus the certificate authority would have to maintain the public key certificates in a directory server that can be accessed by authorized persons and computers.

Exhibit 3 shows how subscribers might use such a repository. Certificates could be retrieved on demand along with their current status. Additional information, such as E-mail addresses or fax numbers, could also be available on demand.

The repository would work as follows:

- The message originator creates a message, generates a digital signature, and sends the message.

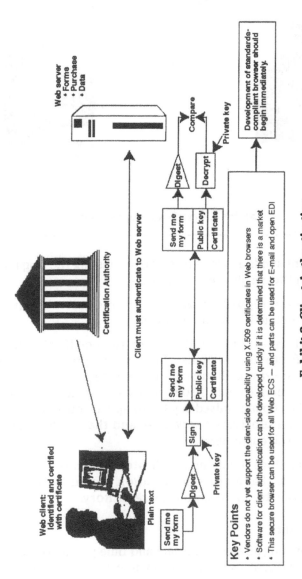

**Key Points**

- Vendors do not yet support the client-side capability using X.509 certificates in Web browsers
- Software for client authentication can be developed quickly if it is determined that there is a market
- This secure browser can be used for all Web ECS — and parts can be used for E-mail and open EDI

**Exhibit 2. Client Authentication.**

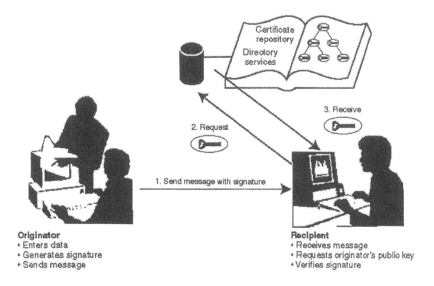

**Exhibit 3. Certificate Repository.**

- The recipient sends a signed message requesting the originator's public key from the certificate repository.

- The certificate repository verifies the requester's signature and returns the public key to the recipient.

The certificate authority could also use the certificate repository to maintain a certificate revocation list (CRL), which provides notification of certificates that are revoked pursuant to a suspected compromise of the private key. This service could also require that the authority report such compromises via a compromised key list to special customers — possibly those enrolled in a subscribed service — and that such notifications be made available to all customers.

Finally, transactions involving certificates issued by other certificate authorities require that a cross-certification record be maintained and made publicly available in the certificate repository.

## Electronic Postmark

A service providing an electronic date and time postmark establishes the existence of a message at a specific point in time. By digitally signing the postmark, the postmarking authority assures the communicating parties that the message was sent, was in transit, or received at the indicated time.

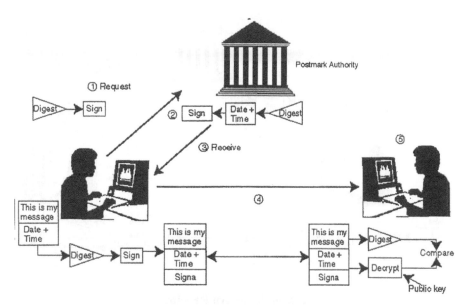

**Exhibit 4. Electronic Postmark.**

This service is most useful when the recipient requires the originator to send a message by a specified deadline. The originator would request the postmark authority to postmark the message. The authority would receive a digest of the message, add a date and time token to it, digitally sign the package, and send it back to the originator, who would forward the complete package (i.e., signed digest, time stamp, and original message) to the recipient as shown in Exhibit 4.

Electronic postmarking functions as follows:

- The originator sends a request to the postmark authority to postmark a message or document (i.e., a digital digest of the message or document).
- The postmark authority adds date and time to the message received and affixes its digital signature to the entire package.
- The postmark authority sends the package back to the originator.
- The originator sends the original message or document plus the postmarked package to the recipient.
- The recipient verifies the postmark authority signature with the authority's public key and reads the message or document.

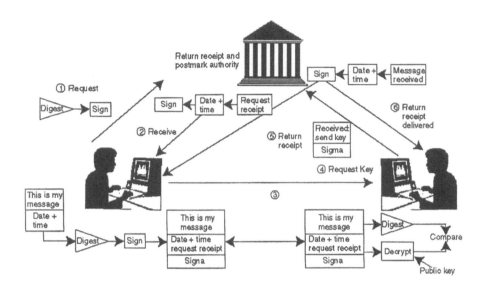

**Exhibit 5. Return Receipt.**

## Return Receipts

This service reports one of three events: that a message has transited the network, that it has been received at the recipient's mailbox, or that the recipient has actually decoded and opened the message at a specific date and time. In the latter instance, the transaction delivered to the recipient that has been encrypted might be set up only to be decrypted with a special one-time key, as shown in Exhibit 5. This one-time key could be provided by the postmark authority upon receipt of an acknowledgment from the recipient accompanied by the recipient's digital signature.

Here is how return receipt might work:

- The originator sends a message digest to the return receipt and postmark authority (the authority) with a request for a postmark and return receipt.
- The authority receives the message digest, adds date and time, encrypts the result, attaches a message to the recipient to request the decryption key from the authority upon receipt of the message, and affixes its digital signature to the package.
- The authority returns the postmarked, receipted package to the originator, who sends it to the recipient.
- The recipient receives the message package and makes a signed request for the decryption key from the authority.

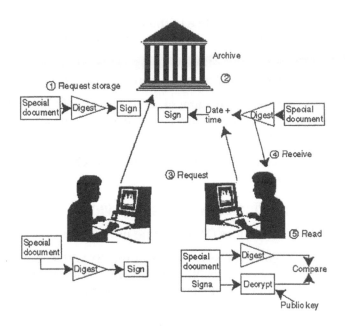

**Exhibit 6. Storage and Retrieval.**

- The authority receives the recipient's request, verifies the recipient's digital signature, and sends the decryption key to the recipient, who then decrypts and reads the message.

- The authority simultaneously forwards the return receipt to the originator.

## Storage and Retrieval Services

These services include transaction archiving where copies of transactions are held for specified periods of time, as illustrated in Exhibit 6. The service might also include information (i.e., documents, videos, or business transactions) that can be sealed, postmarked, and held in public storage to be retrieved via any authorized access. Likewise, encrypted information (i.e., documents, videos, or business transactions) can be sealed, postmarked, and further encrypted and held in sealed storage for indefinite periods of time. Each of these storage and retrieval capabilities must carry legal standing and the stamp of authenticity required for electronic correspondents.

Storage and retrieval works as follows:

- The originator sends a request to the archive to archive a document or message for a specified period of time and designates this information as publicly retrievable.

- The archive adds date and time to the message, verifies the identity of the originator, affixes a digital signature to the package, and archives the package.

- A customer requests the document from the archive.

- The archive retrieves the document, adds a date and time stamp to the package, affixes another digital signature to the new package, and sends it to the recipient.

- The recipient verifies the first and second archive signatures and reads the message.

## USE OF THESE COMMERCIAL EXCHANGE SERVICES

Electronic Commerce Services (ECS) may be used in one of three ways:

- The originator sends a message to the authority with a request for service, the authority provides the service and returns the message to the originator, and the originator then forwards the message to the recipient.
- The originator sends a message to a value added network (VAN), which then forwards the message to the authority with a request for services. The authority provides the service and returns the message to the value added network, which then forwards the message to the recipient.

- The originator sends a message to the authority with a request for service and the address of the recipient. The authority then forwards the message directly to the recipient.

All these services could be provided by a single authority, by a hierarchy of authorities, or by a network of authorities, each specializing in one or more of these services.

## AVAILABLE TECHNOLOGIES FOR ELECTRONIC COMMERCE

Currently, three major technologies are capable of providing electronic commerce services — E-mail, the World Wide Web, and open EDI. Typical of advanced technologies, security elements are the last to be developed and yet are essential if these technologies are to be deemed trustworthy for electronic commerce.

The issues of confidentiality, confirmation of identity, time certainty, and legal protection apply to all these technologies. The solutions — certification, key repositories, postmarking, return receipts, and storage and retrieval — are equally applicable to each of these technologies. Although the state of universality and interoperability varies among these technologies, they are all in a relative state of immaturity.

## Secure E-mail

Electronic messaging's most classic manifestation is E-mail. Because of its capacity for handling attachments, E-mail can be used to transfer official business, financial, technical, and a variety of multimedia forms.

## DMS and PEM.

Both the Department of Defense standard for E-mail, which is based on the ITU's X.400 standard for E-mail (called the Defense Message System or DMS), and the Internet E-mail standard, the simple mail transfer protocol (SMTP), have made provisions for security. The DMS uses encapsulation techniques at several security levels to encrypt and sign E-mail messages. The security standard for the Internet is called Privacy Enhanced Mail (PEM). Both methods rely on a certificate hierarchy and known and trusted infrastructure. Neither method is fully developed.

## Secure World Wide Web

The phenomenal growth of the Web makes it a prime candidate for the dissemination of forms and documents. Organizations see the Web as a prime tool for services such as delivery of applications and requests for information. However, Web technology has two competing types of security: one at the application layer that secures hypertext transfer protocol (HTTP) formatted data (known as SHTTP), and one at the socket layer that encrypts data in the format in which it is transported across the network.

In addition, vendors do not yet support either client-side authentication or the use of X.509 certificates. Although software for such activities as client authentication can be developed relatively quickly, vendors have to be convinced that there is a real market for such products. This technology is about to emerge and, although it will emerge first to support Web applications, it will also speed the development of E-mail and EDI security services.

## Secure Open EDI

Until now, EDI has been used in closed, value-added networks where security and integrity can be closely controlled. Signing and encryption have been proprietary to the EDI product in use or to the value-added EDI network provider.

By contrast, open EDI, running across open networks, requires adherence to the standards that are still being developed and a yet-to-be-developed infrastructure that can ensure trusted keys. To date, the various schemes to accelerate the use of open systems for EDI have not captured the imagination of EDI users and providers.

## THE OVERRIDING ISSUE: A PUBLIC KEY CERTIFICATE INFRASTRUCTURE

The suite of services and technologies described in this chapter depend on trusted public keys and their bindings to users. Users could be completely assured of the integrity of keys and their bindings if they were exchanged manually. Because business is conducted on a national and international scale, users have to be assured of the integrity of the registration authority and the key repository in an inevitably complex, electronic way.

One as-yet-unresolved issue is whether such an authority or authorities should be centralized and hierarchical or distributed. The centralized, hierarchical scheme would mean that certification authorities (and purveyors of the accompanying services) would be certified by a higher authority that, in turn, might be certified by yet a higher authority — and so on to the root authority. This kind certification would create a known chain of trust from the highest to the closest certification authority. This scheme is often referred to as the Public Key Infrastructure (PKI).

The alternative assumes that the market will foster the creation of a variety of specialized certification authorities to serve communities of interest. A complicated method of cross-referencing and maintaining those cross-references in the certificate repository for each community of interest would then develop.

The outcome of this debate is likely to result in a combination of both methods, such as several hierarchies with some kind of managed cross-referencing to enable public key exchanges between disparate communities of interest when required. Following are some of the issues yet to be resolved:

- Agreement on the exact contents of certificates.
- Definition of the size of prime numbers used in key generation.
- Establishment of the qualifications required for obtaining a certificate.
- Definition of the identification and authentication requirements for certificate registration.
- Ruling on the frequency with which certificates are renewed.
- Agreement on the legal standing and precedence for such technology.

## CONCLUSION

Groups such as the Internet Engineering Task Force (IETF), the Federal Government Public Key Infrastructure (PKI) users group, and even the American Bar Association are tackling these knotty issues.

In fact, with toolkits now available that allow the user to become his or her own certificate authority, everyone can get into the act. Private companies such as VeriSign are establishing themselves as certification authorities so that users will give their public keys and certificates credence. The National Security Agency wants to become the certificate authority for the U.S. federal government. The U.S. Postal Service is intent on offering electronic commerce services to businesses and residences by acting as the certificate authority and provider.

An infrastructure will emerge, and it will probably work for users very similar to the way that it has been described in this chapter.

# Chapter 11

# An Overview of the Telecommunications Policy Process

*Leo A. Wrobel*

Corporate network managers grapple with many choices in new network services — and getting rates as low as possible. A company cannot create a new communications network without understanding regulation and the new levels of competition ushered in by the Telecommunications Reform Act. This chapter discusses what communications managers need to know about the structure of regulation bodies, who sets service rates, and how to negotiate with commissioners and carriers.

## INTRODUCTION

The current regulatory environment in the U.S. has built itself over the years piece by piece. By attempting to drive this process in the future, the public can foster innovation and bring the information superhighway to life. This chapter looks back at the past of the regulatory environment and ahead to what lies in store.

Most people know that Alexander Graham Bell invented the telephone. But Mr. Bell's invention may never have succeeded without the work of another man, Theodore Vail, who formalized the concept of the Bell System that controlled the telephone marketplace for three quarters of a century.

The turn of the century brought with it competition in the telephone business. The good news was that customers had a choice of telephone providers, and the bad news was that if customers did not subscribe to the same network, they could not talk to each other. A customer using the red network phone could not talk to someone on the blue network.

Under the Theodore Vail concept, one company would own all the telephone services and control the telephone call from one end to another. Vail had the concept of a vertical monopoly, in which the phone company would actually own the customer's phones, the telephone lines in their homes, and the long-distance lines.

## THE BEGINNING OF COMPETITION

In the early 1950s, a rubber coupling was invented that fit over a telephone handset so that other people in the area could not hear what the person using the telephone was hearing. The telephone company sued the company that made the couplings. Because the phone company had tariffs in place that commanded the force of law, anyone using one of these "hush-a-phones" could legally have their phone service terminated. The manufacturer fought AT&T at the Federal Communications Commission (FCC) and won the right to have its equipment connected to the phone system in 1956. In some ways regulatory activism was necessary, even then.

Three years later the FCC took an even bolder step in deciding that telephone companies were "common carriers" and that they had an obligation to serve all segments of the population. Some companies required special lines or special services or wanted to have private lines dedicated to their specific use. (Because these lines were not available to the public, they were in fact called private lines.) The commission decided that it would be permissible for companies other than the monopoly phone companies to provide these private lines to corporations.

In 1968 another milestone was reached in the Carterphone decision. The Carterphone was an acoustically coupled device designed to connect a phone to a two-way radio. Even though the device was passive (i.e., did not electronically connect to the phone network), AT&T sued. The owner of the Carterphone company was an ambitious entrepreneur with an aggressive legal team. They convinced the commission that the Carterphone was not a threat to the market and that AT&T was trying to preclude competition. The commission ruled that the Carterphone could be connected to the network, as well as other devices that were "privately beneficial and not harmful to the public network."

### Long-Distance Competition

Over the years, the FCC has allowed more inroads into what had been the exclusive telephone monopoly. In long distance, the commission allowed MCI Communications Corp. to tariff a service that allowed connection to the switched network on one end of a private line, allowing the caller to circumvent AT&T's long-distance network. To AT&T, this was an illegal intrusion into its market by "cream skimmers." To MCI, the actions AT&T took to preserve its monopoly on switched service was more evidence of an attempt to control the marketplace in violation of antitrust laws.

AT&T protested, the FCC agreed with AT&T, MCI appealed, and the Court of Appeals in 1977 ruled that MCI's actions were lawful. AT&T was compelled to connect MCI (and other competitors) to the switched marketplace.

In 1984, after a 10-year antitrust suit, Judge Harold Greene of the D.C. Federal District Court approved an agreement between the U.S. Department of Justice and AT&T that split the Bell System into AT&T and seven "Baby Bells" — NYNEX, Bell Atlantic, Bell South, Ameritech, Southwestern Bell, U.S. West, and Pacific Bell. This agreement molded today's calling environment, with competitive long-distance services and far greater consumer choice. Today the availability and cost of services is far superior to what was available ten years ago, before these profound changes.

## Results of the Telecommunications Reform Act of 1996

Today, equally profound changes are taking place. The Telecommunications Reform Act of 1996 promises to be just as far reaching as the AT&T divestiture was 10 years ago.

### Telephone Companies in the Entertainment Business

AT&T, for example, is already carrying "Primestar" satellite direct television under its name. Many of the Bell operating companies (i.e., the Baby Bells) are delivering cable TV services in both their areas and in other companies' service areas.

### Entertainment Companies in the Telephone Business

The near future may hold the "Internet channel" from cable TV providers. Motorola, for example, is rolling out hundreds of thousands of cable modems designed to allow users to surf the Internet at 10M bps, which is more than 150 times faster than an ISDN line, and more than 300 times faster than the fastest modem technology available today. Cable companies and competitive local exchange carriers are also making heavy investments in switching technology to go after the local telephone company monopoly.

### Competitive Local Exchange Carriers (CLECS)

Users who want single providers can get one for local, long-distance, private line, and Internet services from competitive local exchange carriers. Billions are being spent building out local networks, usually with vastly superior technology. The availability of this leading-edge technology at truly competitive prices will be unsurpassed as a milestone in development of the nation's telecommunications infrastructure.

### Foreign Entrants

More ventures, such as the recent announcement of British Telecom's acquisition of MCI, can be expected as position jockeying continues between the giant telecommunications companies worldwide. These events only scratch the surface at the highest levels when attempting to explain the major paradigm changes taking place right now. Smart technologists are honing their skills to take advantage of these remarkable opportunities before their competition does.

## WHO CREATES TELECOMMUNICATIONS POLICY?

Some of players who create telecommunications policy include:

- AT&T.
- The Baby Bells.
- MCI, Sprint, and other IXC.
- Competitive access providers.
- The FCC.
- The courts.
- State regulatory commissions.
- Consumer groups (i.e., lobbyists).
- Congress.
- Cable companies.
- Cellular companies and wireless services.
- Bellcore.
- Large institutional users.

## THE RATE-SETTING PROCESS: WHO SETS THE PRICE?

For a company to take advantage of all the unique opportunities happening right now, it needs to understand the basics of how rates are constructed. Rate cases are divided into two parts:

- **Revenue.** Revenue determines how much money the telephone company should be allowed to earn.
- **Rate design.** Rate design determines who has to pay. In most rate cases, it is the utility vs. everyone else in the revenue portion of the case, because everyone believes that holding rates down in general will help their special interest when it comes to rate design.

In determining how much revenue the utility is entitled to, the commissions are restricted by court decisions that say that the return must be high enough to attract investors into the enterprise. The components of the revenue requirements part of the rate case can be broken down into the formula:

$$RR = (v - d)^*r + e$$

where:

RR = revenue requirement
v  = the value of the rate base
d  = the amount of depreciation of the rate base
r  = the rate of return
e  = expenses

This is a "cost plus" formula, in which the telephone company is granted the opportunity to recoup all of its expenses and get a return on its investment. In a major rate case, virtually every element and subelement of this formula is hotly contested. It can be expected that cost will be an overriding factor in any new custom network integrating advanced and emerging network services that a company designs and requests.

### The Rate Base

The "v" in the "cost plus" formula is the value of the rate base. The rate base is the investment made by the utility in the plant that serves the customer. Thus, items such as telephone poles, wires, switches and buildings are in the rate base. To be included in the rate base, the plant must be "used and useful." For example, if there is an old switch being kept in a switch building, but it is only used perhaps once every two years, it would not generally be considered used and useful. In most commissions, the evaluation of the rate base is made on an original cost basis — in other words, how much the company paid for the copper wire at the time of purchase.

Depreciation recognizes that as rate base equipment is used, it loses its value. The utility has to account for that loss in value and recover enough revenues so that the plant can be replaced at the appropriate time. In a time of rapidly changing equipment, depreciation has to recognize that the plant may still be able to function, but have very little market value. For example, as the telephone companies move from copper to optical fiber, depreciation also has to recognize that it may be cheaper simply to write off the copper wire in the ground. Depreciation is a very complex area in a rate case and should be handled by a highly qualified expert.

### RATEMAKING

Once the regulators determine how much revenue the regulated company should earn, they have to figure out who is going to pay that revenue. In telephone rate cases, there are literally hundreds of services that have to be priced, which can be unbelievably complicated. Moreover, companies that are not traditionally active in the regulatory process (unless they are telecommunications companies, of course) are almost always the ones who end up paying the most.

Ratemaking involves figuring up the costs of producing a service, including the profit for that service, and charging accordingly — this is the starting point for most regulators. However, the entire process is not that easy.

Many of the services that are offered by the telephone company are offered on an undivided basis. For example, a telephone company switch may be providing touch-tone service to one phone, business service to another phone, contacting the operator on yet another phone, and providing caller ID to another telephone. Yet each of these services needs to have a price determined out of the general cost of the switch. Thus, ways must be devised to split up the costs, which helps set the price.

## Residual Ratemaking

To preserve universal service, regulators adopted a process known as residual ratemaking. For example, if a cost study demonstrates that the current rates for residential service only cover one-half of the cost, then a strict cost-based system would say that residential rates should therefore be doubled. In the real world, this is probably not a practical option. In addition to the political fallout of such a move, it would harm universal service. Regulators faced with this problem came up with the concepts of "value of service" and "residual ratemaking."

## Value of Service

There are some products, such as three-way calling or call waiting, that do not cost a great deal once they are placed in a switch. Those services are optional. Therefore, those services can be priced based on the perceived value (i.e., value of service) to the subscriber, which is another way of saying that the provider can charge what the traffic will bear.

If the services are priced too high, they will not contribute as much toward maintaining universal service. The revenues obtained from those services allow the telephone company to remain whole, while the favored classes of service — residential and small business — get small increases in their basic line. If households have call waiting, they may see a small increase on their total bill, but most people will not take the time to drop their optional services.

## Access Charges

Possibly the largest contributors to residual ratemaking are the long-distance carriers (i.e., the IXC), who pay for residual ratemaking through their access charges. Access charges were devised at divestiture to make sure that the local companies were not harmed by the divestiture from AT&T. They were originally calculated on a revenue replacement basis, which included a hefty contribution to universal service.

### Long-Run Incremental Cost (LRIC)

One of the ways of showing that a plan does not have a major impact on the concept of universal telephone service is by calculating the long-run incremental cost (LRIC) of service and including a contribution to universal service on top of that cost. That is how commissions do it. However, LRIC costs are very different when the dynamics of fiber optics are considered. In the world of fiber-optic transmission, there is no need to lay additional cable to provide additional capacity. The basic concept is to determine how much more one unit of output costs to produce.

For example, how much more does it cost to carry one more passenger on an airplane? There may be some cost associated with the additional fuel and the passenger's meal, but assuming that all of the other passengers tickets have already paid for the flight, one additional passenger should have a very small cost. If a utility commission and potential network providers could be made to see such logic, consumers would all be better off.

## DRAFTING A CUSTOM TARIFF OR AGREEMENT WITH A CARRIER

A tariff is the contract between the telephone company (i.e., the carrier) and the customer companies. Although it is debatable whether there will even be tariffs in the future (as of the time of this writing, the FCC is trying to get carriers to retract tariffs), they are still important. Companies need to have some kind of contractual agreement with their carriers, whether in the form of a contract, a tariff or both.

It is important to remember that a tariff commands the weight of the law and preempts contractual law. That means the carrier can change a company's contract if a ruling at the state or federal level changes the rules for the tariff. An AT&T Tariff 12, for example, could change in 24 hours if the FCC rules against the terms in it as part of a broader issue, which is all the more reason to stay in the loop with regard to matters of policy.

Tariffs are similar to very detailed contracts. However, a tariff is actually a law. The carrier cannot lawfully deviate from its tariff, and the customer is bound to pay the tariff charge.

Although this seems reasonable on the surface, there can be some unexpected side effects. For example, the customer and the carrier agree on a specific price for telephone service to the customer's plants and the carrier promises to file that tariff with the appropriate regulatory bodies. The customer's bills change to reflect the agreement, and the customer operates for several years believing that it is paying the right amount. Suddenly, someone discovers that the revised tariff was never filed. The customer is now liable for all of the payments that should have been made under whatever tariff was the true lawful tariff. This is binding even if the provider company has gone out of business.

Customers should be especially careful in their understanding of the tariff because it is the rule book through which services will be purveyed.

## INFLUENCING A REGULATORY BODY

Regulatory bodies include the FCC, state public utility commissions, Congress, and courts. The most active are the state commissions and FCC. A wide variety of influences will apply to each commission, and they will each respond to those influences in a general manner. However, there are a number of factors that a commissioner may be taking into account that go beyond the narrow confines of any particular case.

The commissioner is influenced by many different parties that may include the general public, the governor, the legislature, the utilities, the interveners, the staff, the other commissioners, the press, or the courts. Commissioners are also limited — no commissioner can be an expert in everything their commission does all of the time. As one commissioner put it, it is like being the coach of the football team, the basketball team, the track team, the baseball team, the swimming team, the choir, and the debate team all at once. It can be done, but only with the help of many other people, and those people would have to be experts in their areas. Thus, it is helpful to know who helps the commissioners and what their interests and positions are.

In most commissions, the commissioners are assisted by aides who work directly for them. The aides help summarize the positions of the parties, privately assist the commissioners in understanding the issues, and may meet with people when the commissioner is unable to.

The amount of influence of the staff and the aides varies from state to state. In some states, the staff is extremely influential on the decisions of the commission; in others, the staff may be out of favor and other parties may have more influence.

### Negotiating a Price with the Commissioner

A business trying to negotiate a price with the commissioner should show a return to the carrier over the price of the contract and a contribution to universal service. Commissioners will not approve a solution based only on reduced cost for fear that the business will pass the costs along to its customers. An organization should concentrate on networking solutions that not only grow the business, but also create growth, jobs, and national competitiveness. These are ideals that commissioners can endorse and approve. An organization should make its money through building business, not cost cutting.

**Negotiating with the Carrier**

Once a company has made initial contact with a carrier through a request for information (RFI) or request for proposal (RFP), the carrier goes back to headquarters and establishes what it can provide for the company and at what price. The business should do a little "homework" to determine what network elements are available and what prices are generally being imposed for them.

The interests of the business and the carrier are not necessarily the same; however, this is not necessarily a bad thing. The carriers want to maximize their long-term profits and market share and the company seeks advanced services at rates as low as possible. If the carrier builds a custom network for a company, it may resell the same network to other companies, which creates new revenue opportunities. The company for whom the network was originally built has access to new, enabling technology first.

The company should make sure that at each stage of their cost studies, the carriers employ only long-run incremental cost principles, not just numbers from an arbitrary tariff. The company should start with the carrier's cost and negotiate from there. It is exceedingly difficult to get the carriers to release these costs, however. A basic nondisclosure agreement often sets the carrier's mind at ease.

The company should require the carrier to desegregate (i.e., unbundle) their services into the smallest possible network components. The company may not need all of the services that the carrier wants to bundle together. The carrier's progress should be monitored, and even after the services are approved by the commission, the company should ensure that someone is constantly checking the carrier's performance under the contract. The agreement between the company and the LEC may be in the form of a contract, a tariff or both.

**Converting "Feature Packages" Business Requirements to a Custom Tariff**

All of the conditions are right for the new network when the company finds a willing trading partner, an accommodating utility commission, and an environment ripe for change. A detailed business analysis should be performed at this stage. All of the business processes should be condensed into a digestible white paper for executive management that can be used to justify the money required for the new network and measures the results of the innovations using traditional return-on-investment methodology.

For example, the team creating the white paper comes up with several business processes (e.g., imaging, multimedia, network management, and native LAN connectivity) that would make the operations departments a runaway success. Each of these processes should be described in the paper and numbered as Feature Package 1, Feature Package 2, Feature Package 3, and so on. This exercise will:

- Articulate the business need to management.
- Become the basis for the request for information that will be sent to the carriers.
- Articulate the business need to the carrier.
- Allow the carrier to craft a custom response based on business, not technology, objectives.
- Show a utility commissioner why the business needs a certain technology and correlate it to something that equates to growth, jobs, and cost rather than just technology.

This features package can be crafted into the company's ideal network. It is possible to create a network that does not just spur revenue, but creates competition and new technology that everyone benefits from.

# Chapter 12

# Business Aspects of Multimedia Networking

*T. M. Rajkumar and Amitava Haldar*

Despite the ready availability of multimedia applications, most organizations have been unable to meet the requirements for effectively and efficiently distributing multimedia information. By reviewing the business issues involved in the design of multimedia networks and implementation of multimedia applications, this chapter prepares managers to deliver multimedia applications over the corporate network while providing for guaranteed quality of service.

## INTRODUCTION

As a highly effective method of communication that simultaneously provides several forms of information to the user — audio, graphics and animation, full-motion video, still images, and text — multimedia offers a departure from the communication confines present in other singular-media applications. Advances in multimedia technology and widespread acceptance of the technology in the business community are driving the need to effectively and efficiently distribute multimedia applications.

Users today have easy and inexpensive access to multimedia-capable equipment. The explosive growth of the CD-ROM applications such as multimedia databases, and the World Wide Web indicate the ease with which multimedia applications proliferate in an organization. Despite this ready availability, however, most multimedia applications are currently not distributed and work on single desktop computers. Most organizations have been unable both to keep up with the requirements to distribute multimedia information and to realize the goal of network computing — to build an infrastructure that supports a cooperative enterprise environment. This chapter identifies common multimedia applications and business considerations in effective distribution of multimedia information.

## BUSINESS DRIVERS OF MULTIMEDIA APPLICATIONS

The primary function of multimedia in most applications is as an interface; it allows an unhindered and manageable flow of information to the user that is consistent yet flexible in design and enables the user to accommodate varied work flows. Multimedia must therefore not be a barrier to information transfer; it must be conducive to it.

The following several technology advances have improved multimedia's ability to effectively transfer information and are driving the development of multimedia applications:

- Availability of multimedia-authoring applications.
- Continuously decreasing cost/memory of computer systems.
- Sustained improvements in microprocessor designs that enable multimedia-compression algorithms to be committed to silicon.
- Availability of network and communications equipment that facilitates the storage, management, and transfer of multimedia objects.
- Availability of improved input/output devices such as scanners, voice- and handwriting-recognition systems, and virtual reality.

The most important business driver of multimedia applications is teleconferencing, which saves organizations travel costs by enabling geographically dispersed individuals and groups to communicate in real-time. Multimedia applications development is also driven by the need to access information on the World Wide Web, demand for information and training systems, improved customer services such as advertising and public advice systems, and improved enterprise effectiveness such as correspondence management.

## APPLICATIONS OF NETWORKED MULTIMEDIA

For the purposes of this chapter, the applications of networked multimedia are divided into two categories:[1]

- People-to-people applications, which assist in interpersonal communication.
- People-to-information server applications, in which the user generally interacts with a remote system to receive information or interact with a server. For example, in a WWW application, clients interact with a web server to provide information to the user.

In addition, networked applications are also classified on the basis of time; they are either immediate or deferred. Immediate applications, in which a user interacts with another person or computer in real-time, must meet latency or delay requirements. Deferred applications imply that the user is interacting with the other user or server in a manner that does not

**Exhibit 1. Categories of Networked Multimedia Applications**

|  | Immediate | Deferred |
|---|---|---|
| People-to-People | Telephony, Multimedia Conferencing | E-mail, Voice Mail |
| People-to-Information Server | WWW Browsing, Video-on-Demand | File Transfer |

have latency or delay requirements. Messaging applications such as E-mail and voice mail are people-to-people applications in the deferred category.

A useful test for determining whether an application is immediate or deferred is whether the user is only working on the one application (which would make the application immediate) or can move to other applications during its use (making the application deferred). Exhibit 1 depicts the categories of networked multimedia applications.

The following sections examine multimedia applications and their networking requirements. The focus is on immediate applications, because they place greater demands on the network system than do deferred applications.

## PEOPLE-TO-SERVER APPLICATIONS

### Video-on-Demand

Video-on-demand applications let users request a video from a remote server. In a business setting, this approach is applicable for downloading training videos and viewing them on the desktop. If the videos are stored on a server, video-on-demand can be used for just-in-time training.

Because the disk requirements to download and store a video (before presentation) are expensive, video-on-demand has strict real-time requirements on transmissions but tolerates an initial delay in the playback of the data.[2] Transmission guarantees require that the bandwidth be available for the entire duration of the video. The delay requirements are not stringent, because some data can be buffered at the receiving end.

### WWW Browsing

The World Wide Web is a system that allows clients to retrieve and browse through hypertext/hypermedia documents stored on remote servers. Currently most material on the Web is text- or graphic-based; the data storage and transmission requirements associated with audio and video allow only a few users to add these features. Video access is also awkward because the video player that supports the video format (i.e., software plug-in) must exist on the client.

Many businesses, however, use the Web to provide organizational information and to support access to databases (mostly internal to the company). The Web creates different challenges for business organizations, which must conduct comprehensive capacity planning (i.e., of bandwidth, types of applications, and security) before roll out. It is bandwidth and the number of simultaneous users accessing the service that play a critical role in Web site management. Applications providing multimedia data require greater bandwidth that supports transmission-delay requirements.

## PEOPLE-TO-PEOPLE APPLICATIONS

Two common people-to-people applications are multimedia conferencing and groupware.

### Multimedia Conferencing

Multimedia conferencing is used by many businesses to support the collaborative efforts of growing numbers of virtual groups and organizational teams. The benefits of multimedia conferencing include:

- Reduction or elimination of costly business trips.
- Facilitation of collaborative work such as computer-aided design/ computer-aided manufacturing (CAD/CAM).
- Increased productivity resulting from the ability to meet deadlines and less chance for miscommunication.

### Types of Multimedia Conferencing Systems

There are three main types of multimedia conferencing systems: point-to-point, multipoint, and multicast.

**Point-to-Point Systems.** Point-to-point systems involve two persons communicating interactively from the desktop or groups of people communicating from a conference room. Point-to-point desktop conferencing systems are becoming popular because of the availability of inexpensive, low-overhead digital cameras such as the Quickcam and associated video-conferencing software. These systems let users share screens of data, text, or images.

**Multipoint Systems.** Multipoint conferencing involves three or more locations that are linked either through a local area network or a wide area network and can each send and receive video. Such systems have several unique characteristics, including presentation of multiple media, management and transport of multiple media streams, distributed access to multiple media, high bandwidth requirements, and low-latency bulk data transfer and multipoint communications. Because desktop systems quickly run out of screen space, multipoint conferencing is more effectively conducted in conference rooms with video walls.

**Multicasting Systems.** Multicasting involves the transmission of multimedia traffic by one site and its receipt by other sites. Rather than sending a separate stream to each individual user (i.e., unicasting) or transmitting all packets to everyone (i.e., broadcasting), a multicasting system simultaneously transmits traffic to a designated subset of network users. Many existing systems use broadcasting and let the receivers sort out their messages. This inefficient practice fails to maximize use of network bandwidth and poses potential security problems.

## Groupware

The notion of conferencing is changing to include such features as shared windows and whiteboards enabled by distributed computing. In addition, the use of computer mediation and integration is increasing.

A shared application or conferencing system permits two or more users at separate workstations to simultaneously view and interact with a common instance of an application and content. With such applications, users working on a report, for example, can collectively edit a shared copy. In general, documents used in groupware are active (i.e., the document displayed on the screen is connected to content in a database or spreadsheet).

Groupware provides such features as support for group protocols and control, including round-robin or on-demand floor-control policy, and both symmetric and asymmetric views of changes. In symmetric view, a change that is made is immediately shown to other users. In asymmetric view, applicable in applications involving teacher-student or physician-patient interactions, the changes made in one window may not be shown in another window. Groupware systems also support such issues as membership control (i.e., latecomers) and media control (i.e., synchronization of media).

## TECHNICAL REQUIREMENTS FOR NETWORKED MULTIMEDIA APPLICATIONS

The immediate multimedia applications discussed (i.e., video-on-demand, multimedia conferencing, groupware, and web browsing) have several technical requirements.

## Latency

Latency refers to the delay between the time of transmission from the data source to the reception of data at the destination. Associated with delay is the notion of jitter. Jitter is the uncertainty of arrival of data. In the case of multimedia conferencing systems, practical experience has shown

**Exhibit 2. Storage and Communications Requirements
for Multimedia Applications**

|  | Storage | Communications |
|---|---|---|
| Text | 2K bits per page | 1K bps |
| Graphics | 20K bits per page | 10K bps |
| Audio | 20K bits per signal | 20K bps |
| Image | 300K bits per image | (20 Kb compressed) 100 Kbps |
| Motion Video | 150K bps (compressed) for MPEG1 | 0.42M bps for MPEG227M bytes for NTSC quality 150K bps |
| Animation | 15K bps | 15K bps |

that a maximum delay of 150 milliseconds is appropriate.[3] Synchronous communications involve a bounded transmission delay.

## Synchronization

Existing networks and computing systems treat individual traffic streams (i.e., audio, video, data) as completely independent and unrelated units. When different routes are taken by each of these streams, they must be synchronized at the receiving end through effective and expeditious signaling.

## Bandwidth

Bandwidth requirements for multimedia are steep, because high data throughput is essential for meeting the stream demands of audio and video traffic. A minimum of 1.5M bps is needed for MPEG2, the emerging standard for broadcast-quality video from the Moving Picture Experts Group. Exhibit 2 depicts the storage and communications requirements for multimedia traffic streams.

## Reliability

The high data-presentation rate associated with uncompressed video means that errors such as a single missed frame are not readily noticeable. Most digital video is compressed, however, and dropped frames are easily noticeable. In addition, the human ear is sensitive to loss of audio data. Hence, error controls (such as check sums) and recovery mechanisms (i.e., retransmission requests) need to be built into the network. Adding such mechanisms raises a new complexity, because retransmitted frames may be too late for real-time processing.

## Guaranteeing Quality of Service

Quality-of-service guarantees aim to conserve resources. In a broad sense, quality of service enables an application to state what peak bandwidth it requires, how much variability it can tolerate in the bandwidth, the propagation delay it is sensitive to, and the connection type it requires

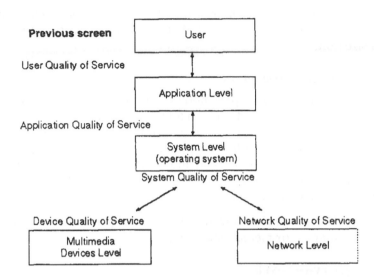

**Exhibit 3. Quality-of-Service Components in Networked Multimedia Applications.**

---

(i.e., permanent or connectionless, multipoint). The principle of quality of service states that the network must reliably achieve a level of performance that the user/application finds acceptable, but no better than that. Network systems can either guarantee the quality of service, not respond to it, or negotiate a level of service that they can guarantee.

Quality of service has several components, which are depicted in Exhibit 3 and described in the sections that follow.[4]

### Application Parameters

Application quality-of-service parameters describe requirements for applications, such as media quality and media relations. Media quality refers to source/sink characteristics (e.g., media data-unit rate) and transmission characteristics (e.g., end-to-end delay). Media relations specifies media conversion and inter- and intrastream synchronization.

### System Parameters

System quality-of-service requirements are specified in qualitative and quantitative terms for communication services and the operating system. Qualitative parameters define the following expected level of services:

- Interstream synchronization, which is defined by an acceptable skew relative to another stream or virtual clock.
- Ordered delivery of data.
- Error-recovery and scheduling mechanisms.

Quantitative parameters are more concrete measures that include specifications such as bits per second, number of errors, job processing time, and data size unit.

### Network and Device Parameters

Network quality-of-service parameters describe requirements on the network, such as network load (i.e., ongoing traffic requirements such as interarrival time), and performance or guaranteed requirements in terms of latency and bandwidth. In addition, traffic parameters such as peak data rate, burst length or jitter, and a traffic model are specified. Traffic models describe arrival of connection requests or traffic contract based on calculated expected traffic parameters.

Device quality-of-service parameters typically include timing and throughput demands for media data units.

### Determining Service Levels

Several different types of service levels can be negotiated, including:

- Guaranteed service, which establishes quality of service within deterministic or statistical bounds.
- Predictive service, which estimates quality of service from past behavior.
- Best-effort service, which is used in the absence of available quality parameters.

### SYSTEM CONSIDERATIONS

Designing networks to support multimedia applications involves more than just networking requirements; attention must also be paid to the entire system. Network configurations, for example, do not treat how the bandwidth is handled once it reaches the desktop. Bus speeds and I/O throughput are part of the link between the data source and the users' screen. There are two possible approaches to handling bus speeds and throughput:

- Faster bus and I/O hardware.
- Desktop LANs that eliminate the workstation bus altogether and replace it with an internal packet switch linking the motherboard and peripheral system.

Bandwidth also is handled through compression techniques for images and video that radically reduce the amount of data transmitted and consequently lower bandwidth requirements. Multimedia information is bursty, meaning that some parts of it require higher bandwidth than others. Dynamic bandwidth allocation is useful to lessen the network burden.

Another consideration involves the accommodation of real-time requirements by the operating system. For example, the jitter and slowdown of a movie player may not be due to availability of resources but to a lack of proper scheduling. A music play program often picks up speed when contending programs terminate. Principal requirements for multimedia-capable operating systems are as follows:[5]

- Operating-system resource management must now be based on quality of service and respond to a new class of service that satisfies time constraints and negotiable service levels.[6]
- Real-time CPU scheduling, memory buffer and file management policies to support real-time processing, and support for real-time synchronization.
- Support for standard applications in addition to real-time multimedia applications.
- Low-overhead task management resulting from the need for frequent switching.

## BARRIERS TO MULTIMEDIA NETWORKING

The extensive bandwidth and storage required to transmit multimedia streams coupled with the insufficient bandwidth of existing networks pose one of the major barriers to multimedia networking. The tendency of existing networks to treat individual streams as independent and unrelated units underscores the challenge of and need for effective synchronization.

Another major roadblock in networking existing applications is caused by proprietary development environments, data formats, and runtime environments, and by incompatible proprietary client-server models. The tight coupling among existing devices, data formats, and application program interfaces (API) makes it even more difficult to devise a standard. Heterogeneous delivery platforms pose networking challenges even when multimedia applications are not involved.

Other related concerns that aggravate existing problems associated with networked multimedia applications result from the lack of uniform standards in the following areas:

- **Data capture and recording.** Uniform data formats for graphics, sound, music, text, video, animation, and still images are needed.
- **Data compression and decompression.** Although there is no predominant standard, several organizations have proposed data compression and decompression standards. Among them are MPEG2 and JPEG (Joint Photographic Experts Group).
- **Media storage and retrieval.** In the case of CD-ROMs, digital video discs are needed for portability across platforms.

- **Edit and assembly.** Content description and container standards are either specified as universal object types or through the conventional method of surrounding dissimilar information types with wrappers. Scripted, structural tagging, identification tagging, and other language constructs have emerged as the conventional tools for cross-platform applications development and parameter passing.
- **Presentation.** Uniform customizable presentation standards are needed for maintaining a common look-and-feel across platforms.
- **Transfer or networking.** Asynchronous transfer mode (ATM) and TCP/IP-NG are emerging standards in this area.
- **Multimedia signaling.** Setting up a multimedia conference automatically, without being routed through a common conference bridge, requires a sequence of signaling events, such as call setup/connect and messages. New approaches are needed to support the capability of originating, modifying, and terminating sessions in a network.

## ISSUES IN MULTIMEDIA SYSTEMS PLANNING

The challenge in networking applications is to develop a strategy that works with existing technology and enables management to provide gradual enhancements to the existing infrastructure. Both scalability and integration must be considered during the planning process. In terms of network management support, the technology chosen should support the entire infrastructure.

### Scalability

The network must be capable of scaling smoothly when new nodes, or applications are added; the goal is to simply add resources to the system rather than change the technology. A desirable form of scalability is that resource costs be linear in some measure of performance or usage.

### Integration

Networked applications are designed along the principles of either vertical or horizontal integration. In vertical integration, a dedicated infrastructure is designed for each application so that, for example, the telephone network is kept separate from the computer network.

In contrast, horizontal integration is based on open standards and provides for complexity, management, and portability. It has the following characteristics:

- Use of integrated networks that handle data, audio, and video and are configured to meet application requirements.
- Use of middleware software to provide, for example, directory and authentication services. Although the underlying network may be

heterogeneous, middleware services provide a set of distributed services with standard programming interfaces and communication protocols.

- The user is provided with a diverse set of applications.[7]

### Application/Content Awareness

In general, vertically integrated networks are application-aware (e.g., videoconferencing networks in general know the media type), and horizontal networks are application-blind (e.g., the Internet). Networks are also sometimes content-aware (e.g., a video-on-demand network knows what video is being downloaded).

### PLANNING STRATEGIES

Several approaches to multimedia systems planning are available.[8] Assuming that network resources will grow to meet the demand of the most-stringent combined user-applications, best-effort schemes are sufficient as currently used. Examples include low-profile, low-cost videoconferences, multimedia E-mail, and downloadable files. This approach, however, does not take the entire multimedia system into account.

Another alternative is to overengineer the networks, making bandwidth shortage a rare problem and access to services almost always available. This approach entails providing the user with the latest technologies and a high cost. In addition, leapfrogging computer power and applications resource requirements makes this approach highly susceptible to problems.

A third and generally more effective approach is to use either quality-of-service parameters or resource reservation, or both. For example, high-profile users (e.g., users of investment banking and medical applications) require that some form of resource reservation occur before the execution of multimedia applications.

### CONCLUSION

As networking evolves and voice, video, and data are handled together, networking systems are expected to handle data streams with equal efficiency and reliability from the temporal, synchronization, and functional perspectives. Technology advancements have made users less tolerant of response delays, unreliable service, and lossy data occurring either at the network or at the desktop system.

For these reasons, it is essential that multimedia networks be designed with all computing resources in mind and provide some resource reservation or quality-of-service guarantee. The task before organizations is to find the most flexible, cost-effective method for delivering multimedia applications over networks while also providing for guaranteed quality of service.[9]

**References**

1. D. Messerschmitt, "The Convergence of Telecommunications and Computing: What Are the Implications Today," *IEEE Communications* 84, No. 8 (1996), pp. 1167–1186.
2. L. Delgrossi, *Design of Reservation Protocols for Multimedia Communications,* Norwalk, CT: Kluwer Academic Publishers, 1996.
3. H. J. Stuttgen, "Network Evolution and Multimedia Communication," *IEEE Multimedia*, Fall 1995, pp. 42–59.
4. K. Nahrstedt and R. Steinmetz, "Resource Management in Networked Multimedia Systems," *IEEE Computer*, May 1995, pp. 52–63.
5. M. Mulhauser, "Services, Frameworks, and Paradigms for Distributed Multimedia Applications," *IEEE Multimedia*, Fall 1996, pp. 48–61.
6. J. F. Koegel Buford, *Multimedia Systems*, New York: ACM Press, 1994.
7. Messerschmidt, pp. 1167–1186.
8. D. Mosse, "Resource Reservations in Networked Multimedia Systems," *ACM Computing Surveys* 27, No. 4 (1995), pp. 610–612.
9. R. Platt, "Standards: New Standards Help Multimedia Get off the Ground," *IEEE Multimedia*, Summer 1996, pp. 78–82.

# Chapter 13

# Integrating the Web and Enterprisewide Business Systems

*Chang-Yang Lin*

This chapter examines the various issues related to enterprisewide business applications in the context of the Web. Managers need to be aware of Web capabilities and limitations, including standards of security, performance, backup, and user management, as well as the processes for integrating the Web and corporate applications. Intranet solutions also are discussed.

## INTRODUCTION

The growth of the World Wide Web, or the Web for short, has been phenomenal since the popular multimedia Web browsers Mosaic and Netscape became available in 1994. Some 1996 figures show that 50% of the Web sites are used by commercial corporations, as compared with 13.5% in the previous year, and that percentage is increasing monthly, as more corporations discover the advantages of maintaining an online presence. Commercial Web sites are still mainly used as marketing tools to provide information about company history, locations, and products, as very few Web sites can respond to information inquiries on enterprise or legacy data that is mostly stored in mainframe computers. As for mission-critical applications (e.g., customer order entry, customer invoicing, billing, and accounts receivable), they are almost nonexistent in the Web sites. This is partially because current Web technology is not mature enough to facilitate effective and risk-free transaction processing over the Internet.

With the remarkable growth of the Web, users, both customers and employees, will inevitably request the ability to access enterprise data via the Web as well as to run Web-based enterprisewide applications. Managers have many issues to consider before setting a plan in motion to satisfy these users' needs. In addition to providing background information on the

Web and its capabilities, this chapter describes the four primary components of the Web. Key terms are examined, including HyperText Transfer Protocol (HTTP), HyperText Markup Language (HTML), and Uniform Resource Locator (URL). The chapter also discusses Web limitations and the "unanswered" business questions; the limitations of current technology are identified. Intranets and their use in corporate settings are examined. The chapter introduces approaches for tying the Web and enterprise systems into a coherent system. The development tools and products for the integration are also identified. Finally, the chapter presents planning issues useful in preparing for Web-based enterprisewide business applications.

## THE WEB AND ITS CAPABILITIES

The World Wide Web is a way of organizing the Internet that allows users to search for and retrieve information quickly and easily in a nonlinear way. This information is structured into small chunks, called pages, and it can be displayed page by page through electronic links. Pages may store information in a variety of formats, including numbers, text, graphic images, video, audio, and programs. Essentially, the Web is a collection of independent, yet interrelated, pages wired together by hypermedia links.

Technically, the Web is a kind of client/server networking technology for the purpose of requesting and providing services. The Web is composed of four components: clients, servers, publishing tools, and communication protocols.

### Web Clients

A Web client acts as a front-end browser for requesting service from the servers. Popular Web browsers include Netscape Navigator, Mosaic, and Microsoft's Internet Explorer. These browsers are generally equipped with graphical user interfaces (GUIs), which make Internet navigation relatively easy.

### Web Servers

A Web server is the back-end distributing system that processes and manages requests for service from the clients. Popular Web servers include Netscape's Commerce Server, Microsoft's Internet Information Server, Process Software's Purveyor, and O'Reilly and Associates' WebSite. These Web servers can be evaluated in terms of such factors as performance, security, and manageability.

### Publishing Tools

The HyperText Markup Language (HTML) is an open platform language used to define Web pages. This language includes a set of tags that must be embedded in the text to make up a hypertext document. Thus, creating an HTML page involves primarily the process of tagging documents; HTML encoding can be done by inserting the code in a standard ASCII text file, inserting tags in a word processing program, or using special software programs that build the code for the user. Such programs allow the user to select, through menus and interactive commands, the desired effects; the program then builds the appropriate HTML code.

Although word processors and other text editors can be used to create Web pages from scratch, tools specifically designed to publish Web pages are available to make working with HTML easier. Examples of these publishing products include Interleaf's Cyberleaf, SoftQuad's HotMetal Pro, InContext Systems' Spider, HTML Assistant Pro, HTMLed, and HotDog. All these products automate at least the tagging process by supporting intuitive what-you-see-is-what-you-get screens (WYSIWYG), menu, toolbar, and drag-and-drop interfaces. In addition, some products such as Cyberleaf are equipped with utility programs able to convert Microsoft Word or Word-Perfect documents into HTML pages. The capabilities of these Web publishing tools can be classified loosely into four groups:

- **HTML Editing** These features are used to enforce HTML syntax rules and to manage the HTML tags for formatting text, designing forms, inserting Universal Resource Links (URLs), and calling up photos, video clips, or sound files.
- **Fundamental Word Processing** These features are used to create and edit the text.
- **Previewing and Testing** These features invoke any Web browser to preview or test HTML pages in WYSIWYG form.
- **Document Conversion** These features convert documents from plain ASCII text files or specific software-dependent files into HTML formats.

Whereas creating simple pages using these publishing tools requires no specific skills, rich and interactive online pages will require extensive knowledge and skills to integrate hyperlinks, multimedia, and embedded objects.

### Communication Protocols and URLs

The Web depends on three protocols to facilitate communications. The Internet protocols include TCP/IP, HyperText Transfer Protocol (HTTP), and Universal Resource Locators (URLs) to communicate over the multiple networks. HTTP is the method that Web servers and Web clients use to exchange HTML pages. This method is built on the concept of hypertext/hypermedia that permits the nonlinear accessing of the pages.

URLs define the unique location where a page or service can be found. An example of URL would be http://home.netscape.com/comprod/index.html.

This URL begins with the letters http as the transfer format, which indicates that the last portion of the address (i.e., index.html) is an HTML page. The section after "://," in this case, home.netscape.com, represents the host computer where the information is stored. This is also referred to as the "home" page or the web site of the Netscape Communications Corporation because it can be used as the starting point to explore other pages in detail. Anyone can publish a home page or start at someone's home page. The rest of this URL is a path name to the file.

URLs do not always begin with the letters http. Other formats are also available, including ftp and News. Together, URLs and Internet protocols enable users to reach, in addition to the Web, other Internet resources, such as E-mail, ftp, gopher, telnet, and discussion groups via Web browsers.

### Search Engines

In addition to the above four components, search engines are constantly being created that help users find the Web sites that store desirable information. WAIS (http://www.wais.com), InfoSeek (http://www.infoseek.com), Yahoo (http://www.yahoo.com), WebCrawler (http://www.webcrawler.com), Lycos (http://lycos.cs.cmu.edu) and SavvySearch (http://guaraldi.cs.colostate.edu:2000) are often used for Web searches. These search engines organize their own databases, start their own search mechanisms to support queries ranging from simple query statements to complex formations and even natural-language queries, and they return a list of URLs. Without these searching machines, finding a list of desirable URLs from the vast, unstructured, uncoordinated Web resources is time-consuming and could take the users months of point-and-click navigation to assemble.

### WEB LIMITATIONS: UNANSWERED BUSINESS QUESTIONS

With its capabilities, the Web has been able to facilitate electronic business transactions. Product promotion, customer support, and electronic publishing are a few examples of functions in which Web technology has been successful. Nevertheless, from a business perspective, four fundamental questions, described below, remain unanswered. These questions have prevented many corporations from carrying out business on the Web.

- **Is the Web navigation mechanism effective?** The Web employs the hypertext mechanism for navigation. For a typical query, the user is often required to do some clicking on the mouse to reach a desirable Web site. Once arrived at a Web site, more clicking is required before information may be obtained. Although searching engines have alleviated some of the difficulty in reaching Web sites, users are still required to do a lot of clicking and bouncing around from page to page following pre-designed links. Such a simple navigation mechanism is not flexible enough to give users more specific information and quicker responses to business queries.

- **Is the Web data structure adequate to support information reporting and query responses?** The Web employs a hypermedia data structure in which information is stored in small chunks, called pages. Text documents and other object-oriented data are fitted into these pages. However, traditional record-based business data and numerical data are not suitable for storage in pages, partially because business data, if stored in pages, cannot be easily accessible on a record-by-record basis. In addition, HTML is just not powerful enough to handle record-oriented business data, nor does it allow user-controlled queries to be easily formulated. Consequently, key information cannot be provided under present Web-based data structure.

- **Can enterprise data or legacy data be available on the Web?** To date, enterprise data — mostly transaction oriented — is stored mainly in mainframe computers. Security and performance concerns are two major reasons why enterprise data is mostly inaccessible from the Web. Methods and techniques are being developed to bring mainframe-based data into the Web. At present, these methods and techniques are not feasible and therefore transaction-related information on order status, invoice, bill of lading, and payment will mostly remain unanswered.

- **Is the Web suitable for mission-critical business applications?** The Web is not set up for on-line transaction processing and has failed to meet the standards of security, performance, backup, and user management. For example, Web technology is inadequate to perform the five security-related tasks (i.e., authentication, certification, confirmation, nonrepudiation, and encryption); therefore, an interactive transaction between trading partners is not reliable. Besides the security concern, other key factors have also contributed to a lack of Web-based mission-critical business applications. These factors include stateless conditions during transaction processing, questionable bandwidth to handle real interactive transactions, and lack of user preparedness for electronic commerce.

## INTRANETS

Despite a lack of legacy data on the Web and immature Web technology for effective transaction processing, an increasing number of corporations are now turning to the Web as their IS solution for addressing business problems within corporations. It is predicted that internal Web or intranet usage will surpass external Internet usage by the year 2000. The key factors for adopting intranets are open platform standards (e.g., HTTP and HTML), ease of installing Web servers and using Web clients, and multimedia capabilities.

The range of intranet applications that can be developed is virtually unlimited. Currently, corporations are deploying intranets as a way to organize their internal communications. Examples of these intranets are:

- Web-based internal E-mail systems.
- Project planning, monitoring, and reporting.
- Forums for brainstorming, collaborations, or problem solving.
- Delivering marketing materials, training materials, or software products.
- On-line customer information queries.
- On-line human resource queries on employee benefits, company policies, personnel information, employee and telephone directories, job listings, and training and education workshops.

One main concern of deploying intranet applications on the Web is security. Currently, several measures are being installed, including firewalls. Most firewall products focus on keeping external Internet users from getting into intranet applications. Others ensure that users are authorized to access the information they seek.

## INTEGRATING THE WEB AND ENTERPRISE SYSTEMS

The process of integrating the Web and enterprisewide systems or building some intranet applications can be approached from two directions. One involves converting enterprise data into hypermedia pages. The other involves building a link between these two systems. Regardless of which approach is used, the goal remains the same; that is, making enterprise data and the various business applications accessible through Web browsers. The use of Web browsers eliminates concerns about heterogeneous hardware and various operating systems over the Internet and intranets as well.

Building links to tie the Web and enterprise systems into a coherent system is much more feasible than converting to hypermedia pages. This is partially because the linkage programs will not interfere with the normal operations of enterprise systems for supporting day-to-day business activities and management decisions. Both researchers and vendors have been placing their emphasis on developing architectures and tools to support the construction of the linkage programs.

### Converting to Hypermedia Pages

Enterprise systems are characterized by a variety of data structures, including traditional flat files, relational databases, IMS databases, object-oriented databases, and special package-related files (e.g., spreadsheet files, song clips, and photo images). Theoretically, this data can all be converted into hypermedia pages to support applications ranging from information inquiry to transaction processing over the Web.

Although current technology is not mature enough to support certain tasks effectively over the Web (e.g., complex interactive transaction processing), migrating key enterprise data to the Web will certainly give customers speedy query responses for such applications as marketing and electronic cataloging.

## Building Linkage Programs

Building the linkage programs to tie the Web and enterprise systems into a coherent system involves two similar approaches: augmenting HTML programs and augmenting enterprise programs.

**Augmenting HTML Programs.** The augmented HTML programs include a data-access subprogram. In addition to the data-access function, many augmented programs may include programs to facilitate interactive input and to merge the enterprise data into pages for presentation. These subprograms may contain SQL statements or procedure codes, called scripts. Examples of these tools or products include DECOUX, SWOOP, OpenUI and OpenWeb, WebDBC, and Open Horizon's Connection for Java.

DECOUX supports an augmented form of HTML that includes embedded SQL statements. SWOOP supports the generation and maintenance of Web systems that store information in an ORACLE relational database. The development tools OpenUI and OpenWeb, WebDBC, and Open Horizon's Connection for Java are based on the function-call models that let developers integrate prebuilt, vendor-driven key components together using C++ or other nonprogramming tools. These tools are now being investigated for applications such as hotel reservation, payroll, and human resource.

### Augmenting Enterprise Programs with Embedded HTML Statements.

Advanced features of HTML, such as forms, are embedded into enterprise programs and are used to capture input transaction data from Web clients. The input data are then fed into enterprise programs for processing. For example, Visual Object COBOL 1.0 by Micro Focus uses CGI to link HTML forms to COBOL programs and therefore let COBOL programs take input from HTML forms.

Besides using the above tools, Java, Sun's object-based open-system language, can be used to create the linkage programs to tie key components together. Furthermore, Java is said to be able to create Web-enabling interactive applications from scratch.

## CHALLENGES AND STRATEGY ISSUES

As commercial Web sites and users continue to grow at an incredible rate, corporations are faced with an opportunity: Incorporating Web technology into enterprisewide applications to improve their competitiveness in the global market. The following is a list of questions and suggested solutions that address this opportunity:

- **How do corporations attract potential customers via the Internet and the Web?** They can build a presence on the Web, and then expand and enhance their Web pages.
- **How do corporations make enterprise data accessible via the Web to enhance service effectiveness for both employees and customers?** They can move enterprise data into a HTML format, use Web technology to connect legacy data, build search and index mechanisms to enterprise data, or develop intranet applications.
- **How do corporations deal with the barriers slowing down the implementation of enterprisewide systems, such as multiplatforms, security, bandwidth, and multiple development tools?** Organizations can plan both external Web and internal Web as an ideal solution for multiplatforms or make intranets a solution for addressing the internal communication concerns. They can also install security tools or firewalls to prevent unauthorized users from reaching vital legacy data or applications and implement systems to track appropriate technologies, such as Web development tools, Web servers, and security tools.
- **What strategies will corporations need to develop to remain competitive?** They can recognize the Web as one part of IS solution, integrate traditional systems and Web-based systems. Managers can support a new intranet development environment. Organizations can prepare for electronic commerce and provide staffing and training for Web technology.

Regardless of Web technology's effectiveness for certain tasks, the rapid growth of the Web and its impact in the global market should not be viewed lightly. Facing these challenges and thus effectively deploying the Web to empower users requires planning. The following sections expand on the previous suggestions, for better planning.

## BUILDING A PRESENCE ON THE WEB

Corporations should position themselves on the Internet's Web by building home pages without any delay. As competitors' presences on the Web increase, one way to guarantee the failure of the above challenges is to adopt a "wait on it" approach.

## EXPANDING AND ENHANCING THE PAGES

Simply migrating paper-based product catalogs to the pages and recording CEO's welcome messages is insufficient to attract potential customers to visit the organization's Web sites repeatedly. Corporations need to think new ways to both enhance and expand the pages. These may include:

- **Making key enterprise data accessible via Web browsers**  Enterprise data always serves as a foundation from which information can be derived. Both predesigned and *ad hoc* queries on key enterprise data must be considered to reflect friendliness and flexibility.
- **Providing additional services and facilities from the pages**  Examples of these services include customer and technical support, downloading reports, forms, policies and procedures, or software products; on-line documentation. Examples of facilities may include a registration form to collect users' information and interests, a special form to allow the users comment on products, and a platform to facilitate interactive communications.

## PLAN INTRANET APPLICATIONS

How the Web is used within a corporation must be planned. Although many applications may be developed based on Web technology, those that involve communication, information sharing, and information distribution should be planned and built first.

## PREPARE FOR ELECTRONIC COMMERCE

As Web technologies continue to mature, the solutions designed to prevent security breaches, stateless transactions, and performance concerns will be gradually available. Thus, corporations must prepare for electronic commerce by making enterprisewide applications — including mission-critical applications — Web-capable. This may include building Web-capable applications from scratch, linking the enterprise data to the Web, and building the linkages between existing enterprise applications and the Web.

Corporations should identify and plan the projects for electronic commerce. Information reporting or inquiry projects may be built first, because linking SQL databases to the Web will be easier to do. Designing special searching mechanisms on enterprise data will also be necessary for fast inquiry response.

Building the linkages between existing enterprise applications and the Web can be performed next. The proven tools and techniques necessary for building such linkages should be evaluated and selected. Depending on the specific needs of the individual corporations, applications to be linked are ranked.

## EDUCATION AND TRAINING

Both developers and users must accept proper training for the emerging Web technology. Overall, developers and users should understand how the Internet and the Web can be accessed, used to gather information, and implemented to create business opportunities. The users who are responsible for publishing must learn HTML tools to create pages. Developers must learn the development tools to reengineer applications on the Web. Developers mastering the tools, including such programming languages as C++ and Java, will be essential for successful Web-enabled transformation.

## CONCLUSION

Web capabilities are extensive and growing more complex and sophisticated at a rapid rate. To keep abreast of such changes, systems developers must consider such factors as security, transfer protocols and languages, and development tools and environments. All capabilities must be evaluated in context of the enterprise — its goals as well as its propensity for risk-taking. Only with a careful weighing of the advantages and disadvantages can an organization move into the technology of the World Wide Web.

# Chapter 14
# Cost Allocation for Communications Networks

*Keith A. Jones*

Data centers, when under efficient management, provide services to a business enterprise that are recovered by a cost allocation system that distributes these costs to customer business units. Operational expenses can be allocated across data communications network infrastructures along the lines of chargeback systems established for the host processing environments.

Most communications managers are already very much aware of all the host system resources that must be charged back to their users. This includes the most common direct system use charge categories (e.g., host CPU, system printer, DASD storage, and tape drive units) as well as indirect resource costs that must be billed (e.g., space, utilities, and technical support services).

Many communications managers may not be as well aware of the resources that must be charged to recover costs across host-linked enterprisewide information networks — or the impact that such networks can have on their host resource costs. Use of these networks can result in new categories of host data center costs that must be recovered through more complex pricing methods. Although managers can readily accommodate any of the more conventional unexpected changes in data center operating expense (e.g., a rise in utility or paper costs) by using an industry-standard strategy that adjusts availability of host access to match available capacity, they are often uncomfortable at the prospect of chargeout across their host network links. This is primarily because they are not as aware of their options for recovering unexpected changes in costs of supporting an enterprisewide data network.

0-8493-9965-3/99/$0.00+$.50
© 1999 by CRC Press LLC

## CHARGEABLE RESOURCES

At first, it is easier for a communications manager to focus on effects to support chargeback of direct network costs on services involving equipment with very short paybacks and high plug-compatibility. The ideal initial resources are modems, terminals, printers, and if already in place, a central help desk telephone line to contact vendors.

The ideal arrangement is to leverage the volume-purchasing power of the central-site data center to obtain the lowest possible direct cost for the business client users. In addition to increasing economies of scale in purchase of hardware, software, and supplies, the data center can offer a central focal point for vendor contacts, negotiations, and coordination of maintenance services — at lower pass-through costs than can be obtained by independent arrangements.

Managers should begin viewing their function as more than just a service bureau for data processing services. The network-linked host data center provides expanded opportunities to offer an enterprisewide range of business information management support services (e.g., computer systems hardware and software purchasing, inventory control, financial analysis, and physical plant engineering).

Especially if existing departments within the organization already offer such basic services, the data center does not have to provide these services directly. Instead, management should increasingly position and present its overall operation as a ready and effective conduit to help enable each business enterprise client to tap into — and leverage — existing packets of expertise within the organization. Communications managers are in a unique position to identify common areas of operational business needs and present both internal and external sources as options to help pool costs.

Regardless of the source of the resources that make up the information enterprise network and host system costs that are to be allocated across the client service base, the primary consideration of the data center manager must be that of defining the categories of use that are to be charged. The chargeable resource categories must be easily understood by the customers who are to be billed and must be measurable by use statistics that can be readily accumulated for the review of customers in their billing statement. This is true regardless of whether the costs are to be allocated according to direct line item unit measure charges or indirect fee assignments.

As with the host chargeback system, it is first of all necessary to be able to identify — and track — all possible network services and resources. Once there is a reasonable assurance that a system of resource accounting procedures has been established that does not allow any network cost or any contingent host system cost to escape unaccounted for, data center managers can consolidate individual categories of network services and resource costs into network cost pools suitable for use in pricing out network chargeback billings.

The definition of these cost pools must be sufficiently detailed to support future strategy for directing patterns of desirable network use in a manner that is predictable and compatible to host cost-efficiency and cost-containment procedures. In other words, categories of resource that are identified to network customers for cost allocation purposes must serve to increase customer awareness of the types of expenses involved in managing the network, regardless of how much is to be billed to recover costs of each resource type.

## NETWORK RESOURCE CATEGORIES

The chargeable resources for enterprisewide network cost allocation can absorb some of the data center resources (e.g., printing, database use, data media, and data center operational services) as well as the resources required for the network. The most important network resource categories are discussed in the following sections.

**Cable.** The costs of cabling to connect enterprisewide network devices can easily be the largest and most complicated category of all network management expenses. Among the available options are:

- *Coaxial cable.* An example is the cable used in IBM 3270 terminals. It is expensive but extremely reliable and compatible with most of the existing network methods. It is often kept in stock by data centers.
- *Unshielded twisted-pair cable.* Also known as telephone wire, this is inexpensive but subject to interference; it often causes host-linkage error.
- *Shielded twisted-pair cable.* Although similar to the unshielded telephone wire, this is wrapped like coaxial cable. It is moderately expensive and moderately dependable.
- *Fiber-optic cable.* This has the widest possible range of applications, and it is the most reliable cable option.
- *Wireless networks.* These are increasingly feasible options, especially when rapid installation is desired and the physical layout of the business enterprise facility is suitable.

**Linkages.** In network terms, these are interconnectors, or plug-compatible interfaces, between networks and host lines. Linkage components include:

- *Plugs.* These include cable connectors and data switches, splitters and sharing devices, wire ribbons, and all other interface linkage hardware. This is typically the most overhead-intensive cost category in network management because it requires inventory control and planning to have every possible plug-type on hand.
- *Modems.* Modems and all other dial-up line management devices as well as communications line multiplexing hardware are most critical to line-speed costs.
- *Wire boxes.* These involve all the business enterprise physical plant or facility-determined access hardware and management.

*Workstations.* This category includes microcomputer configurations that are connected at each local network node or station. The components are:

- *Terminals.* These can include intelligent workstations through gateway servers.
- *Storage.* Storage elements can include the fixed hard disk (if available at the workstation node), diskettes, and any dedicated tape or CD-ROM storage devices.
- *Personal printer.* This is included if a dedicated printer is attached.

*Servers.* This category always comprises an intelligent workstation with the minimum CPU and storage required by the particular network control methods used. It includes:

- *File-server hardware.* This includes the file-server workstation and all network boards that it controls, including LAN boards and host gateway link boards as well as fax boards and other specialized hardware.
- *File-server software.* This includes the network file management control software and shared applications.

**Storage.** High-volume mass storage is frequently needed for backup and archival purposes, which may involve technical support and specialized hardware or software well beyond the usual range of support for LAN administrators. This may include optical memory, imaging, CD-ROM jukeboxes, or other advanced technology with many gigabytes of storage capacity. The need for this technology is increasingly likely if the client network involves graphics, engineering, or any other application requiring intensive backup cycles and complicated version control. The use of high-volume mass storage is usually controlled from a dedicated server that automatically manages files and application software. The client-server may be a minicomputer that functions as a front-end processor to manage enterprise network message requests for real-time access to host programming functions or a backend processor to manage online access to a host database.

**Communications.** This is by far the most cost-intensive network resource. Telecommunications can make or break the network chargeback system, and unfortunately it is an area in which a data center may have limited options.

Much can be learned about network billing from a local telecommunications company, often at great expense.

**LAN Administration Support.** This can include the salaries of the local LAN administrator and the LAN help desk personnel, the costs of training, and the costs of host-based support of LAN inventory, purchasing, billing or any other service provided by the data center. It can also involve both short-term and long-term leasing of network hardware or software, diagnostics, or user training. This category can be large or small, depending on the client. In some cases, clients may prefer to provide some of the LAN technical support; in others, a data center may provide it all.

### Internet Gateway Access

Whether the data center network is SNA or TCP/IP dictates whether it is an option to establish the enterprise's own Internet gateway, which can cost as much as 10 intelligent workstations. That gateway, however, can be cost justified if the enterprise organization does any kind of business on the Internet.

Typically, business on the Internet takes one or more of three forms:

E-mail, user news groups, or a home page on the World Wide Web (WWW, or just the Web). A dedicated gateway requires substantial UNIX-related technical expertise to establish and maintain. A more viable option is a dedicated line to an online service account, which normally costs no more than a single workstation, and internal enterprise customers can still be supported in the three major functional business support areas.

Both a dedicated gateway and a dedicated line can usually be financed using long-term methods. If Internet access is a legitimate enterprise business need, it can be more than easily justified. If not, until the demand (and real need) for Internet access can be precisely predicted, it is often feasible to simply pass through direct charge billing of departmental accounts on online services with Internet access, such as Compuserve, Prodigy, or America Online.

### EXPENSE CATEGORIES

The next step in developing an enterprisewide network cost-allocation system is to assign all expenses into a manageable number of nonoverlapping categories. Most managers can develop a matrix of network resource categories that has a direct correspondence to their host data center

| Expenses \\ Resources | Stations | Servers | Linkages | Storage | Telecom |
|---|---|---|---|---|---|
| **Fixed Costs**<br>Equipment<br>Facilities<br>Insurance<br>Interest<br>Maintenance<br>Salary | | | | | |
| **Variable Costs**<br>Consultants<br>Data Base Support<br>Help Desk<br>LAN Support<br>Paper<br>Supplies<br>Telecom Support<br>Vendors | | | | | |
| **Surcharges**<br>Diagnostics<br>Disaster Recovery<br>Documentation<br>Planning<br>Prevention<br>Tuning<br>Training | | | | | |
| **TOTAL COSTS** | | | | | |

**Exhibit 1. Sample Enpterprisewide Expense Matrix.**

resource assignment matrix. If there is no existing host data center expense matrix to use as a model for defining the network cost allocation expense matrix, the communications manager can begin by grouping the basic categories of network expenses. Exhibit 1 shows a basic network expense assignment matrix.

There are two important considerations. First, each of the categories in the expense matrix must correspond to budget line items that will be forecasted and tracked by a business enterprise financial controller or accountants assigned to audit network costs. Second, expense line items must be defined so they are clearly separated from all other items and there is limited opportunity to assign expenses to the wrong category or, even worse, duplicate direct and indirect costs.

Although the manager should consult with the financial controllers who audit the network before preparing the network cost assignment matrix, the data center manager must usually define how the resource allocation procedures are to be administered, which include assumptions about the methods for measurement and assignment of enterprisewide network resource use and billing obligations. The proposed network resource cost allocation matrix should also be reviewed with the prospective network customers. In addition, the anticipated categories of host-lined data network expenses should be reviewed by the business enterprise organizational management before any pricing strategy or rate structure is determined for the enterprisewide network cost chargeout.

## RATE DETERMINATION

To expand enterprisewide business information services and allocate host system costs across interconnected distributed networks, managers must change their fundamental view from a centralized focus to a decentralized one. This change in focus must include a reorientation to accommodate market-driven as well as demand-driven operations planning.

Communications managers are increasingly in a position of competition with alternative outside vendor sources for every product and service that has traditionally been a vital part of their exclusive business organizational domain. It is therefore necessary for data centers to begin defining their pricing structure on not only what chargeable resources there are but also how each of the resources is charged to help achieve strategic market advantage over the competition.

Data centers can no longer simply apply a straight distribution formula to recover costs but must also factor in potential future costs associated with the risk that new technology will be available at lower cost and that business enterprise users may bypass the data center. Unless the manager is also an expert in both financial management and risk management, this usually means an increasing emphasis on leasing or subcontracting most new services and resources at short-term premium rates, until a sufficient economy of scale can be achieved by bundling enterprisewide data network resource demands to reduce risks as well as costs.

In some cases, host-linked network domains may be large enough to achieve the break- even economies of scale quickly, especially if sufficiently large proprietary data stores are involved. In most cases, however, the process will be more like a traditional tactical penetration to achieve a dominant share of mature, nongrowth market segments, also known as buyer's markets. The management of the central site host data center must go to the business enterprise customer rather than the other way around.

If a data center cannot package centralized services as superior to the competition, not all costs may be recovered. Furthermore, the ultimate determination of what constitutes a chargeable resource is not simply a data center expense that must be recovered but is now also an information network service or resource that a business enterprise customer must want to buy.

The manner of rate determination is directly determined by the network resource allocation strategy and chargeback system cost-control objectives. The most basic consideration determining the rate structure is whether data center management has decided to fully recover network costs on the basis of actual use or to distribute indirect costs of a network resource pool evenly among all of its users. This consideration applies to each network resource category as well as to each category of network customer.

As a basic rule of thumb, the decision of whether to recover costs on the basis of actual use or to distribute costs evenly among business enterprise users is largely determined by the extent to which a resource is equally available for shared, concurrent use or is reserved exclusively for use by an individual network user. If the resource is shared, the rate structure is based on forecasted patterns of use, with sufficient margin to absorb potential error in the forecasted demand as well as the potential probability of drop-off in demand for network services. On the other hand, rate structures can be based on underwriting network capital equipment or financing service-level agreements, which provide greater security for full recovery of all costs from an individual business enterprise customer on the basis of annualized use charges, with provisions for additional setup fees and disconnection fees to recover unforeseen and marginal costs.

As a matter of practical reality, the decision on which of the two methods of rate determination to use must also take into account the availability of dependable enterprisewide network use measurements to support direct line charges. It is also critical to first determine whether the costs that must be recovered will vary depending on the level of use (e.g., the pass-through costs of data transmission over a public telecommunications carrier line) or will be fairly well fixed regardless of whether they are fully used at all times when they are available (e.g., the on-call network technical support cost of labor). It is also important to attempt to define all assumptions on which each resource cost recovery strategy is based; this identifies all the conditions that would necessitate a change in the rate structure and exactly how each cost will be recovered in the event of major changes in enterprise information network use or underlying rate strategy assumptions.

The degree to which the enterprisewide network chargeback pricing can be easily understood by the customer largely determines how effectively all costs are recovered. It is also critical that business enterprise clients be aware of the goals of each rate decision. Depending on how responsibly they use the network, each individual enterprise network customer can help or hurt overall efficiency of the LAN as well as all interconnected LANs and the host.

## SUMMARY

Opportunities exist to broaden the data center's customer base through identifying and establishing chargeback methods for host-linked enterprisewide information networks. These new categories, however, require more complicated pricing methods. Increasing economies of scale make network chargeout a valuable strategy for the communications manager and staff. Managers should:

1. Initially focus on services based on equipment with short paybacks and high compatibility, such as modems, terminals, printers, and a help desk phone line to vendors.
2. Begin viewing their function as more than service bureau for data processing. Instead, the data center manager should position the data center as a resource for where expertise can be found in the organization.
3. Identify and track all network services and resources, including cable, linkages, workstations, servers, storage, communications, and LAN administration support.
4. Establish, if possible, the organization's own Internet gateway.
5. Develop a matrix for defining network cost allocation expenses, to assign all expenses into nonoverlapping categories.

# Section III
# Networking Technology

In the area of communications, the terms networking and technology are closely related to one another. Technology provides the driving force for changes in networking, and communications provided by networks enables researchers at distributed locations to collaborate on projects which, in many instances, are designed to enhance networking. Recognizing the preceding, a handbook covering communications management would be far from complete unless a section was devoted to networking technology.

In this section we will focus our attention upon technologies that have a significant effect upon networking. The first chapter in this section, "New Modem Technologies and Trends," is particularly suitable for inclusion in this section as we can paraphrase Mark Twain by saying that "the demise of modems has been greatly exaggerated." By understanding the features and capabilities associated with new modem technologies, we will be able to use them in a more efficient and effective manner.

The second chapter in this section covers an old technology which is rapidly gaining acceptance due to the growth in multimedia applications. That technology is multicasting, and the chapter "Multicast Networking" provides us with detailed information concerning the application of multicast technology to electronic distribution.

Over the past few years the growth in the use of Frame Relay has reached double digits. While the reliability and near universal availability of Frame Relay contributes to its success, it is not problem free. Recognizing this, the chapter "Frame Relay Testing and Training" is included as the third chapter in this section. After a brief review of Frame Relay, this chapter provides you with a detailed overview of testing methods. In addition, the often overlooked value of training is covered in this chapter which, when combined with testing, can provide you with the tools and techniques necessary to identify and correct network problems when operating in a Frame Relay environment.

Continuing our section on networking technology, the fourth and fifth chapters were selected to provide readers with information concerning methods to more efficiently construct and operate networks transporting multimedia. In the fourth chapter, titled "Working with Images in Client/Server Environments," we are introduced to the basic composition of images which governs their transmission time and data storage requirements. This information is then used to illustrate how several techniques can be employed to manage the storage and transmission challenges associated with the use of images in a client/server environment. Picking up where the prior chapter ends, the fifth chapter, titled "Voice and Video on the LAN," looks at specific LAN technologies for integrating voice and video. In this chapter the use of ATM, LAN switches, and hybrid ATM networks are discussed.

Everyone looks favorably upon a technology which enables you to perform a networking operation that may not be possible without the use of the technology, which can translate to savings on your networking budget. One such technology is inverse multiplexing and is covered in the chapter "Inverse Multiplexing ATM, Bit by Bit." In this chapter we will examine how we can aggregate two or more T1 or E1 transmission facilities to access an ATM wide area network in a manner such that WAN access does not become a bottleneck between linking a LAN to an ATM wide area network transmission facility.

In the seventh and eight chapters in this section we will turn our attention to evolving technologies that enable the bandwidth limitations of the proverbial *last mile* loop from telephone company central offices to subscribers to be overcome. In the chapter "Hybrid Fiber/Coaxial Networks" we will examine how cable TV can be used as a high speed data delivery transmission facility. In the chapter "Choosing Asymmetrical Digital Subscriber Lines" we will examine how evolving technology permits the standard telephone wire connection to support data delivery at a megabit per second data rate. Since both technologies provide the bandwidth necessary to move multimedia to the home or office, the next chapter in this section, entitled "Multimedia Networking Technologies," represents a logical follow-on to those chapters. In "Multimedia Networking Technologies" we will examine a variety of networking technologies associated with both LANs and WANs and their suitability for distributing multimedia information.

In concluding this section we will focus our attention upon security and Windows NT. In the chapter entitled "Computer System and Data Network Security" we will first examine the six basic functions of data security. This will be followed by methods we can use to enhance network security, and, in the event our best efforts should fail, how we can recover from unauthorized access to include data misuse and damage. In concluding this section we will turn our attention to Windows NT. In the chapter "Windows NT Architecture" we will obtain an appreciation for the composition and function of Windows NT core modules. In this chapter we will become familiar with the manner by which Windows NT supports security and networking, and how its modular design provides users with both portability and scalability. Due to the growing influence of this operating system, the concluding chapter in this section will provide us with the foundation to make intelligent decisions concerning the use of this operating system.

-

# Chapter 15

# New Modem Technologies and Trends

*Nathan J. Muller*

Not too long ago, the general consensus was that modems would be supplanted by ISDN terminal adapters connected to digital lines. Now, not only is modem use growing, but new technologies such as sound boards, message centers, and fax capabilities have revitalized this market segment.

## INTRODUCTION

Traditionally, modems have been used for transferring files, accessing bulletin boards, and connecting users to the Internet. Today, there are multifunction modems that include sound boards, message centers, and fax capabilities. There are also modems that work over wireless and cable television (CATV) networks, and modems that are capable of supporting a voice conversation and data transfer simultaneously over the same line. Very soon there will be modems that double the current speed of 28.8K bps to 56K bps, facilitating multimedia communication.

Even with all these innovations, modems still perform the same basic functions — modulation and demodulation. They convert (i.e., modulate) the digital signals generated by standalone or networked PCs into analog signals suitable for transmission over dialup telephone lines or voice-grade leased lines. Another modem, located at the receiving end of the transmission, converts (i.e., demodulates) the analog signals back into their original digital form.

## THE EVOLUTION OF PACKAGING

For years, modems have been available in external, rackmount, or internal versions. But even in packaging, there is plenty of room for innovation.

## External Modems

External modems are standalone hardware devices that connect to a microcomputer's communications port via telephone cabling. They are equipped with front-panel status indicators that inform users of modem activities. Rackmount modems are full- or half-cards that reside in an equipment frame. From there, the individual modems connect to the various PCs. External modems typically reside on an office desk, while the rackmount versions are located in a convenient equipment cabinet or wiring closet for easy troubleshooting and maintenance.

## Internal Modems

Internal modems, which insert into an available expansion slot inside the computer, are best suited for users who rely extensively on the wide area networkwide area network (WAN) to do their jobs. For users who require only occasional access to the WAN, companies can save money by equipping a communications server with a pool of modems that can be shared by many users on a first-come, first-served basis.

## PCMCIA Cards

Another type of internal modem is the size of a credit card and standardized by the Personal Computer Memory Card International Association (PCMCIA). Both wireline and wireless modems are available as plug-in cards to the PCMCIA Type II slots in portable computers. There are even multifunction PCMCIA cards that combine the modem and LAN adapter (Ethernet or Token Ring) on the same card, giving users more connectivity options without requiring an additional card and using up the second PCM-CIA slot included with most laptop and notebook computers.

There are also PCMCIA cards that connect to various wireless messaging services. They have a built-in antenna and can even act as standalone receivers when the computer is turned off. Some cards are programmable, allowing users to access or receive messages from different wireless services, including those based on cellular digital packet data (CDPD) cellular digital packet data and packet radio services such as ARDIS and RAM Mobile Data. Some wireless modems can automatically identify the type of modem protocol used at the receiving end and adjust their own operation and speed accordingly.

## CDPD Modems

Like wireline modems, wireless modems are packed with functionality. There are CDPD modems, for example, that work with any DOS- or Windows-based computer, supporting V.22bis, V.23, V.23bis, V.42bis, Group 3 fax and V.17 wireline fax and data protocols, plus Microcom's MNP-10 cellular protocol or Paradyne's Enhanced Cellular Throughput (ECT) protocol.

## Other Multiport Modems

Another new way vendors are packaging modems is by integrating them with integrated services digital network (ISDN) terminal adapters. This allows users to communicate with conventional dialup services at up to 28.8K bps and also take advantage of ISDN when possible — all without cluttering the desktop or having to use up scarce slots in the PC.

Multiport modems of this kind are being introduced for the corporate environment. U.S. Robotics, for example, offers two models that dynamically support both digital and analog connections. Aimed at telecommunications managers who use a lot of perfectly good analog lines on their networks, the company's 8-port MP/8 I-Modem and 16-port MP/16 I-Modem can handle analog and ISDN calls, making them suitable for companies that are rolling out ISDN connections to analog users. The modems actually determine whether they are connected to an analog or digital line and operate in that mode automatically. The MP modems act as a front end to existing terminal servers. With a channel-aggregation feature, users can add up to 64K bps of bandwidth over each ISDN link during Internet access or other tasks that call for additional bandwidth.

## Multimedia Extensions (MMX) Technology

The next step in modem packaging is to eliminate the need for dedicated hardware altogether. Intel is trying to do precisely this with its native signal processing (NSP) initiative that embeds software emulation of modem and sound card hardware in the Pentium chip. Known as MMX technology, the idea is to allow any Windows application to have access to features implemented in a special driver — to send and receive E-mail and faxes or to play sound files — with no modem or specialized hardware, aside from the main CPU. In effect, NSP will give every Pentium PC the ability to manage basic communications and multimedia tasks, which in turn will let software developers add these features to their applications without having to worry about whether customers have the necessary hardware.

Intel's MMX technology is what makes native signal processing on the Pentium platform feasible. A 100-MHz Pentium would have to dedicate 60% of its resources to V.34 modem processing. With MMX, a 200-MHz Pentium would need to use only 20% of its resources, which is insignificant to most users.

## Host Signal Processor Modems

Motorola is about to enter the emerging market for host signal processor (HSP) modems, which rely heavily on software and the processing power of the host PC. Rather than relying on its own digital signal processor (DSP), this type of modem is based on a less-expensive application-specific integrated circuit (ASIC) and takes advantage of a PC's central Pentium chip for processing power. Motorola plans to introduce an HSP product line geared toward remote access, telecommuters, and mobile workers. The product line will eventually go beyond analog modems to include ISDN terminal adapters and digital subscriber line modems. HSP technology has been around for several years, but has only recently become feasible because of the growing availability of faster desktop computers based on the Pentium chip.

## MODEM FEATURES

In an effort to distinguish theirs from others on the market, modem manufacturers are continually redesigning their products to incorporate the latest standards, enhancing existing features, and adding new ones. Advancements in modulation techniques, error correction, data compression, and diagnostics are among the continuing efforts of modem manufacturers.

### Modulation Techniques

The modulation technique has a lot to do with the speed and reliability of data transmission. Modems convey information by exchanging analog symbols, each of which represents multiple bits.

The symbol rate for modems operating over ordinary phone lines is limited to about 3,400 bps. When a modem has data to transmit, a bit sequence is selected from a pool of available symbols to represent that particular sequence. By packing more data bits into one symbol, modems can achieve higher bit rates. For example, the V.34+ specification squeezes up to 9.8 bits per symbol, vs. only 8.4 bits for V.34. Under ideal line conditions, this equates to 33.6K bps for V.34+ modems and 28.8K bps for V.34 modems.

Increasing the size of the symbol pool allows the modem to adjust to a range of noise conditions, which results in an overall higher speed. The V.34+ offers 1,664 symbols, whereas V.34 offers only 960. The higher number of symbols makes it easier for the receiving modem to differentiate data from noise, which also results in more reliable transmission.

Both V.34+ and V.34 modems use adaptive techniques that enable them to learn about the quality of the line and make adjustments. For example, the sending and receiving modems exchange a set of signals to determine the maximum transmission rate on a particular circuit before user data is actually sent. They also compensate for signal loss detected on a line. If the line exhibits signal loss, the modem can guess how a signal is likely to be degraded across a circuit and boost the signal accordingly to offset the impairment.

These techniques do not guarantee higher speeds and error-free transmission. They only optimize performance on a line-by-line basis.

## Speed

Regardless of manufacturer or standards, the advertised data rate of most modems does not always coincide with the actual data rate. This is because the quality of the connection has a lot to do with the speed of the modem.

If the connection is noisy, for example, a 28.8K-bps modem may have to step down to 24K bps (i.e., "fall back") to continue transmitting data. Likewise, a 19.2K-bps modem more frequently operates at 9.6K bps when the line gets too noisy.

Although some modems are able to sense improvements in line quality and automatically step up to higher data rates (i.e., "fall forward"), consistently noisy lines may mean that the user is not getting the return on investment that was anticipated at the time of purchase. If the 19.2K-bps modem works at only half the data rate most of the time, then the user has paid double the price for what is essentially a 9.6K-bps modem.

## Error Correction

Networks and telecommunications carriers often contain disturbances with which modems must deal or, in some cases, overcome. These disturbances include attenuation distortion, envelope delay distortion, phase jitter, impulse noise, background noise, and harmonic distortion — all of which negatively affect data transmission. To alleviate the disturbances encountered with transferring data over leased lines (without line conditioning) and dialup lines, most products include an error-correction technique in which a processor puts a bit stream through a series of complex algorithms before data transmission.

The most prominent error-correction technique has been the Microcom Networking Protocol (MNP), which uses the cyclic redundancy check (CRC) method for detecting packet errors, and requests retransmissions when necessary.

Link access procedure B (LAP-B), a similar technique, is a member of the high level data link control (HDLC) protocol family, the error-correcting protocol in X.25 for packet-switched networks. LAP-M is an extension to that standard for modem use and is the core of the International Telecommunications Union (ITU) V.42 error-correcting standard. This standard also supports MNP Classes 1 through 4. Full conformance with the V.42 standard requires that both LAP-M and MNP Classes 1 through 4 are supported by the modem. Virtually all modems currently made by major manufacturers conform with the V.42 standard.

The MNP is divided into nine classes. Only the first four deal with error recovery, which is why only those four are referenced in V.42. The other five classes deal with data compression. The MNP error recovery classes perform the following functions:

- MNP Classes 1 to 3 packetize data and, the manufacturer claims, ensure 100% data integrity.
- MNP Class 4 achieves up to 120% link throughput efficiency via Microcom's Adaptive Packet Assembly and Data Phase Optimization, which automatically adjusts packet size relative to line conditions and reduces protocol overhead.

### Data Compression

With the adoption of the V.42bis recommendation by the ITU in 1988, there is a single data compression standard — Lempel-Ziv. This algorithm compresses most data types, including executable programs, graphics, numerics, ASCII text, or binary data streams. Compression ratios of 4:1 can be achieved, although actual throughput gains from data compression depend on the types of data being compressed. Text files are the most likely to yield performance gains, followed by spreadsheet and database files. Executable files are most resistant to compression algorithms because of the random nature of the data.

### Diagnostics and Other Features

Most modems perform a series of diagnostic tests to identify internal and transmission line problems. Most modems also offer standard loopback tests, such as local analog, local digital, and remote digital loopback. Once a modem is set in test mode, characters entered on the keyboard are looped back to the screen for verification.

Most modems also include standard calling features such as automatic dial, answer, redial, fall back, and call-progress monitoring. Calling features simplify the chore of establishing and maintaining a communications connection by automating the dialing process. Telephone numbers can be stored in nonvolatile memory.

Other standard modem features commonly offered include fall back and remote operation. Fall back allows a modem to automatically drop, or fall back, to a lower speed in the event of line noise, and then revert to the original transmission speed after line conditions improve. Remote operation, as the name implies, allows users to activate and configure a modem from a remote terminal.

### SECURITY

Many businesses have become increasingly aware of the importance of implementing a thorough network security strategy to safeguard valuable network data from intruders. Modems that offer security features usually provide two levels of protection: password and dial-back. Password protection requires the user to enter a code, which is verified against an internal security table. Many modems can store multiple passwords.

The dial-back feature offers a higher level of protection. Incoming calls are prompted for a password, and the modem either calls back the originating modem using a number stored in the security table or prompts the user for a telephone number and then calls back.

Security procedures can be implemented before the modem handshaking sequence, rather than after it. This effectively eliminates the access opportunity for potential intruders. In addition to saving connection establishment time, this method uses a precision high-speed analog security sequence that is not even detectable by advanced line monitoring equipment.

For the highest level of security, some modems even support the Data Encryption Standard (DES). Although DES has been around since 1977, it is still one of the most effective means of protecting data. DES-based encryption software uses an algorithm that encodes 64-bit blocks of data and uses a 56-bit key. The length of the key imposes a difficult decoding barrier to would-be intruders because 72 quadrillion (72,000,000,000,000,000) keys are possible.

## TRANSMISSION TECHNIQUES

Modems use two types of transmission techniques: asynchronous or synchronous. The user's operating environment determines whether an asynchronous or synchronous modem is required.

During asynchronous transmission, start- and stop-bits frame each segment of data during transfer to distinguish each bit from the one preceding it. Synchronous transmission transfers data in one continuous stream; therefore, the transmitting and receiving data terminal equipment (DTE) must be synchronized precisely to distinguish each character in the data stream.

### PC-to-PC or PC-to-Mainframe

Most mainframes and minicomputers use synchronous protocols, whereas PC-to-PC communications are typically asynchronous. Users who require both PC-to-PC and PC-to-mainframe communications can purchase modems that support both types of transmissions. The software that comes with the modem usually supports several emulation techniques for file transfers between hosts and PCs.

Those who require more out of the PC-to-host link than simple file transfer can look to such software as Attachmate Corp.'s Extra Personal Client

6.1and Wall Data Inc.'s Rumba Office 95/NT 5.0. Both products offer advanced data-query capabilities. These and other host-access suites offer a variety of connection types and methods within one product, usually installed off a single CD-ROM. At a minimum, such products can connect to an IBM 3270 or AS/400 host without having to depend on IBM's DOS-based drivers.

## Wireless Modems

Wireless modems are required to transfer data over public wireless services and private wireless networks. These modems come in a variety of hardware configurations: standalone, built-in, and removable PCMCIA card.

Newer modems are programmable and therefore capable of being used with a variety of wireless services using different frequencies and protocols. There are even modems that mimic wireline protocols, allowing existing applications to be run over the wireless network without modification.

## Private Wireless Networks

Private wireless networks operate in a range of unique frequency bands to ensure privacy. Using radio modems operating over dedicated frequencies within these frequency bands also permits the transmission of business-critical information without interference problems. Furthermore, the strategic deployment of radio modems can provide metropolitan area coverage without the use of expensive antenna arrays.

Such modems are designed to provide a wireless, protocol-independent interface between host computers and remote terminals located as far away as 30 miles. Most provide a transmission rate of at least 19.2K-bps point-to-point in either half- or full-duplex mode. Some radio modems even support point-to-multipoint radio network configurations, serving as a virtual multidrop radio link that replaces the need for expensive dedicated lines (see Exhibit 1). In this configuration, one modem is designated as the master, passing polling information and responses between the host and terminals over two different frequencies.

In multidrop configurations, a radio network is capable of supporting one type of asynchronous or synchronous polling protocol. Because such modems perform no processing or interpreting of the protocol, the host (or front-end processor) must generate all required protocol framing, line discipline, node addressing, and data encapsulation. Depending on the vendor, these modems may be equipped with an integral repeater to maintain signal integrity over longer distances.

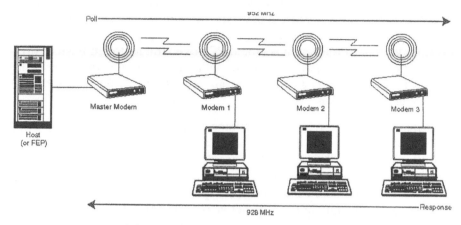

**Exhibit 1. Radio Modem Configuration.**

## Multifrequency Modems

Regardless of the transmission technology or the hardware configuration used, the modem must be tuned to the frequency of the service provider's wireless network to operate properly. Until recently, modems were offered in different versions, according to the wireless network the modem would connect to. This delayed product development and inflated the cost of manufacturing, which was passed on to users in the form of higher prices for equipment.

To overcome these problems, chip manufacturers have developed programmable chipsets that are not limited to a specific network's radio frequency. Newer wireless modems are computer configurable. Within specified frequency ranges, the transmit and receive frequencies are independently selectable via software.

## Multimedia (Hybrid) Modems

Not only can modems be programmed for multifrequency use, they can provide seamless integration of multiple media — wireline and wireless — through a common programmable interface. This is accomplished with a chipset that supports both wireline and wireless communications. Special software used with the chipset provides a method for connecting cellular phones to modems, which is important because cellular phones lack dial tones and other features used by modems on the wireline phone network. The software makes it appear that those features exist.

## Cable Modems

Although today's computers powered by Pentium and PowerPC chips are better equipped than ever to handle multimedia and video, they face a bottleneck that, in most cases, offers top speeds of no more than 28.8K bps or 33.6K bps over dialup lines. A new type of modem, the cable modem, has emerged for delivering entertainment and information services, including Internet access, to television sets and PCs over the installed base of ordinary twisted-pair wiring. Using traditional coaxial cable installed by CATV operators, these modems can deliver speeds of up to 1,000 times that of today's analog modems.

Cable modems are really not modems in the conventional sense. They modulate and demodulate signals like a conventional modem, but otherwise they are more like routers that are designed for installation on CATV networks, which themselves operate much like Ethernet LANs. These cable modems, as well as the cable operators' plant equipment, are even being managed using the familiar simple network management protocol (SNMP).

**Upstream Interference.** Typically, a cable modem sends and receives data in two slightly different fashions. In the downstream direction (from the network to the user), the digital data is modulated and then placed on a typical 6-MHz television carrier. There are several modulation schemes, but the two most popular are quadrature phase-shift keying (QPSK), which provides up to 10M bps, and quadrature amplitude modulation (QAM), which can provide up to 36M bps. This signal can be placed in a 6-MHz channel adjacent to TV signals on either side without disturbing the cable television video signals.

The upstream channel (from the user to the network) is more complicated. Typically, in a two-way activated cable network, the upstream channel is transmitted between 5 and 40 MHz. This tends to be a noisy environment with lots of interference from ham radio, CB radios, and impulse noise from home appliances or office machines. In addition, interference is easily introduced in the home, due to loose connectors or poor cabling. Because cable networks are tree and branch networks, all this noise gets added together and increases as the signals travel upstream.

Most manufacturers will use QPSK or a similar modulation scheme in the upstream direction because it is a more robust scheme than higher-order modulation techniques in a noisy environment. The drawback is that QPSK is slower than QAM.

## ROLE OF DIGITAL SIGNAL PROCESSING

Multifunction modems use programmable digital signal processing (DSP) technology to turn a computer into a complete desktop message center, allowing the user to control telephone, voice (recording and playback), fax, data transfers, and E-mail. Typical features include multiple mailboxes for voice mail, caller ID support, call forwarding, remote message retrieval, phone directory, and contact database.

In some cases, the modem is actually on a full-duplex sound card. By plugging in speakers and a subwoofer, the user can even enjoy a stereo-sound speakerphone. A separate connection to a CD-ROM player allows the user to work at the computer while listening to music. However, these DSP-based products cannot be used as modems and sound cards simultaneously because the processor can take on only one identity at a time.

With DSP, the modem can be easily upgraded to the latest communications standards and new capabilities can be added simply by loading additional software. For example, a 14.4K-bps modem can be upgraded to 28.8K bps by installing new software instead of having to buy new hardware. Likewise, a 28.8K-bps modem can be upgraded to 33.6K bps in the same way, often at no extra charge from the vendor.

## Digital Simultaneous Voice and Data

A new type of modem — digital simultaneous voice and data (DSVD) — allows the user to send voice and data at the same time over a single telephone line. Interference is avoided by having voice and data use different frequencies.

The biggest advantage of DSVD is that users no longer need to interrupt telephone conversations or install a separate line to transmit data or receive faxes. Multimedia modems typically include full-duplex speakerphone, fax, and 16-bit stereo audio capabilities, in addition to advanced modem functionality.

## 56K-bps Modems

Until now, 33.6K was thought to be the practical modem speed over standard phone lines. A new class of modems that can transmit data at 56K bps employs technology that takes advantage of the fact that for most of its length, an analog modem connection is really digital.

When an analog signal leaves the user's modem, it is carried to a phone company central office where it is digitized. If it is destined for a remote analog line, it is converted back to an analog signal at the central office nearest the receiving user. However, if the receiving user has a digital connection to the carrier's network, the modem traffic is converted at only one place, where the analog line meets the central office. When the traffic is converted from analog to digital, noise is introduced that cuts throughput. But the noise is less in the other direction, from digital to analog, allowing the greater downstream bandwidth (see Exhibit 2).

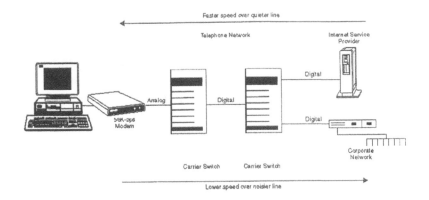

**Exhibit 2. 56K-bps Modem.**

Because it is already in digital form, the traffic is free of impairments from noise introduced when an analog modem signal is made digital within the carrier network. From an analog source, the top speed is quite a bit lower than 56K bps because the traffic is subject to impairment from noise.

A fully digital ISDN basic rate interface line offers up to 128K bps in both directions, but the service is far more expensive than an analog phone line. In addition, ISDN is not universally available and can still be difficult for users to set up with their equipment. Although the new 56K-bps modems are not meant to challenge ISDN, they will fulfill a role as a more economical alternative and significantly cut into the ISDN market.

Among the vendors of 56K-bps modems are U.S. Robotics and Rockwell International. Although U.S. Robotics was the first to introduce a 56K bps modem using its X2 technology, the semiconductor division of Rockwell International followed shortly with a different technique to obtain a 56K bps operating rate. In early 1998 U.S. Robotics held approximately 60 percent of the 56K bps modem market and an International Telecommunications Union (ITU) standard for 56K bps modem technology was being finalized. Until that standard is actually implemented on a worldwide basis, either the U.S. Robotics or Rockwell modem should be considered, based upon the type of modem supported by the destination to be dialed. For example, if the Internet service provider uses Rockwell technology, Rockwell 56K bps modems should be acquired.

## CONCLUSION

Once thought to be an outdated technology that would be supplanted by ISDN terminal adapters connected to digital lines, modems are not only growing in use, they are undergoing a surge in innovation as well. Not only has ISDN not met industry projections in terms of availability, but the carriers appear not to be encouraging its use, as evidenced by significant price hikes.

Higher-speed modems, the advent of cable modems that work over CATV networks, and new technologies that rely more on a computer's CPU for carrying out modem functions have all combined to breathe new life into this market segment. Although today's new-generation modems will not replace the need for ISDN in all cases, they certainly will give many potential ISDN users reason to consider the modem as a practical and economical near-term alternative.

# Chapter 16
# Multicast Networking
*C. Kenneth Miller*

In a business environment where efficient information delivery is critical to staying competitive, multicast network technology offers a new method of electronic distribution. Multicast networking enables group-oriented applications such as videoconferencing, dataconferencing, electronic software distribution, and database updates.

## INTRODUCTION

Multicast transmission is the sending of one message to many, but not all, receivers. Multicast network infrastructures are becoming available in all kinds of data networks, including wide area, satellite, and wireless. This new infrastructure is being used for group-oriented data networks.

Broadcast transmission is the sending of one message to all receivers and has been used extensively in LAN environments. Broadcast traffic over WANs should be avoided, however, because it can flood the WAN with unwanted traffic, or broadcast storms.

Multicast provides the mechanism for one-to-many transmission over WAN without creating broadcast storms. Multicast network infrastructures can be created at layer 2 (i.e., the link layer) or at layer 3 (i.e., the network layer). The primary layer 3 multicast transport technique is multicast IP, which many router vendors support. Layer 3 multicast transport is independent of the underlying network architecture.

Different physical and link layer architectures support multicast and broadcast services. For example, satellite data transmission is a broadcast architecture that easily supports multicast services. Other network infrastructures are multicast LANs, multicast frame relay, and multicast SMDS.

## MULTICAST LANS

Every station on the LAN listens to all transmissions. Nodes on a LAN have MAC addresses, which are sometimes called physical addresses because they designate a physical node on the network. MAC addresses are global, which means that each one is unique.

0-8493-9965-3/99/$0.00+$.50
© 1999 by CRC Press LLC

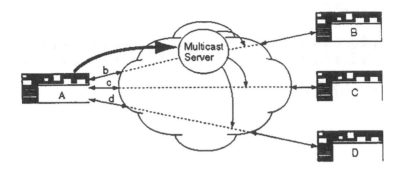

**Exhibit 1. One-way Multicast.**

MAC addresses come in three varieties: individual (unicast), multicast, and broadcast. Unicast addresses identify end points in point-to-point communications. The MAC broadcast address is the all address. MAC multicast addresses are primarily used for mapping to upper-layer multicast addresses.

MAC broadcast frames are usually filtered by bridges and routers, confining them to the LAN and preventing broadcast storms.

### Multicast Frame Relay

Frame relay is a layer 2 protocol designed for use over WAN. Frame relay is a connection-oriented protocol, which means that it emulates actual physical links with PVCs and SVCs. PVCs and SVCs represent point-to-point connections with DLCIs and do not usually have the facility for one-to-many connections. However, the Frame relay Forum recently released specifications for one-way, two-way, and N-way multicast services over Frame relay.

### One-Way Multicast

One-way multicast is suitable for electronic distribution of information from an information service provider. (See Exhibit 1.) A multicast server in the network maps the multicast data link connection identifiers to the individual data link connection identifiers. Individual DLCIs are also present from the members of the group to the multicast transmitter.

### Two-Way Multicast

Two-way multicast enables migration of old IBM SDLC multidrop configurations to a Frame relay environment. (See Exhibit 2.)

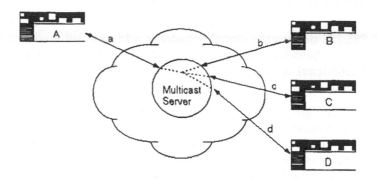

**Exhibit 2. Two-way Multicast.**

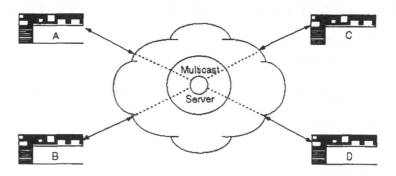

**Exhibit 3. N-way Multicast.**

### N-Way Multicast.

N-way multicast allows any node to be either a transmitter to the group or a receiver. N-way multicast (see Exhibit 3) was designed for teleconferencing applications.

### Multicast Switched Multimegabit Data Service

SMDS was developed by Bellcore for LEC to provide high-speed connectivity between LANs in a metropolitan area. SMDS is a subset of the IEEE 802.6 MAN standard and is offered as a service by several carriers.

SMDS uses a connectionless network architecture in which all nodes can communicate to all other nodes on the network, similar to LANs. All packets sent on the network are available for reception by all nodes, which means that SMDS can support multicast, unicast, and broadcast services.

## COMPARING BROADCAST AND MULTICAST IP

IP supports broadcast as well as multicast services. The IP address 255.255.255.255 defines the global broadcast address and is mapped into the MAC global broadcast address on the LAN to which it is attached. The IP global broadcast address is not usually forwarded by routers out of a local network.

A second category of IP broadcast address is the network broadcast address. In this case, the network portion of the Class A, B, or C IP address is sent to the desired network destination; the host portion is the all 1s broadcast address. Network broadcast addresses are forwarded by routers to the designated network, where they are mapped into that network's MAC broadcast address. For example, the Class C IP address 206.42.32.255 is the network broadcast address for network 206.42.32.

Network broadcast addresses can provide so-called directed broadcast services to a particular network or subnetwork over an internetwork.

### The IP Multicast Protocol

Multicast IP is a new technology that provides network layer routing of IP Class D group address packets in TCP/IP networks. Multicast IP operates over any network architecture, and the multicast groups can be set up and torn down within seconds. Multicast IP is destined to be the dominant means for providing multicast services in data networks of all kinds including mixed network environments or intranets.

### Class D Addressing

Multicast IP uses Class D IP addresses, as shown in Exhibit 4. IP Class A, B, and C addresses are used for point-to-point (unicast) communications and consist of network and host components. Class D addresses, by contrast, have only one component that identifies the multicast group.

Class D addresses occupy the range from 224.0.0.0 to 239.255.255.255 and can be assigned semipermanently or temporarily for the length of time a group is in place. Groups may be set up and torn down in seconds.

Hosts that belong to a group need to support RFC 1112, which is the standard for host extensions for IP multicasting. RFC 1112 specifies the IGMP that is used by members of a multicast group to inform the nearest router supporting multicast routing of their presence in a particular group. The router is responsible for updating routing tables so that multicast packets with the Class D address associated with that group are forwarded to the subnetwork that includes members of the group.

The IGMP dialog is shown in Exhibit 5. Two messages are provided in the dialog: the IGMP query and the IGMP response. Queries are sent to the all

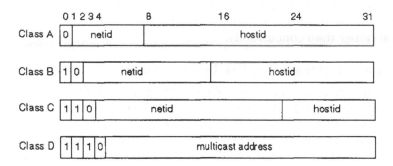

**Exhibit 4. IP Address Types.**

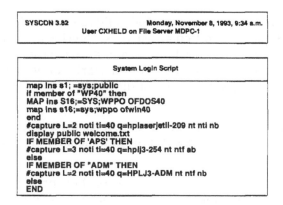

**Exhibit 5. IGMP Dialog.**

hosts' multicast group address — 224.0.0.1 — and carry an IP time-to-live of 1. Hosts respond to queries with host membership reports for each host group to which they belong.

There are two techniques for reducing the number of concurrent reports and the total number of reports transmitted. A host can start a report delay timer or it can send a report that other members of the same group on the network can overhear.

### Starting a Report Delay Timer

When a host receives a query, it can start a report delay timer rather than sending reports immediately for each of its group members on the network interface of the query. Timers are set to different, randomly chosen values between zero and D seconds. A report is generated for the corresponding host group when a timer expires. Thus, reports occur over a D-second interval rather than concurrently.

## Sending a Report that Other Members Overhear

To ensure that other members of the same group overhear the report, it is sent with an IP destination address equal to the host group address being reported and with an IP time-to-live of 1. If a host hears a report for its group on the network, the host stops its own timer and does not generate a report for that group. Thus, usually only one report is generated for each group on the network, by the member host whose delay timer expires first. The multicast routers receive all IP multicast datagram, therefore they need not be addressed explicitly. The routers need not know which hosts belong to a group, only that at least one host belongs to a group on a particular network.

Multicast routers send queries periodically to refresh their knowledge about memberships on a particular network. Queries are usually sent at intervals of approximately one minute to minimize overhead traffic on the network. However, when a multicast router starts up, it may often issue several closely spaced queries to obtain knowledge of local group membership quickly.

Similarly, when a host joins a new group, it issues a report immediately without waiting for a query in case it is the first member of the group on the network.

New members notify the nearest router of their presence in a group almost instantly, whereas notification of leaving a group depends on query timeout, which can be a minute or more. A new version of IGMP is being proposed that provides for explicit host leave group reports, to speed up the notification to routers of hosts leaving a group.

## The Multicast Backbone

The Mbone of the Internet is based on multicast IP and covers 3,000 subnetworks. It is predicted that the Internet will be fully multicast IP enabled soon.

The Mbone uses computers to provide the multicast routing capability, and multicast packets are tunneled through unicast links to tie together the islands of multicast networks. It is used mostly by Internet researchers for videoconferencing and dataconferencing.

Two applications used on the Mbone are based on the ALF lightweight session model originated by Internet researchers. ALF dictates that the best way to meet diverse multicast application requirements is to leave as much flexibility as possible to the application in the application layer. This means that connectivity is viewed as unreliable, using the UDP connectionless transport layer.

Two prominent ALF model applications come from Lawrence B. Livermore Laboratory, which provides the Visual/Audio Tool in multimedia videoconferencing. In addition, the Mbone enables a whiteboard application that lets users of a multicast group electronically write on a whiteboard. All members of the group can see what each member has written. Whiteboarding is essentially an electronic dataconference that allows group members to brainstorm visually.

Other videoconferencing tools that provide use over the Mbone are being used in some universities; however, they are not yet commercially available. The Mbone is still in the research stage.4

### Multicast Routing Protocols

Multicast routing protocols are required to perform optimal routing through router networks, just as unicast routing protocols such as IGMP, OSPF, and RIP are needed to perform optimal unicast routing in router networks. Multicast routing protocols should efficiently minimize the necessary traffic for routing multicast data in the network or internetwork.

There are three predominant multicast routing protocols: DVMRP, Multicast OSPF, and PIM.

**DVMRP.** DVMRP is the oldest multicast routing protocol and uses a technique known as reverse path forwarding. When a router receives a multicast packet (i.e., one with a Class D destination address), it floods the packet out of all paths except the one that leads back to the packet's source, as shown in Exhibit 6. This allows the packet to reach all subnetworks, possibly multiple times. If a router is attached to a set of subnetworks that do not want to receive packets destined to a particular multicast group, the router can send a prune message back up the distribution tree to stop subsequent multicast packets from being forwarded to destinations where there are no members.

DVMRP periodically refloods to reach any new hosts that want to receive a particular group. There is a direct relationship between the time it takes for a new receiver to get the data stream and the frequency of flooding.

DVMRP implements its own unicast routing protocol to determine which interface leads back to the source of the packets for a particular group. This unicast routing protocol is similar to Routing Information Protocol and is based purely on hop count. As a result, the path that the multicast traffic follows may not be the same as the path the unicast traffic follows.

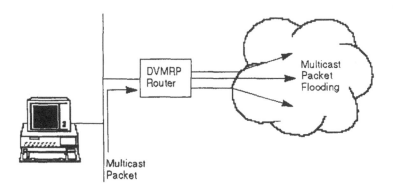

**Exhibit 6. DVMRP Flooding.**

DVMRP is an inefficient multicast routing protocol because of scaling problems. The periodic flooding with broadcast traffic generates significant overhead in the network, and early versions of the protocol did not implement pruning.

Nevertheless, DVMRP has been used to build the Mbone and has been implemented by some router companies. Bay Networks, Inc. (Santa Clara, CA) has chosen DVMRP as its first offering to support multicast routing, and 3Com Corp. (Santa Clara, CA) is planning to implement it in the next few months.

**Multicast Open Shortest Path First (MOSPF).** MOSFP is an extension of the OSPF unicast routing protocol. OSPF is a link state routing protocol, which means that each router in a network understands all of the available links in the network. Each OSPF router calculates the routes from itself to all possible destinations.

MOSPF includes multicast information in OSPF link state advertisements. MOSPF routers learn which multicast groups are active on which subnetworks.

MOSPF builds a distribution tree for each source/group pair and computes a tree for active sources sending to the group. The tree states are stored, and trees must be recomputed when a link state change occurs or when the timer for the store of the link expires.

The main disadvantage of Multicast OSPF is that it works only in networks supporting OSPF. Multicast OSPF, authored by Proteon, Inc. (Westborough, MA) has been implemented in routers available from Proteon and Xyplex, Inc. (Littleton, MA).

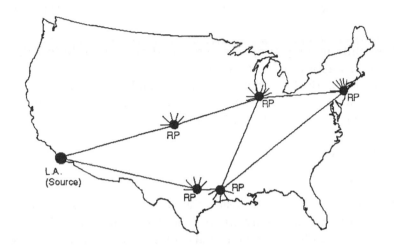

**Exhibit 7. Sparse Mode Topology Showing Rendezvous Points.**

---

**Protocol Independent Multicast (PIM).** PIM works with all existing unicast routing protocols and supports two types of traffic distribution topologies: dense and sparse. Dense mode is most useful when:

- Senders and receivers are in close proximity to one another.
- There are few senders and many receivers.
- The volume of multicast traffic is high.
- The multicast groups do not change very often.

Dense mode PIM uses reverse path forwarding and is similar to DVMRP. Sparse mode PIM is most useful in network topologies scattered over a large geographic area when:

- There are a only a few receivers in a group.
- Senders and receivers are geographically separated by WAN links.
- The groups change often.

Sparse mode PIM is designed for environments where there are many data streams destined for group members, as shown in Exhibit 7. Each stream goes to a relatively small number of group members. For this topology, reverse path forwarding techniques waste bandwidth.

Sparse mode PIM defines a RP. Receiving members of the group join to a particular RP to create a shared distribution tree. There can be many RPs in a single group. Sources must register with all RPs in a group. Once the data stream begins to flow from sender to RP to receiver, the routers optimize the path automatically to remove any unnecessary hops. Sparse mode PIM assumes that no hosts want the multicast traffic unless they specifically request it.

PIM simultaneously supports dense and sparse mode for different groups. PIM was authored by Cisco Systems, Inc. (San Jose CA) and researchers from the University of Southern California, Lawrence B. Livermore Laboratory, and Xerox Parc. Work is continuing in the Internet community to improve multicast routing protocols.

## APPLICATIONS

### Dynamic Groups

Groups defined by Class D addresses can be created and torn down in seconds. (Groups that are easily created and torn down are referred to as dynamic.) Changes to the group can also be performed in seconds, which is useful in many applications.

### Videoconferencing

Videoconferencing is a temporary group setup that may exist for the duration of a meeting of any length. It is essentially an electronic meeting.

### Dataconferencing

Dataconferencing is the same as videoconferencing without the video. Dataconferencing often involves a whiteboard, such as the program used by the academic community in the Mbone.

### Real-Time Distribution of Multimedia Information

There are several new services that provide real-time business news to the desktop. Some of the information provided includes audio, video, and data. Subscribers to these services are constantly entering and leaving the group, therefore the ability to change the size and composition of the group dynamically is very important for this application.

**Multicast File Transfer.** There are several multicast file transfer applications that involve one-to-many transmission of information in the form of files.

*Subscription-based Information Delivery.* Subscription-based information delivery is a service that distributes information electronically using a multicast network and a multicast file transfer program. The information might be, for example, news in text and image form or financial trend analysis in audio form.

Information is in the form of files that need guaranteed delivery. Dynamic groups are important in this application because subscribers are constantly changing.

Electronic subscription delivery of information could become a popular service once the Internet is fully multicast enabled. Today, much time is wasted searching for information on the Internet, even with the advent of sophisticated browsing tools. Consumers have newspapers and magazines delivered as print subscriptions; they should be able to receive the equivalent electronically.

*Electronic Software Distribution.* Software is usually distributed at the time of its release. As the number of hosts on networks grows, software updates become more of a burden, which has led to great interest in the electronic distribution of software using a multicast file transfer program that is guaranteed.

Because distribution of software is not a daily or even a weekly event, it is desirable to terminate the group right after the transfer.

*Distributed Publishing.* National newspapers and other print publications use regional printing facilities to reduce shipping costs. They send information using a series of point-to-point transfers. Multicast file transfer is a more efficient and less costly solution. In this application, the membership group is relatively static.

*Kiosk Applications.* Kiosks are being planned to provide a number of new services, most of which need to be updated with information common for all of the kiosks. For example, the U.S. Department of Transportation is sponsoring a project to implement kiosks at various urban and suburban locations. Information about traffic will be periodically downloaded to the kiosks so that travelers can obtain information about traffic patterns. These kiosks would also be used to disperse information of general public interest, such as facts about major sporting events such as the Olympic games.

Kiosks may also be placed in retail stores as a means of showcasing products using multimedia presentations. The latest fashions and sales promotions can be downloaded into the kiosks using multicast networks and a file transfer program.

*Database Updates.* Linked databases in remote locations can be updated easily using a multicast file transfer program on a multicast network infrastructure.

## VENDOR OFFERINGS

There are not many network infrastructures on a wide area basis that support multicast. There are, however, a number of companies providing low-cost videoconferencing products, and many of them support multicast IP or plan to support it. Intel Corp. (Santa Clara, CA), Connectix Corp. (San Mateo, CA), PictureTel Corp. (Danvers, MA), Insoft, Inc. (Mechanicsburg, PA), and Xing Technology Corp. (Arroyo Grande, CA) all have PC-based videoconferencing products.

Multicast file transfer products are available from StarBurst Communications Corp. (Concord, MA) and Legent, a division of Computer Associates International, Inc. (Islandia, NY).

## CONCLUSION

Multicast network technology and the associated applications are poised to dramatically change the use of networked PCs. Videoconferencing and dataconferencing over IP data networks will become common as network speeds increase and multicast IP router networks become pervasive. Multicast file transfer over multicast IP networks makes electronic information delivery on a subscription basis a reality and electronic delivery of information more like the model for printed information delivery.

Multicast file transfer also facilitates software maintenance by providing the ability to easily distribute software updates. Other distributed applications such as groupware and E-mail directory updates can also benefit, proving that multicast technology will be a major component of information distribution in the not-too-distant future.

# Chapter 17

# Frame Relay Testing and Training

*Steve Greer, Peter Luff, and Sean Yarborough*

Because it provides efficient, cost-effective transfer of bursty, bandwidth-intensive applications, frame relay is now the main access protocol for wide area network communications. This chapter discusses the advantages and disadvantages of frame relay, as well as the reasons why training and testing are important.

## INTRODUCTION

Frame relay — a network access protocol for high-speed, bursty data applications — has been a data communications buzzword for the past five years, but only recently has it begun to serve its purpose. According to Vertical Systems Group, a consulting group in Dedham MA, the number of U.S. public frame relay network subscribers, which was only 590 in the early 1990s, is projected to increase to 8,210 by the late 1990s. The main catalyst for this explosion is the need for high-speed, LAN interconnection.

Frame relay networks provide companies with cost-effective and efficient transfer of such bursty bandwidth-intensive applications as file transfer, E-mail, graphics, and imaging applications. Frame relay decreases the cost of LAN interconnection through the use of statistical multiplexing, which allows many subscribers to utilize the bandwidth on a single circuit. The cost savings is a direct result of the reduction in the use of dedicated leased lines, which tend to be underutilized because bursty transmission is sporadic.

LANs have become so ubiquitous that subscribers expect to be able to communicate across multiple interconnected LANs just as easily as when they communicate over a single LAN. Frame relay addresses LAN interconnection extremely well (i.e., up to T1 speeds), so subscribers can enjoy the same quality data transmission over the WAN that they have come to expect over the LAN.

0-8493-9965-3/99/$0.00+$.50
© 1999 by CRC Press LLC

It is important that service providers and subscribers understand Frame relay technology and its advantages and disadvantages. For example, Frame relay has no inherent error correction. It assumes that a network successfully transmits data and avoids errors. As a result, users need to test the network for errors and comprehensively train employees on Frame relay technology to reduce errors. This chapter briefly reviews the features of Frame relay technology and explains some of the important tests to perform on Frame relay devices and the network.

## ADVANTAGES OF PACKET-SWITCHING FRAME RELAY NETWORKS

The main advantage of frame relay is that it is a packet-switching technology. Packet-switching networks send data from source to destination based on each packet's unique destination address. Once the data is packetized, it can be statistically multiplexed.

Statistical multiplexing allows many subscribers to share the same bandwidth by assuming that not all subscribers will be using the bandwidth at the same time. This avoids high-cost, point-to-point connections such as dedicated leased lines that employ circuit switching. Leased lines are expensive because they are rented and dedicated for exclusive use 24-hours a day, seven days a week. With leased lines, subscribers pay for bandwidth whether it is being used or not. Statistical multiplexing provides multiple data connections through the network simultaneously, and no single customer pays for exclusive privileges. This results in a significant cost advantage over circuit-switched networks.

A second advantage of Frame relay is that its variable-length frames and its low overhead provide excellent network throughput and low delay of data. The variable-length frames allow Frame relay to encapsulate protocols well. Frame relay is protocol independent, so its payload can carry a variety of higher-layer LAN protocols, such as the IP. Because the network does not concern itself with error correction and flow control, overhead in the Frame relay network is low. Therefore, the network uses most of its resources switching user data.

Frame relay realizes another advantage through the CIR. The CIR represents the data traffic level that the network plans to support under typical network conditions; it is agreed upon by the service provider and the subscriber. The advantage of a CIR for the customer is that once it is agreed upon, the service provider should be capable of transmitting at or below the CIR. For example, if an average of 56K-bps throughput is required between two sites, then the CIR should be equal to or greater than 56K bps. Typically, data traffic sent below the CIR passes through the network at a high priority, and data sent in excess of the CIR has a lower priority. This low-priority traffic is the first to be dropped when subscribers create network congestion. The CIR serves as the basis of a well-planned network as well as a billing mechanism.

Finally, frame relay has worldwide industry support from manufacturers, standards organizations, and service providers. This is important because it ensures that there is a high level of interoperability between devices of different manufacturers in different countries.

## DISADVANTAGES OF FRAME RELAY

Although frame relay carries data more efficiently because it has no inherent error correction utilities, this lack of frame management can be detrimental. Frames can be errored because of transmission impairments in the network (i.e., a bit error corrupts a frame, which is then dropped by the network).

In Frame relay, the error correction is left up to the user's intelligent devices (i.e., a router), which can discover discrepancies and request a retransmission. In addition, the reliable deployment of technologies such as T1, DDS, and fiber optics decreases the need for error correction within the network.

Network problems can occur when subscribers exceed the CIR. As previously mentioned, the CIR is the amount of data traffic, agreed upon by the service provider and the subscriber, the network is planned to support under normal network conditions. When too many subscribers exceed the CIR, then a situation may develop in which the network becomes congested and begins to drop frames to alleviate the congestion.

For example, 20 banks are all connected to a Frame relay network. During the day, they all transmit under their CIR for routine electronic communication. At 2:00 p.m., however, all of these banks send their daily transactions to another location for processing, which causes network congestion. If only one bank transmits over the CIR, network congestion probably will not occur. It is the aggregate of many banks transmitting over their CIR that causes congestion and dropped frames.

Frame relay frames are variable in length; therefore, they cause variable delay in the network. For example, a short frame can be switched quickly by the Frame relay network. However, longer frames take longer to process and switch. This creates a variable transit time between long and short frames. Integrated data, voice, and video applications cannot be delayed; therefore, these applications are not best suited to Frame relay. They are better suited to integrated switched digital networks (ISDN) or cell relay technology, such as ATM.

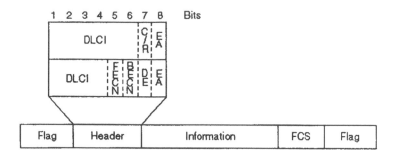

Key:
BECN    backward explicit congestion notification
C/R     command/response
DE      discard eligibility
DLCI    data link connection identifier
EA      extended address
FCS     frame check sequence
FECN    forward explicit congestion notification

**Exhibit 1. The Frame Relay Frame.**

## ANATOMY OF THE FRAME RELAY FRAME

Frame relay's packet-switched technology is based on its older relative, X.25. In a packet-switched network, data is subdivided into individual packets, each with a unique identification and destination address. These packets, or frames, as they are called in frame relay, are variable in length. Each frame contains a header, information field, frame check sequence (FCS), and two flags. (See Exhibit 1.)

### The Frame Header

The header of a frame contains information on connection identification. Connection identification is managed by the data link connection identifier (DLCI). The DLCI is an identifier (i.e., address) associated with each permanent virtual circuit (PVC). A PVC is the path that is set up by the service provider routing data from point A to point B. Once a PVC is defined, it requires no setup operation before data is sent and no disconnect operation after data is sent.

### The DLCI

The DLCI is usually 10 bits long, but it can be extended. Each DLCI indicates a different PVC or end point for data. In other words, the DLCI must be unique for specific destinations. For example, for San Francisco, the DLCI is 45; for New York, it is 49. These values ensure the proper routing of information within a network (see Exhibit 2). The DLCI can be extended to

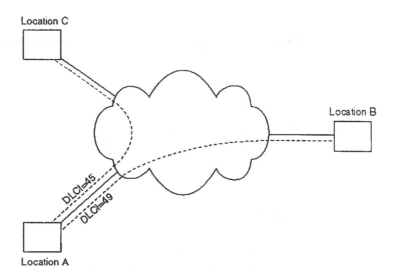

**Exhibit 2. Sample DLCI Values.**

increase addressing capabilities. There are two, one-bit Extended Address fields in the header that indicate if another octet has been added for extended DLCI purposes.

**Congestion Control**

Also within the header are congestion control bits, which identify whether congestion is present. These congestion bits are important because they inform the user of potential errors in the network. If congestion overloads a particular switch, frames will be discarded by the network. There are three main types of congestion control bits: forward explicit congestion notification (FECN), backward explicit congestion notification (BECN), and discard eligibility (DE). (See Exhibit 3.)

The header also includes the Command/Response field. This one-bit field is used by many HDLC-based protocols to indicate whether a frame carries a command or a response. It is passed transparently through the Frame relay network.

**The Information Field**

The information field contains variable numbers of octets (up to 4,096 octets for some implementations) and encapsulates many protocols, including TCP/IP, internetwork packet exchange (IPX), sequenced packet exchange (SPX), SNA, and X.25. The information field is the largest part of

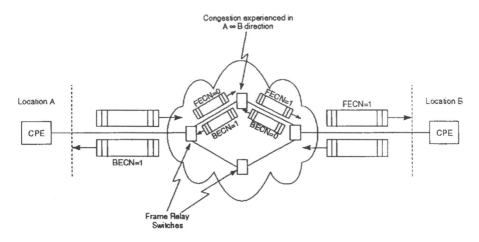

**Exhibit 3. Congestion Control.**

---

the frame and contains the encapsulated protocol header as well as user data.

### The FCS Field and Flags

The FCS field is used for error detection. The transmitting end devices (i.e., routers) apply a complex algorithm to the data in the frame and then place the result in this field as the frame is sent to the receiving equipment (i.e., the router at the far end). Each node along the way recalculates the FCS based on the received data and compares the result to the FCS within the frame. If the results are not identical, then the frame is discarded by the switching node or the end device.

Flags serve as eight-bit idle codes that delineate frames on the circuit.

### Local Management Interface

The local management interface (LMI), a signaling protocol, was instituted by Cisco Systems, Inc. (Menlo Park, CA), Digital Equipment Corp. (Maynard, MA), Northern Telecom, Inc. (McLean, VA) and StrataCom, Inc. (San Jose, CA). It allows the subscriber and the network devices to share information on the status of DLCI on the link.

In addition, the LMI provides a mechanism for the network to recognize that end devices are operating correctly. The LMI proposal was accepted with minor additions by the ANSI and the ITU. These standards organizations slightly modified and standardized the LMI, which is now represented by ANSI T1.617, Annex D, and ITU Q.933, Annex A.

## THE IMPORTANCE OF TESTING

Frame relay networks sacrifice function for speed by relying on intelligent devices and an efficient network to prevent errors and retransmissions. With such a reliance on the network, it is imperative that users test the physical medium, the PVC, and the internetwork, both out of service and in service, when implementing frame relay. Specifically:

- Out-of-service testing is performed when a circuit is taken offline, or when no subscribers are active on the circuit being tested.
- In-service testing can be done while a circuit is active.

The testing of the transmission facilities, as well as testing the internetwork service, ensures that the service itself, the internetwork devices, and the physical media provide seamless network performance for customers.

### Testing the WAN Facilities

Users need to carefully test the transmission facilities before implementing a Frame relay network. There are three parts to a comprehensive test strategy: testing the transmission facilities between the subscriber and the POP switch, testing the PVC through the network, and conducting a lost frames analysis.

**Bit Error Rate Testing.** To test the transmission facilities between the subscriber and the POP switch, an out-of-service BER test should be performed. This test examines the transmission facilities by evaluating the percentage of bits received in error compared to the total number of bits received.

Typically, the BER test set generates one or more complex sets of pseudorandom bit patterns and then transmits these patterns along network segments at rates dependent on the facilities. The BER test set provides the stimulus as well as the receiver to monitor the response of the transmission segment being tested. This test can pick up bit errors, bipolar violations (BPV), cycle redundancy check (CRC) errors, and other errors that may cause the network to drop frames. When these errors occur, an end device requests retransmission, which costs money and consumes valuable bandwidth.

Because the pseudorandom patterns used in BER test do not pass through the switches, this test is useful only between the customer and the POP switch. However, because of frame relay's lack of error correction utilities, BER testing is vital. A clean transmission line must be ensured before any additional investigation can be done.

**PVC Testing.** Once the transmission facilities are verified, the PVC should be tested. This test verifies end-to-end connectivity between two or more subscribers on a specific PVC,

This test is performed by generating and receiving a variety of Frame relay traffic loads with the proper DLCI and LMI support over each valid PVC. The test should be able to transmit frames with control of various header bits, like DLCI, FECN, BECN, and DES test results indicate that the transmission facilities are operating with minimal errors and the correct link management parameters and that the network is properly routing frames across the PVC being tested.

When testing transmission facilities, PVC, and LMI, monitoring of layer-two and layer-one (i.e., transmission facility and PVC phenomena is also important. For example, users can determine that a bipolar violation (BPV) at the physical layer (layer one) coincides with a FCS error on a layer-two analysis, which indicates a transmission facilities problem and not a Frame relay problem.

**A Lost Frames Analysis.** Another important feature of Frame relay testing is determining if any transmitted frames are lost. This test is performed by placing a sequential counter in the data field of the test frames. The test set receiver tracks gaps in the test frames' sequence count. There are usually several reasons the network may be dropping frames: FCS errors are occurring, the attempted throughput exceeds the CIR, too many frames per second are being transmitted, or the network may be experiencing congestion.

This test also discovers dribbling errors that cause network bottlenecks and the determination of critical thresholds of Frame relay devices. The lost frame analysis gives customers a final assurance when verifying network performance because it can discover errors that previous tests did not catch.

## Frame Relay Internetwork Service Testing

The most important reason to test the internetwork service is the increasing number of premium services being offered. These premium services, such as the end-to-end management of network services, rely on LAN/WAN analysis at the higher-level functions that only internetwork testing can verify.

Internetwork service testing begins with the Frame relay devices themselves. These devices generate and receive the Frame relay frames. Simultaneous monitoring of both sides of these devices can be done to verify that LAN traffic to the router is correctly forwarded and encapsulated in Frame relay. This verification of connectivity across the router also ensures correct configuration. The user should test all routers before installation on the network and before calling the provider's wide area support group when switch problems occur.

**The Echo Test.** Another internetwork device test that can be performed to verify connectivity across the network is the echo test. The echo test's key applications are for implementation and installation of routers when establishing connectivity, for in-service measurements on in-service and out-of-service equipment, and for performing round-trip delay measurements through the network.

The echo test eliminates the need to take down the service when testing network connectivity. In an echo test, the test equipment bounces (pings) a packet across the network to the far-end router (or host) and awaits a response. It checks the connections through the WAN by monitoring both the outgoing ping packet and the returning response from the remote host.

**Simultaneous Monitoring of the WAN and LAN.** Simultaneous monitoring of the WAN and LAN should also be performed. By looking at encapsulated LAN protocols, users can verify that customer traffic is correctly addressed, encapsulated, and transmitted over the WAN. In the opposite direction, users should track packets to ensure that Frame relay information is removed and that they are correctly routed to their destination on the LAN.

Multiport analysis provides the ability to test an internetwork at various access points simultaneously. For example, users could access LAN segments. Once the link is established, users can stress the circuit using a traffic generator.

### Commissioning the Frame Relay Service

Once the testing of the Frame relay devices and network is complete, users can concentrate on commissioning the Frame relay service. This application focuses on emulating the DCE and DTE by generating Frame relay packets to see how the network reacts to these packets.

First, the test should provide for Annex D ANSI signaling protocol LMI emulation to imitate network conditions. This action ensures that the network can process the frames across the LAN and the WAN. Once this is accomplished, the user can monitor layer-two and LMI signaling statistics. The test equipment should then stress test the line by generating frames to ensure that the network stands up to agreed communication rates. The commissioning process verifies and sectionalizes inside and outside the Frame relay cloud.

### End-to-End Analysis

Finally, users want to take advantage of the verification of end-to-end LAN/WAN connectivity. End-to-end analysis ensures the integrity of the entire internetwork. With this application, users can generate traffic to remote LANs to verify connectivity or capacity handling. In addition, users can monitor both local and remote trends in network operation to plan for network changes and expansion.

### TRAINING ISSUES UNIQUE TO FRAME RELAY

One aspect that is often overlooked in technical articles, books, and magazines is the training of personnel in technology, network applications, and troubleshooting methodology. Yet training is extremely important when implementing a new technology such as frame relay.

### THE PROVIDER'S PERSPECTIVE

From the service provider's perspective, training is critical in overcoming a technician's lack of protocol or packet-switching knowledge. These technicians, who must install the Frame relay equipment and services, may know how to install DDS or T1 links, but they may have limited protocol experience and most likely have never been exposed to Frame relay. Frame relay training provides the technology background these technicians need. It also provides the installation and troubleshooting background they need to maintain the service.

Training can point out to the technician the prospective problems that occur when testing Frame relay and how to solve them. For example, the physical layer may work but the service may not. This is often caused by switch configuration problems, such as the switch not being configured, being configured incorrectly, or the provider and subscriber configuring their switches incompatibly.

### THE SUBSCRIBER'S PERSPECTIVE

From the subscriber's point of view, training issues on Frame relay technology are less critical, but training on its test applications may be more important. These technicians are comfortable working with circuits and services focused on protocols. For example, an IS department professional may have extensive experience with the technology and the testing of X.25. However, Frame relay, unlike X.25, has no error correction, which introduces a series of testing issues. Although the technology may be similar, the test applications are different.

For subscribers, Frame relay training provides technology specifics, such as how Frame relay applies to their particular network, taking issues like CIR, DLCI connections, and link management into account.

The traditional classroom setting is still popular in many companies. If the company does not have a training department, the data communications manager should consider sending technicians on staff to an outside organization whose specific purpose is to increase workers' comprehension or knowledge level of technology or product use. These sessions can take the form of seminars, classroom sessions, field training, video, distance learning (i.e., teleconferencing), or auditorium-style lectures. Computer-based training might also be available, which provides a self-paced environment that can cover multiple knowledge levels at the same time. As microprocessor technology and memory storage become more advanced, users are able to run complex instruction disks on their personal computers. They can take in the training at their own pace, at home, in the office, or on the road.

### The Benefits of Training

Training offers a critical advantage to an organization through increased production, reduced cost, and maximized efficiency with respect to Frame relay network performance parameters. Training helps employees avoid pitfalls encountered during a new installation. It does this by increasing employee knowledge levels about Frame relay technology and then having them apply this knowledge to everyday work and even future upgrades.

In addition, training enables users to test and manage a Frame relay network from the first day of implementation. This kind of knowledge about the network decreases downtime and outages, as well as return trips to the subscriber's premises.

The key to reducing cost and downtime of a Frame relay network is to plan and implement training before circuit implementation, because the training offers insight on potential problems before they actually occur. Subsequently, service providers and subscribers save money as downtime is reduced because the job was completed efficiently the first time. Training is an expense, but it provides a company with a return on investment through knowledgeable employees who can efficiently run a frame relay network.

### CONCLUSION

Frame relay is now the main access protocol for WAN communications and will likely stay that way for the rest of the decade. But that is not the end for frame relay. The future of Frame relay lies in its capability as an access network for ATM-based services, which many consider to be the communication services of the future. Hybrid frame relay/ATM networks will provide the transition between the two networking technologies. Eventually users will run integrated multimedia applications and services over their ATM networks, making full use of technologies for which Frame relay helped pave the way.

# Chapter 18

# Working with Images in Client/Server Environments

*Gilbert Held*

Careful planning is required so that the burgeoning use of image-based applications results in enhanced user productivity rather than decreased network performance. The several techniques reviewed help tailor an image's characteristics to the intended application to optimize network bandwidth and server storage availability.

## INTRODUCTION

Advances in monitor display technology coupled with the development of multimedia software and increased capacity of disk drives are just some of the several factors contributing to a rapid increase in the use of images in client/server environments. Today it is common to find pictures of employees in a personnel database, images of houses and interiors in a real estate database, and the results of CAT and MRI scans in a hospital patient database.

Although the adage "one picture is worth a thousand words" contributes to the increased use of images, the storage and transmission of images can rapidly diminish network resources. Using images in client/server environments has to be carefully planned so that the resultant application is effective both in terms of cost and of operations. If it is not, the potential adverse effect to network performance will decrease the productivity of all network users — those using image-based applications as well as those using other client/server applications. Inappropriate use of images can also result in inefficient use of disk storage, necessitating costly disk drive upgrades or the acquisition of a hierarchical storage management system whose use introduces delays as migrated files are moved back to disk storage on the receipt of a user access request.

Appropriate use of images is therefore vital to enhancing user productivity and the effective use of network bandwidth and storage.

## AN OVERVIEW OF IMAGING

Two basic types of images are used in computer applications: raster and vector. A raster image consists of a grid of equally sized pieces referred to as pixels and records a color element for each pixel. Raster images include those taken with a camera and scanned photographs. In comparison, vector images are images resulting from a collection of geometric shapes that are combined to form an image and are recorded as mathematical formulas. Computer-aided design (CAD) drawings represent an example of a vector image.

Vector data cannot reproduce photo-realistic images. As a result, most computer-based applications require pictures of persons, places, or things using raster-based images. This discussion of techniques for using images effectively in a client/server environment is therefore limited to raster-based images.

### Storage and Color Depth

A color is associated with each pixel in a raster-based image. That color can vary from a simple black or white denotation to the assignment of one color to each pixel from a palette of more than 16 million colors.

The assignment of a color to a pixel is based on the use of one or more bits per pixel to denote the color of each pixel, a technique referred to as the color depth of the pixel. For example, a black and white raster image would use one bit per pixel to denote the color of each pixel, with each pixel set to 1 to denote black and 0 to denote white. For a 16-level gray scale raster image, each pixel would require 4 bits to indicate the pixel's gray level (24 = 16). Exhibit 1 indicates the correspondence between the number of bits per pixel (i.e., color depth) and the maximum number of colors that can be assigned to a pixel. Note that the use of 24 bits per pixel is referred to as true color and represents the maximum number of colors the human eye can distinguish when viewing a raster image.

### Data Storage

The amount of storage required for an image depends on its size, resolution, and color depth. The size of an image references its vertical and horizontal size typically expressed in inches or millimeters. The resolution of an image references the number of pixels per inch or per millimeter, and the color depth represents the number of bits per pixel required to define the color of each pixel in the image. Thus, the total amount of data storage can be expressed in bytes as follows:

**Exhibit 1. Correspondence between Bits per Pixel and Maximum Number of Colors**

| Bits Per Pixel (Color Depth) | Maximum Number of Colors |
|---|---|
| 1 | 2 |
| 2 | 4 |
| 8 | 16 |
| 16 | 32,768 or 65,536 (depends on format) |
| 24 | 16,777,216 |

**Exhibit 2. Data Storage Requirements for 3.5 × 5-Inch Photograph**

| Data Storage (Bytes) | Color Depth |
|---|---|
| 196,875 | 1 bit (black and white) |
| 393,750 | 2 bits (4 colors/4-level gray scale) |
| 787,500 | 4 bits (16 colors/15-level gray scale) |
| 1,575,000 | 8 bits (256 colors/256-level gray scale) |
| 3,150,000 | 16 bits (32,768 or 65,536 colors) |
| 4,725,000 | 24 bits (16,777,216 colors) |

$$\text{Data storage} = \frac{\text{length} \times \text{width} \times \text{resolution} \times \text{color depth}}{8}$$

The computation of data storage can be illustrated through the example of using 3.5 × 5 inch photographs in a visual database. A scanner is used to digitize each photograph using a resolution of 300 dots per inch. Then, without considering the effect of the color depth of the scanned images, each photograph would require 3.5 in. × 5.0 in. × 300 × 300/(8 bits/byte) or 196,875 bytes of storage.

Exhibit 2 compares the data storage requirements for a 3.5 × 5 inch photograph scanned at 300 dpi using different color depths.

In examining the data storage required for the 3.5 × 5 inch photograph, note that the maximum number of colors supported based on the indicated color depth is indicated in parentheses to the right of the color depth. As indicated by the entries in the table, the use of color significantly affects the data storage required for an image. This effect governs not only the number of images that can be stored on a visual database, but also the ability of users to work with stored images. Concerning the latter, the memory requirement of a workstation to display an image is proportional to the amount of storage the image requires. Thus, physically large images scanned at a high resolution with a high color depth may not be viewable, or only partially viewable at a time, on many workstations.

## Color-Depth Tradeoffs

Careful selection of a color depth appropriate to the particular image-based application supported can result in significant savings in data storage and the time required to transmit images. For example, in a personnel database, a color depth of one or a few bits would probably be sufficient for pictures of employees. Note from the preceding table that the use of black and white images requires 196,875 bytes to store a 3.5 × 5 image, whereas the use of a 24-bit color depth results in a data storage requirement approximately 24 times greater. This means that the use of black and white pictures of employees could reduce the data storage requirements of a personnel database containing employee images by a factor of 24. For an organization with hundreds or thousands of employees, these savings could translate into a significant amount of disk storage becoming available for other applications, or the reduction in equipment required to support an image-based application.

Although few image applications use black and white, significant savings in data storage and transmission time can be achieved by selecting an appropriate color and color depth. In the real estate field, for example, the use of digital cameras is expanding. Many real estate professionals now take pictures of their listings and enter them into a central database for viewing by clients or other members of the organization. Although most digital cameras can support a 24-bit color depth, use of that color depth does not provide any appreciable viewing difference of a home, room, or swimming pool over the use of an 8-bit color depth. Thus, selecting an 8-bit color depth can reduce data storage of color images by a factor of three from the default 24-bit color depth used by many digital cameras.

## Data Transmission

Images also affect client/server operations because of transmission time. To illustrate the effect of image storage on transmission time, the example of a 3.5 × 5 inch photograph stored on a server connected to a 10Base-T Ethernet local area network (LAN) is used. There are 39 workstations and one server connected to the LAN for a total of 40 network devices.

Ethernet is a shared access network, meaning that at any one time only one user can transmit or receive information. Thus, although each device can transmit or receive data at 10M bps, on the average, the devices obtain the use of 10M bps/40 or a 250K-bps data transmission capability. Assuming the photographs were stored using a 24-bit color depth, then each image would require 4.75M bytes of data storage. Storage would actually be slightly more than that amount because images are stored using special file formats that add between a few hundred to approximately a thousand bytes of overhead to each file. Using a storage of 4.75M bytes and an average transmission capability of 250K bps, the time required to download the image from a server to a client workstation would be 4.75M bytes × 8 bits per byte/250K bps or 152 seconds. Thus, on the average it would take almost 2.5 minutes to download each photograph.

Displaying the image on a monitor would result in a slight increase in time because the server would have to access and retrieve the file containing the image from its disk storage system, and an image display program operating on the workstation would require some time to display the image. In any event, 2.5 minutes is not an appropriate waiting period for a guard attempting to verify personnel entering a building, a real estate broker attempting to show a client a series of pictures of homes, or a doctor attempting to view a previously performed MRI scan of a patient.

## MANAGING STORAGE AND TRANSMISSION REQUIREMENTS

Several techniques have been developed to manage the storage and transmission challenges associated with the use of images in a client/server environment. They are presented in the sections that follow.

### File Format

One of the most effective methods for reducing image storage requirements and transmission times is to use an appropriate file format when storing the images. Today, most imaging programs support a wide range of raster file formats, such as the CompuServe GIF, Joint Photographic Experts Group's JPG, Truevision's TGA, Aldus Corp.'s TIF, and Microsoft Windows's BMP. Some of those file formats store scanned images on a pixel by pixel basis, using one to three bytes per pixel for storing the color depth. Other file formats include a built-in data compression feature that compresses the scanned image before storing it.

Although it is tempting to select a file format with a built-in compression capability to reduce data storage and the transmission time required to move images from a server to client workstations, the various compression methods have important differences. For example, CompuServe's GIF file format uses the Lempel Ziv Welch (LZW) lossless compression method, whereas Aldus Corp.'s TIF file format supports six different types of compression, including the Joint Photographic Experts Group's JPG lossy compression method.

A lossless compression method is fully reversible and does not result in the loss of any details on an image. In comparison, a lossy compression method groups blocks of pixels and considers two blocks to be equivalent for compression purposes if they differ by only one or a few pixels. Thus, decompression can result in the loss of a few pixels per block of pixels. Lossy compression can significantly reduce the data storage requirements of images. Although this compression method would not be suitable for

**Exhibit 3. Comparison of Data Storage
Required for Four Different File Formats**

| File Format | Data Storage |
|---|---|
| TIF no compression | 2.4M bytes |
| GIF LZW compression | 1.8M bytes |
| JPG least compression | 1.365M bytes |
| JPG moderate compression | 163K bytes |

storing some images, such as a chest X-ray where every pixel is important, it is highly effective for storing pictures of personnel, homes, and other objects for which the loss of a few pixels does not significantly alter the image's usability.

To illustrate the potential differences in data storage obtained through the use of different file formats, the same photograph was scanned several times and stored each time with a different format. The first scan was accomplished specifying the TIF file format without compression. The resulting file required 2.4M bytes of data storage. Next, the same image was stored using the CompuServe GIF file format, which includes built-in LZW compression. The resulting data storage required for the photograph was reduced to 1.8M bytes. Although a reduction of 600K bytes is significant, LZW compression is fully reversible and does not represent the best method of compression for storing many images.

To illustrate the potential of data storage reduction that can be obtained through the use of lossy compression, the photograph was rescanned two additional times. The first time the image was scanned using the JPG file format specifying least compression, which results in two blocks of pixels being considered as equal if they only differ by one pixel. The resulting scan required 1.365M bytes and yielded a reduction of 435K bytes in storage from the GIF file format. Next, the image was scanned and saved using the JPG file format specifying moderate compression, where two blocks of pixels are considered to be the same even if they differ by up to four pixels per block. As a result of using a moderate level of lossy compression, the amount of data storage was reduced to 163K bytes — a reduction of more than 2M bytes in the storage of the image using a noncompressed file format. Exhibit 3 provides a comparison of the data storage required for storing the same photograph using four different file formats.

If each file was stored on a server on the previously described Ethernet LAN, it would take 1.365M bytes x 8/250K bps or approximately 44 seconds to retrieve the image stored using a JPG file format and least compression. In contrast, the retrieval of the image stored using a JPG file format and moderate compression would require 163K bytes x 8/250K bps or approximately 5.2 seconds. Thus, the use of a moderate level of lossy compression can significantly reduce client retrieval time as well as server data storage requirements.

## Cropping

Another technique that provides an effective mechanism for reducing image storage and transmission requirements is cropping. Cropping involves eliminating portions of an image that are not applicable to the application. For example, if images are required for an employee database, a large portion of the background of the scanned photograph can be cut out.

## File and Image-Type Conversions

Two additional techniques for enhancing the use of images in a client/server environment are file and image-type conversions.

**File Conversion.** Many times software provided with a scanner or digital camera limits the user to storing images with one file format. Thus, the use of an image management program that provides a file conversion capability may provide the ability to significantly reduce the data storage for an image. By converting from one file format to another as well as specifying the use of an appropriate image compression method for the application, users can significantly reduce the storage requirements for an image.

**Image-Type Conversion.** The second conversion method involves a change in the image type. Here image type is used to denote the use of color depth with an image. For example, assume a photograph is scanned using 24-bit true color. Three bytes would then be used to store color information for each pixel. If the photograph is being used in a personnel file, the image could probably be converted to 16 color requiring 4 bits per pixel or 256 color requiring 8 bits per pixel to store color detail information. Thus, converting a one-inch 300 dpi image requiring 90,000 pixels from true color to a 256-color image type would reduce its data storage requirement to 180,000 bytes.

## CONCLUSION

Although the use of images in applications has the potential to enhance user productivity, it also can adversely affect network bandwidth and server storage availability. Effectively using images in network-based applications requires the careful consideration of the use of different image file formats, compression methods, cropping, and image type. By carefully considering each of these image-related features, the characteristics of the image can be tailored to the application. Doing so can significantly reduce the amount of storage required for the image as well as the transmission time from servers to client workstations.

# Chapter 19
# Voice and Video on the LAN

*Martin Taylor*

Voice and data convergence in the LAN is about to become a hot topic in the industry, thanks to advances in switching and processors, as well as the H.323 standard. This chapter first looks at the business reasons for considering the deployment of voice and video over the LAN and then discusses the technical issues and requirements.

## INTRODUCTION

Most desktops in enterprises today are equipped with two network connections: a LAN connection to the PC or workstation for data communications, and a phone connection to the PBX for voice communications. The LAN and the PBX exist as two separate networks with little or no connectivity between them. Each has evolved to meet the very specific and differing needs of data and voice communications, respectively.

Despite much talk in the industry about the convergence of computers and communications, LANs and PBXs have not really moved any closer together during the last decade. In the mid-1980s, some PBX vendors sought to bring data services to the desktop via ISDN technology, but the advent of PCs requiring far more than 64K-bps communications bandwidth favored the emerging LAN standards of Ethernet and Token Ring. So far, most LAN vendors have not attempted to support voice communications on the LAN. But all this is about to change.

There are three key factors at work today that suggest that voice and data convergence in the LAN is about to become a hot topic in the industry:

- The widespread acceptance of advanced LAN switching technologies, including ATM, which makes it possible for the first time to deliver reliable, high-quality, low-delay voice transmissions over the LAN.
- The emergence of the first standard for LAN-based videoconferencing and voice telephony, H.323, which removes objections about the use of proprietary protocols for voice and video over the LAN.

0-8493-9965-3/99/$0.00+$.50
© 1999 by CRC Press LLC

- The deployment of the latest generation of Intel processors, featuring MMX technology, which makes high-quality software-based, real-time voice and video processing feasible for the first time, and the new PC hardware architectures with Universal Serial Bus that permit voice and video peripherals to be attached without additional hardware inside the PC.

This chapter first looks at the business reasons for considering the deployment of voice and video over the LAN, and then discusses the technical issues and requirements.

## THE VALUE OF VOICE AND VIDEO ON THE LAN

There are essentially two main kinds of motivation for considering voice and/or video on the LAN: the need to support new types of applications that involve real-time communications, and the desire to improve the overall cost-effectiveness of the local communications infrastructure.

### New Types of Applications

Desktop videoconferencing, real-time multimedia collaboration, and video-based training are all examples of new kinds of applications that can benefit from the delivery of voice and video over the LAN.

The uptake of desktop videoconferencing has been held back by a combination of high costs and the difficulty of delivering appropriate network services to the desktop. Standards-based H.320 desktop videoconferencing systems require costly video compression and ISDN interface hardware, as well as the provision of new ISDN connections at the desktop alongside the LAN and the phone system. New systems based on the H.323 standard and designed to run over the LAN will leverage the processing power of the latest PCs and the existing switched LAN infrastructure, to lower cost and simplify deployment dramatically.

Desktop videoconferencing may be used either to support internal meetings and discussions between groups located at remote sites, or to support direct interaction with customers and clients. For example, some enterprises in the mortgage lending business use videoconferencing to conduct mortgage approval interviews with potential borrowers, so as to greatly reduce the overall time to complete a mortgage sale.

Real-time collaboration applications, involving any mix of video and voice with data conferencing to support application sharing and interactive whiteboarding, provide a new way for individuals and small groups to collaborate and work together remotely in real-time. This emerging class of applications, typified by Microsoft NetMeeting, is being evaluated by many enterprises, particularly for help desk applications.

By contrast, video-based training is already widely used in enterprise LANs. By delivering self-paced video learning materials to the desktop, training needs can be met in a more timely and less disruptive fashion than traditional classroom methods.

The growing popularity of these kinds of applications should be noted by network planners and designers. A preplanned strategy for local LAN upgrades to support voice and video will reduce the lead time for the deployment of these applications, and enable the enterprise to move swiftly when the application need has been identified, to obtain the business benefits with the least possible delay.

**Infrastructure Efficiencies**

A single local communications infrastructure based on a LAN that handles data, voice, and video has the potential of costing less to own and operate than separate PBX and data-only LAN infrastructures.

The average capital cost of a fully featured PBX for large enterprises is between $700 and $750 per user, according to a leading U.S. telecommunications consultancy, TEQConsult Group. Furthermore, this is expected to rise slightly over the next few years as users demand more sophisticated features from their phone system. It is not difficult to see how a switched LAN that has been enhanced to handle voice could provide a solution for telephony at a fraction of this cost.

Most large PBX installations are equipped with additional facilities such as voice mail and Interactive Voice Response systems for auto-attendant operation. These systems are typically connected directly to the PBX via proprietary interfaces, and they too represent major capital investments. With voice on the LAN, such voice processing applications could be based on open server platforms and leverage the low-cost processing power and disk storage that is a feature of today's PC server market, thereby lowering the system's capital cost still further.

Separate PBX and LAN infrastructures each incur their own management and operational costs. For example, moves, adds, and changes require separate actions to patch physical LAN and voice connections, and to update LAN logon and voice directories. With telephony provided over a voice-enabled LAN supporting combined directory services, the management effort required to administer moves and changes would be substantially reduced.

These cost-of-ownership benefits come with a raft of usability improvements for telephony. The PC (with phone handset attached) becomes the communications terminal for making and receiving phone calls, and the processing power and graphical user interface of the PC can be leveraged to provide point-and-click call launch and manipulation. Features of PBXs such as call transfer, divert, and hold, which are hard to invoke from a phone keypad, become very easy to use from a Windows interface.

Incoming callers can be identified on the PC display by matching Calling Line Identifier with directory entries. And with voice mail and E-mail supported on a unified messaging platform such as Microsoft Exchange or Lotus Notes, all messages are accessible and manageable via a single user interface.

These usability benefits for voice telephony over the LAN extend also to videoconferencing — a single consistent user interface may be applied to both video and voice-only calls.

## LAN TECHNOLOGIES FOR INTEGRATED VOICE AND VIDEO

The LAN technologies in widespread use today — Ethernet, Fast Ethernet, FDDI, and Token Ring — were not designed with the needs of real-time voice and video in mind. These LAN technologies provide "best-effort" delivery of data packets, but offer no guarantees about how long delivery will take. Interactive real-time voice and video communications over the LAN require the delivery of a steady stream of packets with very low end-to-end delay, and this cannot generally be achieved with the current LAN technologies as they stand.

### Asynchronous Transfer Mode (ATM)

At one time, there was a belief that ATM networking to the desktop would be embraced by LAN users to solve this problem. ATM is a networking technology that was designed specifically to handle a combination of the low-delay steady stream characteristics of voice and video and the bursty, intermittent characteristics of data communications.

The ATM Forum, the industry body responsible for publishing ATM specifications, has developed a number of standards that enable desktops connected directly to ATM networks to support existing LAN data applications as well as voice telephony and videoconferencing. The ATM Forum standards for the support of voice and video over ATM to the desktop typically avoid the use of traditional LAN protocols such as IP, and instead place the voice or video streams directly over the ATM protocols.

While it is clear that ATM to the desktop provides an elegant and effective solution for combining voice, video, and data over the LAN, this approach does imply a "forklift" to the LAN infrastructure and the end station connection. The cost and disruptive impact of such an upgrade tend to limit its appeal, and as a result desktop ATM is not expected to be widely adopted.

However, the ability of ATM to provide Quality of Service — that is, to deliver real-time voice or video streams with a guaranteed upper bound on delay — makes ATM an excellent choice for the LAN backbone where voice and video over the LAN is needed.

## Shared and Switched LANs

It is generally accepted that shared LANs are unsuitable for handling real-time voice and video because of the widely varying delays observed when multiple stations are contending for access to the transmission medium. The CSMA/CD access method used in shared Ethernet is particularly poor in this respect. Token Ring, on the other hand, is based on a token-passing access method with multiple levels of priority. Stations waiting to send data packets can be preempted by other stations on the ring with higher priority voice or video packets to send. As a result, Token Ring has excellent potential to handle real-time voice and video traffic, although this potential has yet to be realized in currently available networking products.

LAN switching does much to overcome the limitations of shared LANs, although today's products are still a long way from providing an answer for voice and video over the LAN. It is now cost-effective to provide users with dedicated 10M-bps Ethernet connections to the desktop, and 100M-bps Fast Ethernet uplinks from the wiring closet to the backbone.

However, despite the vast increase in bandwidth provision per user that this represents over and above a shared LAN scenario, there is still contention in the network leading to unacceptable delay characteristics. For example, multiple users connected to the switch may demand file transfers from several servers connected via 100M-bps Fast Ethernet to the backbone. Each server may send a burst of packets that temporarily overwhelms the Fast Ethernet uplink to the wiring closet. A queue will form in the backbone switch that is driving this link, and any voice or video packets being sent to the same wiring closet will have to wait their turn behind the data packets in this queue. The resultant delays will compromise the perceived quality of the voice or video transmission.

The only way to overcome this problem is to find a way of treating real-time voice and video packets differently from data packets in the network, and to give them preferential treatment when transient data overloads cause queues to form on busy network links. In practice, this means that LAN packets must be tagged with some kind of priority information that enables switches to identify which packets need to jump the queue.

The IEEE 802, which oversees standards for LAN technologies, has initiated a project identified as 802.1p, which is concerned with Traffic Class Expediting in LAN switches.

The principal problem faced by 802.1p is that there is no spare information field in the standard Ethernet packet format that could carry the required priority tag. As a result, it has been necessary to propose a new Ethernet packet format with an additional 4 bytes of information in the packet header that can contain a 3-bit priority tag field (offering 8 levels of priority), together with some other information concerned with Virtual LANs.

With the new Ethernet packet format containing a priority tag, end-station applications can identify real-time voice or video packets by assigning them a high priority value in the tag. LAN switches that have been enhanced to process the priority tags can separate high- and low-priority traffic in the switching fabric and place them in separate queues at outgoing switch ports. The LAN switches need to implement a queue scheduling algorithm that gives preference to the higher-priority queues on outgoing ports, and by this means it is hoped that real-time voice and video can be carried over the LAN without incurring unacceptable delays during periods of heavy data traffic.

As of July 1997, the 802.1p standard was still in draft form and the standard is not expected to be completed until 1998. Ethernet switches that support the 802.1p priority tags with multiple internal queuing structures will require a new generation of switching silicon, and the earliest we could expect to see products that conform to the standard would be late 1998 or into 1999. Surprisingly, we may see Token Ring switches that handle multiple priority levels before that time, leveraging the capabilities of the existing Token Ring standard that supports 8 levels of priority.

### Hybrid ATM Networks

The discussion of ATM described how it offers guaranteed Quality of Service for real-time voice and video streams. Today, ATM is increasingly used as a LAN backbone for pure data applications because it offers greater scalability and fault tolerance than other LAN technologies. Ethernet and Token Ring LANs are connected to ATM via "edge switches" equipped with ATM uplinks, typically supporting the ATM Forum standard for carrying LAN traffic over ATM, know as LAN Emulation.

It is possible to enhance ATM edge switches to enable desktops connected via Ethernet or Token Ring to enjoy the benefits of ATM Quality of Service across the LAN backbone. Two techniques have been proposed to achieve this.

The first technique, known as "Cell-in-Frame," extends the native ATM signaling protocols over dedicated Ethernet connections from the edge switch to the end station. The voice or video application in the end station places the voice or video stream in ATM cells using the ATM Forum standards for native ATM transport, and then encapsulates the ATM cells in

Ethernet packets for transport to the edge switch for onward transmission onto the ATM network. Effectively, this is ATM to the desktop, but using physical Ethernet with standard Ethernet adapter cards as a kind of physical transport layer for ATM traffic.

The second technique makes use of an emerging standard protocol for end stations to request Quality of Service for IP-based voice or video applications, known as the Resource Reservation Protocol, or RSVP. The enhanced edge switch intercepts RSVP requests originated by end stations and converts them into ATM signaling to request the setup of connections across the ATM backbone with the appropriate Quality of Service. The edge switch then distinguishes between IP packets containing data and those containing voice or video, using the information provided by RSVP, and steers voice and video packets onto ATM connections that have Quality of Service.

At the time of writing, the technique described here for RSVP-to-ATM mapping enjoys somewhat broader industry support than Cell-in-Frame, perhaps because of its relationship with Internet technology.

Until LAN switches supporting 802.1p priority tagging have proven themselves capable of meeting the very stringent end-to-end delay requirements for real-time voice and video communications, hybrid approaches based on ATM in the backbone and switched Ethernet or Token Ring to the desktop are likely to find acceptance as the solution of choice for voice and video over the LAN.

### Standards for LAN-based Voice and Video Applications

Standards for voice and video over the LAN fall into two categories: those designed for native ATM protocols, and those intended for general-purpose LAN protocols, particularly IP.

Standards for native ATM protocols, such as the ATM Forum's Voice Telephony over ATM (VTOA) are appropriate only for ATM-connected desktops, or desktops running Cell-in-Frame over Ethernet.

Standards for applications that run over IP are applicable both to ATM-connected desktops as well as desktops in general Ethernet or Token Ring environments. The most important standard in this space is H.323, which was developed by the International Telecommunications Union. While H.323 is designed to be independent of the underlying networking protocol, it will most often be deployed running over IP.

H.323 references other existing standards for the digital encoding and compression of voice and video signals, and describes how audio and video streams are carried in the payload of IP packets with the aid of the Real Time Protocol (RTP), which provides timing and synchronization information. H.323 also covers the handling of data streams for application sharing, shared whiteboarding, and real-time file transfer (referencing the T.120 standard), and includes signaling based on ISDN messaging protocols for call setup and teardown.

The H.323 standard is flexible and accommodates any combination of real-time voice, video, and data as part of a single point-to-point or multi-point conference call. It may be used with a voice stream alone as the basis of a LAN telephony solution. H.323 enjoys the broadest support in the industry as a proposed standard for Internet telephony.

### Additional Components: Gateways and Gatekeepers

Creating a LAN infrastructure that can consistently deliver voice and video streams with sufficiently low delay is an absolute prerequisite for integrating voice and video on the LAN, but it is by no means the complete answer to the problem. There are two other key components of a complete voice and video solution, which in H.323 parlance are known as the *gateway* and the *gatekeeper.*

An H.323 gateway provides interconnection between voice and video services on the LAN, and external voice and video services typically provided over circuit-switched networks such as ISDN and the public telephone network. The gateway terminates the IP and RTP protocols carrying the voice and video streams, and converts them to appropriate formats for external networks. For videoconferencing, the conversion is most likely to be to H.320, another ITU standard that specifies how voice and video are carried over ISDN connections. For voice-only connections, the conversion will be to the G.711 standard for digital telephony. This allows voice inter-working with any phone on a public network or connected to a PBX.

An H.323 gatekeeper is a pure software function that provides central call control services. While it is possible to run H.323 voice and video communications over the LAN without a gatekeeper, in practice this function is extremely useful. At the most basic level, the gatekeeper provides directory services and policy-based controls applied to the use of voice and video communications. For example, the gatekeeper can bar stations from accessing certain types of external phone numbers at certain times of day. The gatekeeper can be thought of as the "server" in a client/server model of LAN-based telephony and videoconferencing.

At a more sophisticated level, the gatekeeper may be able to support supplementary services, including call transfer, hold and divert, hunt groups, pick-up groups, attendant operation, etc. — features that are typically found in high-end PBXs for controlling and managing voice calls. While the H.323 standard does not explicitly describe how supplementary call control features may be supported, the standard does provide a framework for the addition of these advanced capabilities.

## CONCLUSION

This chapter has explained the value of voice and video integration on the LAN in terms of both application-driven needs and the desire for infrastructure efficiencies. It has looked at the technology issues surrounding the transport of real-time voice and video streams over LAN infrastructures, and concluded that ATM backbones provide a solution in the near term, with the possibility later of a solution based entirely on switched Ethernet or Token Ring.

Finally, some additional functional elements have been described, such as gateways and gatekeepers, that are an essential part of a complete solution for voice and video over the LAN. Over the last decade, the open standards-based environment typified by PCs and LANs has revolutionized the way data is handled and processed in enterprise environments. Now, this open and standards-based approach is set to tackle the challenge of voice and video, formerly the exclusive domain of the PBX. The history of LAN evolution is set to repeat itself, and one can expect the traditional proprietary mainframe PBX to diminish in importance to the enterprise, giving way to client/server telephony and videoconferencing, just as the mainframe computer has been pushed into the background by client/server techniques for data processing.

# Chapter 20
# Inverse Multiplexing ATM, Bit by Bit

*Robin D. Langdon*

In the time division multiplexing (TDM) environment, there are many applications that require greater than T1/E1 bandwidth, but where the jump to T3/E3 is not possible due to cost or availability of service. The technology to bridge the bandwidth gap between TDM and ATM WANs is known as inverse multiplexing, which allows multiple T1 or E1 lines to be aggregated to form a single multimegabit virtual or "clear" channel.

## INTRODUCTION

Not long ago, the deployment of ATM was considered a wildfire market — ATM would be available on the desktop, would be used in LAN backbones, and would provide transparent LAN-to-WAN interconnection at almost infinitely scalable bandwidths with all the benefits that classes of service could provide. However, the enthusiasm for ATM might be judged to be on the wane.

Completely dismissing ATM would be premature. ATM might be having trouble competing with switched and fast Ethernet for the desktop, but it has firmly established a home in corporate and carrier backbones, where it is experiencing strong growth. On the access side of the public arena, however, ATM's migration into the WAN has been and is projected to be slow. Based on industry forecasts, ATM service revenues in the public network will remain relatively small when compared to alternative switched data network services such as frame relay. A new access option, inverse multiplexing over ATM, is becoming a reality for corporate users who want the benefits of ATM bandwidth but want to avoid the high costs of ATM service and implementation.

## ATM'S POSITION IN THE MARKETPLACE

For end users and carriers, the real issue is what to do when the local network needs to expand to the enterprise network and runs into the bottleneck of the

0-8493-9965-3/99/$0.00+$.50
© 1999 by CRC Press LLC

public WAN's access bandwidth. ATM outside the backbone and in the wide area is a possible solution, if ATM had a larger presence in the public network. ATM service is by no means ubiquitous, nor is it expected to become so in the next several years. ATM in the WAN may not even be available for those customers who need it or are willing to pay for it.

Some network managers, even those running their corporate backbones at ATM's OC-3c rates, may not be able to justify the steep price tags (relative to access alternatives) or backhauling expenses associated with OC-3c or DS3WAN connections. Although T1 ATM prices are coming down to the point where they are equal to or less than the prices of traditional T1 lines (especially in areas where the carriers are trying to encourage users to experiment with ATM services), the bandwidth lost to ATM cell overhead and partially filled cells reduces the available bandwidth to the point where the inefficiencies of T1 ATM may be too high a burden for an application to bear.

To complicate ATM's position in the marketplace, it is also faced with formidable competition from frame relay — a service that has no cell overhead, is ubiquitous, is priced attractively, and has tremendous market momentum. Like ATM in the LAN, ATM in the WAN must compete against alternative technologies that are less expensive, readily available, or easier to use.

## INVERSE MULTIPLEXING FOR ATM

T1 inverse multiplexing, or imuxing, is a process in which a single data stream is split across multiple T1 lines in a round-robin fashion; the T1s are logically combined to form a single virtual data channel that is the aggregate of the T1 bandwidths (minus a small amount for overhead). From the point of view of the device providing the data stream, it is communicating via a single, high-speed WAN channel at some multiple of the T1 rate — that is, at the bandwidth of a fractional T3 service, but using readily available, less expensive T1 services.

The similarities between inverse multiplexing and ATM are significant when planning for current and future network implementations. ATM and inverse multiplexing topologies can both provide the ability to link individual sites by clear channel broadband data pipes. Both imuxing and ATM provide scalability, and both seamlessly link LANs and WANs in enterprise networks. Inverse multiplexing and ATM complement each other and can work together hand-in-hand.

Where the rate of a traditional T1 is insufficient and T3 is too expensive or is unavailable, T1 inverse multiplexing is an efficient and immediate cost-effective solution to provide increased bandwidth. The concept of inverse multiplexing can be applied to ATM cells, where an ATM cell stream

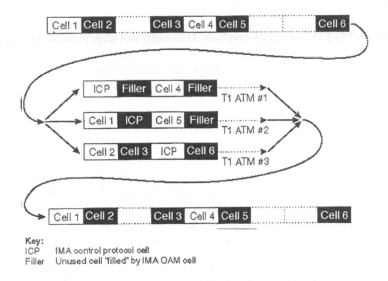

Key:
ICP   IMA control protocol cell
Filler   Unused cell "filled" by IMA OAM cell

**Exhibit 1. Cell-based Inverse Multiplexing for ATM (IMA).**

---

is transmitted across multiple T1/E1 links; alternatively, it can also allow ATM cell traffic to be transported across the existing T1/E1 network infrastructure as a bitstream. In either case, users avoid having to pay for the excessive bandwidth of a T3 or OC-3c line that they may not need. The customer also avoids the price, in dollars or bandwidth, of T1 ATM service.

There are two variations of inverse multiplexing for ATM: cell-based and bit-based. Each has its own strengths, discussed at greater length in the following sections.

### Cell-Based ATM Inverse Multiplexing

The very nature of public carrier networks demands a stable, standardized mechanism for transport. The ATM Forum's evolving standard for inverse multiplexing for ATM (IMA) will play a crucial role in the acceptance and implementation of ATM inverse multiplexing.

IMA is a new user-to-network interface (UNI) being specified by the ATM Forum. The physical interface (PHY) committee of the ATM Forum defines standard mappings of ATM cells onto existing physical layer media; UNIs and PHYs are usually inseparable. In this case, the IMA UNI rides on top of existing T1 or E1 ATM PHY, performing inverse multiplexing via a cell-based control protocol, which is a major departure from the normal PHY definition. (See Exhibit 1.)

IMA is expected to be widely accepted in both the user and equipment vendor communities. Within the carriers' networks, IMA can be used instead of T1ATM for point-to-point trunking between frame relay/ATM switches, greatly improving bandwidth without upgrading to DS3 or OC-3c. On the customer premises, the IMA specification promises vendor interoperability, giving users maximum flexibility in the equipment selection process.

However, the definition of a specification is a long and painstaking process. The IMA specification is still being formulated. Once the standard is defined, the normal maturation process for a new technology will set in. Early adopters of IMA will have to accept a number of adjustments as new hardware, software, and protocols are rolled out. Those customers for whom the risk in cost and reliability of deploying a new technology is too high will have to wait until the dust settles. Multivendor, interoperable NxT1 ATM may take a while to become a reality.

There are users who have network requirements that cannot wait either for stabilized IMA solutions or for high-speed ATM (i.e., DS3 and OC-3c) to become available or more cost-effective in the public network. They need solutions to their networking challenges sooner rather than later. Until the new IMA specification is finalized, they see themselves as having no stable means of interconnecting their ATM networks via inverse multiplexing.

## NXT1 ATM INVERSE MULTIPLEXING — CLEAR CHANNEL ATM

An alternative to IMA allows users to take full advantage of inverse multiplexing's NxT1 (e.g., multiple independent T1 connections) bandwidth for their ATM networks. ATM cells can be inverse multiplexed bit-by-bit, meaning that ATM traffic can be transported transparently over traditional fractional T3/E3 and T1/E1 circuit facilities. This technique is called clear channel ATM (CCA).

Unlike IMA, clear channel ATM is a specification already approved by the ATM Forum. Clear channel ATM is another way of referring to the ATM Forum's transmission convergence sublayer (cell-based TC) specification, also known as ATM over HSSI (high speed serial interface). Cell-based TC specifies a standard format for transmitting cells over any clear-channel bitstream interface. In other words, ATM transports at the bit level, instead of at the cell level. Connectors, clocking, modem control, and status are not addressed by cell-based TC, but are defined by other standards. At the physical layer, V.35, HSSI, or any other type of connector that could accept the ATM bitstream can be used. What is defined by the cell-based TC specification is the bit order and how "start-of-cell" is determined; then, cells are simply placed bit-by-bit onto the transporting technology (see Exhibit 2).

**Exhibit 2. Clear Channel (bit-by-bit) ATM Inverse Multiplexing.**

Clear channel ATM means that an ATM bitstream can be carried over any WAN data circuit, including inverse multiplexed data circuits. Having an HSSI port available for the traffic flow is not necessary; a V.35 port will do, and it is even possible to use an ATM DS3 or OC-3c UNI directly from an ATM switch. By using cell-based TC in conjunction with a readily available UNI (e.g., on an inverse multiplexer with a direct UNI connection to an ATM switch), the difficulties and long maturation created by the process of defining yet another UNI are eliminated.

It usually takes time for a new user-to-network interface to migrate into customer premises equipment, appearing most often first in ATM switches, and then in other devices such as routers and network interface cards (NICs). There are no guarantees that a vendor will even choose to support it. In the ATM switch, a new UNI means that the switch must handle a new interface, address the conversion from one rate to another, and buffer cell traffic moving between old and new UNIs. Despite the UNI deployment taking place in the ATM switch, actual switching is not required in this instance. Because ATM switches tend to be expensive, the addition of a new UNI can mean interface upgrades and reconfigurations.

**Alternatives to Adding a New UNI**

The functions of a cell-based TC imux need not be deployed in a switch because only cell buffering and rate conversion are required. By leaving the switching functions where they belong — in the ATM switch — a more inexpensive and lower-risk solution can be deployed. In the case of clear channel ATM inverse multiplexing, a readily available ATM interface such as a DS3 or OC-3c becomes an ATM "DTE port," which then transports the data stream via multiple T1 or E1 circuits. By converting the traffic from DS3 or OC3 to lower NxT1 rates, and by providing the necessary buffers, the need for a "new" UNI is eliminated.

Clear channel ATM lets users keep their options open with regard to WAN access and ATM transport. They can use the DS3 and/or OC-3c UNI interfaces they have available on their backbone ATM switches without having to deploy a new UNI. Users do not even need to use an ATM switch. With a clear channel ATM inverse multiplexer, a single device such as a

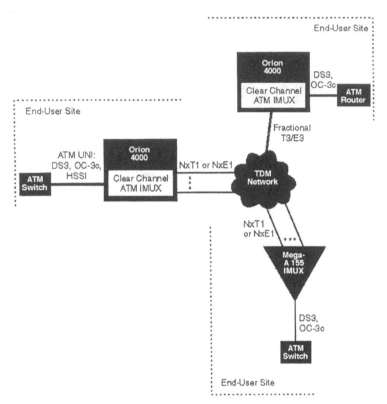

**Exhibit 3. Private Network/Corporate Intranet: Interconnecting ATM Site Backbones with NxT1/E1 TDM Service.**

---

high-speed workstation or server equipped with an OC-3c or DS3 ATM NIC can connect directly into the CCA imux.

### Support for Non-ATM and Multimedia Traffic

Network managers can build private networks and intranets between two or more sites with ATM backbones by using multiple, private line T1 or E1 WAN circuits in a virtual fractional T3 or E3 pipe. It is not necessary to make any changes to the backbone ATM switches that are being interconnected (see Exhibit 3). When they wish to upgrade to a different type of transport (i.e., IMA or higher-speed ATM), they can upgrade without changing their user UNI interface, thereby protecting their original ATM investment.

For those network environments where ATM is required for some, but not necessarily all, applications, clear channel ATM imuxing can be used to

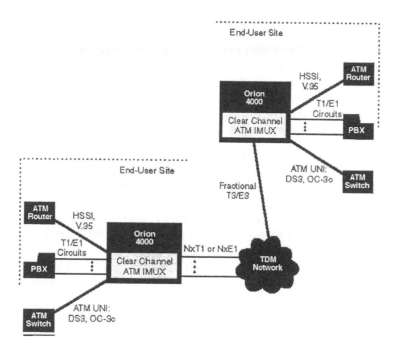

**Exhibit 4. Simultaneously Supporting TDM and ATM Traffic over M13 Service.**

combine ATM traffic over the same fractional T3/E3 links used for non-ATM traffic. In Exhibit 4, a channelized DS3 link in an M13 (multiplexer DS1 to DS3) network can support both traditional non-ATM traffic (including imuxed router traffic and T1 tail circuits from a PBX), as well as specific multimedia applications being run over ATM. Users need not convert all of their WAN access connections to ATM to support what may be a relatively small set of applications; the ATM traffic can be transported transparently over NxT1 links within the channelized DS3 that is used for other types of traffic. It is not an either/or scenario. Users do not have to cut over from TDM to ATM WAN access; they can have both at the same time, over facilities with which they are already familiar. NxT1/E1ATM access can be added incrementally, making the migration to ATM less expensive and less risky.

## Compatibility and Cost Savings

If a carrier is using inverse multiplexing to provide multimegabit-per-second frame services, clear channel ATM could be provided with the same equipment in the infrastructure. An ATM service can be offered using the existing transport technology. Other than adding inverse multiplexers that support clear channel ATM, the carrier's customers need not change their ATM backbone equipment. Neither does the carrier need to change its service facilities, nor retrain and retool to support a new inverse multiplexing technology. The carrier is using the same bit-based inverse multiplexing technology that it does for frame relay, the only difference being that the imux now has an ATM interface facing the customer premises, instead of the imux's customary HSSI or V.35 interface. Circuit provisioning is identical, requiring no retraining other than how to address the expected ATM protocol and interfacing issues.

A carrier's ability to offer virtual ATM transport in the form of NxT1/E1 clear channel ATM imuxing allows it to serve more customers, particularly those who are not quite ready for high-speed DS3 or OC-3c ATM service. A clear channel ATM NxT1 link can provide significantly higher-speed access to a switched ATM service than single T1/E1 links, using readily available lines and without higher bandwidth's price tag. The UNI interfaces already deployed at the customer premises and within the service provider's cloud remain unchanged, and the carrier can now expand its ATM offerings to more than just those few customers in selected geographical areas that can access or afford DS3 and OC-3c bandwidth.

## CONCLUSION

Using clear channel ATM inverse multiplexing does not preclude a user from upgrading to IMA when it is available or affordable, or to DS3 or OC-3c when the user's applications environment demands even greater bandwidth. A benefit of clear channel ATM inverse multiplexing is that both of the technologies that are combined into a solution — a DS3 or OC-3c UNI, with bit-based NxT1/E1 multiplexing — are readily available and well understood. Whether support for IMA is added to a clear channel ATM inverse multiplexer, or the inverse multiplexer is replaced by a higher-speed ATM access device, there is no need for the user or the carrier to restructure the network.

Although it is still undetermined as to the ultimate role that ATM will play, it is clearly an important technology with significant benefits. It is also a technology that will exist in concert with the installed base of TDM WAN access devices for a long time. Clear channel ATM inverse multiplexing leverages both bit-based inverse multiplexing and ATM technologies, and is perhaps the best example of how simply and seamlessly ATM and TDM can coexist — to the benefit of end users and carriers alike.

# Chapter 21
# Hybrid Fiber/Coaxial Networks

*Bill Koerner*

Hybrid Fiber/Coaxial (HFC) cable networks can deliver interactive services such as telephony and high-speed data services. HFC networks use fiber transmitters, fiber nodes, RF amplifiers, and taps to distribute signals to subscribers and set-top boxes (or cable modems) to return signals to the cable company. This chapter explains HFC network management system requirements.

## INTRODUCTION

Telecommunications reform, the Internet, and high-speed data services have revolutionized the definition of communication services. Services rich in multimedia content have the highest demand and require the highest bandwidth to live up to customer expectations.

HFC networks currently offer the best network alternative to deliver these services, but traditionally have never been managed like their telco counterparts. This chapter examines the requirements for managing the HFC cable network, its relationship to the services being offered, and ideas for and challenges of managing the network.

## OVERVIEW OF HFC NETWORKS

When cable TV came about in the 1940s, the intent was to provide TV signals to those who could not receive them from the standard antenna. As more people signed up for cable service, the cable operators simply extended the cable to reach the new customers.

Unfortunately, as they extended the cable, the signal also became weaker, because signal loss is directly proportional to the length of the cable. To overcome the losses, cable operators inserted amplifiers in the transmission network, thus allowing the cable operator to now provide service to more customers. Unfortunately, once again, the amplifiers also

0-8493-9965-3/99/$0.00+$.50
© 1999 by CRC Press LLC

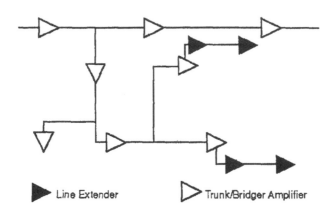

Line Extender    Trunk/Bridger Amplifier

**Exhibit 1. Tree and Branch Architecture.**

added noise and distortions to the original signals; thus there is a theoretical limit to the number of customers the cable operators could service.

Throughout the 1980s, amplifier manufacturers improved not only the noise and distortion characteristics, but also the frequency range. It was now possible to extend the transmission networks farther and offer more channels. Exhibit 1 shows a typical example of what came to be known as the "tree and branch architecture."

Advances in fiber optic technology made it possible to use laser transmitters, receivers, and fiber optic cable to distribute the cable TV signal to neighborhoods, and then use the existing RF network to distribute the signals to the subscribers. Thus was born the HFC cable network.

The HFC network allowed the cable operator to reduce the number of RF amplifiers needed, which increased the quality of the signal provided and overall network reliability. With the RF network reduced to just a few amplifiers, it was also now easier to support higher frequencies (i.e., more channels). Most current HFC designs support up to 750 MHz of bandwidth, which roughly translates to 110 channels. Exhibit 2 shows an example of a HFC network.

## REQUIREMENTS FOR MANAGING HFC NETWORKS

Since the early days of cable TV, the intent has mostly been to deliver analog television signals to subscribers. Higher frequencies meant that cable operators could offer more channels, thus the cable network explosion during the 1980s and 1990s.

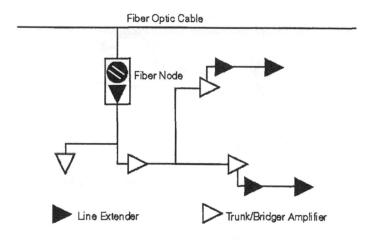

**Exhibit 2. HFC Network Architecture.**

With the newly available bandwidth, several cable operators discovered that they could offer other services that generated additional revenue. Digital Music Express, a CD-like audio service, allowed the cable operator to offer 30 digital radio channels. Pay-per-view allowed the cable operator to offer newly released movies and sports events to subscribers by programming (authorizing) the set-top box for subscribers that ordered the additional service.

### Achieving Interactivity

Until this point, most cable networks only worked in one direction, called the downstream path. Basically, the cable signals are broadcast to all set-top boxes, and the set-top controls what the customer is authorized to use.

Some cable plants also have, or are being designed for, a return path, or an upstream path (see Exhibit 3). This design is what makes the HFC network interactive — the ability to pass data either way — and is setting the stage for many types of services, ranging from telephony to high-speed data services, energy management, and Internet access.

Most return paths are designed to work in the 5 MHz to 40 MHz frequency range (mostly because that spectrum is not being used for other channels). The return path, however, offers some serious challenges for reliable operation of two-way services. Examples of common problems encountered (for both upstream and return path) with a HFC network are also shown in Exhibit 3.

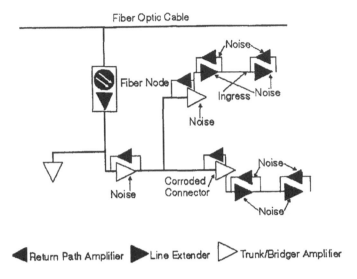

**Exhibit 3. HFC Network with Impairments.**

**Distortion.** With any active components, distortion is unavoidable. In the case of HFC network, the main cause of distortion comes from multiple carriers (i.e., frequencies) in amplifiers.

If the combined signal strength is too strong, the amplifier will go into compression and generate distortion products. These will cause the existing carrier levels to be distorted by multiples and combinations of other carriers.

**Carrier Levels.** As previously stated, if the carrier levels are too high, they will cause the amplifiers to generate distortion products. If they are too low, then the carrier-to-noise ratio will be too low (i.e., not enough signal strength at the receiving end).

The frequency response of the amplifiers can also cause variation of the carrier levels, thus the lower frequencies may be fine and the higher frequencies will have a low (bad) carrier-to-noise ratio.

**Corroded Connectors.** HFC networks are constructed either above ground (on telephone poles) or underground. In both environments, the connectors (between the cable and the amplifiers) will corrode or degrade with time, either from water seeping into the connection or from other types of wear — everything from animals chewing on the connectors to varying tension on the cable.

This type of destruction can either let other signals in (known as "ingress") or distort the signals passing through it, most noticeably the

60 Hz power supply used to power the amplifiers. This distortion causes 60 Hz and other multiples (usually 120 Hz) distortion across all frequencies.

**Ingress.** Although the cable network is a closed network, there are still external signals that can get into, and interfere with, upstream traffic. Ham radio has components at 7, 14, and 21 MHz; shortwave radio has components at 6,10, 12 and 15 MHz; arc welders produce broadband noise that can last for long time periods (minutes); lightning produces broadband noise that can last for several seconds. Home wiring (as when consumers decide to wire up their entertainment system) is responsible for common causes of noise imposed on the return path.

**Noise Funneling.** The return path also experiences a phenomenon referred to as noise funneling, where the collective noise of all the return path amplifiers collects, or funnels, back into the fiber node. This phenomenon can be difficult to troubleshoot, because it will be difficult to determine which amplifier is causing the significant noise problem.

### "Digital" Requires Monitoring

Until this time, cable operators had no method equivalent to methods used by the telcos to monitor their network. Cable companies usually relied on subscribers to call in when there was a problem — either no cable signal at all (an outage), snowy images (low levels or carrier/noise problems), or multiple pictures (crossmod, microreflections, or other distortion problems).

With analog TV signals, a wide variety of problems could exist, yet the picture was still visible, thus there was no real need to put in elaborate monitoring systems. With the advent of new, digital-based services, however, there is no graceful fading of the services — they either work or they don't. Digital modulation is more resistant to network problems, but it eventually will reach a point where it won't work.

To ensure delivery of quality services, it becomes necessary to manage both the HFC network and the services that run on top of it.

### SERVICES RUNNING ON THE HFC NETWORK

To illustrate the relationship between the HFC network and the services that run on top of it, a few examples are given of the services delivered over HFC and how they might correlate to problems with the network.

### Analog Video Service

As mentioned previously, there are many types of problems that can occur in the HFC network and still allow viewing of analog video. These problems could include signal levels that decrease as a function of frequency or distortion products that superimpose several channels onto one. These problems are well known and characterized, and most HFC networks are optimized to minimize their effects.

### Digital Services

These are the new services that will take advantage of the broadband capabilities of the HFC network. What is unknown is how the HFC impairments will affect the digital services.

Recent studies have looked at several different HFC networks to test their ability to support digital services. The tests (done by Cable Television Laboratories, Inc.) used a RF T1 modem to determine the performance factors from five different cable plants. Measurements were compared against ITU-TSS G.821 performance objectives.

What these studies concluded was that the return path is a hostile environment. One cable plant defect can make the entire reverse spectrum unusable.

The field testing emphasized the critical importance of conducting a comprehensive and thorough plant hardening effort and maintaining precise gain alignment. The most troublesome conditions were caused by impulse noise, usually observed with cold temperatures, high wind conditions, increased precipitation (including thunderstorms), and combinations of all of these weather variables.

Under these conditions, the integrity of the transmission path (both downstream and the return path) was affected, resulting in increased error seconds, severely error seconds, and poor availability. This does not rule out the ability of the HFC network to deliver the services; it merely indicates that a well-characterized HFC network, along with a comprehensive network management system, is required to offer the new services that meet subscriber expectations.

### IDEAS FOR MANAGING THE HFC NETWORK

One method for managing communications networks such as HFC is the TMN model.

### Telecommunications Management Network (TMN) Model

Briefly, the TMN model breaks the operation process into five distinct layers:

- Business management.
- Service management.
- Network management.
- Element management.
- Network elements.

Each of these layers is connected, and each affects the ability to offer services to subscribers. For each layer, the management systems must incorporate the following five functions:

- Fault management.
- Configuration management.
- Performance management.
- Security management.
- Accounting management.

Communications between the layers are handled by a standard protocol — CMIP.

The TMN model offers a structured approach to meet the new requirements of HFC management discussed in the previous section. Specifically for the HFC network, the following items should be addressed:

- Monitor status of HFC network (fault management).
- Monitor status of head end equipment (fault management).
- Manage head end equipment (configuration, performance, security, and accounting management functions).
- Monitor QOS into the head end.

**Example: High-Speed Data Services over HFC**

To illustrate the management approach, an example of high-speed data services over a HFC network is illustrated in Exhibit 4. The data service is very similar to a standard network service found in many corporations, where PCs have access to each other and a main server complex.

In this example, the real difference is in the network medium and the signal conversion system (which converts Ethernet traffic into RF packets). Instead of 10-BaseT, FDDI or a T1 line, the distribution network is HFC.

In the traditional data network, there would be routers, bridges, and hubs to segment the traffic over the network. These devices have some monitoring capability to indicate the traffic going through them and the number of packets that were resent.

These devices also are part of the management system and have their own management application that can control the type and amount of traffic flowing through them. Typically, this is through the use of MIB and SNMP. Thus, when a problem occurs with a device, it can be used to troubleshoot the data network problems.

**HFC Equipment**

In the HFC environment, the network uses fiber transmitters, fiber nodes, RF amplifiers and taps to distribute the signals to the subscribers and set-top boxes, or cable modems, to return the signals to the head end.

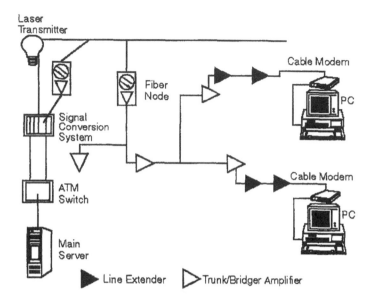

**Exhibit 4. HFC Network with High Speed Data Service.**

No similar management strategy currently exists for the HFC environment. Most HFC equipment currently does not have monitoring capability built in.

### Status Monitoring Systems

Many of the HFC devices support an external transponder, or telemetry equipment, that is managed by a status monitoring system. The communication between the status monitoring system and the transponders is through a proprietary protocol. The communication path is through the HFC network to the transponders and through the return path, or telephone line, for the return communication.

The status monitoring system plays an important role in establishing similar capabilities for the HFC network. In the example shown in Exhibit 4, transponders could be placed in the fiber node, trunk or bridge amplifiers, and line extenders. With these transponders, the status monitoring system would be able to indicate the status of those devices in near real time.

The types of parameters the transponders can measure include AGC levels for the amplifiers, RF levels of various carriers, temperature inside the amplifier or node housing, and laser power level. These parameters allow the monitoring system to predict the current health of the HFC network.

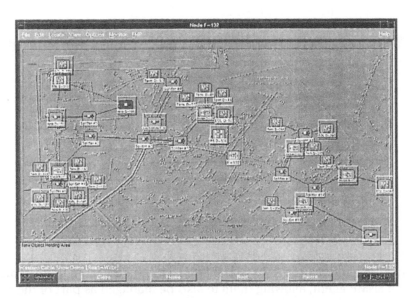

**Exhibit 5. Status Monitoring System Represented in Network Management System.**

Some specialized monitoring modules, called end-of-line monitors, can perform more detailed measurements on the RF carriers. These parameters are tuned more for analog video (i.e., carrier/noise ratio, depth of modulation, carrier level variation over time) than they are for digital services, but still can be used as a diagnostic tool when problems in digital services occur.

Exhibit 5 shows an example of bringing the status monitoring information into a standard network management system, such as HPOV platform. This example shows a fiber node and the associated RF devices to service a 500-home area. Color is used to indicate the status of the managed objects — red for critical, yellow for major or minor, green for normal, and blue for unmanaged.

Note that although the status monitoring system typically has a proprietary protocol to communicate with the transponders (shown as managed objects in Exhibit 5), they can still be represented in a standard management environment, either through proxy agents or through a mediation device (discussed in more detail later).

## Standard Management Capabilities

Most of the components used for the high-speed data service currently support standard management capabilities. The server complex and ATM

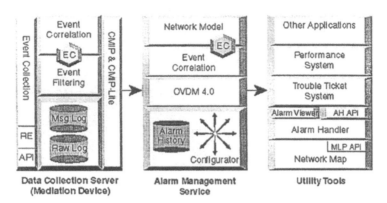

**Exhibit 6. Fault Management Platform.**

switches typically have SNMP capabilities. Home PCs can support some sort of a SNMP agent, allowing them to also be managed as part of the service.

The signal conversion systems and cable modems are relatively new and may not support SNMP capability for the first revisions. Thus, the high-speed digital service could be managed similar to a corporate application, with management products like Hewlett-Packard's Network Node Manager or Operations Center.

## Monitoring Non-Standard Services

For those services (or pieces of services) that do not offer standard management capability, it is still necessary to at least monitor the fault status. Most equipment used in the head end will either have some sort of alarm capability or be controlled by a PC application that will have alarm capability, typically through a RS-232 serial port. These types of devices could still be incorporated as part of a management system through the use of a mediation device.

Exhibit 6 shows the FMP from Hewlett-Packard. It incorporates a mediation device as the first interface to the network management system.

This mediation device is used to map RS-232, SNMP, and CMIP devices into a standard X.733 alarm messaging format. Also built into the mediation device is event correlation, which allows the management system to correlate related alarms (e.g., HFC outages and critical alarms in services) before forwarding onto the network management system. This would, for example, allow only one alarm to be forwarded when hundreds of alarms may be logged into the mediation device.

At the network management layer (shown as alarm management service and utility tools in Exhibit 6), another layer of event correlation takes place. This layer correlates alarms from other head ends or from other types of managed object classes (i.e., head end equipment) to develop root-cause analysis. This is the event correlation that would allow the user, for example, to correlate alarms from the high-speed data service with alarms from the HFC network.

### Manager/Agent Application for Controlling HFC Equipment

Up to this point, this chapter has discussed monitoring the status of equipment in a HFC network. The other aspect of a management system is to control the equipment — that is, some sort of manager/agent application.

Most head end equipment currently either has no management application or has a PC-based application that was designed to be a standalone application. In order for the network management system to control the devices, there needs to be some way to program the devices, either directly or through an agent application.

If the head end devices have some sort of PC application for control, it may be possible to login from a remote terminal on the network management station and control the devices that way. That would allow for centralized control, but does not meet the requirements of the TMN model.

For those devices that do not have a manager/agent application, or some sort of MIB, they cannot be automatically managed by the network management system. Equipment vendors will have to develop a manager/agent application for their devices.

### CONCLUSION

Management for HFC networks is in its infancy stage. A majority of the equipment vendors are in the process of developing a network management strategy for their devices and services, which will include the development of a manager and agent application.

### SNMP vs. CMIP

Currently, most vendors are leaning toward the use of SNMP to control their devices. Because of the widespread acceptance of SNMP in the computer network and systems management, there are hundreds of development tools that make the development task much easier than CMIP. CMIP does have some performance capabilities that far exceed SNMP, and some equipment used with a HFC network (e.g., telephone switches, SONET gear) may use CMIP instead of SNMP.

For the short-term (i.e., over the next five years), the management protocols used will probably include SNMP, TL-1, CMIP, and other, non-standard forms. Thus the network management system used will have to be flexible, one that can handle many protocols yet provide a common, standards-based operating environment.

With the network management system, it will be possible to present the management information for all network elements and services in one consistent GUI and provide for centralized management. With the integrated information, it will be possible to proactively monitor the HFC network, and eventually predict when the HFC network will need maintenance or when it will start to affect the digital services, thus allowing for a reliable, high-speed communications network for many types of services.

# Chapter 22
# Choosing Asymmetrical Digital Subscriber Lines

*Gilbert Held*

Digital subscriber lines (DSLs) enable high-speed transmissions — including interLAN communications, videoconferencing, and mainframe access — over existing copper twisted-pair local loops. By determining the availability, operating rate of the service, and the capability of the carrier's internal broadband network, users can decide whether DSL service is a cost-effective transport replacement for their current service.

## INTRODUCTION

Although essentially all long-distance communications in North America are now transported via fiber-optic cable, the majority of what is referred to as "the last cable mile" — the 18,000-foot local loop from the telephone company central office (CO) to subscribers — continues to be twisted-pair copper cable. Because of the high cost of installing fiber cable from telephone company central offices to individual residential and business subscribers, communications carriers are exploring methods that enable high-speed transmission to occur over their existing copper twisted-pair local loops. The result is the development of a series of digital subscriber lines.

Although several DSL products, including high data-rate digital subscriber lines (HDSL), single-line digital subscriber lines (SDSL), and very high data-rate digital subscriber lines (VDSL) are discussed in this chapter, the focus is on asymmetrical digital subscriber line (ADSL) technology, because it is the most practical transmission facility. In addition, ADSL is being used in a series of field trials conducted by telephone companies around the world.

0-8493-9965-3/99/$0.00+$.50
© 1999 by CRC Press LLC

## ASYMMETRICAL DIGITAL SUBSCRIBER LINES (ADSL)

ADSL is a technology for use over telephone twisted-pair loops in which data rates between 1.544 and 6M bps, and in some cases up to 8M bps, can be obtained from the carrier's central office to the subscriber (referred to as downstream transmission), while a transmission rate of 640K bps to 800K bps is obtained in the opposite direction (referred to as upstream transmission). Because the operating rate differs in each direction, this technique is referred to as asymmetrical transmission.

ADSL modems use either discrete multitone (DMT) or carrierless amplitude/phase (CAP) modulation. DMT was standardized by the American National Standards Institute (ANSI) as standard T1.413. CAP was developed by Paradyne, formerly a unit of AT&T and now an independent company. Although DMT is standardized, CAP is presently deployed in a number of field trials throughout the world for high-speed Internet access and has received high marks for its performance. It is quite possible that communications carriers will select both of the competitive methods to obtain an ADSL capability.

### Discrete Multitone (DMT) Operation

DMT permits the transmission of high-speed data over conventional copper twisted-pair wire without adversely affecting voice communications. Through the use of frequency division multiplexing (FDM), a copper twisted-pair subscriber line is subdivided into three parts by frequency. One channel is assigned for downstream data transmission and a second is assigned for upstream data transmission. The first two channels have a variable amount of bandwidth based on the results of the ADSL modems communicating with one another. The third channel, which uses a fixed spectrum of bandwidth from 0 to 4 KHz, is used for normal telephone operations. Thus, an ADSL line simultaneously supports the bidirectional transmission of high-speed data and conventional voice connection.

In Exhibit 1, the ADSL modem is shown with two digital connections, one to a LAN and another to a mainframe. An ADSL modem can support virtually unlimited digital connections; however, most modems used in field trials have been limited to two to four connectors. The ADSL modem supports multiple digital devices through the use of time-division multiplexing (TDM), which can be used to subdivide the upstream and downstream data channels by time into independent digital connections.

Under the DMT standard, the frequency spectrum above 10 KHz is subdivided into a large number of independent subchannels. Because the amount of attenuation at high frequencies depends on the length of the subscriber line and its wire gauge, an ADSL modem based on DMT technology installed at a central office must first determine which subchannels are usable. The modem transmits tones to the remote modem installed at the

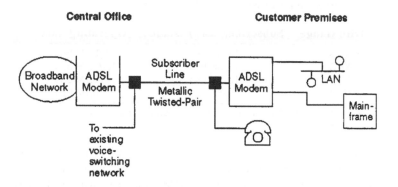

**Note:**
An ADSL modem converts digital data into frequency tones above 4 KHz. As a result, the 0 to 4 KHz bandwidth of twisted-pair cable can continue to be used for voice communications.

**Exhibit 1. Using an Asymmetrical Digital Subscriber Line.**

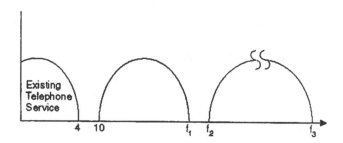

**Exhibit 2. ADSL Modem Use of the Copper Twisted-Pair Frequency Spectrum.**

customer's premises, where the tones are analyzed. The remote modem responds during this initiation process at a relatively low data rate, which significantly reduces the possibility of the signal analysis performed by the remote modem being misinterpreted.

On receipt of the returned signal analysis, the ADSL modem located in the telephone company's central office will use up to 256 4-KHz-wide subchannels for downstream transmissions. Through a reverse learning process, the remote modem will use up to 32 4-KHz-wide subchannels for upstream transmission. Exhibit 2 illustrates the use of the copper twisted-pair frequency spectrum by an ADSL modem. In Exhibit 2, f1, f2, and f3 are variables based on the results of the ADSL modem's discrete multitone handshaking process; however, the actual limit for f3 is 1.1 MHz, which represents the maximum usable bandwidth on a copper twisted-pair cable.

**Exhibit 3. Generalized ADSL Performance**

| Wire Gauge | Subscriber Line Distance | Operating Rate |
|---|---|---|
| 24 AWG | 18,000 feet | 1.5/2.0M bps |
| 26 AWG | 15,000 feet | 1.5/2.0M bps |
| 24 AWG | 12,000 feet | 6.1M bps |
| 26 AWG | 9,000 feet | 6.1M bps |

*Note:* AWG is the American Wire Gauge standard for measuring connectors.

**Benefits of DMT.** One of the main benefits of DMT is its ability to take advantage of the characteristics of twisted-pair wire, which can vary from one local loop to another. This makes DMT modulation well suited for obtaining a higher data throughput than is possible through the use of a single carrier transmission technique. Because the transmission rate varies depending on the wire gauge and cable length as well as the physical characteristics of the cable, ADSL performance can vary considerably from one local loop to another. Ignoring bridge taps, which represent sections of unterminated twisted-pair cable connected in parallel across the twisted-pair cable under consideration, various tests of ADSL lines provide a general indication of their operating rate capability, which is summarized in Exhibit 3.

## Carrierless Amplitude/Phase (CAP) Modulation

CAP modulation is a derivative of quadrature amplitude modulation (QAM), which was developed by Paradyne when it was a subsidiary of AT&T and which is used in most modems today. Unlike DMT, which subdivides the bandwidth of the twisted-pair wire into 4 KHz segments, CAP uses the entire bandwidth in upstream and downstream channels.

Under CAP, serial data is encoded by mapping a group of bits into a signal constellation point using a two-dimensional, eight-state trellis coding with Reed-Solomon forward error correction. Reed-Solomon automatically protects transmitted data against impairments due to crosstalk, impulse noise, and background noise.

In the CAP modulation process, once a group of bits are mapped to a predefined point in the signal constellation, the in-phase and quadrature filters implement the positioning in the signal constellation. Because this technique simply adjusts the amplitude and phase without requiring a constant carrier, the technique is referred to as "carrierless."

The ADSL modem developed by Paradyne uses a 256-point signal constellation for downstream operations. This constellation pattern is in the 120 KHz to 1,224 KHz frequency range and produces a composite signaling rate of 960K baud, with 7 bits packed into each signal change. Although the resulting downstream operating rate is 6.72M bps, the use of the Reed-Solomon forward error correction code reduces the actual payload to 6.312M bps, plus a 64K-bps control channel. In the upstream direction, the Paradyne ADSL modem uses a CAP-16 line code in the 35-KHz to 72-KHz frequency band to obtain a composite signaling rate of 24K baud across 16 subchannels. By packing 3 bits per signal change, an upstream line rate of 72K bps is obtained, of which 64K bps is available for data. Similar to an ADSL DMT modem, an ADSL CAP modem can use time-division multiplexing to derive multiple channels on the upstream and downstream channels.

### ADSL Developments and Field Tests

Although the ANSI DMT standard defines an operating rate of 6M bps on local loops up to 12,000 feet in length, some vendors now offer rates approaching 8M bps downstream and up to 800K bps upstream. This additional data rate is accomplished through an automatic rate adaptation capability that correlates the connected data rate to distance and line noise, enabling additional bandwidth to be gained — which translates into a higher operating rate.

In the US, GTE Telephone Operations (Stamford CT) began testing the use of ADSL technology as part of a public data trial in the Dallas-Fort Worth area during 1996. This trial tests downstream data transmission at operating rates of up to 4M bps and upstream transmission at data rates up to 500K bps. The testing involves the Irving Public Library system, several bookstores, and area GTE employees. ADSL modems used during this trial are provided by Western Technologies of Oswego IL and Aware, Inc. of Bedford MA.

On the West Coast, U.S. WEST (Olympia WA) is testing ADSL-based services through its ENTERPRISE business unit and will use equipment from several vendors before deciding on which equipment to deploy commercially. Other communications carriers are expected to announce field trials as well as commercial deployment of ADSL technology soon.

### ADDITIONAL DSL TECHNOLOGIES

In addition to ADSL, three related technologies warrant a degree of discussion:

- High data-rate digital subscriber line (HDSL).
- Single-line digital subscriber line (SDSL).
- Very high data-rate digital subscriber line (VDSL).

HDSL modems are used on either end of one or more pair of twisted-pair wires to obtain a T1 or E1 operating rate. Currently, a T1 operating rate requires two lines and E1 requires three. HDSL is primarily used on college campuses to provide a T1 or E1 link to interconnect LANs.

SDSL represents HDSL over a single telephone line and is used where multiple lines do not exist or would be expensive to install.

VDSL modems for twisted-pair access operate at data rates from 12.9 to 52.8M bps on 24-gauge cable. Because of the higher operating rate, the maximum transmission distance supported by VDSL is limited to under 4,000 feet. Higher rates over shorter distances may limit VDSL's ability to support communications carrier customers.

VDSL standards may not be finalized for several years. There are four VDSL line coding methods — discrete multitone, discrete wavelet multitone, carrierless amplitude/phase modulation, and simple line coding. DMT for VDSL is similar to the technology used in the ADSL standard, with more carriers (supporting ADSL) being the primary difference between the two. Discrete wavelet multitone coding represents a multicarrier system that uses wavelet transformers for individual carriers. The carrierless amplitude/phase modulation method under consideration is similar to Paradyne's CAP, representing a version of suppressed carrier quadrature amplitude modulation. The fourth coding technique, simple line coding, represents a baseband signaling and filtering system.

Based on the higher transmission capacity of VDSL, it will probably be deployed by communications carriers to businesses as a mechanism for asynchronous transfer mode (ATM) connectivity. The ATM Forum, which produced a 51.84M-bps standard for a private user-to-network interface, is currently examining the potential delivery of ATM via VDSL transmission.

## CONCLUSION

From the viewpoint of a corporate network manager, ADSL is probably the only digital subscriber line technology that will be offered by enough carriers in the next few years to deserve consideration for interconnecting geographically separated locations. Although two different types of ADSL technology, based on either DMT or CAP modulation, are being considered by communications carriers, from the perspective of the end user the most important factors are:

- Availability of service.
- Operating rate of the service.
- Ability of the carrier's internal broadband network to provide connectivity.

The availability of ADSL will govern whether or not the technology can be used to interconnect LANs, provide remote access to mainframes, support videoconferencing between locations, or perform other communications functions. Although it may be possible, for example, to use an ADSL connection in one location and a conventional T1 connection in another location for communications, carriers still have not addressed the conversion of data between different transmission facilities.

The second area of concern is the operating rate of ADSL service. Because the transmission rate varies — depending on line quality, the distance of the user's location from a carrier's central office, and the wire gauge of the wire pair — users cannot fully appreciate its transmission capability until an ADSL line becomes operational. Vendor specifications should be used as a guide and ADSL should be considered for applications that require a high data transmission capability but that can also be effectively performed if only a fraction of that capability is actually achieved.

Thus, videoconferencing or LAN access to the Internet are two applications for which ADSL may prove effective, even if the user achieves half or even a quarter of the theoretical ADSL rate due to a bad subscriber loop, long subscriber wire distance from the carrier's central office, or a similar factor.

A third area that should be examined before considering ADSL service is the scope of the carrier's internal broadband network. The user should determine whether the network interconnects only the ADSL offerings of that carrier, if it provides connectivity to other carriers, and if it provides connectivity to other data services offered by that carrier. By doing so, the user can determine if it will be possible to use ADSL services as a transport mechanism for such data services as X.25 and frame relay.

By contacting their communications carrier, users can ascertain when ADSL may be deployed in their areas and its projected cost. By asking the carrier key questions concerning the availability of the service in different areas where an organization may have offices, the operating rate of the service, and the capability of the carrier's internal broadband network, users can determine if ADSL service will be suitable for trial. If so, a test plan should be developed to compare ADSL with traditional T1 service to determine if it can be used as a cost-effective transport replacement.

# Chapter 23
# Multimedia Networking Technologies

*T. M. Rajkumar and Amitava Haldar*

A host of technologies are emerging to help organizations support the enterprisewide delivery of new multimedia applications. Some of these technologies work well at the workgroup or local area network level, and others work at the backbone or wide area network level. This chapter reviews many of the technologies in these two groups and evaluates their suitability for distributing multimedia information.

## INTRODUCTION

Multimedia applications involving databases, the World Wide Web and desktop videoconferencing challenge IS organizations to implement networking technologies that support a wide variety of information forms. Multimedia applications place different demands on the network than do traditionally supported discrete media (such as text and data). They require support for continuous, delay-sensitive media such as audio and video that need connection-oriented links. Because most networks today support connectionless links, they are poorly suited to support multimedia data.

A host of technologies are emerging to support enterprise multimedia applications. Some of them work well at the LAN or workgroup level, and others work at the WAN or backbone level. This chapter discusses the multimedia networking technologies within these two groups and their suitability for distributing multimedia information.

## LAN TECHNOLOGIES

Because traditional LAN technologies such as Ethernet and Token Ring are designed to process data packets and operate in contentious mode, they cannot meet the demands placed on the LAN by multimedia applications. Several technologies have been proposed to support multimedia on the LAN, including asynchronous Ethernet, FDDI, Fast Ethernet, and ATM.

### Asynchronous Ethernet

In contrast to packet-switched technologies, asynchronous transmission guarantees timely delivery of information, avoiding delay and jitter. The premise behind asynchronous Ethernet is that voice (not audio or video) is the critical component in multimedia communications.[1] Hence, this technology is most important at locations where videoconferencing is the primary multimedia application.

To ensure that voice receives priority, a special asynchronous ISDN 6.144M-bps line is added to the standard Ethernet technology. This additional bandwidth is sufficient for a multipoint videoconference with six participants, each using 384K bps and additional bandwidth for such ancillary functions as white boarding. In addition, asynchronous Ethernet is easy to add to existing Ethernet networks, because all that is required is an asynchronous Ethernet hub and cards for the computers involved in videoconferencing. On segments where such asynchronous capability is not required, it need not be added.[2]

**Suitability for Multimedia Traffic.** Asynchronous Ethernet is a shared-media approach with limited multicasting support for audio only. It is not suited for full-motion video (i.e., the Moving Picture Experts Group or Motion Picture Experts Group standard), but it supports H.261 video (the teleconferencing standard). It provides truly asynchronous support for voice.[3] From a business perspective, asynchronous Ethernet is only suitable as a small workgroup solution and where multimedia needs are not great. The technology should be viewed as a transitionary step to ATM technology.

### Fast Ethernet

The IEEE 802.3 or 100Base-T is rapidly becoming the technology of choice for providing bandwidth to users because it uses the same CSMA/CD technique as the widely used 10Base-T Ethernet. The high-speed 100Base-T offers 100M-bps performance for a small increase in cost for network adapters and hubs. In addition, it allows existing 10M-bps cards to share the same network, providing for easy transition.

This Fast Ethernet technology has limitations however. It needs a repeater every 250 meters as opposed to the every 2,500 meters required by 10Base-T systems. Because the regular ISA bus architecture is not fast enough to handle the 100M bps of bandwidth 100Base-T provides, the technology needs PCs with PCI buses.

100Base-T supports three different signaling schemes that require specific types of repeaters. It may require four wires as opposed to the standard UTP wiring existing in some organizations. The availability of mitigating technologies minimizes these problems.

100Base-Tx also has a new duplexing feature, allowing it to boost network speed to 200M bps. In general, the network adapter must always be listening on the receiving pair of wires to check for a collision. When Ethernet switching is used, a dedicated 100 Mbps is available to the adapter, avoiding the need to check for collisions. In this way, the UTP wiring can be used and 200M-bps bandwidth is available. This option is typically used for the server and not for each desktop.

**Suitability for Multimedia Traffic.** Ideally, 100Base-T is a workgroup solution, because the 100M-bps bandwidth is shared among the different users. It relies on appropriate use by every user station, and it cannot make any delay guarantees or provide QOS considerations. This high-speed Ethernet technology is useful because it provides backward compatibility with existing 10Base-T networks, making it easy to configure, install, and manage. In addition, a new set of gigabit Ethernet standards expected by mid-1997 should allow groups employing the technology to use increased bandwidth in the near future.

## 100VG-AnyLAN

A second alternative high-speed Ethernet solution is the 100VG-AnyLAN option. This technique does not use the standard CSMA/CD access technique, but rather a new DPA technique. DPA enables the system to assign priorities and ensures on-time delivery of multimedia information.

100VG-AnyLAN also depends on more intelligence in the hub. Under DPA, a node wishing to transmit sends a request-to-send to the hub. If the message is a priority message, a special bit stream sent over two pairs of wiring indicates this to the hub. The hub continuously scans and grants the requests based on their priority. The hub also sends a notice to the receiving node that it is about to receive a message. It then routes the packet from the sending node to the receiving node or nodes. Implementing the priority 100VG-AnyLAN thus requires use of all four wires, which can be costly to implement. The primary advantage of 100VG-AnyLAN over 100Base-T4 is that it also supports Token Ring technology.

**Suitability for Multimedia Traffic.** 100VG-AnyLAN supports multimedia better than Ethernet, because it assigns priority to multimedia traffic and supports multicasting. It is particularly more suited than 100Base-T, because with a small number of workstations (i.e., less than 30) it can support delays of less than 10 microseconds.[4]

Despite these advantages, 100VG-AnyLAN does not provide QOS guarantees or support for existing (i.e., Ethernet) infrastructure. From a business perspective, 100VG-AnyLAN is useful for organizations that have invested heavily in Token Ring systems. For these groups of organizations, 100VG-AnyLAN provides an efficient way of supporting multimedia at the workgroup level.

## FDDI

Because of its speed, FDDI is used extensively as the backbone to interconnect LANs. FDDI uses a token-passing method to provide 100M-bps of bandwidth. It can also be spread over larger distances (i.e., 200K meters) than bus-type networks and supports up to 500 stations on a ring.

FDDI uses two counter rotating rings for data transfer. The use of two rings ensures against failure of the ring when a single node fails. FDDI has extensive network management support, and its cost has fallen to $1,500 to $3,000 per hub.

## FDDI II

FDDI II provides a circuit-switched service while maintaining the token-controlled packet-switched service of the original FDDI. This is done by imposing a fixed-frame structure on the original FDDI and regularly repeating time slots in the frame (i.e., asynchronous transmission). FDDI II provides the continuous sustained data rate needed for multimedia traffic, but total bandwidth still remains at 100M bps.

**Suitability for Multimedia Traffic.** FDDI II adds constant bit rate traffic to FDDI to support multimedia. Its bandwidth is sufficient for LANs and supports multicasting. To bring FDDI II to the desktop is a costly proposition, however. Like FDDI, FDDI II is used mostly at the backbone to interconnect LAN systems. It is also incompatible with FDDI in the sense that a station with FDDI cannot read a FDDI II frame; the reverse, however, is possible.

## ASYNCHRONOUS TRANSFER MODE

ATM is a technology that serves equally well at the LAN and WAN levels. The following sections provide a general description of this still-emerging technology and specifics on its LAN emulation technology.

ATM uses fixed-size 53-byte cells (i.e., a 48-byte information field and a 5-byte header field) and breaks all traffic into these cells to ensure quicker switching and multiplexing. It provides point-to-point and point-to-multipoint connections through virtual circuits. ATM currently supports speeds as high as 155M bps and 622M bps and will reach 10G bps

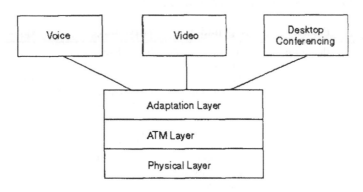

**Exhibit 1. ATM Layer Architecture.**

in the future. It operates as a DS3 or T3 line (i.e., 45M bps) or possibly a DS1 line (i.e., 1.544 Mbps).

### ATM Architecture

ATM functionality corresponds to the physical layer and data link layer of the OSI model; the architecture is depicted in Exhibit 1. In the physical layer, information is transferred from one user to another by cell-based asynchronous transmission or, more frequently, by an externally framed synchronous transmission structure, typically a SONET structure. Thus in the latter option, the ATM cells are carried inside a SONET structure (i.e., 90 columns and 9 rows of 8-bit bytes) with a bit rate of 51.84M bps (i.e., one frame is transmitted every 125 microseconds — the sampling interval used in digitizing voice for telephone systems).

The ATM layer multiplexes cells over the physical link. The major function of this layer is to complete the ATM cell structure and set up the cell streams for transmissions of outgoing process, receive the incoming cells, and send them to the corresponding stream. The cells are distinguished by the VCI and VPI in the cell header. A table in the switch helps the ATM layer place the cell in the appropriate output link. A generic flow control is used for media access by the user network interface to control the amount of traffic entering the network.

The ATM adaptation layer has the job of adapting higher-level data into the format needed by the ATM layer. When the necessary adaptation is completed, many different kinds of traffic can be carried over the same system, enabling ATM networks to aggregate network traffic to cut costs while simultaneously providing flexible service provisioning.[5] AAL identifies four service classes based on the following three parameters:

**Exhibit 2. Quality and Application Classes in ATM**

| Name | Priority | Negotiation | Advantage | Applications |
|------|----------|-------------|-----------|--------------|
| Constant Bit Rate | High priority | "Contract basis" for maximum data rate | No cell loss | Real-time audio and video |
| Variable Bit Rate | Medium to high | Peak cell rate and sustained cell rate | QOS guaranteed for cell loss and bandwidth availability | Not for LAN traffic but for most others |
| Available Bit Rate | Medium | Negotiates bandwidth availability and cell loss | Reliable delivery of bursty data | LAN traffic |
| Unspecified Bit Rate | Low to medium | No QOS | Efficient use of bandwidth | Noncritical applications |

- The timing relation between source and destination (i.e., yes/no).
- Constant, variable, or available (C, V, A) bit rate.
- Connection mode (connection-oriented or connectionless).

**Suitability for Multimedia Traffic.** ATM's greatest advantage is its ability to specify QOS by applications. This allows ATM switches to efficiently allocate network resources among applications with very different needs. For example, LAN data traffic may be able to tolerate delay but no loss, and desktop video can drop frames but tolerates no delay. Choices of quality and the class of applications that can exploit them are shown in Exhibit 2.

ATM also has several other advantages, including:[6]

- Network resources given on demand (i.e., statistical multiplexing).
- Easy transition from the existing network.
- AAL-specific adaptability.
- Easy network management.
- Reduced error checking means that it works only on low rate links.

The problems associated with ATM technology include:

- The need for traffic parameters to be stated on start-up.
- The need to resolve interoperability issues. The PNNI standard has just been defined and approved by the ATM Forum (a standards group for ATM).
- The need for switching architectures capable of supporting the high data rates of broadband applications.

## LAN Emulation

As seen in Exhibit 3, ATMs and LANs differ in their basic nature; ATMs are inherently connection-oriented while LANs are connectionless. The

**Exhibit 3. Comparison of ATMs and LANs**

| ATM | LANs |
| --- | --- |
| Connection oriented | Connectionless |
| Leads to inefficient use of network resources when broadcast and multicasting is used | Broadcast and multicast achieved through shared media |
| Hierarchical addresses | Address format based on serial number in adapter card |
| User setup needs speed and traffic characteristics for QOS | Because it is impossible to specify traffic characteristics, there is no guarantee of service |

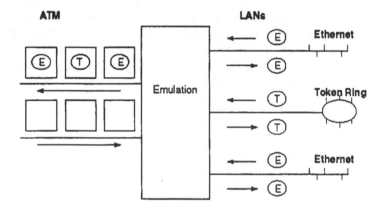

**Exhibit 4. LAN Emulation.**

aim of LANE is to make the ATM switch invisible to legacy LANs. It also provides a way to protect existing investments in bus and Token Ring networks.[7]

As shown in Exhibit 4, LANE provides a mechanism for tying legacy networks to ATM networks and using them without modification to software. It allows ATM's connection-oriented fabric to mimic a connectionless system and makes two separate LANs appear as one big LAN. LANE does this by emulating the MAC layer protocol so that the ATM network looks like just another MAC sublayer similar to either Ethernet or Token Ring. Because of this, it is not possible to mix Token Ring and Ethernet medias on the same LANE. However, they can be emulated separately and bridged. LANE provides mechanisms to map the media access address to the ATM address and vice versa and to multicast the same information to different systems on the network.[8]

The ATM switch itself does not emulate. It basically sets up a virtual connection and switches 53-byte cells as usual. By separating the physical and logical infrastructure into multiple segments, this virtual connection provides significant benefits in terms of increased security and scalability.[9]

**Suitability for Multimedia Traffic.** Although LANE is attractive, it lacks robustness as defined currently, because a single broadcast server is used to do all multicasts and broadcast. Hence, the system is exposed to a single point of failure. The current LAN emulation service does not specify the interaction between LAN emulation service components LNNI, a specification necessary to ensure interoperability. The ATM Forum is working on this aspect and a standard is expected shortly.

Because different types of networks (i.e., Ethernet or Token Ring) must still be bridged or routed, LANE is only useful at the workgroup level and cannot be used at the WAN level. In addition, LANE does not allow applications to take advantage of the QOS characteristics that are the greatest benefit of ATM. LANE's greatest benefit lies in the protection of investments in the existing infrastructure; as such, it serves as an important step in the ATM migration strategy for many organizations.

## WAN TECHNOLOGIES

As is the case for LANs, several technology options are available for supporting multimedia communication on the WAN. Chief among these transport technologies are the IP, frame relay, SMDS, fiber channel, and ATM.

### Frame Relay

Frame relay typically connects at speeds of T-1 lines and is an evolution of standard X.25 networks. Like X.25, it combines packets into frames and allocates bandwidth to multiple data streams. Frame relay uses the LAP-D frame structure with a data link connection identifier to route the data. Its payload is as high as 4K bytes and it handles Ethernet data without segmentation. It does not provide for error checking or flow-control mechanisms.

Frame relay connections are either PVC or SVC. PVC establishes a fixed path through the network for each source/destination node and remains defined for long periods of time. SVCs are defined and used only for the specific sessions. Multicasting services can be added over PVC lines, and the bandwidth assigned to each PVC is the committed information rate.

Frame relay over ATM lets a frame relay site communicate directly with an ATM site so that frames can be sent through the ATM backbone. Edge devices convert frame relays to ATM cells and vice versa. This allows LANs to be interconnected through ATM switches or IP to be transmitted over frame relay.

**Suitability for Multimedia Traffic.** Frame relay is not suitable for voice or video traffic because it does not provide for latency or constant bit rate transmission. The protocol does not add substantially to the delay itself, but it cannot guarantee a set delay. Frame relay provides for committed information rate on PVC lines and has been tested for videoconferencing with limited success. It is a popular mechanism for providing wide area data interconnections. Frame relay and ATM together enable a company to handle both low-speed and high-speed multimedia networking over the WAN. Frame relay is currently more affordable than ATM because it has been available longer.

## Internet Protocol

The TCP/IP has become the backbone of the WAN for carrying data services. The problem for carrying multimedia data with IP is the delay associated with the routing of the packets from one node to another. IP does not allocate a specific path nor guarantee a specific bandwidth to the multimedia application. Several technology options are being developed to resolve these problems, including Classic IP over ATM, RSVP, MPOA, and NHRP.

**Classic IP over ATM.** Classic IP over ATM uses the bandwidth of ATM to provide IP services without changing the fundamental nature of the protocol. The technology uses 9,000-byte frames at the higher layers and reduces packet overhead, which is advantageous for bulk data transfers. Classic IP over ATM also uses a modified version of IP's address resolution protocol ARP to find ATM's VCI/VPI connectionless correspondence to the IP network address.

**Suitability for Multimedia Traffic.** Classic IP over ATM aims to expand and use the huge bandwidth of ATM switches, but it fails to provide for QOS considerations. Because the approach shifts a lot of work to the router feeding the ATM switch, the TCP/IP network may be congested and slow regardless of the speed of the switch. In addition, the fact that two separate routing/switching structures are trying to find the best path adds to a lot of confusion.[10]

## RSVP

A better option for carrying multimedia using IP is to use the IETF's RSVP, which should be available in mid-1997. To support a mix of voice, data, and video, RSVP confirms QOS parameters with the networking devices using vendor-specific APIs.

RSVP operates through allocation of the following types of resources:[11]

- Active resources (such as a CPU that is a service provider).
- Passive resources, which are the system capabilities used by the active resources. They include main memory or bandwidth (i.e., link throughput).

In addition to reserving and allocating resources so that traffic flows follow QOS specifications, RSVP uses proper service disciplines and allocation strategies for multimedia delivery and adapts to resource changes.

**Suitability for Multimedia Traffic.** RSVP essentially allows a router-based network to mimic a circuit-switched network on a best-effort basis. Best effort suffices if there is adequate bandwidth; otherwise quality suffers. RSVP tries to ensure that the bandwidth is reserved and available. It has the advantages of working over both physical network architectures (Ethernet and Token Ring) and matching well with the new IPV6, which allows applications to label packets with traffic patterns. Packets belonging to a particular traffic flow from an application are easily switched.

RSVP thus allows the user to provide QOS to the network workstation without extending ATM to the workstation. Multicast extensions such as the MBone are separate extensions from RSVP. Because the Internet is so widely available, however, and despite the presence of delay and jitter, RSVP is being used as an experimental multimedia communications platform.

**Multiprotocol over ATM.** MPOA allows ATM switches to route LAN-based traffic between subnetworks, eliminating the router bottlenecks. In addition, IP switching is becoming available. It removes all ATM overhead and uses just the switching feature of ATM, enabling routing to be bypassed. IP switching is still an experimental technology and should be viewed with caution.

## NHRP

Another technology designed to allow multimedia to be carried over IP is the NHRP being developed by the IETF. NHRP aims to eliminate or bypass some or all of the routers used by Classic IP over ATM by directly connecting to the ATM fabric. Disjoint IP subnets are viewed as one logical NBMA. Each NBMA has a server that resolves IP addresses to NBMA addresses using dynamic address-learning mechanisms. Once addresses are resolved, a node then connects to the destination node with the required QOS parameters.

Although NBMA servers reduce the number of hops, they may increase the response time by a round-trip time (a critical factor for some applications).

NBMA servers add network management complexity and introduce additional points of failure in the system.

### Switched Multimegabit Data Service (SMDS)

SMDS is a connectionless service to interconnect LANs that enables access at T1 and T3 speeds. It can slice up to 9K bytes of data into fixed 53-byte cells (same as ATM) that are then switched through the network. Because it supports up to 9K bytes, it allows entire LAN frames to be encapsulated and provides reliable interconnections between LANs. The advantages of SMDS include scalability, bandwidth on demand, connectionless service, and multicasting support for some protocols.

**Suitability for Multimedia Traffic.** Because SMDS is packet-based, the delivered data stream can experience delays. This delay is not large and is less than 30 microseconds. In addition, SMDS does not provide for any synchronization of the data. The application is responsible for multiplexing audio and video and synchronizing the data at either end. The choice of 53-byte cells was made to provide a migratory path to ATM technology, rendering SMDS an interim technology.

### Fiber Channel

Fiber channel is a new technology that integrates the channel technology of mainframes and networking fiber technology. Fiber channel provides a single standard for network storage and data transfer and moves device interconnection and switching to a fabric. Each network node is responsible only for the single point-point connection between itself and the fabric. The fabric is responsible for routing between nodes, error detection and correction, and flow control. It supports distances of up to 10K meters at speeds of 266M bps to 4G bps.

**Suitability for Multimedia Traffic.** Applications that are compatible with ATM run on fiber channel, which offers an even shorter delay than ATM. Because fiber channel integrates both storage devices and networking, it is ideal for use on servers such as video servers. To bring the technology to the desktop is costly, however, running roughly $2,000.

Because of its limit of 10K meters, fiber channel is really more suited to LANs or MAN. Unlike ATM technology, the entire standard for fiber channel has been formalized and interoperability is not an issue. Exhibit 5 compares the ATM and fiber channel technologies.

### Suitability of WAN-based ATM

As previously discussed, ATM has been designed from the ground up to carry multimedia traffic on the WAN.

**Exhibit 5. Comparison of ATM and Fiber Channel**

|                                 | ATM       | Fiber Channel  |
|---------------------------------|-----------|----------------|
| Congestion Handling             | Discards  | Not an option  |
| Multivendor and Multiprotocol   | Struggles | Handles easily |

Although ATM provides the capability necessary for delivering multimedia traffic, much of the backbone or desktop connections have not been implemented. Making a desktop unit ATM-capable costs around $1,000. ATM on the WAN costs an average of $100,000/month when traffic exceeds 1.54M bps. Another issue that must be resolved is the interoperability of the switches from different vendors. Standards (in addition to PNNI) are still evolving to provide this and other capabilities. PNNI automatically disseminates network topology and resource information to all switches in the network and enables QOS-sensitive cell switching.

Despite these issues, ATM's support for real-time and data applications, quality of service, and multicasting, and its low delay and jitter make it the perfect match for multimedia communications. ATM's ability to be the transmission system for multiservice networks — those designed to carry voice, data, and video — provides profound advantages to a business by reducing the costs for equipment and support.[12] Because ATM also allows great flexibility and every other multimedia technology provides an access path to it, ATM is the logical long-term choice networking solution.

## CONCLUSION

Each available multimedia technology should be considered one of the many tools in the manager's kit. Each technology can be mixed and matched to suit the enterprise's networking needs (e.g., bandwidth, priority, and availability) and budget. Cooperation between network architectures and application architectures is important for predetermining traffic patterns and proactively managing bottlenecks.[13]

Almost all multimedia networking technologies provide for interconnection and incremental deployment. Because early implementations of any technology may mean interoperability issues have yet to be resolved, cautious integration is prudent.

Developing a strategic plan for multimedia networking that meets the goals and objectives of all users should encompass both computers and communications needs. Because voice and video communications will in all likelihood be a part of the network plan, users of these applications should be included in the planning and implementation team. To reduce the disruption that accompanies a technology transition, careful attention should be paid to migration planning.

Resource planning and project planning software help estimate the network resources needed to deliver a multimedia solution. Implementation should also take place in stages. For example, a workgroup solution may first be installed and pilot-tested before introducing the backbone technology. Network management is another area that mandates careful planning. It should encompass planning for configuration management (i.e., network element administration to provide services), fault management (i.e., detecting and isolating faults in network elements), and performance management (i.e., monitoring performance and managing traffic).

**References**

1. N. J. Muller, "Multimedia over the Network," *Byte*, March 1996, pp. 73–80.
2. N. J. Muller, pp. 73–80.
3. H. J. Stuttgen, "Network Evolution and Multimedia Communication," *IEEE Multimedia*, Fall 1995, pp. 42–59.
4. Stuttgen, pp. 42–59.
5. D. Ruiu, "Testing ATM Systems," *IEEE Spectrum*, June 1994, pp. 25–27.
6. J. N. Rodriguez, "ATM: The New Communication Era," *IEEE Computer*, May 1995, pp. 11–14.
7. N. Kavak, "Data Communication in ATM Networks," *IEEE Network*, May/June 1995, pp. 28–37; R. Jeffries, "ATM LAN Emulation: The Inside Story," *Data Communications*, Sept.21, 1994, pp. 95–100.
8. I. J. Hines, *ATM: The Key To High Speed Broadband Networking*, New York: M&T Books, 1996; W. Goralski, *Introduction to ATM Networking*, New York: McGraw-Hill, 1995.
9. N. Kavak, "Data Communication in ATM Networks," *IEEE Network*, May/June 1995, pp. 28–37.
10. R. Jeffries, "ATM LAN Emulation: The Inside Story," *Data Communications*, Sept. 21, 1994, pp. 95–100; W. Goralski, *Introduction to ATM Networking*, New York: McGraw-Hill, 1995.
11. K. Nahrstedt, and R. Steinmetz, "Resource Management in Networked Multimedia Systems," *IEEE Computer*, May 1995, pp. 52–63.
12. R. Madge, "Technology's Real-World Edge," *Information Week*, Sept. 16, 1996, p. 178.
13. E. Horwitt, "IP over ATM," *Network World*, April 15, 1996, pp. 40–42, 45.

# Chapter 24
# The Basics of Computer System and Data Network Security

*C. Warren Axelrod*

Complete security against unauthorized computer access, misuse, and damage is, by all practical measures, not economically feasible. Reducing and limiting such breaches, however, is achievable. This chapter discusses the security functions, avoidance, deterrence, prevention, detection, recovery, and correction, and provides examples of preventive measures in each area of risk.

## PROBLEMS ADDRESSED

One primary goal of a computer system and data network security program is to prevent unauthorized access to computer systems and facilities. Another goal, should unauthorized access occur, is to prevent the misuse of, or damage to, computer and network assets. If, despite security precautions, an incident of such unauthorized access causes damage, the data security department should act immediately to recover from the intrusion and to prevent recurrence.

The complete protection of computer systems and data networks has become increasingly complex, expensive, and restrictive as computer systems move from centralized mainframes and minicomputers to distributed client-server architectures and as data networks provide broader access to an exploding population of end users. Consequently, complete protection is seldom economically justifiable. Data center and data network managers must accept some tradeoffs and compromises. Although absolute protection is not feasible, the occurrences of breaches of security and damage to assets can be reduced through careful evaluation of risks and implementation of preventive measures. This chapter brings together fundamental security concepts to provide data center managers and data network managers with

0-8493-9965-3/99/$0.00+$.50
© 1999 by CRC Press LLC

an overview of the data security function. Examples of preventive measures are provided for each area of risk discussed.

## BASIC SECURITY FUNCTIONS

There are six basic data security functions. The first three — avoidance, deterrence, and prevention — address the organization's need to control the level of access and limit the distribution of access authority. The last three — detection, recovery, and correction — respond to unauthorized intrusions or destruction of assets.

Avoidance is the elimination of a threat to assets or the removal of assets from potential danger. Deterrence is the discouragement of behavior that threatens computer assets. Prevention is the implementation of measures to protect assets in the event of an attempted security breach.

In response to an attempted or actual security breach, detection is the deployment of means to recognize intrusion or damage and to raise an alarm during the breach. Recovery includes determining the extent of the damage and returning the system to operating condition. Correction is the introduction of new measures or the improvement of existing measures to avoid similar security breaches in the future.

## SECURITY VIOLATIONS

Computer systems and data networks must be secured against three types of violations: unauthorized access, misuse, and damage.

Unauthorized access is the gaining of illicit entry — physically or electronically — to the computer facility, the system software, or the data. Misuse is the manipulation of computer and network assets against the interests of the organization, whether or not any damage results. Damage is the adverse modification or destruction of physical or electronic computer and network assets. Damage is essentially an extreme form of misuse, and whether an attempt to misuse a system results in damage is often a matter of chance. Some forms of misuse may leave a computer system or network physically and logically intact but can cause irreparable financial damage to an organization.

Exhibit 1 indicates the type of violation addressed by each security measure. These measures are arranged according to the six basic security functions. The major areas of risk are discussed in the following sections.

## AVOIDANCE

Avoidance is a strategy that prevents unauthorized access, misuse, and damage. The strengths and weaknesses of avoidance methods are discussed in the following sections.

**Exhibit 1. Security Functions by Type of Breach**

| Security Function | Avoidance | Deterrence |
|---|---|---|
| Unauthorized Access | — Screen employees before hiring and assignment to computer and network functions. | — Install highly visible access controls (e.g., guards and cameras). |
| | — Locate computer and network facilities in remote or nondescript buildings. | — Implement search procedures for mail, especially packages. |
| | — Do not advertise locations or means of access to computer and network facilities. | — Implement well-monitored sign-in and sign-out procedures for facilities. |
| | — Limit the number of systems accessible to users. | — Take strong action in the event of attempted unauthorized access. |
| | | — Do not disclose known weaknesses in access control. |
| Misuse | — Restrict availability or data, programs, and documentation. | — Install very apparent measures for monitoring use of systems and networks (e.g., security software to report each use by person and type of use). |
| | — Limit the number of copies of data programs, and documentation. | — Question even small deviations from expected use patterns. |
| | — Limit the number of staff members with access to systems, networks and facilities. | — Take strong, well-publicized action for even minor infringements. |
| | — Limit physical access to essential areas only. Limit knowledge on a need-to-know basis. | |
| | — Limit use of systems to essential use only. | |
| | — Reduce overlap of applications. | |
| Damage | — Disperse computer and network facilities, both long-range and short-range, so that damage to one component cannot affect others. | — Use the same measures as for misuse with even stronger actions and sanctions for attempted or successful destructive activities, be they willful or negligent. |
| | — Design software architecture and network topology with independent modules so that damage to one does not affect others. | — Accidental damage with no evidence of negligence should be dealt with sternly. |
| | — Minimize procedural linkages to reduce the domino effect. | |
| | — Expand knowledge of critical systems and networks beyond one individual. | |

## Avoiding Unauthorized Access

The top row of Exhibit 1 illustrates how abusive access to a system or facility can be avoided by keeping potential abusers and target systems as far apart as possible. An organization should be particularly careful in its screening of individuals, such as those under consideration for employment, who might be given access to the system. Potential employees should be subject to intensive background investigations to ensure that all statements with regard to previous experience and education are accurate and complete. Several specialized firms perform independent checks and can verify statements regarding education, employment history, and criminal records. Character references should be obtained and verified. Personal impressions are valuable also; it is advisable to have several staff members meet with job candidates to obtain their impressions.

## Screening Nonemployees

In addition, the screening process should extend to all nonemployees who are granted access (e.g., consultants, vendor staff, service personnel and, increasingly, customers), though not to the same degree as potential employees.

In cases of personnel working for other firms, it is more reasonable to perform a check on the organization providing the service staff and to ensure, through contractual language, that the service organization takes full responsibility for its own staff. Checks on a service organization should include an investigation of that company's employee screening procedures and a review of references from companies with which the service organization has recently conducted business. It is also important to ensure that suitable confidentiality and vendor liability clauses are included in consulting and service agreements.

When customers are granted direct access to the organization's computer systems via the company's or a third party's data network, the usual credit checks and business viability verifications need to be performed. In addition, due diligence examinations to uncover any previous fraudulent customer activities should be conducted. The extent of such checks should be based on an evaluation of the magnitude of the assets at risk, the probability of recovering such assets if stolen, and an assessment of the probability that a customer would risk reputation and possible legal action if caught.

A standard security policy is that anyone who has not been screened should not be given system access. For example, frequent deliveries or pickups should be conducted in nonsensitive areas in all cases in which delivery personnel have not been screened. In addition, information regarding the location and nature of computer installations should be restricted whenever possible. Limiting the number of persons who know the systems' location and function also limits the risk of unauthorized access.

## Maintaining a Low Profile

Although it is not practical to provide the kind of stringent security necessary for sensitive military facilities, it is reasonable to encourage low profiles for computer facilities and data networks. Large signs indicating the company name or the nature of the facility should certainly be avoided in all cases. Inside buildings, the organization should avoid using signs indicating the location of the data center, or can instead use signs with nondescriptive language (e.g., facilities management). The slight inconvenience caused to authorized persons is more than compensated for by the barrier put before unwelcome visitors.

Another desirable, but not always practical, approach to avoiding unauthorized access is to limit the number of computer systems and potential points of access. This reduces the number of targets and simplifies the task of protecting them. Concentrating resources in this manner, however, can increase the magnitude of a potential loss if unauthorized access were to be obtained.

From a marketing perspective, it may be desirable to advertise easy customer access to services offered on organizations' computer systems. However, the specific whereabouts of computer and network facilities should be restricted information.

## Distributed Environments

Organizations have increasingly begun to distribute their computing facilities throughout the organization, sometimes situating the facilities externally, with other firms, or individuals outside the organization (e.g., customers and business partners). This distribution limits the amount of protection that a centralized IS function can provide to the organization's computer resources. In such a distributed environment, security measures must extend to terminals, workstations, and other remote devices that are connected to the organization's central facilities, because these remote facilities are often not within the direct physical control of the organization itself. Security measures should also be applied to the links among systems and devices — not only to private and public networks, but also to network equipment and facilities.

The methods that should be used to control access to remote facilities and networks is an extension of those used for a central facility; however, the measures are more difficult to implement and manage. The difficulty of protecting physically isolated equipment is caused by the equipment's remote location — which, ironically, was intended originally to facilitate access to users.

The screening process is much more critical in a distributed environment because the number and variety of individuals with authorized access is generally much larger than for centralized systems. Not only are the users scattered around the organization, they may be employees of other firms, such as service providers and business partners, or private individuals, as with retail customers. Nevertheless, it is necessary to ensure that users who can gain authorized access to any device or network are rigorously screened. As with centralized facilities, the persons given access to remote and networked facilities should be restricted to essential uses only.

Obvious designations as to the existence and purpose of remote devices and network equipment should be avoided. Authorized users should be advised not to make any documentation available to or accessible by others with access to the physical area. In addition, they should not leave their terminals or workstations in an operating condition that would allow someone else to gain access easily.

### Avoiding Misuse

Basically, system misuse can be avoided by restricting the activities of those who have gained or are allowed access to the system, network, or facilities. The fundamental premise of avoiding misuse is that, if the system, network, or facilities are difficult to access, some potential acts of misuse cannot occur. If the organization severely limits the number of people who can enter facilities or gain access to systems and networks and limits authorized users to necessary functions and features, they reduce the occurrences of misuse. This concept applies whether the systems are centrally located or widely dispersed. The data network exposure becomes more significant for dispersed systems.

The trend is toward much broader access to an organization's computer systems. Examples are students and staff having direct access to college computer systems, customers and suppliers connecting into companies' systems, and private citizens accessing government data. Again, the organization might be able to be somewhat selective in determining who gets access privileges, but it would appear that such restrictions are becoming less viable. The real key to avoidance of misuse is the building of impenetrable firewalls between what is available to general users and those components of the system which, if misused, do not affect the underlying systems.

Limiting the availability and accessibility of software copies, information about related systems, and overlapping application programs restricts the end users' environments to those processes in which end users have direct interest. Strict adherence to separation-of-duties policies and restricting applications by discrete functional areas also help organizations avoid the misuse of computer and network assets and facilities.

## Avoiding Damage

As shown in Exhibit 1, some of the recommendations for avoiding damage conflict with those for avoiding access and misuse. For example, avoidance of access favors limiting the number of facilities, thereby reducing the number of targets that have to be protected. But if more systems are placed in a single facility, the probable extent of any damage is increased. IS functions therefore must strike a balance between the two conflicting principles. A compromise is to operate as few facilities as is feasible and to ensure that they are sufficiently dispersed that an extensive disaster (e.g., an earthquake) or regional electrical or telephone power failure is less likely to affect a number of critical facilities.

Another conflict is between limiting the employees' knowledge of systems to avoid misuse and informing employees sufficiently about the system so that one individual cannot alter the software or data to the organization's disadvantage without another being able to recognize and remedy the alteration. The avoidance of damage is to reduce the potential spread of a damaging event. Consequently, data center managers and network managers should aim for as much physical, logical, and procedural separation of systems and data networks as possible, so that any damage would be contained.

## DETERRENCE

The advantages and disadvantages of deterrence — the discouragement of behavior that threatens computer assets — are discussed in the following sections.

### Deterring Unauthorized Access

The deterrence of attempts at unauthorized access can be achieved through a combination of highly visible warnings and well-publicized consequences. Warning notices provide obvious indications that all attempts to access a facility, system, or network will encounter the organization's rigorous screening methods. Publicized consequences let potential intruders know that any perpetrators who are apprehended will be penalized according to company policy or prosecuted to the full extent of the law.

### Deterring Misuse and Damage

Controls that monitor actual use of systems after access has been gained are effective deterrents of illicit and unauthorized actions because they increase the probability of detecting potential misusers. Monitoring actual use is complex, however, because the range of possible damaging activities is very large, whereas controlling access involves monitoring a single activity, namely, gaining entry. The actions taken against those caught attempting misuse or damage should be sufficiently severe to deter individuals contemplating similar activities.

## PREVENTION

Preventing unauthorized access, misuse, and damage takes various forms. The advantages and drawbacks to each are discussed in the following sections.

### Preventing Unauthorized Access

The standard method for preventing unauthorized logical access to a computer system or data network is the password sign-on procedure. This method, which is the most common and well-known, is vulnerable to a knowledgeable violator but is extremely effective against novice intruders. Although the visibility of access controls can be an effective deterrent, it is usually less effective in preventing unauthorized access. The most effective preventive measures are generally those that are hidden, as they are much more difficult to identify and break.

Increasingly, the trend is to extend access to more and more end users, of whom many — such as customers — are not under the direct control of the organization responsible for the systems. The major online services (such as America Online, Compuserve, and Prodigy) and Internet access providers are only too eager to grant ready access to expand their customer base, and service providers are falling over themselves to offer their wares over these services. In such a situation the goal must be to control access rather than prevent it. In the past, banks sent out millions of unsolicited credit cards without careful analysis of potential customers' credit worthiness, and bad debts skyrocketed. To some extent, the online services and access providers are doing much the same by blanketing the population with disks and offers of free service. In reality, the risk is not of the same order as with credit cards, but there is the potential for fraud and worse. The service providers have come up with methods to limit their potential exposure by, for example, obtaining a credit card number in advance so that services can be billed with relative assurance that they will be paid for.

It is when money transactions begin to take place over these networks that the real need for security and control come to the fore, and significant efforts are being made to ensure secure and fraud-free money transactions. Realistically, such transactions are not much different from the millions of transactions that take place each day over telephone lines except that, as the human element is replaced by computer-based services, there is a greater need to have systems and procedures to protect against unauthorized transactions.

Completely preventing unauthorized access to communications networks can be particularly difficult to achieve technically. Networks using dedicated private lines are the most readily protected because at least the end equipment can be guarded physically, and dedicated lines provide less opportunity for an unauthorized person to gain access. Public telephone lines are the most vulnerable because essentially anyone can attempt to dial in. Some techniques (e.g., callback systems, which break the connection and dial back the end user at a specific number) provide somewhat greater security but are complex and relatively costly. Most of these techniques are highly restrictive of computer facilities' normal operations and therefore are often undesirable. Nevertheless, many of the most highly publicized computer break-ins have been accomplished over public networks, which suggests that some technical measures should be taken to restrict access and to ensure that only authorized users are allowed to use the systems.

In addition, it is advisable to limit both the physical and logical points of access. This not only allows better monitoring and control but can greatly reduce the cost of protection. Whatever access controls are in place, provisions should be made for backup in the event that one method fails as a result of staff unavailability, power or equipment failure, or negligence.

### Preventing Misuse and Damage

Preventing misuse of and damage to a computer system or data network after an intruder has gained access depends on the system's or network's ability to isolate and control potentially damaging functions. Such prevention measures include security software that allows only authorized personnel to access, change, or copy specific data and programs.

Networks are particularly vulnerable to misuse and damage because they present difficulty in protecting components and communications media from access. One way to prevent misuse of the data carried on a network is to use encryption. The computer industry has devoted a great deal of work to encryption techniques, which code the messages transmitted through the network. The encrypted messages can be understood only when decoded with a key; while encrypted, the data is meaningless to those lacking the key. Access to the key must be restricted to authorized persons. There has been considerable controversy surrounding encryption, as the U.S. government has been advocating a method using the so-called

"Clipper" chip, whereby government agencies can have access to the keys for all public and private communications.

Aside from physical damage, network equipment can be rendered useless if the switch settings are changed or, as such devices become more sophisticated and software controlled, if the programs are deleted or modified. In some cases, the same type of security access measures that are available for computer systems are also available for high-end communications devices.

Logical security measures should be backed up to guard against accidental or deliberate destruction of the primary system, and they should be installed on backup systems to ensure security if a disaster backup plan is invoked.

## DETECTION

Detection methods have their strengths and weaknesses, as discussed in the following sections.

### Detecting Unauthorized Access

Access controls are not foolproof. Given that breaches do occur, misuse or damage to the system can be prevented if intrusions are detected. A variety of techniques can be employed for detecting physical or logical access.

**Physical Access.** Common detection systems for physical access to facilities include video cameras connected to television monitors and videocassette records at guards' desks. Such systems are common in banks, offices, metropolitan apartment buildings, and stores selling valuable products or located in dangerous areas. The very presence of such systems may be a deterrent to potential intruders because it is clear that offenders could be identified through the videotape. In darkened areas, where standard video cameras may not work, other technologies (e.g., infrared or ultrasonic cameras and sensors) can record or detect intrusions.

**Logical Access.** Remote or local logical access to a computer system or data network can be detected and sometimes traced using the various software packages that check and record all attempts to gain logical access to systems and networks and warn of any unauthorized or atypical attempts. Security programs are available separately or as options with other software from computer and communications equipment manufacturers and software vendors.

## Detecting Misuse

System misuse can be difficult to detect because a perpetrator may not leave any easily detected evidence, especially if he or she has changed nothing (e.g., databases may be accessed, read, and copied but not modified). Because of this detection problem, a category of EDP audit software has been designed to monitor attempted system misuse. Such software can detect and report unauthorized attempts to access programs and data as well as determine whether the system has been used in unauthorized ways. Audit software has traditionally been available for mainframes and large networks and is now available for local area networks connecting microcomputers, workstations, and network and file servers.

Previously, organizations expressed little interest in acquiring software to detect unauthorized access to, and misuse of, microcomputer-based systems. It was believed that physical controls (e.g., locks and keys) and logical controls (e.g., passwords) were adequate. Highly publicized computer virus attacks, however, have raised organizations' awareness that, even when physical access is prevented, a virus can be introduced into a system from a diskette or communications line. Several available software packages are designed to detect such misuse and remove its cause.

## Detecting Damage

Software can also help determine whether misuse of the system has caused damage to programs or data. In general, such programs and procedures are invoked when an access attempt is known to have been made or when there is a suspicion that someone has been tampering with the programs or data.

Routine software checks should ensure that updated versions of the programs have not been installed after the last official installation date, that unauthorized programs or versions of programs are not present, and that no programs that should have been installed are missing. If any of these situations occur, all production programs should be reloaded from a protected source as soon as possible. Copies of earlier versions of all production programs should be retained in a secure place for restoration purposes.

These procedures, however, often do not detect computer viruses, which can remain dormant and therefore undiscovered until they are triggered into action. There is also a real danger that earlier versions of programs contain viruses. Unless a virus announces its existence, damage (e.g., lost data) may be blamed on such other causes as hardware failure or operator error. If an incident of damage cannot be fully explained, the data center manager or data network manager should be aware of the possibility that viruses may be present and should seek to remove them.

Mechanisms within the application programs should check the integrity of the data on a continuing basis. For example, such mechanisms should determine whether any change in the number of items or bytes in a data file or database is consistent with the number added or subtracted by any process. There should be a check to ensure that, if a file or database has been closed and then opened some time later, the number of items in the file or database has not changed during an inactive interim period. Although these are relatively simple tests, they can be effective in detecting damage. A more complete test of each system component is extremely time-consuming and expensive and is usually reserved for instances in which personnel are relatively certain that damage has occurred. In such cases, the intent of the process is to determine the nature and extent of the damage rather than its occurrence.

Frequently, damage to programs or data is detected only by chance, e.g., when a previously stable process does not complete successfully or when users discover that some information produced by the system is incorrect or inconsistent. In such cases, it is necessary to determine quickly whether the aberration is due to error, misinterpretation, or damage.

For the physical protection of facilities, a range of detection devices is available for smoke, fire, flooding, and other physical threats. Such devices, however, only signal the presence of an active, readily detectable, damaging agent. In general, they do not detect preliminary damage that might lead to fires or flooding (e.g., the slow deterioration of materials or structural decay). Such damage can be detected early only through a program of regular inspections and tests by experts.

## RECOVERY

Should the worst happen and damage occur, a data center's ability to recover is of critical importance.

### Recovering from Unauthorized Access

If the access security controls are damaged during an attempted breach — whether or not the attempt succeeds — it is vital to reinstitute security control quickly. For example, if a door lock is destroyed during a break-in, it must be quickly replaced to eliminate the vulnerability resulting from an unlockable door. At the very least, the previous access controls should be restored. If the break-in indicates deficiencies in the previous mechanisms, however, they should be modified, as described in the section on correcting access control deficiencies.

### Recovery from Misuse and Damage

A recovery process should bring the misused or damaged system back to its condition before the event that caused the damage. If the misuse or damage continues, measures must be instituted immediately to halt the abuse, even if they are only interim measures. A contingency plan should be written, tested, and periodically reviewed before any damaging event ever takes place so that the organization is fully equipped to enact effective recovery procedures.

## CORRECTION

There are several issues concerning corrections measures.

### Correcting Access Control Deficiencies

If unauthorized access occurs, the controls in place are either inadequate or inadequately enforced. In such cases, changes must be made to the access controls or procedures to ensure that the same type of unauthorized access can be prevented in the future.

To some extent this is "closing the barnyard door after the horse has fled." However, it may also be construed as recognition of the fact that the competition between security methods and those motivated to break them is ongoing. No sooner is a more sophisticated security method created than someone is working on a method to break it. This results in a continuous escalation of security measures. Often an organization does not realize that its security measures have been outwitted until an actual break-in occurs.

### RECOMMENDED COURSE OF ACTION

Among the options available to data center and network managers, preventive security measures are the most effective. They may prevent access by unauthorized users or prevent authorized users from causing damage through negligence. An effective overall security program should include controls and procedures for handling all phases of a potential security breach.

When initiating a security program for a particular system or network, data center and network managers should define the system security according to the estimated value of resources to be protected, the most vulnerable routes for access or damage to resources, and the feasibility of protecting those routes without severely compromising the primary functions of the system. This chapter defines all possible areas in which security can be implemented to prevent damage. The guidelines defined here should be modified and implemented according to the requirements of a particular system.

Chapter 25
# Windows NT Architecture
*Gilbert Held*

Windows NT is a sophisticated operating system for workstations and network servers. This chapter helps network managers to understand the communications capability of workstations and servers running on Windows NT, and database administrators to determine the suitability of this platform for a structured query language (SQL) database server.

## INTRODUCTION

Windows NT is a 32-bit, preemptive multitasking operating system that includes comprehensive networking capabilities and several levels of security. Microsoft markets two version of Windows NT: one for workstations — appropriately named Windows NT Workstation — and a second for servers — Windows NT Server. This chapter, which describes the workings of the NT architecture, collectively references both versions as Windows NT when information is applicable to both versions of the operating system. Similarly, it references a specific version of the operating system when the information presented is specific to either Windows NT Workstation or Windows NT Server.

## ARCHITECTURE

Windows NT consists of nine basic modules. The relationship of those modules to one another, as well as to the hardware platform on which the operating system runs, is illustrated in Exhibit 1.

### Hardware Abstraction Layer

The hardware abstraction layer (HAL) is located directly above the hardware on which Windows NT operates. HAL actually represents a software module developed by hardware manufacturers that is bundled into Windows NT to allow it to operate on a specific hardware platform, such as Intel X86, DEC Alpha, or IBM PowerPC.

0-8493-9965-3/99/$0.00+$.50
© 1999 by CRC Press LLC

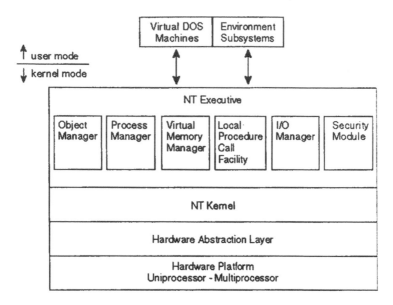

**Exhibit 1. Windows NT Core Modules.**

HAL hides the specifics of the hardware platform from the rest of the operating system and represents the lowest level of Windows NT. Thus, HAL provides true hardware platform independence for the operating system.

Using HAL, software developers can create new software without a lot of knowledge about the hardware platform. This allows software developers to provide enhanced performance capabilities, such as additional device drives. Hardware vendors can provide the interface between the operating system and the specific hardware.

**Kernel**

The kernel represents the core of the Windows NT operating system. All operating systems have a kernel. The key difference between the Windows NT kernel and those found in other operating systems is the tasks managed.

The Windows NT kernel manages thread dispatching. (A "thread" is a basic item that can be scheduled by the kernel.) The kernel is also responsible for scheduling and processor synchronization when the hardware platform has multiple processors.

To perform scheduling, the Windows NT kernel attempts to dispatch threads for execution in a way that promotes the most efficient use of the processors in the hardware platform. The actual dispatching of threads is based on their priority, with Windows NT supporting 32 priority levels to maximize processor use.

The kernel always resides in real memory within the hardware platform's RAM and is nonpayable to disk. When NT controls a multiprocessor platform, the kernel will run on all processors at the same time and communicate with each other to govern the distribution of threads.

### The NT Executive

The NT Executive can be considered a common service provider because it is responsible for providing a set of services to all other operating system components. The Windows NT Executive is the highest level within the kernel mode of the operating system.

As indicated in Exhibit 1, the Executive consists of six core modules that provide an interface between users and computers (represented by Virtual DOS Machines and Environment Subsystems) and the kernel. Virtual DOS Machines support DOS or 16-bit Windows 3.X applications. Windows NT provides support by creating virtual machines and then implementing the required environment within such a machine, resulting in the term "virtual DOS machines."

In comparison, "environment subsystems" are environments that may be required to operate on top of Windows NT. Examples of currently supported environment subsystems include OS/2, POSIX, and Win32 (the Windows NT subsystem).

### Object Manager

The object manager names, retains, and provides security for objects used by the operating system. In a Windows NT environment, an object represents physical items as well as the occurrence of defined situations. Thus, an object can represent directories, files, physical hardware ports, semaphores, events, and threads. An object-oriented approach is used to manage objects. If network managers are using Windows NT, they can view the status of event objects through the NT Event Viewer, which is provided in the operating system as an administrative tool.

### Process Manager

In a Windows NT environment, a process represents an address space, a group of objects defined as a resource, or a set of threads. Thus, each of these entities is managed by the process manager. In doing so, the process manager combines those entities into a "virtual machine," on which a program executes. Here the term "virtual machine" represents a set of resources required to provide support for the execution of a program. Windows NT permits multiple virtual machines to be established, allowing multiprocessing capability.

**Virtual Memory Manager**

Windows NT uses a special file on the hardware platform's hard disk for additional memory beyond available RAM. That file is referred to as a virtual memory paging or swap file and is automatically created when the operating system is installed.

The Virtual Memory Manager manages the use of virtual memory as a supplement to physical RAM. For example, when one program cannot completely fit into RAM because of its size or the current occupancy by other executing programs, the Virtual Memory Manager might swap one program currently in memory to disk to enable another program to execute, or it could swap portions of the program requesting execution between RAM and the hard disk to execute portions of the program in a predefined sequence.

Although the operation of the Virtual Memory Manager is transparent to programs using it, network managers can change the paging file size. To do so, they would first select the System icon in the Control Panel and then select the Virtual Memory entry from the resulting display. This action results in the display of a dialog box labeled Virtual Memory. Exhibit 2 illustrates the Virtual Memory dialog box with its default settings shown for a Pentium processor.

Although Windows NT automatically creates a virtual memory paging file and assigns an initial file size based on the capacity of the system's hard disk, the operating system does not know what applications the network manager intends to run or the size of those applications. Thus, if network managers frequently work with applications that require a large amount of memory, they should consider raising the default setting.

In Exhibit 2, Windows NT provides a pseudo constraint on the sizes of the paging file. That constraint is in the form of a range of values defined for the size of the paging file; however, that range is a recommendation and is not actually enforced by the operating system. For example, to set the initial size of the paging file to two megabytes, the user would type "20" into the box labeled Initial Size and then click on the Set button. Similarly, if users want to raise the maximum size of the paging file to 100 megabytes, they would enter that value in the appropriate location in the dialog box and click on the Set button.

**Local Procedure Call Facility**

Programs that execute under Windows NT have a client/server relationship with the operating system. The Local Procedure Call Facility is responsible for the passing of messages between programs.

```
┌─────────────────────────────────────────────────────────────────────┐
│  ┌──────────────────────────────────────────────────────────────┐   │
│  │ ═      Virtual Memory                                         │   │
│  │                                              ┌──────────────┐ │   │
│  │ Drive  [Volume Label]    Paging File Size [MB]│     OK       │ │   │
│  │ C:    [MS-DOS 62]            43 - 93          └──────────────┘ │   │
│  │                                              ┌──────────────┐ │   │
│  │                                              │   Cancel     │ │   │
│  │                                              └──────────────┘ │   │
│  │                                              ┌──────────────┐ │   │
│  │                                              │    Help      │ │   │
│  │                                              └──────────────┘ │   │
│  │  ┌─Paging File Size for Selected Drive──────────────┐         │   │
│  │  │  Drive:            C: [MS-DOS_62]                 │         │   │
│  │  │  Space Available:  1414 MB                        │         │   │
│  │  │  Initial Size [MB]:  [ 43 ]                        │         │   │
│  │  │  Maximum Size [MB]: [ 93 ]    ┌── Set ──┐          │         │   │
│  │  └──────────────────────────────────────────────────┘         │   │
│  │  ┌─Total Paging File Size for All Drives────────────┐         │   │
│  │  │  Minimum Allowed:    2 MB                         │         │   │
│  │  │  Recommended:        43 MB                        │         │   │
│  │  │  Currently Allocated: 43 MB                       │         │   │
│  │  └──────────────────────────────────────────────────┘         │   │
│  │  ┌─Registry Size────────────────────────────────────┐         │   │
│  │  │  Current Registry Size:        2 MB               │         │   │
│  │  │  Maximum Registry Size [MB]   [ 8 ]               │         │   │
│  │  └──────────────────────────────────────────────────┘         │   │
│  └──────────────────────────────────────────────────────────────┘   │
└─────────────────────────────────────────────────────────────────────┘
```

**Exhibit 2. Virtual Memory Dialog Box.**

## I/O Manager

The Input/Output (I/O) Manager is responsible for managing all input and output to and from storage and the network. To perform its required functions, the I/O Manager uses four other lower-level subsystems — the Cache Manager, file system drivers, hardware device drivers, and network drivers.

The Cache Manager provides a dynamic cache space in RAM that increases and decreases based on available memory. File system drivers provide support for two file systems, the file allocation table (FAT) and the high performance file system (HPFS). The FAT file system provides backward support for DOS and 16-bit Windows 3.X-based programs, whereas the HPFS enables support of the new file system for Windows NT 32-bit applications.

The hardware device drivers used in Windows NT are written in C++ to provide portability between hardware platforms. This allows a driver developed for a CD-ROM, a plotter, or another hardware device to work with all Windows NT hardware platforms.

Network drivers represent the fourth lower-level I/O Manager subsystem. These drivers provide access from Windows NT to network interface cards, enabling transmission to and from the network and the operating system.

**The Security Module**

Windows NT includes a comprehensive security facility built into the operating system. Once the user turns on power to the hardware platform, this facility is immediately recognizable. Unlike Windows 3.X, Windows 95, or DOS, Windows NT prompts the operator for a password before allowing access to the computer's resources.

Windows NT security works by the log-on process and a local security subsystem that monitors access to all objects and verifies that a user has appropriate permission before allowing access to an object. The log-on process is linked to the Security Reference Monitor, which is responsible for access validation and audit generation for the local security subsystem. Another component of the Security Module is the Security Account Manager. The Security Account Manager maintains user and group information on a secure database.

**WINDOWS NT NETWORKING**

One of the biggest advantages associated with the use of Windows NT is its built-in support of many transport protocols. The Windows NT networking architecture was established in a layered design that follows the seven-layer ISO Open System Interconnection (OSI) Reference Model. Exhibit 3 illustrates the general correspondence between Windows NT layers and OSI Reference Model layers.

The environment subsystems represent virtual DOS machines as well as 32-bit applications operating on top of NT. At the presentation layer, the Network Provider module is required for each network supported through a redirector. At the session layer, the Windows NT Executive uses a server and redirector to provide capability for a server and workstation, respectively. Both components are implemented as file system drivers and multiple redirectors can be loaded at the same time, so that a Windows NT computer can be connected to several networks. For example, NT includes redirectors for NetWare and VINES, enabling an NT workstation or server to be connected to Novell and Banyan networks.

At the transport layer, the transport driver interface (TDI) provides a higher-layer interface to multiple transport protocols. Those protocols,

**Exhibit 3. Correspondence Between Windows NT and OSI
Reference Model Layers**

| OSI Reference Model Layers | Windows NT Layers | | | |
|---|---|---|---|---|
| Application | Environment Subsystems | | | |
| Presentation | Network Provider | | | |
| Session | Executive Services | | | |
| | Server | | Redirector | |
| Transport | Transport Driver Interface | | | |
| Network | NetBEUI | DLC | TCP/IP | NSLink (SPX/IPX) |
| Data Link | NDIS | | | |
| | NIC Drivers | | | |
| Physical | NIC | | | |

which represent operations at the network layer, include built-in NT protocol stacks for NetBEUI, used by the LAN Manager and LAN Server operating systems; Data Link Control (DLC), which provides access to IBM mainframes; TCP/IP for Internet and intranet applications; and NWLink, which represents a version of Novell's SPX/IPX protocols. Through the use of TCP/IP, a Windows NT computer can function as a TCP/IP client, whereas the use of NWLink enables a Windows NT computer to operate as NetWare client.

At the data link layer, Windows NT includes a built-in Network Device Interface Specification (NDIS). NDIS enables support for multiple protocol stacks through network interface card drivers. Thus, NDIS allows a network interface card to simultaneously communicate with multiple supported protocol stacks. This means that a Windows NT computer could, for example, simultaneously operate as both a TCP/IP and a NetWare SPX/IPX client.

## UPGRADE ISSUES

The key differences between NT 3.5 and 4.0 are speed and user interface. Windows 4.0 added the Windows 95 user interface to NT. In addition, a recoding of the operating system makes it slightly faster than 3.51. However, because the difference in cost between a Pentium and Pentium Pro microprocessor is a few hundred dollars, it may be more economical to purchase the more powerful processor and retain the familiar Windows 3.51 interface. This could eliminate the costs associated with retraining employees.

Conversely, if an organization has already migrated to Windows 95 or is planning to migrate to that operating system, the network manager may want to consider Windows NT Version 4.0. Its use of the Windows 95 interface may be well known to some or most of the organization's employees who will be using NT, which should minimize training costs while providing a slightly improved level of performance.

## CONCLUSION

The modular design of the Windows NT architecture makes it both portable and scalable. Windows NT's hardware abstraction layer allows the operating system to run on different hardware platforms. Currently, Windows NT runs on Intel X86 and Digital Equipment Corp. (DEC) Alpha. Until the new release of NT this operating system supported the MIPS RISC (reduced instruction set computing), and the PowerPC series of microprocessors jointly manufactured by IBM Corp. and Motorola.

Besides being highly portable, Windows NT supports scalability, which allows the operating system to effectively use multiple processors. Thus, when network managers evaluate Windows NT Server as a platform for different applications, it is important for them to note that they have several options for retaining their investment as applications grow.

For example, because of its scalability, network managers could replace a uniprocessor Intel Pentium motherboard with a dual- or quad-processor motherboard. If this replacement does not provide the necessary level of processing power, network managers might consider migrating hardware to a high-level DEC Alpha-based computer. If that migration is required and the applications continue to grow, network managers could use multiple processors to ensure scalability.

# Section IV
# Interoperability and Standards Issues

Interoperability is one of the most important considerations when designing and expanding a network. By obtaining the ability to use products from different vendors we are able to literally break the umbilical cord which previously tied organizations to a single vendor. By obtaining hardware and software that is interoperable, the ties that previously bound organizations to a single vendor regardless of price, delivery schedule, or performance no longer are applicable. This in turn made the communications industry a more competitive industry, fostering price competition and innovation to the benefit of the end user. Although interoperability is important, it would not be possible without standards. Thus, interoperability and standards go hand in hand, and are the focus of this section.

The first two chapters in this section provide us with detailed information covering two versions of Ethernet that operate at 100 Mbps. In the first chapter, "Introduction to 100BASE-T: Fast (and Faster) Ethernet," we will become familiar with the four versions of 100BASE-T to include the type of wiring required and their physical layer signaling system. This chapter also introduces us to the auto-negotiation feature of Fast Ethernet which enables us to use 10BASE-T hubs and end stations with a 100BASE-T hub. Although we primarily think of 100BASE-T when we hear the term Fast Ethernet, there are actually two Fast Ethernet standards. The second standard is known as 100VG-AnyLAN and is the focus of the second chapter in this section titled "A Better Fast Ethernet: 100VG-AnyLAN." In this chapter we will be introduced to the demand priority protocol of 100VG-AnyLAN and why it is better suited for multi-media applications on a LAN than the CSMA/CD access protocol used by 100BASE-T.

Recognizing the importance of Fiber Channel, two chapters in this topic are included in this section. The chapter titled "Applications and Business Issues of Fiber Channel" provides us with an introduction to the economics and technology associated with the use of transport technology. This chapter is followed by the chapter titled "Fiber Channel Architecture, Layers, and Services" which provides us with detailed information covering Fiber

Channel's OSI style layering structure, scalability, and topologies it supports, enabling you to use this networking technology in a variety of networking situations.

The importance of the World Wide Web can be noted by billboard advertisements and TV commercials, with most organizations now including their Web address for viewers to note. In the fifth chapter in this section we turn our attention to the software which enables the Web to function. In the chapter "Linking to the World Wide Web" we are introduced to the Hyper-Text Transmission Protocol which makes Web transmission possible, Universal Resource Identifiers which make hyperlinks possible, and the HyperText Markup Language which enables standardized Web pages to be created.

Along with Web addresses, one's email address is becoming as prevalent as a person's telephone number. With email providing near instantaneous delivery of messages at a fraction of the cost of Postal Service mail, literally billions of email messages are transmitted daily. While it may be a simple decision to decide to implement email, there is a considerable debate over the use of different email protocols. In the sixth chapter in this section, "X.400 Vs. SMTP," we are introduced to the key decision criterions we should consider in selecting an email protocol. In this chapter such issues as functionality, security, systems management, message management, human resources requirements, and performance are compared and contrasted for X.400 and SMTP.

In concluding this section we turn our attention to a topic which every user of the Internet must consider. That topic is the pending use of all available IP addresses under the current version of the Internet Protocol, IPv4. In the chapter "IPv6: The Next Generation Internet Protocol" we are introduced to the features of this new protocol to include its addressing scheme which will enable this new protocol to support communications requirements that could materialize over the next several centuries.

# Chapter 26

# Introduction to 100BASE-T: Fast (and Faster) Ethernet

*Colin Mick*

Fast Ethernet (100BASE-T), an extension to the IEEE802.3 Ethernet standard to support service at 100M bps, is virtually identical to 10BASE-T, in that it uses the same media access control (MAC) layer, frame format, and carrier sense multiple access with collision detection (CSMA/CD) protocol. Network managers can use 100BASE-T to improve bandwidth and still maximize investments in equipment, management tools, applications, and network support personnel.

## INTRODUCTION

Fast Ethernet (100BASE-T) is an extension to the IEEE802.3 Ethernet standard to support service at 100M bps. It is virtually identical to 10BASE-T, in that it uses the same media access control (MAC) layer, frame format, and carrier sense multiple access with collision detection (CSMA/CD) protocol. This means that network managers can use 100BASE-T to improve bandwidth and still make maximum use of investments in equipment, management tools, applications, and network support personnel.

100BASE-T is designed to work transparently with 10BASE-T systems. Switches (high-speed, multiport bridges) are used to connect existing 10BASE-T networks to 100BASE-T technology. By building networks with 100BASE-T and 10BASE-T linked with switches and repeating hubs, network designers can build networks that provide four levels of service:

- Shared 10M-bps service
- Dedicated (switched) 10M-bps service
- Shared 100M-bps service
- Dedicated 100M-bps service

0-8493-9965-3/99/$0.00+$.50
© 1999 by CRC Press LLC

Operating at higher speeds with the same frame size and the CSMA/CD protocol requires that 100BASE-T collision domain diameters be smaller — typically about 200 meters. In 100BASE-T, larger networks are built by combining collision domains by way of switches. Fiber (100BASE-FX) links are used to support long (i.e., 412 meters in half duplex, 2 kilometers in full duplex) cable runs. Within a single collision domain, port density is increased by using modular or stacking hubs.

The 100BASE-T standard (IEEE802.3u, 1995) currently defines four physical layer signaling systems:

- 100BASE-TX supports operation over two pairs of Category 5 unshielded twisted pair (UTP) or shielded twisted pair (STP) cables.
- 100BASE-T4 supports operation over four pairs of Category 3, Category 4, or Category 5 UTP or STP cables.
- 100BASE-T2 supports operation over two pairs of Category 3, Category 4, or Category 5 UTP or STP cables.
- 100BASE-FX supports operation over two 62.5-micron multimode fibers.

Products for 100BASE-TX and 100BASE-FX are available from a wide range of manufacturers. Products for 100BASE-T4 are supported by a smaller group of manufacturers and no products have yet been offered for 100BASE-T2.

In addition, the Fast Ethernet standard has recently added support for full-duplex operation and flow control. Full-duplex operation is broadly available in current 10BASE-T and 100BASE-T products.

## HOW IT WORKS: AN ISO VIEW

Exhibit 1 depicts an ISO seven-layer diagram comparing 10BASE-T and 100BASE-T. Both 10BASE-T and 100BASE-T defined operations at the lower half of the data link layer (known as the Media Access or MAC layer) and the physical layer. Extension of the Ethernet standard to 100M-bps operation required one small change to the MAC layer operation specified in the IEEE802.3 standard. Originally, timing was defined in absolute terms (i.e., an external reference clock). As a result, timing specifications were defined in milliseconds, nanoseconds, and picoseconds. To support 100M-bps operation, timing was respecified relative to the internal clock of the MAC. This meant that specifications were defined in bit times.

Several changes were made at the physical layer. In 10BASE-T, coding (i.e., conversion of data bits to symbols) is done in the PLS layer, directly below the MAC. A mechanical interface called the attachment unit interface (AUI) is situated directly below the PLS. Below the AUI is the PMA layer, which converts the digital symbols into analog symbols that can be

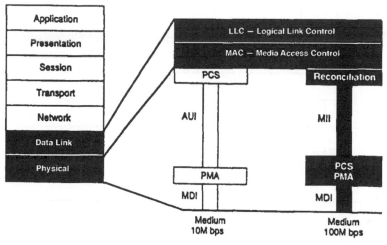

**Exhibit 1. 100M bps Standards Model.**

sent across the wire and a media-dependent interface (MDI) — a socket for connecting the cable.

100BASE-T puts the coding, called the physical coding sublayer (PCS), below the mechanical interface. This was done to make it possible to offer a variety of coding systems that could be packaged in a transceiver along with the analog/digital circuitry for connection via the mechanical interface. The mechanical interface used for 100BASE-T is called the Media Independent Interface (MII). It is similar to the AUI, but offers a larger data path and the ability to move management information between the PHY and the MAC. A simple mapping function, called the Reconciliation Sublayer, handles linking the MII to the MAC. As noted previously, 100BASE-T currently supports four signaling systems (see Exhibit 2): 100BASE-TX, 100BASE-T4, 100BASE-T2, and 100BASE-FX.

Two 100BASE-T signaling systems — 100BASE-TX and 100BASE-FX — are based on the transport protocol/physical medium dependent (TP/PMD) specification developed by the ANSI X3T12 committee to support sending fiber distributed data interface (FDDI) signals over copper wire (see Exhibit 3). TP/PMD uses continuous signaling, unlike the discrete signaling used with 10BASE-T. In 10BASE-T, when a station is finished sending a

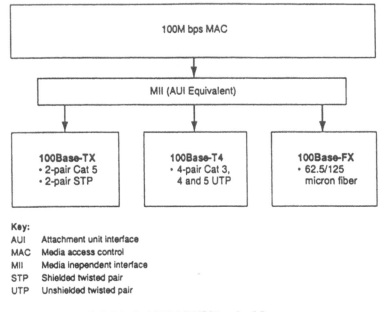

Key:
AUI   Attachment unit interface
MAC  Media access control
MII   Media inependent interface
STP   Shielded twisted pair
UTP   Unshielded twisted pair

**Exhibit 2. 100BASE-T Physical Layers.**

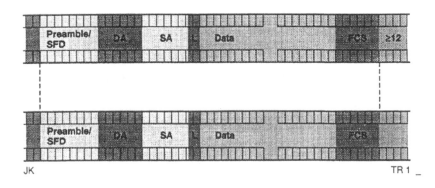

**Exhibit 3. 100BASE-T (TX and FX) Frames.**

frame, it sends a few idle signals and then goes quiet, except for a link pulse, which is sent every 16 ms to indicate that the link is still good.

In TP/PMD, a continuous stream of idle symbols is sent when data is not being transmitted. To ease the transition between data and idle signals, a JK symbol sequence is added to the front of a data frame and a TR symbol sequence is added to the end of the frame before transmission of idle symbols

**Exhibit 4. 10BASE-T-FX**

---

- Uses 2-strand, 62.5/125 micron fiber
- Connector: MIC, ST, SC (converters available)
- Uses FDDI TP/PMD specification
  - Continuous signaling scheme
  - 4B5B coding scheme
- Transmits over 1-fiber and receives over 1-fiber
- 100M bps data rate
- Full and half duplex
- Detects and signals far end faults

---

begins. The JK, TR, and idle transmission patterns must be added to Ethernet frames when they are transmitted via the TP/PMD specification.

Both 100BASE-TX and 100BASE-FX use 4B5B coding. This means it takes 5 baud (signal transitions on the wire) to transmit 4 bits of information. This is vastly more efficient than the Manchester coding used for 10BASE-T, which requires 2 baud to send each bit across the wire.

Exhibit 4 summarizes the attributes of 100BASE-FX. It uses two strands of 63.5-micron fiber. All standard connectors are listed in the specification — different manufacturers support different types of connectors. 100BASE-FX uses the FDDI TP/PMD specification with continuous signaling and 4B5B coding. The data clock runs at 125 MHz, providing a signaling rate of 100M bps with the 80% efficiency of 4B5B coding. One fiber is used for transmitting data, the other for receiving data. It can support both half-duplex and full-duplex operation and has automatic link detection.

## 100BASE-TX

Exhibit 5 summarizes the attributes of 100BASE-TX. It operates over two pairs of Category 5 UTP or STP, and uses Category 5 certified RJ-45 connectors. It uses the 125-MHz data clock, continuous signaling, and 4B5B coding of 100BASE-FX, but adds signal scrambling and MLT-3 conditioning to deal with noise problems associated with sending high-frequency signals over copper. 100BASE-TX uses exactly the same connector pinouts as 10BASE-T. It transmits over one pair and receives over the other. It supports half-duplex and full-duplex operation.

## 100BASE-T4

100BASE-T4 (see Exhibit 6) is a more complex signaling system because it must support a 100M-bps data rate over cable certified for operation at 16 MHz. This is accomplished by increasing the number of cable pairs used for data transmission and using a more sophisticated coding system. 100BASE-T4 starts with the two pairs used for 10BASE-T — one for transmit

- Uses 2-pair Category 5 twisted pair cable
- Connector: Category 5 certified RJ-45 (IEC 603-7), or DB-9
- Uses FDDI TP/PMD specification
  - Continuous signaling scheme
  - 4B5B coding scheme
  - Scrambled symbols
  - MLT-3

- Transmits over 1-pair and receives over 1-pair
- 100M bps data rate
- Full and half duplex modes
- Identical connector pin-out

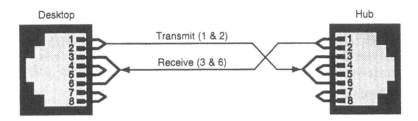

**Exhibit 5. 100BASE-TX.**

- Uses 4-pair Cat 3, 4, or 5 cable
- Transmits over 3-pair
- Connector: Standard RJ-45 (IEC 603-7)
- Uses an 8B6T coding scheme
- Signaling: 100M bps = 3-pair x 25 Mhz x (133% for 8B6T encoding)
- Half Duplex

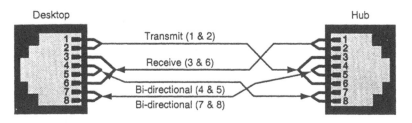

**Exhibit 6. 100BASE-T4.**

and one for receive — and adds two additional pairs that are used bidirectionally. This means that when transmitting, 100BASE-T4 always transmits over three pairs (one dedicated and two bidirectional) while listening for collisions on the remaining pair. It uses a much more sophisticated coding system called 8B6T.

Unlike other coding systems that use binary (0, 1) codes, 100BASE-T4 uses ternary (+1, 0, −1) codes, which enable it to pack 8 bits of data into 6

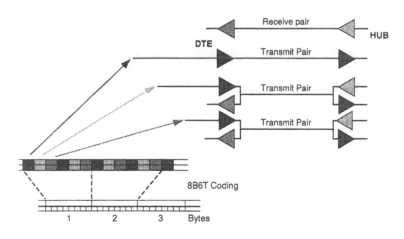

**Exhibit 7. 100BASE-T4 Signaling.**

ternary symbols. By using 8B6T coding and three wire pairs for transmission, 100BASE-T4 provides a 100M-bps data transmission rate with a clock speed of only 25 MHz (8 bits transmitted as 6 ternary symbols over three wire pairs at 25 MHz.)

This process is diagrammed in Exhibit 7: 1 byte (8 bits) of data is encoded into 6 ternary symbols, which are transmitted sequentially across three wire pairs. Unlike 100BASE-TX and 100BASE-FX, 100BASE-T4 does not support full-duplex operation.

**100BASE-T2**

100BASE-T2 provides a more robust and noise-resistant signaling system capable of operating over two pairs of Category 3, Category 4, or Category 5 UTP, or over STP links and supporting both half-duplex and full duplex operation. It uses an extremely sophisticated coding system called PAM5X5, which employs quinary (five-level — +2, +1, 0, –1, –2) signaling. In addition, it uses hybrid circuitry to enable simultaneous bidirectional transmission of 50M-bps data streams over each of the two wire pairs (see Exhibit 8).

Because of its robust encoding, 100BASE-T2 emits less noise during use and is less susceptible to noise from external sources. When used with 4-pair Category 5 cable bundles, it can coexist with other signaling systems. A single four-pair bundle can carry two 100BASE-T2 links, one 100BASE-T2 link, and one 10BASE-T link, or one 100BASE-T link and one voice (telephone) link.

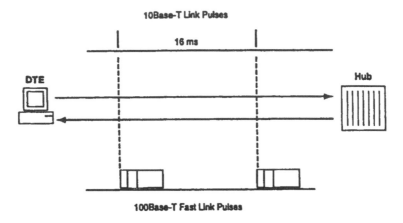

10Base-T Link Pulses

16 ms

DTE

Hub

100Base-T Fast Link Pulses

**Exhibit 8. Media-Independent Interface (MII).**

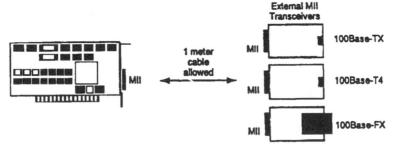

- Single Interface to provide for media flexibility
  - Similar to an AUI
  - 40-pin connector
  - Nibble wide data path and station management interface
  - Command and status registers

External MII Transceivers

1 meter cable allowed

MII

MII

MII

MII

100Base-TX

100Base-T4

100Base-FX

**Exhibit 9. 100BASE-T Auto Negotiation (2).**

## Media-Independent Interface (MII)

The Media-Independent Interface is a mechanical interface to the Ethernet MAC, similar to the AUI, which is used to connect transceivers (see Exhibit 9). The MII supports a nibble-wide data path, a station management interface, and command and status registers. It uses a 40-pin connector, similar in appearance to mini-small computer systems interface (mini-SCSI) connectors.

### Auto-Negotiation

Auto-Negotiation provides automatic link testing and configuration for UTP signaling systems. All 100BASE-T systems using UTP or STP go through Auto-Negotiation prior to establishing a link. During this start-up process, 100BASE-T systems on each side of a link:

- Check the link.
- Exchange coded information defining the abilities of each link partner (e.g., 10BASE-T half duplex operation, 10BASE-T full-duplex operation, 100BASE-TX half-duplex operation, 100BASE-TX full-duplex operation, 100BASE-T2 half-duplex operation, 1000BASE-T2 full-duplex operation or 100BASE-T4 operation).
- Go to an internal lookup table to determine the highest common operation mode.
- Configure themselves as per the table.
- Turn off Auto-Negotiation.
- Open the link.

If one end of the link is a 10BASE-T system that does not support Auto-Negotiation, the partner is automatically configured for 10BASE-T half-duplex operation (default mode). When confronted with another networking technology that uses the RJ-45 connector (e.g., Token Ring), Auto-negotiation will automatically fail the link.

Auto-Negotiation is based on the link pulse used in 10BASE-T. For Auto-Negotiation, the link pulse is divided into 33 fast link pulses that are used to carry pages of coded information between link partners.

### Full Duplex Operation

Full-duplex operation supports simultaneous signaling in both directions over dedicated links by turning off the CSMA/CD collision detection circuitry. It provides some increase in bandwidth over links that have a high proportion of bidirectional traffic, such as switch-switch and switch-server links. In addition, full-duplex operation increases the maximum length of fiber links. Whereas a half-duplex link is limited to 412 meters by the need to detect collisions, full-duplex operation supports links of up to 2 kilometers because no collision detection is required. This increased link length is only useful for fiber links, signal attenuation limits, and copper link length to 100 meters for both half- and full-duplex operation.

### Flow Control

Flow control provides a method for controlling traffic flows between intermediate devices (primarily switches and routers) and between intermediate devices and servers to avoid dropping packets. Currently two-speed (10/100 or 100/1000) operation requires large buffers to reduce the

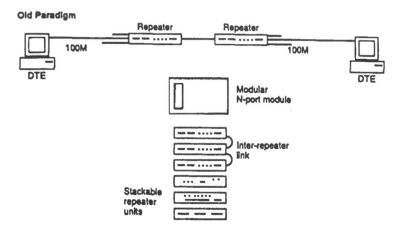

**Exhibit 10. Repeater Connection Styles.**

probability of dropping packets when a continuous stream of packets is sent from a high-speed to a low-speed device (e.g., 100M bps to 10M bps, or 1000M bps to 100M bps). In such a scenario, when the buffers fill, the intermediate device drops the unbuffered packets.

Flow control provides a management alternative to having large buffers. When a buffer approaches full, the receiving device can send a flow control packet back to the sending device to stop the incoming packet stream. When the buffers of the receiving device empty, packet transmission starts again. This eliminates dropped packets and allows manufacturers to build switches with smaller buffers, which reduces costs.

**Repeaters and Repeater Connections**

Repeaters provide for shared media operation in 10BASE-T and 100BASE-T via the CSMA/CD protocol. 10BASE-T networks have a collision domain diameter of 1000 meters. This permits building large, single-collision domain networks using hierarchical, cascaded repeating hubs to increase port density. 100BASE-T does not permit hierarchical cascading of hubs because the maximum collision domain for UTP is slightly more than 200 meters (see Exhibit 10).

Two techniques can be used to build large, single-collision domain networks (i.e., increase port density). One technique is to use modular hubs, where ports can be added by inserting additional multiport cards into the hub chassis. A second is to use stackable hubs — stand-alone repeaters that can be connected via high-bandwidth stacking ports that do not impact the collision domain.

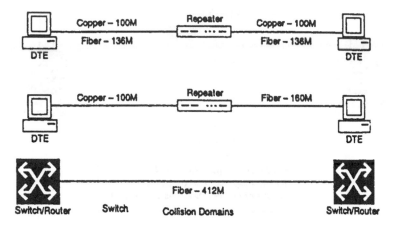

**Exhibit 11. 100BASE-T Topologies.**

## Topology Rules

Topology rules for half-duplex 100BASE-T networks are shown in Exhibit 11. Copper links are limited to 100 meters by the U.S. cabling standard EIA/TIA-568-A. A collision domain containing two copper links can contain one class I repeater and two 100-meter copper links; or two class II repeaters, two 100-meter copper links, and a 5-meter copper inter-repeater link. A collision domain containing a class I repeater with two fiber links can support two fiber links of 136 meters, for a collision domain diameter of 272 meters. A collision domain containing a class I repeater can also support one copper link of 100 meters and a single fiber link of 160 meters.

A fiber DTE-DTE half-duplex collision domain (e.g., a switch-to-switch or switch-to-server) can support a 412-meter fiber link. Links of up to 2 kilometers can be supported over fiber by operating in full-duplex mode, which turns off the CSMA/CD portion of the protocol and requires a dedicated link (see Exhibit 12).

## Gigabit Ethernet

Work to extend the Ethernet family to 1000M-bps (gigabit) operation is well underway. The first products using the new technology were demonstrated at Networld + Interop Las Vegas in May 1997, and the first products start shipping during the summer of 1997. Initial products will support operation over 62.5-micron multimode fiber (1000BASE-SX), 50-micron single-mode fiber (1000BASE-LX), or short lengths (to 25 meters) of coaxial cable (1000BASE-CX). The operation of these products is being defined in a supplement to the IEEE 802.3 standard entitled 802.3z

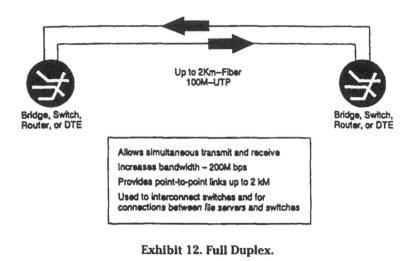

**Exhibit 12. Full Duplex.**

It is scheduled for completion in 1998. A second supplement, entitled 802.3ab, will define gigabit Ethernet over 100-meter, four-pair Category 5 copper links (1000BASE-T). It is scheduled for completion in late 1998.

## IMPACTS ON NETWORK DESIGN

Fast Ethernet is a family of 100M-bps signaling systems for use with the standard Ethernet MAC layer. The family consists of four signaling systems (100BASE-TX, 100BASE-T4, 100BASE-T2, and 100BASE-FX) and technologies that support automatic start-up (Auto-Negotiation), shared media operation (Repeaters), full-duplex operation, and flow-control to manage traffic flow.

Fast Ethernet devices work seamlessly with legacy Ethernet systems: they have the same MAC layer, the same frame format, and the same CSMA/CD protocol for shared media operation. Auto-Negotiation ensures that all 100BASE-T devices operating over copper links automatically configure themselves to operate with link partners. This makes 100BASE-T a very economical technology for adding high-bandwidth links to legacy systems.

Higher-speed operation reduces the diameter of 100BASE-T shared media collision domains to approximately 200 meters for copper. Collision domains can be extended through the use of fiber and connected via switches to build large, complex networks. Full-duplex operation improves bandwidth for bidirectional links and increases the maximum length of fiber links to kilometers. Port density within a single collision domain is expanded through the use of modular and stackable hubs.

100M bps is not the endpoint for Ethernet. 1000M-bps (gigabit) devices were demonstrated in the spring of 1997 and began shipping in the summer of 1997. Targets for gigabit Ethernet operation are 700 meters for full-duplex single mode fiber links, 25 meters for short-haul copper coax links, and 100 meters for Category 5 copper links.

# Chapter 27
# A Better Fast Ethernet: 100VG-AnyLAN

*Gilbert Held*

100VG-AnyLAN is an increasingly attractive transport mechanism for upgrading LANs because it is affordable, available, and easily interfaces with Token Ring and Ethernet.

## INTRODUCTION

Although ATM networking has received a considerable amount of attention, its use as a transport mechanism for local area networks at an economical price may require a wait until the turn of the century. In the interim, one of three successors to the Ethernet — 100VG-AnyLAN — appears to provide network users with a high-speed local area networking capability to support emerging multimedia applications and alleviate existing network bottlenecks. 100VG-AnyLAN is designed from the ground up to interconnect with essentially any type of LAN, such as Ethernet, Token Ring, FDDI, and even ATM, when it becomes available for use. An understanding of the operational capability of 100VG-AnyLAN can assist network managers in developing a LAN upgrade strategy. This chapter provides network managers and users with information required to determine how 100VG-AnyLAN can be used in future networking plans and how its functionality and operational capability can satisfy networking requirements.

## FAST ETHERNET EVOLUTION

The IEEE 802 Committee was originally limited to developing standards for operating rates up to 20M b/s, and the ANSI was tasked with developing standards exceeding that data rate. In 1992, the IEEE Obtained an additional level of responsibility and requested proposals for "Fast Ethernet," designed to raise the Ethernet operating rate from 10M b/s to 100M b/s. This request resulted in two initial proposals.

0-8493-9965-3/99/$0.00+$.50
© 1999 by CRC Press LLC

## 100BaseT

One proposal, now referred to as 100BaseT, was developed by a consortium that included Synoptics Communications, Inc., 3Com Corp., and Ungermann-Bass, Inc. This proposal retained the CSMA/CD access proposal, but it does not support prioritization or the multiplexing of time-sensitive traffic. As a result, it is difficult to support a large number of concurrent LAN sessions that include multimedia applications. In addition, the CSMA/CD access protocol cannot distinguish between different types of network traffic, which makes connection with other CSMA/CD networks difficult.

## 100VG-AnyLAN

A second 100M-b/s proposal was developed by AT&T Microelectronics and Hewlett-Packard Co. This proposal, referred to as 100VG-AnyLAN, replaced the CSMA/CD access protocol by a demand-priority scheme that supports Ethernet, Token Ring, FDDI, and other types of LANs. In addition, 100VG-AnyLAN can transport data at 100M b/s for distances up to 100 meters using category 3 unshielded twisted-pair cable, a capability that enables it to support a significant installed base of wiring.

Although the IEEE was supposed to select only one Fast Ethernet proposal, it has not done so to date. 100VG-AnyLAN has become the IEEE 802.12 standard, while the CSMA/CD proposal has become an addendum to the IEEE's 802.3 Ethernet standard, 802.3e.

## Asynchronous Ethernet

A third Fast Ethernet proposal — asynchronous Ethernet — was developed by National semiconductor. It also supports the CSMA/CD access protocol. However, this LAN technique only supports an operating rate of 16M b/s and results in multiplexed 64K-b/s ISDN channels being carried within the bandwidth. This proposal has not yet received as much interest as the other proposals.

## HUB ARCHITECTURE

100VG-AnyLAN was designed as a hub-centric network architecture. A central hub, known as a level 1 or "root" hub, functions as an inverted tree base in establishing a 100VG-AnyLAN network. From this hub, other hubs or nodes form a star topology, fanning out underneath the root hub as illustrated in Exhibit 1. All hubs located in the same network segment must be configured to support the same frame format — IEEE 802.3 Ethernet or IEEE 802.5 Token Ring. Through the attachment of a bridge or router to a hub port, the 100VG-AnyLAN network can be extended to interconnect

Level 1 "Root" Hub

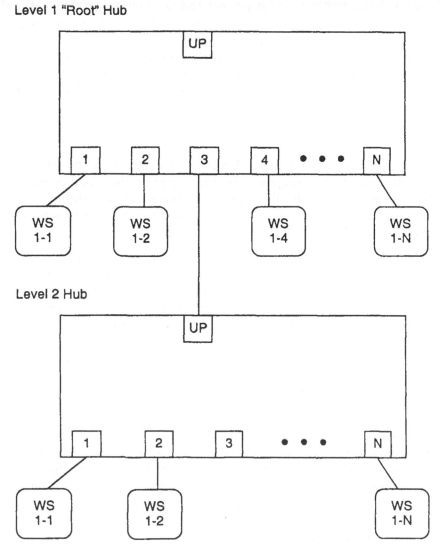

Level 2 Hub

**Key:**
WS Workstation Hub–Level Port

**Exhibit 1. 100VG-AnyLan Topology.**

with other Ethernet or Token Ring networks, FDDI, and ATM-based networks, or a WAN transmission facility.

Each hub in a 100VG-AnyLAN network has one uplink port (labeled "up" in Exhibit 1) and "n" downlink ports (labeled 1 through N). The uplink port on each hub is reserved for connecting lower-level hubs to an upper-level hub, whereas the downlink ports are used to connect an upper-level hub to workstations, bridges, routers, and other network devices, including lower-level hubs. Up to three levels of cascading can be used on a 100VG-AnyLAN network.

## Hub Operation

Each hub port can be configured to operate in one of two modes — normal or monitor. Ports configured to operate in their normal mode forward only those packets specifically addressed to the attached node. In comparison, ports configured to operate in the monitor mode forward every packet received by the hub.

Devices connected to nodes gain access to a 100VG-AnyLAN network through the use of a centrally controlled access method, referred to as "demand priority." Under the demand-priority access method, a node issues a request — referred to as a demand — to the hub it is connected to, thus transmitting a packet onto the 100VG-AnyLAN network. Each request includes a priority label assigned by the upper-layer application. The priority label is either normal, for normal data packets, or high, for packets carrying time-critical multimedia information. Naturally, high-priority requests are granted access to the network prior to normal-priority requests.

The level 1, or "root," hub continuously scans its ports using a round-robin sequence for requests. Lower-level hubs connected as nodes also perform a round-robin scanning process and forward node requests to the root hub. The root hub determines which nodes are requesting permission to transmit a packet, as well as the priority level associated with the packet. Each hub maintains a separate list for both normal- and high-priority requests. Normal-priority requests are serviced in their port order until a higher-priority request is received. Upon receipt of a higher-priority request, the hub will complete any packet transmission in progress and then service the high-priority packet before servicing the normal-priority list.

To prevent a long sequence of high-priority requests from abnormally delaying low-priority requests, the hub also monitors node request-to-send response times. If the delay exceeds a predefined time, the hub automatically raises the normal-priority level to a high-priority level.

Level 1 "Root" Hub

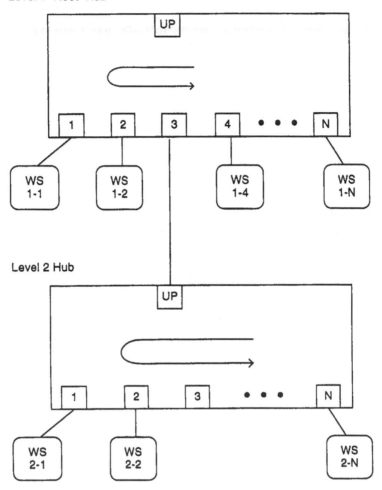

Level 2 Hub

**Note:**
*If all ports have normal-priority requests pending, then:*
*Level 1 scan 1-1, 1-2, 1-3, 1-4,...1-N*

*Level 2 scan 2-1, 2-2, 2-3,...2-N*

*Level 1 resulting packet order sequence*
*     1-1, 1-2, 2-1, 2-2, 2-3,...2-N, 1-4,...1-N*

**Exhibit 2. 100VG-AnyLAN Hub Round Robin Scanning.**

## Round-Robin Scanning

Exhibit 2 illustrates an example of the 100VG-AnyLAN hub round-robin scanning process. Assuming all ports initially have normal-priority requests pending, the packet service order begins at the level 1 hub's first port (1-1). Next, the level 1 hub's second port is serviced (1-2). When the third port is examined, it inserts the round-robin sequence generated by the level 2 hub. That is, it inserts the packet order sequence 2-1, 2-2, 2-3, ...2-N. This sequence is then followed by adding the remaining level 1 hub ports. Thus, the inserted packet order sequence is followed by the sequence 1-4, ...1-N. If at time $t$ equals 0, nodes 2-1 and 1-4 generate high-priority requests, then the packet service order at the level 1 hub would be revised, becoming 2-1, 1-4, 1-1, 1-2, 2-2, ...2-N, 1-5, ...1-N.

## Network Layers

As 100VG-AnyLAN was developed to comply with IEEE network modes, its design resulted in the separation of network functions into sublayers. Exhibit 3 illustrates the relationship of the IEEE 802.12 DTE reference model to the well-known ISO/OSI model.

Similar to other IEEE LAN standards, 802.12 subdivides the International Standards Organization data link layer into two sublayers — LLC and MAC. Information is transmitted over the LLC sublayer in either IEEE 802.3 or 802.5 frame formats, whereas the MAC sublayer uses the demand-priority mechanism to access the network. The 802.12 model differs from the Ethernet and Token Ring models in its subdivision of the physical layer into four sublayers.

## PMI Sublayer Functions

The PMI sublayer is responsible for performing four key functions before passing data to the PMI sublayer. Those functions are quartet channeling, data scrambling, 5BGB encoding, and the addition of a preamble and "start" and "end" frame delimiter to frames, which prepares them for transmission by the lower sublayer. Exhibit 4 illustrates the functions performed at the PMI and PMD sublayers.

**Quartet Channeling.** Quartet channeling is the process of first sequentially dividing MAC frame data octets into 5-bit data quintets. Next, each 5-bit quintet is distributed sequentially among four channels. The rationale for the use of four channels is that they represent a transmission pair for a 4-UTP demand-priority network.

As indicated in Exhibit 4, channel 0 data is transmitted on twisted-pair wires 1 and 2, channel 1 data winds up being transmitted on wires 3 and 6, and so on. When 2-pair or fiber optic cable is used, 100VG-AnyLAN specifies the use of a multiplexing scheme that is incorporated at the PMD sublayer.

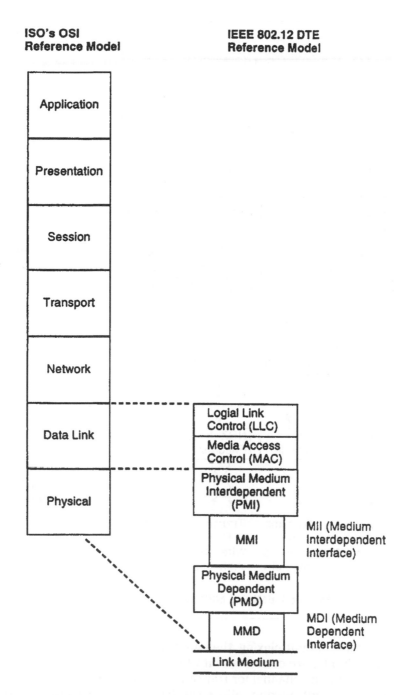

**Exhibit 3. IEEE 802.12 Reference Model Compared to OSI Reference Model.**

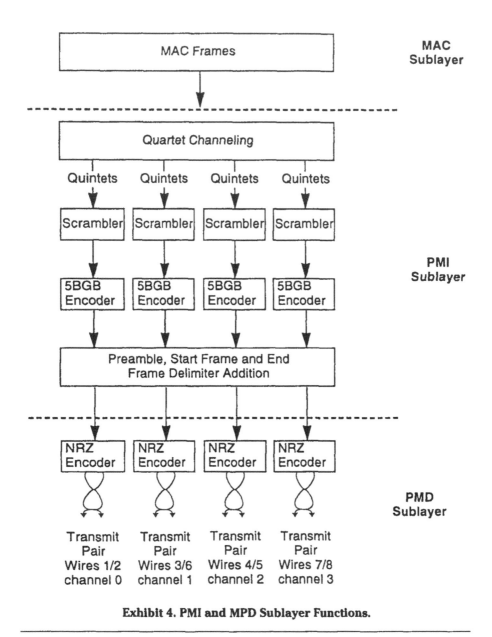

**Exhibit 4. PMI and MPD Sublayer Functions.**

Through the use of multiplexing, the four channels illustrated in the lower portion of Exhibit 4 are converted into two channels for transmission on 2-pair wire, or to one channel for transmission on fiber optic cable. Thus, the addition of multiplexing tailors the PMD sublayer to the physical medium used by the network.

**Data Scrambling.** The scrambler used at the PMI level reduces the potential effect of radio frequency interference and signal crosstalk between cable pairs. To accomplish this, the scramblers randomize the bit patterns on each transmission pair, eliminating the potential for long repetitious strings of 0s and 1s. Each of the four scramblers uses a different scrambling mechanism that ensures the randomness of the resulting data.

**5BGB Encoding.** The mapping of scrambled 5-bit data quintets into 6-bit symbols is performed by the 5BGB encoders shown in Exhibit 4. The encoding process results in the creation of a balanced data pattern that contains equal numbers of 0s and 1s, providing guaranteed clock-transition synchronization for receiver circuits. In addition, the 5BGB encoding process provides an added error-checking capability. This results from the fact that 5BGB encoding supports the use of only 16 symbol patterns. Thus, invalid symbols can be detected as error conditions.

**Data Addition.** The last function performed by the PMI layer is adding the preamble and starting and ending frame delimiters to each channel. This preprocesses the data into a format that can be transmitted across the network. The actual placement of data onto the network is performed by the PMD sublayer.

## PMD Sublayer

PMD sublayer functions include NRZ encoding, link medium operation, and link status control. In addition, if the transmission medium is 2-pair or fiber optic cable, the PMD sublayer will also perform channel multiplexing. The remainder of the functions discussed in this section use 4-pair unshielded twisted- pair cable cabling.

**NRZ Encoding.** NRZ encoding is a two-level signaling mechanism (0 and + voltage) used to represent the values of data transmitted on the copper 4-pair unshielded twisted-pair cable. Under NRZ encoding, successive 1 bits are represented by a continuous + voltage level. Thus, to differentiate one "1" from a succeeding "1," NRZ encoding requires the use of clocking circuitry.

**Link Medium Operation.** Link medium operation permits a 4-UTP 100VG-AnyLAN network to operate in both full- and half-duplex. F-DX communications use two channels for transmission from the hub to a node, and the remaining two channels are used for transmission from the node to the hub.

F-DX communication is required when link-status information is transmitted between a hub and a node. In comparison, normal data flow is

**Exhibit 5. PMD Link Status Control Signaling**

| Tone Pattern | Meaning when Received by a Node | Meaning when Received by a Hub |
|---|---|---|
| 1-1 | Idle | Idle |
| 1-2 | Incoming Data Packet | Normal-Priority Request |
| 2-1 | Reserved | High-Priority Request |
| 2-2 | Link Training Request | Link Training Request |

accomplished via a half-duplex operation, where all four channels are used to transmit data from the node to the hub or from the hub to the node.

**Link Status Control.** Link status control requires a full-duplex transmission mode of operation. When operating in F-DX, two frequency tones — referred to as tone 1 and tone 2 — are used to communicate the link status between the hub and the node. In actuality, the tones are generated by producing a pattern of 1s and 0s at a specific signaling rate to produce a tone. For example, tone 1 is generated by transmitting a 30MHz alternating pattern of sixteen 1s followed by sixteen 0s, resulting in a frequency of approximately 0.9375 MHz. In comparison, tone 2 is generated by transmitting a 30MHz alternating pattern of eight 1s followed by eight 0s, resulting in a frequency of approximately 1.875 MHz.

Through the use of a combination of tones, control signals are transmitted by the hub and the node. Exhibit 5 lists the link status control signals supported at the PMD sublayer.

The "idle" status, when received by a node, indicates that the hub has no pending packets. When received by the hub, an idle status indicates no requests are pending. An "incoming data packet" status indicates to a node that data may be destined to that port from the hub. This instructs the node to stop sending control tones on channels 2 and 3 so it can receive the packet. The normal-priority request indicates to the hub that the node is requesting to transmit a normal-priority packet. In comparison, the high-priority request indicates to the hub that the node is requesting to send a high-priority packet. The last signal permissible, link training request, indicates to the node or hub that link initialization is being requested.

## CONCLUSION

100VG-AnyLAN network adapter cards are expected to be available for under $400, providing a cost-effective, high-speed LAN transmission infrastructure. In comparison, ATM adapter cards are many years away from commercial production and are expected to cost in excess of $1,250 per network adapter card when they become available. Because of the affordability of 100VG-AnyLAN and its ability to directly interface with existing

Ethernet and Token Ring networks (and indirectly to FDDI and ATM), it is a very attractive method of satisfying high-speed organizational LAN communications requirements. Thus, network managers should place 100VG-AnyLAN on the top of their list of emerging technologies to explore for satisfying organizational requirements.

# Chapter 28
# Applications and Business Issues of Fiber Channel

*Ed Frymoyer*

For data communications managers looking for a networking technology that offers scalable bandwidth, connectivity, distance and protocol multiplexing, and guaranteed delivery, fiber channel is an economical solution. Fiber channel is designed to improve information flow, not just transport data or bits. This chapter discusses the economics and technology fundamentals of fiber channel as a transport technology.

## INTRODUCTION

Occasionally, new technologies transform ways of thinking — this is sometimes called a paradigm shift. Fiber channel is an example of such a technology.

Fiber channel is a high-speed information connection for all classes of computers across a wide range of system protocols, extensible in speeds up to gigabit rates and beyond. An industry initiative, which started in 1988, has produced a defined standard and an increasing number of practical installations in enterprises. This chapter examines fiber channel technology, benefits, and applications.

## HOW FIBER CHANNEL DIFFERS
## FROM OTHER TRANSPORT TECHNOLOGIES

Fiber channel is an OSI technology that was developed independently, without any predefined structure and methodology. More than 60 companies helped define fiber channel — it is probably the most democratic standard ever designed.

0-8493-9965-3/99/$0.00+$.50
© 1999 by CRC Press LLC

Fiber channel offers:

- channel reliability and performance.
- use with multiple applications.
- the ability to share media.
- improved networking capabilities.

Fiber channel is designed to improve information flow, not just to transport data or bits. The emphasis is on interconnection of information by providing access, flexibility, application layer friendliness, data integrity, high availability, distance insensitivity, and seamless extension to higher rates as needed.

### Shared Storage, Computing, and Network Resources

Although a sophisticated structure is necessary for such flexibility and performance, fiber channel enables a change of the computing paradigm. Fiber channel links both storage and computing resources. By linking local and distributed storage locations with the same access time (i.e., latency) as local-to-local locations, fiber channel creates a flattened memory space — the virtual local disk. Because performance is the same with local or distance storage or shared computer resources, fiber channel enables true mainframe downsizing using open systems client/server methodologies. The costs and user-friendliness of fiber channel can be compared with those of distributed personal computing methods. Fiber channel provides high-bandwidth multiple applications over a wide range of computer equipment, from the desktop to the glass house.

ATM and FDDI, among other transport technologies, are designed as frame or cell-based transports for physically carrying data over a networked structure. Applications must be adapted to the cell or frame transport methodology. As opposed to a physical connection construct such as FDDI or ATM, fiber channel is a systems-level technology. It also easily becomes a server technology; allowing high-performance sharing of storage, computing, and networking resources. Exhibit 1 compares the maximum data rates of various data communications technologies.

A primary advantage of fiber channel architecture is that it enables multiple server functions. One interconnect board (known as an N_Port or channel in the standard's parlance) can inherently provide multifunctionality. Combined with a switched fiber channel network, this allows rapid access to distributed mass storage, distributed computing, and multiple networking resources. Fiber channel is thus unique as a transport technology whose structure provides all these functions. Because fiber channel is a clustering technology, it allows sharing of computing and storage resources over the same connections in a high-bandwidth, low-latency,

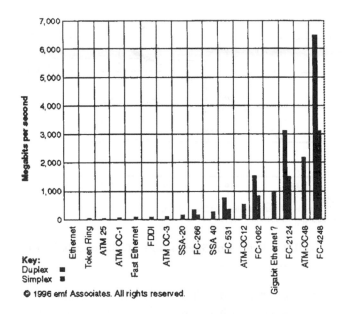

**Exhibit 1. Maximum Data Rate by Technology.**

time-multiplexed manner. Fiber channel implies multiple services, multiple applications, and fully scalable physical and logical service.

## Fiber Channel Economics

The high-volume economics of SCSI and Ethernet determine the cost structure of fiber channel. Costs for these technologies, at speeds much lower than fiber channel, are well under $100 per connection. Gigabit fiber channel has matured rapidly — connectivity will soon be available for the same price of Ethernet in 1993. Currently, fiber channel connections — adapter boards with optical — are $1,000 to $2,500 (this is the original equipment manufacturer price). Soon prices with copper connections will be well under $500, and by the year 2000, will be under $100 for the simplest copper connection.

To be useful, a technology must have the appropriate high-volume economics and the business incentives necessary to achieve the volume. fiber channel economics can be compared with those of SCSI mass-storage serial upgrades based on 30M- and higher volume SCSI connections. The cost of these connections is, at most, $200 for a high-volume adapter board and much less for embedded connections such as those on disk drives. Long-term, fiber channel must provide much higher cost performance at the same cost as SCSI for both hosts and peripherals. The Ethernet network-connec-

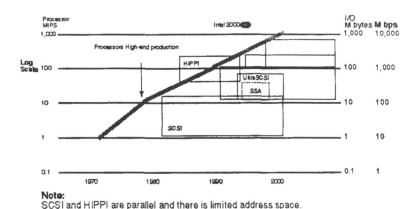

**Exhibit 2. Processor Speeds and I/O Standards Rates.**

tion market is comparable in volume with the SCSI market. The costs of Ethernet connections are far less than $100 per port in volume.

Fiber channel promises to approach these costs within the next few years, and seems to be ahead of the experience curve for gigabit connections. Gigabit at Ethernet prices seems achievable.

### Processor Speeds

The speed of processors and associated MIPS are rising at 35% per year. By the end of the decade, workstations and high-end PCs will be at 1,000 to 2,000 MIPS performance based on new processor development trends. (Exhibit 2 shows processor speeds and I/O standards rates for several technologies.) Intel has announced its goal of 2,000 MIPS by the year 2000 for its widely used series of processors and RISC successors based on the HP/PA RISC technology. Similar trends are evident from IBM, Motorola, and Apple PowerPCs, in addition to Sun SPARC workstations.

The rate of information I/O must keep up with processor performance increases. Whether it takes an information connection operating at 1/10, 1/2, or full MIP rate to match the processor, there is a significant gap. Most channel and networking technologies do not track increased processor performance. Fiber channel meets the speed requirements and is also scalable to accommodate future rates. SSA is a very limited, short-term solution aimed at serial SCSI only. ATM has promise on the wide area, but complexity and high costs make it unsuitable for serial memory busses. Exhibit 3 illustrates the difference in processor speeds among several data communications technologies.

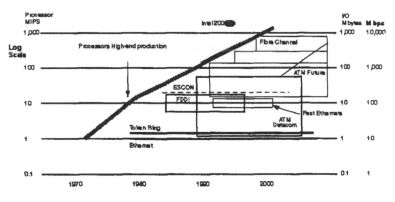

**Exhibit 3. Processor Speed and Data Communications Technologies.**

## FIBER CHANNEL AS A SERVER TECHNOLOGY

When fiber channel is used as a server technology, the same interconnection can rapidly time-multiplex several functions with only one external I/O channel required. The server functionality of fiber channel offers great promise in the long term. New paradigms of computing and interconnection are possible with a technology that can share storage, computing, and network resources. The greatest advantage of fiber channel is the single I/O connection that provides the capability to create resource sharing in multiple dimensions.

When combined with management services such as MIBs and SNMP, fiber channel has the structure to work in a highly distributed environment. Not only does fiber channel offer rate scalability, it also provides multiple server functions on the same structure, which makes it the most cost-effective interface in many situations. A single adapter board can provide the multiple functionality. The connection is fast enough that time multiplexing is an effective strategy. The server function not only implements distributed low-latency, high-bandwidth clustering, but also enables setting up object-oriented exchanges between diverse classes of computers.

## NETWORKING

Fiber channel is also a network. TCP/IP, the main methodology used for networks, is carried seamlessly over fiber channel. Fiber channel can connect up to 16M users in a single fiber channel domain. Fiber channel supports traditional peer-to-peer message routing. In addition, because fiber channel is faster than other networks, a very practical methodology of transporting Ethernet, ATM, FDDI, and other networks is possible. SONET-to-Fiber Channel connections for private data lines or Fiber Channel-to-ATM for public data switching are effective ways of providing connections between local fiber channel high-speed data islands to remote sites.

Systems management through SNMP is built into the fiber channel standard. A number of methodologies including OpenView or NetWare can be used to provide the information gathering in addition to SNMP. Several vendors are creating management products to work with fiber channel networks. Fabric services such as a name server are built into the standard. Broadcast, multicast, and hunt groups are part of the architecture. Near-term extensions of the standard provide for up to 256 virtual subchannel connections to any one user; asynchronous services have been defined and will be part of the formal standard soon.

## APPLICATIONS

Fiber channel has been successful with high-rate OLTP database applications and in distributed graphics/video simultaneous editing. For example, Sun Microsystems installed its SPARC servers in Fingerhut, a large catalog sales company. Fingerhut needed a distributed client/server solution that would provide for more than 500 simultaneous users being connected and a transaction rate of more than 8,000 IOPS. Fiber channel connected to several parallel NFS connections provided performance better than any competitive system.

AT&T needed rapid ad generation for its long-distance unit. Advertisements were created by agencies in New York and Boston and needed to be turned around much faster than the typical four to five weeks required with existing technology. After transmission by D3 lines (45M bps), extensive real-time editing was required at the New Jersey headquarters. For the video, 270M bps was required, and additional amounts were required for voice interaction and whiteboard display. Originally, AT&T attempted to use an internal ATM network to do the job, but concluded that it would be several years before the required performance could be achieved.

AT&T has selected Ancor Communications' gigabit-per-second fiber channel switching fabric and now estimates that the time savings would pay for the network investment within a year. Editing of ads can now be done in 7 to 10 days. Similar gains in productivity and performance using fiber channel can be expected in other business areas.

## CONCLUSION

Fiber channel is actually both a channel and a network. It offers channel features such as simplicity and guaranteed performance in addition to network features like distance and protocol multiplexing.

Network administrators in search of more bandwidth may wish to explore fiber channel as the solution for bandwidth-intensive applications. By combining the speed and performance of channel communication with the extended reach and flexibility of a network, fiber channel offers reliable, high-throughput communication.

Fiber channel is poised to become the most important new information connection technology. In an information economy where access, management, cost, and exploitation of information assets are the most critical business issues, such a technology is essential.

# Chapter 29
# Fiber Channel Architecture, Layers, and Services

*Ed Frymoyer*

Fiber Channel technology combines the attributes of a channel and a network medium. This chapter explains how Fiber Channel works with existing interfaces, its use as a high-speed backbone in a LAN, and its messaging structure. Three topologies with guidelines for use are also explained.

## INTRODUCTION

Fiber Channel is an OSI technology that provides flexibility, application layer friendliness, data integrity, and high availability. Fiber Channel technology provides a seamless application and systems interface without the need for the computer system to support the intricacies, buffering, and management of high-performance information interconnection features.

## FIBER CHANNEL LAYERS

Fiber Channel's OSI-style layering structure is based on practical separation of the functional layers (see Exhibit 1). Fiber Channel layers include:

- **FC-0.** This is the lowest level of the FC physical standard, covering the physical characteristics of the interface and media.
- **FC-1.** This is the middle level of the FC physical standard. It defines the 8- to 10-bit encoding/decoding and transmission protocol.
- **FC-2.** This is the highest level of FC physical standard, defining the rules for signaling protocol and describing transfer of frames, sequences, and exchanges.
- **FC-3.** This is the hierarchical level in the Fiber Channel standard that provides common services. Layer FC-3 is not currently used but is available for future applications, such as disk striping (i.e., multiplexing data

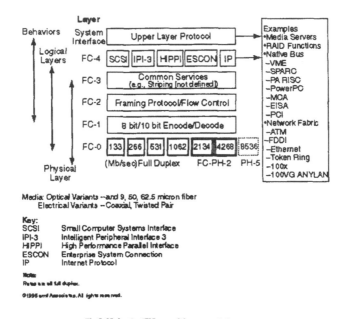

Exhibit 1. Fiber Channel Layers.

over multiple disk drives to improve performance) or data management.

- **FC-4.** This is the hierarchical level in the Fiber Channel standard that specifies the mapping of upper layer protocols to levels below.

The FC-0 (physical) layer and the encode/decode layers are physically and functionally separated from the link control and feature selection (FC-2) and application interface (FC-4) layers. The high-speed serial functions (i.e., optical and electrical) are separated from the parallel processed FC-2 and the software/firmware dependent FC-4.

In contrast to 802.x transport technologies that include a physical layer that is media connection only and a MAC layer that is a combination of high-speed and low-speed functions, Fiber Channel offers a more practical approach by providing clean separations.

There are no sublayer physical definitions of the layers. A clean interface can be made to computer systems as well as to important peripherals such as mass storage, media storage, medical devices, process equipment, data gathering devices (e.g., real-time sensors), and other systems. The upper layer protocol is usually the systems bus or processor I/O function. This arrangement allows easy reuse of system's software drivers with a minimal update to handle the speed of Fiber Channel, which can range up to 100M bps using optical fiber. Functionally, the information form and structure look the same. Specifically, current FC-4 layers address SCSI, IPI-3, HIPPI, block MUX, Enterprise ESCON, and traditional TCP/IP.

Future applications may use a streamlined form of Fiber Channel that provides tighter coupling between the Fiber Channel I/O and the native bus of the computer/processor. The technology is still developing. Clustering protocols are being developed with Direct Memory Access-to -direct memory access connections. The protocols also offer the reliability of TCP/IP and less than 25 microsecond latency, which is much better than any other serialized system with the distance reach of Fiber Channel. This level of latency is useful in distributed systems, but not in very closely coupled systems such as backplane-connected processors.

## Channel Networking

Fiber Channel provides links to other LAN technologies by means of straightforward bridging/routing methodologies. This combination of channel and network connectivity is called *channel networking* and is unique to Fiber Channel.

A Fiber Channel connection may support one or more of the defined sets of application layer (FC-4s). Fiber Channel implementations may be very simple — as in only serial SCSI — or very complex, as for multiple FC-4 support. Also, the link may support one or more transmission rates.

## Chip Coding

A combination of hardware and firmware achieves the management, link control, buffering, and feature set implementation of layers FC-2, 3, and 4. Single and multiple chip implementations are available. The complexity of this adapter board hardware depends on how many FC-4s are supported of feature sets supported. Whether implementation is as a set of chips (i.e., microcontroller, memory, and the range firmware) or a single chip, the developer can use readily available CMOS processes.

The encode/decode function (FC-1) is the interface between the parallel process and the serial process. The 8-bit to 10-bit encoding provides a balanced set of 10 bits derived from a transmitted set of bits. The a conversion provides balanced set of bits in which there is only one more 1 than 0 for each set of 10 bits. Also, there are at most five 1s or 0s sequentially between each transition from 1 to 0 or vice versa. This coding has made it very easy for chip manufacturers and to build serialize–deserializer chips and hardware. In addition, all single-bit errors in a 10-bit segment are detectable.

Fiber Channel uses the 8-bit/10-bit methodology because it is easy to implement and provides an extremely balanced serial data stream for all possible idle inputs. The guaranteed transitions in the 8-bit/10-bit coding structure provide a multiplexed serial stream from which it is very easy to recover timing. The balanced serial data stream also reduces electromagnetic and radio frequency interference problems.

The output of the FC-1 layer is a parallel 10-bit signal. Some implementations have this layer on the physical interface chip, but this must combine functionality with the CMOS in FC-2 chips. The higher rates are in the extensions of the Fiber Channel standard; 2G bps and 4G bps are already approved for FC physical layer 2.

### Physical, Behavioral, and Logical Subsets

The classification into physical, logical, and behavioral subsets is useful for the development of interoperability profiles. Because of the range and complexity of the Fiber Channel standard, profiles that define the physical, logical, and behavioral choices for a specific market or application are needed. Some of the first were defined and published by the Fiber Channel Systems Initiative (FCSI) and its participants (Hewlett-Packard, IBM, and Sun Microsystems) and provide the baseline for interoperable implementations by almost all of today's hardware for serial SCSI and TCP/IP. FCSI's goal was to create an open systems supply of interoperable pieceparts and systems.

### MESSAGE STRUCTURE DEFINITION

In addition, Fiber Channel defines message structure to allow disassembly of and reassembly messages from the application layer of the transmitting side to the same level at the receiving side. These are called Fiber Channel exchanges, sequences, and frames.

### Exchanges

An exchange refers to an application layer's functional communication between users. Examples are a SCSI connection or a TCP/IP session. Several exchanges can be active simultaneously.

### Sequences

In Fiber Channel lexicon, a sequence is a related set of frames (one or more) within the context of a specific exchange. Sometimes a sequence is called the Fiber Channel information unit (though not specifically defined by the standard).

### Frame

A frame is a set of bytes containing control (i.e., routing) and data elements. A frame is the atomic unit in Fiber Channel. Frame overhead is a fixed 36 bytes. Frames are variable from 36 bytes (control information

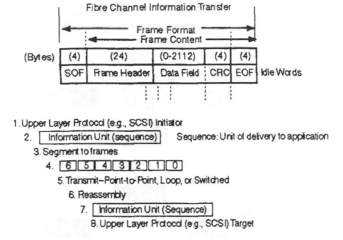

**Exhibit 2. Fiber Channel Information Transfer.**

only) to 2,112 bytes long, which allows it to be very efficient for normal-size exchanges between computers as well as to and from mass storage connections. Exhibit 2 illustrates framing, message assembly, and message disassembly.

Fiber Channel further defines classes of messages that encompass both circuit connection (class 1) and packet connection (classes 2, 3, 4). Class 2 guarantees delivery and acknowledgment, a unique feature in packetized protocol technologies that improves transfer efficiency because:

- the receiver does not need to guess about delivery.
- packets cannot be dropped without notification to the sender; the receiver sends back an acknowledgment indicating the data has been received and whether or not is has been corrupted (i.e., a CRC Check).

Many small-scale implementations use class 3 (i.e., packetized datagram-unreliable) because it is simpler to implement and relatively reliable.

## SCALABILITY AND GUIDELINES FOR USE

Forms of Fiber Channel connection include point-to-point loop, arbitrated, and switched fabric (see Exhibit 3). Users should select the connection that fits their application without device-cost impact. Topologies are designed to be interconnectable and upgradable.

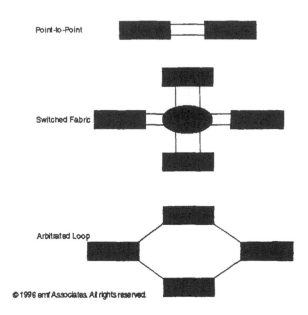

Point-to-Point

Switched Fabric

Arbitrated Loop

**Exhibit 3. Fiber Channel Topologies.**

## Point-to-Point Connections

Point-to-point links provide a dedicated high-bandwidth connection, such as the one from a disk array to a server. Some forms provide high availability, fault tolerant access for two-server/two-disk-array applications.

## Fiber Channel Fabrics

In the switched fabric topology, traffic between Fiber Channel ports passes through an intermediary switch called a fabric that combines cross-bar and packet-switching capabilities. Multiple switches can be linked together to form larger fabrics.

Like other switched media (e.g., Fast Ethernet switching hubs ATM switches), capacity in switched fabric topologies is scalable. New switch modules are added to connect additional devices and the aggregate throughput increases to accommodate the increased load.

Fabrics can also interconnect devices with different speed and Fiber Channel media, so the speed and cost of the Fiber Channel link can be selected to match the anticipated traffic from the bridge or router.

Fiber Channel fabrics provide multicast services without requiring external frame replication servers, although the size of a multicast packet is limited to the maximum frame size of the fabric (generally 2K bytes). Available fabrics support datagram, acknowledged connectionless, and connection-oriented service classes. In the future, some fabrics will support a virtual circuit-oriented class of service, in which multiple circuits with guaranteed bandwidth can be established by a single port.

## Arbitrated Loop

In the arbitrated loop topology, up to 126 nodes can be connected in a shared-media topology. Instead of a circulating token or a collision sense mechanism, a simple arbitration mechanism ensures fairness. Star topologies with passive hubs provide robustness; some hub ports may be equipped with a loop bypass circuit to ensure continued loop operation if the port is offline.

Current implementations use TwinAxcess operating at a gigabit, which has ample capacity for interconnecting disk drives that can source on the average less than 20M bytes or network connections with 10M bps and a certain number of 100M-bps LANs (Ethernet).

Low cost is the primary advantage of the arbitrated loop topology. Only half the number of transceivers are required compared with fabric connections, and no switch is required. However, because bandwidth is shared among all nodes on an individual loop, the number of devices will be limited if many have high-traffic requirements.

## Fiber Channel Application Interconnection

Fiber Channel can be viewed as an application-to-application connection using a common adapter port, such as a workstation, PC, storage array, disk drive, or any other appropriate peripheral (this port is known as the N_Port in Fiber Channel lexicon) and a common interconnection technology (i.e., point-to-point, loop, or switched). Exhibit 4 illustrates simultaneous multiplexed connections among applications using Fiber Channel.

Many applications can benefit from the economies of scale of other applications, with the incremental costs being small for both the hardware and software elements. For little additional complexity, a connection can be both serial SCSI and TCP/IP. Examples include multiple video connections (being investigated by digital video and digital movie studios), clustering and disk file access, and interactive medical applications that require streaming of data from an imaging device (e.g., MRI) and simultaneously sending the data via TCP/IP to a doctor's office in the same facility.

## CONCLUSION

Because of its unique architecture, Fiber Channel can offer the high-performance, low-cost connection required by bandwidth-intensive applications.

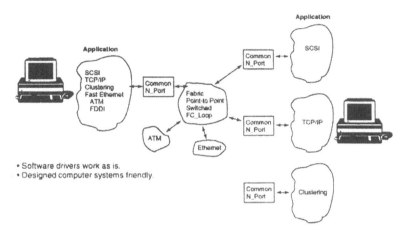

**Exhibit 4. Simultaneous Multiplexed Connections.**

By combining the attributes of a channel and a network, Fiber Channel enables data transfer rates that are up to 250 times faster than many network protocols. Now that computers are faster and better able to handle large amounts of data, a network interconnection is needed that can handle higher speeds. Fiber Channel is emerging as the information connection technology that enables reliability and performance at record speeds.

# Chapter 30
# Linking to the World Wide Web

*John P. Slone*

The World Wide Web gives users almost instant access to hyperlinked documents, images, and graphics from sites around the globe. The key technologies used to define, deploy, and retrieve Web-based information are discussed in this chapter.

## A WINDOW TO THE WORLD

The World Wide Web has been described as the world's most successful client/server application. The WWW, also known to its supporters as the Web, is a tool for retrieving network-accessible information residing on servers all over the world.

The WWW can best be exploited when it is accessed through LAN-attached workstations and when it is used to access information held by LAN-attached servers. Similarly, Web technology can be used to enhance the usefulness of a local area network, whether or not the LAN is connected to the Internet.

This chapter gives an overview of the World Wide Web, including its fundamental concepts, the protocols and specifications that make Web hyperlinks possible, and the software requirements for accessing Web-related information.

## HYPERLINKS

The wealth of information available on the WWW is far greater than what can be contained within a single computer, which creates the need to link information from different sources. That linkage mechanism is known as "hypermedia." Hypermedia is an extension of the simpler concept known as hypertext, or linked text.

Linked text is nothing new. Text linkages have existed for centuries in such written forms as footnotes, bibliographies, and tables of contents.

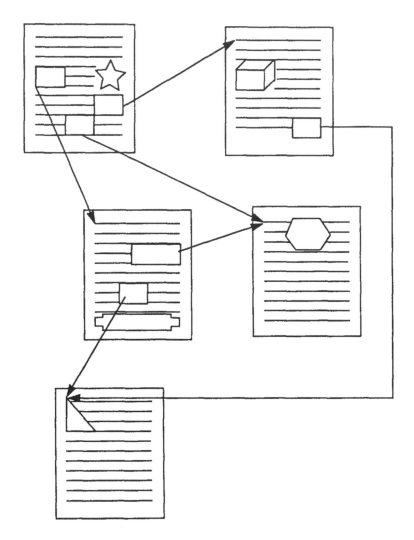

**Exhibit 1. Examples of Text Linkages.**

Hypertext is simply a mechanism for providing these links in a computerized environment.

A familiar example to most end users is the set of Help screens provided with Windows applications. When a user selects Help, a list of topics is presented. The user then selects a topic by clicking on a word or phrase. Within the resulting text, certain words or phrases are highlighted, indicating that more information related to the highlighted text is available for further exploration. Hyperlinks let a user jump to different documents by following the highlighted entries that lead to other Web sites when the user clicks on them. Exhibit 1 illustrates how text linkages flow between documents.

In the WWW, links may point to information objects such as pictures, movies, sound clips, or practically anything else that can be represented digitally. Similarly, links may be established between nontext objects and other objects. For example, it is not uncommon to find links from speaker icons to sound clips, or from small pictures to large pictures.

Hyperlinks in WWW documents often extend around the globe. A</n>single document may contain links to documents in several different countries. It is, in fact, the expansion of these links from document to document on a global scale that enhances the popularity of the Web.

## HOW HTTP ENABLES INFORMATION SHARING

The original designers of the Web recognized that for a global hypermedia system to be effective, it had to be possible for users to execute hypertext links in as little as 100 milliseconds. The World Wide Web accomplishes global Hypermedia linking through the HTTP that is used for information sharing. In its simplest form, an HTTP transaction consists of four phases: connection, request, response, and close.

### Connection

TCP/IP is the most widely used protocol set for internetwork communications. On a TCP/IP network, a TCP/IP connection is established between the client application and the server. A connection request is sent from the client to the server, followed by the return of a connection acknowledgment.

### Request and Response

Upon receipt of the connection acknowledgment, the client issues a request. The request, which is an ASCII string, consists of the wordGET followed by a space and the address of the requested document. The convention used for the document address is called a URL. The response is then returned by the server in the form of an HTML document.

### Close

When the server has returned the entire response, it closes the process by breaking the TCP/IP connection. Optionally, the client may abort the transfer before this point by breaking the connection, in which case the server will not indicate that an error has occurred. This protocol exchange is illustrated as a time-flow diagram in Exhibit 2.

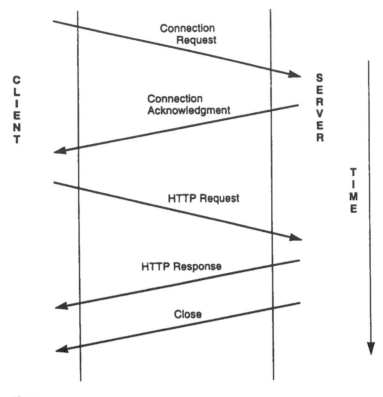

**KEY:**
HTTP  hypertext transfer protocol

**Exhibit 2. HTTP Time-Flow Diagram.**

Web clients are considered well-behaved if they read the response as rapidly as possible without requiring human intervention. Error messages are sent as text in HTML syntax and can only be distinguished from normal messages by their human-readable content. There are no provisions within HTTP for error control or recovery, nor are there any provisions for flow control.

These two facets of the protocol, lack of error control and lack of flow control, allow the protocol to operate efficiently and without the need for either entity to maintain state information. Furthermore, each HTTP transaction is an independent action, unrelated to any transactions that occurred before it or that will occur subsequently.

Extensions to HTTP continue to be developed. Each extension is to be backward compatible with basic HTTP. For example, the capability to perform a search or to allow fill-in forms is accomplished by embedding the variables within the address field.

**Exhibit 3. Universal Resource Identifier (URI) Reserved Characters**

| Reserved Character | Meaning |
| --- | --- |
| Percent sign (%) | Used as an escape sequence identifier. The two characters that follow must represent the hexadecimal value of the character represented by the sequence. |
| Slash (/) | Used to identify hierarchical relationships among the path components. Significance is left to right, with entities to the left representing elements closer to the root. This allows the construction of partial URIs representing relative paths. |
| Hash mark (#) | Used to separate the URI of an object from a fragment identifier that represents a specific portion of that object. |
| Question mark(?) | Used to separate the URI of a object that can be queried (e.g., a database) from the elements that make up a query applied to the object. The complete URI stands for the object that is returned as a result of the query. |
| Asterisk (*) and exclamation point (!) | Reserved for definition as reserved characters within specific schemes. |

## FINDING INFORMATION ON THE WEB

The WWW uses an addressing structure known as a URL, an instantiation of the generic concept of a URI. URI globally identify resources that exist within the scope of any registered name or address space, now or in the future.

### How to Read a Web Address

Despite its impressive capability, the URI concept is remarkably simple. For any given name or address that exists within a naming or addressing scheme, a URI can be created by a simple encapsulation method that tags the address with the scheme's registered identifier. The structure of the resulting URI is as follows: prefix:path.

The prefix is an arbitrary character string registered as the identifier of the particular naming or addressing scheme. The colon is simply a delimiter, and the path follows the convention of the name or address scheme identified by the prefix.

To ensure effective operation across diverse systems and globally interconnected networks, URI have been defined more precisely to identify reserved characters and escape sequences for handling reserved characters. Reserved characters are identified in Exhibit 3.

### Unsafe Characters

Any characters that normally appear within the name or address of an object must be encoded as escape sequences within a URI. In addition, certain characters are considered unsafe characters, and it is recommended that they be encoded to ensure consistent operation across a wide range of systems and networks. Unsafe characters include white-space characters, control characters, and language-specific characters, among others. Once all reserved characters and unsafe characters have been properly encoded and the string has been tagged with the appropriate scheme identifier prefix, the resulting string is referred to as the canonical form of a URI.

### URL Path Structure

A number of formal syntax and semantics specifications have been defined for URL, and more types continue to be defined. Types defined for IPs include HTTP, Gopher, and FTP.

Most URL for objects found on the Internet share a common structure. As with any URI, the structure consists of a scheme identifier prefix followed by a path. The path is subdivided such that the first part represents information specific to the IP.

The Internet protocol part is identified by a leading double slash (//) and terminates at the next slash (/). This part of the path contains at least one element and may contain up to four.

The element that is required is the host's Internet domain name or IP address. (Users will find that most people use the domain name.) A second element that is fairly common in practice is the host's port number. If it is not present, the default port for the protocol specified by the scheme identifier is assumed. For example, port 80 is assumed for HTTP. If the port number is present, it follows the host name, separated by a colon.

The other two elements, which are used much less frequently, are the user name and password. If present, these precede the host name and are separated from the host name by the commercial "at" sign (@). If both elements are present, the user name comes first, and the two are separated by a colon.

The remainder of the path structure uses a hierarchical scheme, with elements (presumably directories or some logical equivalent) separated by slashes. An example of a URL path is as follows:

http://www.ncsa.uiuc.edu/SDG/Software/WinMosaic/HomePage.html

The individual components of the URL are read from left to right. First, note that the scheme identifier, which terminates at the first colon, indicates that HTTP is the protocol that will be used to access the object in question. The part that appears between the double slash and the next occurrence of a slash tells the user that the host on the Internet is known by the name of www.ncsa.uiuc.edu. Because this is an HTTP URL, user names and passwords are not supported, thus it would be meaningless (and perhaps error-producing) to include them. Because no port is identified, the default port of 80 will be used. As such, it would have been equally valid for the URL to be:

> http://www.ncsa.uiuc.edu:80/SDG/Software/WinMosaic/HomePage.html

In this case, though, it would be superfluous to include the port. Ports are typically specified when the server is listening to a nondefault port, as is commonly the case when, for example, it is desirable to operate a server on a nonprivileged port (above 1024).

The remainder of the URL breaks down simply as a hierarchical file structure. Within the root context of the server is a directory called SDG, which in turn has a directory called Software, which has a directory called WinMosaic. Under that directory is a file called HomePage.html, which is the object of interest.

Other Internet URL types (e.g., Gopher and FTP) have similar structures up to the end of the IP part. An example of a Who is gateway that operates on a Gopher server at MIT is as follows:

> gopher://sipb.mit.edu:70/1B%3aInternet%20whois%20servers

The part of the path following the single slash is radically different from what is seen in an HTTP URL. This allows the specification of a path understandable by a Gopher server and serves to illustrate the flexibility of the URL concept.

## HYPERTEXT MARKUP LANGUAGE

Documents returned in HTTP responses are formatted in the HTML syntax. HTML is a proper subset of the more familiar SGML. Documents written in HTML are simple text files with special tags that specify formatting directions.

Tags in HTML are delineated by a pair of angle brackets (<>). Some tags appear in opening/closing pairs. In this case, the closing tag usually has a slash immediately following the left bracket. Exhibit 4 shows tags commonly found in Web documents.

HTML is specified in three versions, two of which have been finalized. Version 1 is the basic, minimal subset required to be understood by all Web clients. It provides basic document formatting, hypermedia linking, and embedded images.

Version 2 also supports inline forms, allowing fill-in forms capabilities including text input fields, scroll-bar option selections, radio buttons,

**Exhibit 4. Commonly Used HTML Tags**

| Tag Type | Tag Identifier | Usage | Example |
|---|---|---|---|
| Title | Title | Specifies the title that appears at the top of a client screen. | < title > This is a Document Title</title > |
| Header size n | Hn | Indicates a header line appearing within the text area of the client screen. The n is an inverse relative size control; smaller numbers indicate larger size fonts. | < h2 > Size 2 Header </h2 > |
| Paragraph | P | Indicates a new paragraph. Usually prints a blank line. | ...end of paragraph< p > Start of next paragraph... |
| Italics | I | Indicates utilized print. | < i > utilized print </i > normal print |
| Bold | B | Indicates bold print. | < b > bold print</b > normal print |
| Anchor reference | a href | Indicates hyperlink point of reference. | <ahref = "http.//your.machine.com/directory/ structure/filename.html">highlighted phrase</a > |
| Anchor name | a name | Names a document fragment. Other references identify this fragment with a hash mark (#) URL structure. | < a aname-"z50" >First line of identified fragment.</a > |
| Image | Img | Identifies an embedded image. | < img src = "[URL of image file]" > |

checkboxes, and other basic form element types. Version 2 HTML is the level most commonly used on the World Wide Web.

Version 3 includes more sophisticated features such as tables, figures, text that wraps around images, and mathematical equations. It is not yet finalized.

WWW clients and servers support other protocols in addition to HTTP, including Gopher, FTP, Telnet, and SMTP.

## WEB SOFTWARE COMPONENTS

### Client Software

Access to the World Wide Web depends on the use of a client application called a browser. The widespread popularity of the Web was brought about largely through the development and no-cost distribution of a browser called Mosaic, developed at the NCSA at the University of Illinois.

Mosaic, which to many people has become synonymous with the Web, is available in versions for Windows, Macintosh, or X-windows platforms. It is available by anonymous FTP from NCSA (ftp.ncsa.uiuc.edu) and numerous other sites.

Besides Mosaic, there are approximately 30 different browser applications available for a variety of platforms, including line-mode terminal browsers and E-mail–based browsers. Most of these browsers are free, although several commercial browser products are gaining popularity because of enhanced features and value-added services, such as help-desk support. Among the more popular browsers are Netscape, from Netscape Communications Corp., and Enhanced Mosaic, from Spyglass, Inc.

## Servers

Considering that the WWW is a client/server application, the availability of no-cost servers is a critical factor in the Web's popularity. The most widely used of the free servers are those provided by NCSA and by EPPL, the ELPP in Geneva, Switzerland. The NCSA server is available for UNIX machines; the CERN server runs on UNIX or VMS.

As with browsers, many servers are available, both as freeware and commercially, and operate on a variety of platforms including Windows and Macintosh. Although it is designed around the client/server paradigm, the World Wide Web is envisioned by many of its proponents as being a peer-to-peer network. Users of the Web, in this vision, are both information providers and consumers.

## Viewers

Although the WWW can be used to access information objects of practically any type — text, image, sound, and video — most of the current crop of browsers are limited to displaying text with inline graphic images. To support the viewing or sound of other object types, external viewers are used. These are separate applications that can be invoked automatically by the browser based on the file extension of the file in which the object is contained.

Each browser application has its own method of configuring the viewers to be used for a given object type. Some rely on manual editing of Windows.INI files, for example, and others provide pop-up menu support.

Several viewers are available as freeware or shareware applications along with browser distributions. Popular viewers for Windows include Lview for JPEG images and WHAM for sound files. For Macintosh, popular viewers include JPEGView for Joint Photographic Experts Group images, SoundMachine for audio, and Sparkle for MPEG video.

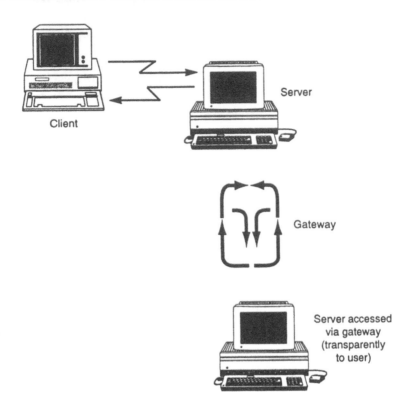

Server

Client

Gateway

Server accessed
via gateway
(transparently
to user)

**Exhibit 5. Gateway Transparency.**

## Gateways

In the same way viewers are used to enhance the usefulness of browsers, gateways are used to enhance the usefulness and extend the reach of servers. From the perspective of the user, gateways are transparent, as shown in Exhibit 5.

Several special-purpose gateways provide features including the ability to perform keyword searches, send mail, or access relational databases. Another popular type of gateway tailors responses depending on where the user clicked within a graphical image. Most servers today support an interface known as the CGI, which allows the development of gateways written in a variety of computer languages capable of supporting practically any requirement.

## HTML Tools

To facilitate the deployment of Web-based information, several HTML conversion and authoring tools have been developed. Most HTML tools provide conversion capability for the more popular word processors, including Word and WordPerfect, and for a wide range of document formats, including postscript, Rich Text Format, FileMaker, troff, LaTeX, BibTeX, Interleaf, and QuarkXPress.

## HOW SECURE IS THE WEB?

World Wide Web security is essentially no different from security for other networked applications. Data privacy, data integrity, and protection from attack are key concerns for business users of the Web. In many ways the solutions are the same as they are for other networked applications. For example, because of the ability to download files using a Web browser instead of an FTP client, procedures for protecting against viruses are essentially the same.

In the early stages of Web development, the Web was used primarily for the purpose of publishing information to as wide an audience as possible. Consequently, data privacy was not a concern initially. More recently, however, people have begun using the Web for distributing information of a more private nature and for buying and selling goods and services across the Internet. These requirements are driving the need for more stringent and specialized security measures.

Security standards for the Web are still being developed. Two primary contenders have been proposed to solve the general problem of securing data flowing between browsers and servers. One approach, known as the SSL, provides for a secure connection at the TCP layer. An alternative to SSL, known as S-HTTP, provides encryption of selected fields within the HTTP protocol packets.

## EMBEDDING WEB TECHNOLOGY IN OTHER PRODUCTS

The WWW has become so popular because it is based on relatively simple protocols that offer sophisticated service — access to a wealth of information spanning the globe. Growth of the Web has continued unabated since its inception, and Web traffic (specifically HTTP packets) has begun to exceed E-mail traffic on the Internet's backbone network, NSFNet.

In addition to mere growth of the numbers, technological capabilities are expected to continue to be enhanced. A second-generation HTTP is under development and is expected to be published in late 1996. HTML will most likely continue to be enhanced, and Web authoring tools, viewers, and gateways will continue to become more sophisticated.

Despite these continuing trends, however, it appears likely that the most important change with respect to the Web will be outside the realm of the Web and Web products. Specifically, Web capabilities are beginning to emerge as a set of embedded features within other products such as operating systems and word processors. Once this happens on a large scale, users will be that much closer to having access to a world of information at their fingertips.

# Chapter 31
# X.400 vs. SMTP

*Gordon L. Preston*

X.400 and SMTP/MIME are the subject of much canonical debate in the messaging community. Although the general consensus is that X.400 offers better functionality than SMTP/MIME as an E-mail protocol, the decision to use X.400 or SMTP/MIME must be based not only on their functionality but also other issues such as security, systems management, message management, human resources requirements, and performance.

## INTRODUCTION

X.400 or SMTP/MIME? No matter what your choice in E-mail protocol, the pros and cons of each technology should be evaluated in the context of the real underlying issue — keeping the network running.

Significant improvements in network management tools, utilities, and techniques are essential before a large, integrated network can begin cost-effective operations. The lack of adequate management tools at the application layer is a major impediment to implementing economical enterprise-wide messaging systems. Operating such networks requires highly skilled software engineers who understand large-scale global enterprise networks.

This chapter covers the issues of operating a reliable messaging environment using either X.400 or SMTP as protocols to transfer E-mail. First, however, the basic features and philosophies of X.400 and SMTP/MIME are explained, including a brief look at the state of electronic mail (E-mail) today and the development process for each protocol.

Exploring critical networking issues requires an understanding of the basic features and philosophies of X.400 and SMTP/MIME, including a brief look at electronic mail (E-mail) today and the development process for each protocol.

## X.400 BACKGROUND

X.400 is based on a formal messaging model created in standardization groups in the International Telecommunications Union–Telecommunications Standards Sector (ITU-TSS). It is the international standard for message

0-8493-9965-3/99/$0.00+$.50
© 1999 by CRC Press LLC

handling. It is a full-feature, store-and-forward message-handling system designed to process multimedia and complex business documents.

In particular, X.400's specification of robust message delivery and non-delivery notification schemes makes it well suited to support electronic commerce transactions. X.400 is a commercially viable and secure message-handling technology supported by a worldwide infrastructure and officially sanctioned by various governments, telecommunication vendors, and public service providers. In addition, X.400 is designed to address not only messaging, but also directory, security, and network management.

## SMTP BACKGROUND

Transmission Control Protocol/Internet Protocol (TCP/IP) is the *de facto* standard network protocol offering a connectionless-mode network service in the Internet suite of protocols. Simple mail transfer protocol (SMTP) is the application-level protocol offering message-handling service. However, because SMTP has its roots in the primarily academic and research and development background of the Internet Engineering Task Force (IETF), its use has been in a relatively benign and open environment without the need for rigidly enforced network performance, security, and message-delivery criteria.

## SMTP/MIME

Messaging by SMTP has been greatly enhanced with the development of Multipurpose Internet Mail Extensions (MIME). This is the official proposed standard format for multimedia Internet mail encapsulated inside standard Internet Request for Comment (RFC) 822 messages.

In simpler terms, MIME provides a way to exchange multimedia E-mail among many different computer systems. It is a collection of specifications that describe how mail user agents (MUAs) can identify arbitrary document types and message body types so the interface can decide how best to display the incoming data to the user. All the information about the attachment is embedded in the message itself. The MUA redefines the structure and contents of RFC 822 message bodies. Users can send word processor documents, spreadsheets, audio files, images, and textual data to someone else regardless of the platform, mail transport agent (MTA), or network operational system that is used by the sender or receiver.

## ELECTRONIC MAIL

E-mail is by far the most popular application carried over the Internet. Internet mail is based on various RFCs, including RFC 822 for SMTP.

E-mail with SMTP has become very popular in research, development, and engineering environments because of their use of UNIX. UNIX and engineering environments usually have TCP/IP and SMTP interconnection protocols bundled in with their operating systems. The Internet has proved to be eminently successful in providing information services to a widely diverse worldwide community with more than 9.4 million host computers on the Internet. One hundred and twenty nine countries now have direct connectivity to the Internet and 39 million users are reachable by E-mail. (A full report is available at http://www.nw.com/zone/WWW/report.html.)

## THE X.400 AND SMTP/MIME DEVELOPMENT PROCESS

X.400 was designed as a total international messaging environment from the beginning, whereas SMTP developed as an outgrowth of earlier experimental work on the Defense Advanced Researched Projects Agency (DARPA) Network. X.400 provides a complete set of internationally agreed-to standards; approved SMTP/MIME RFCs do not have the same level of official international agreement and approval. The unified design of X.400 as a total messaging environment is also reflected in its clean design interfaces with other international standards required to provide a messaging service — namely, directory (X.500), management (X.700), and security (X.900) services.

SMTP is an outgrowth of the Internet and the Internet Engineering Task Force (IETF). As a quasi-official body with no set membership, the IETF is not necessarily representative of all potential customers' needs. It has primary responsibility for the development and review of potential Internet standards from all sources. The IETF's working groups pursue specific technical issues, frequently resulting in the development of one or more specifications that are proposed for adoption as Internet standards. Most IETF members agree that the greatest benefit for all Internet community members results from the cooperative development of technically superior protocols and services.

SMTP/MIME, although capable of interfacing with these other international standards, does not work with the same level of designed interoperability as does X.400. This lack of designed interoperability will directly (and negatively) impact system operational maintenance and management costs.

## THE SMTP VS. X.400 DEBATE

There is no right or wrong answer when it comes to making a choice between X.400 and SMTP. The choice of technology depends on each organization's particular needs and which strength or weakness of different technologies is most important to them. An organization that wants to

**Exhibit 1. Strengths and Weaknesses of SMTP/MIME**

| Strengths | Weaknesses |
|---|---|
| Very popular in the marketplace with millions of users worldwide | Lacks functionality |
| Low cost | Sendmail is free |
| Available on numerous platforms | Implementations differ |
| Text body parts keep everything simple | Too simple for some uses |
| Runs over IP, which comes with UNIX | Limited security |
| Simple addressing | Questionable for financial transactions |
| Simple message routing with DNS | Uses DNS |
| Simplicity and flexibility of the format of RFC #822 messages | Simplicity and flexibility of the format of RFC #822 messages |
| Numerous gateways available | Lack of structure |

share similar technology with as many people as possible can effectively use SMTP/MIME. If security, increased functionality, and operational features such as guaranteed message traceability are most important, then X.400 is the answer.

## SMTP/MIME CHARACTERISTICS

SMTP/MIME supports the transmission of sophisticated information, including images and video, yet it is simple in its design and extensible in nature because of its unique content-type/subtype body part identification mechanism. In short, SMTP/MIME provides a low-cost solution for messaging backbones.

Each part of a multimedia message identifies what type of information is carried in the message part. An entire MIME message, as opposed to an individual part of a multimedia message, can also have a type. For example, a message might have the type "text/plain" and consist of entirely plain text. A MIME message containing parts of different types has the umbrella type "multipart/mixed." Many types and subtypes have been defined to include audio, image, external data source reference, and partial messages.

The simplicity and flexibility of SMTP/MIME are its main strengths because it can easily be implemented on all systems. Its weaknesses include no support for non-ASCII character sets, limited header structure, and an unstructured message body.

Exhibit 1 summarizes the strengths and weaknesses of SMTP/MIME.

## X.400 CHARACTERISTICS

The ITU-TSS has developed an ambitious set of standards for electronic messaging called the X.400 message-handling system (MHS) and the X.500 directory services standards. X.400 has a very complete set of functional characteristics and can accommodate any type of messaging from simple interpersonal text to attached graphics, voice, and video clips. X.435 is defined for electronic commerce, using basic MHS components. X.400 is based on a functional model consisting of a few main components:

- **User agents (UAs)** Used on the desktop for message creation/reading.
- **Message store (MS)** Stores messages until recipient chooses to read them.
- **Message transfer agents (MTAs)** Stores and forwards messages within and between networks.
- **Access units (AUs)** Interfaces to other messaging entities (i.e., voice, facsimile, telex, physical delivery).

An X.500 directory is a collection of entries that contain information about things such as countries, organizations, people, computers, security, and application programs. The directory is a collection of one or more directory system agent (DSA) computers, each of which holds information for some portion of the directory.

Users access the X.500 directory via a computer process referred to as a directory user agent (DUA). Specific protocols have been developed to control directory access and the exchange of information with distributed directories.

X.500 is absolutely essential for implementing the address translation, document conversion, and sophisticated message routing needed for large-scale E-mail integration efforts. Directory synchronization is the basis for implementing transparent user addresses between systems.

X.400/X.500 systems are used by most of the world's telecommunication service providers. The U.S. government is implementing a global X.400 messaging system for the military called the Defense Message System (DMS). NATO is also working toward implementing an X.400-based messaging system. This system defines a military message-handling system (MMHS) using X.400, similar to DMS. The militaries of Australia, Canada, the United Kingdom, and New Zealand are also implementing X.400-based MMHS. X.400 is the preferred technology for backbone messaging services of several large commercial companies in the U.S. and is widely used in Europe.

The strengths and weaknesses of X.400 are summarized in Exhibit 2.

## INDUSTRIAL-STRENGTH MESSAGING REQUIREMENTS

X.400 has superior functionality defined in the standards, although many of these enhanced functions, such as multimedia and security, have yet to be deployed commercially. Electronic commerce using X.435 is still waiting for large industry segments to take advantage of this defined standard. Additionally, features such as delivery notifications, delivery to alternate recipients,

**Exhibit 2. Strengths and Weaknesses of X.400**

| Strengths | Weaknesses |
|---|---|
| Rigorous standards process through ITU | Rigorous standards process through ITU |
| International standard for message handling | Expensive |
| Functionality | Complex to understand and configure |
| Robust message delivery and non-delivery schemes | Not widely accepted by commercial marketplace |
| Well suited for electronic commerce | Lack of robust user agents from popular vendors |
| Strong security standards defined | Security implementations lagging |
| Works well with X.500 directory services | X.500 complex to implement |
| Predictable performance | Overhead is significant |

and receipt notifications are critical to "industrial strength" messaging systems needed by large commercial organizations or a system such as DMS.

SMTP, as defined by RFC 822, lacks the functionality required for backbone messaging systems or a highly complex network such as DMS. However, several improvements have taken place over the past few years. Functionality enhancements defined under MIME to extend SMTP and provide for messages with enclosed software objects such as images, video, audio, and binary file data have greatly enhanced Internet mail use for large organizations. Privacy Enhanced Mail (PEM) RFCs address many shortcomings with regard to security. These RFCs define data confidentiality, authenticity, integrity and nonrepudiation, message encipherment, and digital signatures.

One of the questions being asked by messaging system architects is: Can SMTP/MIME meet the messaging requirements of a large global enterprise? A "qualified" yes is the answer; assuming further extensions to MIME would be required, primarily in the areas of message management. Members of the IETF have shown great resiliency in further enhancing messaging functionality over the Internet when the need arises. IETF members could develop the missing pieces to make SMTP/MIME functionally similar to X.400.

## Critical Comparison Factors

The most important comparisons between X.400 and SMTP/MIME concern functionality, security, systems management, message management, management manpower requirements, and performance.

## Functionality

X.400 is more advanced in this respect, but developers are working to improve SMTP/MIME to match X.400's functionality.

## Security

Message security capabilities provided by the X.400 standards are far superior to SMTP/MIME. However, there are very few large-scale implementations that take advantage of the numerous security-related features specified within the standards.

Internet security is a major concern for many users. Although security options (such as software for trusted and privacy enhanced mail) exist, they are not widely and uniformly deployed.

Besides lacking security, SMTP/MIME lacks reliable audit trails. Spoofing, a process by which someone masquerades as another correspondent, is easily done via Internet mail. A user is also allowed to send a message through a rE-mailer service so that the original address is not attached to the message when it arrives at its final destination. It is therefore almost impossible to audit messages.

## Systems Management

X.400 has greater potential in this respect. The entire area of management — including message management, component management, and complete MHS management — needs more attention. The experience of E-mail managers in large organizations demonstrates the need for many additional management tools for a large, complex messaging network.

## Managing a Messaging System

Managing complex, enterprisewide messaging systems is difficult for several reasons:

- A lack of standards for message management.
- Interoperability — network managers have to deal with X.400, SMTP, proprietary LAN protocols, and legacy systems.
- The large number of components. An enterprisewide messaging system is composed of many different kinds of components, each with its own specific behavior characteristics (i.e., MTAs, UAs, directories, and gateways.)

Much work has been done on developing standards to govern the individual components associated with X.400. Although very little agreement has been reached on how to manage these various components. The network administrator must have tools and utilities available to manage day-to-day network operations. A fully deployed messaging system such as DMS with 2 million users will carry several million messages per day.

## Industry Standards for E-mail Management

Significant work has started on developing industry standards specific to E-mail management. A joint International Federation Information

Processing (IFIP) group examined the overall problem of messaging management. A similar IETF task force led to the development of RFC 1566 (also known as the Mail and Directory Management MIB, or MADMAN MIB), which defines a class of managed objects that can be deployed within any vendor's messaging architecture. The MADMAN MIB, however, is oriented to the Internet and SMTP, and therefore lacks the ability to model some of the more complex features present in X.400-based systems.

Simple network management protocol (SNMP) and SNMP version 2, both of which are associated with the SMTP/MIME environment, are the leading protocols for managing network transport functions. However, SNMP does not work across non-TCP/IP transports. The management information base (MIB) is a definition of the managed object (i.e., what can be managed remotely). The MADMAN MIB is complete with approved standard definitions, but very limited in functionality (i.e., monitoring only). SNMP and the MIB definitions are only 5% of the puzzle, however.

The ITU-TSS and the International Standards Organization/International Electrotechnical Commission (ISO/IEC) are currently working on the following MHS management documents:

**General:**

| | |
|---|---|
| MHS Management Model and Architecture | X.460 |
| MHS Management Information | X.461 |

**Management Functions for MHS:**

| | |
|---|---|
| Logging | X.462 |
| Security | X.463 |
| Configuration | X.464 |
| Fault Management | X.465 |
| Performance Management | X.466 |

### EMA Requirements for Messaging Management

The Electronic Messaging Association (EMA) is working on a framework that will allow management of multivendor messaging systems. The EMA's work leverages the IFIP's work and is aligned with the MADMAN MIB definitions. The effort is broad in scope because it also addresses the area of message tracing and standardizing a set of tasks for message management across a multivendor environment. The EMA's Messaging Management Committee has characterized requirements for messaging management in the following four major categories:

- **Operational management** Deals with finding outages and fixing them as well as doing routine maintenance. Statistical analysis of traffic and components is accomplished. There is little difference between the two technologies — X.400 and SMTP/MIME — in this area.

- **Configuration management** Deals with managing the addition and deletion of components in the messaging system. It includes tasks such as dynamic updating of message routing tables, starting and stopping messaging system components, and discovering and depicting messaging system components across the network. Both X.400 and SMTP/MIME are lacking in this respect.
- **Administration management** Provides a means of managing subscribers, distribution lists, and accounting information. It includes facilities for security administration. Control throughout some portions of the Internet is loose. No person or group has authority over some functional subnetworks, such as Usenet, as a whole. Every administrator controls their own subnetwork. This is different from the X.400 assignment and demarcation of responsibilities, which are vested in management domains, with accountability for performance and control being highly defined. X.400 is superior in this area.
- **Network management** Is the process of keeping the underlying networking layer healthy. X.400 and SMTP/MIME are equal in this category.

### Message Management

X.400 is more sophisticated than SMTP/MIME, but still needs significant improvements. The ability to track a message through messaging systems is central to the establishment of a trusted delivery infrastructure for any complex commercial usage. Maintaining unique identification of a message as it crosses intersystem boundaries represents a significant challenge that no previous standardization activity has addressed.

### Human Resources Requirements and Support Costs

Much work is needed in this area for both X.400 and SMTP/MIME technologies. The largest messaging networks can carry several million messages per day. Network administrators do not have time to stop and analyze trouble spots — there is too much traffic coming. They need utilities to shunt aside a problem message and let the traffic flow continue. It also takes very knowledgeable software engineers to accomplish this work, and they are expensive.

Managing these distributed messaging systems from a single, centralized, administrative control system is difficult and costly. One major Fortune 500 corporation estimates that it spends approximately $40 per user, per year to acquire messaging hardware and software vs. $200-$300 per user, per year in operating costs to manage and administer the messaging network.

A study by Creative Networks, Inc. indicated messaging support costs, including end-user support, to be:

- $4,189 annual cost per desktop user.
- $5,426 annual cost per mobile user.

A key cost factor is the amount of end-user support required. Companies lose approximately $684 per user annually to downtime, $764 to lost productivity, and $1,198 to lost revenues due to messaging system problems. Problems with E-mail cut productivity in environments where jobs depend on computer-based information. A typical downtime incident takes 6.3 hours of staff time to resolve.

The need for a resident administrator at each major site can significantly increase the cost of managing large-scale messaging systems. In addition to being on call to deal with system failures or changes in configuration, administrators find themselves subject to normal corporate cost-containment efforts. They are called to manage high levels of ongoing expenses in training as well as in development of complex internal procedures for managing the messaging network across different departments and dissimilar platforms. A major business imperative is to improve the reliability of electronic messaging while reducing the costs of maintaining the messaging infrastructure.

## Performance

There is no preferred technology from a performance standpoint. Engineering benchmarks are needed to demonstrate the performance of all components and the overall network. Performance bottlenecks must be identified and corrected by the system administrator, but additional tools are desperately needed. Further analysis and modeling of both X.400 and SMTP-based networks is needed. SMTP-based networks carry large volumes of information, but with very limited functionality. X.400-based networks also carry significant traffic loads and provide very reliable service. X.400 can be engineered to deliver reliable and predictable performance. Both technologies suffer in performance when encryption is added. However, there is overhead involved that requires additional bandwidth.

## Commercial Use

X.400 is preferred over SMTP/MIME by large organizations needing guaranteed network services. X.400 has gained international acceptance and is used by most European Postal, Telegraph, and Telephone (PTT) services and telecommunication providers throughout the world. The International Civil Aviation Organization standardized on X.400 because of the greater flexibility and enhanced features that are available.

The most effective means of tying messaging systems together still is the old tried-and-true X.400 backbone. Numerous large commercial and government organizations need a robust and reliable messaging network. Vendors of X.400 components have not experienced significant revenues selling X.400 components because there are still too many unresolved issues; namely, lack of management tools and utilities, plus fully developed directory services. Although SMTP/MIME vendors have made significant sales, SMTP/MIME also has the same problems with lack of management tools and directory services.

In forums such as the Electronic Messaging Association, customers repeatedly state they want the benefits and capabilities offered by X.400 messaging. It is this demand that has led to changes in the current SMTP systems to attempt to offer the same functionality provided by X.400.

## CONCLUSION

X.400 is a better protocol than SMTP/MIME for building a sophisticated network. The standards definitions are very complete for functionality and most networking requirements. X.400 has numerous security features and guaranteed message delivery and notification. These are extremely important for large, predictable, commercial messaging networks.

SMTP/MIME functionality is missing some important messaging requirements such as delivery notifications, delivery to alternate recipients, and receipt notifications. In fairness, these elements probably could be added, but further work is needed. SMTP grew up in the UNIX environment to provide simple text messaging. Numerous features have been added over time, but the entire process has been an *ad hoc* development — not the planned architectural development process that the international standards bodies followed with X.400.

In the long run, X.400 and SMTP/MIME are expected to converge on a single set of standards, or at least sufficient development of bridging technology to enable the seamless coexistence of both technologies. The National Institute of Standards and Technology (NIST) has a special interest group working on coexistence and convergence profiles that will promote coexistence as a step toward convergence. This further effort strengthens the belief that the few functionality differences between X.400 and SMTP/MIME are not critical in choosing between the two.

From a standards perspective, the most critical missing ingredient in providing a robust, reliable network is the lack of management tools and utilities. This is where development attention needs to be focused, rather than on functional differences between the protocols. It does not matter which technology is chosen, nor how robust the individual components are, if the network cannot be managed. Users must be able to easily manage the overall network to provide the type of messaging environment that everyone is striving for.

Chapter 32

# IPv6:
# The Next-Generation
# Internet Protocol

*Gary C. Kessler*

The only way to cope with the changes on the Internet — the number of hosts, types of applications, and growing security concerns — is to implement a new version of the Internet protocol to succeed IPv4. The IETF formed the IPng Working Group to define this transitional protocol, and the result was IPv6 — designed as an evolution from IPv4, rather than as a radical change.

## INTRODUCTION

The Internet is historically linked to the ARPANET, the pioneering packet-switched network built for the U.S. Department of Defense in 1969. Starting with four nodes that year, the ARPANET slowly grew to encompass many systems across the US, and connected to hosts in Europe and Asia by the end of the 1970s. By the early 1980s, many regional and national networks across the globe started to become interconnected, and their common communications protocols were based on the TCP/IP suite. By the late 1980s, the number of host systems on these primarily academic and research networks could be counted in the hundreds or thousands. In addition, most of the traffic was supporting simple text-based applications, such as E-mail, file transfers, and login.

By the 1990s, however, users discovered the Internet and commercial use, previously prohibited or constrained on the Internet, was actively encouraged. Since the beginning of this decade, new host systems are being added to the Internet at rates of up to 10% per month, and the Internet has been doubling in size every 10-12 months for several years. By January 1997, there were more than 16 million hosts on the Internet, ranging from PC-class systems to supercomputers, on more than 100,000 networks worldwide.

The number of connected hosts is only one measure of the Internet's growth. Another way to quantify the change, however, is in the changing applications. On today's Internet it is common to see hypermedia, audio, video, animation, and other types of traffic that were once thought to be anathema to a packet-switching environment. As the Internet provides better service support, new applications will spark even more growth and changing demographics. In addition, nomadic access has become a major issue with the increased use of laptop computers, and security concerns have grown as a result of the increased amount of sensitive information accessible via the Internet.

## IPV6 BACKGROUND AND FEATURES

The IP was introduced in the ARPANET in the mid-1970s. The version of IP commonly used today is IPv4, described in RFC 791.

Although several protocol suites (including OSI) were proposed over the years to replace IPv4, none succeeded because of IPv4's large and continually growing installed base. Nevertheless, IPv4 was never intended for today's Internet in terms of the number of hosts, types of applications, or security concerns.

In the early 1990s, the IETF recognized that the only way to cope with these changes was to design a new version of IP to become the successor to IPv4. The IETF formed the IPng Working Group to define this transitional protocol, ensuring long-term compatibility between the current and new IP versions and support for current and emerging IP-based applications.

Work started on IPng in 1991 and several IPng proposals were subsequently drafted. The result of this effort was IPv6, described in RFCs 1883 to 1886; these four RFCs were officially entered into the Internet Standards Track in December 1995.

### Differences Between IPv4 and IPv6

IPv6 is designed as an evolution from IPv4 rather than as a radical change. Useful features of IPv4 were carried over in IPv6 and less useful features were dropped. According to the IPv6 specification, the changes from IPv4 to IPv6 fall primarily into the following categories:

- **Expanded addressing capabilities** The IP address size is increased from 32 bits to 128 bits in IPv6, supporting a much greater number of addressable nodes, more levels of addressing hierarchy, and simpler autoconfiguration of addresses for remote users. The scalability of multicast routing is improved by adding a scope field to multicast addresses. A new type of address, called anycast, is also defined.

- **Header format simplification** Some IPv4 header fields have been dropped or made optional to reduce the necessary amount of packet processing and to limit the bandwidth cost of the IPv6 header.
- **Improved support for extensions and options** IPv6 header options are encoded to allow for more efficient forwarding, less stringent limits on the length of options, and greater flexibility for introducing new options in the future. Some fields of an IPv4 header are optional in IPv6.
- **Flow labeling capability** A new QOS capability has been added to enable the labeling of packets belonging to particular traffic "flows" for which the sender requests special handling, such as real-time service.
- **Authentication and privacy capabilities** Extensions to support security options, such as authentication, data integrity, and data confidentiality, are built into IPv6.

### Improved Terminology of IPv6

IPv6 also introduces and formalizes terminology that, in the IPv4 environment, are loosely defined, ill-defined, or undefined. The new and improved terminology includes:

- **Packet** This is an IPv6 PDU, comprising a header and the associated payload. In IPv4, this would have been termed "packet" or "datagram."
- **Node** This is a device that implements IPv6.
- **Router** This is an IPv6 node that forwards packets, based on the IP address, not explicitly addressed to itself. In former TCP/IP terminology, this device was often referred to as a gateway.
- **Host** This represents any node that is not a router. Hosts are typically end-user systems.
- **Link** This is a medium over which nodes communicate with each other at the data link layer (e.g., an automated teller machine, a frame relay, a SMDS, a WAN, or an Ethernet or Token Ring LAN).
- **Neighbors** These are nodes attached to the same link.

### IPV6 HEADER FORMAT

The format of an IPv6 header is shown in Exhibit 1. Although IPv6 addresses are four times the size of IPv4 addresses, the basic IPv6 header is only twice the size of an IPv4 header, thus decreasing the impact of the larger address fields. The fields of the IPv6 header are:

- **Version** This represents the IP version number (4 bits). This field's value is 6 for IPv6 and 4 for IPv4. This field is in the same location as the version field in the IPv4 header, making it simple for an IP node to quickly distinguish an IPv4 packet from an IPv6 packet.

**Exhibit 1. IPv6 Header Format**

| Version | Priority | Flow Label | |
|---|---|---|---|
| Payload Length | | Next Header | Hop Limit |
| Source Address | | | |
| Destination Address | | | |

**Exhibit 2. Sample Values of Next Header Field**

| Value | Contents of the next header |
|---|---|
| 1 | Internet Control Message Protocol (ICMP) |
| 6 | Transmission Control Protocol (TCP) |
| 17 | User Datagram Protocol (UDP) |
| 43 | Routing header |
| 44 | Fragment header |
| 58 | Internet Control Message Protocol version 6 (ICMPv6) |
| 59 | Nothing; this is the final header |
| 60 | Destination Options header |
| 89 | Open Shortest Path First (OSPF) |

- **Priority** This enables a source to identify the desired delivery priority of the packet (4 bits).
- **Flow label** This is used by a source to identify associated packets needing the same type of special handling, such as a real-time service between a pair of hosts (24 bits).
- **Payload length** This is the length of the portion of the packet following the header, in octets (16 bits). The maximum value in this field is 65,535; if this field contains zero, it means that the packet contains a payload larger than 64K bytes and the actual payload length value is carried in a jumbo payload hop-by-hop option.
- **Next header** This identifies the type of header immediately following the IPv6 header and uses the same values as the IPv4 protocol field, where applicable (8 bits). The next header field can indicate an options header, higher layer protocol, or no protocol above IP. Sample values are listed in Exhibit 2.

- **Hop limit** This specifies the maximum number of hops that a packet may take before it is discarded (8 bits). This value is set by the source and decremented by one by each node that forwards the packet; the packet is discarded if the hop limit reaches zero. The comparable field in IPv4 is the TTL field; it was renamed for IPv6 because the value limits the number of hops, not the amount of time that a packet can stay in the network.
- **Source address** This is the IPv6 address of the originator of the packet (128 bits).
- **Destination address** This is the IPv6 address of the intended recipients of the packet (128 bits).

## IPV6 ADDRESSES

To accommodate almost unlimited growth and a variety of addressing formats, IPv6 addresses are 128 bits in length. This address space is probably sufficient to uniquely address every molecule in the solar system.

IPv6 defines three types of addresses:

1. A unicast address specifies a single host.
2. An anycast address specifies a set of hosts, such as a set of FTP servers for a given organization. A packet sent to an anycast address is delivered to one of the hosts identified by that address, usually the "closest" one, as defined by the routing protocol.
3. A multicast address also identifies a set of hosts; a packet sent to a multicast address is delivered to all the hosts in the group.

There is no broadcast address in IPv6 as in IPv4, because that function is provided by multicast addresses.

IPv4 addresses are written in dotted decimal notation, where the decimal value of each of the four address bytes is separated by dots. The preferred form of an IPv6 address is to write the hexadecimal value of the eight 16-bit blocks of the address, separated by colons (:), such as FF04:19:5:ABD4:187:2C:754:2B1. The leading zeros do not have to be written and each field must have some value.

IPv6 addresses often contain long strings of zeros because of the way in which addresses are allocated. A compressed address form uses a double colon (::) to indicate multiple 16-bit blocks of zeros; for example, the address FF01:0:0:0:0:0:0:5A could be written as FF01::5A. To avoid ambiguity, the "::" can only appear once in an address.

An alternative, hybrid address format has been defined to make it more convenient to represent an IPv4 address in an IPv6 environment. In this scheme, the first 96 address bits (six groups of 16) are represented in the regular IPv6 format and the remaining 32 address bits are represented in

**Exhibit 3. Address Prefix Allocation (From RFC 1884)**

| Allocation | Prefix (Binary) | Fraction of Address Space |
|---|---|---|
| Reserved | 0000 0000 | 1/256 |
| Unassigned | 0000 0001 | 1/256 |
| Reserved for NSAP Allocation | 0000 001 | 1/128 |
| Reserved for IPX Allocation | 0000 010 | 1/128 |
| Unassigned | 0000 011 | 1/128 |
| Unassigned | 0000 1 | 1/32 |
| Unassigned | 0001 | 1/16 |
| Unassigned | 001 | 1/8 |
| Provider-Based Unicast Address | 010 | 1/8 |
| Unassigned | 011 | 1/8 |
| Reserved for Geographic-Based Unicast Addresses | 100 | 1/8 |
| Unassigned | 101 | 1/8 |
| Unassigned | 110 | 1/8 |
| Unassigned | 1110 | 1/16 |
| Unassigned | 1111 0 | 1/32 |
| Unassigned | 1111 10 | 1/64 |
| Unassigned | 1111 110 | 1/128 |
| Unassigned | 1111 1110 0 | 1/512 |
| Link Local Use Addresses | 1111 1110 10 | 1/1024 |
| Site Local Use Addresses | 1111 1110 11 | 1/1024 |
| Multicast Addresses | 1111 1111 | 1/256 |

common IPv4 dotted decimal; for example, 0:0:0:0:0:0:199.182.20.17 (or::199.182.20.17).

## Address Prefix Allocation

One of the goals of the IPv6 address format is to accommodate many different types of addresses. The beginning of an address contains a 3- to 10-bit format prefix defining the general address type; the remaining bits contain the actual host address, in a format specific to the indicated address type. Exhibit 3 represents an address prefix allocation (from RFC 1884).

## The Provider-Based Unicast Address

The provider-based unicast address is an IPv6 address that might be assigned by an ISP to a customer. Exhibit 4 shows a provider-based unicast address format. This type of address contains a number of subfields, including the following:

- **Format prefix** This indicates the type of address as provider-based unicast. It is always 3 bits, coded "010."
- **Registry identifier** This identifies the Internet address registry from which the ISP obtains addresses.

- **Provider identifier** This identifies the ISP. This field contains the address block assigned to the ISP by the address registry authority.
- **Subscriber identifier** This identifies the ISP's subscriber. This field contains the address assigned to this subscriber by the ISP. The providerID and subscriberID fields together are 56 bits in length.
- **Intrasubscriber** This contains the portion of the address assigned and managed by the subscriber.

**Exhibit 4. Provider-Based Unicast Address Format**

| 3 bits | 5 bits | n bits | 56-n bits | 64 bits |

## IPv4-Compatible Addresses

Another particularly important address type is the one that indicates an IPv4 address. With more than 16 million hosts using 32-bit addresses, the public Internet must continue to accommodate IPv4 addresses even as it slowly migrates to IPv6 addressing,

IPv4 addresses are carried in a 128-bit IPv6 address that begins with 80 zeros (0:0:0:0:0). The next 16-bit block contains the compatibility bits, which indicate the way in which the host/router handles IPv4 and IPv6 addresses. If the device can handle either IPv4 or IPv6 addresses, the compatibility bits are all set to zero (0) and this is termed an "IPv4-compatible IPv6 address"; if the address represents an IPv4-only node, the compatibility bits are all set to one (0xFFFF) and the address is termed an "IPv4-mapped IPv6 address." The final 32 bits contain a 32-bit IPv4 address in dotted decimal form.

## Multicast Addresses

IPv6 multicast addresses provide an identifier for a group of nodes. A node may belong to any number of multicast groups. Multicast addresses may not be used as a source address in IPv6 packets or appear in any routing.

All multicast addresses, as shown in Exhibit 5, begin with 8 ones (0xFF). The next 4 bits are a set of flag bits (flgs); the 3 high-order bits are set to zero; and the fourth bit (T-bit) indicates a permanently assigned ("well-known") multicast address (T = 0) or a nonpermanently assigned ("transient") multicast address (T = 1). The next 4 bits indicate the scope of the address, or the part of the network for which this multicast address is relevant; options include node-local (0x1), link-local (0x2), site-local (0x5), organization-local (0x8), or global (0xE).

**Exhibit 5. Multicast Address Format**

| 8 | 4 | 4 | 112 bits |

The remaining 112 bits are the group identifier, which identifies the multi-cast group, either permanent or transient, within the given scope. The interpretation of a permanently assigned multicast address is independent of the scope value. For example, if the World Wide Web (WWW) server group is assigned a permanent multicast address with a group identifier of 0x77, then:

- FF01:0:0:0:0:0:0:77 would refer to all WWW servers on the same node as the sender.
- FF02:0:0:0:0:0:0:77 would refer to all WWW servers on the same link as the sender.
- FF05:0:0:0:0:0:0:77 would refer to all WWW servers at the same site as the sender.
- FF0E:0:0:0:0:0:0:77 would refer to all WWW servers in the Internet.

Finally, a number of well-known multicast addresses are predefined, including:

- **Reserved multicast addresses** These are reserved and are never assigned to any multicast group. These addresses have the form FF0x:0:0:0:0:0:0:0, where x is any hexadecimal digit.
- **All nodes' addresses** These identify the group of all IPv6 nodes within the given scope. These addresses are of the form FF0t:0:0:0:0:0:0:1, where t = 1 (node-local) or 2 (link-local).
- **All routers' addresses** These identify the group of all IPv6 routers within the given scope. These addresses are of the form FF0t:0:0:0:0:0:0:2, where t = 1 (node-local) or 2 (link-local).
- **The DHCP server/relay-agent address** This identifies the group of all IPv6 DHCP servers and relay agents with the link-local scope; this address is FF02:0:0:0:0:0:0:C.

## IPV6 EXTENSION HEADERS AND OPTIONS

In IPv6, optional IP layer information is encoded in separate extension headers that are placed between the IPv6 basic header and the higher-layer protocol header. An IPv6 packet may carry zero, one, or more such extension headers, each identified by the next header field of the preceding header and each containing an even multiple of 64 bits (see Exhibit 6). A fully compliant implementation of IPv6 includes support for the following extension headers and corresponding options:

- **The hop-by-hop options header** This header carries information that must be examined by every node along a packet's path. Three options are included in this category. The pad1 option is used to insert a single octet of padding into the options area of a header for 64-bit alignment, whereas the padN option is used to insert two or more octets of padding. The jumbo payload option is used to indicate the length of the

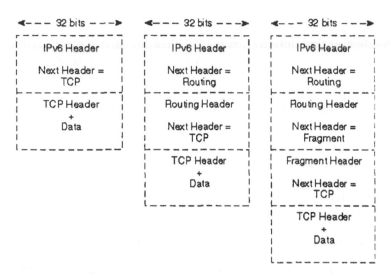

**Note:**
The left-hand column represents a TCP segment encapsulated in IP without additional options, the middle column represents a TCP segment following a routing header, and the right-hand column represents a TCP segment fragment following a fragment header following a routing header.

**Exhibit 6. IPv6 Extension Header Examples.**

---

packet when the payload portion is longer than 65,535 octets. This option is employed when the payload length field is set to zero.

- **The routing header** This header is used by an IPv6 source to list one or more intermediate nodes that must be visited as part of the packet's path to the destination; this option is functionally similar to IPv4's loose and strict source routing options. This header contains a list of addresses and an indication of whether each address is strict or loose. If an address is marked strict, it means that this node must be a neighbor of the previously addressed node; if an address is marked loose, this node does not have to be a neighbor of the previous node.
- **The fragment header** This header is used by an IPv6 source to send packets that are larger than the MTU on the path to the destination. This header contains a packet identifier, fragment offset, and final fragment indicator. Unlike IPv4, where fragmentation information is carried in every packet header, IPv6 only carries fragmentation/reassembly information in those packets that are fragmented. In another departure from IPv4, fragmentation in IPv6 is performed only by the source and not by the routers along a packet's path. All IPv6 hosts and routers must support an MTU of 576 octets; it is recommended that path MTU

discovery procedures (per RFC 1981) be invoked to discover, and take advantage of, those paths with a larger MTU.

- **The destination options header** This header carries optional information that has to be examined only by a packet's destination node(s). The only destination options defined so far are pad1 and padN, as described above.
- **The IP AH and IP ESP** These are IPv6 security mechanisms (a section on IPv6 security appears later in this chapter).

With the exception of the hop-by-hop option, extension headers are only examined or processed by the intended destination nodes. The contents of each extension header determine whether or not to proceed to the next header and, therefore, extension headers must be processed in the order that they appear in the packet.

## IPV6 QUALITY-OF-SERVICE (QOS) PARAMETERS

The priority and flow label fields in the IPv6 header are used by a source to identify packets needing special handling by network routers. The concept of a flow in IP is a major departure from IPv4 and most other connectionless protocols; flows are sometimes referred to as a form of connectionless virtual circuit because all packets with the same flow label are treated similarly and the network views them as associated entities.

Special handling for nondefault quality of service is an important capability for supporting applications that require guaranteed throughput, end-to-end delay, and jitter, such as multimedia or real-time communication. These QOS parameters are an extension of IPv4's TOS capability.

The priority field allows the source to identify the desired priority of a packet. Values 0 through 7 are used for congestion-controlled traffic, or traffic that backs off in response to network congestion, such as TCP segments. For this type of traffic, the following priority values are recommended:

- Zero is recommended for uncharacterized traffic.
- One is recommended for "filler" traffic (e.g., Netnews).
- Two is recommended for unattended data transfer (e.g., E-mail).
- Three is recommended for reserved traffic.
- Four is recommended for attended bulk transfer, such as FTP or HTTP.
- Five is also recommended for reserved traffic.
- Six is recommended for interactive traffic (i.e., telnet).
- Seven is recommended for Internet control traffic (i.e., routing protocols and SNMP)

Values 8 through 15 are defined for noncongestion-controlled traffic, or traffic that does not back off in response to network congestion, such as real-time packets being sent at a constant rate. For this type of traffic, the lowest priority value (8) should be used for packets that the sender is most willing to have discarded under congestion conditions (e.g., high-fidelity video traffic) and the highest value (15) should be used for those packets that the sender is least willing to have discarded (e.g., low-fidelity audio traffic).

The flow label is used by a source to identify packets needing nondefault QOS. The nature of the special handling might be conveyed to the network routers by a control protocol, such as the RSVP, or by information within the flow packets themselves, such as a hop-by-hop option. There may be multiple active flows from a source to a destination, as well as traffic that is not associated with any flow (i.e., flow label = 0). A flow is uniquely identified by the combination of a source address and a nonzero flow label. This aspect of IPv6 is still in the experimental stage and future definition is expected.

## IPV6 SECURITY

In the early days of TCP/IP, the ARPANET user community was small and close, and security mechanisms were not the primary concern. As the number of TCP/IP hosts grew, and the user community became one of strangers (some nefarious) rather than friends, security became more important. As critical and sensitive data travels on today's Internet, security is of paramount concern.

Although many of today's TCP/IP applications have their own devices, security should be implemented at the lowest possible protocol layer. IPv4 has few, if any, security mechanisms, and authentication and privacy at lower protocol layers is largely absent. IPv6 builds two security schemes into the basic protocol.

### IP Authentication Header

The first mechanism is the IP authentication header (RFC 1826), an extension header that can provide integrity and authentication for IP packets. Although many different authentication techniques are supported, use of the keyed message digest 5 (MD5, described in RFC 1321) algorithm is required to ensure interoperability. Use of this option can eliminate a large number of network attacks, such as IP address spoofing. This option is also valuable in overcoming some of the security weaknesses of IP source routing.

IPv4 provides no host authentication. It can only supply the sending host's address as advertised by the sending host in the IP datagram. Placing host authentication information at the Internet layer in IPv6 provides significant protection to higher-layer protocols and services that currently lack meaningful authentication processes.

### IP Encapsulating Security Payload

The second mechanism is the IP encapsulating security payload (ESP, described in RFC 1827), an extension header that can provide integrity and confidentiality for IP packets. Although the ESP definition is algorithm-independent, the DES-CBC is specified as the standard encryption scheme to ensure interoperability. The ESP mechanism can be used to encrypt an entire IP packet (tunnel-mode ESP) or just the higher-layer portion of the payload (transport-mode ESP).

These features add to the secure nature of IP traffic while actually reducing the security effort; authentication performed on an end-to-end basis during session establishment provides more secure communications even in the absence of firewall routers.

## ICMPV6

The ICMP provides error and information messages that are beyond the scope of IP. ICMPv6 is functionally similar to ICMPv4 and also uses a similar message format and forms an integral part of IPv6. ICMPv6 messages are carried in an IPv6 datagram with a next header field value of 58.

ICMPv6 error messages include:

- **Destination unreachable** This is sent when a packet cannot be delivered to its destination address for reasons other than congestion.
- **Packet too big** This is sent by a router when it has a packet that it cannot forward because the packet is larger than the MTU of the outgoing link.
- **Time exceeded** This is sent by a router when the packet's hop limit reaches zero or if all fragments of a datagram are not received within the fragment reassembly time.
- **Parameter problem** This is sent by a node that finds some problem in a field in the packet header that results in an inability to process the header.

ICMPv6 informational messages are echo request and echo reply (used by IPv6 nodes for diagnostic purposes), as well as group membership query, group membership report, and group membership reduction (all used to convey information about multicast group membership from nodes to their neighboring routers).

## MIGRATION TO IPV6

When IPv4 became the official ARPANET standard in 1983, use of previous protocols ceased and there was no planned interoperability between the old and the new. This is not the case with the introduction of IPv6.

**Exhibit 7. Common Short-Term Scenario where an IPv4 Network Interconnects IPv6 Networks.**

Although IPv6 is currently being rolled out for the Internet backbone, there is no scheduled date of a flash cut from one to the other; coexistence of IPv4 and IPv6 is anticipated for many years to come. The sheer number of hosts using IPv4 today suggests that no other policy even begins to make sense. IPv6 will appear in the large ISP backbones sooner rather than later, and some smaller service providers and local network administrators will not make the conversion quickly unless they perceive some benefit from IPv6.

The coexistence of IPv4 and IPv6 in the network means that different protocols and procedures need to be accommodated. In one common short-term scenario, IPv6 networks will be interconnected via an IPv4 backbone (see Exhibit 7). The boundary routers will be IPv4-compatible IPv6 nodes and the routers' interfaces will be given IPv4-compatible IPv6 addresses. The IPv6 packet is transported over the IPv4 network by encapsulating the packet in an IPv4 header in a process is called tunneling. Tunneling can also be performed when an organization has converted a part of its subnet to IPv6. This process can be used on host-host, router-router, or host-router links.

Although the introduction of IPv6 is inevitable, many of the market pressures for its development have been rendered somewhat unnecessary because of parallel developments that enhance the capabilities of IPv4. The address limitations of IPv4, for example, are minimized by use of CIDR. Nomadic user address allocation can be managed by the DHCP servers and relay agents. QOS management can be handled by the RSVP protocol. And the IP authentication header and encapsulating security payload procedures can be applied to IPv4 as well as to IPv6.

This is not meant to suggest that IP vendors are waiting. IPv6 has already started to appear in many new products and production networks. Support for IPv6 on several versions of UNIX have been announced by such organizations as Digital Equipment Corp., IBM Corp., INRIA, or The French National Institute for Research in Computer Science and Control), Japan's WIDE Project, Sun Microsystems, Inc., the SICS, and the U.S. Naval Research Laboratory.

Other companies have announced support for IPv6 in other operating environments, including Apple Computer, Inc.'s MacOS, FTP Software, Inc.'s DOS/Windows, Mentat's STREAMS, Novell, Inc.'s NetWare, and Siemens Nixdorf, Inc.'s BS2000. Major router vendors that have announced support for IPv6 include Bay Networks, Inc., Cisco Systems, Inc., Digital Equipment Corp., Ipsilon Networks, Penril Datability Networks, and Telebit Corp.

### 6bone Trials

One of the important proving grounds of IPv6 is the 6bone, a testbed network spanning North America, Europe, and Japan, which began operating in 1996. The 6bone is a virtual network built on top of portions of today's IPv4-based Internet, designed specifically to route IPv6 packets. The goal of this collaborative trial is to test IPv6 implementations and to define early policies and procedures that will be necessary to support IPv6 in the future. In addition, it will demonstrate IPv6's new capabilities and will provide a basis for user confidence in the new protocol.

For most users, the transition from IPv4 to IPv6 will occur when the version of their host's operating system software is updated; in some cases, it means running dual-stacked systems with both versions of IP. For larger user networks, it may make sense to follow the model of the larger global Internet — in particular, to predesign the IPv6 network topology and addressing scheme, to build a testbed IPv6 network with routers and a DNS, and then slowly to migrate applications, users, and subnetworks to the new backbone. The lessons learned from the 6bone activity are useful for individual networks as well as for the Internet backbone.

### CONCLUSION

The transition to IPv6 has already started, even though most Internet and TCP/IP users have not yet seen new software on their local systems or on local networks. Before IPv6 can be widely deployed, the network infrastructure must be upgraded to employ software that accommodates the new protocol.

In addition, the new address format must be accommodated by every TCP/IP protocol that uses addresses. The DNS, for example, has defined an AAAA resource record for IPv6 128-bit addresses (IPv4's 32-bit addresses use an A record) and the IP6.INT address domain (IPv4 uses the ARPA address domain). Other protocols that must be modified for IPv6 include DHCP, the ARP family, and IP routing protocols such as the RIP, OSPF protocol, and the BGP. Only after the routers and the backbones are upgraded will hosts start to transition to the new protocol and applications be modified to take advantage of IPv6's capabilities.

# Section V
# Organizational Communications Services

Prior to the 1990s most persons would associate the term "communications services" with leased lines, X.25 packet switching, and the PBX connection furnished by the local telephone company. During the 1990s the rapid growth in electronic messaging and the use of the Internet resulted in organizations in effect becoming service providers and offering a variety of communications services to their employees and customers. Two of those services that account for the vast majority of organizational communications services are the creation and operation of virtual private networks and electronic mail facilities, both of which are topics covered by chapters in this section.

The first chapter included in this section, entitled "Overview of Virtual Private Networks," introduces us to the VPN concept, explaining the key advantages associated with the construction of a virtual private network designed to provide voice, high speed data, and even cellular services under one service umbrella. This chapter acquaints us with different VPN billing options, network management alternatives, access arrangements, and the different types of data services that can be included under a VPN agreement.

In the second chapter in this section we examine virtual networking with respect to the Internet. In the chapter titled "Using the Internet as a Virtual Private Network," we turn our attention to a different type of virtual networking. In this chapter we will examine the economics associated with the use of the Internet as a virtual network in comparison to the use of leased lines to interconnect geographically separated corporate locations. Once this is accomplished we turn our attention to the issues of authentication and encryption and various methods that can be employed to protect organizational data as it flows between corporate locations via the publicly accessible Internet.

In the third, fourth, and fifth chapters in this section we examine electronic mail as an organizational communications service. In the third chapter we focus our attention upon obtaining an overview of the features and services to look for when shopping for a corporate E-mail system. This chapter, which is titled "Popular E-mail Systems," provides a list of over 30 features to consider when selecting a corporate E-mail system, and then examines many of those features with respect to several of the leading E-mail systems on the market.

Building upon the information provided in the third chapter, the next two chapters are focused upon specific vendor products. In the fourth chapter, entitled "Novell Messaging Products," we turn our attention to Novell's GroupWise messaging suite. In the fifth chapter which is titled "An Introduction to Microsoft Exchange Server," we examine the electronic messaging features and capabilities from Microsoft Corporation.

The ability to provide an organizational communications services capability depends upon many factors; however, the key factor that cannot be overlooked is the regulatory environment. If government rules and regulations provide competition among telecommunications companies, the number of new offerings and lowering of prices can be expected to increase. This in turn can be expected to provide organizations with the ability to continue to expand their role in acting as a provider of communications services. Due to the importance of the regulatory process, this section concludes with the chapter titled "The 1996 U.S. Telecommunications Act and Worldwide Deregulation."

# Chapter 33
# Overview of Virtual Private Networks

*Nathan J. Muller*

Virtual private networks — carrier-provided networks that function like private networks — are an increasingly attractive alternative for obtaining private network functionality without the overhead associated with acquiring and managing dedicated private lines. Understanding the features and business benefits of VPNs and their access options is the first step in implementing this cost-effective method of transporting voice and data traffic across regional, national, and international locations.

## INTRODUCTION

Carrier-provided networks that function like private networks are referred to as VPNs. By relying more on VPNs, corporations minimize the operating costs and staffing requirements associated with private networks. In addition, they gain the advantages of dealing with a single carrier instead of with the multiple carriers and vendors required for a typical private network. This relieves organizations of the costs associated with staffing, maintenance, and inventory without sacrificing control, service quality, and configuration flexibility.

AT&T introduced the first VPN service in 1985. Its SDN was offered as an inexpensive alternative to private lines. Since then, VPNs have added more functionality and expanded globally. Today, the Big Three carriers — AT&T (SDN), MCI (Vnet), and Sprint (VPN Service) — each offer virtual private networks. In the case of AT&T, various services — including high-speed data and cellular calls — may be combined under one service umbrella, expanding opportunities for cost savings within a single discount plan.

## THE VPN CONCEPT

VPNs let users create their own private networks by drawing on the intelligence embedded in the carrier's network. This intelligence is actually derived from software programs residing in various switch points throughout the network. Services and features are defined in software, giving users greater flexibility in configuring their networks than is possible with hardware-based services. In fact, an entire network can be reconfigured by changing a few parameters in a network database.

The intelligence inherent in virtual private networks lets network managers control many operating parameters and features within their communications environments. For example, the flexible-routing feature allows the network manager to reroute calls to alternate locations when a node experiences an outage or peak-hour traffic congestion. This feature is also used to extend customer service business hours across multiple time zones. The location-screening feature lets network managers define a list of numbers that cannot be called from a given VPN location. This helps contain call costs by disallowing certain types of outbound calls.

Originating call screening is a feature that gives network managers the means to create caller groups and screening groups. Caller groups identify individual users who have similar call restrictions, and screening groups identify particular telephone numbers that are allowed or blocked for each caller. Time intervals are also used as a call-screening mechanism, allowing or blocking calls according to time-of-day and day-of-week parameters.

With a feature called NNX sharing, VPN customers reuse NNXs (i.e., exchange numbers) at different network locations to set up their seven-digit on-net numbering plans. This provides dialing consistency across multiple corporate locations. Another feature, partitioned database management, lets corporations add subsidiaries to the VPN network while providing for flexible, autonomous management when required by the subsidiaries to address local needs. The VPN can even transparently interface with the company's private network or with the private network of a strategic partner. In this case, the VPN caller is not aware that the dialed number is a VPN or private network location, because the numbering plan is uniform across both networks.

VPNs provide several other useful features, including ANI data, which is matched to information in a database containing the computer and telecommunications assets assigned to each employee, for example. When a call comes through to the corporate help desk, the ANI data is sent to a host, where it is matched with the employee's file. The help desk operator then has all relevant data available immediately to assist the caller in resolving the problem.

## MAKING THE BUSINESS CASE FOR VPNs

An increasing number of companies are finding virtual private networks to be a practical alternative method for obtaining private network functionality without the overhead associated with acquiring and managing dedicated private lines. There are several other advantages to opting for a virtual private network, including:

- The ability to assign access codes and corresponding class-of-service restrictions to users; these codes are used for internal billing, to limit the potential for misuse of the telecommunications system, and to facilitate overall communications management.
- The ability to consolidate billing, resulting in only one bill for the entire network.
- The ability to tie small remote locations to the corporate network economically, instead of using expensive dial-up facilities.
- The ability to meet a variety of needs (e.g., switched voice and data, travel cards, toll-free service, and international and cellular calls) using a single carrier.
- The availability of a variety of access methods, including switched and dedicated access, 700 and 800 dial access, and remote calling card access.
- The availability of digit translation capabilities that permit corporations to build global networks using a single carrier. Digit translation services perform seven-to-10-digit, 10-to-seven-digit, and seven-to-seven-digit translations and convert domestic telephone numbers to IDDD numbers through 10-to-IDDD and seven-to-IDDD translation.
- The ability to have the carrier monitor network performance and reroute around failures and points of congestion.
- The ability to have the carrier control network maintenance and management, reducing the need for high-priced in-house technical personnel, diagnostic tools, and spares inventory.
- The ability to configure the network flexibly, through on-site management terminals that enable users to meet bandwidth application needs and control costs.
- The ability to access enhanced transmission facilities, with speeds ranging from 56K bps to 384K and 1.536M bps, and plan for emerging broadband services.
- The ability to combine network-services pricing typically based on distance and usage with pricing for other services to qualify for further volume discounts.
- The ability to customize dialing plans to streamline corporate operations. A dealership network, for example, assigns a unique four-digit code for the parts department. Then, to call any dealership across the country to find a part, a user simply dials the telephone-number prefix of that location.

The intelligence embedded in the virtual network at the carriers' serving offices also gives users more flexibility in selecting equipment. PBXs from various vendors connect to a VPN service provider's POP through various local access arrangements. The private network exists as a separate entity on the VPN service provider's backbone network, with the service provider assuming responsibility for translating digits from a customer-specific numbering plan to the service provider's own numbering plan, and vice versa. All routing and any failures are transparent to the customer and, consequently, to each individual user on the network.

## Billing Options

One of the most attractive aspects of virtual private network services is customized billing. Typically, users select from among the following billing options:

- The main account accrues all discounts under the program. In some cases, even the use of wireless voice and data messaging services qualifies for the volume discount.
- Discounts are assigned to each location according to its prorated share of traffic.
- A portion of the discounts is assigned to each location based on its prorated share of traffic, with a specified percentage assigned to the headquarters location.
- Usage and access rates are billed to each location, or subsidiaries are billed separately from main accounts.
- Billing information and customized reports are accessed at customer premises terminals or provided by the carrier on diskette, microfiche, magnetic tape, tape cassette, or CD-ROM as well as in paper form.
- A name substitution feature allows authorization codes, billing groups, telephone numbers, master account numbers, dialed numbers, originating numbers, and credit card numbers to be substituted with the names of individuals, resulting in a virtually numberless bill for internal distribution. This prevents sensitive information from falling into inappropriate hands.

AT&T, MCI, and Sprint all offer rebilling capabilities that use a percentage or flat-rate formula to mark up or discount internal telephone bills. Billing information is even summarized in graphical reports, such as bar and pie charts.

Carrier-provided software is available that allows users to work with call detail and billing information to generate reports in a variety of formats. Some software even illustrates calling patterns with maps.

Electronic invoicing also is available. AT&T, for example, provides this capability by linking its SDN Billing Advantage with EDIView, its EDI offering.

## NETWORK MANAGEMENT

Each of the major VPN service providers offers various management and reporting capabilities through a network management database that enables users to perform numerous tasks without carrier involvement.

The network management database contains information about the network configuration, usage, equipment inventory, and call restrictions. On gaining access to the database, the telecommunications manager sets up, changes, and deletes authorization codes and approves the use of capabilities such as international dialing by caller, workgroup, or department. The manager also redirects calls from one VPN site to another to allow, for example, calls to an East Coast sales office to be answered by the West Coast sales office after the East Coast office closes for the day. Once the manager is satisfied with the changes, they are uploaded to the carrier's network database and take effect within minutes.

Telecommunications managers access call detail and network usage summaries, which are used to identify network traffic trends and assess network performance. In addition to being able to download traffic statistics about dedicated VPN trunk groups, users receive five-, 10-, and 15-minute trunk group usage statistics an hour after they occur; these statistics are then used to monitor network performance and carry out traffic engineering tasks. Usage is broken down and summarized in a variety of ways — such as by location, type of service, and time of day. This information is used to spot exceptional traffic patterns that may indicate either abuse or the need for service reconfiguration.

Through a network management station, the carrier provides network alarms and traffic status alerts for VPN locations using dedicated access facilities. These alarms indicate potential service outages (e.g., conditions that impair traffic and could lead to service disruption). Alert messages are routed to customers in accordance with preprogrammed priority levels, ensuring that critical faults are reviewed first. The system furnishes the customer with data on the specific type of alarm, direction, location, and priority level, along with details about the cause of the alarm (e.g., signal loss, upstream failed signal, or frame slippage). The availability of such detail permits customers to isolate faults immediately.

In addition, telecommunications managers can request access-line status information and schedule transmission tests with the carrier. The network management database describes common network problems in detail and offers specific advice on how to resolve them. The manager submits service orders and trouble reports to the carrier electronically through the management station. Telecommunications managers can also test network designs and add new corporate locations to the VPN.

## ACCESS ARRANGEMENTS

A variety of access arrangements available from the VPN service providers are targeted for specific levels of traffic, including a single-voice frequency channel, 24-voice channels through a DS1 link, and 44-voice channels through a T1 link equipped with bit-compression multiplexers, in addition to a capability that splits a DS1 link into its component DS0s at the VPN serving office for connection to off-net services. The same DS1 link is used for a variety of applications, from 800 service to videoconferencing, thereby reducing access costs. Depending on the carrier, there may be optional cellular and messaging links to the VPN as well. Even phone card users can dial into the VPN, with specific calling privileges defined for each card. All of a company's usage can be tied into a single invoicing structure, regardless of access method.

The architecture of the VPN makes use of software-defined intelligence residing in strategic points of the network. AT&T's SDN, for example, consists of an ACP connected to the PBX through dedicated or switched lines. The ACPs connect with the carrier's NCP, where the customer's seven-digit on-net number is converted to the appropriate code for routing through the virtual network.

Instead of charging for multiple local access lines to support different usage-based services, the carriers allow users to consolidate multiple services over a single T1 access line. A user who needs only 384K bps for a data application, for example, fills the unused portion of the access pipe with 18 channels of voice traffic to justify the cost of the access line. At the carrier's cross-connect system, the dedicated 384K-bps channel and 18 switched channels are split out from the incoming DS1 signal. The 384K-bps DS0 bundle is then routed to its destination, whereas the voice channels are handed off to the carrier's Class 4 switch, which distributes the voice channels to the appropriate service.

## DATA NETWORKING OVER THE VPN

Although obtaining economical voice traffic has traditionally been the primary motivation behind the move to VPN service, a variety of low-speed and high-speed VPN data services are available as well.

### Low-Speed Data Services

AT&T has been especially aggressive in offering its SDN customers the means to access a wide array of AT&T EasyLink messaging services. The offering, AT&T SDN EasyLink Solutions, enables customers to use their SDN networks to connect directly to electronic messaging features from AT&T EasyLink Services, including electronic mail, shared folders, text-to-fax

(MailFAX), electronic data interchange, Telex, and a variety of information services.

SDN EasyLink Solutions includes the following services:

- **AT&T SDN Electronic Mail.** This worldwide public messaging service offers secure transport and feature-rich functionality that supports access from a variety of computer platforms. The service provides worldwide electronic mail delivery to many systems, including X.400 gateways and the Internet.
- **AT&T SDN Shared Folder.** This service is an electronic bulletin board service within SDN Electronic Mail that automatically downloads new information to each user's mailbox whenever the user queries the system for new mail.
- **AT&T SDN MailFAX.** This service lets users send electronic mail documents from a computer to a receiver's fax machine. Service features include automatic retry, fax broadcast, and customized logos and signatures.
- **AT&T SDN Enhanced FAX.** The enhanced fax service provides secure store-and-forward delivery of facsimile transmissions worldwide.
- **AT&T SDN Electronic Data Interchange.** This EDI service provides message transport, storage, and tracking for the electronic exchange of business documents such as purchase orders or invoices in standard data formats.
- **AT&T SDN Telex.** This service connects users to the worldwide telex network and the extensive community of Telex subscribers in numerous industries, including international commerce, banking, and shipping.
- **AT&T SDN Information Services.** These information services give users fast and cost-effective access to a broad spectrum of online news services, interactive research databases, bulletin boards, and research-on-demand services.

## High-Speed Data Services

VPNs also are capable of supporting such bandwidth-intensive applications as LAN interconnection, image transfers, and videoconferencing. These services are offered under AT&T's SDDN, MCI's VPDS, and Sprint's VPN Premiere.

AT&T's SDDN, for example, offers high-speed data networking in conjunction with SDN's advanced call-handling capabilities. SDDN shares the network capabilities of ACCUNET SDS for reliable transport of data at rates of 56K bps and higher. (Low-speed data is transported over SDN using dial-up modems or PBX data connections.) SDN supports low-speed dial-up modem connections and higher-speed connections through a PBX, T1 multiplexer, or D4 channel bank. AT&T's SDDN offering supports 56K- and

64K-bps service, 64K-bps clear channel, and 384K- and 1.536M-bps connections utilizing the ISDN PRI. These high transmission speeds are achieved by stacking contiguous 64K-bps clear channels. Users take full advantage of virtual networking by combining and routing their voice and data traffic in a single T1 access line to the SDN/SDDN network.

Users access SDDN with DDS lines for data transmission at rates of up to 56K bps using dial-up modems or DSUs with an optional auto-dial or re-dial capability; alternatively, access is obtained through AT&T ACCUNET T1.5 lines. Customer premises equipment (e.g., intelligent multiplexers and PBXs) interprets ISDN PRI messages for call setup, detection of facility failures, and reinitiation of call setup in response to abnormal call disconnects. Real-time restoration is achieved within seconds of a service disruption so that critical data applications remain operational; SDDN also supports SDN network management capabilities such as call screening, flexible routing, periodic traffic reports, and customer-initiated testing. SDDN is well-suited for applications that:

- Have high-speed or high-volume data transmission requirements.
- Have a time window for completion (e.g., applications performed during the night, morning, or other specified time periods).
- Benefit from bandwidth-on-demand and usage-based pricing (e.g., applications active for a limited duration, used infrequently, or required for unscheduled events).
- Have restoration requirements (e.g., critical applications that must remain operational in the event of a network failure). Such applications are currently protected through a dial backup capability or spare bandwidth and alternate routing in a T1 multiplexer network.
- Have multiple endpoint destinations (e.g., applications requiring serial or nonsimultaneous communications between an originating point and several endpoints).
- Benefit from networking flexibility (e.g., applications with traffic patterns that demonstrate daily or seasonal variations or that change drastically as the network grows). SDDN eliminates the time and expense required to install additional private lines.

Specific applications that benefit from SDDN include RJE and NJE, CAD/CAE and medical imaging, distributed/shared computing, LAN interconnection, high-speed mainframe communications, PC-to-host and PC-to-PC transfer, peak traffic overflow and private line backup, videoconferencing, and Group IV facsimile.

**Performance Objectives**

VPN performance standards for data are comparable to private line services through the use of high-quality digital transport and an automatic restoration capability. With AT&T's SDDN, for example, performance is measured in terms of network interface availability, network reliability, post dialing delay, call blocking, restoration, and service availability.

**Network Interface Availability.** For SDDN connections, an availability number indicates the percentage of time that all SDDN components are usable for customer applications. The target SDDN network interface-to-network interface (NI-to-NI) availability is 99.9% and includes ACCUNET T1.5 or DDS access links. Without the service restoration feature, the availability figure drops to 99.75%.

**Network Reliability.** Network reliability for SDDN is a measure of line transmission performance given in terms of EFS and SES. An EFS is a second with no bit errors, and an SES is a second with more than one error per 1,000 bits. Reliability objectives for EFS and SES are, respectively, 99.9% and 30 SES per day between AT&T serving offices (SO-to-SO), and 99.75% and 38 SES per day between network interfaces (NI-to-NI).

**Post Dialing Delay (PDD).** Post dialing delay refers to the amount of time from call initiation to call setup and is measured at the originating network interface. The SDDN objective is a four-second average post dialing delay, with 95% of all calls receiving network response within six seconds.

**Call Blocking.** Call blocking is the probability that an unsuccessful call attempt is due to network congestion. The target blocking is 1% during peak busy hours and 0.5% with planned improvements, with fewer than one call per 200 attempts blocked during peak traffic hours.

**Restoration.** The SDDN restoration objective for an NI-to-NI connection is less than 20 seconds for an estimated 99% of all restoration attempts. The stated restoration performance may not be guaranteed, however, in the event of a catastrophic or widespread network failure. The stated objective includes time spent in detection, redialing, and call setup stages in the SDDN network and CPE. A maximum of six seconds is allocated to CPE for failure detection and redialing an SDDN connection in response to a disconnect message.

**Service Availability.** Service availability objectives are improved with the use of diverse access arrangements. The split access flexible egress routing (SAFER) capability, available with AT&T 4ESS software, allows origination and distribution of calls between two toll switches, which minimizes the vulnerability to access link and nodal failures.

## LOCAL VPN SERVICE

A new development in the VPN market is the emergence of local services. Bell Atlantic, for example, is offering a local VPN service in the mid-Atlantic region under the name of Bell Atlantic All@once VPNS. VPNS service allows companies to manage their local and intraLATA calls and save money on interLATA calls using Bell Atlantic's public network as if it were their own private network.

With VPNS, customers can do such things as access their voice network remotely, make business calls from the road or home at business rates, originate calls from remote locations and bill them to the office, and block calls to certain telephone numbers or regions. Uniform pricing and billing plans are also arranged for all of the customer's locations to reduce the administrative costs involved with reviewing billing statements, even if each location uses a different carrier.

Bell Atlantic's service lets large business customers configure components of the public network like a customized private network without the expense of dedicated lines or equipment. Until now, services of this kind could not be used for local calls because they were offered through long-distance companies. Bell Atlantic's service, however, is used for local calls and also works with the customer's existing long distance services. The VPNS service also is compatible with Centrex services, PBX systems, or other customer premises equipment.

Once Bell Atlantic has achieved regulatory approval to deliver interLATA long-distance services, the company plans to expand the VPNS service to include in-region and out-of-region long distance service.

As an integral part of its All@once approach for large businesses, Bell Atlantic consults with companies to assess their communications needs and analyze their local calling patterns to design a solution that optimizes use of the public network. Bell Atlantic estimates that 25% to 75% of local phone traffic could be on a local VPN, where it could be subject to the lower rates that make VPNs attractive to users.

## CONCLUSION

VPNs permit the creation of networks that combine the advantages of both private facilities and public services, drawing on the intelligence embedded in the carrier's network. With services and features defined in software and implemented through out-of-band signaling methods, users have greater flexibility in configuring their networks from on-premises terminals and management systems than is possible with services implemented with manual patch panels and hardwired equipment. These capabilities make VPNs attractive for data as well as for voice — for regional, national, and international corporate locations — and portend success for VPNs long into the future.

# Chapter 34
# Using the Internet as a Virtual Network

*Gilbert Held*

As organizations rapidly established connections to the Internet it became apparent that in many firms duplicate network connections and the expenses associated with maintaining and operating duplicate networks might be minimized by their integration. Managers at many organizations that certify monthly bills for payment began to ask key questions, such as why do we maintain a private network to interconnect our branch offices and corporate headquarters as well as maintain an Internet connection for each location? The answer to this question is actually more complex than it may appear and involves an examination of the advantages and disadvantages associated with virtual networking. Thus, the information presented in this chapter can be used to tailor a response to the previously asked question that can match the advantages and disadvantages of virtual networking against the specific networking requirements of an organization.

## VIRTUAL NETWORKING CONCEPTS

Virtual networking has its origins in the concept of the virtual office during the evolution of the latter occurring in the early 1990s. The virtual office represents a temporary logical grouping of individuals regardless of their location or position in the organization to work on a specific project. Thus, this project concept is also commonly referred to as an organization without boundaries.

The earliest methods used to support the communications requirements of the virtual organization were voice, fax, and electronic mail. By the mid 1990s, a new type of local area network (LAN) known as a virtual LAN was developed in part to support the dynamic assignment of personnel to virtual organizations. A second method of providing communications support for virtual organizations referred to as virtual networking represents the transmission of data between two locations on a mesh structured network that is so large it can be considered to represent a network without boundaries. That network is the Internet and almost all references to virtual networking either implicitly or explicitly reference transmission over the Internet.

## INTERNET ECONOMICS

The first use of the Internet as a virtual network allowed traveling personnel to access the corporate network via dialing the transmission facility of an Internet Service Provider (ISP). Since many ISPs now offer unlimited dial access for a flat rate of $20 per month, the use of the Internet can be economically rewarding even when compared to the low cost of long distance service. For example, even at 10 cents per minute, an hour of access per day for a traveling corporate employee would result in a communications bill of $6 per day or $132 per month based upon 22 working days in the month. Thus, a flat rate of $20 per month for unlimited Internet access could result in significant savings when the Internet is used as a transmission facility to access a corporate computer connected to that network.

Although virtual networking on an individual basis can provide hundreds of dollars of savings, when used as a mechanism to replace or supplement private networks, the resulting cost savings can rapidly escalate to the point where they are truly appealing. To illustrate how the use of the Internet as a virtual network to interconnect corporate locations can result in significant economic savings, let's examine an example of the use of the Internet. Exhibit 1 illustrates the use of the Internet to connect three geographically separated corporate locations.

In examining Exhibit 1 note that each corporate location is shown connected to the Internet via an Internet Service Provider. Most ISPs have access points in major metropolitan areas and will charge approximately $1000 per month for a T1 line connection. This type of transmission facility was originally developed to support the transmission of 24 digitized voice conversations and is now used with T1 multiplexers and routers to mix digitized voice and data or to simply transmit data onto the 1.544 Mbps operating rate of the circuit. In the example shown in Exhibit 1, we will assume that each corporate location uses a T1 connection to the Internet via an ISP to interconnect their LANs via the Internet.

From an economic perspective we can compare the cost of using the Internet to the cost of connecting the three locations shown in Exhibit 1 via two T1 lines. In doing so, let's first assume each location is 500 miles distant from the next location, resulting in 1000 T1 circuit miles being required to interconnect the three locations.

Although the cost of T1 circuits can vary based upon their total mileage, the use of a multi-year contract, and other factors, a monthly cost of $3 per mile provides a reasonable approximation of the cost to include local loop

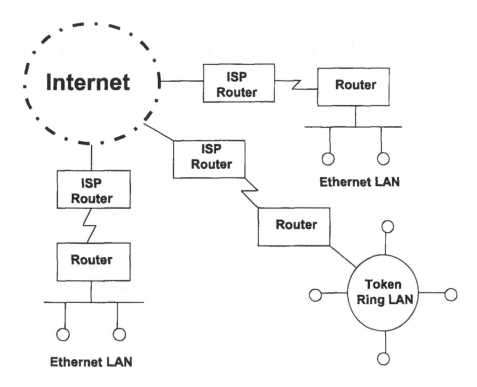

**Exhibit 1. Using the Internet to Interconnect Separate Locations.**

access fees. Thus, interconnecting the three locations shown in Exhibit 1 via a private network consisting of two leased T1 circuits would cost $3,000 based upon a distance of 500 miles between locations. Note that this cost equals the cost associated with connecting three locations via T1 lines to the Internet based upon the reasonable assumption that each location is in a major metropolitan area.

Now let's assume that the locations shown in Exhibit 1 represent Seattle, New York City, and Miami. In this example the circuit mileage would increase to approximately 3,500 miles. At a monthly cost of $3 per circuit mile the use of two T1 circuits to interconnect the three locations via a private network would increase to 3500 x 3, or $10,500. Now let's assume each location is interconnected to each other via the Internet. The cost to connect each location would still be $1000 per month since each location represents a major metropolitan area. Thus, the cost associated with using the Internet would remain fixed at $3000 per month, but the potential monthly savings would now become $7500.

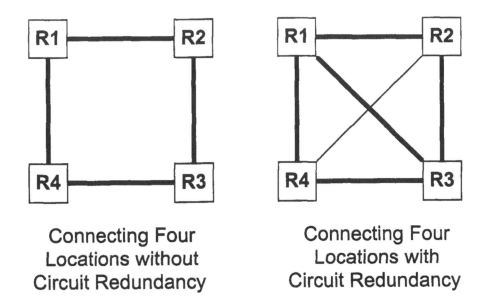

**Connecting Four Locations without Circuit Redundancy**

**Connecting Four Locations with Circuit Redundancy**

**Exhibit 2. Comparing Private Network Router Port Requirements and Reliability.**

The preceding example illustrates a key concept associated with the use of the Internet as a virtual network for interconnecting geographically separated corporate locations. As the distance between locations increases, the potential savings increases.

**Equipment Cost**

Another savings that can be considered when the Internet is used to connect corporate locations concerns the use of router ports. In Exhibit 1 only three serial router ports are required to provide three locations with the ability to communicate with each other. Now assume the number of corporate locations increased to four. Then four routers with one serial port per router would be required to enable communications between any location via the Internet. In comparison, you could connect four locations on a private network with four leased lines as shown in the top portion of Exhibit 2. In doing so each router would require two serial ports. Since router ports can easily cost $1000 or more, the use of a private router based network to interconnect a large number of geographically separated organizational locations can result in the cost of routers considerably exceeding the cost of routers used to provide a similar networking capability via the Internet.

## RELIABILITY ISSUES

Another benefit that can be obtained from the use of the Internet is reliability. Once data reaches an ISP it is transferred onto a mesh structured backbone which contains redundant circuits that provide alternate paths between ISPs. Thus, the failure of a circuit on the Internet backbone is normally transparent to user operations as routers used by ISPs have the ability to select alternate routers. In comparison, additional circuits and router ports would be required to provide a mesh structured private network facility. Exhibit 2B illustrates how four routers would each require three serial ports to support a mesh structure topology that could be used to easily route data around circuit failures. However, this level of reliability would be extremely costly as it would require the installation of additional circuits and additional router ports for each router in the network. Now that we have an appreciation for the advantages associated with the use of the Internet as a virtual network to interconnect geographically separated organizational locations, let's turn our attention to two key issues that may restrict the ability of your organization to use this method of virtual networking — network predictability and security.

### Network Predictability

Currently the Internet can be classified as an unpredictable network. That is, there is currently no assurance that data transmitted from one location will not be adversely affected by network traffic in such a manner that packets are received at the destination with variable time delays between packets. This means that the Internet is better suited for transporting certain types of data streams than other types of data streams. For example, time dependent applications such as SNA logical link control (LLC) type 2 data could be adversely affected by variable time delays, possibly resulting in session timeouts occurring even though a workstation on one LAN accessing a mainframe connected to a distant LAN responded in a timely manner to a mainframe query. Similarly, an attempt to route digitized voice via the use of a specialized gateway that converts voice into a sequence of IP packets would be more suitable for use on an internal private network than for transmission over the Internet. In this example an organization could install ReSerVation Protocol (RSVP) compatible equipment to allocate portions of bandwidth through their internal network for time delay sensitive applications, such as the transport of digitized voice. In comparison, the deployment of RSVP compatible equipment by Internet Service Providers is probably several years away as several key issues remain to be resolved to include how to bill subscribers for reserved bandwidth established between several ISPs.

When considering network predictability as an issue, there are several applications that are very suitable for transport via the Internet. Those applications include electronic mail, file transfer, and Web browsing into a corporate database. Thus, if your organization is considering the use of the Internet as a mechanism to replace a costly leased line based private network and your applications fall into the previously mentioned types of time dependent data transfers that are not adversely affected by the unpredictable nature of Internet transmission, an economic comparison becomes warranted. However, if your organization currently uses a private network for transporting digitized voice conversations or for accessing one or more mainframes using a time dependent protocol such as LLC2, you should probably defer a decision on the use of the Internet as a virtual network until RSVP becomes available and is priced. At that time you would then perform an economic analysis to determine if the potential savings afforded from replacing a private line based network by the use of the Internet is worth the effort. Concerning that effort, another issue that requires careful attention when you move from a private leased line based network to the use of the Internet is security.

## SECURITY CONSIDERATIONS

When using a private leased line based network, most security issues concern the distribution of userIDs and passwords if required for employees to gain access to different computers connected to the network. In such situations, the ability of a hacker from outside the organization to adversely affect security is nonexistent since there is no connection between a public network and the organization's private network. However, once an organization decides to use the Internet as a virtual network to interconnect geographically separated locations, security becomes a key issue as your organization is now exposed to the efforts of millions of persons that could attempt to access your organization's computational facilities. Thus, a mechanism to bar intruders and allow authorized users from one location to access another location becomes necessary. That mechanism can be obtained either through the packet filtering capability of a router or through the use of a firewall.

### Packet Filtering Router

A packet filtering router can be used to restrict access based upon the source address, destination address, and TCP port number contained in a datagram. Here the TCP port number is a numeric value between 0 and 1023 that defines the type of data being transported. For example, Hyper-Text Transport Protocol (HTTP), which conveys Web browser pages, uses port 80. Thus, an example of a filter that would bar all traffic other than Web server traffic through a router from users on the IP network whose address is 192.47.27.0 to the network address 203.171.141.25 would be entered as follows:

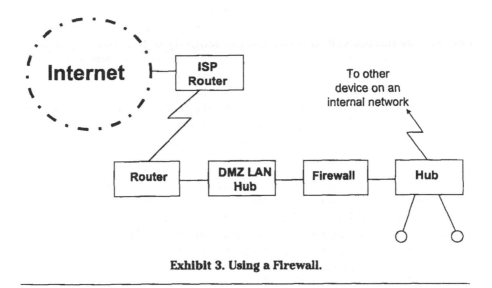

**Exhibit 3. Using a Firewall.**

Permit TCP 80 192.47.27.0 203.171.141.25

Although packet filtering represents a useful mechanism for barring unauthorized access, it has a specific weakness in the fact that IP addresses can be spoofed. In addition, by itself packet filtering does not verify the originator of data nor does it prevent a user that gains access to a network behind the router from using an electronic dictionary in an attempt to gain illegal access to organizational computational facilities. To obtain an enhanced level of security, most organizations that anticipate using the Internet as a virtual network will install a firewall at each location connected to the Internet.

## Using Firewalls

Exhibit 3 illustrates the placement of a firewall to provide an extra level of protection between a corporate LAN and the Internet. In this example, the router is connected to a hub that has only one other connection, that of the firewall. This type of workstation-less hub is commonly called a DMZ LAN as any illegal activity passed by the router is barred by the firewall prior to the activity adversely affecting users.

In addition to performing filtering in a manner similar to routers, firewalls may include a number of additional security related functions and features. Those features can include the authentication of remote users, proxy services, and virus scanning of incoming electronic mail and file transfers. Authentication is usually performed by a one-time password check, using the Bellcore S/Key system or the Security Dynamics Secure ID card. The S/Key system generates via software a one time password that is checked by the firewall to verify the authenticity of the user requesting access. In comparison, the Security Dynamics Secure ID card is a credit card-sized device that generates a pseudo random number every 60 seconds. A user would enter their PIN number and the number generated by the Secure ID card which is transmitted to the firewall. The firewall would use an algorithm to compute the Secure ID card number based upon the provided PIN and consider the requester to be authenticated if the number generated by the firewall matches the transmitted number.

The proxy service capability of a firewall results in the firewall barring direct client-server requests. Instead, the firewall examines each request against a set of predefined rules and, if permitted, acts as an intermediate client and performs the requested server connection. Through the use of proxy services the firewall can check for dictionary attacks, protocol spoofing and other illegal activities and can either terminate the attempts or alert a manager via an E-mail or page to the illegal activity being attempted.

When considering the Internet as a virtual network, the cost of a firewall as an added measure of protection should be based upon your organizational requirements. If you plan to use the Internet only to transfer electronic mail, a virus checker on your mail servers may be both sufficient and considerably less costly than the use of a firewall. If your organization has several servers at each location with important content that requires a high level of protection, then the expense associated with the use of firewalls may be well justified. Thus, a careful analysis of the type of data to be transmitted via the Internet between corporate locations as well as economics and security issues associated with the use of the Internet become important criteria prior to determining if virtual networking is a practical solution for the replacement of a private leased line based network.

## RECOMMENDED COURSE OF ACTION

Using the Internet as a virtual network can save costs. Before using the Internet in such a way, a data center manager should consider the following:

- *Distance between locations to be networked.* The greater the distance between these locations, the greater potential for saving money.
- *The number of locations to be connected.* The larger the number, the greater opportunity for savings. Also, the Internet is a reliable network. For a similarly reliable private network, an organization would have to purchase more equipment. This is another way using the Internet as a virtual network can save cost.

- *Network predictability.* The Internet is not predictable. If your organization wants to use a virtual Internet network for applications other than E-mail, Web browsing, and transferring files, you should not view the Internet as an option.
- *Network security.* By using the Internet as a virtual network, an organization risks exposing vital information to other users of the Internet. Firewalls do protect sites connected to the Internet, but they are still vulnerable to hackers.

By weighing the pros and cons previously listed, a data center manager can decide if using the Internet as a virtual network will save money and still provide the needed security and predictability.

# Chapter 35
# Popular E-mail Systems

*Gary Cannon*

The commercial E-mail industry continues to grow at an impressive rate. There are almost 91 million E-mail users around the world. This chapter discusses what features and services to look for when shopping for a corporate E-mail system, and compares the leading E-mail systems on the market.

## INTRODUCTION

The Internet has grown so rapidly because of users' need to communicate and share information. Although many people were doing just that on commercial networks, the Internet offers more than just E-mail and is less expensive than commercial systems.

The number of E-mail users has grown almost 74% in the past year. More than 47 million people are using LAN E-mail systems, most of which are connected to commercial services. The larger commercial networks cannot accurately estimate how many individual users they support because most users on LANs and larger systems do not have individual accounts on the commercial networks. The majority of users access the commercial systems through corporate gateways.

This number of users continues to grow, and as commercial systems enhance their product and service offerings, there will be continued expansion on the commercial side of the market as well as the Internet.

Many business users rely on E-mail to conduct their day-to-day functions. E-mail ties together many other applications and has contributed significantly to the information explosion.

## ELECTRONIC MESSAGING: A HISTORICAL PERSPECTIVE

For years, telex served as the only form of electronic mail and was strictly the domain of government agencies and big business. About 25 years ago a few operating systems had rudimentary messaging capabilities. IBM

0-8493-9965-3/99/$0.00+$.50
© 1999 by CRC Press LLC

Corp.'s Virtual Machine (VM) system could communicate between active terminals. Digital Equipment Corp.'s Virtual Memory System (VMS) operating system came up with the basics of what would become VMSmail.

At about the same time, General Electric's Information Services Business Division (ISBD) developed the time-sharing concept with Dartmouth University and introduced an internal system known as Cross File (XFL), which allowed employees to send messages to one another when they were working on projects together. XFL developed into a divisionwide utility and each office had an address. Originally, senders wrote out their message on a piece of paper and handed it to the administrator. Sometime during the day the message would be entered into the system and the sender could expect a reply in a day or so. Functionally, the system worked fine. Practically, it took a few years before the organization fully accepted the application and integrated it fully into daily operation.

Over the next few years, more users would get addresses and access to the system directly via asynchronous terminals. Message traffic started to increase and ISBD offered the XFL system to other GE divisions.

Electronic mail was referred to as message switching then, which was a regulated application under the law in the U.S. and would remain so until January 1981, when it was deregulated and computer service companies entered into the E-mail market. A new commercial application was born and several companies jumped into the market, some as service providers and others as the software developers. E-mail as an industry continued to grow steadily until someone discovered the Internet — now almost everyone has an E-mail address.

## PRIMARY ELECTRONIC MESSAGING SYSTEM CATEGORIES

Today there are four primary categories of E-mail systems and users:

- **Online services.** A relatively small number of services provide E-mail to a large number of users. Examples include CompuServe, America Online, and Prodigy. There are an estimated 12 million users of these services worldwide.
- **Commercial services.** These are traditional computer service companies with mostly corporate clients providing connectivity between companies. Examples include AT&T, GE Information Services (GEIS), MCI, and Sprint. There are an estimated 1.5 million users of these services worldwide.
- **Private E-mail.** These E-mail systems are proprietary to companies and large organizations and are maintained and operated by them. Examples include General Motors, Pfizer, and J.C Penney. There are an estimated 70 million users of these services worldwide.
- **The Internet.** An estimated 35 million users worldwide use Internet E-mail.

## FEATURES AND FUNCTIONS

When selecting what features an E-mail system should have, the IS department must keep the users in mind. The E-mail system must serve the users. Reliability and maintenance are also critical. There is no 800 number to call if something goes wrong with the LAN server. The LAN is a proprietary system that has to be repaired in-house. As user communities within companies expand, so does the reliability and service problem. As a company grows, so does its local networks, and soon IS and the network staff are maintaining a worldwide collection of them.

Network managers must also be concerned with connectivity. E-mail users, if they do not already, may soon need to communicate with people outside their immediate community. All the popular E-mail systems today have gateways.

### X.400 and SMTP

X.400 is the international standard for interconnecting unlike messaging systems. The X.400 recommendations were developed and continue to be upgraded by the Telecommunications Standardization Sector of the International Telecommunications Union, an organization charted by the United Nations that represents most of the countries with modern telephone systems. Almost every E-mail vendor offers X.400 software to connect its system to the commercial world. The software is still expensive, but it is reliable and fast, handles attached files well, and offers excellent security. It does, however, have a slight problem with addressing.

Most E-mail system vendors now offer simple mail transfer protocol (SMTP) gateways with their products to connect to the Internet. SMTP is reliable, almost as fast as X.400, does an acceptable job with binary files, has its own addressing problems, and is inexpensive. There is still the directory problem.

The commercial service world also offers proprietary gateways for many private E-mail systems to their public services, which gives the corporate user a window to the E-mail world. For many private E-mail system clients who do not yet need X.400 software, the commercial services offer a gateway to the X.400 world. All of them also provide gateway services to the Internet.

### X.500 Directory Service

All of this connectivity introduces the most serious problem in E-mail today — addressing and directories. Worldwide connectivity does no good if there is no map for getting around.

X.500 is E-mail's atlas. It can interconnect distributed directories, but it is still waiting in the wings. The North American Directory Forum (NADF) has been showing a demo of interconnected X.500 for two years. Commercial service providers are trying to lure corporate clients into using X.500. Some large companies are even experimenting with their own in-house X.500 systems. Because there are still concerns about privacy and security with X.500, many companies are investigating alternatives. This brings additional pressures on the E-mail system vendors to define and offer competent directory services. Companies such as Hitachi are, in addition, introducing directory synchronization products such as SyncWare.

## Features and Services Checklists

Following is a checklist of features users should look for when reviewing E-mail products:

- Editing capability.
- Distribution lists.
- Import/export capability.
- File Transfer Body Part (FTBP) or BP-15 (X.400) ability.
- A spell checker.
- The ability to send forms.
- Function keys.
- Reply options.
- A calendar/scheduler feature.

Following is a checklist of services users should look for when reviewing E-mail products (several of these services are discussed in the section "E-mail Services"):

- Directories.
- Ad hoc entries.
- Fax output.
- Fax input.
- Message notification.
- Delivery options.
- Security.
- Encryption.
- Keyboard combinations.
- On-screen help.
- Computer-based training (CBT).
- Message storage and archive.
- Storage backup.
- Communications protocol.
- Comm port/comm line backup.
- Expansion capabilities.

Following is a checklist of services users should look for to ensure sufficient connectivity in an E-mail system:

- SMTP gateway.
- X.400 gateway.
- Telex.
- Fax.
- Mail API (MAPI).
- Wireless services.
- Pager services.

**Features for Creating Messages**

Fortunately for users, competition in this field is intense and many of the newer E-mail systems have similar features and capabilities. Besides sending and receiving mail, creating messages is the next most important function.

A single function key should initiate this operation and prepare the user to address the message and set options. Most systems set the cursor at the TO: block, and the next keystroke should open the address book and point to the first entry, starting with the letters matching those keyed in.

Identifying the name selection with (in many cases) the return key, the user can set the address book to identify the next entry with further keystrokes. There should be no limit to the number of addresses selected. When the TO: block is filled, then a tab or another keystroke should place the user at the cc: block. This operation is processed in the same way as the TO: block. Many systems also allow for blind copies — these are addressees who receive the message but are not shown in the address block.

**Editing Capability**

After the addressing tasks are completed, the user can proceed to constructing the message text. The majority of E-mail messages are written on the fly and perhaps include some previously prepared text. Full-page editing features are a must. Cut-and-paste manipulation of the text, along with import of existing files, allows the user to create messages efficiently.

It is extremely convenient to have a spell checker in the E-mail system. If the E-mail system is part of a complete office support system such as MS Office or HP Desk, then the spell checker will be available and probably shared between the individual components. That way the user does not have to keep updating separate new-word dictionary files.

## Attaching Files

After the user has completed the text of the message, he or she may want to include some additional files to accompany the message. These can be word processing documents, spreadsheets, drawings, charts, and graphs. Any file that can be stored on the PC, workstation, or mainframe should be able to join the message in transit to its destination. This is a standard capability of most E-mail systems, X.400, and the Internet, although they all handle attached files in different ways. Gateways are improving at allowing attached files to cross these boundaries.

Clicking on the attached file icon or function key should place the user in the directory reserved for attached files. Selecting each with a single keystroke should add the attachments to the file list for this message. Again, there may be no technical limit to the number or size of files, but the speed and reliability of transit may be affected if the files are too large in size.

## File Compression

Many organizations struggle with whether or not to offer file compression. On a commercial service, the cost of the transfer is always important. Equally important is the time of transit. Then the question arises, "does the receiver on the other end have the same compression algorithm?"

Within the corporate environment, file compression should be easier as long as all employees have moved up to the same version of the software. The cost savings of closing the data center and putting every location on LANs is countered with the problem that most LANs operate independently and with differing versions of the software, making E-mail and file transfers more of a challenge.

## Distribution Lists

Associated with addressing are distribution lists. Some systems cannot handle lengthy address lists. This is not necessarily a design flaw; more often, it represents memory limitations of intermediate or receiving systems. A single address entry can add a few hundred bytes to the header; therefore, distribution lists are highly recommended.

Distribution lists can be thought of as header compression techniques. Most commercial services charge for additional message copies, whether they are TO:s or cc:s. Therefore, the use of distribution lists reduces invoices as well as transit times.

In many systems, distribution lists can only be created by the administrator. Other systems allow the user to create and maintain their own distribution lists. In either case, their use is recommended for efficiency.

However, many people overuse the distribution list by, for example, sending everyone a message that not necessarily everyone needs to see.

## Importing Text

The importing feature can be used during message creation to save portions of messages for future use. IS, for example, can use this feature to explain aspects of messaging to users. An IS staffer can save many previously used answers in files on his or her PC and incorporate them in messages to current queries. This expedites the job of IS and ensures that each user gets a complete and accurate response each time. If a new query comes up, IS can use the export feature to save that response for future use.

When importing text, users may also want to search for a particular string to verify that they brought in the correct file. The ability to search the text of the message being created is a handy feature. For frequent E-mail users, it is almost a necessary tool.

## Signature Files

Many users frequently import their signature file, which may consist of, for example, the user's X.400 address, Internet address, and telephone number. Sometimes addresses in the FROM: block of a message get scrambled or expanded by gateways in transit. A signature file contains the correct version of the sender's address. With all the gateways around the world, this is a highly recommended practice.

## Forms

Forms are a special type of import. Some E-mail systems allow forms to be generated that are partially filled out by the sender, with the intent that the recipient fill in the rest and return it or pass it on. Forms usually have special fields that are reserved for alpha or numeric import to assist the user in entering required data. The field size can be specified, and on more sophisticated systems, only certain users can enter particular fields. Most systems with forms are restricted to sharing the forms among users of the same system. Going outside that system usually requires that the form be sent as an attached file, if it is possible at all.

## E-MAIL SERVICES

Various services such as directories, fax gateways, message notification, security, and connectivity are provided with modern electronic messaging systems.

## Directories

Directories are one of the most critical and complex problems facing the messaging industry today. The E-mail population is hovering around 100 million users. This population requires an extensive directory, to say the least.

The X.500 solution, however, has been around for about eight years and acceptance has been very slow. In the short term, most companies are investigating interim solutions.

The bottom line is that the E-mail system should have a flexible directory service that can handle local and remote addresses. Users should be able to enter ad hoc addresses as well as access centrally administered entries from anywhere on the LAN or mainframe E-mail system. When multiple E-mail systems are involved, the gateway system or hub service should contain all entries. Control Data, Soft*Switch, DEC, and Microsoft Exchange all offer this capability. These systems are also X.500 compatible.

## System Directories vs. Local Address Books

The difference between a system directory and a local address book is that the directory contains all the addresses for an entire system that may include other E-mail systems connected via gateways. The address book is what each user maintains on his or her individual PC or workstation. When users need the address for someone not in their address book, they search the system directory.

The directory should be available to all users and the directories of separate post offices should be able to exchange entries. Directory synchronization packages are also starting to appear on the market. Hitachi's SyncWare interfaces with a variety of E-mail system directories and includes an X.500 gateway. Individual users should also be able to load their address book from the system directory.

One feature very helpful to users is the ability to cut and paste into an address book from text. Frequently users get messages with long cc: lists and would like to be able to copy one or more entries into their address books rather than retype the entry. Sometimes messages come through a number of gateways and the FROM: address is about three times as long as when it started out. If the sender includes his or her original address in the text, the receiver can extract it and simply transfer it to an address book.

Another feature that should be required by network-based directories is the ability to handle queries and updates by mail. This feature allows users with the proper access to send queries to the directory to search for particular entries or names, preferably with a mask character. Updating the directory by mail is also a feature needed by remote administrative users, again with the proper security permissions. This feature is not a requirement obvious to LAN users because everyone is connected and can access the directory. However, when there are a variety of systems and directories interconnected via commercial networks or the Internet, query and update by mail is a time saver.

The directory should have a local find capability that allows the user to search either on address or name for an entry. As directories and address books grow in size and scope, these features will be required by all users. Eventually, users will be able to query an X.500 directory for any entry they need.

### Fax Gateways

Even before the Internet, there was the fax. Fax gateways have existed on commercial E-mail services for more than a decade. PCs have added fax gateways within the past seven or eight years. Recently fax modem prices have fallen, so it is affordable for almost every PC and LAN to send and receive faxes. One major convenience of a fax modem for travelers is that they do not have to carry a printer on the road with them.

### Message Notification

PCs now have literally hundreds of applications for users, and most people only spend a short time each day on E-mail. Therefore, when a message arrives, the user may want to be interrupted and notified. Some systems provide a capability that informs the user of new mail. The form of notification, either a flashing indication in the corner of the screen or a simple beep, should be set by the user. This capability should also include a message when the PC is turned on that there is mail waiting.

### Security

As more critical business information is transported via E-mail, security options have become more important to system implementers. Many of these have been a standard part of electronic data interchange (EDI) for years and are starting to show up in the E-mail side of the industry. As the cost for sending files via E-mail decreases, the need for additional security increases.

### Gateways

This may be the most often used capability when selecting E-mail systems. Some companies feel they have to decide between either X.400 or the Internet. Most E-mail systems now come standard with a simple mail transport protocol (SMTP) gateway for Internet, and almost every E-mail system on the market has an X.400 gateway.

For an E-mail system or service to survive, it must provide access to the Internet at least via E-mail. The standard that is quoted most often for E-mail access to the Internet is RFC-822, which specifies the rules for SMTP. This is a democratic procedure for posting proposed specifications on the Internet and allowing people to debate the pros and cons of all or part of the specifications. After a proper time period, the request for comment (RFC) committee decides to make the RFC part of the standing rules of the Internet.

## X.400 Software

The X.400 standard is administered by committee. The ITU-TSS has standing committees that create and maintain the recommendations for telecommunications. The most familiar of these are the X series, including X.25, X.400, and X.500. Each of these has committees made up of representatives from the international telephone companies, U.S. phone companies, and software companies involved in the telecommunications industry. These committees meet periodically to review the status of their efforts and between meetings usually share information via E-mail. When they complete a new version of the recommendations, they gather in a plenary session for approval from the ruling committees and new final versions are published and announced.

The meetings used to occur on a regular four-year cycle, but have recently been changed to an as-needed basis. The recommendations can be purchased from government offices, the UN, or companies associated with the ITU-TSS. There are also supplementary documents available, such as the implementer's guide. It still helps to have a resident expert when designing and writing an X.400 gateway.

Approximately 18 companies around the world actually offer X.400 software. In the US, Digital Equipment Corp. and Hewlett-Packard supply X.400 software for their systems. ISOCOR and OSIware (Infonet Software Services) offer X.400 systems of a more generic nature to interconnect systems from other vendors. Europe has a number of suppliers of X.400 systems, such as Marben and Net-Tel.

## Telex, Fax, and Wireless

Other gateways often required by E-mail systems are telex, fax, and wireless. Telex is still used extensively around the world. All service providers offer a gateway to telex. Some private E-mail systems offer a telex gateway, but this requires a separate service agreement with a telex service provider. This gateway must work both ways, unlike most fax gateways.

ISOCOR offers a fax gateway that permits fax into X.400. The fax user sends a document and, after the connect indication, keys in a code that corresponds to a directory entry in the ISOCOR software. The incoming fax is converted to text and routed to the address in the directory. This is a handy capability for medium-to-large scale service.

With the increase in the use of wireless communications for PCs and the ever-popular pager, many E-mail systems are starting to incorporate gateways for wireless services. This requires a third-party provider, but it does offer the user that last-ditch method for reaching someone away from the office.

### Popular Messaging Systems

The following sections focus on the pros and cons of the leading messaging systems on the market today that can be installed in companies.

**Lotus cc:Mail.** Lotus cc:Mail has dominated LAN-based systems since its introduction a few years ago. cc:Mail provides efficient directory services and most of the features anyone would need. It handles many of the common APIs available and operates on most platforms. Many other E-mail systems imitate cc:Mail, but it has remained the market leader.

**IBM Office Vision 400.** IBM Office Vision had difficult beginnings. It survived mainly on the strength of IBM in the mainframe market. Distributed Office Support System (DISOSS), which eventually became Office Vision/Multiple Virtual Storage (OV/MVS), is a very large system requiring a well-trained, knowledgeable staff. It is not the most user-friendly system and has the limited 8*8 (DGN.DEN) addressing common to SNA Distribution Services (SNADS)-based systems. PROFS, the precursor of OV/VM, is a much more user-friendly system that can use nickname files, includes a calendar feature, and has a more flexible directory system.

The most popular entry in the Office Vision stable is OV/400. The AS/400 platform is quite possibly the biggest seller after the PC. AS/400 is extremely popular in Europe and the U.S. Although OV/400 still uses the SNADS 8*8 addressing, it does have the personal address book feature popular in other systems. OV/400 also has the calendar capability found in OV/VM. Gateways are available for X.400 and the more popular APIs.

**DEC All-in-One.** Digital Equipment Corp. offers two of the older and most popular E-mail systems today. VMSmail, like UNIX Sendmail, is a utility feature in the VMS operating system. It is a command-line-oriented system that is strongly enhanced by the availability of DEC's Message Router system. Even with the overwhelming popularity of full-screen systems, there are still many VMSmail systems active today.

The mainstay for DEC E-mail systems is All-in-One. This is a full-service, full-screen presentation E-mail system. Along with MAILbus, DEC All-in-One supports X.400 and SMTP as well as X.500 directory protocols.

All-in-One can operate on a standalone VAX as well as an entire network of VAXs interconnected via DECnet. With MAILbus, All-in-One interfaces with LANs and other E-mail systems including OV/VM and OV/400 via SNADS. Many companies with multiple E-mail systems use All-in-One and MAILbus as their central hub system. Distributed directory services (DDS) capability, combined with the X.500 protocols, ensure that this system will be around for a while.

**HP Open Desk Manager.** HP Open Desk Manager is the premier system for UNIX-based E-mail on midrange systems. HP mail is based on SMTP and therefore readily interfaces with the Internet. Hewlett-Packard also offers a full X.400 system, which allows it to communicate with commercial service providers. The flexibility of HP Open Desk Manager includes interfaces to cc:Mail and Microsoft Mail, as well as Wang and Office Vision systems. The directory service is extremely flexible and allows for local and remote entries in various formats. The directory allows the user to search on a number of fields in the database, making this a very useful tool.

**Lotus Notes.** Compared with the other products, Lotus Notes is a fairly new arrival. However, with the strength of Lotus, now backed by IBM, Notes will most likely be around for a long time.

Notes is a true workgroup system that incorporates the spreadsheet capabilities of Lotus 1-2-3 with a database/foldering capability that has made it instantly popular. Many people wonder how the two products — Lotus cc:Mail and Lotus Notes — will develop. cc:Mail will probably take over as the E-mail engine for Notes eventually.

**Microsoft Mail.** The dominance of Microsoft in the computer industry has almost guaranteed success for the various E-mail products they offer. The original MSmail for the Macintosh is still popular and one of the most widely used. MSmail for the PC is the old Network Courier, acquired by Microsoft years ago.

Microsoft's new Microsoft Mail Exchange is based on the Windows NT server. It interfaces the older products into the NT systems and includes interfaces to cc:Mail, Lotus Notes, and others. Microsoft Mail uses the X.400 gateway. Other X.400 software vendors also offer gateways for Microsoft Mail. Standard with Microsoft Mail Exchange is the SMTP gateway, which interfaces to the Internet for E-mail. Microsoft is also offering software for direct access to the Internet.

**Fisher TAO.** Fisher International has been a very strong player in the E-mail market with EMCEE. This is a mainframe-based system that runs on the VMS platform. The newer version, EMCEE/TAO, incorporates paging facilities along with calendar and X.400 gateways. It offers the usual SNADS gateway as well as SMTP and LAN message handling system (MHS) connectivity. The company plans to add an X.500 capability, which should significantly enhance its market share.

**Memo.** This mainframe E-mail system was developed by Verimation in Europe for a single client. It became so popular there that they started marketing Memo in the U.S. Two years ago they added X.400, and more recently an SMTP gateway, and the product is still selling. Memo owns a sizeable share of the messaging market primarily in Europe.

**BeyondMail.** Banyan Systems' BeyondMail does not command a large portion of the E-mail market, but it is important to mention because it is the guidepost against which E-mail systems should be measured. Since its introduction about five years ago, BeyondMail has had more functions and features than any of its competitors. It easily accesses documents from other applications such as MS Word, WordPerfect, and Lotus 1-2-3. It has a very flexible and powerful directory service based on Novell MHS. It includes an SMTP gateway and runs on UNIX, which makes it a natural for linking with the Internet. BeyondMail also runs on Windows, DOS, and Mac platforms. There is also a link to calendar and scheduling systems and a rules-based scripting language that helps the user interface with other applications on the LAN.

**QuickMail.** CE Software QuickMail is probably the best known of the Macintosh-based E-mail systems. There are more than 2.5 million users. This product is very popular in the advertising and publishing industries. It also runs on Windows and DOS platforms; however, the Mac is where it shines. QuickMail interfaces well with word processing packages on the Mac and is capable of sending attached files, including drawings. There are many gateways to commercial systems and the Internet, making this a popular and versatile system.

**GroupWise.** Novell is the newest entry into the E-mail market. However, due to the strength of Novell in the industry, GroupWise ranks about third in the LAN market with more than 11% of the mailboxes. GroupWise can link to other systems via MHS and has an SMTP gateway to access E-mail on the Internet. Several X.400 software vendors offer gateways for GroupWise, making the worldwide reach of this system impressive.

## CONCLUSION

This chapter has discussed all of the necessary features to look for in an E-mail package for corporate use. In summary, the leading E-mail packages are described and compared. Most of the different E-mail systems use gateways between each other, so there is little overlap of user populations and almost everyone is able to communicate with each other. Unfortunately, it is still difficult to find someone's address. Among all of the E-mail systems on the market, cc:Mail leads the LAN systems with number of mailboxes installed, and IBM Office Vision is on top of the list of midsize and mainframe systems.

# Chapter 36
# Novell Messaging Products

*Bruce Greenblatt*

Novell, Inc., is the world's leading network software provider, connecting people to other people and the information they need and enabling them to act on it anytime, any place. The company's software products provide the distributed infrastructure, network services, and advanced network access required to make networked information and pervasive computing an integral part of everyone's daily life.

Today's Novell was born from a dying hardware manufacturer called Novell Data Systems. When Novell Data Systems experienced problems with its workstation hardware business during the early 1980s, its source of venture capital, Safeguard Scientific, began looking for someone to salvage the company. Ray Noorda was invited to take a look at the company. He was not impressed by the hardware products, but he did take an interest in the ideas of SuperSet, a foursome of software development consultants that Novell Data Systems had hired in October 1981 to network its CPM Z80 microprocessors. SuperSet and Ray shared the same networking vision. Distributed computing systems could make inroads into applications traditionally implemented on minicomputers and mainframes.

SuperSet demonstrated their newly created file server operating system at COMDEX '82 using nine networked PCs. Ray Noorda stopped by their booth to take a look. By early 1983, Novell Data Systems was reorganized as Novell, Inc., and Ray Noorda joined the company as president. It did not take Ray long to change the focus of the new company to networking. Novell introduced what would become its flagship product later in 1983. The first version of NetWare was network file server software based on the Intel 8086 microprocessor. The company quickly began porting NetWare to other vendors' hardware. SuperSet, with the help of Novell engineers, soon rewrote NetWare in 286 mode and added a variety of revolutionary system fault-tolerant features such as disk mirroring. The revamped product was demonstrated at COMDEX '85 — the same year the company went public.

## DEFINING THE FUTURE OF NETWORKING

In 1994 Ray Noorda stepped down as Novell's president and CEO, naming Bob Frankenberg as his successor. Bob articulated Novell's pervasive computing vision, defining the business of Novell as connecting people with other people and the information they need, enabling them to act on it any time, any place. This vision centers on the idea that soon the smart global network will be as indispensable and easy to access as a telephone providing a near-instant digital link to global network resources. It will be as if all businesses, from the smallest mom-and-pop shop to the largest enterprise, are branch offices of one gigantic worldwide virtual corporation.

Novell is working with other leading technology companies to build the infrastructure to fulfill this global networking vision. As the world leader in networking software, Novell has the technology, partnerships, and strategy to make the networked world a reality. Novell's strategy for forging the future of networking rests on three basic principles: build smart networks; give users network access any time, from any place; and enable heterogeneous networks to be easily connected.

To make the vision real, Novell is now creating systems and services that build the infrastructure for the smart global network; open programmer interfaces that will enable the network to integrate heterogeneous applications, systems, and platforms from all types of developers; and products that enable universal access to the global network. At the core of Novell's strategy for building a smart global network is today's NetWare 4.1, the fastest, most reliable, most scalable, and best-supported networking environment available. NetWare is the ideal platform on which to build smart network services, and the company has started with NetWare Directory Services (NDS). With more than 10 million users, NDS is quickly emerging as the *de ßΣ* standard for networks worldwide.

Other smart networking services are available alongside NDS, including file and print, security, messaging, transaction processing, licensing, management, remote access, host connectivity, database, routing, and telephony. More services will follow soon, including distributed objects and electronic commerce services. Linking today's 2.5 million separate networks into one global network community is the role of NetWare Connect Services (NCS), which became available in late 1995. Through Novell's partnerships with communications providers like AT&T, NCS will enable NetWare sites to connect their NetWare LANs securely to any other NetWare LANs, virtually anywhere in the world. Integrated Internet connections will effectively eliminate the distinction between the net and the user's LAN.

To put NetWare networks directly onto the Internet, customers are able to add a robust NetWare Internet Server that is integrated with NetWare services for the most manageable Internet connection and Web publishing system available. Today, it is hard to develop software that takes full advantage of the network and almost impossible to develop software that takes advantage of a heterogeneous network. Net2000, Novell's revolutionary new set of APIs, will remove these obstacles by giving developers a simple, universal programming interface to the diverse global network. Compatible with developers' favorite toolsets, Net2000 will make building solutions for a global network as easy as building stand-alone desktop solutions today.

As powerful as network applications will be, many people today do not need or want to use a PC. Novell's Nested NetWare extends network access and services to any device with an embedded microprocessor, regardless of its architecture. For instance, one day soon the Nested NetWare computer inside a car will notify the driver by E-mail when it is time for a tune-up. A Nested NetWare vending machine will report its daily stock levels electronically. A Nested NetWare interactive television will connect viewers to the Internet.

With the next century less than 3 years away, networks will become the principal transport medium for global commerce, content, and ideas. By the turn of the century, Novell technology will enable 1 billion connections around the world. And we will all see the biggest boom in productivity since the invention of the personal computer. Clearly, the era of the network is upon us. And Novell is already well down the road toward a world of pervasive computing that connects people with other people and the information they need — enabling them to act on it any time, from any place.

## MESSAGE HANDLING SERVICES

### Global Message Handling Services

Novell's NetWare Message Handling Services (MHS) product family provides a messaging infrastructure service. Because messaging is, by nature, a fully distributed service used on a networkwide basis, the concept of a directory is very important. NetWare Global MHS is Novell's NetWare Loadable Module (NLM)-based messaging product that includes messaging-specific directory support designed to: service environments without NetWare 4.0, integrate NetWare 3.x messaging environments with NetWare 4.0, and propagate message routing information. This approach allows NetWare Global MHS to provide the complete messaging solution customers and MHS application developers need.

NetWare Global MHS is a store-and-forward messaging technology that provides messaging and directory services to any desktop that has file access to a NetWare server (e.g., DOS, Windows, Macintosh, Unix, and OS/2), and to disconnected laptops. MHS is typically used in conjunction with such messaging applications as E-mail, calendaring, and network fax applications. Commercial third-party products include da vinci's eMAIL and Co-ordinator, Coordinate.com's BeyondMail, Reach's MailMAN and WorkMAN, Powercore's WinMail, Infinite's ExpressIT!, Notework's Notework, Futurus' Team, MicroSystems Software's CaLANdar, Campbell Services' OnTime, Castelle's FaxPress, Optus' FACSys, CE Software's QuickMail, Transend's CompletE-mail, and many others. In addition, MHS comes with a starter E-mail package, FirstMail, to enable users to get started with messaging.

Submitting a message to MHS is as easy as creating a text file with appropriate headers and giving MHS access to the new file. The simplicity of this process makes it easy for third parties to develop applications and for system integrators and corporate developers to use the messaging system. For example, an E-mail message may look like this:

```
smf-71
To: Bob Smith@marketing.acme
From: Tim Johnson@engineering.acme
Subject: Q1 Results?

Are the quarterly results in yet?
```

Once a message has been submitted, MHS determines how to route it through the messaging system. Global MHS implements various messaging protocols, including standard MHS protocols, as well as other industry standards (e.g., SMTP, SNADS, and X.400). After sending a message through the messaging system, MHS delivers the message into a file that the recipient's application may access. In addition to the messaging service, Global MHS provides a directory system for use by MHS and its applications. Access to directory information is gained by opening a shared file on the Net-Ware server containing information about individual users on the messaging system. E-mail applications typically use this information to provide point-and-click lists to the users. The naming scheme for MHS is hierarchical, as shown in Exhibit 5-4-1.

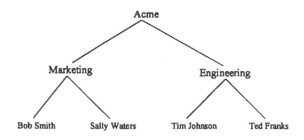

**Exhibit 5-4-1. MHS Naming Scheme.**

For example, Bob Smith's MHS name is formed from this tree: Bob-Smith@marketing.acme. The nodes in the naming tree that are not leaf nodes are called workgroups. Therefore, Acme is a workgroup that contains two other workgroups: marketing.acme, and engineering.acme. This hierarchical naming scheme allows a single unique global name for all MHS messaging users to ensure that no two MHS messaging users in the world have the same MHS name. In addition, this naming scheme is structurally identical to that in NetWare directory services (NDS) and X.500. Applications can also gain access to the directory information. They typically use this information to provide point-and-click lists to users. MHS provides this information in the form of an extract file that contains sorted records in a fixed-length format. Each record contains information about a user of the messaging system (e.g., mail address, phone number, title, and department). Directory information is shared between servers through a subscription mechanism. This mechanism is another characteristic of the NetWare Global MHS directory that logically relates to NDS functions.

The NetWare Global MHS product provides scalable, fully integrated MHS services to NetWare 3.x users. Implemented as a set of NLMs for NetWare 3.x and NetWare 4.x, NetWare Global MHS enables the network operating system to support a complete messaging infrastructure. This approach allows messaging services to be easily installed and also capitalizes on existing NetWare investments. NetWare Global MHS provides built-in directory support, routing, and workgroup-to-workgroup connectivity and it offers optional protocol modules for messaging interoperability with users on SMTP, SNADS, and X.400 systems.

Users and their associated mailboxes can be added to a server in a NetWare 3.x environment through the administrative utility in Global MHS. That server becomes the owner of that user object, and it commands the right to modify or delete the object. MHS propagates the fact that this object exists to other MHS systems by creating MHS directory synchronization messages. In addition to user information, distribution lists and workgroup information are also propagated the same way. To minimize synchronization traffic, only changes in the directory are propagated immediately. MHS also periodically synchronizes the entire directory to ensure that all servers have the same directory information (this is useful to guard against undelivered directory synchronization messages that may have resulted from servers being down for a long period of time or a loss of a communications link). Global MHS also uses directory synchronization messages to synchronize routing information, including server connectivity.

Global MHS uses the user information in the directory for routing purposes. Global MHS routing is a two-step process. The first step is to determine on which server the recipient's mailbox is located. The second step is to examine the connectivity of the network to determine the best path to that server. Messages are then routed accordingly.

NetWare 4.1 implements a variety of new services and functions. The feature that is particularly relevant to MHS is NDS. NDS implements a distributed directory database that takes over the role performed by the Bindery in previous NetWare releases. NDS's schema conforms to the X.500 international standard and is similar to the NetWare Global MHS directory. Names in the directory are hierarchical as shown in the diagram in Exibit 5-1. This is very similar to the MHS naming scheme, with the exception that NDS permits nodes in the directory tree to have a type associated with them (e.g., organization or common name).

Application programming interface (API) access to the NDS directory is broad, providing read and write access to a large number of objects, allowing for yellow-page search operations, comparison of attributes, modification to the schema of the directory, and partition management. In addition to information about users, the directory can contain information about many other types of objects, printers, devices, queues, file volumes, and more. Because the schema is extensible, other types of information can also be added.

To facilitate management of the directory, NDS divides the tree into logical divisions or partitions. The partitions may not overlap, and each node in the tree falls into a partition. Information about each partition is kept in a file on a server. The administrator determines where the master copy of the partition data resides and where replicas of each partition (if any) are to be kept. Making replicas of partitions increases the reliability of the directory and can also increase its performance. If a query to the directory is made and the currently attached server does not have the information locally, it will refer the requester to a server that does have the information. The effect of replicated partitions is similar to that of the Global MHS subscription mechanism.

## MHS Services for NetWare 4.1

Messaging is a network service that provides the basis for automatic data transfer across the network. Novell bundles its industry-standard back-end messaging server, NetWare messaging services, in NetWare 4 as a core network service. Because NetWare 4.1 messaging services are integrated with Novell's NDS, administration of the messaging environment is now accomplished using the same directory for both the network users and messaging users. The same GUI utility, NWAdmin, is used to administer both users in the NetWare 4 environment. This reduces administrative costs and overhead by simplifying management and administration of the messaging system.

MHS Services for NetWare 4.1 is an open platform supporting many popular E-mail client applications: Microsoft Mail, NetWare MHS client applications, and mail-enabled applications based on Common Mail Call (CMC), Vendor Independent Messaging (VIM), and Simple MAPI APIs. MHS Services for NetWare 4.1 is a service that exploits NetWare and Novell's other connectivity products, including TCP/IP, NetWare for SAA, NetWare Connect, and NetWare MultiProtocol Router (MPR).

NetWare MHS offers server-to-server connectivity over IPX and TCP/IP connections, plus asynchronous support for remote servers and dial-in laptops by making using of NetWare Connect clients and servers. Multithreaded operations within NetWare MHS support as many as eight concurrent asynchronous sessions.

The MHS Services for NetWare 4.1 solution exploits the multithreaded nature of NetWare for higher throughput. MHS Services for NetWare 4.1 has very low incremental memory requirements on the NetWare server (250K). Local groups of users are serviced without adding load to the backbone network. The NetWare 4.1 messaging services are fully backward compatible with the SMF v71 API, and ship integrated with NetWare 4.1 at no additional cost.

## GROUPWISE

Not long ago, a messaging system was seen simply as a means for people to exchange E-mail messages. As workgroup computing evolves, however, many agree that the right messaging system can also erase the traditional boundaries of disparate applications, multiple operating system platforms, and multiple geographical locations, thereby extending the scope of workgroup computing and making the virtual workgroup a reality. For a messaging system to provide a solid yet flexible foundation for workgroup computing solutions, the messaging system architecture must be broad enough to support both an organization's current needs as well as its future needs for the next 5 to 10 years. Its architecture must therefore embody five important design principles. The architectural foundation must include the following attributes:

- It must be elegantly simple, yet powerful enough to handle very complex solutions.
- It must be flexible enough to change and expand without affecting the workgroup applications and solutions already dependent on it.
- It cannot be dependent on a specific operating system or environment, but must be open, portable, and full-functioned while operating on multiple existing and new operating systems and environments.
- It must be powerful enough to work under multiple client/server operating models concurrently to provide the best for process load-balancing and data security needs.

- It must be robust enough to support Novell's distributed document processing architecture, as well as open enough to support other industry applications and standards.

The overall effectiveness of workgroup solutions depends in large measure on how much the underlying messaging system architecture embodies these principles. As organizations look for workgroup computing solutions, they should carefully consider both the workgroup applications and the messaging system architecture that will provide the workgroup-enabling foundation for those applications.

### GroupWise Positioning

Before explaining the details of the GroupWise messaging system architecture, it is important to position GroupWise in the workgroup software industry. Workgroup software represents a broad category of applications and services that help groups of people work together more efficiently. The depth of GroupWise encompasses several groupware categories, including electronic messaging, calendaring and scheduling, and office automation. For today's workgroup communication needs, simple E-mail is not enough anymore. GroupWise provides the messaging services required for a strong workgroup computing foundation, including the following:

- Support for multiple message types (e.g., mail messages, schedule requests, task assignments, scheduled calendar notes, phone messages, and custom messages)
- Workflow routing for collaborative work
- Full message status tracking for knowing when messages are delivered, opened, deleted, accepted, declined, or delegated, and for tracking the progress of routed messages

The open messaging environment (OME) electronic messaging strategy guides the development direction of GroupWise. The OME strategy incorporates strengths from today's GroupWise products and services and those services available in MHS. The convergence of these technologies will strengthen the already robust messaging services in GroupWise.

### Integrated Messaging Services

At the heart of GroupWise's unique design is the integration of E-mail, scheduling, calendaring, and task management services into a single application. The strategy behind this messaging service integration is twofold. First, integration of the messaging services for E-mail and scheduling eliminates duplication of back-end messaging resources, including user directories, message transport, and especially the message stores. Second, combining all of these services together under a single interface provides more consistent ease of use and reduced training costs for the end-users. GroupWise is designed to work as seamlessly in heterogeneous computing environments as in those organizations that have standardized on a single OS platform.

Bringing the messaging system to desktop applications is a major objective within the Novell electronic messaging strategy. E-mail APIs (e.g., MAPI and CMC) allow desktop applications such as word processors and spreadsheet programs to make calls directly into an API-compliant E-mail system. In other words, the desktop application has become mail-enabled. For endusers, mail-enabling means the ability to mail the documents, spreadsheets, or graphics they are working on without leaving their current applications. GroupWise brings more than just E-mail functions to the desktop application. GroupWise can message-enable an application by bringing the combined ability of E-mail, calendaring, scheduling, and task management into the applications that people use most. Message-enabling means attaching an agenda to a meeting request, routing a document for review, and checking the calendar, all without leaving the applications where users do most of their work. Message-enabling means bringing the GroupWise collaborative services (e.g., workflow routing, status tracking, and task management) to desktop applications. GroupWise does not to force people into an unfamiliar work environment, but adds messaging ability to the applications they currently use.

In addition to message-enabling applications, GroupWise provides a messaging system on which message-aware applications can be built. Although a message-enabled application uses the messaging system client to perform messaging functions, a message-aware application can directly use the message transport, user directory, and message store of the underlying messaging system. GroupWise is open enough to support the message-aware applications of the future. As organizations move up to the advanced messaging capabilities of GroupWise, they must be able to provide interoperability with existing E-mail systems (e.g., Lotus cc:Mail, NetWare Global MHS, or IBM OfficeVision/VM), including both message exchange and directory synchronization.

GroupWise gateways also provide connectivity to public and standards-based messaging systems (e.g., X.400 and SMTP/MIME) for communication outside the organization. GroupWise is designed to fit seamlessly into an organization's overall messaging system and to work well with all of its components.

As today's organizations become more mobile, people want the flexibility of not being tied down to the office workstation. An important part of the Novell GroupWare strategy is to offer the widest range of mobile computing options, giving people the freedom to access their messages and information from whatever device best suits their needs. Laptop computers, telephones, and pagers can all act as interfaces to the GroupWise messaging system.

Directory synchronization is completely automatic and an integral component of the administration program. GroupWise also supports directory exchange (import/export) with major network directories from within the administration program, as well as custom directory exchange capabilities through the GroupWise API Gateway. Administration and maintenance typically constitute a large portion of the overall cost of operating a messaging system. As additional improvements in administration and management services are developed, all GroupWare products will eventually be supported by the same administration and management platform.

## GroupWise 4.1 Electronic Messaging Architecture

This section provides a technical overview of the core engine technology and administration services that bring the GroupWise 4.1 electronic messaging system to life. Before moving on to these subjects, however, it is important to understand the basic components of the GroupWise messaging system. GroupWise is a store and forward-based messaging system. The major message handling and administrative components within the GroupWise system are the client, the post office, the Message Server, the gateways, and the domain.

The client is the end-user application. The Post Office is the directory structure on a network file server that provides the message storage area for a specific group of users. The message server is the message transport agent (MTA) within the GroupWise system that provides routing services among post offices and through gateways. The gateway is the connection and translation software for communicating between GroupWise and other messaging systems. The domain is the basic administration unit consisting of the post offices and gateways directly serviced by a message server (see Exhibit 5-4-2).

The GroupWise core engine (shared code) technology lies at the heart of the GroupWise system's simple yet powerful architecture. All GroupWise clients and message servers share the same base code or core engine. The engine, which defines the core messaging functional ability and services, was created using object-oriented design and coding methods. The core engine's object-oriented design provides unique benefits at several levels throughout the GroupWise messaging system architecture.

All GroupWise message types, including mail messages, calendar items, meeting requests, and task assignments, are defined within the core engine. In other words, all GroupWise clients and message servers can handle multiple message types, making GroupWise able to truly combine E-mail, calendaring, scheduling, and task management into the same LAN-based messaging system. Not only are the various message types defined within the engine, but so are the GroupWise messaging services (e.g., folders, rules, workflow routing, and file attachments). What this means is that all

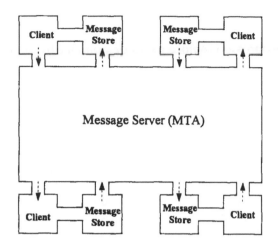

**Exhibit 5-4-2. GroupWise Message Server MTA.**

message types share the same functional ability. Some of the unique functions shared by all message types in GroupWise include the following:

- Rules-based message management applies to meeting requests, task assignments, and calendar notes as well as mail messages.
- Messages of all types are stored in the same folder structure.
- Workflow routing applies to both mail messages and task assignments.
- Files can be attached to any message type, including meeting requests and task assignments.

For example, the cross-message rules function allows users to auto-forward mail and auto-delegate meetings and tasks while they are out of the office.

### GroupWise 4.1 Message Server

The GroupWise 4.1 Message Server is the message transport agent used to distribute messages between post offices (i.e., directories and databases for message storage), domains (i.e., groups of one or more post offices), and gateways to external messaging systems. These messages can be E-mail, calendaring and scheduling requests, and message tracking. The message server also handles updates to domains and to databases within domains. The GroupWise 4.1 Message Server is available for Unix, OS/2, NetWare Loadable Modules (NLMs), and DOS. The message server is necessary for GroupWise customers who want to do the following:

- Connect two or more GroupWise post offices
- Connect two or more GroupWise domains

- Install one or more GroupWise gateways to external messaging systems
- Support GroupWise remote users or connect to remote GroupWise sites
- Provide maximum security for message transfer

Features of the message server include compatibility with all major networks, automated maintenance for UNIX, OS/2, and NLM message servers, electronic messaging capabilities, security, flexible configuration, and directory synchronization. The UNIX, OS/2, and NLM message servers automatically clean up problems encountered in the message database without any effort on the part of the administrator. When the message server finds a problem in the database, it notifies the administrator with an E-mail message describing the problem and the actions taken to resolve the problem. Because additional server threads are used for maintenance, messages continue to flow through the system while the automatic maintenance is active. The message server also provides error checking to ensure that messages are not lost in transit.

With the message server, users can communicate with other users in their organization, whether or not they are using GroupWise. They can send messages to other users in their department, building, or a distant office within a matter of seconds. With GroupWise's connectivity solutions, they can also communicate with almost any other E-mail user in the world. The message server adds security to a messaging system. If users specify secure mode, the message server will take control of all database updates. The GroupWise 4.1 Client will still have read access to databases, but will not be able to write to or delete databases.

GroupWise lets users configure their messaging system flexibly. Group-Wise provides direct links, in which message servers in two domains can directly exchange messages, and a gateway link, in which two domains are linked through another messaging system. With the message server, users can integrate the GroupWise messaging system with other messaging systems and enable communication between local and wide area networks. The message server provides simple, effective directory synchronization. When users add, modify, or delete other users, groups, or resources in one domain, the message server sends a message to all other domains informing them of the change. The other domains then handle updates to each directory. Directory synchronization is done continuously, without any effort on the part of the administrator.

The capability for both the client and message server to perform the same processing functions also offers unique load-balancing ability. The GroupWise message server includes a threshold feature that lets the administrator determine what level of processing the client should handle before turning over processing duties to the message server. For example, the client can process small transactions quickly and efficiently with no perceptible performance degradation for the end-user, while freeing the message server to process other transactions (e.g., message routing).

At the same time, a user does not want to wait for the client to process a message to all the people in a department or organization. The administrator can set a threshold that lets the client process small transactions (e.g., message delivery to one or two recipients), while passing all large transactions to the message server for processing. This load-balancing function keeps the client and message server running at maximum efficiency and improves the overall message processing speed.

An aspect of the core engine technology is the ability to support multiple processing models concurrently. For example, for single-post office systems that do not require a server for message routing, the client can perform all message-processing functions. For systems with message servers, the client and message server can share processing responsibilities, or all processing can be forced to the message server for security reasons. Each domain (i.e., message server and associated post offices) within the GroupWise system can use the client and server model that best suits that domain's needs.

Communication between the GroupWise clients and message servers is message-based (i.e., store and forward). Client/server interprocess communication (IPC) support will be implemented with OME. Although some messaging systems limit the client/server connection to one method or the other, GroupWise will offer the flexibility of using either or both. The message-based communication model provides a fundamentally simple, yet powerful design for cross-platform interconnectivity. Transaction messages are placed in a queue relative to the client's post office. The message server, which may or may not be running on the same platform as the client, can then pick up and process the transaction. All the client and message server need to work under this transaction model is network file access to the post office.

The client/server engine will also support IPC connections for those network configurations that support direct client/server protocols. In this configuration, the client will pass all transaction requests directly to the message server, which will process the requests on behalf of the client.

## GroupWise Gateways

How servers communicate and distribute messages among similar and dissimilar messaging systems is becoming a critical issue for many organizations. The need to communicate with people outside an organization's network or messaging system is driving organizations to look for far-reaching connectivity solutions. GroupWise gateways are designed specifically to provide reliable and consistent connectivity and interoperability solutions. All GroupWise gateways provide the same level of basic services and support multiple message types. In addition, most GroupWise gateways provide pass-through messaging and directory synchronization services.

Not only must a gateway connect GroupWise with another messaging system, it must also preserve the integrity of the information flowing between the two systems. GroupWise gateways must effectively handle messages that are not natively supported in other systems. For example, if a gateway connects to an E-mail-only system, the gateway is intelligent enough to convert all meeting requests and task assignments into the other system's E-mail message format without losing any of the scheduling or task information.

If the gateway is connecting to a combined E-mail and scheduling system (e.g., IBM OfficeVision or DEC All-In-One), the gateway can convert Group-Wise meeting requests into a message format that the other system understands. The gateway can also receive meeting requests from the other system. Not only is the meeting information preserved, but so is the ability to accept or decline the request. The OfficeVision Gateway also supports busy searches between the GroupWise and OfficeVision calendaring systems.

Pass-through messaging lets GroupWise connect with another physically separate GroupWise system, using a different intermediary messaging system as a transport. Pass-through messages are encapsulated in the other system's message format and then unencapsulated when they reach the remote GroupWise system. This encapsulation or tunneling preserves all messaging functions (e.g., message status tracking, attachments, priorities, and calendar-busy searches). It also maintains administrative functions (e.g., directory synchronization) between the two GroupWise systems.

Many GroupWise gateways also provide directory synchronization between GroupWise and a different messaging system. For example, the GroupWise cc:Mail Gateway automatically updates the cc:Mail directory with changes made in the GroupWise directory, and vice versa. A long list of GroupWise gateways built on the same core engine technology provides consistency of gateway functional ability, integrity of exchanged messages, and extensive connectivity to other messaging systems.

## GroupWise Administration

Administration of GroupWise software in NetWare 4.1 environments is achieved using the native NWADMIN program provided with NetWare. NWADMIN plug-in modules allow seamless administration of the Group-

Wise users and objects. The GroupWise directory will first be synchronized with, and then eventually replaced by, NDS as the directory service in Net-Ware environments. The GroupWise administration architecture supports both a central and distributed administration model. All GroupWise administration can be done centrally by a single person, regardless of system size and the location of the various system components. Administration responsibilities can also be divided among multiple administrators, each with responsibility for a specific domain.

The ability to monitor and diagnose the system is currently missing in most LAN-based messaging products. Novell GroupWise offers support for SNMP management of its message server programs. GroupWise also offers diagnostic and status reporting services with the Admin program. The administrator can monitor the heartbeat, or message flow, of the system and automatically be notified of system problems via mail message, pager, or voice mail.

### GroupWise Telephony Access Server

The GroupWise Telephony Access Server (TAS) enables users to access their personal GroupWise mailboxes remotely without using a computer. As with many messaging systems, GroupWise allows a user to gain access to his or her mailbox through a remote computer, modem, and telephone line. Although remote access to a messaging system by modem helps users be more productive and accessible, it can be limiting because not every user has access to a computer outside the workplace. Now GroupWise is leading the way into the next generation of mobile computing by giving every GroupWise user the ability to receive and send messages anywhere, anytime, using a standard touch-tone telephone.

After accessing TAS, GroupWise users can read and send messages and listen to calendar information. Users can also take advantage of extensive message search capabilities, and can even have messages or calendar information sent to a fax machine. To access TAS, a user simply calls the TAS telephone number supplied by the GroupWise administrator. TAS then prompts the user for his or her personal TAS ID and password. The Group-Wise administrator assigns the TAS ID and a numerical password. If desired, the user can change the password after accessing TAS using the originally assigned password. If a user forgets the correct TAS ID, inputting his or her first and last name will prompt TAS to give the correct ID (the user must, of course, also know the password to gain access). Once the ID and password are verified, the TAS voice presents the user with a menu of options. If the user does not respond within a specific amount of time, TAS automatically repeats instructions and gives additional assistance.

If the user chooses to hear new messages from the inbox, TAS first tells the user how many new messages there are. For each message, TAS indicates who sent the message and reads the subject line. The user can then listen to the message or skip to the next one. When listening to a message, the user has the option of listening to attachments as well. Before reading an attachment, TAS indicates approximately how long it will take to read it. The user can reply to, forward, or delete any message. For scheduled meetings, tasks, and notes, the user can also accept, decline, or delegate the message. If the user asks to listen to calendar information, TAS prompts the user to input the day and then gives the user the option to listen to the day's appointments, notes, or tasks, or to listen to all three categories combined.

If the optional GroupWise Fax/Print Gateway is installed at the user's master system, the user can instruct TAS to send any message, along with its attachments, to a fax machine. The user can also choose to have his or her personal calendar faxed in one of three formats: planner day view, trifold day view, or week view.

A user can search for a specific message by indicating the message location (e.g., in-box or out-box), the message type (e.g., mail, calendar, or both), and a key word. TAS looks for the key word in the subject, to, and from lines of all messages meeting the search criteria and reports how many matches it finds. The user can then choose to listen to just the subject or to the entire text of the matching messages.

When sending a message, replying to a message, or forwarding a message, the user simply talks into the telephone handset. TAS records the user's voice and appends the sound file to the message. To address the message, the user can input the recipient's TAS ID or the recipient's first and last name. The subject line of a TAS message is always Audio Telephone Message. A recipient can listen to a TAS message on his or her PC if it has a sound card installed, or by dialing into TAS. Users can find out if and when messages have been delivered, opened, and deleted. They can also check to see whether meetings they have scheduled, tasks they have assigned, or calendar notes they have sent have been accepted, declined, or delegated.

Administering the telephone access server is simple and straightforward. After installing the TAS software, the administrator sets up the server from within the GroupWise Admin program by providing the necessary information for software and database location, telephone line setup, and user access. To set up the telephone lines, the administrator indicates how many lines will be used and selects the language for each line. After setup and activation of the server, the administrator can disable a specific telephone line at any time to control access and perform maintenance.

The administrator can also control who can use the TAS service. Access to TAS can be granted to individual users, to an entire post office, or to a whole domain. The administrator can also specify a pattern for automatically assigning TAS IDs as users are granted access. Systems requirements users can access TAS through any standard touch-tone telephone. The TAS software should be run as an OS/2 process on the network where the master GroupWise system is installed. Although it is possible to run TAS on the same machine as the message server, it is recommended that TAS be run on a dedicated machine.

As with all GroupWise gateways, TAS requires a GroupWise message server in the master GroupWise system. The message server is the message transport agent within GroupWise and provides message routing services among post offices, gateways, and services like TAS.

## GROUPWISE 5

GroupWise 5 is a powerful new groupware product that integrates a variety of groupware functions (e.g., messaging, calendaring and scheduling, online discussions, information storage, and retrieval and workflow) into a single environment. These functions are built on a proven set of information and communications management services that provide all users in the office, on the road, or at home access to the information they need to collaborate and make decisions.

Today's organizations face an environment that grows more complex and competitive with each passing year. Organizations must do more and more work with fewer resources than ever before. As competition increases, profits and budgets come under pressure. To remain competitive and thrive in this environment, many organizations are looking for software solutions that can increase efficiency while better leveraging one of the organization's most vital resources: information.

During the last decade, software companies have done much to increase the efficiency of individuals by providing applications that let them create and process information at the desktop. Now organizations are looking to expand individual efficiency to teams and workgroups through networked applications. People and organizations are looking for improved access to information and better ways to collaborate anytime, anywhere.

### Empowering People to Act on Information

It is a fundamental truth in business: people need information to do their jobs effectively. For example, they need to know answers to the following types of questions.

- How many of part A are currently in inventory?
- What does sales think of the new marketing plan?
- How has this problem been solved in the past?

The frustrating part for many organizations is that the information people need to make sound, informed decisions usually exists somewhere in the organization if only the right people could find it, process it, understand it, and use it when they needed to. Novell GroupWare is helping organizations take advantage of their networking infrastructure to empower people to act on information anytime, anywhere. Novell GroupWare does this today by offering a family of leading-edge collaborative computing products, including GroupWise, InForms, SoftSolutions, MHS, and Collabra Share for GroupWise. Building upon this foundation of proven technology, Novell is delivering its next-generation groupware solution, called Group-Wise 5. GroupWise 5 has helped individuals, teams, and workgroups in an organization better share and act on information, simultaneously shortening and improving the decision-making cycle.

A typical workday consists of a flood of notes and faxes, voice mail and E-mail, each demanding some action be taken. Users drown in the sheer volume of information that comes in multiple forms and from multiple channels. Today's typical PC user faces a daunting information feast-or-famine situation. On the one hand, an explosion in computer use has created information overload, where users routinely face mountains of raw data without structure or context for that data. As a result, people spend too much time sorting, sifting, and processing information and not enough time acting on it.

With all of this seemingly available information, however, people at all levels of the organization are starved for the vital information they need to act to make a decision. Users must ask where the important items are located. How do users access these pieces of information, store them, communicate and manage them so they can make effective business decisions in a timely fashion? How do messaging systems increase the productivity of individuals and workgroups? And how do these systems decrease the time it takes to execute a business process? GroupWise 5 addresses this dilemma.

## Solutions to the Problem

GroupWise 5 solves this dual problem of data overload and information starvation by providing the following groupware solutions:

- A work management framework. The GroupWise 5 Desktop provides an optimized and flexible framework in which users interact with other members of a team or workgroup. The desktop offers new and powerful tools to profile, organize, share, communicate, and act on information.
- A Universal In Box to manage all kinds of incoming messages and data.
- A Universal Out Box to track all outbound messages and data.

- Shared folders to provide central repositories for all kinds of information.

From this desktop, users can access each of GroupWise 5's groupware functions, including messaging, scheduling, calendaring, documents management, electronic forms, workflow, and online discussions. Information management services of GroupWise 5 provide new and flexible tools to view corporate data, as well as a method for storing information that leads to high availability and usability. GroupWise 5 leverages existing corporate data by enabling timely access to it.

Communications management services of GroupWise 5 facilitate the movement of information among members of a workgroup without corrupting or compromising the information. Common administration and management of GroupWise 5 reduces the cost of ownership and leverages the existing network services by letting organizations manage their groupware applications and their network from a common point of administration.

**Business Solutions**

GroupWise 5 reduces the cost of ownership and leverages the existing network services by letting organizations manage their groupware applications and their network from a common point of administration. Group-Wise 5 empowers both the individual and the team or workgroup. Specifically, GroupWise 5 enables the following:

- Knowledge workers to accelerate their decision-making processes
- Enterprisewide and departmental workgroups to accelerate the execution of tasks and business processes
- Power users and applications developers to create custom groupware applications tailored to solve unique business or reengineering objectives
- System administrators to easily manage their groupware services, custom applications, and networks at the same time

GroupWise 5 can be used to solve a wide variety of information and communication challenges an organization might face, including the following:

- Leveraging existing information currently tied up in company databases and electronic files anywhere on the network
- Automating business processes (e.g., lead tracking, sales, expense reporting, and purchasing)
- Making individual and group scheduling faster and easier
- Accelerating information access for sales or support personnel
- Replacing less effective meetings with online discussions

The first components of GroupWise 5 were available in the second half of 1996; however, the foundation of GroupWise 5 is available today in the following products that are market-tested: GroupWise, InForms, SoftSolutions, MHS, and Collabra Share for GroupWise. In fact, current customers of these products have driven the requirements for GroupWise 5 described in the following sections.

### The GroupWise 5 Desktop

The GroupWise 5 Desktop gives users new tools to help them more efficiently collaborate with others, manage information, and make decisions. These new tools include a Universal In Box, a Universal Out Box, and shared folders. The revolutionary GroupWise 5 Desktop will be available on a variety of client platforms, including MS Windows, Windows 95, Macintosh, Power Macintosh, and UNIX.

At the heart of the GroupWise 5 Desktop is the Universal In Box. This in-box replaces the many competing in-boxes a typical user manages (e.g., voice mailbox, E-mail in-box, fax machine, pager) with a single in-box for all types of information. As a result, users spend less time processing in-box contents and only have to learn one interface to manage all types of incoming information. The GroupWise 5 Desktop provides a framework for how work gets done in an organization.

GroupWise 5 can help users effectively manage day-to-day work, as well as automate multistep business processes. The GroupWise 5 Desktop provides streamlined access to a complete set of groupware features (e.g., messaging, calendaring and scheduling, information storage and retrieval, and custom groupware applications). The GroupWise 5 Universal In Box accepts E-mail messages, schedule requests, delegated tasks, voice mail, faxes, pages, electronic forms, and many other types of data. The GroupWise 5 Desktop is truly unique because of the various forms of information that the Universal In Box can handle. For each of these data types, GroupWise 5 does the following:

- Maintains native attributes. For example, a voice message appears in the Universal In Box as a voice message and maintains its native attributes (e.g., caller identification)
- Profiles and manages information in the same way regardless of data type

Users can apply GroupWise 5's message-handling functions and server-based rules not only to E-mail but to all data types supported by the Universal In Box (e.g., a voice message can be sorted, delegated, routed, and copied). The GroupWise 5 Universal Out Box provides complete message tracking and user accountability. GroupWise 5 Shared Folders lets members of a team or workgroup easily share information related to a particular topic or project. At any time, users can see if messages have been received, opened, deleted, or delegated. They can even retract messages that have not already been opened. The message tracking offered with GroupWise 5 is especially important as groupware solutions are expanded to transport delegated tasks, appointments, and other workgroup activities.

Through the GroupWise 5 Desktop, users can also access information stored in shared folders. These folders let members of a team or workgroup easily share information related to a particular topic or project. Any type of information supported by the Universal In Box (e.g., messages, voice mail, documents, or faxes) can be stored in shared folders. Through the GroupWise 5 Desktop, users can access all their groupware functions. Messaging, calendaring and scheduling, task management, workflow, electronic forms, document management, online discussions, and even custom groupware applications all are available from one screen, with a consistent interface.

At the heart of the GroupWise 5 work management solution is the Universal In Box. It combines many in-boxes into a single point of entry for all types of information. GroupWise 5 dynamically links together objects of any data type received through the Universal In Box with actions taken on those objects. These links form context trails, a powerful way to preserve the relationship between information and actions. With context trails, users can act on information and relate it to tasks, scheduled items, messages, people, and documents in an intelligent way.

GroupWise 5 provides tools that enable users to streamline, prioritize, manage, and automate responses to incoming information. For example, a product development meeting scheduled in GroupWise 5 might be linked to one of the following:

- The original schedule request to attend the meeting
- An E-mail message from the vice-president citing a specific product problem
- Several complaint forms filled out by technical support
- An online discussion for where solutions for the problem have been discussed
- A voice mail recording from a particularly irate customer

Users rushing into the meeting could quickly navigate through these context trails to construct a full understanding of the situation. The GroupWise 5 Desktop provides a framework for how work gets done in your organization. GroupWise 5 can help users effectively manage day-to-day work, as well as automate multistep business processes, such as expense reporting and customer tracking. In a typical workday, users react to information as it arrives on their desktop, responding to a voice mail message, returning a response to an E-mail, delegating a task, or accepting an invitation to a meeting. The number of these demands is often so overwhelming that a day at work is not a set of planned activities but a series of interruptions. GroupWise 5 provides tools that enable users to streamline, prioritize, manage, and automate responses to incoming information, thereby allowing users to better manage interruptions and execute planned activities.

In addition, GroupWise 5 can automate the repetitive tasks associated with certain business processes (e.g., expense reporting). For example, a common expense report might flow from an employee to a supervisor for review and approval, then route to accounting for reimbursement. In this scenario, GroupWise 5 automates and expedites each individual's step in the process, as well as the process as a whole. From the GroupWise 5 Desktop, a user would fill out an intelligent expense report form that performs all calculations. The user would then drag the form onto a workflow icon that would launch the approval and reimbursement process.

The power of the GroupWise 5 Desktop applied to a typical new product development team should be considered. From a single window GroupWise 5 can automate a wide variety of business processes (e.g., sales tracking, customer support, and expense reporting) to obtain the following.

- A shared folder containing all of the E-mail and voice-mail messages, faxes, memos, and other inbound information on the current product development cycle
- An online discussion in which the new product's feature set is discussed with team members in sales, engineering, marketing, and manufacturing from facilities around the world
- Sales history information for previous products in the line

All the information needed to make product development decisions would be readily available without having to switch between programs or dig through a wide variety of sources. The GroupWise 5 Desktop gives individuals and workgroups a powerful work management model designed from the ground up with collaborative computing in mind. It does not dictate how users must go about their work. It is completely customizable and extensible to third-party applications so that users are free to choose the applications they need to shorten decision processes.

Supporting the GroupWise 5 Desktop are information management services that offer users access to all kinds of corporate data and information. The GroupWise 5 information management services allow users to view, query, store, and move corporate data while maintaining its integrity, version control, and security. Even though users are often faced with information overload, it often seems impossible to find the right information on demand — regardless of where it might be stored. In fact, estimates show that the average executive spends approximately 1 month per year waiting for information. Therefore, information management services that speed the process of finding crucial information can save time and money.

GroupWise 5 accelerates decision-making by helping users access vital information, no matter where or how it is stored. Powerful document management features based on SoftSolutions technology can search and retrieve information from native application files (e.g., word processor documents, presentations, and spreadsheets), and integrated InForms technology allows GroupWise 5 users to view and extract information stored in company databases using a familiar forms metaphor. Users can view, collect, circulate, and route information from their GroupWise 5 Desktop.

Effective communications are strategic to collaborative computing. With this in mind, Novell is delivering a robust communications infrastructure that is modular and based on industry standards. GroupWise 5 offers a wide range of background communications services, from one-to-one communications to one-to-many, to many-to-many. These services:

- Offer complete support for remote and mobile users
- Intelligently support the many types of data workgroups need to share
- Connect to external and legacy systems
- Can be scaled to meet the needs of workgroups, departments, or entire enterprises
- Feature a true client/server architecture

Like the other services provided by GroupWise 5, the communications management services support multiple data types, including not only E-mail, documents, and forms, but also voice mail, images, and faxes. And GroupWise 5 optimizes the movement of information over a network. For example, these services give users the option of downloading files or simply moving references or pointers around the network, avoiding the consumption of network bandwidth by large files (e.g., sound or video files).

GroupWise 5 communications services enable today's road warriors to take their offices with them. GroupWise 5 provides mobile users access to their in-boxes and out-boxes by way of remote client software or a standard touch-tone telephone, so they can continue to participate in the workflow of a business process when they are away from the office. In addition, remote client software lets users access data stores and participate in conferences — it even lets them take snapshots of data or forms when on the road and synchronize it when they return to the office. A user is never out of the loop, and a business process does not have to come to a screeching halt.

## SUMMARY

GroupWise 5 represents the culmination of the integration of Novell's MHS product line and its GroupWise product line. At the heart of communications services is the GroupWise 5 message transfer agent. It supports many desktop clients, including MHS SMF70/71 clients, GroupWise 4.1 clients, MAPI 1.0 clients, CMC 2.0 clients, and GroupWise 5 clients. Current

MHS and GroupWise users can easily migrate to GroupWise 5 by replacing their MTA with the GroupWise 5 MTA, moving individual mailboxes to GroupWise 5 one at a time or upgrading entire post offices.

GroupWise 5 communications management services also support popular connectivity standards (e.g., MHS, X.400, and SMTP/MIME). GroupWise 5 provides a host of gateways to a wide variety of existing messaging systems. Users can protect their investment in legacy messaging and data systems as well as connect to the external world of private and public data networks.

The foundation of Novell's GroupWise 5 product family resides in market-tested products that are available today, including InForms, SoftSolutions, MHS, and Collabra Share for GroupWise. Workgroups using these products are already on the path to GroupWise 5. They offer immediate, real-world benefits to organizations by leveraging the value of NetWare by implementing GroupWise and MHS — robust messaging technologies that capitalize on NetWare's system administration and management.

# Chapter 37
# An Introduction to Microsoft Exchange Server

*Lee Benjamin*

Microsoft Exchange Server embraces Internet standards and extends rich messaging and collaboration solutions to businesses of all sizes. As such it is the first client/server messaging system to integrate E-mail, group scheduling, Internet access, discussion groups, rules, electronic forms, and groupware in a single system with centralized management capabilities.

Microsoft Exchange Server provides a complete and scalable messaging infrastructure. It provides a solid foundation for building client/server solutions that gather, organize, share, and deliver information virtually anyway users want it. Microsoft Exchange Server was designed from the ground up to provide users and administrators with unmatched open and secure access to the Internet. Native SMTP support, support for MIME for reliable delivery of Internet mail attachments, and support for Web browsers and HTML ensures seamless Internet connectivity.

Since its introduction in the spring of 1996, customers have been evaluating and deploying Microsoft Exchange Server along with Microsoft Outlook and other clients in record numbers. This chapter offers an overview of how Microsoft Exchange Server can help organizations improve their business processes, work smarter, and increase profits through improved communication. The topics to be covered include:

- Trends in messaging and collaboration
- Infrastructure for messaging and collaboration
- Redefining groupware
- Internet connectivity
- Easy and powerful administration
- Building a business strategy around Microsoft Exchange Server

Microsoft Exchange Server is part of the Microsoft BackOffice integrated family of server products, which are designed to make it easier for organizations to improve decision making and streamline business processes with client/server solutions. The Microsoft BackOffice family includes the Microsoft Windows NT Server network operating system, Microsoft Internet Information Server, Microsoft Exchange Server, Microsoft SQL Server, Microsoft SNA Server, and Microsoft Systems Management Server.

## TRENDS IN MESSAGING AND COLLABORATION

Information, both from within organizations and from outside sources, is becoming one of the most valuable commodities in business today. Never before has so much information been so readily available. Nor have there been such high expectations for how much individuals will be able to accomplish with this information. To take advantage of this information, businesses are rethinking every aspect of their operations and reengineering business processes to react more quickly, become more responsive, provide better service, and unify teams separated by thousands of miles and multiple time zones.

Until now, organizations looking for a messaging system had two choices: either a host-based system that provided beneficial administrative capabilities but was costly and did not integrate well with PC-based desktop applications, or a LAN-based system that integrated well with PC-based desktop applications but was not scalable and was less reliable than host systems.

### Unifying LAN- and Host-Based E-Mail

Microsoft Exchange is not a response to any one single product. Rather, it is the evolution of messaging products in general. For the past 10 years, Microsoft has been a leader in LAN messaging solutions. In 1987, Microsoft released the first version of Microsoft Mail. This product was significant in two ways.

First, as a client/server implementation of messaging, Microsoft Mail was a test platform of what Microsoft Exchange Server would become. Second, Microsoft added a programming layer (API) to the product. One might say that this was the grandfather of MAPI, the Messaging Application Programming Interface upon which Exchange is built. Microsoft Mail for PC Networks now has an installed base of well over 10 million copies. Over the years, customers have told Microsoft what they wanted in their next-generation messaging system. Microsoft Exchange is that product.

Microsoft Exchange Server delivers the benefits of both LAN-based and host-based E-mail systems and eliminates the shortcomings of each approach. It integrates E-mail, group scheduling, electronic forms, rules, groupware, and built-in support for the Internet on a single platform with centralized management capabilities. Microsoft Exchange Server can provide everyone in the organization, from professional developers to administrators to end-users, with a single point of access to critical business information. It makes messaging easier, more reliable, and more scalable for organizations of all sizes.

Technology is not only changing how businesses process and assimilate information, it is affecting how this information is transferred, viewed, and acted upon. Electronic messaging plays a pivotal role in this process. The annual growth in individual electronic mailboxes is phenomenal. It has been estimated that there was an installed base of more than 100 million mailboxes worldwide at the end of 1996. Five key trends have led to this growth:

- *Growth in PC use.* It has been estimated that an installed base of more than 200 million personal computers exists worldwide. Performance increases and price decreases have expanded the demand for PCs both at home and in the workplace. In addition, the rapid acceptance of the Internet by companies as a marketing vehicle indicates that the PC has reached the mainstream for more than just recreational or business uses.
- *Adoption of the graphical user interface.* The intuitive, icon-based graphical user client interface has made E-mail applications easier to use and has made it possible to create more sophisticated messages than with previous MS-DOS and host-based E-mail applications.
- *Integration of messaging in the operating system.* As messaging functionality has been integrated into the operating system, every application has become "mail-enabled." Users are able to easily distribute documents and data from within applications without having to switch to a dedicated E-mail inbox. Messaging functionality in the operating system also provides a platform for critical new business applications such as forms routing and electronic collaboration.
- *Client/server computing.* Client/server computing combines the flexibility of LAN-based systems — for easier management and extensibility — with the power and security of mainframe host-based systems. In addition, client/server technology has made electronic messaging systems "smarter" so they can anticipate problems that previously required human intervention, thus reducing overall support costs.
- *Growth of the Internet.* The growth of the Internet is perhaps the most important platform shift to hit the computing industry since the introduction of the IBM personal computer in 1981. The most explosive expansion is expected to be in the use of Internet technologies to improve communication within organizations.

Anticipating these trends, Microsoft Exchange Server was developed to unify host-based and LAN-based environments that have historically been separate. Microsoft Exchange Server incorporates both messaging and information sharing in a unified product architecture. By taking advantage of client/server technology, organizations receive the scalability benefits of host-based environments and the flexibility of LAN-based environments.

### The Microsoft Exchange Product Family

The Microsoft Exchange product family consists of:

- The Microsoft Outlook family of clients (Outlook, Outlook Express, and Outlook Web Access) for Microsoft Exchange Server, which includes E-mail, rules, public folders, sample applications, native Internet support, rapid and easy electronic forms, and an application design environment that makes it easy for users to create groupware applications without programming. These clients are based on protocols such as MAPI, IMAP4, POP3, and LDAP. Outlook is the premier client for Microsoft Exchange Server and is available for Windows 95 and Windows NT. A version of Outlook is also available for the Windows 3.x and Apple Macintosh System 7.x operating systems. Other clients such as POP3 and Web-based clients can also access Microsoft Exchange Server.
- Microsoft Exchange Server, which consists of core components that provide the main messaging services — message transfer and delivery, message storage, directory services, and a centralized administration program. Optional server components provide seamless connectivity and directory exchange between Microsoft Exchange Server sites linked over the Internet, via X.400 or other messaging systems. Microsoft Exchange Server supports SMTP and X.400 as standards to ensure reliable message transfer for systems backboned over the Internet or other systems. It also provides outstanding NNTP (Network News Transport Protocol) and Web access and integration, enabling customers to easily access all types of Internet information.

Microsoft Exchange Server must also be a platform for an assortment of business solutions, which organizations of all sizes can implement to meet a wide range of key challenges, including:

- Making it easy for salespeople and support technicians to find product information
- Improving an organization's access to market information
- Allowing users to receive timely and accurate information regarding sales and product activity
- Making individual and group scheduling fast and easy
- Improving customer tracking

- Allowing all technicians and engineers to share common customer technical issues
- Continuing to expand the network and add new applications while maintaining complete compatibility with existing systems

## INFRASTRUCTURE FOR MESSAGING AND COLLABORATION

Microsoft Exchange Server combines the best features of both host-based and LAN-based E-mail systems with some additional benefits all its own. The result is a messaging system that is easy to use and manage and that moves messages and files through the system quickly, securely, and reliably, regardless of how many users or servers the organization has.

### Universal Inbox

The Universal Inbox in the Microsoft Outlook Client lets users keep all messages, forms, faxes, and meeting requests in one location, where they can be easily accessed. Users can search and sort these items using a wide range of criteria — such as addressee, topic, or date of receipt — to quickly locate the information they need.

In addition, server-based rules automatically process incoming messages, including those from the Internet, even when the user is out of the office. These rules can be configured to file incoming messages in appropriate folders or to respond immediately with specified actions, such as forwarding messages to another person, flagging them for special attention, or generating a reply automatically.

### Tight Integration with Desktop Applications

Because Microsoft Outlook is tightly integrated with the Microsoft Windows operating system and the Microsoft Office family of products, it is easy for users to learn and use. Microsoft Outlook actually ships with both Exchange Server and Microsoft Office 97. With new features such as "journaling" (which allows a user to find a file based on when that file was used, rather than by file name), Outlook can keep track of what users do every day.

### Fast, Secure, and Reliable

Microsoft Exchange Server takes full advantage of the robust client/server architecture in Windows NT Server to get messages to their destinations quickly, whether across the hall or around the world. It also provides tools for easily tracking messages sent to other users of Microsoft Exchange Server and via the Internet to users on other systems, to confirm that they arrived and that they were read. Support for digital encryption allows users to automatically secure messages against unauthorized access, and digital signatures guarantee that messages get to their recipients without modification.

In addition to these security features, Microsoft Exchange Server also takes advantage of the security features built into Windows NT Server to prevent unauthorized users — inside or outside the organization — from accessing corporate data.

### Remote Client Access

Local replication is the ability to do two-way synchronization between a server folder and a copy of that folder on a local or portable machine. Local replication is initiated by creating an offline folder — a snapshot or "replica" — of the server-based folder the user wishes to use while disconnected from the server. (The use of offline folder synchronization is discussed further in a subsequent section.)

### Scalable

Built on the scalable Windows NT Server architecture that supports the full array of Intel and Digital Alpha-based servers, Microsoft Exchange Server scales to meet a range of requirements — from those of a small, growing office to those of a multinational corporation.

It is easy to add users to existing servers and new servers to an organization as it grows. Routing and directory replication occur automatically between the new and existing servers at each site. Plus, optional connectors are available to connect computers running Microsoft Exchange Server to the Internet and X.400 systems.

### REDEFINING GROUPWARE

In addition to E-mail, which allows users to send information to each other, Microsoft Exchange Server and Microsoft Outlook support groupware applications that help users share information by retrieving it wherever it might be — without the traditional complexities of navigating through a maze of network servers or jumping between multiple screens and applications.

A built-in suite of groupware applications in Microsoft Exchange Server gives users a headstart with group scheduling, bulletin boards, task management, and customer tracking. Because these applications are designed to integrate tightly with the Windows operating system and Microsoft Office, Microsoft Exchange Server provides an ideal platform for integrating business solutions with desktop applications.

While some Microsoft Exchange Server applications are ready to go right out of the box, and many more are also available on the Web, you can also easily customize them using Microsoft Outlook and extend them using popular development tools such as the Visual Basic programming system, the Visual C++ development system, Java, and ActiveX components.

The concept of discussion groups and bulletin boards are nothing new to Internet users. With the Microsoft Exchange Internet News Service, the complete set of Internet newsgroups are easily available to users through public folders. Organizations can make public folder information available to internal or external users of the Web without storing information in redundant locations or manually reformatting information into hypertext markup language (HTML) format, via Outlook, Outlook Web Access, or any NNTP newsreader client. Users can also access newsgroups hosted on Exchange Server using the native NNTP protocol.

Microsoft Exchange Server also allows users to communicate with each other and to share information from any time zone or location. This is especially important for mobile users, who need to break through traditional organizational boundaries to communicate with the enterprise. Group scheduling and public folders help users work together more effectively, whether they are across the hall, across the country, or around the globe.

**Group Scheduling**

A full-featured personal calendar, task manager, and group scheduler in its own right, Microsoft Outlook has been incorporated into Microsoft Exchange Server to provide a fully extensible system that can act as a rich foundation for business-specific, activity-management applications. It takes full advantage of the advanced client/server architecture and centralized management features in Microsoft Exchange Server.

Microsoft Outlook is a tool for scheduling group meetings, rooms, and resources. To schedule a meeting, users can overlay the busy times of all the attendees in a single calendar to automatically schedule a meeting, conference room, and any other resources required. The Microsoft Outlook contact-management features provide users with easy access to the names and phone numbers that are part of their daily work.

**Public Folders**

Public folders make it easy for users to access information on a related topic all in one place. Documents can be stored in public folders for easy access by users inside and outside an organization. These folders are easy to set up without programming; relevant documents can be dragged into the folder. Microsoft Exchange Server uses these public folders as containers for groupware and custom applications.

## Bulletin Boards

Support for bulletin boards enables organizations to easily share information throughout the enterprise. Information is organized so that users can easily find what they need, leave messages, and communicate about the topic.

It is interesting to note that Internet users have been working with bulletin boards for many years using Usenet Newsgroups. Microsoft Exchange Server uses the same Internet Standard, called NNTP. Sample bulletin board folders, which are easily customizable, are included with Microsoft Exchange Server.

## Outlook Forms

Electronic forms are easy to create and modify in Outlook so users can send and receive structured information. Traditionally advanced features such as drop-down lists and validation formulas are easy to get at and use. More sophisticated capabilities are accessible from Outlook's rich programming extensibility interfaces. In addition, Outlook forms are automatically rendered to the Web so any user can get to them.

## Public Folder Replication

One of the key strengths of Microsoft Exchange Server is its ability to distribute and synchronize shared information through the Microsoft Exchange Server replication system. It is possible to have multiple synchronized copies of folders in different locations regardless of whether users are connected over a LAN or WAN, or the Internet or X.400 backbone.

Replicating information in this way means that synchronized copies of a public folder can reside on multiple servers, distributing the processing load and improving response time for users accessing information within the folder. It also means synchronized copies of a public folder can reside at several geographically separated sites, significantly reducing the amount of long-distance WAN traffic necessary to access information. If a server holding one copy of a public folder becomes unavailable, other servers holding synchronized copies of the same folder can be accessed transparently, greatly increasing the availability of information for users and resulting in a highly reliable system.

Microsoft Exchange Server offers users the unique benefit of location-independent access to shared information. With replication, the physical location of folders is irrelevant to users, and Microsoft Exchange Server hides the sophistication of public folder replication. Users need not be aware of where replicated folders are located, the number of replicated copies, or even that replication occurs at all. They simply find information more easily than ever before.

With the Microsoft Exchange Internet Mail Service users can replicate public folders and groupware applications throughout a distributed organization, even if they do not have a wide area network. Managing public folder replication is very easy. Using the graphical Microsoft Exchange Server Administrator program, system managers need only select the servers that will receive replicas of the public folders.

### Offline Folder Synchronization

Microsoft Exchange Server allows users to automatically perform two-way synchronization between a server folder and a copy of that folder on a local PC. For example, a user can create an offline folder — a snapshot or "replica" — of a customer-tracking application to take on a business trip and update it based on interactions with customers during the trip. Then, when the user reconnects to the server — either remotely by modem or by connecting to the LAN upon returning to the office — the folders can be bidirectionally synchronized with the server. Changes, including forms and views, made on the local machine are updated to the server, and changes to the server-based folders automatically show up on the user's PC. Offline folder synchronization lets users maintain up-to-date information without having to be continuously connected to the network.

Creating an offline folder is different from simply copying a server folder to the hard disk, because an offline folder remembers its relationship with the server folder and uses that relationship to perform the bidirectional update. Only changes — not the whole folder — are copied, which helps minimize network traffic.

Microsoft Exchange Server supports multiple simultaneous offline folder synchronization sessions from many different locations. Built-in conflict resolution for public folders ensures that all the changes are added. The owner of the folder is notified if there is a conflict and can choose which version to keep. With the powerful server-to-server replication technology in Microsoft Exchange Server, this information can then be automatically replicated to users of your system around the world.

### Easy-to-Create Groupware Applications

Microsoft Exchange Server delivers a scalable set of tools that lets almost anyone — even users who have never programmed — develop custom groupware applications. It also gives professional programmers all the power they need to build advanced business software systems. Microsoft Exchange Server includes these key development features for both users and programmers:

- *Fast applications development without programming.* Users can build complete groupware applications — such as a customer-tracking system or an electronic discussion forum — without programming. Assuming they have the appropriate permissions, users can simply copy an existing application (including forms, views, permissions, and rules) and modify it as they wish with the functionality available in the Microsoft Outlook Client. They can easily modify existing forms or create new ones with a menu choice to Design Outlook Form, which requires no programming knowledge.

• *Central application management.* Once users complete an application, they will usually hand it off to the Microsoft Exchange Server administrator for further testing or distribution to others within the organization. The Microsoft Exchange Server replication engine manages the distribution of the application or any new forms that may have been revised or created for existing applications. One can also replicate these applications from one Microsoft Exchange Server site to another over the Internet by using the Microsoft Exchange Internet Mail Service.

Both of these capabilities translate into reduced cycles for creating, modifying, and distributing groupware applications. That means end-users can build applications that are valuable to them without having to wait for a response from their IS departments. Even if an application turns out to be less useful than the creator hoped it would be, the development cost is minor.

The IS department can also benefit because it can customize those applications that do turn out to be worthwhile, since forms created or modified with Microsoft Outlook are extensible with Visual Basic Script programming system. In addition, Outlook Forms can be further extended with other programming tools such as Visual C++, ActiveX Controls, and Java. By using the Microsoft Exchange Server replication engine, revisions and new applications can be deployed inexpensively as well.

The speedy application design and delivery process made possible by Microsoft Exchange Server enables the people who have the best understanding of the functionality needed to respond quickly to market requirements. As a result, an organization can reduce the costs of adapting and rolling out those applications. Whenever an application is rolled out within an organization, it is usually only a matter of time before the applications developer hears from users about how it could be improved. Many applications provide limited functionality — once the barrier is reached, they cannot be customized any further and require redesign from scratch with a more powerful tool.

Thus, forms designed by end-users can be customized by professional developers using the full power of Visual Basic Script. Other workgroup application design tools either require a high degree of programming skill or quickly run out of steam, as a particularly useful application requires additional functionality. Microsoft Exchange Server opens the door between end-user application design and the full power of the Windows APIs available through more powerful programming languages.

Exchange Server takes these forms even further by automatically rendering them to the Web as HTML forms. By leveraging a technology known as ActiveServer Pages, included with the Microsoft Internet Information Server, forms and the information in them can be seen by any user accessing Exchange from a browser anywhere on the World Wide Web (if they have the appropriate permissions of course).

### MAPI: Messaging Application Programming Interface

The MAPI subsystem is the infrastructure on which Microsoft Exchange Server is built. Messaging client applications communicate with service providers running on the server through the MAPI subsystem. Through broad publication of Microsoft messaging APIs, and because of the robust messaging and workgroup functionality defined in them, MAPI has become a widely used standard throughout the industry for messaging and groupware clients and providers.

MAPI-compliant clients span a variety of messaging- and workgroup-based applications and support either Windows 32-bit MAPI applications on Windows 95 or Windows NT, and 16-bit MAPI applications running on Windows 3.x. Each of these types of applications can access the service provider functionality needed without requiring a specific interface for each provider. This is similar to the situation where applications that use the Microsoft Windows printing subsystem do not need drivers for every available printer.

Messaging applications that require messaging services can access them through any of five programming interfaces:

- Simple MAPI (sMAPI)
- Common Messaging Calls (CMC)
- ActiveMessaging (formerly known as OLE Messaging and OLE Scheduling)
- MAPI itself
- (In the near future) Internet Mail Access Protocol, or IMAP

Client requests for messaging services are processed by the MAPI subsystem — either as function interface calls (for sMAPI or CMC) or as manipulations of MAPI objects (for OLE Messaging or MAPI itself) — and are passed on to the appropriate MAPI-compliant service provider. The MAPI service providers then perform the requested actions for the client and pass back the action through the MAPI subsystem to the MAPI client.

Third-party programming interfaces that can be built upon MAPI are frequently employed. Because MAPI is an open and well-defined interface, a proprietary third-party API can be implemented on top of MAPI without having to revise the MAPI subsystem itself. Thus, customers and vendors can implement their own MAPI solutions that meet their particular needs without incurring the development costs that would otherwise accrue on other messaging infrastructures.

## INTERNET CONNECTIVITY

Extensive built-in support for the Internet in the Microsoft Outlook Clients, as well as the Microsoft Exchange Internet Mail Service, Microsoft Exchange Internet News Service, and Outlook Web Access, makes it easy for organizations to use the Internet as a communications backbone, to make Internet newsgroup data available to their users through public folders, and to make messaging and public folder information available to the ever-growing numbers of Internet Web users.

The Microsoft Exchange Internet Mail Service provides high-performance multithreaded connectivity between Microsoft Exchange Server sites and the Internet. It also supports MIME and UUENCODE (and BINHEX for Macintosh) to ensure that attachments arrive at their destinations intact. Built-in message tracking helps ensure message delivery. Standards-based digital encryption and digital signatures ensure message security.

These capabilities make it possible for organizations to use the Internet as a virtual private network to connect Microsoft Exchange Server sites over the Internet and to route messages using the TCP/IP SMTP or X.400 protocols. You can easily control who sends and receives Internet mail by rejecting or accepting messages on a per-host basis.

### Integrated Internet Support

The Microsoft Outlook Clients include built-in Internet mail standards to allow users, connected locally or remotely, to reach other Microsoft Exchange Server sites and virtually anyone else using any Internet service provider. Native MIME support allows files to be transported reliably over the Internet. Support for Post Office Protocol, Version 3 (POP3), PPP, and IMAP4 ensures compatibility with all SMTP E-mail systems.

The Microsoft Exchange Inbox — a version of Microsoft Exchange Client that does not include Microsoft Exchange Server–specific functionality — is built into the Windows 95 operating system. This feature makes Internet mail easy to set up and access. Any user with an Internet mailbox via POP3 can use the Internet Mail Driver for Windows 95 in the Microsoft Exchange Inbox. Similarly, any client that supports POP3 can connect to a Microsoft Exchange Server. Outlook Express is an Internet Mail and News Client that ships with Microsoft Internet Explorer 4.0 and supports the SMTP/POP3, LDAP, NNTP, and IMAP4 protocols.

### Direct Connections over the Internet for Mobile Users

The Microsoft Exchange Inbox and Microsoft Outlook clients can also leverage the Internet in another way — as an alternative to dialup connections.

Outlook clients and Microsoft Exchange Server both have built-in support to connect to each other securely over the Internet. Mobile users can use a local Internet service provider (ISP) to connect to the Microsoft Exchange Server site located back in their organizational headquarters. Once this connection is established, users have full access to all server-based functionality, including directory services, digital signature and encryption, group scheduling, free/busy checking, and public-folder applications.

### Support for Internet Newsgroups and Discussion Groups

As previously mentioned, the Microsoft Exchange Internet News Service can bring a Usenet news feed to Microsoft Exchange Server, from which administrators can distribute the feed to users through the public folder interface in Microsoft Exchange Server. Items within a newsgroup are assembled by conversation topic — the view preferred by most discussion group users. Users can then read the articles and post replies to be sent back to the Internet newsgroup.

Using the standard Microsoft Exchange Client Post Note feature, users can post a new article or a follow-up to an article or send a reply to the author of an article. Users have all the composition features of the Microsoft Exchange Inbox for composing posts to discussion groups. As with E-mail, however, the extent to which these composition features can be viewed by other users depends on the encoding format used.

The Internet News Connector automatically uses UUENCODE or MIME to encode outgoing and decode incoming post attachments. Thus, when users see an attachment in a post, they need only double-click and watch the attachment pop up. There is no waiting for the decoder to process the file.

### Outlook Web Access

This capability provides a different, but equally important, kind of integration with the Internet. Outlook Web Service translates the information stored in Microsoft Exchange Server folders into HTML and makes it available — at the document or item level — as a uniform resource locator (URL) to any user with a Web browser. This capability teams up with the Microsoft Internet Information Server (IIS), which hosts the URL. As a result, organizations with documents or discussions they want to make available to Web users inside or outside their organization can accomplish this without storing the information in two different places, manually changing its format into HTML, or requiring that everyone use the same kind of client.

## EASY AND POWERFUL CENTRALIZED ADMINISTRATION

While Microsoft Exchange Server offers the tight integration with desktop applications previously available only with LAN-based E-mail systems, it also offers the centralized administrative capabilities previously available only with host-based systems. Its easy-to-manage, reliable messaging infrastructure gives administrators a single view of the entire enterprise.

### Easy-to-Use Graphical Administration Program

Microsoft Exchange Server includes a number of tools that help administrators reduce administration time while keeping the system running at peak performance. The graphical Administrator program lets administrators manage all components of the system, either remotely or locally from a single desktop. Built-in intelligent monitoring tools automatically notify the administrator of a problem with any of the servers and can restart the service or the server if necessary. Microsoft Exchange Server integrates tightly with Windows NT Server monitoring tools as well, so administrators can even create new user accounts and new mailboxes in one simple step for those users.

### Information Moves Reliably

To keep the right information flowing to the right people, users need to be able to count on reliable message delivery. Using powerful monitoring and management tools, Microsoft Exchange Server helps ensure that the entire organization enjoys uninterrupted service. It even seeks out and corrects problems based on administrator guidelines. If a connection goes down, Microsoft Exchange Server automatically reroutes messages as well as public folder and directory changes, balancing them over the remaining connections. This greatly simplifies administration and ensures reliable and efficient communication.

### Microsoft Exchange Server Components

Let's take a closer look at Microsoft Exchange Server components: private folder, public information store, directory, directory synchronization agent (DXA), and message transfer agent (MTA) objects reside in the server container on Microsoft Exchange Server.

Each server installation of Microsoft Exchange Server automatically contains an instance of the directory, the information store, and the MTA. These Windows NT-based services control directory replication and mail connectivity within a site. Directory and public folder replication between sites, as well as mail connectivity between sites and with other mail systems, are controlled through the Administrator program.

**Private Folders: Central Storage for Private User Data.** Private folders provide central storage for all the mailboxes that exist on that server. Users have the option to store messages locally, but server-based private folders are recommended for security, management, and backup purposes. Synchronizing server folders to the local machine is the best of both worlds and is the default configuration for people who travel with their computer.

**Public Information Store: Centrally Replicating Global Access Store.** O n each server, the public information store houses data that can be replicated throughout the organization. Using the Administrator program to customize this replication, you can allow some data to be replicated everywhere, while other data is replicated only to key servers in each site. Data replication can be tightly controlled because rich status screens, available at all times, enable the administrator to track the replication of data throughout the enterprise.

**Exchange Directory Replication and Synchronization.** The Microsoft Exchange Server directory provides a wealth of customizable end-user information and covers all the routing information required by a server. Automatic replication of directory information between servers in a site eliminates the need to configure servers.

Directory synchronization has been perceived as the single biggest weakness in LAN-based messaging. Microsoft Exchange Server changes this perception with a process that keeps directories automatically synchronized on a daily basis. This makes it possible to communicate quickly and easily with users on a wide range of messaging systems such as Microsoft Mail for PC Networks, Microsoft Mail for AppleTalk Networks, Lotus cc:Mail, and optionally other messaging systems.

**Message Transfer Agent.** The MTA delivers all data between two servers in a site and between two bridgehead servers in different sites. The MTA is standards-based and can use client/server remote procedure calls (RPCs), Internet Mail (SMTP), or X.400 to communicate between sites.

All transport objects that enable connectivity to other sites and other mail systems reside in the Connections Container in Microsoft Exchange Server. These objects can be accessed directly through the Administrator program. The Connections Container on a Microsoft Exchange Server site houses four objects that enable site-to-site connectivity: Microsoft Exchange Site Connector, Microsoft Exchange Internet Mail Connector, Microsoft Exchange X.400 Connector, and the Remote Access Service (RAS) Connector.

## Single Interface for Global Management

All objects are created and managed through the Administrator program using the same commands. A Microsoft Exchange Server installation can be implemented using a wide range of connectivity options that are all managed through a single interface. The exchange of all site-to-site information — from user-to-user messaging to data replication to route monitoring — is handled through mail messages. This single administration infrastructure greatly simplifies management of the rich functionality of Microsoft Exchange Server.

**Microsoft Mail Connector.** The Microsoft Mail Connector, included standard with Microsoft Exchange Server, provides seamless connectivity to Microsoft Mail Server for PC Networks, Microsoft Mail Server for AppleTalk Networks, and Microsoft Mail Server for PC Networks gateways. It uses a "connector" post office that is structured as a Microsoft Mail 3.x post office. Each Microsoft Exchange Server site appears to Microsoft Mail Server as another Microsoft Mail post office. A Microsoft Exchange Server site can connect directly to an existing Microsoft Mail post office, allowing you to replace — not just supplement — an existing Microsoft Mail MTA. No additional software is required.

**Lotus cc:Mail Connector.** The Microsoft Exchange Connector for Lotus cc:Mail also provides messaging connectivity and directory synchronization. Customers can co-exist and send information easily between these E-mail systems, and then later migrate when they are ready with the Lotus cc:Mail migration tools that are also included.

**Microsoft Exchange Internet Mail Service.** The Internet has long used several E-mail standards. RFC 821 (also known as Simple Message Transfer Protocol, or SMTP) defines how Internet mail is transferred, while RFC 822 defines the message content for plain-text messages. RFC 1521 (Multipurpose Internet Mail Extensions, or MIME) supports rich attachments such as documents, images, sound, and video. Microsoft Exchange Internet Mail Connector supports all three standards. It also enables backboning between two remote Microsoft Exchange Server sites using the Internet or other SMTP systems, making it an important component for customers who rely on SMTP connectivity to communicate with members of their own organization, as well as other organizations.

**Microsoft Exchange X.400 Connector.** The X.400 Connector supports three different connectivity options — TCP/IP, TP4, and X.25 — between Microsoft Exchange Server and other X.400-compliant mail systems, and between two different Microsoft Exchange Server sites over an X.400 backbone. The X.400 Connector supports both 1984 and 1988 X.400 communication and includes support for the latest X.400 protocol, File Transfer Body Part (FTBP). The X.400 Connector also enables backboning between two remote sites using a public X.400 services, such as MCI or Sprint.

**Dynamic Dialup (RAS) Connector.** The RAS Connector object is a special-case site connector. It uses dial-up networking (also known as RAS, or Remote Access Services) instead of a permanent network connection, thereby enabling dial-up connectivity between two Microsoft Exchange Server sites. The administrator configures when the connections should be made, and Microsoft Exchange Server connects to the other site at that time. This connector is also standards-based, using the Internet Point-to-Point Protocol (PPP). The Dynamic Dialup Connector can be automatically invoked by the Internet Mail Service and the Internet News Service so companies can participate in the Internet without the added cost of a permanent connection.

## Client Support

Microsoft Exchange Server supports clients running the Windows NT and Windows 95, Windows 3.1, Windows for Workgroups, MS-DOS, and Macintosh System 7 operating systems so that users work within a familiar environment. It uses the built-in network protocol support of Windows NT Server, specifically TCP/IP and NetBEUI. In addition, its network-independent messaging protocol enables Microsoft Exchange Server to work cooperatively with existing network systems such as Novell NetWare.

You can also install and use the Microsoft Outlook Client for Windows 3.x on a Novell NetWare 3.x client running a monolithic IPX/SPX NETx, ODI/NETx, ODI/VLM, or LAN Workplace for DOS (version 4.2 or later) with no modification to the client. Microsoft Exchange clients communicate with the Microsoft Exchange Server computer by using DCE-compatible remote procedure calls, which are forwarded within an IP or SPX packet using the Windows Sockets interface.

## Manage all Components from a Single Seat

Because the connectors for Microsoft Mail, Lotus cc:Mail, the Internet, and X.400 systems all function as core parts of Microsoft Exchange Server rather than as add-on applications, they take advantage of the message routing, management, and monitoring features built into Microsoft Exchange Server. They also integrate with the administrative tools provided in Windows NT Server. By using and extending tools found in Windows NT Server, Microsoft Exchange makes use of strong authentication, provides an easy-to-use backup facility that does not require the system to be shut down to save data, and features an extensive dial-in facility that can manage up to 256 connections on a single server.

Monitoring tools include extensions to Windows NT's Performance Monitor, as well as both Server and Link Monitors that inform network administrators when there is a problem or delay in the system. Microsoft Exchange Server makes use of the Windows NT Event Log to store all types of information on the operating status of the system. This monitoring capability lets the administrator set up an automatic escalation process if a service stops. For example, if the MTA service stops, the monitoring system can be configured to automatically restart it or to notify specific individuals who can determine an appropriate action.

### Easy Migration

Built-in migration tools make it easy to convert user accounts to Microsoft Exchange Server. These tools work with the existing system and the Administrator program to copy and import addresses, mailboxes, and scheduling information from existing systems. It is also easy to automatically upgrade client software from the server. Migration tools are included for Microsoft Mail for PC Networks, Microsoft Mail for AppleTalk Networks, Lotus cc:Mail, Digital All-in-One, IBM PROFS/OV, Verimation MEMO, Collabra Share, and Novell Groupwise.

### BUILDING A BUSINESS STRATEGY AROUND MICROSOFT EXCHANGE SERVER

Businesses of all types and sizes can implement Microsoft Exchange Server as their information infrastructure. It supports all E-mail, information exchange, and line-of-business applications that help organizations use information to greater business advantage. Microsoft has worked closely with customers throughout the development of Microsoft Exchange Server to help ensure that it meets the needs of even the largest and most complex systems. The following are some common examples of how customers are implementing Microsoft Exchange Server.

### Downsizing

Many large organizations will migrate their E-mail systems from a host mainframe to a client/server system based on Microsoft Exchange Server. Microsoft Exchange Server provides the security and robust operations capabilities of the mainframe in a more flexible, inexpensive, scalable, and manageable implementation. It also includes migration tools that make it easy to move users from existing LAN-based and host-based E-mail systems.

Customers who are downsizing operations can develop applications for Microsoft Exchange Server using popular languages and development tools not applicable for mainframe computers. These customers require the flexibility that only a family of clients such as Outlook can offer.

### Connecting Multisystem Environments

Customers with multiple personal computing and network platforms can use Microsoft Exchange Server to link all their users together. Organizations can benefit from the simplified administration of having just one server and a single client interface that supports all popular computing platforms. In addition, Microsoft Exchange Server allows organizations to use the Internet as a communications backbone to connect to and share information with other geographic locations of their own organization as well as with other companies.

### Upgrading Current Microsoft Mail Systems

Many customers have built powerful messaging systems — including electronic forms and mail-enabled applications — with Microsoft Mail. All of their existing messaging investments will seamlessly migrate to Microsoft Exchange Server, allowing them to gain the new capabilities that Microsoft Exchange Server offers without losing access to their mission-critical applications already in place. Customers of other LAN shared-file system based E-mail systems will enjoy the same benefits.

The real test of Microsoft Exchange Server capabilities is in real-life business solutions. The following are just a few of the solutions that can be implemented using the Microsoft Exchange product family.

**Customer-Support Systems.** Organizations have always struggled with the costly problem of duplicating efforts because individuals do not know that others have already tackled the same issues. A customer-support system can remedy this problem by allowing support technicians to document and share their experiences and acquired knowledge with their colleagues in other support centers. This sharing helps keep organizations from "reinventing the wheel," because all employees can see and use the information and ideas generated by others. It also allows technicians to automatically route product bug reports to the engineering staff at the home office.

**Customer Account Tracking.** Providing superior customer service with distributed sales teams requires excellent communication among all team members and a shared history of customer contact. Inconsistent communication with customers is one of the main reasons companies lose customers to competitors.

An account-tracking system improves the management of customers by enabling account managers to see at a glance whenever anyone in the company has made contact with a customer account. A customer-tracking system also helps identify solid new sales opportunities and pinpoint customer problems that require immediate attention. Because many account managers travel extensively, this information must be accessible both from the office network and from remote locations such as hotel rooms, airports, or home.

**Sales Tracking.** Today, every organization that manufactures a product worries about the high cost of carrying large inventories of finished goods and supplies. A sales-tracking application can help businesses make better manufacturing planning decisions by helping sales managers and marketing executives get up-to-the-minute information, including sales volumes by region, product, and customer. This information makes it possible to identify regions or products that require special attention and to make more informed projections of demand for each product.

**Product Information Libraries.** The key to excellent customer service is providing customers with the right information, right now. A product information library application can help organizations improve customer service by providing salespeople with up-to-date, correct information.

This online library must contain a variety of interrelated information, including word-processing documents, spreadsheets, presentation graphics slide shows, E-mail messages from product managers, and, increasingly, multimedia elements such as images, sound clips, and videos. Sales reps can have read-only access to this library, while product managers at any location can change and modify those items that pertain to their particular products.

Such an electronic library of product information eliminates the need to continually distribute new printed product information to the sales force, which in turn eliminates the problem of disposing of expensive inventories of obsolete brochures and data sheets when products change.

**A Market and General Information Newswire.** Today's rapid business pace requires that managers stay in constant touch with business trends that will affect their markets and customers. A newswire application provides an easy way for employees to stay in touch with important trends, the needs of customers, and their competitors without a separate specialized application.

## SUMMARY

By integrating a powerful E-mail system, group scheduling, groupware applications, Internet connectivity, and centralized administrative tools all on a single platform, Microsoft Exchange Server makes messaging easier, more reliable, and more scalable for organizations of all sizes. Microsoft Exchange Server is also a highly extensible and programmable product that allows organizations to build more advanced information-sharing applications or extend existing applications easily, based on existing knowledge. In addition, it provides the centralized administrative tools to keep the enterprise running securely behind the scenes.

As a result, Microsoft Exchange Server can help organizations save time and improve all forms of business communications, both within and beyond the enterprise. By the time this chapter goes to press, the next version of Microsoft Exchange Server will already be available. New functionality in its clients, more integration with the Internet and Web, and greater scalability and performance are just a few of the improvements in store for customers.

Microsoft Exchange Server was designed to handle today's messaging and collaboration requirements. It is built on existing Internet standards and is designed to easily adopt new and emerging technologies to provide the best platform to its customers. Messaging is an evolutionary technology and Microsoft Exchange Server provides the foundation for any organization's messaging and collaboration growth.

# Chapter 38
# The 1996 U.S. Telecommunications Act and Worldwide Deregulation

*Keith G. Knightson*

Deregulation of the telecommunications market is under way in many countries, including the U.S., the U.K., the nations of the European Union, and Japan. This chapter examines various deregulation initiatives and the measures being taken by the 1996 Telecommunications Act to ensure fair competition among telecommunications companies.

## DEREGULATION AND COMPETITION

There is a big difference between deregulation and the practical establishment of a competitive market. The term *deregulation* usually means the elimination of a monopoly in a public market. The dominant carrier who held the monopoly before deregulation is often referred to as the incumbent.

The intent of deregulation is to create an open and competitive market. The problem in actually creating such competition is the difficulty that newcomers (i.e., new entrant carriers) have in competing with a well established incumbent. Unless this problem is addressed, deregulation may not result in competitive supply, and incumbents will retain *de facto* monopoly positions.

The initiatives being undertaken by the various national regulatory authorities, including the Federal Communications Commission (FCC), are concerned with the practical aspects of establishing an open marketplace subsequent to actual deregulation.

0-8493-9965-3/99/$0.00+$.50
© 1999 by CRC Press LLC

## PROBLEMS WITH DEREGULATION

Many countries have been deregulated for years — the U.S. since 1974, the U.K. since 1983, and Japan since 1985. The European Union has set a target date of 1998 for a fully open European market. Many countries that have been deregulated for some time have, based on their experiences, instituted new telecommunications acts or amendments.

In most cases, the original basis for interconnection between competing organizations depended solely on bilateral negotiations between the parties concerned. In all cases, the various national regulatory bodies usually retain the power to arbitrate and issue orders when negotiations between an incumbent carrier and a new entrant carrier fail to reach an agreement. This hands-off approach has led to:

- Protracted interconnection negotiation periods.
- Anticompetitive practices.
- Lack of free and fair conditions for potential new entrant carriers and their suppliers.

This situation is part of the natural process of developing competition. Drastic changes, such as those involved in moving from a total monopoly to fair competition, are bound to produce unforeseen consequences and associated growing pains.

Incumbents, even if forced by license or statute, do not voluntarily grant interconnection to competing network operators. Without regulatory arbitration, negotiations simply break down. The Ministry of Posts and Telecommunications in Japan and OFTEL, the national regulator in the U.K., have learned this lesson from experience. The new 1996 US Telecommunications Act addresses these issues.

## THE 1996 U.S. TELECOMMUNICATIONS ACT

The 1996 Telecommunications Act and the accompanying FCC commentary were published in August 1996. The principle goals of the act include:

- Opening the local exchange and exchange access markets to competitive entry.
- Promoting increased competition in telecommunications markets that are already open to competition, including the long- distance services market.

The act directs the FCC and its state colleagues to remove not only statutory and regulatory impediments to competition, but also the operational impediments. Incumbents are mandated to take steps to open their networks to competition, including providing interconnection and offering access to unbundled elements of their networks.

## Interconnection

The FCC identifies a minimum set of five technically feasible points at which incumbent local exchange carriers (LECs) must provide interconnection, including:

- The line side of a local switch.
- The trunk side of a local switch.
- The trunk interconnection points of a tandem switch.
- Central office cross-connect points.
- Out- of-band signaling facilities, such as signaling transfer points, necessary to exchange traffic and access call-related data bases.

In addition, the point of access to unbundled elements also is technically a feasible point of interconnection. The FCC also anticipates and encourages parties, through open, multilateral negotiation and arbitration, to identify additional points of technically feasible interconnection.

## Unbundled Access

Section 251 of the Telecommunications Act also requires LECs to provide access to network elements on an unbundled basis at any technically feasible point, including:

- Local loops.
- Local and tandem switches (including all vertical switching features provided by such switches).
- Interoffice transmission facilities.
- Network interface devices.
- Signaling and call- related data base facilities.
- Operations support systems functions.
- Operator and directory assistance facilities.

Section 251 also states that the commission will consider, at a minimum, whether:

- Access to such network elements is necessary.
- The failure to provide access to such network elements would impair the ability of the telecommunications carrier seeking access to provide the service that it intends to offer.

The lack of a clear standard is not sufficient reason to deny access. Public standardization at agreed-upon interface points are in the interests of all parties.

**Local Loop.** A local loop situation can be quite complex because of the variety of transmission techniques and concentration points. However, the FCC requires incumbents to provide access regardless of technology or concentration. Thus, this requirement embraces integrated digital loop carrier (IDLC), two- wire and four- wire voice grade loops, and two-wire and four-wire voice grade loops conditioned to provide such services as integrated services digital networks (ISDN), asynchronous digital subscriber lines (ADSL), high bit-rate digital subscriber lines (HDSL), and DS1- level signals.

IDLC carries aggregated loop traffic from the point of concentration in the LEC's loop facilities directly to the switch via a multiplexed circuit. ADSL provides a high-speed downstream data path, a medium-speed upstream data path, and an analog voice path. HDSL provides 768K-bps data over two-wire and 1.544M bps over four-wire. Therefore, the granularity of unbundling is clearly an important issue.

On the question of this granularity, the FCC declines to define a loop in terms of specific elements or functions, relying on the fallback position of "technically feasible points." However, that raises the subject of subloop unbundling, which would provide carriers with access at various points along the loop between the local exchange and the customer premises. Additionally, this would enhance competition because the competitor would only need to purchase loop facilities that they could not provide over their own feeder infrastructure.

## COORDINATING INTERCONNECTIVITY

The FCC will monitor the mechanics of achieving the desired level of interconnection and unbundling. Nondiscriminatory access to public telecommunications networks will be established through:

- Planning and design of coordinated public telecommunications networks.
- Ensuring public telecommunications network interconnectivity.
- Ensuring the ability of users and information providers to seamlessly and transparently transmit and receive information between and across telecommunications networks.

The Telecommunications Act states that the FCC can participate, in conjunction with the appropriate industry standards-setting organizations, in the development of interconnectivity standards that promote access to:

- Public telecommunications networks used to provide telecommunications service.
- Network capabilities and services by individuals with disabilities.
- Information services by subscribers of rural telephone companies.

The Network Reliability and Interoperability Committee was established under this mandate.

**Network Reliability and Interoperability Committee (NRIC)**

The charter of NRIC, set by the FCC, is to ask the council to provide recommendations for the FCC and for the telecommunications industry that will ensure optimal reliability, interoperability, and accessibility to public telecommunications networks. The objective of the recommendations is to ensure that users and information providers can seamlessly transmit and receive information between and across telecommunications networks. The charter asks the council to continue to report on the reliability of public telecommunications networks. The NRIC has organized two working groups to gather and analyze information.

**Focus Group 1.** The council has organized focus group 1 to identify technical and engineering barriers to network accessibility and interconnectivity and to identify ways to eliminate them. Focus group 1 documents and evaluates the processes by which coordinated network planning and design occur, and will evaluate options for optimizing these processes. The group considers security issues and methods by which the FCC could oversee coordinated network planning. The FCC will provide focus group 1 with conferencing resources, including a Web site, so that it can make work files available electronically.

**Focus Group 2.** Focus group 2 assesses the effectiveness of the standards-setting process and determines what role is most appropriate for the FCC. Focus group 2 uses conference resources provided by Committee T-1, an ANSI-accredited standards development organization sponsored by the Alliance for Telecommunications Industry Solutions, to make work files available.

**Task Groups**

Four task groups have been established within focus group 1 to address planning, implementation, operations, and user interoperability.

**Task Group 1 — Planning.** Task group 1 addresses the issue of planning by:

- Identifying the differences between planning for network architectures and network implementations.
- Identifying the differences between the planning of national and regional services.
- Examining the transition of architectures, products, and services from a proprietary to a public status.
- Evaluating the impacts that protecting competitive information has on the planning and design of products and services.
- Examining timing issues relative to matching the availability of network products and services.
- Developing a recommendation on the FCC's role for coordinated network planning.

**Task Group 2 — Implementation.** Task group 2 addresses implementation issues by:

- Monitoring information sharing.
- Monitoring the interconnection environment.
- Acting as an industry liaison to improve implementation processes.

**Task Group 3 — Operations.** Task group 3 addresses issues of operations by:

- Investigating operations systems access (i.e., functionality, interfaces, security, reliability, and measurements).
- Overseeing performance monitoring.
- Determining security requirements (i.e., ID authorization, auditing, access control, partitioning, and measurements).
- Investigating signaling (i.e., congestion control, interoperability, reliability, synchronization, and security).
- Confirmation of interoperability by testing and certification.

**Task Group 4 — User Interoperability.** Task group 4 monitors interoperability by ensuring that:

- There are increased interconnections.
- There are Internet interconnections.
- Asynchronous transfer mode service is available to users.
- There are service interconnection definitions.
- There are adequate standards for vendor compatibility.

## WORLDWIDE DEREGULATION ACTIVITIES

### Japan's Interconnection Rules

The Telecommunications Council Report indicates that the bilateral negotiation process in Japan has been plagued by problems. Negotiations for frame relay service and virtual private networks service between long-distance new common carriers and Nippon Telegraph and Telephone Corp. (NTT) have taken an unduly long period of time. Thus, interconnection between suppliers with essential facilities, such as NTT's local communications network and other suppliers, has become a very important issue to a telecommunications policy dedicated to fair and effective competition.

As a consequence, the Japanese government created the "Deregulation Action Program" to clarify the basic rules for interconnection to the NTT local communications network. Japan recently established a "set points of interconnection" very similar to those enumerated in the 1996 U.S. Telecommunications Act.

### Europe's Open Network Provision

The European community created a directive to establish the internal market for telecommunications services through an open network provision (ONP). The directive states that ONP should include harmonized conditions with regard to:

- Technical interfaces, including the definition and implementation of network termination points.
- Usage conditions, including access to frequencies.
- Tariff principles.

The requirements are published in the ONP standards list. This list is divided into those elements that are formally referenced (i.e., mandatory in the context of ON) and those still considered voluntary. These are known as the reference list and the indicative list, respectively.

The European Telecommunications Standards Institute (ETSI) is the driving force in the development of telecommunications standards for Europe. The ONP mandates ETSI to produce standards to meet its evolving requirements. Most ETSI standards are equivalent to or extensions of international standards.

### The U.K. — A Framework for Action

The UK established two methods of addressing anticompetitive behavior.

First, generic interconnection regimes will be set up, as opposed to case-by-case interconnection conditions. Second, all deliberations will take place in the public domain because:

- Publication of cases will promote better understanding of policies and the interpretation of license conditions and legislative provisions, and of what is considered to be conduct or circumstances requiring enforcement or remedial action.
- Publicity of cases in which companies were uncooperative and acted unfairly may discourage others from following suit.

### SUMMARY

Countries experiencing deregulation concur that a framework based solely on bilateral negotiations between carriers does not function effectively and that something more needs to be done to level the playing field.

New initiatives are being taken in many regions around the world to address network interconnection in a more generic, consistent, and controlled way. The new provisions for interconnection within the recent 1996 US Telecommunications Act, the European Community's Open Network Provision Directives, and Japan's Basic Rules for Interconnection are ample evidence of worldwide efforts to reintroduce regulation based on collaboration and consensus.

Typically, these initiatives have two major components:

- The establishment of formal points of interconnection.
- The identification of standards to be used at the points of interconnection.

To offset discriminatory practices, the U.S. and Japan enumerated a preliminary minimum set of obligatory interconnection points and accessible network elements selected from an unbundled architecture. Europe appears to be heading in the same direction.

The 1996 US Telecommunications Act and the new activities initiated by the FCC will be of great benefit to the consumer in offering a wider choice of services and suppliers at a lower cost. However, there is still a considerable way to go before a truly open and fully competitive environment will be realized.

# Section VI
# The Internet
# and Internetworking

In this section we will focus our attention upon two of the most rapidly evolving areas in the field of communications, the network of interconnected networks known as the Internet and the application of Internet technology for private networks. Although the Internet has its origin in research sponsored by the United States Department of Defense, today it represents a rapidly growing commercial communications medium which delivers electronic mail, advertising, and on-line sales. The importance of the Internet can be judged by advertisements in print and on radio and television, with most advertisers now placing their Web address in their commercials. The rapid introduction of new technologies for supporting Internet applications resulted in many private networks adopting multimedia, electronic mail, real-time audio, and other Internet developed technologies. This in turn facilitates the operation of private networks which can take advantage of the economics of scale associated with the development of technologies oriented towards the large customer base on the Internet. Recognizing the importance of the Internet as both an information delivery and sales mechanism along with its role in providing technologies for use on private networks, this section contains 13 chapters selected to provide us with detailed information covering different aspects of the Internet and internetworking.

The first chapter in this section, "The Internet Engineering Task Force," provides us with detailed information on the evolution of the Internet, how Internet standards are developed, and the role of different Internet working groups whose efforts facilitate interoperability and security. After obtaining a solid overview of the role of the Internet Engineering Task Force, the second chapter in this section introduces us to the legal environment of the Internet. In this chapter, "The Legal and Regulatory Environment of the Internet," we are introduced to the applicability of contract law, intellectual property rights, torts and negligence, and criminal law as they apply to the Internet. This chapter also discusses the need for system administrators to place appropriate notices and disclosures on their systems, and describes strategies you should consider to ensure your effort in the monitoring and control of your system does not turn into a legal problem.

Prior to Windows 95 most persons had to purchase a TCP/IP protocol stack in order to use FTP or a Web browser. Since the introduction of Windows 95 with its built-in TCP/IP protocol stack and the availability of numerous freeware stacks for other operating systems, we tend to view TCP/IP as free. In the third chapter in this section, "The Hidden Cost of Free TCP/IP," we will examine the critical issues associated with the use of free TCP/IP software and obtain an appreciation for the cost of support, network management, and updates that may make free software an expensive proposition.

Although the Internet can be used for transferring files, sending audio and video information, and countless other activities, the key component that provides this capability is the Internet server. In a series of three chapters in this section we will examine how to choose and equip an Internet server, its support requirements, and methods required to ensure your Internet connection rate provides an appropriate level of access to your Web server.

The fourth chapter in this section, "Choosing and Equipping an Internet Server," describes how to select an Internet server and the application software which provides it with its capability. The fifth chapter, "Supporting a Web Site," introduces us to the communications link, hardware platform, software, and personnel issues that must be examined. In concluding our server examination the sixth chapter in this section, "Selecting a Web Server Connection Rate," illustrates the calculations necessary to determine the speed of the connection from your Internet Service Provider to the LAN containing your Web server such that the guesswork associated with connecting a Web server to the Internet is eliminated.

Recognizing the importance of security, five chapters are included in this section to provide you with information concerning the type of illegal activity you can expect to encounter and methods to protect your organization's computational facilities from those threats. In the seventh chapter, "Criminal Activity on the Internet," we will become acquainted with the legal and ethical aspects of many types of Internet criminal activities. The eighth chapter, "An Introduction to Internet Security and Firewall Policies," provides us with information concerning the protection of traffic on a network via the use of a firewall. This chapter is followed by the chapter titled "Firewalls: An Effective Solution for Internet Security." This ninth chapter expands our knowledge concerning the use of firewalls as a security mechanism and acquaints us with their selection factors. Thus, that chapter provides a lead-in to the tenth chapter in this section, "Selecting an Internet Firewall." This chapter provides a detailed examination of the different functions and features vendors incorporated into this category of communications equipment as well as the cost and support issues you should consider to obtain a device that satisfies your organization's security requirements. In concluding this 'section within a section' focused on Internet security, the chapter "A New Security Model for Networks and the Internet" reviews basic security issues and introduces type enforcement as a mechanism for establishing data security.

In concluding this section we will turn our attention to the application of Internet technology for facilitating private network operations. The twelfth chapter in this section, "An Intranet Primer," introduces us to the benefits of intranets and their challenges in terms of management, data integrity, security, maintenance, and development. In the last chapter in this section, "Virtual Networking Management and Planning," we will examine the issues that must be evaluated to ensure the use of a virtual network provides the level of performance necessary for satisfying organizational requirements.

# Chapter 39
# The Internet Engineering Task Force

*Gary C. Kessler*

The key to the success of communication over the Internet is the use of a standard set of protocols, based on transmission control protocol/Internet protocol (TCP/IP). The Internet Engineering Task Force (IETF) is the group that oversees the Internet standards process. This chapter focuses on the history of the IETF, its organization and function, and its role in developing Internet security specifications.

The Internet is one of the best success stories of anarchy or socialism in modern history. The Internet has proven to be an example of cooperation between countries, commercial entities (often in competition with each other), government agencies, and educational institutions for the sole purpose of enhancing communication. Yet, even this loose cooperative requires some central administrative authority for such things as operational guidelines, protocol specifications, and address assignment.

The key to the success of communication over the Internet is the use of a standard set of protocols, based on the transmission control protocol/Internet protocol (TCP/IP). The Internet Engineering Task Force (IETF) is the group that oversees the Internet standards process. This chapter focuses on the history of the IETF, its organization and function, and, in particular, its role in developing Internet security specifications.

## THE EVOLVING ADMINISTRATION OF THE INTERNET

The Internet began as a project funded by the U.S. Department of Defense (DoD) as an experiment in the use of packet switching technology. Starting with only four nodes in 1969, the Advanced Research Projects Agency network (ARPANET) spanned the continental United States by 1975 and expanded to other continents by the end of the 1970s.

0-8493-9965-3/99/$0.00+$.50
© 1999 by CRC Press LLC

In 1979, the Internet Control and Configuration Board (ICCB) was formed. The charter of the ICCB was to provide an oversight function for the design and deployment of protocols within the connected Internet. In 1983, the ICCB was renamed as the Internet Activities Board (IAB). With a charter similar to that of the ICCB, the IAB evolved into a full-fledged *de facto* standards organization, dedicated to ratifying standards used within the Internet. The chairman of the IAB was called the "Internet Architect." This individual's primary function was to coordinate the activities of numerous task forces within the IAB, each of which focused on a specific architectural or protocol issue.

In 1984, the ARPANET was split into two components: the ARPANET, which was used for research and development, and MILNET, which carried unclassified military traffic. With this division, the designation of TCP/IP as the official protocol suite, and subsequent National Science Foundation (NSF) funding, the modern Internet was born.

In 1986, the IAB was reorganized to provide an oversight function for a number of subsidiary groups. The Internet Research Task Force (IRTF) was put into place to oversee research activities related to the TCP/IP protocol suite and the architecture of the Internet. The activities of the IRTF are coordinated by the Internet Research Steering Group (IRSG). The IETF was formed to concentrate on short-to-medium term engineering issues related to the Internet.

The U.S. Internet had historically received funding from government agencies, such as the DoD, the Department of Energy, the National Aeronautics and Space Administration (NASA), and the NSF. By the end of the 1980s, it became apparent that this funding would decrease over time. In addition, the introduction of commercial users and an increasing number of commercial Internet service providers foreshadowed the loss of a dominant central administration that, in turn, threatened the long-term process for making Internet standards.

### The Internet Society

In January 1992, the Internet Society (ISOC) was formed with a charter of providing an institutional home for the IETF and the Internet standards process. ISOC provides a number of services in support of this role, including sponsoring conferences and workshops and raising funds from industry, government, and other sources. Although headquartered in the United States, the ISOC is an international organization providing administrative support for the international Internet. Included in this administrative structure is the IAB, IETF, IRTF, and the Internet Assigned Number Authority (IANA).

To reflect its new role as a part of ISOC, the Internet Activities Board was renamed the Internet Architecture Board in June of 1992. ISOC provides support for the IETF and IRTF, as they have historically been a part of the IAB.

The relationship between ISOC and the IETF has changed slightly each year, as they determine exactly what their relationship should be. In June 1995, the ISOC Board of Trustees confirmed that its primary goal remains to "keep the Internet going." It is still committed to providing services that facilitate the standards process as carried out by the IETF.

## INTERNET ENGINEERING TASK FORCE OVERVIEW AND CHARTER

The IETF provides a forum for working groups to coordinate technical developments of new protocols. Its most important function is the development and selection of standards within the Internet protocol suite.

When the IETF was formed in 1986, it was a forum for technical coordination by contractors for the U.S. Defense Advanced Research Projects Agency (DARPA) working on the ARPANET, Defense Data Network (DDN), and Internet core gateway system. Since that time, the IETF has grown into a large open international community of network designers, operators, vendors, and researchers concerned with the evolution of the Internet architecture and the smooth operation of the Internet.

The IETF mission includes:

- Identifying, and proposing solutions to, operational and technical problems in the Internet.
- Specifying the development or usage of protocols and the near-term architecture to solve technical problems for the Internet.
- Facilitating technology transfer from the IRTF to the wider Internet community.
- Providing a forum for the exchange of relevant information within the Internet community between vendors, users, researchers, agency contractors, and network managers.

Exhibit 1 shows the general hierarchy of the IETF.

Technical activity on any specific topic in the IETF is addressed within working groups, which are organized roughly by function into nine areas. Each area is led by one or more Area Directors, who have primary responsibility for that one aspect of IETF activity. Together with the Chair of the IETF, these technical directors compose the Internet Engineering Steering Group (IESG).

The IAB is a technical advisory group of the Internet Society. Its responsibilities include:

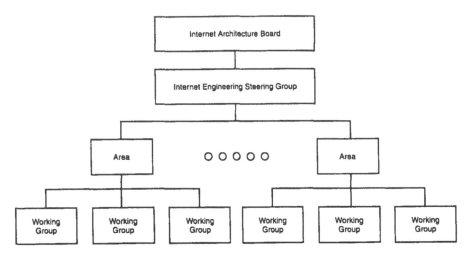

**Exhibit 1. Internet Engineering Task Force Organization.**

- *IESG Selection:* The IAB appoints a new IETF Chair and all other IESG candidates, from a list provided by the IETF Nominating Committee.
- *Architectural Oversight:* The IAB provides oversight of the architecture for the protocols and procedures used by the Internet.
- *Standards Process Oversight and Appeal:* The IAB provides oversight of the process used to create Internet Standards. It also serves as an appeal board for complaints of improper execution of the standards process.
- *RFC Series and IANA:* The IAB is responsible for editorial management and publication of the Request for Comments (RFC) document series and for administration of the various Internet assigned numbers.
- *External Liaison:* The IAB acts as a representative of the interests of the Internet Society in liaison relationships with other organizations concerned with standards and other technical and organizational issues relevant to the worldwide Internet.
- *Advice to ISOC:* The IAB acts as a source of advice and guidance to the Board of Trustees and Officers of the Internet Society concerning technical, architectural, procedural, and, where appropriate, policy matters pertaining to the Internet and its enabling technologies.

## INTERNET ENGINEERING TASK FORCE STRUCTURE AND INTERNET STANDARDS PROCESS

The IETF provides a central focus for technical aspects of the Internet. The work is undertaken by a number of functional areas, as seen in Exhibit 2,

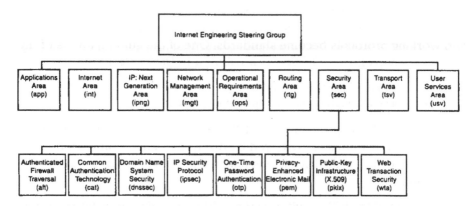

**Exhibit 2. Internet Engineering Steering Group, IETF Areas, and Security Area Working Groups.**

within the IETF that have general responsibilities and the areas are comprised of individual working groups (WGs) with specific tasks.

The WGs form the backbone of the IETF. Each WG is formed with a relatively narrow focus, rather than looking at large problems. In addition, the WGs usually start with or quickly define a limited number of options by which to achieve their goals. When formed, each WG defines a charter with a specific set of goals and milestones. Each WG also maintains an Internet electronic mail discussion list and an online archive.

The working groups conduct business during IETF plenary meetings, meetings outside of the IETF, and through electronic mail. The IETF holds week-long plenary sessions three times a year. These meetings include working group sessions, technical presentations, network status reports, working group reports, and an open IESG meeting. Proceedings of each IETF plenary are published, which include reports from each area, each working group, and each technical presentation as well as a summary of all current standardization activities. Meeting reports, working group charters and mailing list information, and general information on current IETF activities are available online through anonymous file transfer protocol (FTP) and the World Wide Web (WWW).

Unlike most other "standards" groups, the plenary sessions and proceedings are not the only place where important work is accomplished and documented. Most final decisions are made through E-mail or, at the very least, are circulated by E-mail. One reason for this apparent looseness is that WG meetings and discussions are open to anyone within the Internet community (which includes just about everyone) with something to contribute.

In another departure from other standards groups, the IETF WGs do not require unanimity before progressing with work. Furthermore, only proven and working protocols become standards. One of the guiding forces of the Working Groups is the IETF Credo, attributed to David Clark:

> We reject kings, presidents, and voting.
> We believe in rough consensus and running code.

The effect of this principle is that there is no formal voting within the WGs. Instead, disputes are resolved by discussion and demonstrations of working models. These discussions take place at the plenaries and on the discussion lists.

The result of the WG activities is the publication of various Internet documents. The IETF publishes two types of documentation:

- *Internet-Drafts.* An Internet-Draft (ID) is a working document, and is referred to as a "work in progress." IDs have no official status and expire after six months; they are not archived beyond their expiration date. The IETF Secretariat distributes the announcement for new Internet-Drafts.
- Request *for Comments.* Requests for Comments (RFCs) are the literature of the Internet. In particular, they are the series of documents that provide an historical record of the IAB. RFCs are edited, assigned a number, and announced by the RFC Editor. The four categories of RFC are:
  - *Historic,* which refers to an RFC that is important for historic purposes, but is unlikely to become (or remain) an Internet standard either due to lack of interest or because it has been superseded by later work. Examples include the Common Management Information Services over TCP/IP (CMOT) specification (RFC 1189) and the Border Gateway Protocol version 3 (BGP-3; RFCs 1267 and 1268).
  - *Experimental,* referring to an RFC that describes experimental work related to the Internet that is not a part of an operational service offering. Examples are the Stream Protocol Version 2 (ST2; RFC 1819)and Unsolicited Address Resolution Protocol (UNARP) (RFC 1868).
  - *Informational,* which refers to RFCs that provide general, historical, and tutorial information for the Internet community; these are usually produced by a standards organization or other group or individual outside of the IESG. Examples are the Novell IPX Over Various WAN Media (IPXWAN) specification (RFC 1634) and A Primer on Internet and TCP/IP Tools (RFC 1739).
  - *Standards Track,* referring to RFCs that are intended to become Internet standards.

The Standards Track RFCs contains three classes:

1. A *Proposed Standard* is a complete, credible specification that has a demonstrated utility for use on the Internet. A Proposed Standard has an expiration date from between six months and two years of the publication date, by which time it must be elevated to a higher status, updated, or withdrawn.
2. A *Draft Standard* is written only after there have been several independent, interoperable implementations of a specification. Draft Standards usually reflect some limited operational experience, but indicate enough knowledge that the specification seems to work well. A Draft Standard has an expiration date from between four months and two years of the publication date, by which time it must be moved to a different status, updated, or withdrawn. Examples are the HyperText Markup Language (HTML) version 2 (RFC 1866) and Relative Uniform Resource Locators (URLs; RFC 1808).
3. An *Internet Standard* is "the real thing" and refers to specifications with demonstrated operational stability; examples are IP (RFC 791; also known as STD 5) and TCP (RFC 793; also known as STD 7). An RFC can stay as a Standard forever or may be reclassified as Historic.

## INTERNET ENGINEERING TASK FORCE SECURITY AREA WORKING GROUPS

The IETF Security Area (SEC) is comprised of eight working groups, as shown previously in Exhibit 2. Each working group has its own charter, goals, major accomplishments, and publications. As shown in Exhibit 3, each WG also maintains an Internet discussion list, where most of its work is done, as well as an on-line file archive. Additional up-to-date information about the WGs, including a list of area directors and WG chairs, can be found in the archive.

### Authenticated Firewall Traversal Working Group

The Authenticated Firewall Traversal (AFT) Working Group is chartered to specify a protocol for application-layer support for firewall traversal. The working group intends to specify a traversal protocol supporting both TCP and user datagram protocol (UDP) applications with a general framework for authentication of the firewall traversal. To promote interoperability, the group also proposes a base authentication technique for use within the general authentication framework.

The output of the AFT WG consists of one or more Standards Track RFCs describing the traversal protocol, the base authentication methods, and a reference implementation of the protocol. The working group's initial work along these lines was the design and Internet-Draft specification of the SOCKS protocol and authentication methods in late 1994.

**Exhibit 3. Security Area Working Group Mailing List and Archive Information**

| Working Group | General Discussion | Archive |
|---|---|---|
| Authenticated Firewall Traversal | aft@unify.com | ftp://ftp.unify.com/ietf/aft |
| Common Authentication Technology | cat-ietf@mit.edu | ftp://bitsy.mit.edu/cat-ietf/archive/ |
| Domain Name System Security | dns-security@tis.com | ftp://ftp.tis.com/pub/dns-security |
| IP Security Protocol | ipsec@ans.net | ftp://ftp.ans.net/pub/archive/ipsec |
| One Time Password Authentication | ietf-otp@bellcore.com | ftp://ftp.bellcore.com/pub/ietf-otp/archive |
| Privacy-Enhanced Electronic Mail | pem-dev@tis.com | pem-dev-request@tis.com |
| Public-Key Infrastructure (X.509) | ietf-pkix@tandem.com | ftp://ftp.tandem.com/ietf/mailing-lists/current |
| Web Transaction Security | www-security@nsmx.rutgers.edu | http://www-ns.rutgers.edu/www-security |

*Note:* To subscribe to these discussion lists (other than pkix), send an E-mail message to listname-request with the word subscribe in the message body. To subscribe to the pkix list, send a message to listserv@tandem.com and place subscribe your_E-mail ietf-pkix in the message body.

**Common Authentication Technology Working Group**

The Common Authentication Technology (CAT) Working Group has a charter to define strong authentication mechanisms for a variety of protocol callers in such a way that the specifics of the underlying security mechanisms are transparent to those callers. By separating security implementation tasks from the tasks of integrating security data elements into caller protocols, those tasks can be partitioned and performed separately by implementers with different areas of expertise. This provides leverage for the IETF community's security-oriented resources and allows protocol implementers to focus on the functions that their protocols are designed to provide, rather than on characteristics of security mechanisms. The CAT WG seeks to encourage uniformity and modularity in security approaches, supporting the use of common techniques and accommodating evolution of underlying technologies.

The CAT working group has pursued several interrelated tasks to achieve these goals. They are working toward agreements on a common service interface allowing callers to invoke security services and a common authentication token format, incorporating a means to identify the mechanism type in conjunction with the authentication data elements that should be interpreted. They are also examining suitable underlying mechanisms to implement these security functions. Two candidate architectures under consideration are Kerberos V5, based on secret-key technology and contributed by MIT, and ITU-T Rec. X.509-based public-key Distributed Authentication Services, being prepared for contribution by Digital.

The following RFCs have been published as a result of the work of the CAT WG:

- 1507: Distributed Authentication Security Service (DASS).
- 1508: Generic Security Service Application Program Interface (GSS-API).
- 1509: Generic Security Service API: C-bindings.
- 1510: The Kerberos Network Authentication Service (V5).
- 1511: Common Authentication Technology Overview.

The CAT WG has also written several Internet-Drafts on FTP security extensions; Kerberos V5, public-key, and other GSS-API mechanisms; and single-use authentication mechanisms with Kerberos.

**Domain Name System Security Working Group**

The Domain Name System Security (DNSSEC) Working Group has a charter to specify data integrity and authentication enhancements to the domain name system (DNS) protocol to protect against unauthorized modification of data and masquerading of data origin. The specific mechanism to be added to the DNS protocol is a digital signature. The digital signature service will enable DNS resource records to be "signed." Upon verification of the signatures, remote sites can have confidence in the accuracy of the records received.

The DNSSEC WG is exploring two primary issues with the aim of finding resolutions. The first issue is determining whether the resource records should be signed by the primary or secondary servers, or both, or by the start of authority (SOA) for the DNS zone; this issue is relevant because there are servers for sites that are not connected with Internet protocol (IP). The second issue is specifying the mechanism for the distribution of the public keys necessary to verify the digital signatures.

The DNSSEC WG is also operating under two working assumptions. First, backwards compatibility and co-existence with DNS servers and clients that do not support the proposed security services is required. Second, data in the DNS is considered public information, meaning that discussions and proposals involving data confidentiality and access control are explicitly outside the scope of this working group.

The DNSSEC working group has produced Internet-Drafts for DNS security extensions and a definition for mapping autonomous systems number into the DNS.

**Internet Protocol Security Protocol Working Group**

The Internet Protocol Security Protocol (IPSEC) Working Group has a charter to develop mechanisms to protect IP client protocols. A Network Layer security protocol will be developed that provides cryptographic security services supporting combinations of authentication, integrity, access control, and confidentiality. Newly defined IP Authentication Header (AH) and IP Encapsulating Security Payload (ESP) protocol formats will be independent of the cryptographic algorithm. Initial work is towards host-to-host security, followed by subnet-to-subnet and host-to-subnet security.

Protocol and cryptographic techniques will also be developed to support the key management requirements of the Network Layer security. The key management will be specified as an Application Layer protocol, independent of the lower layer security protocol, and will initially support public key-based techniques. Flexibility in the protocol will allow eventual support of Key Distribution Center (KDC), such as Kerberos, and manual distribution approaches.

The IPSEC WG has been responsible for the publication of several RFCs:

- 1825: Security Architecture for the Internet Protocol.
- 1826: IP Authentication Header.
- 1827: IP Encapsulating Security Payload.
- 1829: The ESP DES-CBC Transform.
- 1828: IP Authentication using Keyed MD5.

In addition, the IPSEC WG has published several Internet-Drafts including The Photuris Session Key Management Protocol, Internet Security Association and Key Management Protocol (ISAKMP), Simple Key-Management For Internet Protocols (SKIP), ICMP Security Failures Messages, X.509 Encoding of Diffie-Hellman Public Values, Encoding of an Unsigned Diffie-Hellman Public Value, Certificate Discovery Protocol, and SKIP Algorithm Discovery Protocol. Additional work for 1996 and 1997 includes definition and interoperability testing of the ESP and AH, and the definition and testing of the Internet Key Management Protocol (IKMP).

## One-Time Password Authentication Working Group

The goal of the One-Time Password Authentication (OTP) Working Group is to prepare an Internet standard for one-time passwords. The basis for the group's effort will be the technology in the Bellcore S/KEY system and related interoperable packages (e.g., logdaemon). The bulk of the work of this WG is currently taking place.

## Privacy-Enhanced Electronic Mail Working Group

The work of the Privacy-Enhanced Electronic Mail (PEM) Working Group is an outgrowth of the work performed by the IETF's Privacy and Security Research Group (PSRG). At the heart of the Privacy Enhanced Mail (PEM) specification is a set of procedures for transforming RFC 822 (Simple Mail Transfer Protocol) messages in such a way as to provide integrity, data origin authenticity, and, optionally, confidentiality. PEM may be employed with either symmetric or asymmetric cryptographic key distribution mechanisms. Because the asymmetric (i.e., public-key) mechanisms are better suited to the large-scale, heterogeneously administered environment characteristic of the Internet, only those mechanisms have been standardized to date. The standard form adopted by PEM is largely a profile of the ITU-T X.509 (Directory Authentication Framework) recommendation.

PEM and related specifications are described in several RFCs written by members of this working group:

- 1319: The MD2 Message-Digest Algorithm.
- 1320: The MD4 Message-Digest Algorithm.
- 1321: The MD5 Message-Digest Algorithm.
- 1421: Privacy Enhancement for Internet Electronic Mail: Part I: Message Encryption and Authentication Procedures.
- 1422: Privacy Enhancement for Internet Electronic Mail: Part II: Certificate-Based Key Management.
- 1423: Privacy Enhancement for Internet Electronic Mail: Part III: Algorithms, Modes, and Identifiers.
- 1424: Privacy Enhancement for Internet Electronic Mail: Part IV: Key Certification and Related Services.

- 1847: Security Multiparts for MIME: Multipart/Signed and Multipart/ Encrypted.
- 1848: MIME Object Security Services.

Future work will include PEM compression.

## Public-Key Infrastructure (X.509) Working Group

Many Internet protocols and applications employ public-key technology for security purposes and require a public-key infrastructure (PKI) to manage public keys securely for widely distributed users or systems. ITU-T Rec. X.509 constitutes a widely accepted basis for such an infrastructure by defining data formats and procedures related to the distribution of public keys through certificates digitally signed by Certification Authorities (CAs). RFC 1422 specified the basis of an X.509-based PKI, targeted primarily at satisfying the needs of PEM. Since RFC 1422 was issued, application requirements for an Internet PKI have broadened tremendously, and the capabilities of X.509 have advanced with the development of standards defining the X.509 version 3 certificate and version 2 Certificate Revocation List (CRL).

The charter of the Public-Key Infrastructure (X.509) (PKIX) Working Group is to develop Internet standards needed to support an X.509-based PKI. The goal of this PKI is to facilitate the use of X.509 certificates in multiple applications that use the Internet and to promote interoperability between different implementations choosing to use X.509 certificates. The resulting PKI is intended to provide a framework that supports a range of trust or hierarchy environments and a range of usage environments.

Candidate applications to be served by this PKI include, but are not limited to, PEM, GSS-API mechanisms, IP Security protocols, Internet payment protocols, and World Wide Web (WWW) protocols. The work of this group does not preclude use of noninfrastructural public-key distribution techniques or of non-X.509 PKIs by such applications. The PKIX WG also coordinates with the IETF White Pages (X.500/WHOIS++) project.

The PKIX WG will focus on tailoring and profiling the features available in the X.509 v3 certificate to match more closely the requirements and characteristics of the Internet environment. Other topics to be addressed may include:

- Alternatives for CA-to-CA certification links and structures, including guidelines for constraints.
- Revocation alternatives, including profiling of X.509 v2 CRL extensions.
- Certificate and CRL distribution options (X.500-based, non-X.500-based).
- Guidelines for policy definition and registration.

- Administrative protocols and procedures, including certificate generation, revocation notification, cross-certification, and key-pair updating.
- Naming and name forms (i.e., how entities are identified).
- Generation of client key pairs by the PKI.

### Web Transaction Security Working Group

The goal of the Web Transaction Security (WTS) Working Group is to develop requirements and a specification for the provision of security services to World Wide Web transactions using the HyperText Transfer Protocol (HTTP). This work is proceeding in parallel to, and independently of, the development of nonsecurity features by the HTTP Working Group (IETF Applications Area).

The WTS WG's current goal is to prepare an HTTP Security Requirements Specification and an HTTP Security Protocol Specification. Two Internet-Drafts have been published to date: the Secure HyperText Transfer Protocol (SHTTP) and a specification for the use of the GSS-API for Web Security. Both will eventually be forwarded for publication as RFCs.

### CONTACTING THE INTERNET SOCIETY AND IETF

The addresses and telephone numbers for the Internet Society, the IETF, and other groups are:

Internet Society

12020 Sunrise Valley Drive, Suite 210
Reston VA 22091
(703) 648 9888 (voice)
(800) 468 9507 (voice, U.S. only)
(703) 648 9887 (fax)
info@isoc.org
ftp://ftp.isoc.org/
gopher://info.isoc.org/11/isoc
http://www.isoc.org

IETF Secretariat

c/o Corporation for National Research Initiatives
1895 Preston White Drive, Suite 100
Reston VA 22091
(703) 620 8990 (voice)
(703) 758-5913 (fax)
ietf-secretariat@cnri.reston.va.us
http://ietf.cnri.reston.va.us/
IAB information: http://www.iab.org/iab/iab.html
IANA information: http://www.iana.org/iana/
IESG information: http://www.ietf.cnri.reston.va.us/iesg.html

# Chapter 40

# The Legal and Regulatory Environment of the Internet

*Lawrence D. Dietz*

---

Laws pertaining to the Internet are emerging as the system matures. Large end-user organizations are discovering the true nature of technology's influence on business relationships. This chapter discusses the critical areas of the law and legal liabilities for organizations doing business over the Internet, and uses examples of recent cases to demonstrate possible outcomes of legal action.

## INTRODUCTION

The legal environment of the Internet has often been compared with the Wild West in the days of the American frontier. This analogy is used to convey the wide open and freewheeling atmosphere that pervades this area of the law. The Internet, like many other technological phenomena, is developing along several parallel directions. The main line is the technology direction — those facets of networking, computing, software, and database, which, when combined, add up to the ability to access the array of interconnected computers known as the Internet.

The second area of development is the nature of business on the Internet. How can information be exchanged? How can goods or services be bought or sold? What aspects of today's business rules can be effectively employed as rules for tomorrow's net-based business?

It is only after business transactions are in process or, more properly, when business transactions do not turn out according to the expectations of the participants that the law enters into the picture. Astute managers do not resort to the law to correct a problem; rather, the law is supposed to be used as a guideline to avoid problems or to minimize the consequences if things go wrong.

Therefore, it follows that the law of the Internet is an emerging and evolving beast. Large end-user organizations are turning to technology first and then are immersed in the process of figuring out how to use that technology. Once the technology is employed, the true nature of its influence on business relationships can be determined. The deeper and more mission-critical the use of technology is, the more severe the effects are if something goes awry. When it is clear that a simple business solution will not work to resolve a problem, lawyers are called.

## DEFINING THE SITUATION

To understand the sheer magnitude of the dilemma of law on the Internet, it is useful to look at the Internet through an analogy. John Anderson, the former Presidential candidate, speaking at the annual RSA Conference in Redwood City, California in January 1995, compared the Internet with interstate highways. He pointed out how, back in 1955, no one could have foreseen the economic fallout of the interstate highway network. Originally set up during the Eisenhower administration as a key part of its Civil Defense strategy, the interstate highway network spawned not only a multibillion dollar auto and truck industry, but had a profound effect on shipping and on population concentration. No one could have looked at the way highways would either spur or destroy commerce and communities.

At present, the Internet and its subsequent progeny are similarly unknown and unpredictable. From a legal perspective, this situation becomes particularly perplexing. When stripped to its core, the purpose of a legal system is to form a bulwark upon which a set of governing behaviors can be determined. The split of law into civil and criminal areas has historically been used to divide the legal world into two segments: a part that deals with interaction among parties (i.e., civil law) and a part that governs an individual's (or organization's) behavior with respect to society (i.e., criminal law).

From a U.S. perspective, civil law may be further divided into multiple areas: areas of legal specialty and jurisdictions. As law relates to the Internet, areas of consequence are:

- Contract law.
- Intellectual property.
- Torts and negligence.
- Criminal law.

Before addressing each one of these areas in turn, it is important to point out that laws are not enforced in a vacuum. A critical aspect of the law is jurisdiction. Jurisdiction has two dimensions: the party and the law. The first jurisdictional issue is: does the court have the power to control an individual or entity? In the United States, a court's jurisdiction may be a city, county, state, several states, or the entire country.

The second question is one of subject matter or rules. Plaintiffs (i.e., the parties bringing a suit) determine where they will bring the action; that is the legal forum. If the plaintiffs and defendants (i.e., those charged by the action) are from different locations and if the matter at hand occurred in yet another location, various procedures are set in motion by both sides to decide which set of rules (i.e., body of law) will be applied by the court. This is especially true in a federal court that, although located in one state, will often be compelled to follow the law of another. This jurisdictional issue is called diversity of citizenship, whereby the law of one state may be applied to adjudicate a dispute in a court of another state.

There is no greater challenge to jurisdiction than that of an indefinable web of computers and the various media that link them. The Internet is conceptually stateless and countryless, so jurisdictional issues are wide open. Some of the key aspects of litigation, such as forum shopping (i.e., picking the best place to bring the action), is discussed in a later section. Moreover, courts need two kinds of jurisdiction to try a case: personal jurisdiction over the parties and subject matter jurisdiction over the matter. One is not enough; both are necessary.

The next sections highlight significant areas of the law and how they relate to the Internet and its security and integrity.

## Contract Law

The Internet may become not only a transportation medium for business transactions, but the subject matter as well. Existing rules of law and terms and conditions that govern business transactions, such as the UCC, must be modified to bend to the Internet way of doing business.

A number of reforms have been under way for several years on different fronts. A key area of contract law that is evolving is EDI. Organizations can employ EDI to replace paper transactions. If so, clear terms and conditions must be extended to encompass new concepts of contractual relationships. Key terms, such as acceptance, rejection, and remedies for breach of contract, must be couched in terms appropriate for the Internet world. Potential failures or compromises of Internet-based transactions, failure to perform by Internet service providers, as well as action or inaction by suppliers and customers must be considered in developing contracts between organizations using EDI.

Areas of particular interest to Internet security practitioners include the use and acceptance of digital signatures in lieu of written signatures. A digital signature is the use of an algorithm as a substitute for an individual's authorized, holographic signature. The purpose of the signature is to commit the signer. It is an authentication of the signer's intent and proof of his or her acceptance or authoring of the document at hand.

The main reason behind the push for digital signatures is the UCC. Used by 49 states (the exception is Louisiana), the UCC requires both parties to sign a writing for transactions in excess of $500. As a side note, there are other branches of the law, such as real estate, where a signed writing is also required for the transaction to be valid. Digital signatures could be employed in a number of other areas in which the legitimization of documents is important.

## Intellectual Property

Intellectual property is made up of several key components: patents, trademarks, copyrights, and trade secrets. For the most part, intellectual property is a part of state raft; that is, federal law controls its validity and use. Only trade secrets are governed by state law. From the perspective of the Internet security practitioner, a fair number of rules are already in place. Violations or, more commonly, infringement of intellectual property rights can occur throughout large end-user organizations. The availability and convenience of E-mail and the Internet as a transportation medium increase the reach of a potential infringer. The literally unlimited horizons of the Internet raise the stakes for intellectual property problems.

The astute practitioner will bolster him or herself through aggressive policies and extensive education. Employees and others with access to an organization's intellectual property should be placed under contractual control not to use that property improperly. As with other aspects of employee-related legal issues, notice and consent are critical. Organizations must be obligors on notice as to what information is a trade secret, and they must place conspicuous notice on copyright or trademarked items.

Organizations must remember that the Internet is another way in which employees can transport protected property to unauthorized parties. They must guard against the possibility of this occurring as they would with more traditional vulnerabilities.

## Torts and Negligence

In cases involving the Internet and in others involving negligence, courts will apply (and will instruct jurors to apply) classic test factors. The common law test applied in these situations has the following elements:

- **Gravity of the harm:** how extensive was the damage?
- **Likelihood to occur:** given the surrounding circumstances, how likely was the event to happen?
- **Cost to prevent:** Given the size of the potential harm and its likelihood, what would have the cost been to prevent the harm and how reasonable would it have been to expend those funds?
- **Duty of care:** What responsibility did the defendant have to the plaintiff? For example, because banks hold their depositors' money and are considered fiduciaries, they are held to a higher standard of care than a simple vendor of stationery goods would be.
- **Standard of care:** What do other similar persons or organizations do under the same circumstances? Do 95% or more of similar victims of a crime perpetuated over the Internet employ firewalls? How sophisticated is the victim as an Internet user or provider?

These factors will continue to be the yardsticks by which negligence actions will be measured.

Product liability is an area within tort law in which products used in Internet applications are included. By way of analogy, the New Jersey Supreme Court in Roberts v. Rich Foods, Inc., 139 N.J. 365 (1995) found that a computer used in a motor vehicle was defective. This computer was used by truck drivers to record mileage and fuel data. The court judged it as defective, because the device could be operated while the vehicle was in motion. It was reasoned that operating the computer would divert the driver's attention from operating the vehicle, so that if there was an accident, the design of the computer would be a factor in that accident, and liability of the computer manufacturer for improper design had to be considered.

### Criminal Law

Criminal law is a creature of the government. The plaintiff is the government or "The People." To be guilty of a crime, one must have "broken the law" or violated a particular statute. Typical criminal law statutes require a voluntary or involuntary action (i.e., *actus reus*) in legal jargon and an intent (i.e., *mens rea*). Usually, Internet and other computer crime laws require voluntary acts (as opposed to involuntary or unconscious acts) and purposeful intent. Therefore, government prosecutors must be able to prove both. This proof must be to the higher standard known as "beyond a reasonable doubt," which contrasts with civil law, where the standard is preponderance (i.e., majority) of the evidence.

Often, as with other laws, computer crime laws are shaped out of well-known past rules. For example, criminal harassment activity, stalking, and similar behavior have been a part of the legal landscape for some time. In

June 1995, the State of Connecticut joined the ranks of computer crime pioneers by amending its existing harassment law to include a "computer network" as a means by which a defendant could employ with "the intent to harass, annoy, alarm, or terrorize." Details can be found in the Connecticut General Statutes, sections 53A to 182b, and 183.

Another important aspect of Internet criminal law that is currently being addressed is the issue of sentencing guidelines. Sentencing guidelines are issued by various jurisdictions and are used by judges in dealing with the post-trial punishment of defendants who have been found guilty. Among the aspects of sentencing guidelines is "sexual abuse or exploitation."(For reference, look at the United States Sentencing Guidelines, Section 2G2.2[b][4].) The First Circuit Court, based in Boston, MA, felt that the transmission of child pornography over the Internet (in this case, AOL) did not constitute sexual abuse or exploitation under the guidelines. The case in question was United States v. Chapman, 60F.3d 894 (1st Cir. 1995).

In this case, according to the court, there was "considerable evidence" that the defendant used AOL to transmit child pornography on a number of occasions. The court concluded that these transmissions were not abuse or exploitation under the guidelines; therefore, these transmissions should not be considered a factor in deciding an appropriate sentence.

The Computer Fraud and Abuse Act of 1986 serves to protect computer systems, particularly federal computers. United States Code Section 1030 (a)(5)(A) states that its penalty provisions apply to "anyone who intentionally accesses a Federal interest computer without authorization, and by means of one or more instances of such conduct, alters, damages, or destroys information in any such Federal interest computer or prevents authorized use of any such computer or information ..." and thereby causes loss of $1,000 or more.

It is important to note that the term "Federal interest computer" broadens the scope of the law to more than just federal government computers. It would logically include contractors to the federal government and perhaps computers privately owned by U.S. federal government employees that are being used for the benefit of the federal government. It is also interesting to note that loss of use receives protection under the statute as well as damage or alteration.

The most well-known conviction under this statute, upheld on appeal, was the case of the Cornell graduate student, Robert Morris (son of the NSA cryptographer), who was convicted for releasing the "worm," a computer virus that replicated itself over the Internet, causing multiple crashes. Among those computers affected were a significant number of "Federal interest computers." The appeals court's opinion may be read at

United States v. Morris, 928 F.2d 504 (2d Cir.), certiorari denied by the Supreme Court in 502 U.S. 817 (1991).

### Export Control and International Traffic in Arms Regulations (22 CFR, Parts 120 through 128 & 130)

These regulations are used to control export of anything that could harm the security of the United States. This includes weapons, weapons systems, and cryptography. Vendors seeking to export must secure an export license. The approval process weaves a circuitous route among the Departments of Commerce, Defense, and State. Although the process has been a thorn in the side of U.S. software exporters, it has spawned a specialized consulting niche. This niche has been addressed by a number of independents, most recently by RSA Data Security, in Redwood City, CA. RSA recently announced a new division in the company, which will be headed by a former employee of the NSA, to assist companies in obtaining export licenses. There are also a number of independent consultants, such as Cecil Shure, president of CSI Associates, in Washington, DC, who specialize in exporting.

In fairness, the Clinton administration has been sending a number of signals that it is willing to relax the draconian regulations under certain circumstances. Among these, are the vendor's willingness to give the government access to key-breaking information when the government asks for it, or as a part of the approval cycle. This is both good news and bad news for vendors. On the positive side, the approval process may, at last, be getting more export friendly. On the negative, non-US customers may not be willing to employ a product knowing that the U.S. government is able to "read their mail."

## LIABILITY ISSUES

Anyone can be named in a lawsuit or charged with a crime. The "who" can be an individual or an organization. Ancillary potential plaintiffs and defendants in Internet matters can include suppliers, customers, government agencies, and trade associations, to name a few possible candidates.

### An International Perspective

In an unusually frank spirit of cooperation, the forum for suit was broadened in Europe to allow defamation plaintiffs domiciled in a Brussels Convention country to pursue remedies either where the publication originated or where the harm occurred. The choice of litigation could therefore be based on a greater likelihood of success under that country's laws or the reputation for plaintiff sympathy. (Plaintiffs choose where to bring actions; defendants merely respond.) Reference for the European Court of Justice is C-68.93 and the U.K. reference is *Shevill v. Presse Alliance*

*CA* (1992) All ER. The defendant was a French publisher, and the action was brought in the U.K. because the plaintiff felt that the U.K. was a more sympathetic jurisdiction. The court noted that circulation was greater in France than in the U.K., but that was not material to the selection of forums.

## A Role in the Events

In general, a party cannot be found liable unless it had some part in the problematic acts. For purposes of the law, the party can just as easily be an organization (government or private) as well as an individual. Of particular interest to the Internet community is the issue of publisher liability. One who creates or edits the "news" is far more likely to be found culpable if there is a liability issue than one who merely distributes or transmits the news.

A New York case, Stratton Oakmont Inc. vs. Prodigy Services Co., No. 31063/94, 1995 WL 323710, 23 Media Law report 1794 (N.Y. Supreme Court 1995), was decided against the on-line service. The facts involved comments posted by an unidentified bulletin board user in October 1994. These comments on "Money Talk" contained allegedly libelous statements about Statton, an investment banking firm. Stratton sued both the poster and Prodigy.

The rationale behind this decision covered a number of relevant points. Prodigy employed moderators for the panels. These "Board Leaders" had a number of responsibilities over the bulletin board. These leaders were charged with enforcing the content guidelines set up by Prodigy (the guidelines themselves were considered another reason why Prodigy had control over content) and could use a special delete function to remove offending material. The court also noted that Prodigy employed software to screen postings for offensive language. Another critical aspect of this case was that the Board Leader of Money Talk was found to be an agent of Prodigy and that agent liability attached.

The opposite ruling (that is, finding that the service provider was not a publisher) was the 1991 case in the Southern District of New York, Cubby Inc. vs. CompuServe Inc., 776 F. Supp. 135 (S.D.N.Y. 1991). In this case, the court felt that CompuServe did not post any guidelines, take any role in controlling content, or promote itself as a family-oriented service, as Prodigy had.

Organizations can be found liable for the actions of their employees or agents under the legal doctrine of *respondeat superior*. Simply stated, employers can be liable for the acts of their employees acting within the scope of their employment. Therefore, software developers who accidentally unleash a virus or worm, as Morris did, may bring liability upon their employers. In addition, plaintiffs will continue to search for defendants with money. Often employers have more financial wherewithal than their employees and become the targets of legal action.

Some areas of the law look to what management actually knew or should have known given "due diligence" of the reasonable person under similar circumstances. Intentional acts by employees that can or should have been prevented by more direct action by management may also result in liability applying to the organization, even for intentional acts.

Another rule of law, which is that intentional criminal acts are a bar to liability, may also be applied in Internet security cases; however, there are no guarantees. Juries have often gone against facts that appear to be overwhelming and appellate jurisdictions have often labored to reach a decision based on abstract theories of society goodness. The absence of historical precedent makes legal actions by and about the Internet perfectly positioned for inconsistent decisions. Security practitioners who go down this uncharted road do so at their peril.

### Product Liability

Anyone in the "stream of commerce" can be included as a party in a product liability matter. Included in the stream of commerce are designers, developers, manufacturers, distributors, representatives, and retailers. An aggressive plaintiff and competent counsel will seek to embroil any potential defendant in litigation. This is especially true if the defendant has significant financial resources or a track record of trying to settle rather than litigate matters. This will undoubtedly be an important aspect of future Internet legal activity.

## LIABILITIES AND AVAILABLE REMEDIES

The ultimate purpose of remedies is to put the aggrieved party back into the position that he or she would have been in if the wrongdoer had not acted in the way that he or she did. Remedies can also be used to deter future negative behavior and compensate the plaintiff for wrongs against society committed by the defendant.

### Money Damages

A court can award substantial sums of money to the aggrieved parties. Their rationale can be real or imagined. Amounts can be rational or irrational. Experts are often used to "prove up" damages. The role of the expert witness is to clarify facts for the court. As shown in a recent, celebrated criminal trial in Los Angeles, scientific, expert testimony does not necessarily ensure victory for the presenter. In addition to damages as a result of the defendant's act or failure to act, damages can be awarded based on a "bad intent" on the part of the offender. These punitive damages can often be twice or three times the amount of actual damages.

## Injunctions

An injunction is simply a court order prohibiting a party (or parties) from doing a specific action. To get an injunction during the pre-trial phase, plaintiffs have to demonstrate (among other things) that they will suffer irreparable harm if the injunction is not invoked, that the plaintiff is likely to win on the merits of the case (which will result in a permanent court ruling), and that the court will be able to enforce the injunction.

## Criminal Liability

Remedies in criminal cases are spelled out by the statute that was violated and the sentencing guidelines that jurisdictions often issue to accompany the laws. The most common punishments include fines, community service, and incarceration. Incarceration can take many forms: county, state, or federal prisons; and a growing number of other more innovative programs such as confinement to one's home.

Courts have sometimes gone to great lengths in computer-related crimes to remove a convicted defendant's access to the tools of the computer trade. The incorrigible nature of some defendants and the magnitude of the harm they caused, combined with their lack of remorse, have often induced judges to impose heavier and more creative sentences than in comparable cases of non-computer-related crimes.

## Lawyer Liability

Lawyer liability is a phrase that the author uses to describe other harm. Time spent with and money spent on attorney's fees are not trivial. In the days of downsizing and rightsizing, employee productivity is zealously guarded. Time spent that does not either increase revenue or decrease costs is wasted time. The effort and resources needed to pursue and win a legal action should be considered before the action is undertaken. Fees for attorneys, as well as other expenses, such as court costs and expert fees, are substantial. Often plaintiffs have to spend an inordinate amount of time educating their counsel about the nature of their businesses and the nature of this action. Combine this time investment with the uncertain nature of law as related to the Internet and the general lack of computer literacy in the legal profession and there are the makings of a true disaster in terms of the expenditure of resources vs. the likelihood of benefit or gain.

This approach could be applied to computers as well. Given the seemingly pro-right wing and pro-conservative American electorate and the noncommittal nature of leading politicians and their desire to win the family vote, a strong push to repeal such infringements is not likely to come from elected officials. Rather, it will be up to pioneering plaintiffs, perhaps aided by the EFF or CPSR or other similar rights advocates to step up to employ legal action to block enforcement.

Such activity is not unprecedented. The California proposition 187 limiting educational and other entitlements of immigrants, which, although passed by the electorate, was blocked due to potential constitutionality problems, could be a model for such protestations. However, computer and information freedom does not have a readily identifiable homogenous group of affected persons who will take direct, immediate, and costly action, at least not at this time. Furthermore, championing of pornography is not a popular view that will capture the hearts and minds of the electorate or the media.

## AVOIDING PROBLEMS

System administrators must be mindful of the need for notice and disclosure. They must ensure that users or subscribers are fully aware of who has access to the system. They must indicate clearly how monitoring and control may be or is exercised on the system. Employee handbooks should spell out exactly what employees are expected to do in terms of use of the company's information resources. All employees should sign an acknowledgment that they have read the rules, understand them, and agree to be bound by them.

### Prosecution of Hackers

It is important to remember that a criminal prosecution is run by the office of the local DA, not by the victim. The goal of the DA is to get a conviction, not to ensure that the victim is compensated; nor is his or her goal to prevent similar occurrences in the future. A decision to proceed with prosecution is also a decision to cooperate fully with law enforcement authorities. Cooperation may require a significant amount of time, money, and resources from the company. This commitment may not fit with the company's goals of minimizing bad publicity, fixing the leak, and controlling the course of legal events.

Should the decision be made to proceed, it is important to be mindful of the rules of evidence and the critical need to keep a pure chain of custody. One person's opinion that a piece of evidence is damning does not mean that it is and, more importantly, it does not mean that it will be admissible and, if it is, that it will be understood by the trier of fact, whether judge or jury.

It is important to recognize that experts may be needed and that they may come from the ranks of the company or the company's suppliers. Victims may not be in a position either to recommend, to supply, or to compensate needed experts, and the District Attorney's budget may not permit hiring the "right" kind of talent.

History has shown that a defendant with financial muscle is not to be taken lightly. Should the defendant be well funded, he or she might not get convicted, and might turn around and sue the plaintiff for defamation or malicious prosecution.

Before opting for a criminal prosecution, a lot of good information can be found in a Government Printing Office document: the Criminal Justice Resource Manual, prepared by the Department of Justice. It contains good advice concerning the types of computer crimes, evidence, likely perpetrators, and other related material.

Companies contemplating this type of prosecution should also be sensitive to the track record of the local DA with respect to this type of white-collar crime case. Obviously, some jurisdictions (such as Austin, TX; Boston, MA; and Santa Clara, CA) are better venues for technology-related cases due to the high population of computer literate potential jurors and high-tech companies.

It is critical to remember that when the lawyer is called, whether a civil counsel, corporate counsel, or the local DA, someone loses time, resources, and money.

## CONCLUSION

An organization should determine its goals early on in the process and balance the practical results that it wants to achieve against the legal hurdles that will have to be navigated to get them. Often, compromise is a faster, cheaper, and better alternative than pursuing legal remedies. Simple themes are always better than complex ones.

Chapter 41

# The Hidden Costs of Free TCP/IP

*Walker, Richer & Quinn, Inc.*

As free TCP/IP software becomes increasingly available, data center managers have new choices to make. Evaluations must consider whether free software provides the connectivity, features, performance, and ease of use required in today's organization. In addition, "free" software can incur costs in unexpected areas. This chapter uncovers the critical issues when the decision is being made to use free TCP/IP software, discusses interconnectivity issues when introducing a vendor's TCP/IP software into the organization, and examines the implications for an AS/400 environment.

## INTRODUCTION

The growth in TCP/IP is explosive. All major hardware vendors, including IBM, have endorsed TCP/IP. By 1998, it is projected that 59% of all midrange systems, including UNIX and AS/400s, will be running TCP/IP, and desktop installations of TCP/IP will rise to more than 50%. As TCP/IP becomes the established networking standard, management tools and new applications will become even more important, along with proven reliability and strong technical support. Free TCP/IP stacks may be satisfactory for a casual user, but they are less likely to fulfill the needs of complex corporate environments, now and in the future.

Even though a free protocol suite may appear to fill all the organization's needs, many data center managers have been surprised to discover that that is not always the case, particularly in corporate environments. Not only do free suites usually lack the robust functionality of purchased TCP/IP software, but they also often involve hidden costs. Because an application is only as reliable as the protocol suite it runs on, it pays to review some considerations, outlined in this chapter, before selecting a product.

0-8493-9965-3/99/$0.00+$.50
© 1999 by CRC Press LLC

In addition, companies that analyze TCP/IP stacks should look at both architecture and applications when they choose a stack for their complex enterprises. Architecture makes a difference to the ultimate functioning of the stack in such areas as mobile connectivity and configuration flexibility. Kernel applications, those that are critical to the smooth functioning of an enterprise network that are integrated into TCP/IP, vary widely among stacks. This chapter discusses the importance of kernel applications and identifies specific issues for the data center manager to examine.

Finally, AS/400 vendors and customers have been paying close attention to the proliferation of TCP/IP. Many organizations have opted for the promise of open networking with less expensive implementations and information sharing with other systems, across a common backbone network. Unfortunately, with the promise comes compromise. This chapter illustrates the differences between TCP/IP and IBM's proprietary networking technology, Advanced Peer-to-Peer Communication (APPC) and illustrates the limitations of TCP/IP in an AS/400environment. The chapter concludes with suggestions for maximizing the benefits of TCP/IP without sacrificing the comprehensive nature of an APPC connection.

## SELECTING FREE TCP/IP PROTOCOL SUITES

If the organization is considering a particular TCP/IP implementation, data center managers must ask questions to determine whether the software is designed for the needs of large, corporate networks. Free data communications protocol suites, also known as stacks because they involve more than one protocol, should be examined closely; the following sections discuss critical questions data center managers must ask to uncover possible pitfalls. (Exhibit 1 offers a checklist for identifying high-value TCP/IP software.)

**Exhibit 1. A TCP/IP Checklist for Identifying High-Value TCP/IP Software**

---

Software designed for corporate environments:

- Full corporate connectivity with TCP/IP, UDP, LAT, IPX/SPX, SLIP, CSLIP, and PPP.
- VxD/DDL design for performance and reliability.
- Management tools (SNMP MIB II, an event viewer, and diagnostics).
- Support for all existing name and address resolution protocols and current dynamic addressing.
- Full-featured applications, such as VT420/320, FTP client and server, TN3270E and TN5250, Internet and intranet applications.
- NFS capabilities.
- Open connectivity — 100 percent Windows Sockets compliance to ensure compatibility with third-party and Internet shareware/freeware applications.
- Ease of use remote and mobile computing — with features optimized for remote computing (dynamic link recovery, reductions in protocol overhead, increased throughput).

---

A product backed by a company with solid experience in host systems, networking, and desktop programs. Knowledgeable and ongoing free technical support that includes online services and fax-on-demand information. Complete, easy-to-read documentation. Limited site license agreements that allow free updates for at least one year. Favorable ratings in independent comparisons by industry publications and evaluators.

## What Are the Costs of Using a Stack That Is Not Designed for Complex, Heterogeneous Environments?

For the casual user, a free TCP/IP stack may provide all the necessary functionality. If the organization has several networks and users, however, the requirements may far outstrip what a free stack can provide. In this situation, data center managers must consider a stack that is compliant with current standards, that does not sacrifice access to legacy systems, and that delivers the required capabilities for mission-critical computing. Capabilities include:

- **Full-enterprise connectivity.** True open computing means networking all the organization's systems, so software must include not only TCP/IP but also UDP, LAT, NS/VT, IPX/SPX, SLIP, CSLIP, and PPP. Selected software should also connect to UNIX, Digital, IBM, and HP hosts. Otherwise, the costs of adding connectivity can mount fast.
- **Full-featured applications.** The data center manager must check for advanced VT420, TN3270E, TN5250 emulation, FTP client and server, and Internet and intranet applications, to name a few. Accepting a stack without these applications means the organization will have to pay extra for them.
- **Ease of use.** If the software is not easy to use, the organization must commit additional resources to training and support. Command-line driven operations are not intuitive, so other features to look for include graphical operations and context-sensitive help. If the interface has a familiar look, users can become productive much sooner.

## What Is the Cost of Using a Stack That Lacks a Robust Networking Architecture?

Costs result from a multitude of inefficiencies. Areas the data center manager should examine closely are performance, name and address resolution, remote and mobile computing, and open connectivity. Managers should:

- Look for networking software that offers a combined VxD/DLL design. A cooperative implementation can give the superior performance of VxDs and the reliability of a DLL. Of course, the true test is in the organization's own environment; managers must be sure the stack works with all hardware, including notebook computers, and all applications. The alternative could be a hodge-podge of fixes, which not only cost more but also affect performance.

- Be sure the host name and address resolution protocol currently in use is supported. For example, some implementations ignore DNS. The support must provide access to all applications that the organization plans to run. If not, the data center manager could be in for a significant amount of work. He or she will have to map all the nodes in the network to their specific addresses manually, which can be a significant drain on the budget. Dynamic network address assignment is another consideration. For example, some stacks support only DHCP, whereas organizations may also use BOOTP. In this case, the stack must support both.

- Consider developing needs, especially in the area of telecommuting and mobile computing, because today enterprise connectivity increasingly means connecting from anywhere. Free stacks are not likely to be designed with the specialized features needed to support connections to enterprise computers in remote offices or hotel rooms, or over cellular connections. Data center managers must look for a stack that is optimized for these uses, including dynamic link recovery to re-establish a lost connection, and features that reduce costly overhead and increase throughput. Without these optimizations, the organization could have to pay for additional software for these users, as well as incur unnecessary charges for telephone or cellular connections. In addition, establishing one standard inside and outside the office for all connections will simplify support. These optimizations provide efficiencies on internal networks, as well.

- Check support for open computing standards such as Windows Sockets(WinSock), because most corporate computing environments do have a mix of hardware and software. Most vendors claim to support WinSock, but only a stack that is 100% WinSock compliant has passed all the Windows Sockets API Tester(WSAT) without error. This achievement is the data center manager's assurance that the stack will work reliably with applications designed to the WinSock standard, including third-party and Internet freeware/shareware applications. No assumptions should be made about any vendor's support; the manager should feel free to ask for information about its WSAT results. Ensuring that applications are supported can save money, and spare staff the resulting frustration when network applications fail due to poor WinSock compatibility.

## What Is the Cost of Support?

If the data center manager has past experience with free software bundled with other products, he or she is aware of the shortcomings. Anyone who has telephoned vendor help lines for popular PC products knows there may be a considerable wait before the call is even answered. Time, according to the old expression, is money.

Support costs are not trivial. According to a recent report on the costs of software ownership by Dataquest, the average annual support costs for networking and communication software for the Microsoft Windows environment are nearly twice as much as the initial product street price. This figure is high, compared to office suites, such as Microsoft Office, with support costs that are less than half than the initial product price.

The higher costs for networking support are easy to understand when the support policies offered by leading software firms are examined. One major vendor that includes a free stack with its operating system charges $35 per incident for networking technical support. This charge applies from day one; the vendor excludes networking questions from the 90-day free support policy it typically offers for other software.

One alternative is to purchase a support plan. Again, the same vendor offers a support plan for larger organizations at $25,000 a year, for up to 150 incidents a year, with an additional $1,500 for 10 additional incidents. This means that free stacks can be very expensive to support, especially in the long term. Data center managers should look for a company that includes free support past the 90-day warranty period and that offers online help and fax-on-demand services.

### What Is the Cost of Network Management?

Networking software is very different from word processing or spreadsheet software. Those programs are unlikely to bring down the entire network if they fail. However, even with the best networking software, the network will inevitably go down on occasion. When that happens, data center managers need diagnostic tools to get the network up and running again quickly, and they need monitoring capabilities to avoid future problems. Free stacks typically lack desktop monitoring and diagnostic tools.

If the organization needs critical features such as diagnostic and monitoring capabilities, file sharing and/or IP addressing, a stack with these features must be purchased, because these features are written to the kernel, not to the WinSock API. Managers cannot simply plug in desktop management tools, NFS, or BOOTP from one vendor and use them on another's stack. This means an industrial-strength TCP/IP tool is the solution.

### What Is the Cost in Waiting for Updates?

When a TCP/IP stack is bundled with a personal operating system customers may have to wait for a new version of the operating system before enhancements are added to the TCP/IP software. Historically, that can mean long waits. Yet in the TCP/IP and Internet world, new specifications and applications are being added all the time.

Networking vendors should be able to respond more quickly, delivering upgrades, feature enhancements, and patches faster, so your corporate network will not suffer while awaiting the next release of an operating system.

Once these questions have been considered and answered, the organization must test the selected stack. There is no substitute for trying software in the actual environment. With sufficient evaluation, following the criteria outlined in this section, the TCP/IP stack will provide the reliability, scalability, and flexibility required by corporate networks for their mission-critical applications. While such high-value software may initially cost more, it is an investment that will save time and money in the long term.

## KERNEL APPLICATIONS: THE SILENT TCP/IP ISSUE

Conventional wisdom says that all TCP/IP stacks are created equal. Whether they are embedded into operating systems, available free as shareware, or sold as part of a TCP/IP application suite, they are all interchangeable.

This view takes into account only that portion of the TCP/IP stack that has to do with Windows Sockets (WinSock). WinSock is an open API that functions like a standard wall outlet, giving developers the freedom to write TCP/IP-based applications and plug them in without having to worry about the peculiarities of the underlying TCP/IP stack. Common WinSock applications include Internet browsers, FTP clients, PC X servers, and VT420, TN3270, and TN5250 connectivity products. Written to the WinSock API, these applications should work with any TCP/IP stack.

WinSock is just the surface of the TCP/IP stack, however, and it is not the only portion of the stack to which applications are written. Below the WinSock layer, TCP/IP stacks are largely proprietary, with different architectural approaches to how they meet user needs. In addition, many applications that are important to the smooth functioning of an enterprise network are integrated into TCP/IP below WinSock. These "kernel" applications are the TCP/IP issues that are largely ignored, and the silence is costing companies both money and time.

## KERNEL APPLICATIONS MAKE A DIFFERENCE

Many applications can be written only to the kernel; network management tools are one example. This means that a vendor's management tools will work only with its own stack. Therefore, a data center manager who is interested in being able to manage hundreds or thousands of desktops running TCP/IP will most likely want to select the stack that has the best network management applications built in. An organization cannot simply purchase and patch in applications to a free kernel. This is also the case with many other applications, including:

- Dynamic IP assignment via DHCP/BOOTP/RARP.
- Communications via SLIP/CSLIP, PPP, ISDN, and FDDI.
- Video and data conferencing via IP multicasting.
- IP-based security.
- NetBIOS support.
- Network/desktop management via SNMP MIB II.
- Remote and mobile optimizations, including scripting.

The number of network-critical applications that exist at the kernel level is substantial, and because an industry standard kernel interface does not exist, there is no way to pick and choose among kernel-based applications to optimize a stack. If the organization now, or in the future, plans to use any of these applications, data center managers need to carefully evaluate their TCP/IP stack decision.

## SPECIFIC KERNEL ISSUES

Kernel applications affect a large organization in a variety of ways. They can affect future flexibility, network overhead, and administration time, to name just a few. When looking at stacks and deciding which kernel applications are important, managers should:

- Beware of stacks that force the organization into one standard over another, such as BOOTP vs. DHCP for dynamic address assignment. It is very expensive for a company that has standardized on BOOTP servers to replace all servers to support DHCP.
- Review the kernel applications that can affect network overhead. The way one stack handles handshaking with the host, for example, can significantly affect the number of packets put over both serial and Ethernet networks, and FTP and NFS caching reduces the overhead on serial lines.
- Look for stacks that provide dynamic link recovery and progressive acknowledgment, especially if the organization supports mobile and remote users.
- Determine how difficult it is to configure different desktops for different ways of connecting. Can the data center set up one client with an Ethernet connection and another with a serial PPP connection with little hassle? Configuration flexibility is an important kernel-level issue, especially when configuring large numbers of users, or remote users.
- Consider how security is implemented. This is one rapidly changing area that differs markedly from stack to stack. The most useful stack will support emerging security standards such as Kerberos, CHAP/PAP, IP-based security standards, and FTP firewall passthrough authentication. Is the NFS client implementation flexible? Does it provide easy access

to NFS data and devices? Are NFS connection set-ups simple? Look for a stack that allows for tuning NFS parameters for better performance and that provides administration tools that help manage NFS connections.

- Determine whether kernel applications keep up with WinSock applications. For example, as multipoint data and video conferencing becomes more common, your stack will need to support IP multicasting, a kernel-based feature. Many free stacks are enhanced only when the operating systems they are embedded in are upgraded, thus limiting the timely implementation of new technologies.
- Evaluate network management tools. Does the stack come complete with diagnostic and monitoring tools, such as statistics for packet counts, trace utility, IP route tables, and ARP cache? SNMP MIB II agent and private MIB support are important, as well as event/fault logging, Finger client and server, and multimedia Ping. These allow for better administration and control of enterprisewide networks.

Other areas of kernel concern include memory resource management and scripting. TCP/IP implementations vary radically, with potential impact on an organization in a wide range of areas.

## MATCHING REQUIREMENTS TO NEEDS

What people are finding in the real world of heterogeneous systems, enterprise-wide networks, and large corporate environments is that their requirements for a stack far outstrip what a free stack can provide. Many of these requirements are implemented within the architecture or the applications at the kernel level.

Enterprise customers are the market that looks for vendors who provide quality support, that take ownership of problems and respond quickly and helpfully. This means reliable support that does not require a credit card number or funneling the question through a single support contract. Support also means help for moving from proprietary transports to TCP/IP, from people who understand the desktop, networking, and host issues involved. If a PC's network connection suddenly stops working, can the help desk get the information it needs to get it back on line quickly? The answer lies in the quality of the kernel applications — and in the quality of support provided.

## MPTN ELIMINATES THE COMPROMISES OF TCP/IP IN AS/400 ENVIRONMENTS

The AS/400 world has been watching the proliferation of TCP/IP with great interest. A number of sites have been seduced by the promise of open networking with less expensive implementations and information sharing with other systems, across a common backbone network. Unfortunately, with the promise comes compromise.

**Exhibit 2. Terminology**

| Basic Functions | APPC | TCP/IP |
|---|---|---|
| File Transfer | SQL | FTP |
| Terminal Services | Display Station Pass Through | Telnet |
| Printing | Display Station Pass Through | LPR/LPD |
| File Services | Shared Folders | NFS |

The purpose of this chapter is twofold: To briefly illustrate the differences between TCP/IP and IBM's proprietary networking technology, Advanced Peer-to-Peer Communication (APPC) and to illustrate the limitations of TCP/IP in an AS/400environment, and suggest workarounds so the organization can get the benefits of TCP/IP without sacrificing the comprehensive nature of an APPC connection.

Exhibit 2 shows how TCP/IP and APPC connections are categorized into four critical areas. Because the table shows that TCP/IP and APPC provide similar functionality, it might be assumed that only the names of their respective functions are different. For example, TCP/IP provides terminal services with Telnet, whereas APPC provides terminal services with Display Station Pass Through (DSPT).

## Limitations of TCP/IP

To better understand the compromise associated with TCP/IP, however, the data center manager needs to look beyond Exhibit 2 and explore the actual implementation of the functions. With TCP/IP connections, there are limitations with three of the four functions listed: file transfer, terminal services, and printing. Combined, these limitations make up the compromise in a TCP/IP connection. Although the constraints are subtle and in some instances pose no real problem, data center managers should consider them carefully before taking the plunge into TCP/IP.

**File Transfer Limitation.** In the AS/400 world, most file transfers incorporate SQL query capabilities. In the TCP/IP world, the common file transfer protocol, FTP, does not allow for SQL queries. This results in the inability to selectively download on a filed record basis. In addition, FTP does not handle packed fields or binary numbers appropriately. To circumvent these problems, managers need to send the output of a query to a disk file and transfer the resulting file to the PC. This workaround is not elegant, but it does accomplish the task at hand.

**Terminal Services Limitation.** Although this limitation is subtle, it can pose larger problems. The terminal services provided by Telnet do not allow for Device Name Mapping. Telnet has no method for assigning a specific device name to a TN5250session. Instead, sites are randomly assigned a device name from a pool of available names. Unfortunately, for those sites that require specific naming, there is no workaround at this time. This is the only noteworthy difference between terminal services provided by Telnet and terminal services provided by Display Station Pass Through.

**Printing Limitation.** In the APPC world, 3812-to-PCL conversion takes place at the PC. In the TCP/IP world, using LPR/LPD, 3812-to-PCL conversion occurs on the host. Because host CPU cycles are typically in short supply, having the AS/400 CPU perform printer conversions can bog down the system. With short print jobs, there is no noticeable performance degradation on the host. However, with large jobs or numerous print jobs, slightly slower performance can be expected from the AS/400. Although this limitation is also subtle, it's a good idea to remember that AS/400 CPU cycles are being used for a task that used to be performed by the CPU of the PC, and manage your printing accordingly.

In spite of these limitations, TCP/IP offers both the benefits of open networking and a common protocol for sharing information with multi-vendor systems. The goal is to find a solution that capitalizes on the merits of TCP/IP, without trading off the functionality needed to maintain productivity. That solution can be found in Multi-Protocol Transport Networking. MPTN is an open architecture from IBM that enables integration of AS/400 systems into a multi-vendor connectivity environment. MPTN is available in Version 3 Release 1 of OS/400 as "AnyNet."

The primary advantage of MPTN is that this new interface allows the use of APPC to communicate over TCP/IP networks. This means that the full capability of an APPC connection is available over the existing TCP/IP backbone. Effectively, this links a client PC directly to the AS/400, providing transparent access to functions such as AS/400 printing and file transfer. In essence, it enables the functions typically associated with DSPT, but over a TCP/IP connection. In contrast, TN5250 supports terminal functions via TCP/IP, printing is handled by LPR/LPD, and file transfer is handled by FTP.

Exhibit 3 shows a graphical representation of MPTN at the PC and the AS/400. MPTN can be thought of as a translation layer between APPC and TCP/IP. This translation layer must exist on both the client and host to accomplish the connection. As far as end users are concerned, they are communicating via APPC. To the network it just looks like another TCP/IP packet.

## CONCLUSION

TCP/IP offers the benefits of open networking and connecting multi-vendor systems together with a single protocol. There has been a recent proliferation of free data communications protocol suites, with many distinct advantages. However, because an application is only as reliable as the protocol suite it

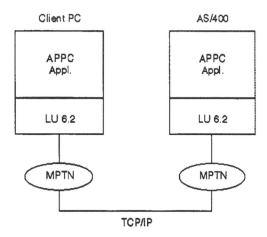

**Exhibit 3. MPTN at the PC and the AS/400.**

runs on, several issues must be carefully considered before selecting a product.

Data center managers should also examine architecture features, such as mobile connectivity, and applications, such as those critical to the smooth functioning of the enterprise, when they choose a TCP/IP stack for their complex organizations. For organizations with an AS/400, still more protocol limitations must be considered, such as file transfer, terminal services, and printing. Above all, the decision to use TCP/IP free software is the result of careful evaluation of organizations' equipment and goals against the costs of sustaining such software.

# Chapter 42

# Choosing and Equipping an Internet Server

*Nathan J. Muller*

The key to truly reaping the benefits of the Internet lies within the server. A server should provide ease-of-use and security and support such basic applications as E-mail and newsgroups. This chapter describes how to choose an Internet server and application software that best fits the needs of different users and organizations.

## INTRODUCTION

The Internet is a global collection of servers interconnected by routers over various types of carrier-provided lines and services. It comprises more than 4 million hosts on about 100,000 networks in 160 countries. Approximately 30 million people have access to the Internet, a number that is expected to grow to 200 million by the turn of the century. The Internet comprises databases that have a combined capacity that can only be measured in terabytes — more information than has ever been printed on paper. It is accessed and navigated by PCs and workstations equipped with client software such as Mosaic and Netscape.

## INTERNET AND INTRANET SERVICES

One of the most popular and fastest-growing services on the Internet is the World Wide Web, also known as WWW or simply "the Web." The Web is an interactive, graphically-oriented, distributed, platform-independent, hypertext information system. Browser software such as Netscape and Mosaic make it easy for users to find information published on Web servers, which can be configured for public or private access. When configured for private access, companies can create VPN or "intranets" to facilitate information exchange among employees, customers, suppliers, and strategic partners.

0-8493-9965-3/99/$0.00+$.50
© 1999 by CRC Press LLC

Of all the services that can be accessed over the Internet, the Web holds the greatest promise for electronic commerce. Using catalogs displayed on the Web, customers can order products by filling out forms transmitted through E-mail. Often the transactions include buyers' credit card numbers, which requires a secure means of transmission. Other electronic commerce applications include online banking and stock trading.

With a Web server, an organization can leverage Web technology for internal communication on an intranet by producing online documentation of corporate materials, automating sales force activities, providing training-on-demand, or using data warehousing capabilities to analyze large amounts of data or complex data.

The factor driving these activities is the same in every case: providing users access to information. As companies use the Web to deliver new services, they need solutions that are capable of storing, managing, and organizing all of their existing data. Furthermore, these mechanisms need to tie into existing applications and be reliable, scalable, and open.

Early Web implementations focused on providing access to static data, mostly in the form of simple text and graphics. As Web-based interactions become more complex, the next step is the creation of real-world applications that can manipulate, input, modify, analyze, and apply this content to everyday tasks. The need for live, online applications that can manipulate dynamic, constantly changing data is driving the Web into the next phase of its evolution.

## PLATFORM CONSIDERATIONS

The key to delivering services over the Internet is the server. The Internet is a true client/server network. Integrating into this client/server environment requires servers with strong connectivity capabilities suitable for high-traffic and mission-critical applications. The server must have ease-of-use functionality that allows corporate users to access information quickly and easily. The server must have security features that enable users to share confidential information or conduct encrypted electronic transactions across the Internet. Finally, the server must be able to support the many applications that have become the staple of the Internet, including electronic mail and newsgroups.

### Processor Architecture

A high-performance server is a virtual requirement for any company that is serious about establishing a presence on the Internet. There are basically two choices of processor architectures: RISC-based or CISC-based. RISC processors are usually used on high-end UNIX servers; CISC processors, such as Intel's Pentium Pro, are used on Windows NT machines. The performance of the Pentium Pro rivals that of RISC processors and costs less.

Because of the volume of service requests — sometimes tens of thousands a day — the server should be equipped with the most powerful processor available. The more powerful the processor, the greater the number of service requests (i.e., page lookups, database searches, and forms processing) the server will be able to handle.

**SMP Servers.** Servers with SMP enable the operating system to distribute different processing jobs among two or more processors. All the CPUs have equal capabilities and can handle the same tasks. Each CPU can run the operating system as well as user applications. Not only can any CPUs execute any job, but jobs can be shifted from one CPUs to another as the load changes. This capability can be very important at high-traffic sites, especially those that do a lot of local processing to fulfill service requests.

Some servers come equipped with multiple RISC or CISC processors. Users should be aware, however, that the added cost of an SMP server is not merely a few hundred dollars per extra processor. There are costs for additional hardware resources as well — such as extra RAM and storage space — that can add several thousand dollars to the purchase price. However, as needs change, users can upgrade SMP servers incrementally without having to buy a new system. In this way, performance can be increased and the original hardware investment can be protected. This requirement is especially critical in the rapidly evolving Internet market in which organizations want to implement new applications on their servers that require increasing database and search performance.

### Operating System: UNIX vs. NT

When choosing a server, the operating system deserves particular attention. The choices are usually between UNIX and Windows NT. Although some vendors offer server software for Windows 3.1 and Windows 95, these are usually intended for casual rather than business use.

Most Internet servers are based on UNIX, but Windows NT is growing in popularity and may overtake UNIX in the near future. A Windows NT server offers comparable performance and functionality to a UNIX server and is easier to set up and administer, making it the platform of choice among developers of new sites.

Like UNIX, Windows NT is a multitasking, multithreaded operating system. As such, NT executes software as threads, which are streams of commands that make up applications. At any point during execution, NT's process manager interrupts (or preempts) a thread to allow another thread some CPUs time. Also like UNIX, Windows NT supports multiple processors.

If the server has more than one CPUs, NT distributes the threads over the processors, allowing two or more threads to run simultaneously.

### Fault Tolerance

If the server is supporting mission-critical applications over the Internet, several levels of fault tolerance merit consideration. Fault tolerance must be viewed from both the systems and subsystems perspectives.

**Site Mirroring.** From the systems perspective, fault tolerance can be implemented by linking multiple servers together. When one system fails or must be taken offline for upgrades or reconfigurations, the standby system is activated to handle the load. This is often called site mirroring. An additional level of protection can be obtained through features of the operating system that protect read and write processes in progress during the switch to the standby system.

**Hot Standby.** At the subsystem level, there are several server options that can improve fault tolerance, including ports, network interfaces, memory expansion cards, disks, tapes, and I/O channels. All must be duplicated so that an alternate hardware component can assume responsibility in the event of a subsystem failure. This procedure is sometimes referred to as a hot-standby solution, whereby a secondary subsystem monitors the tasks of the primary subsystem in preparation for assuming such tasks when needed.

If a component in the primary subsystem fails, the secondary subsystem takes over without users being aware that a changeover has taken place. An obvious disadvantage of this solution is that companies must purchase twice the amount of hardware needed, and half of this hardware remains idle unless a failure occurs in the primary system.

Because large amounts of data may be located at the server, the server must be able to implement recovery procedures in the event of a program, operating system, or hardware failure. For example, when a transaction terminates abnormally, the server must be able to detect an incomplete transaction so that the database is not left in an inconsistent state. The server's rollback facility is invoked automatically, which backs out of the partially updated database. The transaction can then be resubmitted by the program or user. A roll-forward facility recovers completed transactions and updates in the event of a disk failure by reading a transaction journal that contains a record of all updates.

**Load Balancing.** Another means of achieving fault tolerance is to have all hardware components function simultaneously, but with a load-balancing mechanism that reallocates the processing tasks to surviving components when a failure occurs. This technique requires a UNIX operating system equipped with vendor options that continually monitor the system for errors and dynamically reconfigures the system to adapt to performance problems.

**Hot Swapping.** Hot swapping is an important capability that allows the network administrator to remove and replace faulty server modules without interrupting or degrading network performance. In some cases, standby modules can be brought online through commands issued at the network management workstation or automatically upon fault detection.

**Uninterruptible Power Supply.** To guard against an onsite power outage, an UPS can provide an extra measure of protection. The UPS provides enough standby power to permit continuous operation or an orderly shutdown during power failures, or to change over to other power sources such as diesel-powered generators. Some UPSs have SNMP capabilities, so network managers can monitor battery backup from the central management console. For example, using SNMP, every UPS can be instructed to test itself once a week and report back if the test fails.

## INTERNET APPLICATION SOFTWARE

An Internet server must be equipped with software that allows it to run various Internet applications. Some server software supports general communications for document publishing over the World Wide Web. Often called a communications server or Web server, this type of server can be enhanced with software specifically designed for secure electronic commerce. Server software is available for performing many different functions, including implementing newsgroups, facilitating message exchange (i.e., E-mail), improving the performance and security of communications, and controlling traffic between the Internet and the corporate network.

Sometimes a server is dedicated to a single application such as E-mail, newsgroups, or electronic commerce. Other times, the server supports multiple Internet applications. The specific configuration depends on such factors as available system resources (i.e., memory, disk space, processing power, and port capacity), network topology, available bandwidth, traffic patterns, and the security requirements of the organization.

### Communications Software

A communications server enables users to access various documents and services that reside on it and retrieve them using the HTTP. These servers support the standard multimedia document format — the HTML — for the presentation of rich text, graphics, audio, and video. Hyperlinks connect related information across the network, creating a seamless web. Client software such as Mosaic and Netscape is used for navigation. Some vendors offer servers preconfigured with these Internet protocols, allowing them to be quickly installed and put into operation.

A key service performed by any Internet server is the translation of complex IP addresses to simpler server domain names. When a user requests the URL of a certain Web page, for example, the DNS replies with the numeric IP address of the server the user is contacting. It does this by checking a lookup table that cross-references server domain names and IP addresses.

For example, the domain name ddx might stand for "dynamic data exchange." This domain name might translate into the IP address 204.177.193.22. The translation capability of the IDNS makes it easy for users to access Internet resources by not requiring them to learn and enter long strings of numbers. To access the Web page of DDE, the user would enter the URL as http://www.ddx.com, which contains the domain name ddx.

## Commerce Software

A commerce server is used for conducting secure electronic commerce and communications on the Internet. It permits companies to publish hypermedia documents formatted in HTML and to deliver them using HTTP. To ensure data security, the commerce server provides advanced security features through the use of the SSL protocol, which provides:

- *Server authentication.* Any SSL-compatible client can verify the identity of the server using a certificate and a digital signature.
- *Data encryption.* The privacy of client/server communications is ensured by encrypting the data stream between the two entities.
- *Data integrity.* SSL verifies that the contents of a message arrive at their destination in the same form as they were sent.

As with other types of Internet servers, vendors offer commerce servers preconfigured with the protocols necessary to support electronic commerce.

## News Software

A news server lets users create secure public and private discussion groups for access over the Internet and other TCP/IP-based networks using the standard NNTP. The news server's support of NNTP enables it to accept feeds from popular Usenet newsgroups and allows the creation and maintenance of private discussion groups. Most newsreaders are based on NNTP; some support SSL for secure communication between clients and news servers.

A news server should support the MIME, which allows users to send virtually any type of data across the Internet, including text, graphics, sound, video clips, and many other types of files. Attaching documents in a variety of formats greatly expands the capability of a discussion group to serve as a repository of information and knowledge to support workgroup collaboration. Colleagues can download documents sent to the group, mark them up, and send them back.

## Mail Software

Client/server messaging systems are implemented by special mail software installed on a server. Mail software lets users easily exchange information within a company as well as across the Internet. Mail software has many features that can be controlled by either the system administrator or each user with an E-mail account.

The mail software should conform to open standards, including HTTP, MIME, SMTP, and POP3. MIME lets organizations send and receive messages with rich content types, thereby allowing businesses to transmit mission-critical information of any type without loss of fidelity. The SMTP ensures interoperability with other client/server messaging systems that support Internet mail or proprietary messaging systems with Internet mail gateways. The POP3 ensures interoperability with such popular client software as Zmail, Eudora, Pegasus Mail, Microsoft Exchange client (with the Microsoft "Plus" pack), and most other Internet-capable mail products.

## Proxy Software

To improve the performance and security of communications across the TCP/IP-based Internet, many organizations use a proxy server. This kind of software offers performance improvements by using an intelligent cache for storing retrieved documents.

The proxy's disk-based caching feature minimizes use of the external network by eliminating recurrent retrievals of commonly accessed documents. This feature provides additional "virtual bandwidth" to existing network resources and significantly improves interactive response time for locally attached clients. The resulting performance improvements provide a cost-effective alternative to purchasing additional network bandwidth. Because the cache is disk-based, it can be tuned to provide optimal performance based on network usage patterns.

The proxy server should allow dynamic process management, which allows the creation of a configurable number of processes that reside in memory waiting to fulfill HTTP requests. This feature improves system performance by eliminating the unnecessary overhead of creating and deleting processes to fulfill every HTTP request. The dynamic process management algorithm increases the number of server processes, within configurable limits, to efficiently handle periods of peak demand, resulting in faster document serving, greater throughput delivery, and better system reliability.

### Firewall Software

An application-level firewall acts as a security wall and gateway between a trusted internal network and such untrustworthy networks as the Internet. Access can be controlled by individuals or groups of users or by system names, domains, subnets, date, time, protocol, and service.

Security is bidirectional, simultaneously prohibiting unauthorized users from accessing the corporate network while also managing internal users' Internet access privileges. The firewall even periodically checks its own code to prevent modification by sophisticated intruders.

The firewall gathers and logs information about where attempted break-ins originate, how they got there, and what the people responsible for them appear to be doing. Log entries include information on connection attempts, service types, users, file transfer names and sizes, connection duration, and trace routes. Together, this information leaves an electronic footprint that can help identify intruders.

### WEB DATABASE CONSIDERATIONS

Internet servers are the repositories of various databases. These databases may be set up for public access or for restricted intracompany access. In either case, the challenge of maintaining the information is apparent to IS professionals charged with keeping it accurate and up to date.

Vendors are developing ways to ease the maintenance burden. For example, database management vendors such as Oracle Corp. offer ways of integrating an existing data warehouse with the Internet without having to reformat the data into HTML. The data is not sent until a request is received and validated.

In addition, the server supports HTTP-type negotiation, so it can deliver different versions of the same object (e.g., an image stored in multiple formats) according to each client's preferences. The server also supports national language negotiation, allowing the same document in different translations to be delivered to different clients.

The database server should support the two common authentication mechanisms: basic and digest authentication. Both mechanisms allow certain directories to be protected by user name/password combinations. However, digest authentication transmits encrypted passwords and basic authentication does not. Other security extensions that may be bundled with database servers include HTTP, S-HTTP and SSL standards, which are especially important in supporting electronic commerce applications.

## Maintenance and Testing Tools

The maintenance of most Web databases still relies on the diligence of each document owner or site administrator to periodically check for integrity by testing for broken links, malformed documents, and outdated information. Data base integrity is usually tested by visually scanning each document and manually activating every hypertext link. Particular attention should be given to links that reference other Web sites because they are usually controlled by a third party who can change the location of files to a different server or directory or delete them entirely.

**Link Analyzers.** Link analyzers can examine a collection of documents and validate the links for accessibility, completeness, and consistency. However, this type of integrity check is usually applied more as a means of one-time verification than as a regular maintenance process. This check also fails to provide adequate support across distributed databases and for situations in which the document contents are outside the immediate span of control.

**Log Files.** Some types of errors can be identified by the server's log files. The server records each document request and, if an error occurred, the nature of that error. Such information can be used to identify requests for documents that have moved and those that have misspelled URL, which are used to identify the location of documents on the Internet. Only the server manager usually has access to that information, however. The error is almost never relayed to the person charged with document maintenance, either because it is not recognized as a document error or because the origin of the error is not apparent from the error message.

Even with better procedures, log files do not reveal failed requests that never made it to the server, nor can they support preventive maintenance and problems associated with changed document content. With a large and growing database, manual maintenance methods become difficult and may eventually become impossible.

## Design Tools

New design tools are available that address the maintenance and testing issue by providing the means to visualize the creation, maintenance, and navigation of whole collections of online documents. Where traditional Web tools such as browsers and HTML editors focus on the Web page, these tools address the Web site, which may be either physical or logical in structure. These tools include a system to identify which pages are included in the site and another to describe how the pages are interconnected. The construction of a site is facilitated by providing templates for creating pages and scripts and linkage to tools for editing and verifying HTML documents.

In addition to offering high-level views of a site — either graphical or hierarchical — the design tools check for stale links (either local or remote), validate the conformance level of HTML pages, and make broad structural changes to the site architecture by using a mouse to drag and drop sections of the Web hierarchy into a different location.

**Agents or Robots.** Although design tools address document creation and maintenance at the site level, they do not comprehensively address the maintenance needs of distributed hypertext infrastructures that span multiple Web sites. This task can be handled by special software known as agents or robots. These programs can be given a list of instructions about what databases to traverse, whom to notify for problems, and where to put the resulting maintenance information.

For example, the agent or robot may be tasked to provide information about the following conditions that typically indicate document changes:

- *A referenced object has a redirected* Uniform Resource Locator. (i.e., a document has been moved to another location).
- *A referenced object cannot be accessed.* (i.e., there is a broken or improperly configured link).
- *A referenced object has a recently modified date.*(i.e., the contents of a document have changed).
- *An owned object has an upcoming expiration date.* (i.e., a document may be removed or changed soon).

To get its instructions, the agent or robot reads a text file containing a list of options and tasks to be performed. Each task describes a specific hypertext infrastructure to be encompassed by the traversal process. A task instruction includes the traversal type, an infrastructure name (for later reference), the "top URL" at which to start traversing, the location for placing the indexed output, an E-mail address that corresponds to the owner of that infrastructure, and a set of options that determine what identified maintenance issues justify sending an E-mail message.

## COMMON GATEWAY INTERFACE

An Internet server should support the CGI, which is a standard for interfacing external applications with information servers, such as HTTP or Web servers. Gateway programs handle information requests and return the appropriate document or generate one spontaneously. With CGI, a Web server can serve information that is not in a form readable by the client (i.e., an SQL database) and act as a gateway between the two to produce something that clients can interpret and display.

Gateways can be used for a variety of purposes, the most common being the processing of form requests, such as database queries or online purchase orders.

Gateways conforming to the CGI specification can be written in any language that produces an executable file, such as C and C+. Among the more popular languages for developing CGI scripts are PERL and TCL, both derivatives of the C language.

An advantage of using PERL and TCL is that either language can be used to speed the construction of applications to which new scripts and script components can be added without the need to recompile and restart, as is required when the C language is used. Of course, the server on which the CGI scripts reside must have a copy of the program itself — PERL, TCL, or an alternative program.

## CONCLUSION

The client/server architecture of the Internet and its use of open protocols for information formatting and delivery makes it possible for any connected computer to provide services to any other computer. With this capability, businesses can extend communications beyond organizational boundaries and serve the informational needs of all users.

The type of services that are available depends on the application software that runs on one or more servers. A server may be dedicated to a specific Internet application or multiple applications, depending on such factors as system resources and the specific needs of the organization. A careful evaluation of the hardware platform, operating system, and application software in terms of features and conformance to Internet standards ensures that the current and emerging needs of the organization and its users are met in an efficient and economical manner.

# Chapter 43
# Supporting a Web Site
*Gilbert Held*

The popularity of the World Wide Web is beyond dispute, with over 25 million persons now surfing the Web on a daily basis. As organizations continue to "step forward" and establish a presence on the Web, management will rapidly note that in many cases the initial cost estimate represents the proverbial tip of the iceberg. In this chapter our goal is to become aware of the entire iceberg by focusing attention upon the economics associated with supporting a Web site. To do so we will turn our attention to the communications link, hardware platform, software, and personnel that may be required to support a Web site. This will provide you with a firm indication of the true potential cost that can be associated with supporting the presence of your organization on the Web.

## COMMUNICATIONS

The connection of a Web server to the Internet is commonly accomplished via the use of a leased line between your server site and an Internet Service Provider (ISP). At your server site your Web server is normally connected to a local area network (LAN), and the LAN is connected to a router which in turn is connected to the leased line routed to the ISP. Exhibit 1 illustrates the previously described method used to connect a Web server to the Internet.

In examining Exhibit 1 it is important to note that some ISPs will provide a router and arrange for the installation of a leased line for a single monthly fee. If the ISP is also a communications carrier it can provide both the leased line and the router which may result in a slight reduction in the total monthly cost due to the elimination of a middleman. Examples of ISPs that are also communications carriers include AT&T, MCI, Sprint, and several of the local Bell Operating Companies (BOCs).

The router provides the ability to move traffic destined to a different network off the LAN hub to the ISP which forwards data to the Internet. Similarly, the router also accepts inbound data and places such data onto the local network via a connection to the hub. Most ISPs allow customers to purchase a router; however, they will only guarantee support for certain

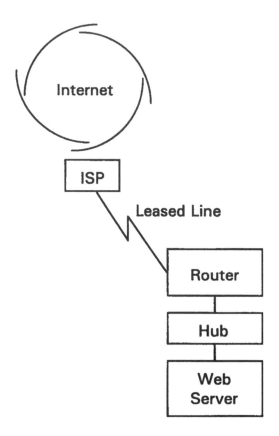

**Exhibit 1. Connecting a Web Server to the Internet.**

products. This means that if you obtain a non-supported product and a problem arises, the ISP will not be able to test the connection from their location to your router's wide area network interface.

The actual leased line can range in scope from a Dataphone Digital Service (DDS) 56 Kbps line to a fractional T1 operating in increments of 56 or 64 Kbps up to 784 Kbps, or a full T1 operating at 1.544 Mbps. Thus, the actual cost for communications will vary based upon the type of transmission facility installed. Although most ISPs bill monthly based upon the transmission capacity of the leased line, several ISPs introduced a new type of measured transmission service during 1996. One example of this measured service is offered by BBN Planet which will install a T1 line and bill your organization based upon the average utilization of the transmission facility over a 24-hour per day period on a monthly basis. Although this measured usage billing mechanism can provide significant savings for organizations that need the ability to support periodic surges in network traffic from a relatively low base of usage, if you have a consistent high level of usage a more conventional fixed rate plan may be more appropriate.

Returning to Exhibit 1, note that the Web server is shown as only one of two devices connected to the LAN hub, with the other device being the router. This type of connection represents a communications isolated connection to the Internet since there is no possible access from the Internet to other corporate computers that may reside on an internal corporate network. Since many organizations either have other devices connected to the network to which the Web server is connected or use a multiport router to connect multiple networks to the Internet via a single Internet communications connection, security then becomes a very important issue to consider.

## SECURITY ISSUES

Almost all routers include a filtering capability that can be used to enable or disable the flow of packets based upon source address, destination address, and TCP's "well-known" port. Here the term "well-known" port represents a numeric that identifies the type of application data being transported within a TCP packet. For example, a value of 25 is used for the Simple Mail Transport Protocol (SMTP) used to transport electronic mail, while a value of 80 is used for the HyperText Transport Protocol (HTTP) used to transport Web browser data. Thus, by configuring the router to disable all traffic on TCP port 25 you could disable the flow of electronic mail.

Although router filtering is useful, it cannot prevent repetitive attacks against your computer resources. For example, if your Web server is also configured to support the file transfer protocol (ftp), a hacker could guess an account name by repetitively using the entries in an electronic dictionary to first obtain an account name, and could then reuse the dictionary to discover a password associated with the account. Preventing this so-called dictionary attack as well as providing additional levels of security beyond router filtering requires the use of a firewall.

## THE FIREWALL OPTION

Exhibit 2 illustrates the use of a firewall to protect an internal corporate network connected to the Internet by the use of a two-LAN port router. In this example the Web server can be considered to reside on the public access network while the corporate internal network obtains protection from the use of a firewall.

The actual cost of a firewall can range from approximately $2500 to well over $30,000, with the more expensive products providing authentication, encryption, and a digital signature capability, features not included in low cost products. In addition to the one-time cost of the firewall, most vendors

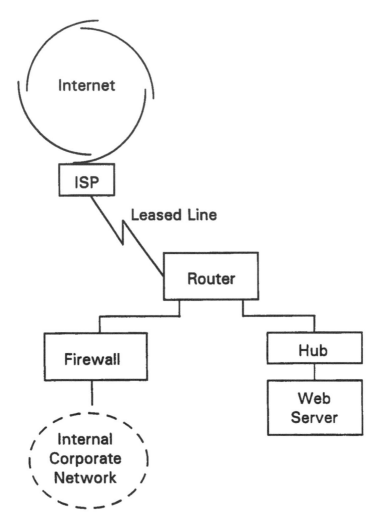

**Exhibit 2. Using a Firewall to Protect an Internal Corporate Network.**

market a separate yearly maintenance fee that provides support and software upgrades. Concerning the actual configuration and operation of a firewall, it can require a minimum of a day or two to set up. Thereafter, the level of support will vary based upon the dynamics of the organization. If your organization frequently changes policies and rules, you can expect a member of your communications staff to be devoted to reconfiguring and testing the firewall. If your organization rarely changes rules and policies once they are established, you can probably expect an existing employee to devote only a few hours every few weeks to maintaining the firewall.

Now that we have an appreciation for the communications involved in supporting a Web site, let's turn our attention to the hardware platform.

## HARDWARE

A Web server can be established on a variety of platforms, ranging from older Intel 486 computers to the latest Sun Microsystem Solaris workstations, Intel Pentium and Pentium Pro, and Digital Equipment Corporation's Alpha-based systems. Although Sun Solaris-based computers probably represented the majority of Web server platforms established during 1994 and 1995, the introduction of Pentium and Pentium Pro microprocessors and Microsoft's Windows NT Server resulted in the "Win-Tel" combination of Windows NT Server operating on an Intel-based Pentium or Pentium Pro becoming a very popular platform.

Most organizations establishing a Web presence look upon themselves as explorers charting virgin territory since there is no practical method to anticipate usage. This means that an effective hardware platform will represent one that is expandable to satisfy an increased level of usage if the site should grow in popularity. One commonly used type of platform is a multiprocessor server with a Redundant Array of Inexpensive Disks (RAID) storage subsystem. In early 1997 ARL, DEC, Dell and IBM offered multiprocessor capable motherboard systems that could support 2, 4, 6, and eventually 8 Pentium or Pentium Pro processors. Thus, if a single Pentium Pro should prove inadequate you can add additional processors instead of having to consider the use of a UNIX-based minicomputer or a mainframe. Concerning disk storage, most multiprocessor capable servers support RAID storage subsystems that include drive-bys into which you can easily install additional drives while the server continues to operate. Due to the modular design of most modern Web server hardware platforms, upgrades can usually be accomplished in hours instead of days. Thus, hardware support can usually be accomplished by existing personnel. Unfortunately, this is usually not the case with software which we will examine next.

## SOFTWARE

There are three areas you must consider when planning support requirements for software. Those areas include the operating system, server software, and applications software.

## OPERATING SYSTEM

Most modern operating systems now are changed on almost a yearly basis. Since few organizations are comfortable with simply upgrading their OS without prior testing, many organizations first upgrade a test platform and test that software upgrade for a period of time prior to migrating the upgrade to their production computer. Web servers are no exception to this test first policy, which means you may have to consider acquiring a test server if your organization plans to test software prior to installing new products on a production server.

The value of a test platform was recently noted by a series of problems associated with a service pack for a popular operating system. This service pack, which represents a minor release designed to correct bugs, introduced a new one that caused Web servers to freeze. Fortunately, several organizations noted this problem on their test server and did not apply the service pack release to their production server.

The personnel support required for the operating system to include maintaining administrative accounts usually requires only a few hours per week and may be able to be performed by existing personnel. The real effort that will more than likely require additional employees involves support for Web server software and the application programming effort involved in creating and maintaining Web pages on the server.

## SERVER SOFTWARE

The installation and operation of a Web server software program is normally a relatively simple non-time consuming process. What turns this process into a half to full time position is when you add access controls to different directories on your Web server and have a dynamic environment that requires frequent backups. Under such circumstances you may require an employee to devote a considerable amount of time to maintaining Web accounts, performing tape backups onto a backup server, and performing other administrative actions. Quite often many organizations will assign hardware, operating system, and Web server support to one individual on a full time basis and designate a second employee as a backup.

## APPLICATION PROGRAMMING

The scope of the application programming effort required to support a Web server can vary considerably based upon the type of Web pages you plan to construct, whether or not you will use CGI scripts and JAVA applets, and the presence or absence of a database server that will be linked electronically to your Web server. For a simple Web site that uses only Hyper-Text Markup Language (HTML) to create static Web pages that are only periodically changed, you may only require the effort of one person to create and maintain application software on your Web server. As the complexity of the Web site increases, the level of support can increase in tandem. In fact, based upon the experience of this author in installing, configuring, and managing approximately 30 Web sites, you can expect the necessity to add a full time programmer to support the creation and testing of JAVA applets, and another person for database queries. Thus, a commercial Web site that requires the establishment of accounts and uses CGI scripts, JAVA applets, and an electronically linked database server could require at least four full time staff members to support all software related activities. One person would maintain the operating system and Web server software, while three additional employees would be assigned to the application programming development effort.

## RECOMMENDED COURSE OF ACTION

It is important to note that no two Web sites, unless they are mirrored, are equal. This manes that the level of support required to install, configure, operate, and maintain a corporate presence on the World Wide Web can vary from organization to organization based upon the type of server you will operate, the level of Web page design, and the possible linkage of your server's pages to a back-end database. Thus, readers should view the information presented in this chapter as general guidelines that can be used to note the potential level of support associated with communications, hardware, and software aspects associated with establishing and maintaining a Web server. In addition, this chapter indicates the various options for communications, hardware, and software you can consider which will have a bearing on the total cost associated with a Web site. By carefully considering your requirements and evaluating those requirements against the information presented in this chapter, you can determine the general level of support and cost associated with establishing and maintaining a Web site. This in turn will allow you to note the true shape of the iceberg in terms of cost and support, instead of just noting the proverbial "tip of the iceberg!"

# Chapter 44
# Selecting a Web Server Connection Rate
*Gilbert Held*

Determining the best operating rate for a WAN connection to the Internet is a common problem for organizations wishing to obtain a presence on the World Wide Web. Some simple calculations can help network managers compare and balance user requirements against the cost of providing an Internet connection.

## PROBLEMS ADDRESSED

If the operating rate of the Internet connection is too slow, anyone trying to access an organization's server from the Internet may get frustrated and terminate their access of information from the corporate Web server site. At the opposite extreme, if an organization's Internet access connection operating rate exceeds the bandwidth required to support an acceptable level of access, you may be wasting corporate funds for an unnecessary level of transmission capacity.

As this chapter shows, with knowledge of the ways in which a Web server can be connected to the Internet, as well as knowledge about some of the transmission constraints associated with a Web server connection, it is possible to determine an appropriate Web server connection rate.

## BASICS OF CONNECTING TO THE INTERNET

Exhibit 1 illustrates the typical method by which Web servers are normally connected to the Internet. A Web server resides on a local area network, with the LAN connected via a router to an IAP. The IAP has a direct connection to a backbone network node on the Internet, commonly using a full T3 or SMDS connection to provide Internet access for a large group of organizations that obtain Internet access through its connection facilities.

Although an Ethernet bus-based LAN is shown in Exhibit 1, in actuality any type of local area network that can be connected to a router (and for which TCP/IP drivers are available) can be used by the Web server. Thus,

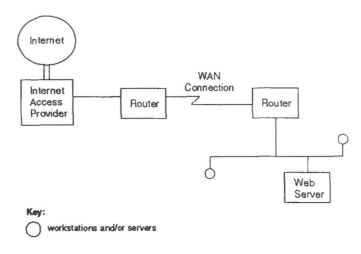

**Exhibit 1. Web Server Connection to the Internet.**

other common LANs used by Web servers include Token Ring and FDDI as well as the numerous flavors of Ethernet, such as 10Base-T, 100Base-T, and 100VG-AnyLAN.

### Analog vs. Digital Leased Lines

The actual WAN connection between the IAP and the customer can range in scope from low-speed analog leased lines to a variety of digital leased lines. Only a few access providers offer analog leased line connection options. When offered, the actual operating rate of the WAN connection is commonly limited to 19.2K bps or 24.4K bps, based on bandwidth constraints of a voice-grade analog leased line that limits modem-operating rates. Concerning digital leased line operating rates, IAP recommend and offer 56K-bps, Fractional T1 in increments of 56K- or 64K-bps, full T1, fractional T3, and full T3 connectivity.

### Connection Constraints

Although the WAN operating rate can constrain users from accessing information from an organization's Web server, another less recognized but equally important constraint exists — that is, the traffic on the local area network on which the Web server resides. Although the focus of this chapter is on determining an appropriate WAN operating rate to connect a Web server to the Internet, it also examines the constraints associated with LAN traffic that affect the ability of the server to respond to information requests received from the Internet.

## WAN Connectivity Factors

Three key factors govern the selection of an appropriate operating rate to connect a Web server to the Internet through a wide area network transmission facility. Those factors include:

- The composition of the Web pages residing on a server.
- The types of pages retrieved by a person accessing the Web server.
- The number of "hits" expected to occur during the busy hour.

A typical Web page consists of a mixture of graphics and text. For example, a university might include a picture of "Old Main" on the home page in the form of a GIF file consisting of 75,000 bytes of storage supplemented by 500 characters of text that welcomes Internet surfers to the university home page. Thus, this university home page would contain 75,500 bytes that must be transmitted each time a member of the Internet community accesses the home page of the university.

By computing the data storage requirements of each page stored on the Web server and estimating the access distribution of each page, it is possible to compute the average number of bytes transmitted in response to each Internet access to the organization's Web server.

For example, assume an organization plans to develop a Web server that stores four distinct Web pages as well as a home page, providing Internet users with the ability to access two types of data from the home page. The construction of a two-tier page relationship under the home page is illustrated in Exhibit 2.

This example used to compute an appropriate WAN operating rate is for illustrative purposes only. Although the Web home page is always initially accessed, from the home page users typically access other server pages using hypertext links coded on the home page. Similarly, upon accessing different server pages, a user who wants to jump to other pages on the server is constrained by the links programmed on each page. Thus, the data transmitted in response to each page an Internet user accesses, as well as the sequence of pages accessed, will more than likely differ from organization to organization.

## PERFORMING THE REQUIRED COMPUTATIONS

Assume that an organization has already determined that when Web pages are arranged in a tier structure, access to a home page at the top of the tier represents 40% of all accesses, while the remaining 60% is subdivided by remaining tiers. Furthermore, the organization's Web page structure is to be constructed in two tiers below the home page, with the data storage associated with each page to include text and graphics as well as the access percentage of each page, as listed at the bottom of Exhibit 2.

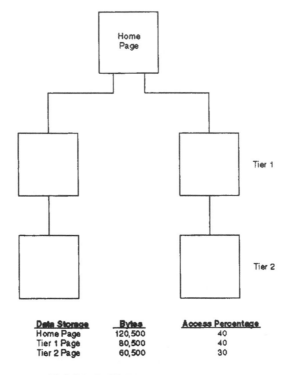

| Data Storage | Bytes | Access Percentage |
|---|---|---|
| Home Page | 120,500 | 40 |
| Tier 1 Page | 80,500 | 40 |
| Tier 2 Page | 60,500 | 30 |

**Exhibit 2. Web Page Relationship.**

After determining the data storage required for each Web page and the distribution of Internet access by page, it is possible to compute the average number of bytes that will be transmitted from the Web server in response to each "hit" on the organization's server. Here the term "hit" refers to an access request to a Web page on the server via the HTTP using a URL that represents a file stored on the server, which equates to the contents of a Web page.

Using the information from Exhibit 2, the average data transmission rate resulting from a hit on the organization's server is computed as follows:

$$120,500 \times .40 + 80,500 \times .30 + 60,500 \times .30 = 90,500$$

Thus, each hit on the organization's Web server results in a requirement to transmit 90,500 bytes of data from the server to the Internet via the WAN connection to the IAP.

### Hit Estimation

Perhaps the most difficult estimate to make is the number of hits that are expected to occur during the busiest hour of the business day. Access to an organization's Web server depends on a large number of variables, many of which are beyond the control of the organization.

For example, although a company can control advertising of its Web's URL in trade publications, it may be difficult (if not impossible) to inhibit robot search engines from visiting the site, retrieving each page available for public access on the company's server and indexing the contents of the server's Web pages. Once this index is placed onto the database of a search engine, access to the company's Web server can result from persons invoking a Web search using Lycos, Alta Vista, or a similar search engine.

Unfortunately, because of limitations associated with many search engines, forward references to an organization's Web server may not be relevant and can alter the distribution of page hits as many persons, upon viewing your home page, may click on the "back" button to return to the list of search matches provided by a search engine query and select a different match. If the organization was a tire distributor named Roosevelt Tires, for example, many Web search engines would return the home page URL in response to a search for the word "Roosevelt," even though the person was searching for references to one of the presidents and not for an automobile tire distributor.

Many IAP can furnish statistics that may be applicable for use by an organization. A major exception to using such average statistics is if an organization is placing highly desirable information on the Web server, such as the results of major sports events like the Super Bowl or World Series as they occur. Otherwise, the information concerning busy hour hits the company's IAP supplies can be considered to represent a reasonable level of activity that will materialize.

Returning to the estimation process, assume the organization can expect 660 hits during the busy hour. Although this hit activity may appear to be low in comparison to the tens of hundreds of thousands of hits reported by well-known URL representing popular Web server sites, during a 24-hour period you are configuring the operating rate of the WAN connection to support $24 \times 660$ or 15,840 hits, based upon a busy hour hit rate of 660.

According to statistics published by several IAP, during 1995 the average number of hits per Web site when the top 100 sites are excluded is under 5,000 per day. Thus, if an organization is the typical business, college, or government agency, it may be able to use a lower WAN operating rate than determined by this example.

After determining the number of hits the Web site will support during the busy hour and the average number of bytes that will be transmitted in response to a hit, it is possible to compute other WAN operating rates. For this example, each hit results in the transmission of 90,500 bytes, and the

WAN operating rate is sized to support 660 hits during the busy hour. Thus, the results obtained are:

660 hits per hour × 90,500 bytes per hit × 8 bits60 minutes per hour
× 60 seconds per minute = 132,733 bps

## LAN BANDWIDTH CONSTRAINTS

Based on the preceding computations it would be tempting to order a 192K-bps Fractional T1 as the WAN connection to the IAP, because the next lower fraction of service, 128K bps, would not provide a sufficient operating rate to accommodate the computed busy hour transmission requirement for 132,733 bps. However, before ordering the fractional T1 line, the business needs to consider the average bandwidth the Web server can obtain on the LAN it is connected to.

If the average bandwidth exceeds the computed WAN operating rate, the LAN will not be a bottleneck that should be modified. If the average LAN bandwidth obtainable by the Web server is less than the computed WAN operating rate, the local area network will function as a bottleneck, impeding access via the WAN to the Web server. This means that regardless of any increase in the operating rate of the wide area network connection, users' ability to access the organization's Web server will be restricted by local traffic on the LAN.

If this situation should occur, possible solutions are segmenting the LAN, creating a separate LAN for the Web server, migrating to a higher-speed technology, or performing a network adjustment to remove the effect of a portion of local LAN traffic functioning as a bottleneck to the Web server.

### Determining the Effect on Local Traffic

To illustrate the computations involved in analyzing the effect of local traffic, assume the LAN shown in Exhibit 1 is a 10M-bps 10Base-T network that supports 23 workstations and one file server in addition to the Web server, resulting in a total of 25 stations on the network. This means that on the average, each network device will obtain access to 1/25 of the bandwidth of the LAN, or 400,000 bps (10M bps/25).

However, the bandwidth of the LAN does not represent the actual data transfer a network station can obtain. This is because the access protocol of the network will limit the achievable bandwidth to a percentage of the statistical average.

For example, on an Ethernet LAN that uses the CSMA/CD protocol, collisions will occur when two stations listen to the network and, noting an absence of transmission, attempt to transmit a frame at or near the same time. When a collision occurs, a jam signal is transmitted by the first station that detects the high voltage resulting from the collision, causing each station with data to transmit to invoke a random exponential backoff algorithm.

This algorithm generates a period of time the network station delays attempting a retransmission; however, the frequency of collisions, jams, and the invocation of backoff algorithms increase as network utilization increases. For an Ethernet LAN, network utilization beyond a 60% level can result in significant degradation of performance, which can serve as a cap on achievable transmission throughput. Thus, the average bandwidth of 400,000 bps previously computed should be multiplied by 60% to obtain a more realistic level of average available bandwidth obtainable by each station on the LAN to include the Web server.

In this example, the Web server will obtain on the average 240,000 bps of LAN bandwidth (i.e., 400,000 bps x .6). Since the average LAN bandwidth obtainable by the Web server exceeds the computed WAN operating rate, no adjustment is required to the LAN. If the Web server was connected to a Token Ring LAN, the average bandwidth of 400,000 bps should be multiplied by 75%, since a Token Ring LAN does not have its performance seriously degraded until network utilization exceeds 75%.

## MAKING WEB PAGE ADJUSTMENTS

As described thus far, network managers need to consider the LAN bandwidth obtained by the Web server as well as the WAN operating rate to effectively select a wide area network connection method to an IAP. When computing the WAN operating rate, it is important to note that the rate depends on:

- The number of hits expected to occur during the busy hour.
- The storage in bytes required to hold each page (which represents data that has to be transmitted in response to a page hit).
- The distribution of hits on the pages that are placed on the company's Web server.

The first and third factors are obtained by an estimation process. However, a company has a high degree of control over the composition of its server's Web pages, and this fact can be used as an effective tool in adjusting the WAN connection's ability to support the estimated number of hits expected during the busy hour.

Because initial access to a company's Web server is through its home page, that page will have the highest distribution of hits on the company server. Thus, if the estimate of busy hour traffic is low, it is possible to increase the selected WAN operating rate to support additional hits by reducing the transmission associated with each home page hit. Methods include replacing GIF images with their equivalent JPEG images that require less storage, cropping images to reduce their data storage requirements, or eliminating all or some images on the home page.

## RECOMMENDED COURSE OF ACTION

The selection of an appropriate wide area network operating rate to connect a corporate Web server to the Internet depends on three key factors, of which two — the expected number of hits during the busiest hour and the distribution of hits per server page — can only be estimated. This means that the WAN operating rate's ability to service expected traffic will only be as good as two traffic-related estimates.

However, by planning ahead the organization can adjust the third factor — the data storage on the server's home page — and obtain the flexibility to alter the selected WAN operating rate to support additional hits during the busy hour.

By following the methodology presented in this chapter, network managers and others involved in corporate Web page creation will be able to remove a large degree of the guesswork associated with connecting a Web server to the Internet. In addition, they should be able to rapidly adjust the capacity of a wide area network connection to support additional Web server hits if such an adjustment should become necessary.

# Chapter 45
# Criminal Activity on the Internet
*Edward H. Freeman*

The development and widespread use of the Internet and E-mail has changed the methods by which organizations distribute information. The Internet has also exposed organizations to new types of criminal activity, including privacy and copyright violations, fraud, libel, and several forms of industrial espionage. This chapter discusses the legal and ethical aspects of crime on the Internet and offers specific, practical suggestions that organizations and individuals can use to reduce potential problems.

## PROBLEMS ADDRESSED

Within the last five years, the Internet has developed into an efficient and inexpensive method to distribute and receive information. Organizations can conduct business on an instantaneous basis throughout the world. People around the world who have special interests can learn new skills, discuss common concerns, and exchange information quickly and informally.

Unfortunately, problems with criminal activity and privacy have been created with the development of the Internet. Long-time users are often disturbed with the rapid growth of the Internet. "The Internet...is becoming a tacky bazaar of junk mail, small-time scams, and now, lawyers and lawsuits."[1] The rapid development of the Internet and E-mail technology has created new legal ramifications for traditional criminal law.

This chapter discusses the development and current condition of the Internet. Criminal activity and how the courts and other government agencies have related this activity to the Internet and E-mail are addressed. The chapter defines what is necessary to prove or disprove charges of criminal activity on the Internet. Such associated issues as privacy, fraud, and copyright infringement, are also discussed. Examples from court cases are offered, as well as specific, practical steps that both organizations and individuals can take to reduce or prevent potential problems.

0-8493-9965-3/99/$0.00+$.50
© 1999 by CRC Press LLC

# THE INTERNET AND INTERNETWORKING

## HISTORY AND SCOPE

The Internet was born during the mid-1970s from an attempt to connect a Defense Department network with a series of radio and satellite networks. To transmit a message from one computer to another, the sender simply had to address the message correctly and send it over the network. The communicating computers, not the network, were responsible for ensuring that the communication was successfully completed.[2]

The development of inexpensive desktop computers and workstations has changed the scope of the computer and communications market. Organizations now expect the capability to transmit large quantities of documents and data. Certain communications (e.g., business and medical documents) must be transmitted confidentially. Other Internet items (e.g., commercial databases, bulletin boards and advertising materials) are designed to be readily available to the public. Transmissions require a technology that screens unauthorized users and charges authorized recipients for the services that are provided. Users frequently use different brands and models of computers and operating systems, so the network must be capable of operating on numerous systems.

The Internet transmits messages between users on many networks. Communications are sent between users on the individual networks, and the Internet is used to establish the proper connection.

The Internet is not a corporation. Authority for Internet operations and policy rests with the Internet Society (ISOC), a voluntary membership organization whose purpose is to promote information exchange on the Internet. ISOC has directors who work to standardize technology and allocate resources. The Internet Architecture Board and the Engineering Task Force are volunteer organizations that establish communication and network standards for the Internet. The Community Emergency Response Team serves as a central clearinghouse to which incidents can be reported. Individual networks and their management contribute their experience and ideas to develop Internet standards. If a network accepts Internet standards and considers itself so, then it will be a part of the Internet.[3]

Access to the Internet is open to anyone with a computer and a modem. The Internet itself does not collect fees from participating networks nor from individual or corporate users. Member networks establish their services and collect fees from users. Users pay the networks directly for Internet access.

The Internet is designed so that the individual user can get desired information easily, even though the request for information may pass through several networks. The user does not need any special computer background and is often unaware of the complexity of Internet communications.

Organizations and individuals pay for access to a regional network, which in turn pays a national provider for access. Internet service, of course, is not free, but occasionally the fees are not directly passed on to users, especially when government or advertising is involved. Fees are paid to the individual network or data provider, not to the Internet. Currently more than 20 million Internet users exist throughout the world, and use is growing at a phenomenal rate.

## PRIVACY AND E-MAIL

E-mail allows individuals and organizations to send messages to each other. Many corporations, government agencies, and universities have introduced E-mail as an efficient alternative to the paper flow that clogs their mail rooms. Recipients of E-mail can read and delete messages without printing them. This procedure eliminates much of the clutter created by paper documents.

E-mail is frequently used for correspondences not related to business. Few employers would object if an employee occasionally sends personal messages to co-workers on the office E-mail system. A more serious question is whether an organization has the right to read an employee's E-mail and take disciplinary or legal action based on its contents. In the business environment, employees have been fired when their employers read their E-mail messages. [+][4] Who owns E-mail sent through an organization's network: the writer, the recipient, or the organization? Can an organization routinely monitor messages transmitted over the network?

Outside the business environment, problems related to E-mail security also exist. At the 1994 Winter Olympics in Lillehammer, Norway, three American reporters logged on to figure skater Tonya Harding's E-mail account in the Olympic village's computer service. Although they did not read any messages, serious problems with privacy and journalistic integrity were brought into public forum.[5]

The word *privacy* does not appear anywhere in the U.S. Constitution. The Fourth Amendment provides that: The right of the people to be secure in their persons, houses, papers and effects, against unreasonable searches and seizures, shall not be violated, and no warrants shall issue, but upon probable cause, supported by oath or affirmation, and particularly describing the place to be searched, and the persons or things to be seized.

The restrictions in the Fourth Amendment apply only against government employees but do not restrict the activities of private employers or individuals. The Supreme Court has held that electronic listening by a government agency against its employees violated the Fourth Amendment only when the individual had a reasonable expectation of privacy.[6] In a military setting, in which security measures were extremely tight, the court held that the expectation of privacy that an engineer had in materials kept in his desk was not objectively reasonable.[7]

How does the standard of a reasonable expectation of privacy for government employees apply to computer-related material? In *Williams vs. Philadelphia Housing Authority*, Williams, an attorney with the Philadelphia Housing Authority, alleged that his supervisor violated his Fourth Amendment rights by removing a computer disk from his desk while he was on leave. The disk contained Housing Authority documents written by Williams as well as personal items. Williams had been told to clear his desk before he went on leave.

The court decided that Williams did not establish a claim for unreasonable search and seizure. By retrieving the disk, the supervisor acted in her official capacity. Because the disk contained both work-related and personal documents, the court concluded it was reasonable that the supervisor reviewed the personal material in her search of official documents.

## ELECTRONIC COMMUNICATIONS PRIVACY ACT OF 1986

The Electronic Communications Privacy Act of 1986[8] (ECPA) addresses unauthorized surveillance of E-mail by parties outside the government. ECPA provides criminal sanctions for unauthorized access to electronic communications. It also restricts the actions of service providers when they handle information contained in stored messages. The ECPA makes it a federal felony to intercept, disclose or use an electronic communications that is being transmitted. Exceptions occur when:

- One party to the message (the originator, the addressee, or the intended recipient) gives actual or implied consent for another party to read the message.
- A government agency with a warrant or administrative subpoena requests the information.[9]
- The provider of service (network operator) accesses the message in the normal course of operations, specifically for mechanical or service quality control checks.

Most observers agree that an organization that develops a network specifically for its employees can monitor its employee's communications and take specific legal action based on the contents of the message. An employee was recently dismissed for including inappropriate language and vulgar jokes in an E-mail message. Another employee was dismissed when his employer learned from E-mail messages that he had been previously employed as a stripper.

Both organizations and employees should understand their rights and responsibilities when E-mail is involved. Employees should realize that their personal and business communications can be electronically monitored in the workplace without specific notification. A potentially damaging or embarrassing message should never be sent on the E-mail network.

If an organization does choose to monitor messages, the following guidelines should be established:

- **Monitoring should be conducted only for a short period and only for a specific purpose.** Such actions should be considered only in extreme circumstances and should only be used when no other viable alternative exists.
- **Information and documents gathered should not be used for any other purpose.** Employees should not be disciplined for using E-mail for nonbusiness-related messages.
- **The procedures used should conform with legal requirements.** In addition, they should be conducted in a manner consistent with the terms of the organization's employee handbook.

The organization should realize that routine monitoring of employee messages can have a devastating effect on employee morale. If employees are concerned about the privacy of their E-mail, they will simply stop using the system. As a result, an expensive and crucial investment in the network will not fulfill its function, and the organization will not receive the many benefits of E-mail.

Both organizations and employees should be aware that E-mail messages are discoverable in legal proceedings. This means that such messages can be subpoenaed and presented as evidence in court. Employees and organizations should be aware that a backup of existing E-mail is taken regularly on a regular basis, so that deleted messages are retained indefinitely when the computer system is backed up nightly. Individuals should not write anything on E-mail that they would not say or write publicly.

## LIBEL

The Internet is a public network available to any person who has access to a computer and a modem. Anybody can log on to the Internet and send messages to other users. Control of Internet messages is more difficult because users can hide their identities by using false names.

Libel is a written, printed, or pictorial statement that damages a person by defaming his character or reputation, damaging him in his occupation, or exposing him to public ridicule. In the real world, freedom of speech is limited by the laws of libel. To date, the few libel suits involving electronic services have been settled out of court, so little legal precedent exists.

Can a network be held liable for a libelous message sent by a subscriber? In *Cubby vs. CompuServe*,[10] the Plaintiff sued CompuServe because a third party had allegedly posted a libelous message on the CompuServe network. The court ruled that CompuServe could not be sued for libel. Networks do not exercise editorial control over the messages that they transmit.

Although the matter has not been decided in the courts, it appears that an individual could be held liable to sending libelous E-mail messages. An article in *The Nation* states, "the Internet is not a free space when it comes to libel; it is subject to the same libel law as any publication."[11]

## FRAUD

The increasing popularity of the Internet and its bulletin boards has led to new methods of conducting old fraudulent activities. A *New York Times* article announced, "the scammers, swindlers and sharpies who hunt for unwary investors on the phone and through the mail are now prowling online computers services. But in cyberspace, where the police are few and dubious offers can be sent for under $2, such chicanery carries special twists."[12]

In one specific case, a posting on a Prodigy bulletin board claimed that E.T.C. Industries, an electric car company, was "primed for breakout".The note omitted the fact that its author was doing public relations for the company and was the son of its president. The Commissioner of Securities in Missouri issued a cease-and-desist order against E.T.C.

The Interactive Services Association and the North Securities Administrators Association are currently drafting rules that may restrict this sort of illegal activity. Investors should be especially careful about their reaction to such tips.

The Internet is especially vulnerable to credit card fraud. Kevin Mitnick, who was arrested by FBI agents in February, 1995, was able to steal thousands of credit-card numbers from an Internet service provider. Ivy James Lay, an MCI employee in North Carolina, programmed a microcomputer to capture more than 50,000 credit card numbers. He sold the numbers to a network of dealers, resulting in more than $50 million in fraudulent charges.[13]

Organizations must take specific steps to safeguard computers that are connected to the Internet. Firewall software screens outside requests for information so that only certain, registered computers can access the internal network through the Internet. Although firewalls are not hacker-proof, they do offer substantial protection. In addition, encryption techniques can be used when sensitive information must be sent outside the internal network.

## SOFTWARE PIRACY

Computer networks make it easy to copy programs and store them on computer bulletin boards. Bulletin board subscribers can then download these programs without paying for them. Many of these programs are freeware (i.e., programs donated by their creators) or shareware (i.e., programs available on a trial basis to potential users, who are expected to pay for the software if they choose to continue using it). Often, however, downloaded software is copyrighted material.

More than $1 billion worth of software is illegally downloaded every year. In one case, Windows 95 software was available for downloading nine months before it was released to the public. In another incident, David LaMacchia, a student from the Massachusetts Institute of Technology, was indicted for conspiracy to commit wire fraud after he allegedly established a bulletin board containing copyrighted versions of Excel 5.0 and WordPerfect for Windows 6.0.[14]

On Dec.28, 1994, the federal court dismissed the indictment, basing the decision on two factors. LaMacchia did not make a profit on his actions, as required under the copyright act. Further, his actions did not constitute wire fraud, which would have required a fiduciary relationship between LaMacchia and the copyright owner. The court was extremely critical of his actions and called for congressional action to remedy the problem.[15]

Software developers and their trade group, the Software Publishers Association, have prosecuted several individuals, bulletin boards, and companies for illegally copying software. The federal government has indicted several bulletin board operators in the past for charging users to download pirated software. Successful prosecution is often difficult because bulletin board operators are often young students who do not charge customers and simply cannot afford to pay more than a token judgment. Most judges or juries would simply not punish operators severely. Organizations and individuals should avoid potential liability by avoiding the use of copyrighted, downloaded software.

## FLAMING

Computer users express various opinions on the Internet. On occasion, the anonymity of the network encourages vulgar, verbal tirades known as *flaming*. For some users flaming is simply a harmless method of self-expression. Most recipients ignore such messages; however, operators occasionally remove an offensive user from the bulletin board. A set of standards (known as *netiquette explains what is considered acceptable* behavior for Internet users.[16]

What happens when flaming goes beyond any decent standards of proper behavior? In San Jose, a pedophile made contact on a bulletin board with a police detective posing as a young teenage boy. When they arranged to meet, the pedophile was arrested. More than 100 similar incidents have occurred.[17]

As one system operator said, "the Internet is expanding at logarithmic rates. A million new users will bring a few sociopaths. Until recently, [there was] complete anarchy with self-regulation. Now some human will have to look at everything and decide what to post."[18] Unfortunately, even a single flamer can destroy the good nature and style of a bulletin board. A single individual with criminal intent can cause tremendous problems. A bulletin board operator is often forced to censor or eliminate messages from a particularly annoying or offensive user.

From a legal standpoint, a bulletin board operator has the absolute right to censor message or ban a user for any reason or even for no reason. Just as a newspaper is not required to print every opinion, a bulletin board or network operator is not required to allow all opinions.

## FREE SPEECH

Individuals log on to bulletin boards to obtain information or simply to talk to others. It is often difficult to control access to the bulletin board. This has led to several cases in which the limits of free speech as they relate to cyberspace have been challenged.

Ohio police confiscated a $3,000 computer belonging to Mark Lehrer, charging that children had seen pornography on his bulletin board. Lehrer did have pornographic files available, but he restricted access to users over 18 and required that users send a copy of their driver's license. A few explicit photos were in the nonrestricted area because of a filing error. Local police recruited a 15-year-old to gain access to the files and then arrested the operator. Lehrer entered a guilty plea to a misdemeanor charge of possessing a criminal tool, specifically his computer.

In a similar matter, an uninvited Tennessee hacker broke into a California bulletin board that featured pornographic materials. The operator was charged with violation of obscenity laws, not by lenient California standards but in accordance with standards established in Tennessee. For the first time, a bulletin board operator was prosecuted where the obscene material was received instead of at its point of origin. The operator was convicted and the case is currently on appeal.[19]

The concept of free speech on the Internet, especially when users in different states are involved, will eventually be decided by the courts. At issue is a 1973 Supreme Court ruling[20] that states obscenity must be judged by local community standards. Should alleged obscenity on a California bulletin board be judged by the standards of another state, which may be much stricter than in California? This is typical of the type of problem that can develop in cyberspace, in which state borders are essentially meaningless.

Internet users have all types of political beliefs; some users are libertarian in their views regarding the Internet (i.e., they believe in keeping the government out of cyberspace). This viewpoint is in opposition to the common belief that children should not be exposed to pornography. An early solution to this dilemma is not likely.[21]

## HACKERS AND PASSWORD PROTECTION

E-mail can transmit hundreds of pages of text throughout the world in a few minutes. Most experts recommend, however, that particularly sensitive information (e.g., medical and financial records) be sent by alternative means. This is due in part to the lack of security on the Internet.

Although a user needs a password to send E-mail, typically no real barriers to entering another user's area and reading that person's mail exist. Hackers are expert network users who specialize in illegal access and manipulation of user areas. In 1993, there were 1334 confirmed hacking incidents on the Internet.[22]

By using privacy-enhanced mail (PEM), Internet users can use cryptography to decode and encode their messages. Under PEM, each user is given two numbers, known as keys, that lock and unlock computerized messages. One number is the public key, which is freely distributed. The other number is the private key, which is kept secret.

A user can send secure mail by typing in the recipient's public key, which is public information. The recipient then has to apply his private key to decode the message, so only that person can read the message. The system can also verify the sender's private key signature; the recipient can unlock it using the sender's public key. Messages are then secure as long as a user's private key is kept secret.[23]

To protect E-mail and other data, the following recommendations will prove useful to individuals and organizations:[24]

- **Passwords should be changed frequently.** A password should never be written down, especially next to a terminal.
- **Passwords should never be given out to anyone, especially if someone claims to be an employee of the computer network.** Such requests should be reported to the system administrator.
- **Passwords should never be included in E-mail messages.**

- **English words should not be used as passwords.** Hackers can run dictionary programs that attempt every word in the English language as a password.
- **Passwords that contain personal information (e.g., nicknames, children's names, spouse's names, or birth dates) should be avoided.** A hacker can determine a user's password based on personal information.
- **Immediate steps should be taken to disable an employee's password when that employee leaves the organization.**
- **Many organizations require that users change their passwords on a regular basis and not reuse them.** If a user feels that a password is no longer secure, the system administrator should be contacted for a new password. If an employee does choose to take this action, it should never be used as an indication that the employee is less than scrupulous with his or her use of the computer network.

Until a more secure method of transmitting E-mail is developed, users should remain cautious about what they send and store on the Internet. It is often a good idea to rely on alternative means of sending messages.

## RECOMMENDED COURSE OF ACTION

The Internet and E-mail have drastically changed the ways in which society does business. As with any new technology, problems can develop. The following recommendations should be beneficial in reducing problems:

- **Individuals should be extremely careful of what they send in E-mail.** If a document should not be left in clear view on a desk overnight, an alternate method to transmit the document should be used.
- **Policies should be clearly defined.** If an organization chooses to ban personal messages from its E-mail system, this policy should be explicitly spelled out to all employees.
- **Organizations should respect the privacy of their employees.** E-mail should not be read unless a crucial reason for doing so is evident. If such actions are necessary, they should be conducted on a short-term basis. Employee privacy and corporate personnel procedures should be honored.
- **Organizations should be extremely careful to ensure that software is purchased from legitimate vendors.** Illegal copies of copyrighted software are frequently downloaded from bulletin boards. Use of this software could be disastrous to an organization.

Organizations and individuals must take serious steps to ensure that communications are secure and confidential. Common sense, restraint, and a high level of integrity should be exercised by all parties involved.

**References**

1. "Newsletter Faces Libel Suit for 'Flaming' on Internet," *Wall Street Journal*, April 22, 1994, p. B1.
2. Krol, E., *Whole Internet*, Sebastapol, CA: O'Reilly & Associates, Inc., 1994, p. 13.
3. Harowitz, S., "Building Security into Cyberspace," *Security Management*, June 1994, p. 54.
4. Nelson, C.L. "Employers Have No Right to Snoop Through Mail," *Computerworld*, June 27, 1994, p. 135.
5. "Hacked Off," *Sporting News*, March 7, 1994, p. 6.
6. *Katz vs. U.S.* 389 U.S. 347, 88 S.Ct. 507, 1967.
7. *Schowengerdt vs. U.S.*, 944 F.2d 483, 9th Cir. 1991.
8. 18 *U.S.C.* §2510 *et sequation.*
9. 18 *U.S.C.* §2703.
10. *Cubby vs. CompuServe*, 776 F. Supp 135, SDNY 1991.
11. Wiener, "Free Speech on the Internet," *The Nation*, June 13, 1994, p. 825.
12. "Cyberspace Swindles: Old Scams, New Twists," *New York Times*, July 16,1994, p. A35.
13. Cortese, "Warding Off the Cyberspace Invaders," *Business Week*, March 13, 1995, p. 92.
14. "Crimes of the Net," *Newsweek*, Nov.14, 1994, p. 46.
15. Gunn, "Law and Disorder on the Internet," *PC Magazine*, March 14, 1995, p. 30.
16. Fisher, S. *Riding the Internet Highway*, Indianapolis IN: New Riders Publishing, 1993, pp. 33–37.
17. "Seeking Victims in Cyberspace," *U.S. News & World Report*, Sept.19, 1994, p. 73.
18. Wiener, "Free Speech on the Internet," *Nation*, June 13, 1995, p. 69.
19. Ness, "Big Brother @ Cyberspace," *Progressive*, December 1994, p. 22.
20. *Miller vs. California*, 413 U.S. 15, 1973.
21. "Who Speaks for Cyberspace?" *The Economist*, Jan.14, 1995, p. 69.
22. Kierman, "Internet Wide Open to Hacker Attack," *New Scientist*, April 2, 1994, p. 8.
23. "Protecting E-mail," *Technology Review*, August/September 1992, p. 11.
24. Wilson, "Computing Insecurity," *Chronicle of Higher Education*, Feb. 16, 1994, p. A25.

# Chapter 46
# An Introduction to Internet Security and Firewall Policies

*William Hugh Murray*

This chapter is an introduction to security on the Internet. It describes the characteristics, applications, and protocols of the network. It also describes and explains the peculiar vulnerabilities that arise from these characteristics and the attacks that exploit them. This chapter offers strategies, tactics, and mechanisms for protecting the traffic on the network. It places special emphasis on firewalls and encryption and strategies for using them.

## INTRODUCTION

Any attempt to describe anything as dynamic, not to say unstable, as the Internet, is likely to make one look foolish. Describing the Internet can be liken to five blind men trying to describe an elephant. However, the elephant remains an elephant, it does not change during the examination and discussion. On the other hand, descriptions of the Internet that are only three years old are already so out of date as to be inaccurate if not dangerously misleading.

The Internet is already the most complex artifact in history. It may turn out to be important, or it may not. On the chance that it is or will be important, it makes sense to try to understand it, no matter how difficult and uncertain an explanation is likely to be.

## THE CHARACTERISTICS OF THE INTERNET

The Internet can be defined and described, in part, in terms of its characteristics. Although it is possible for a network to have some of these characteristics without having them all, they are related in subtle ways.

0-8493-9965-3/99/$0.00+$.50
© 1999 by CRC Press LLC

## Public and Open

Perhaps one of the most important characteristics of the Internet, at least from a security point of view, is that it is essentially public and open. It is public in the sense that, like the phone system, anyone can use it. One may have to go to a pay phone, a kiosk, or the public library, but anyone can use it. Libraries have been known to hand out user IDs with the same frequency as library cards. No requirements exist to be able to use the Internet, i.e., anyone can use it. In addition, as in broadcast TV, radio, or magazine advertising, most of the traffic is public. Its value increases with the number of people who see it. Although it has not always been so, most of the servers and services available on the Internet do not know or care who their users are. No user identification or authentication is required. The servers may count the accesses and they might like to know the demographics of those who visit, but otherwise, the greater number of visits, the more successful the site is considered.

Similar to it being public, the Internet is open. Like the postal system and for the price of a postage stamp, anyone can send a message. For the price of an accommodation address, anyone can receive a message. Although there may be an agreement to pay, no other permission is required and, as a rule, payment in advance is not required. The Internet is also open in the sense that with a minimum of notice to or cooperation of others a connection can be made. A node at the edge of a network can be added easily and unilaterally, creating a new connection between networks. Therefore, it is difficult, nearly impossible, to know what the network looks like.

Although only a small percentage of the traffic on the Internet is sensitive to disclosure and most applications and services are free, almost all traffic is sensitive to contamination and most services are sensitive to interference. Moreover, although many who offer public information on the Internet want many people to see it, they want it to get through in tact; they do not want it modified, they do not want it broken, and they do not want to be responsible for what they did not say. The public and open nature of the Internet makes this more difficult to achieve. It also makes it more difficult to achieve confidentiality and accountability for that traffic and those applications that require them.

## Inclusive Network of Networks

By definition, an internetwork is a network that connects networks. Therefore, the Internet is a network of networks. It is one collection of all networks, and the economic advantage of a connection is so great as to be irresistible. Moreover, although isolated networks may exist in the short term, in the long term, the internetwork will be one. Isolated networks that persist will be sparse, small, and temporary as not to be significant.

**Mesh Topology**

The Internet has a mesh topology, which means that, except at the edges, most nodes are connected to two or more other nodes. In addition, there are multiple paths between any two points on the network, because the topology maximizes the potential that a message will get through and maximizes the total message carrying potential (i.e., bandwidth) of the network. On the other hand, at least by default, users do not know what path their traffic will follow or what nodes and links their messages will traverse.

**Flat**

Ideally, the Internet is flat, as opposed to hierarchical. Information flows directly from the origin to the destination rather than in, to a central switching point, and then back out to the destination. Therefore, the cost to send a message between any two points on the network is the same as between any other two points. The time required for a message to move between any two points is roughly the same as for any other two points chosen at random. Finally, the bandwidth between any two points is roughly the same as for any other two points.

As expected, messages flow more quickly between nodes that are close together. However, it is possible for a part of a message to circle the globe, even when addressed to a nearby node. So, at least on average, across all randomly chosen pairs of nodes, the Internet is flat.

**Broadcast**

A node that desires to send a message to another node broadcasts that message to the remainder of the network. Depending on the routing algorithm used, the originating node may prefer nodes that it thinks are in the direction of the destination. However, it is possible for a message to traverse the globe even when addressed to a nearby node. Other nodes that receive the message look at the destination address in the message and forward it in the general direction of that destination. This is similar to a point-to-point network in which the path between two points is determined in advance and dedicated, at least for the instant, to carrying that message. Although every packet does not pass every node and it is possible for users to influence the path that their traffic follows, few users have the necessary special knowledge to take advantage of this capability. They do not know how to exercise the control or to distinguish one path from another. Such control, if used, would limit the paths and bandwidth available to the traffic and be achieved at the cost of a reduction in the chances that the traffic would get through quickly.

### Different Types of Internet Connections

Three kinds of connections are available on the Internet.

**Packet-Switched.** Related to the idea of broadcast is that of packet-switched. A message is broken into packets, each packet is labeled as to its origin and destination and then is broadcast onto the network. Other nodes forward the packet in the general direction of the destination. It is possible that adjacent packets in a message will follow different paths to the destination. This is the opposite of circuit-switched networks, such as the voice network, in which a circuit or path is determined in advance and all parts of the message follow the same path. In a packet-switched network, an intervening node may see only a part of a message. On the other hand, it increases the number of nodes that may see a part of it.

**Peer-Connected.** Nodes on the Internet are "peer connected." No node dominates or controls another. Thus, by default, all nodes behave as if they trust all other nodes as themselves. The implication is that the level of trust is equal to that of the least trusted node.

**Any-to-Any Connection.** Like the postal system, and except as otherwise restricted, any device connected to the Internet can send a message to any other device. There is no requirement for an answer but, at a minimum, the destination device must recognize the message and make a decision about it. For example, at MIT the softdrink vending machines are connected to the Internet. If the addresses are known, they may be queried from anywhere in the world.

### Increasing Interoperability

If connectivity is the ability to send a message to any node, interoperability is the ability to get a meaningful answer back. Already, the Internet is better at answering questions than most individuals are at asking questions. The Internet can provide a report of freeway traffic in Los Angeles, hotel availability in London, or the schedule of every opera house in the world for the next two years. It can also locate all the bed and breakfast lodgings in most places in the world, and get an index to the treasures of the Vatican Library or of the British Museum. Individuals can locate and download graphics, moving images, and general and specialized software. A query on "Mona Lisa" returns references to both 1000 different prints of Da Vinci's La Gioconda and a sound clip of the Nat King Cole song. If the necessary software is unavailable to interoperate with another system at a particular layer, software can be downloaded at another.

As protocols and interfaces become more standard, they become more useful. As the use of a standard increases, so does the propensity to comply with it. The less standard an interface, the more it must include information about its intended or productive use.

### No Central Authority

Although there are authorities such as the IAB and the IETF, which make architectural and design decisions for the Internet, no one is obliged to follow them. The individual networks are independently owned and operated. There is no central authority that is responsible for the operation of the entire network. Because the network is global, it is not even subject to the authority of any single nation state.

## INTERNET PROTOCOLS

The Internet can also be defined and described in terms of the communication protocols that it employs. One, somewhat pure, definition is that the Internet is that collection of interconnected networks that employ TCP/IP suite of protocols. A more practical definition is that the Internet is that set plus those networks connected to it by appropriate gateways. (For purposes of this definition, a gateway is a node that translates traffic from one protocol to another.)

### The Internet Protocol

The fundamental protocol of the Internet is IP, the Internet protocol. IP is the network layer protocol for the TCP/IP Protocol Suite. It is fundamental in the sense that all other protocols are built on it. It is connectionless, best-effort, packet-switched, and unchecked. "Best effort" means that the network will do its best to deliver the packet, but there are no guarantees. "Unchecked" means that there is no redundancy in the protocol to enable either the sender or the receiver to know whether the packet was received correctly. There is no acknowledgment of the receipt of the message. The receiver cannot be sure that the message comes from where the origin address of the packet says that it comes from.

IP is to the Internet as the post card is to the postal system, limited in capacity, function, and intent. However, just as a message of any length can be sent by using multiple post cards, or by using one post card to acknowledge or to check on another, IP packets can be composed in such a way as to compensate for all of these limitations. These compositions make up the higher-level protocols.

### The Transmission Control Protocol

The TCP, is the standard IP for the transfer layer. It defines how IP packets are sent back and forth between a sender and a receiver to provide many of the things that IP does not. However, even TCP does not provide security or the reliability of origin and destination. Both the sender and the receiver know that they are talking to someone that is orderly and well behaved, but they do not know for sure that it is their intended party, and they do not know if any one is listening in.

### The Oldest and Most Widely Used Protocols

The following are among the oldest and most widely used protocols on the Internet:

- **Telnet.** This was originally intended for connecting host-dependent terminals to remote systems or applications. Today, it is used by terminal emulator programs on workstations.
- **File Transfer Protocol.** FTP is used to move files from one system to another.
- **Simple Mail Transfer Protocol.** SMTP is used for E-mail.

The applications of these protocols are discussed in subsequent sections.

### Other Common Protocols

In addition to those protocols previously discussed are the following:

- **Serial Line Internet Protocol.** The SLIP is used to exchange IP traffic with a device, usually a workstation, that is running the proper protocols but without a separate address. It is used to connect workstations to hosts or to Internet service providers through the dial-switched network. It is analogous to an extension cord or a remote.
- **Point-to-Point Protocol.** The PPP is similar to SLIP, but is associated with leased lines. It is usually used to connect a single system to a boundary or "edge" node.
- **Network Time Protocol.** The NTP is used to set and synchronize the system clocks of Internet nodes. It is able to synchronize all systems in a network to within milliseconds of each other, i.e., to within the accuracy and precision of the system clocks themselves.
- **Secure Protocols.** Recently, secure versions of these protocols have been specified, and reference implementations of these protocols are available for Unix systems. Additional implementations should be available in 1996.

## INTERNET APPLICATIONS

Recall the analogy that describing the Internet can be liken to five blind men trying to describe an elephant. For most of the blind men, the Internet elephant looks like its applications. The Internet is open as to its applications. No real limit to the number of applications exists, and new ones are added every day. However, some applications are sufficiently significant that a description of those applications describes how the net looks to most users.

## E-mail

The most widely used application on the Internet is E-mail. Recent statistics suggest between 50 and 100 million users, and a 1 billion users are estimated as early as 2000. E-mail rivals television, copiers, and facsimile machines in its rate of growth. Moreover, as was the case with copiers and facsimiles, it is becoming difficult to remember how business was conducted before E-mail.

Internet E-mail uses the SMTP, and the MIME protocol. MIME runs on top of SMTP to permit the exchange of files, programs, sounds, images, and moving images. E-mail is the most interconnected and interoperable application. Even those networks that have resisted connection to the Internet at other levels are connected at the E-mail layer.

In addition, E-mail is the most ubiquitous application in the Internet; it interoperates with many of the others. Several servers are on the Internet that accept mail messages, convert them into requests for other services, convert the answers to those mail messages, and send them back to the requester. Thus, a user that has access to E-mail functionality, has access to all of the information on the network (i.e., Internet).

## Logging on to a Remote System

One of the earliest and most obvious of Internet applications was to create a session between a terminal on one system and an application on a remote system. This kind of application used a client process on the origin system, the Telnet client. It IS-IS initiated by entering the command, telnet, on the originating system. The parameters of the command specify the target system and any nondefault characteristics of the connection request. The request is responded to by the telnet server, a started process (a daemon in Unix parlance) on the target system. The protocol is also called telnet. The user on the origin system sees a prompt from the answering server process, for example, the operating system or an application, on the target system. The user is usually expected to logon, that is, send a user identifier (i.e., user ID) and authenticating data (i.e., a password) to the target system. However, for the target system, the user identifier and password are optional.

## File Transfer

The FTP is used to exchange file system objects between systems. It is symmetric, and works in either direction. Either system may initiate a transfer in either direction. The FTP process (daemon in Unix parlance) must have access to the file system. That is, in systems with closed file systems, the process or the user on whose behalf it is operating must possess the necessary access rights (e.g., read, write, or create) to the file object or directory on which it wants to operate.

A convention called, "anonymous FTP," permits the protocol to be used for public applications. The user can logon to the system with a user ID of anonymous, which requires no password. By convention, users are requested to put their origin system and user ID in the password field. However, the value in this field is not checked or validated in any way; a blank will work as well as the truth.

## VULNERABILITIES ON THE INTERNET

The vulnerabilities on the Internet are closely related to its characteristics, its protocols, its uses, and its history. In addition, because the Internet is a broadcast network, messages are vulnerable to disclosure, replay, and interference.

The large number of components on the Internet makes it vulnerable to flaws in the implementation of those components. Because there may be many instances of a flaw, elimination of them is extremely difficult. A recent example of such a flaw was an instance of incomplete parameter checking in the Unix system logging routine, syslog. This error permitted a very long log entry to exceed the space provided for it, overlay program space, and get itself executed.

Many components in systems peer-connected to the Internet contain "escape" mechanisms. These are invoked by an otherwise unlikely character sequence to cause what follows this escape sequence to be handled, not by the component itself, but by the environment in which it runs, often with the privilege of the "escaped from" component. A famous escape mechanism, exploited by the infamous "All Souls" worm, was the debug feature of the sendmail mail handler. This option was invoked by an escape sequence in a message that caused what followed it to be passed through to Unix to be executed as a command. The worm used this feature, among others, to copy and execute itself.

Because nodes are peer connected and trust each other, compromise of one may result in compromise of many, perhaps all. In a peer connected network, the level of trust in the network is equal to that of the least trusted node or link.

Many of the vulnerabilities described in the preceding paragraphs are features rather than flaws. In other words, they are desired and valued by some users and managers. Because of their value, their total elimination is unlikely.

Every node on the Internet has a system manager or privileged user. This user is not subject to any controls intended to ensure that users and their systems are orderly and well-behaved. In single user systems, the only user is a peer of the privileged user in the multi-user system. That user is assumed to have the same motivation, training, and supervision as the manager of a multi-user system. The vast number of such users ensures that at least some of them will be disorderly and unreliable. Because they are all peers and because the systems are peer connected, it makes little difference which of them are trustworthy.

The Internet is so large and complex that no one, not the designers, not the implementers, not the operators, and not the users, fully apprehends it, much less comprehends it. Everyone are the blind men. Nonetheless, its immense scope and size make it unlikely that it will ever be perfect. Attackers look on it as a "target rich" environment. Although most nodes on the network are implemented, configured, and operated so as to resist attack, the great number of them ensures that there will always be some that are vulnerable to attack.

Finally, two of the vulnerabilities on the Internet, insecure links and insecure nodes, are fundamental. In other words, they are inherent to the Internet, nature, use, intent, or at least its history. Contrary to popular belief, they are not the result of errors, flaws, or failures on the part of the designers, implementers, or operators of the network. Rather, these insecure links and nodes are the result of attempts to have the greatest chance of getting a message from point *A* to point *B* in the least amount of time. They are never going to go away; it is not simply a matter of time. Indeed, at least for the next five years, they are likely to get worse. That is, vulnerabilities will be increase faster than the ability to fix them. Moreover, the number of insecure links and nodes in the network are both growing at a much faster rate than the number of secure ones. This vulnerability is certain and extremely resistant to change.

## ATTACKS ON THE INTERNET

The conditions for a successful attack include necessary access, special knowledge, work, and time. Because of its nature, all of these things are somewhat more available on the Internet than on other networks. Because the Internet is open, almost anyone can gain access. Most of the special knowledge in the world is recorded, encapsulated, and available on the Internet, mostly for the taking; although. Every now and then permission is required. Even much of the necessary work to launch a successful attack has been encapsulated in computer programs. Thus, they can be perpetrated by those who lack skill and special knowledge and who are not prepared to do the work themselves.

### Eavesdropping

As packets move through the net, they can be observed by privileged users of the nodes or by using special equipment to listen in on the links. These attacks are easily automated.

### Packet and Password Grabbers

A packet grabber is an automated eavesdropping attack, a program that copies packets as they move through an intermediate node (i.e., a node between the origin and destination). A password grabber is a special case of a packet grabber that identifies and stores for later use user IDs and passwords as they pass through an intermediate node. Because, at least as a general rule, unprivileged processes cannot look at traffic in transit, password grabbers must be installed by privileged users. However, recent experience suggests that they are often placed in penetrated systems. Writing password grabbers requires special knowledge and work. However, now, so many copies of those programs exist that the attack can be used even by those without the knowledge and not prepared to do the work. The Internet has so may password grabbers that passwords in the clear are not sufficiently reliable for commercial or other sensitive applications, and the problem moves from the category of an attack to that of a pervasive problem.

### Address Spoofing

The origin address on the IP packet is not reliable. The sending system can set this address to any value that it wishes. Nonetheless, by convention and for convenience, many systems rely on this address to determine where a packet came from and to decide how to treat it. Packets carrying the origin address of recognized systems may be treated as though they had originated on a trusted system. Again, with sufficient work and knowledge, it is possible to write a program to exploit this trust. Toolkits for building this kind of attack have been written and distributed within the hacker community.

### Trojan Horses

A Trojan Horse attack is in one in which a hostile entity, for example, armed warriors, is concealed inside a benign or trusted one, for example a gift horse, to get it through a protective barrier or perimeter, in the original case, the walls of the city of Troy. In computer science, it usually refers to a malicious program included in another program or even in data. Although most systems are vulnerable to this kind of attack to some degree or another, and it has always been a concern, until the proliferation of desktop computers and viruses, it was not a problem.

As previously discussed, both node-to-node connectivity and trust and open file systems make the Internet particularly vulnerable. Trojan Horses can and do travel over any of the popular protocols and in any of the popular object types. For example, they can travel in files over FTP, as documents over MIME, or in arbitrary objects called by HTML scripts fetched from WWW servers by browsers. Although some browsers and interpreters (e.g., HotJava) are designed to resist such attacks, most are not. Even in situations in which the browser or interpreter is resistant, it is always possible to dupe some users in a large population.

Trojan Horses are easily executed because they have attractive names or descriptions or the names of frequently used programs. They may require a minimum of user cooperation. For example, the PRANK (virus) was implemented as an MS Word macro and could spread in any Word document. Simply asking Word to open an infected document would contaminate that copy of Word and any document that it subsequently opened. If an infected document were attached to an E-mail message, an act as simple as double clicking the icon for the document would be sufficient to execute the macro. Because such a macro can contain and call an arbitrary program, there is no limit to the sophistication of the program or the contamination it can cause.

Trojan Horse attacks are of special concern on the Internet because they compromise trust of end-point nodes, of the net, and of applications on the net.

### Browsing

Browsing is going through the network to look at available, public, accidentally, and erroneously available data in search of something of value. Specifically, in an attack sense, this search method looks for special data that will reduce the cost of an attack against other nodes. For example, many systems implement or provide directory services. These directory services return the names of enrolled users, i.e., user identifiers. The information returned by these public services is used by the attacker to identify targets and thereby reduce the cost of attack. Attackers also use browsing to identify and download attack programs.

### Exhaustion

When confronted with good security and when all other attacks fail, an attacker can always fall back on trying all possible combinations of data (e.g., user identifiers and passwords) until he or she finds one that gets through. Traditional systems resisted such attacks by disconnecting disorderly devices (i.e., devices that failed to successfully logon). Because the Internet is a broadcast network, there is no connection to break. A system must look at every packet addressed to it and make a determination as to what to do with it. It is possible to spread the attack over time or across addresses so as to disguise the attack as errors or noise.

## Denial of Service

Denial of service attacks are those that cause failures by overloading or consuming all available resources. On the Internet, this class of attack includes "spamming" or overloading a target with unwanted traffic. Although the target is not damaged in any permanent way, it may be unable to provide critical services to those intended to use it.

## DEFENDING AGAINST ATTACKS ON THE INTERNET

A vast number of options exist that the implementers, operators, and users of the net can do to limit these vulnerabilities and the attacks against them. However, in considering them, keep in mind that these vulnerabilities are fundamental to the nature of the Internet. The only way to eliminate all of the risk is to either eliminate the Internet or alter it so fundamentally that it will lose its identity. Clearly, neither of these options are viable. Rather, the defenses should be balanced against the vulnerabilities so as to preserve essential trust. Discussions of some broad categories of defense mechanisms follow in the subsequent section.

### Isolation and Compartmentation

Of course, the most obvious defense against network attacks is simply not to attach, to connect, or to participate in a network. Not only is this defense effective, it is also demonstrable to the satisfaction of third parties. However, the value of the security obtained rarely compensates for the lost value of connecting or participating in a network. Moreover, it has often been said that sensitive defense systems are safe because they are not connected to public networks.

Because the value of connecting to a network is high and because the cost of that connection is low, isolation is difficult to maintain. Even a very small system or a single desk-top workstation can form a connection between networks.

### Policies

In the presence of known connections, people can provide protection. They can recognize attacks and take timely and appropriate action. However, for this to be effective, it must be planned and pervasive. If management wishes to rely on individuals', in advance, it must tell them what action to take. A policy is an expression of management's intention. It should contain a recapitulation of the user behavior that management relies on. It should also clearly delineate the responsibilities of employees and managers. Finally, it should specifically address the responsibility to report anomalies.

### Bastions

Bastions are "projecting" fortifications. They are strong systems that can be seen from the outside (i.e., the public network), but which are designed to resist attack (e.g., by recognizing only a very limited repertoire of application specific commands). Bastions normally hide the generality and flexibility of their operating systems from the network. A full-function gateway system that can be seen from the public network is called a bastion host. Such a gateway must be able to protect itself from its traffic. Finally, because most protective mechanisms can be bypassed or circumvented, all applications and services that can be seen from the network should be able to resist their traffic.

### Filters

Filters are processes that pass some traffic while rejecting some other traffic. The intent is to pass safe traffic and to resist attack traffic. Filters may operate on headers or content. Many filters operate on the basis of the origin address in the header. They pass traffic that appears to have originated on recognized or trusted systems. They may also operate on a combination of origin, protocol, and destination. For example, they may pass mail traffic from unknown origins to the mail port on the post office machine and reject outside traffic addressed to the Telnet port on the same machine. Filters are important. For further information see the subsequent section.

### Wrappers

Wrappers are proxy programs or processes. They can be viewed as traffic filtering programs. They are designed to protect the target from unintended traffic, known attacks, or to compensate for known weaknesses. They often assume the name of the process that they are intended to protect (i.e., common functions or known targets). For example, suppose that a privileged program is known to have a flaw or an escape mechanism that can be exploited by a packet or a message. A wrapper can be given the name of that program, placed ahead of it in the search order, and used to protect against messages of the dangerous form. After eliminating all messages of the dangerous form, the remainder are passed to the "wrapped" program as normal.

Using a wrapper is a preferable alternative and it presents a lower risk to cure a vulnerability than patching or replacing the vulnerable program. They have been employed to great advantage in Unix systems in which it is often easier to use the wrapper than to find out whether the particular version of Unix or one of its subsystems that is being used has a particular problem. The most famous wrappers are a collection known as COPS. These are used to protect Unix systems from a set of known attacks and vulnerabilities.

## FILTERS: THE MOST POPULAR DEFENSE

Filters are the most popular defense to ward off network attacks. The intent is to pass normal traffic while rejecting all attack traffic. Of course, the difficulty is in being able to recognize the difference between the two. Filters are normally based on the origin, the destination, and the kind of traffic. Traffic is permitted to flow from trusted or known sources to safe or intended destinations. Of course, most destinations will ignore traffic that is not addressed to them but will certainly listen to attack traffic that is addressed to them. Filtering on destination address can protect the system from seeing attack traffic at the expense of protecting it from all traffic.

### Filters Implemented by Using Routers

In part, because networks are usually connected to each other through routers, routers are a favorite place to filter traffic. The same logic that is used by the router to decide where to send traffic can be used to reject traffic (i.e., to decide to send it to the "bit bucket." For example, only those packets that appear to have originated on systems whose addresses are recognized (i.e., on a list of known systems) may be accepted.

### Packets by Address: IP Address and Port

A filter must have criteria by which to decide which traffic to pass and which to reject. The criteria must appear in the packet. The most frequently used criteria are the IP origin and destination addresses. Typically, this is expressed as an address pair. In other words, traffic appearing to originate at $A$ and addressed to $B$ may pass this router. Although it could say all traffic originating at $A$ may pass or all traffic intended for $B$ may pass, this is significantly less rigorous or secure.

The origin and destination are usually expressed as IP addresses and may be further qualified by port. That is traffic originating on the mail port of $A$ may pass to the mail port on $B$, but to no other port.

### Protocols

The protocol is also visible in the packet and is useful for routing and security purposes. For example, the filter may pass traffic in the SMTP protocol to pass to the mail server, while not allowing other IP traffic addressed to the same service to pass. Because the intent of the traffic is more obvious in the higher-level protocols, filtering by protocol can be very effective and useful.

## FIREWALLS

It is beyond the scope of this chapter to provide instruction on how to build or even to operate a firewall. Within the allotted space, it is difficult to simply convey an understanding of their nature and use. A basic definition and discussion follows.

The *American Heritage Dictionary* defines a firewall as "a fireproof wall used as a barrier to prevent the spread of a fire." By analogy, a network firewall is a traffic-proof barrier used to prevent the spread of disorderly or malicious traffic. More specifically, a firewall is a special collection of hardware and software that connects two networks and that is used to protect each of the assumptions as to which side of the firewall a fire will start on.

Like most analogies, this one is instructive even at the extremes where it begins to break down. In the analogy, a firewall is assumed to resist fire equally in both directions. It is symmetric; it does not have to treat fire on one side of the wall differently from fire on the other. It must resist fire, but it must pass people. However, it is easy to distinguish people from fire, and all people and all fire, on either side of the wall, are treated the same. The task of the network firewall is to distinguish between threatening and non-threatening traffic and to do so differently depending on which side the traffic originates. In the presence of fire, a firewall need not pass people; resisting fire is more important than passing people. However, the network firewall will rarely be permitted to reject all traffic in the name of rejecting all attack traffic. It will usually be required to pass legitimate traffic, even in the presence of known attack traffic.

Moreover, a firewall is not is a box; it is not a product that can be purchased off the shelf. At time of this writing, more than 40 vendors offer products that are described, at least in part, as firewalls. Although similarities among them exist, there are also fundamental differences in their approaches. Even given a complete understanding of company requirements and security policy, gaining sufficient knowledge about tens of products to decide which one is most appropriate is a major challenge.

### Firewall Policy Positions

Four fundamental policy positions are available to network operators. The firewall policy will be the result of these postures and of the applications on the network.

**Paranoid.** The first of these positions is called paranoid. It is motivated by extreme caution and probably fear, and characterized by the absence of a connection to the Internet.

**Prudent.** The second position is called prudent or restrictive. It too is motivated by caution, but also by a recognition of the value of connection to the Internet. It is characterized by the fact that everything which is not explicitly allowed is implicitly forbidden. For example, a private Internet user would have to be explicitly authorized to Telnet to a system on the public Internet.

**Permissive.** The permissive posture is the opposite of the restrictive policy. Under this policy, everything that is not explicitly forbidden is implicitly allowed. Obviously, it is the intent of this policy to forbid the necessary conditions for all known attacks. This policy is intended to provide a level of protection with a minimum of interference with applications. This is the policy most likely to be applied when applying a firewall to an existing connection. It is particularly useful if little is known about the applications and if there is a strong desire not to interfere with or break those applications. It is the policy most likely to be recommended by Internet service providers who are motivated to maximize the value of the connection.

**Promiscuous.** The promiscuous policy is that anything goes. Under this policy, there are multiple connections and any legitimate packet can flow from any source to any destination.

### Choosing a Firewall Policy

An interesting questions is why anyone would want to be in postures one or four? Remarkably, position one is the default position for business. Most businesses have not yet connected to the Internet. Position four is the default policy for the Internet; all connections and traffic are tolerated in the name of maximizing the bandwidth and the potential for getting messages through.

If an Internet service provider is asked for guidance on a firewall policy, it will likely recommend that the position should be on the promiscuous side of permissive. The service provider will supply a list of restrictions to address all of the attacks that it knows about. However, this permits exposure to a large set of fundamental vulnerabilities. This is, in part, because the Internet service provider believes in the value of the net and does not wish to deny its clients any benefits without necessity.

This author recommends a position on the paranoid side of prudent or restrictive. In other words, permit only that traffic that is associated with a particular value for which the net is being used. The flow of all other traffic should be resisted.

### A Conservative Firewall Policy

A conservative firewall policy is intended to position an institution or network on the paranoid side of restrictive. The intent is to protect not only against known and expected attacks, but also against those that have not been invented yet. It is driven by fundamental vulnerabilities, rather than by known threats and attacks. It attempts to take only those risks that are necessary to accommodate the intended applications.

In addition, no information about the private network should be available on the public net. Private net addresses should never appear on the public net; they should be replaced or aliased to an address that the firewall owns. Addresses on packets and messages should be re-encoded at the firewall. Similarly, users' internal E-mail addresses should not appear on the public net. These private addresses should be replaced with the name of the site or enterprise at the firewall on the way out and replaced on the way in.

Protocols should not traverse the firewall. Traffic should be decoded and re-encoded at the firewall. For example, a SMTP carrying a message should be decoded into a message and then re-encoded into another SMTP for transmission at the firewall.

Reusable passwords should not traverse the firewall in either direction. Incoming passwords may be replays and are not reliable evidence of the identity of the user. Outgoing passwords may be similar to those used by users on the inside, and their use across the firewall may compromise internal systems. A preference for Secure Telnet or FTP should be made. These protocols provide end-to-encryption for all traffic, including the password. Alternatively, one-time passwords (e.g., SecureID or s-key) could be used. Although these do not protect all traffic, they protect against replays.

Proxies should represent the public net to the private net. For example, when a user of the private net wishes to access a WWW server on the public net, he or she should be transparently routed through the WWW proxy on the firewall. This proxy should hide the user's address from the public net, and protects both nets and the user. The user cannot misrepresent his or her address to the public net, and a process on the public net can directly attack only the proxy, not the user.

Only a limited set of limited applications should be permitted. Under this policy, such a limited application as E-mail is permitted, and such a very general application as telnet is discouraged. Telnet is very general, flexible, and its intent is not obvious. It is vulnerable as a target and useful for attack.

Only those public applications that are intended for use on the public net should be placed on the public net. The public should not be permitted to traverse a firewall simply for the purpose of gaining access to public applications.

---

**Exhibit 1. Encryption on the Internet**

| Application | Encryption |
| --- | --- |
| E-mail | PGP, SecureXchange, PEM, S-MIME |
| File | PGP, RSA Secure, Entrust |
| Application | DES, IDEA, stelnet, sftp |
| Client/Server | Secure Socket Layer (SSL) |
| Gateway-to-gateway | Digital, IBM, TIS |
| World Wide Web | s-http |
| Secure IP | S/WAN |

See http://www.rsa.com for a list of products and vendors.

Applications on the public net should be implemented on dedicated and isolated servers. The server should be dedicated to a single use; it should not rely on the operating system to protect the application. Public servers should not know about the private net. Any connection to the private net should be to an application and over a trusted path. Privileged access to such servers should require strong authentication.

The public should not be granted read and write access to the same resource. For example, if the public can read a web page, they should not be able to write to it. The ability to write to it would permit them to alter or contaminate the data in a manner that could prove embarrassing. If a directory is provided to which the public can send files, they should not be able to read from that directory. If they can both read and write to the directory, they may use it simply as storage in lieu of their own. They may also use it to store contraband data that they would not want on their own systems and which might also prove embarrassing.

## ENCRYPTION

Encryption is the application and use of secret, as opposed to public, codes. It is a powerful defense that can deal with many of the problems related to vulnerable links and even some of those related to insecure nodes. It is inexpensive and effective. In addition, multiple implementations are available. However, it is limited in the open node problems that it can deal with and may require some management infrastructure. Exhibit 1 displays some of the encryption choices available for selected applications on the Internet.

Encryption is used for two fundamental purposes on the net. The first is to preserve necessary confidentiality on the net, which is the traditional use of cryptography. The second is to enable some confidence about with whom one is talking. In other words, if conversation is in a language that can only be spoken by one other, the correct parties are speaking to one another.

Encryption can also be used to resist password grabbers and other eavesdropping attacks.

## USING THE INTERNET IN A RELATIVELY SAFE ENVIRONMENT

The following are recommendations for using the Internet in a relatively safe way. Although few will follow all of these recommendations, there is risk involved in any deviation from the recommendations. Moreover, although complete adherence to these recommendations will not eliminate all vulnerabilities, it will address many of them. Finally, although complete adherence will not eliminate all risks, it following these recommendations provides a reasonable balance between risk and other values.

- **Do not rely on the secrecy or authenticity of any information traversing the internet in public codes.** Names and addresses, credit card numbers, passwords, and other data received from the public net may be replays rather than originals. Amounts and account numbers may have been tampered with.

- **Choose a single point of connection to the Internet.** Although the Internet is inherently mesh connected, and more than one connection may be necessary to avoid single points of failure, the more connections, the more points of attack and the more difficult it is to maintain consistent controls. The fewer the number or points of connection, the fewer the potential points of attack and the easier to maintain control.

- **Connect to the Internet only with equipment dedicated to that purpose.** When computers were expensive, it was economic to put as many applications as possible on the costly hardware. Communication software was added to connect existing multi-use, multi-user systems to the net. Attacks exploited this gratuitous generality. Because of less expensive hardware, hardware connected to the net should be dedicated to that use. All other applications should be run on other systems.

- **Choose application-only connections.** Many of the compromises of the Internet have resulted from the fact that the components were connected at the system layer and that attacks have succeeded in escaping the application to the more general and flexible system layer. If in an attack encounters the E-mail service, it should see nothing else. If it escapes the E-mail application, it should see nothing. Under no circumstances, should it see the prompt of an operating system that knows about any other system. In other words, the operating system should be hidden from the public net.

- **Limit the use of Telnet.** Telnet, particularly to the operating system, is a very general and flexible capability. It can be both used for attack and is vulnerable to attacks. Most of its functions and capabilities can be accomplished with safer alternatives.

- **Use end-to-end encryption for commercial applications on the net.** Although most of the applications and traffic on the public net are public, commercial and other private applications on the public net must be conducted in secret codes.
- **Require strong authentication.** Users of private applications on the public net or of the public net for commercial applications must use strong authentication. Two independent kinds of evidence should be employed to determine the identity of a user, and the authentication data must be protected from capture and replay.
- **Log, monitor, and meter events and traffic.** Given enough time, almost any attack can succeed. It is important to be able to recognize attack traffic and correct for it early. Attacks can usually be recognized by a change, often a sudden increase, from normal traffic patterns. It is useful to know what normal traffic looks like to be able to recognize variances on a timely basis, and to communicate the condition of those variances to managers who can take timely corrective action.

## CONCLUSION

The Internet is as ubiquitous as the telephone and for similar reasons. It gives users such an economic advantage over nonusers so that the nonusers are forced to become users. Pundits are fond of saying that no one is making money on the Internet. This position is fatuous and suggests that tens of thousands of enterprises are behaving irrationally. What is meant is that no one is conducting commerce on the Internet, at least not in the sense that they are selling, distributing, billing, and being paid over the Internet. Of course, many firms are doing one or more of these. Many others are making money, mostly by reducing costs. Many companies are using the Internet because it is the most efficient way to support customers.

The Internet holds out the promise to empower, enrich, and perhaps even ennoble. A minimum level of public trust and confidence must be maintained if that promise becomes a reality. That trust is both fragile and irreparable.

Because fundamental vulnerabilities on the network exist and because all possible attacks cannot be anticipated, a conservative policy and a responsive posture are required.

Chapter 47

# Firewalls: An Effective Solution for Internet Security

*E. Eugene Schultz*

Firewalls are an effective method of reducing the possibility of network intrusion by attackers. The key to successful firewall implementation is the selection of the appropriate system and regular maintenance.

## INTRODUCTION

The Internet has presented a new, complex set of challenges that even the most sophisticated technical experts have not been able to solve adequately. Achieving adequate security is one of the foremost of these challenges. The major security threats that the Internet community faces are described in this chapter. It also explains how firewall — potentially one of the most effective solutions for Internet security — can address these threats, and it presents some practical advice for obtaining the maximum advantages of using firewalls.

## INTERNET SECURITY THREATS

The vastness and openness that characterizes the Internet presents an extremely challenging problem — security. Although many claims about the number and cost of Internet-related intrusions are available, valid, credible statistics about the magnitude of this problem will not be available until scientific research is conducted. Exacerbating this dilemma is that most corporations that experience intrusions from the Internet and other sources do not want to make these incidents known for fear of public relations damage and, worse yet, many organizations fail to even detect most intrusions. Sources, such as Carnegie Mellon University's CERT, however, suggest that the number of Internet-related intrusions each year is very high and that the number of intrusions reported to CERT (which is one of dozens of incident response teams) is only the tip of the iceberg. No credible statistics

0-8493-9965-3/99/$0.00+$.50
© 1999 by CRC Press LLC

concerning the total amount of financial loss resulting from security-related intrusions are available, but, judging by the amount of money corporations and government agencies are spending to implement Internet and other security controls, the cost must be extremely high.

Many types of Internet security threats exist. One of the most serious methods is IP spoofing. In this type of attack, a perpetrator fabricates packet that bear the address of origination of a client host and sends these packets to the server for this client. The server acknowledges receiving these packets by returning packets with a certain sequence number. If the attacker can guess this packet sequence number and incorporate it into another set of fabricated packets that are then sent back to the server, the server can be tricked into setting up a connection with a fraudulent client. The intruder can subsequently use attack methods, such as use of trusted host relationships to intrude into the server machine.

A similar threat is DNS spoofing. In this type of attack, an intruder subverts a host within a network, and sets up this machine to function as an apparently legitimate name server. The host then provides bogus data about host identities and certain network services, enabling the intruder to break into other hosts within the network.

Session hijacking is another Internet security threat. The major tasks for the attacker who wants to hijack an ongoing session between remote hosts are locating an existing connection between two hosts and fabricating packets that bear the address of the host from which the connection has originated. By sending these packets to the destination host, the originating host's connection is dropped, and the attacker picks up the connection.

Another Internet security threat is network snooping, in which attackers install programs that copy packets traversing network segments. The attackers periodically inspect files that contain the data from the captured packets to discover critical log-on information, particularly user IDs and passwords for remote systems. Attackers subsequently connect to the systems for which they possess the correct log-on information and log on with no trouble. Attackers targeting networks operated by ISPs have made this problem especially serious, because so much information travels these networks. These attacks demonstrate just how vulnerable network infrastructures are; successfully attacking networks at key points, where router, firewalls, and server machines are located, is generally the most efficient way to gain information allowing unauthorized access to multitudes of host machines within a network.

A significant proportion of attacks exploit security exposures in programs that provide important network services. Examples of these programs include sendmail, NFS, and NIS. These exposures allow intruders to gain access to remote hosts and to manipulate services supported by these hosts or even to obtain superuser access. Of increasing concern is the susceptibility of WWW services and the hosts that house these services to successful attack. The ability of intruders to exploit vulnerabilities in the HTTP and in Java, a programming language used to write WWW applications, seems to be growing at an alarming rate.

Until a short time ago, most intruders have attempted to cover up indications of their activity, often by installing programs that selectively eliminated data from system logs. These also avoided causing system crashes or causing massive slowdowns or disruption. However, a significant proportion of the perpetrator community has apparently shifted its strategy by increasingly perpetrating denial-of-service attacks. For example, many types of hosts crash or perform a core dump when they are sent a PING or PING packet that exceeds a specified size limit or when they are flooded with SYN packets that initiate host-to-host connections. (PING, is a service used to determine whether a host on a network is up and running.) These denial-of-service attacks make up an increasing proportion of observed Internet attacks. They represent a particularly serious threat, because many organizations require continuity of computing and networking operations to maintain their business operations.

Not to be overlooked is another type of security threat called social engineering. Social engineering is fabricating a story to trick users, system administrators, or help desk personnel into providing information required to access systems. Intruders usually solicit password for user accounts, but information about the network infrastructure and the identity of individual hosts can also be the target of social engineering attacks.

## INTERNET SECURITY CONTROLS

As previously mentioned, Internet security threats pose a challenge because of their diversity and severity. An added complication is an abundance of potential solutions.

### Encryption

Encryption is a process of using an algorithm to transform cleartext information into text that cannot be read without the proper key. Encryption protects information stored in host machines and transmitted over networks. It is also useful in authentication users to hosts or networks. Although encryption is an effective solution, its usefulness is limited by the difficulty in managing encryption keys (i.e., of assigning keys to users and recovering keys if they are lost or forgotten), laws limiting the export and use of encryption, and the lack of adherence to encryption standards by many vendors.

### One-Time Passwords

Using one-time passwords is another way in which to challenge security threats. One-time passwords captured while in transit over networks become worthless, because each password can only be used once. A captured password has already been used by the legitimate user who has initiated a remote log-on session by the time that the captured password can be employed. Nevertheless, one-time passwords address only a relatively small proportion of the total range of Internet security threats. They do not, for example, protect against IP spoofing or exploitation of vulnerabilities in programs.

Installing fixes for vulnerabilities in all hosts within an Internet-capable network does not provide an entirely suitable solution because of the cost of labor, and, over the last few years, vulnerabilities have surfaced at a rate far faster than that at which fixes have become available.

### Firewalls

Although no single Internet security control measure is perfect, the firewall has, in many respects, proved more useful overall than most other controls. Simply, a firewall is a security barrier between two networks that screens traffic coming in and out of the gate of one network to accept or reject connections and service requests according to a set of rules. If configured properly, it addresses a large number of threats that originate from outside a network without introducing any significant security liabilities. Because most organizations are unable to install every patch that CERT advisories describe, these organizations can nevertheless protect hosts within their networks against external attacks that exploit vulnerabilities by installing a firewall that prevents users from outside of the network from reaching the vulnerable programs in the first place. A more sophisticated firewall also controls how any connection between a host external to a network and an internal host occurs. Moreover, an effective firewall hides information, such as names and addresses of hosts within the network, as well as the topology of the network, which it is employed to protect.

Firewalls can defend against attacks on hosts (including spoofing attacks), application protocols, and applications. In addition, firewalls provide a central method for administering security on a network and for logging incoming and outgoing traffic to allow for accountability of user actions and for triggering incident response activity if unauthorized activity occurs.

Firewalls are typically placed at gateways to networks to create a security perimeter, as shown in Exhibit 1, primarily to protect an internal network from threats originating from an external one (particularly from the Internet). This scheme is successful to the degree that the security perimeter

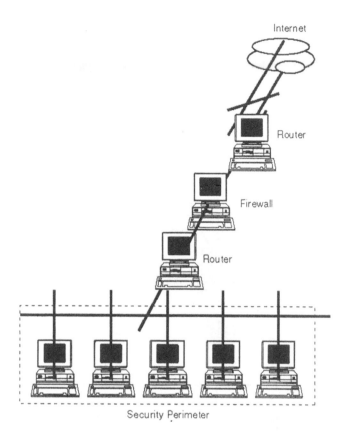

**Exhibit 1. A typical Gate-Based Firewall Architecture.**

is not accessible through unprotected avenues of access. The firewall acts as a choke component for security purposes. Exhibit 1 displays routers that are located in front and in back of the firewall. The first router (shown above the firewall) is an external one used initially to route incoming traffic, to direct outgoing traffic to external networks, and to broadcast information that enables other network routers (as well as the router on the other side of the firewall) to know how to reach the host network. The other internal router (shown below the firewall) sends incoming packets to their destination within the internal network, directs outgoing packets to the external router, and broadcasts information on how to reach the internal network and the external router. This belt-and-suspenders configuration further boosts security by preventing the broadcast of information about the internal network outside of the network that the firewall protects. An attacker finding this information can learn IP addresses, subnets, servers, and other information, which is useful in perpetrating attacks against the

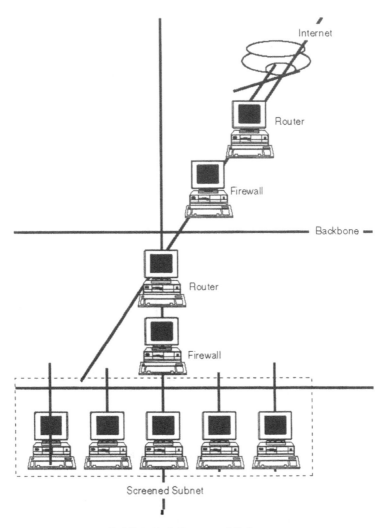

**Exhibit 2. A Screened Subnet.**

network. Hiding information about the internal network is much more difficult if the gate has only one router.

Another way in which firewalls are deployed (though less frequently) is within an internal network — at the entrance to a subnet within a network — rather than at the gateway to the entire network. The purpose of this configuration (shown in Exhibit 2) is to segregate a subnetwork (a screened subnet) from the internal network at large, a wise strategy if the subnet has tighter security requirements than the rest of the security perimeter. This type of deployment more carefully controls access to data and services within a subnet than is otherwise allowed within the network. The gate-based firewall, for example, may allow FTP access to an internal network from external sources. However, if a subnet contains hosts that store information, such as lease bid data or salary data, allowing FTP access to this subnet is less advisable. Setting up the subnet as a screened subnet may provide suitable security control, that is, the internal firewall that provides security screening for the subnet is configured to deny all FTP access, regardless of whether the access requests originated from outside or inside the network.

Simply having a firewall, no matter how it is designed and implemented, does not necessarily protect against externally originated security threats. The benefits of firewalls depend to a large degree on the type used and how it is deployed and maintained.

## USING FIREWALLS EFFECTIVELY

To ensure that firewalls perform their intended function, it is important to choose the appropriate firewall and to implement it correctly. Establishing a firewall policy is also a critical step in securing a system, as is regular maintenance of the entire security structure.

### Choosing the Right Firewall

Each type of firewall offers its own set of advantages and disadvantages. Combined with the vast array of vendor firewall products and the possibility of custom-building firewall, this task can be potentially overwhelming. Establishing a set of criteria for selecting an appropriate firewall is an effective aid in narrowing down the choices.

One of the most important considerations is the amount and type of security needed. For some organizations with low to moderate security needs, installing a packet-filtering firewall that blocks out only the most dangerous incoming service requests often provides the most satisfactory solution, because the cost and effort are not likely to be great. For other organizations, such as banks and insurance corporations, packet-filtering firewalls do not generally provide the granularity and control against unauthorized actions usually needed for connecting customers to services that reside within a financial or insurance corporation's network.

Additional factors, such as the reputation of the vendor, the arrangements for vendor support, the verifiability of the firewall's code (i.e., to confirm that the firewall does what the vendor claims it does), the support for strong authentication, the ease of administration, the ability of the firewall to withstand direct attacks, and the quality and extent of logging and alarming capabilities should also be strong considerations in choosing a firewall.

### The Importance of a Firewall Policy

The discussion to this point has focused on high-level technical considerations. Although these considerations are extremely important, too often security professionals overlook other considerations that, if neglected, can render firewalls ineffective. The most important consideration in effectively using firewalls is developing a firewall policy.

A firewall policy is a statement of how a firewall should work — the rules by which incoming and outgoing traffic should be allowed or rejected. A firewall policy, therefore, is a type of security requirements document for a firewall. As security needs change, firewall policies must change accordingly. Failing to create and update a firewall policy for each firewall almost inevitably results in gaps between expectations and the actual function of the firewall, resulting in uncontrolled security exposures in firewall functionality. For example, security administrators may think that all incoming HTTP requests are blocked, but the firewall may actually allow HTTP requests from certain IP addresses, leaving an unrecognized avenue of attack.

An effective firewall policy should provide the basis for firewall implementation and configuration; needed changes in the way that the firewall works should always be preceded by changes in the firewall policy. An accurate, up-to-date firewall policy should also serve as the basis for evaluating and testing a firewall.

### Security Maintenance

Many organizations that employ firewalls feel a false sense of security once the firewalls are in place. Properly designing and implementing firewalls can be difficult, costly, and time consuming. It is critical to remember, however, that firewall design and implementation are simply the beginning point of having a firewall. Firewalls that are improperly maintained soon lose their value as security control tools.

One of the most important facets of firewall maintenance is updating the security policy and rules by which each firewall operates. Firewall functionality invariably must change as new services and applications are introduced in (or sometimes removed from) a network. Undertaking the task of daily inspections of firewall logs to discover attempted and possibly successful attacks on both the firewall and the internal network that it protects should be an extremely high priority. Evaluating and testing the adequacy of firewalls for unexpected access avenues to the security perimeter and vulnerabilities that lead to unauthorized access to the firewall should also be a frequent, high-priority activity.

Firewall products have improved considerably over the past several years, and are likely to continue to improve. Several vendor products, for example, are not network addressable, which makes breaking into these platforms by someone who does not have physical access to them virtually impossible. At the same time, however, recognizing the limitations of firewalls and ensuring that other appropriate Internet security controls are in place is becoming increasingly important because of such problems as third-party connections to organizations' networks that bypass gate-based security mechanisms altogether. Therefore, an Internet security strategy that includes firewalls in addition to host-based security mechanisms is invariably the most appropriate direction for achieving suitable levels of Internet security.

## CONCLUSION

Internet connectivity can be extremely valuable to an organization, but it involves many security risks. A firewall is a key tool in an appropriate set of security control measures to protect Internet-capable networks. Firewalls can be placed at the gateway to a network to form a security perimeter around the networks that they protect or at the entrance to subnets to screen the subnets from the rest of the internal network.

Developing an accurate and complete firewall policy is the most important step in using firewalls effectively. This policy should be modified and updated as new applications are added within the internal network protected by the firewall and new security threats emerge. Maintaining firewalls properly and regularly examining the log data that they provide are almost certainly the most neglected aspects of using firewalls. Yet, these activities are among the most important in ensuring the defenses are adequate and that incidents are quickly detected and handled. Performing regular security evaluations and testing the firewall to identify any exploitable vulnerabilities or misconfiguration are also essential activities. Establishing a regular security procedure minimizes the possibility of system penetration by an attacker.

# Chapter 48
# Selecting an Internet Firewall

*Marcus J. Ranum*

Internet security risks are, in reality, not that much different from other security problems that organizations face every day. It is the newness of the Internet that makes it seem more different and dangerous than anything else. In approaching Internet security, it should be considered as a fraction of the overall computer security requirements for the entire organization. Most important, computer security should be handled consistently throughout the enterprise. Without such an approach, a secure firewall may be protecting a wide-open network behind it. If the course of Internet security is uncertain, security should be based on comparable approaches for other vulnerable systems that have previously worked.

## INTRODUCTION

Many organizations have or are about to have connections to the Internet, but they are alarmed at the risk of being broken into by hackers, industrial spies, or other electronic miscreants. The magnitude of this threat is difficult to assess in concrete terms. However, it is clear that not being connected to the Internet is a business risk as well, which may result in lost revenue, delays in time-to-market, or poor customer perception. As Internet connectivity becomes a common business infrastructure requirement like the FAX, more and more organizations will face these risks.

## THE RISKS ASSOCIATED WITH INTERNET CONNECTIONS

Internet security risks are, in reality, not that much different from other security problems that organizations face every day. It is the newness of the Internet that makes it seem more different and dangerous than anything else. In approaching Internet security, it should be considered as a fraction of the overall computer security requirements for the entire organization. Most important, computer security should be handled consistently throughout the enterprise. Organizations are every bit as likely to be attacked through dial-up access, social engineering, dumpster diving, or PBX/toll fraud as they are over the Internet. It is unfortunate that organizations may invest a huge amount of money and effort in securing their Internet connection, but have unprotected modem pools without even passwords or dial-back, which allow access into the network behind the firewall. Management support and an architectural view of the organization are essential requirements to achieve a consistent security approach. Without a uniform approach, a secure firewall may be protecting a wide-open network behind it. If the course of Internet security is uncertain, security should be based on comparable approaches for other vulnerable systems that have previously worked.

## Downtime

Probably the most expensive cost resulting from a break-in is downtime: system manager's time, time-to-market, and clean-up costs. In some cases, public embarrassment may also be a significant factor. Before deciding on any actions that may affect the organization's systems security, these questions should be asked:

- What needs protection?
- How likely is it that someone will want to break, steal, or alter the items needing protection?
- If they succeed, what will be the expense?

In some cases, the potential damage might be so high that no justification for Internet connectivity exists. Before reaching that conclusion, existing security practices should be examined. Frequently, organizations that have decided not to connect to the Internet permit dial-in access or have other lax security practices that are every bit as risky than a well-secured Internet connection.

Often, organizations with very restrictive firewalls or no formal Internet security policies have dial-out modems scattered around the network, as individuals who need Internet access simply obtain it through commercial Internet service providers. These links are potentially avenues of attack, like any other Internet links.

## Sophistication of Attacks

Many managers do not understand the level of sophistication that attackers are showing. As a result, they either over- or underestimate the likelihood that their existing security (if they have any) will be compromised. In the recent past, attacks have been increasing in sophistication, including exploiting protocol level flaws and cryptographic flaws, and employing more clever social engineering tactics. A pattern has emerged wherein highly skilled attackers (called ueberhackers) develop tools for exploiting specific weaknesses, and eventually the tools find their way into the hands of less skilled or completely unskilled novices (called ankle biters) who can still employ them to penetrate sophisticated defenses. Attackers are also persistent and understand how to exploit the often tangled interconnections between corporate networks, modem pools, and other networks (such as X.25 networks or PC LAN software). In the last year, at least three cases were reported of firewalls being compromised from the inside by attackers who gained access to management networks through dial-in modems left unattended on users' desktops.

What implications does this have for the would-be connected site? Simply having a firewall in place does not make an organization invulnerable to attack. Other routes of attack into the network must be secured as well, and constant security awareness is mandated. Organizations with extremely critical data should put it behind internal firewalls and should further compartmentalize their networks to make it harder for attackers to succeed once they are in. In some cases, if data is extremely sensitive or mission-critical systems exist, not having an Internet connection, or having it only on a physically isolated network that is separate from the corporate backbone, should be considered.

### Likelihood of Attack

A number of organizations have concluded that security is not a problem for them because "nobody will bother to attack them." However, when an attacker is choosing a target, he or she usually does not bother researching the target to see if they may be valuable; it is easier to smash in and take a look around. As a result, attacks seem to be random. Systems that have important data are ignored in favor of systems that simply catch the attacker's eye. Recently, attackers that broke into a financial database system were observed to completely ignore the financial data (worth millions of dollars) in favor of exploiting a back-door connection to a local university's computing center. The unpredictable nature of attacks makes it difficult to place a value on defenses. For example, a site with a very strong firewall and no important data might come under ferocious attack, and a different site with no security at all in front of mission critical systems may be completely ignored. Unless an organization's data is unimportant and employees' jobs are secure, it is foolish to assume that attackers will ignore any organization.

### HOW TO ASSESS THE RISKS OF INTERNET CONNECTIONS

To assess the risks of Internet connections, three questions should be considered:

- If something happens to the network, will it put the organization out of business?
- What are the Internet services that the organization wants to use?
- Based on the list of Internet services, should any special requirements be considered that may mandate additional security services?

## Mission Critical Networking

The first question to ask when considering Internet connectivity is, "if something happens to the network, will it put the organization out of business?" Connecting to public networks greatly increases that chance of something happening, and that factor must be evaluated in designing an Internet connection. Regardless of whether a security problem could put an organization out of business, the kind of business damage that downtime or system clean-up might cost must be estimated.

Organizations with intellectual property or private data must also consider the potential for disclosure of trade secrets or the liability if a customer's private information is divulged. If an organization, for example, handles patient records, customer financial or credit card information, personal data, customer home addresses and demographic information, corporate attorneys should be consulted for information about effective business practices in the industry, and the data should be protected accordingly.

## Service-Oriented Requirements Analysis

One approach that is effective in determining what a firewall should do is the process of service-oriented requirements analysis. Rather than simply relying on technical details about what a firewall should provide, a list of the network services of which the organization wants to take advantage should be compiled. A typical set of Internet services can include:

- Access to the World Wide Web, including FTP.
- The ability to send and receive E-mail.
- The option of subscribing to USENET newsgroups.
- The ability to Telnet out to remote sites.

## Defining Security Requirements for Services

Based on the list of services to be provided to an organization's users, any special requirements should be considered that may mandate additional security services. The organization should determine what kinds of audit trail or records (if any) are required that relate to transactions traveling through the network. An organization's requirements should be modeled on other "real life" services the organization uses, and the security policies should remain consistent. For example, if a security policy states that users cannot FTP data out, those users should not be able to send E-mail or mail floppy disks with data through the postal system. A consistent approach to security is key to a security program that works, or at least, does what the designers intended it to do.

Another important consideration when approaching security is the growth plan for the organization's network. For example, if a firewall or Internet connection is installed that provides a few services today, will that solution work three years from now? This does not mean that the same hardware will be in place, because the lifecycles of network equipment for Internet connections are fairly short. The basic architecture that is put in place is likely to be viable in the long term.

## DIFFERENT TYPES OF FIREWALLS

A firewall should be thought of as a gap between two networks, filled with something that lets only a few selected forms of traffic through. The designers of the firewall should be able to explain the mechanism that enforces the separation, as well as the mechanisms that carry data back and forth. Another important aspect of a firewall is how well it protects itself against attack. In other words, the firewall itself should not be easy to break into, because breaking into the firewall will give an attacker an entree into an organization's entire network.

### Router Screening

The simplest and most popular form of firewall is router screening. Most commercial routers have some kind of capability built into them to restrict traffic between destinations, while permitting other traffic, for example. Screening routers operate only at the network level and make all their permit or deny decisions based on the contents of the TCP/IP packet header. They are very fast, very flexible, and inexpensive, but they lack the ability to provide detailed audit information about the traffic they transmit. Screening routers have often proved vulnerable to attack, because they also rely on software being correctly configured on the hosts behind them. Many experts, for this reason, prefer to avoid screening routers as a sole defense.

### Dual-Homed Gateway

A second form of firewall is the dual-homed gateway, which is a system with two network interfaces that sits on both the protected network and on the public network. Because the gateway can communicate with both networks, it is an ideal place to install software for carrying data back and forth. Such software agents are called proxies and are usually customized for the service that they are intended to provide. For example, a dual-homed gateway that has a proxy for WWW traffic has some form of agent running on it that manages to make requests to the remote networks on behalf of the user.

### Proxy Firewalls

Proxy firewalls (also known as application firewalls) are attractive to many sites, because the proxies are able to perform a detailed audit of the data passing through them. According to many experts, they are also more secure, because the software proxies can be customized to specifically deflect known attacks to which the host software behind the firewall might be vulnerable. The main disadvantage of proxy firewalls is that they are sometimes not completely transparent, and they do not support protocols for which a proxy has not been developed.

### Dynamic Packet Filtering

Recently, a number of firewalls based on dynamic packet filtering have appeared on the market. A dynamic packet filter firewall is a cross between a proxy firewall and a screening router. To the end user, it looks like it is operating only at the network level, but the firewall is examining the traffic as it passes by, just like a proxy firewall's proxy application does. When a user connects out through the firewall, it records that fact and allows data to come back in (i.e., through the firewall) to the user for the duration of that session. Dynamic packet screening firewalls are an attractive technology that is still evolving, but which shows promise for the future.

### SECURITY COMPROMISES IN FIREWALLS

Firewalls, like many other security systems, are not perfect. The compromise or trade-off that they usually represent is between ease of use and security. The more rigorously the firewall checks the user's identity and activity, the more likely the user is to feel interrupted, pestered, and resentful. When choosing a firewall, user resentment should not be discounted as a factor in the decision-making process. Many sites with firewalls have internal networks festooned with uncontrolled dial-in and dial-out modems installed by users to bypass the firewall by subscribing to commercial online services. If the security system chosen is not useful and easy to use, end users will bypass it, unless there is sufficient authority to prevent them.

Proxy firewalls provide more effective auditing and tighter access control than screening router firewalls, but many do not have sufficient capacity to support network connections faster than ethernet speed. If an organization plans on using ATM networks or T3 lines, the only choice may be to use a screening router type firewall.

## CASE STUDIES

Following below are three situations where firewalls need to be employed, but the nature of those individuals seeking Internet connectivity presents some interesting challenges. The first two, academia and research laboratories, present common difficulties, and the third, electronic commerce applications, presents other obstacles to implementing a secure Internet connection.

### An Academic Organization

Academic organizations, such as universities, typically have the most difficulty setting up a firewall. This may be due to notions of academic freedom and that the user community usually wants to experiment with a variety of features of the network. These users may also tend to resent or circumvent a firewall that interferes with their activities. Moreover, academic organizations often have independent departmental budgets and semi-autonomous use of the campus network, which makes it difficult to enforce a common security approach. If one department in the university installs a security system that interferes with the others, they can and do simply purchase new network links to bypass it. One approach that seems to work for academia is to isolate critical computing systems behind internal firewalls. Systems where student records, loan information, and paychecks are processed should be isolated from the main campus networks by placing them behind screening routers or commercial firewalls.

### A Research Laboratory

Research laboratories are often another difficult case. Scientists expect to use the network for collaboration and research access to late-breaking information. In many cases, however, the research may be economically significant and should be protected. Systems where patent applications or designs for proprietary products reside, for example, should be isolated and protected; or a second network, which is Internet accessible and physically separate from the internal research network, should be considered.

Research laboratories have many of the same problems as academia, because they tend to have user communities that want to be on the cutting edge and they will not tolerate interference. Perhaps more than anything else, it is important to get staff to recognize that intellectual property must be protected. Many research laboratories are connected to the Internet behind commercial proxy-based firewalls that are fairly conservative but which permit access to the Web and other sources of information. Other research laboratories rely on separated networks or isolated systems for storing proprietary information.

### An Electronic Commerce Application

As electronic commerce becomes more important, the need to pass commercial traffic into and out of firewalls will become more crucial. Service-oriented requirements analysis is a useful tool for designing and implementing such systems. For example, suppose that an organization wants to put a Web server on an external network and to provide database access of some sort to a system behind a firewall. In this case, the requirement is to get data back and forth for SQL only. A screening router firewall configured to just allow the SQL data between the outside Web server and the inside server might be chosen. A commercial firewall that permitted some kind of generic proxy or which supported a SQL service might be another option.

## MANAGERIAL ISSUES

Previously discussed have been the common security issues surrounding firewalls. Other managerial issues, such as maintenance, building a firewall (as opposed to purchasing a ready-made one), and answering the question is it secure, must be considered.

### Maintaining Typical Firewalls

Typical firewalls require about an hour of labor power per week to maintain. This hour does not include the other Internet-related time that the firewall administrator (or someone) will expend. Internet connectivity requires someone to act as postmaster for E-mail, Webmaster (potentially), FTP maintainer, and USENET news manager.

Each of these tasks are time-consuming, and each can become a full-time job for an individual. Often, the firewall administrator becomes responsible for a lot of tasks in addition to firewall maintenance. He or she is usually the first person contacted or interrupted when someone detects a problem or cannot get their Web browser to talk to the firewall, for example.

### Building a Firewall

A number of tools are available for building a firewall. Trusted Information Systems, Inc.'s Internet Firewall Toolkit is a freely available reference implementation of a set of firewall application proxies. It is available through anonymous FTP from ftp://ftp.tis.com/pub/firewalls/toolkit.When building a firewall by using a router or a router and the toolkit, the router's built-in screening can be advantageous. Brent Chapman and Elizabeth Zwicky's book on firewalls, Building Internet Firewalls, describes some approaches to setting up a screening router.

An important factor to weigh when deciding whether to build or buy a firewall is the cost of staff time. Having an employee devote a week to building a firewall may not be cost effective. In addition, providing support over the long term will further increase costs.

Before such a variety of commercial firewalls were available, many companies hired consultants to build their firewalls. Today, this is not a cost-effective option, because consultants eventually cost more than purchasing a commercial firewall, and it may not be able to be supported or enhanced over time.

### Is the Firewall Secure?

Is a firewall secure? This is a difficult question to answer, because no formal tests exist that can be easily applied to something as flexible as a firewall. A safe rule of thumb is that the more the firewall lets in and out, the less likely it is to be resistant to attack. The only firewall that is absolutely secure is one that is turned off.

If the quality of a firewall from a particular vendor is worrisome, common sense should be applied. The same kinds of questions that would be asked of vendors about any other mission-critical product purchase should be considered. For example, how long have they been in the business, what is the size of their installed base, and do they have independent experts review their design and implementation. A vendor should be able to clearly articulate how the design of their firewall leads to its security. An organization should be wary of accepting a vendor's hand-waving or insinuations that their competitors' products are insecure.

## COST ISSUES

In addition to managerial concerns, are cost issues. The most commonly asked question is: does more expense buy more security?

### Does More Expensive Buy More Security?

A common misconception about firewalls is that what is gotten is what is paid for, and, therefore, the more expensive a firewall, the more secure it is. Unlike PC hardware, which is a commodity market, the firewall market has not yet settled down enough for consistent and competitive pricing to evolve. Most firewalls available commercially cost between $10K and $20K, but the more expensive offerings can cost as much as $80K and upwards. A firewall buyer should show some healthy skepticism when it comes to cost vs. value. If a firewall costs twice as much as another, the seller should be able to clearly explain why its product is twice as good.

## COSTS AND DELIVERY

Before purchasing a firewall, it is important to be familiar with what typical installations involve and what are the deliverables that can be expected of a vendor.

### A Typical Firewall Installation

Most firewalls used to be sold as consulting packages. When a firewall was sold, part of its cost was installation and support, usually involving a consultant from the vendor arriving onsite and assisting with the installation. Many of the sites that were connecting to the Internet had no local TCP/IP expertise, so the firewall installer's job often also encompassed configuring routing and other tasks like setting up internal domain name servers and sendmail. Some vendors still provide such a level of service, and others simply ship a power-on-and-configure turnkey solution.

Typically, when a firewall is installed, the Internet connection must be ready, but not connected to the protected network. The firewall installer arrives, tests the machine's basic function, and then may lead a meeting in which to work out the details of how the firewall will be configured: what access control policy should be put in place, where E-mail should be routed, and where logging information should be forwarded, for example. Once the installer clearly understands how the firewall should be configured, it is connected to the Internet side and tested for correct operation with the network. Then, the firewall's access control rules are installed and checked, and it is connected to the protected network. Typically, some basic interoperation tests are performed, such as Web access and E-mail sending and receipt. When everything checks out positively, the organization is connected to the Internet.

### What Vendors Typically Provide with a Firewall

Most vendors provide some kind of support period for basic questions pertaining to the firewall. Many provide an installation service such as the one previously described, which is valuable because the organization is given an opportunity to tailor its firewall in a way that makes sense for it, while having a qualified vendor support ready to help. Often, a difficult part of setting up a firewall is getting the various software packages behind the firewall to talk correctly to it. Some vendors provide direct support as far as hooking PC LAN mail systems into the firewall's mailer or configuring domain name servers. If an organization does not have technical skills in these areas, having a vendor that is able and willing to support a custom configuration is a big time and energy saver.

Some Internet Service Providers (ISPs) offer a supported firewall as part of their connectivity service. For organizations that are new to TCP/IP or that are in a hurry, this is an attractive option, because the network support, leased line support, and firewall support are all supplied by the same vendor. The single most important service that vendors can provide with their firewalls is an understanding of how to make a sensible security policy. Unless an organization is certain that it understands what traffic it's letting into and out of its network, it is not safe to just install a firewall that lets users point and click to decide what information to allow through.

Some firewalls can be configured to allow through things that they normally should not, on the assumption that users are experts and know what they are doing. Support from the vendor in getting everything set up with a reasonable baseline helps keep an organization from having a firewall that is accidentally configured to allow an attack through it.

### What Vendors Typically, Do Not Provide with a Firewall

Vendors typically do not configure internal legacy systems to work with the firewall. For example, most firewalls assume that they are talking to Internet on one side and a TCP/IP network on the other. Usually, it is the customer's responsibility to have TCP/IP capable systems on the inside network, which the firewall can interact with. For E-mail, firewalls mostly support only Simple Mail Transfer Protocol (SMTP), and it is the customer's responsibility to have an SMTP compatible system someplace on the inside. Often, it is also the customer's responsibility to know any system specific configuration changes necessary to get that internal SMTP system to forward all Internet outbound mail to the firewall. Unless an organization is buying a firewall from an independent service provider, it is usually the customer's responsibility to have a class C IP network address and domain name allocated.

### CONCLUSION

Choosing a firewall is a lot like choosing a car. The natural assumption is that choosing a car is easy because by the time most drivers can afford one, they already have accumulated a lot of the information needed to be able to assess quickly and easily the cost/benefit performance and convenience tradeoffs that different cars represent. The best way to ensure that a firewall is suitable is to gather enough information so that a choice can be made wisely. Books, such as the following, are also available: *Firewalls and Internet Security: Pursuing the Wily Hacker* by Bill Cheswick and Steve Bellovin, published by Addison-Wesley, and *Building Internet Firewalls* by Brent Chapman and Elizabeth Zwicky, published by O'Rielly and Associates.

# Chapter 49
# A New Security Model for Networks and the Internet

*Dan Thomsen*

Computer security is a matter of controlling how data is shared for reading and modifying. Type enforcement is a new security mechanism that can be used as the basic security building block for a large number of systems where security is an important factor. This chapter discusses basic computer security issues and introduces type enforcement as a method for establishing data security. It also presents the *Sidewinder* firewall system as an implementation of the type enforcement mechanism.

## INTRODUCTION

Type enforcement is a new security mechanism that can be used as the basic security building block for a large number of systems in which security is an important factor. One of the most critical areas requiring protection is the system firewalls. Firewalls are the equivalent of walls around a castle and are under constant attack from external forces. Installing software to protect the network will not be effective if the software runs on a platform that cannot protect itself. It is like building the castle walls on a swamp.

Computer security is a matter of controlling how data is shared for reading and modifying. Only one person using an isolated computer is completely secure. However, people inside and outside of the organization need to share information. Type enforcement allows a computer to be divided into separate compartments, basically having a number of isolated computers inside of a single computer. Because the compartments are in a single computer, the process of sharing information among compartments can be controlled by type enforcement.

Most secure systems are difficult to work with and require extra development time. Type enforcement strikes a balance between security and

0-8493-9965-3/99/$0.00+$.50
© 1999 by CRC Press LLC

flexibility. As a result, new security services can be provided more quickly, because they can build on the security of the underlying operating system. Type enforcement permits the incorporation of security more quickly because it allows the applications to be encapsulated. Each application is protected from:

- Hostile manipulation by outsiders.
- Interference from other applications.
- Erroneous behavior by the application itself.

## SECURITY BASICS

An examination of the potential problems that can arise on a poorly secured system will help in understanding the need for security. Three basic kinds of malicious behavior are:

- Denial of service.
- Compromising the integrity of the information.
- Disclosure of information.

### Denial of Service

Denial of service occurs when a hostile entity uses a critical service of the computer system in such a way that no service or severely degraded service is available to others. Denial of service is a difficult attack to detect and protect against, because it is difficult to distinguish when a program is being malicious or is simply greedy. An example of denial of service is an Internet attack, where a attacker requests a large number of connections to an Internet server. Through the use of an improper protocol, the attacker can leave a number of the connections half open. Most systems can handle only a small number of half-open connections before they are no longer able to communicate with other systems on the net. The attack completely disables the Internet server.

### Compromising the Integrity of the Information

Most people take for granted that the information stored on the computer system is accurate, or, at least, has not been modified with a malicious intent. If the information loses its accuracy, the consequences can be extreme. For example, if competitors hacked into a company's database and deleted customer records, a significant loss of revenues could result. Users must be able to trust that data is accurate and complete.

### Disclosure of Information

Probably the most serious attack is disclosure of information. If the information taken off a system is important to the success of an organization, it has considerable value to a competitor. Corporate espionage is a real threat, especially from foreign companies, where the legal reprisals are much more difficult to enforce. Insiders also pose a significant threat. Limiting user access to the information needed to perform specific jobs increases data security dramatically.

## The Information Bucket

Every security mechanism has the concept of limiting who can have access to data. This concept is called the "information bucket." All related information is placed in the same bucket, and then access to that bucket is controlled. The information bucket is very similar to the access class or the security level in Department of Defense (DoD) systems. For example, most computer systems have the concept of users. Each user gets his or her own bucket in which to work. All user files reside in the appropriate bucket, and the users control who can access their files. In its simplest form, a bucket has a set of programs and a set of files that the programs can access.

A secure system must control at least four factors:

- Who can access a bucket.
- Which programs can run in that bucket.
- What those programs can access.
- Which programs can communicate with other programs.

Communication between programs must be controlled, because programs can send information to other programs, which then write that information into another bucket.

A system is very secure if no overlap exists between buckets, because in this configuration no user is able to read, modify data, or consume system resources from another bucket. However, this situation is equivalent to giving each user a separate computer and not allowing individual users to talk to each other. People in many computing environments need to share information. If the users are responsible for the information resources in their buckets and are careful about sharing their information with others, the system can remain secure.

Security problems arise when the boundaries between buckets are not well defined. For example, if two different buckets can read and write the same file, information can flow between the two buckets. This type of "leaky" bucket is a potential security problem. When leaky or overlapping buckets are combined with a complex system in which a large number of buckets exist, it becomes difficult to know how secure the system is.

For those leaks that are necessary, special programs can monitor data transfers between buckets to ensure that only the proper data is leaving the bucket. These programs are "trusted," in that they guarantee that only the proper data is transferred. Writing a program that performs a guarantee is difficult. The best approach with current technology is to write the program as small as possible, so that it can be analyzed for potential error by a network administrator.

The goal of a secure system is to strike the proper balance between guarding and sharing data. A rough measure of how secure a system is can be obtained by considering these three factors:

- The number of buckets.
- The amount of overlap between buckets.
- The level of trust for the programs protecting data channels (if information is allowed to move between buckets).

The more overlap that exists between buckets, the more information can flow through the system, and the more analysis is required to ensure that the system is secure.

Another consideration for the security of a system is any exception to the bucket policy. For example, many systems allow an administrator to access any bucket on the system. The problem is not that administrators cannot be trusted, but rather that this situation gives attackers an opportunity to gain complete access. Instead of trying to find a leaky bucket, an attacker can try to trick the system into thinking he or she is the administrator.

## TYPE ENFORCEMENT

Type enforcement was first proposed as part of the LOCK system to fulfill DoD requirements for secure systems. Most DoD secure systems in the late 1980s focused on the traditional classification levels of the DoD, such as unclassified, confidential, secret, and top secret. These systems implemented very strict buckets, with a one-way information flow between buckets. However, data and application interactions rarely fall into such a constrained security policy. In the course of an application transaction, data may flow in a complete circle through many different buckets with different security requirements.

The goal of type enforcement is to give each program only the permissions that the program requires to do its job. This concept is called "least privilege." Type enforcement assigns each type of critical program its own bucket. All the files that the program needs to access are placed in the bucket as well. Many programs need the same files, because they are doing the same kinds of tasks. Type enforcement categorizes individual programs and files into general groups that describe the abstract behavior of the components. Programs are grouped into domains, and files are grouped into types. For example, two mail reader programs like Elm and Pine require the same permissions; thus, they are grouped together in the mail reader domain.

**Exhibit 1. Type Enforcement Domain Definition Table (DDT)**

| | File Types | | | |
| Process Domains | Web pages | Mailbox file | Mail Aliases | Public files |
| --- | --- | --- | --- | --- |
| WWW Server | r | | | |
| Mail System | | rw | r | |
| ftp | | | | rw |

r = read; w = write; blank squares indicate no access is allowed

**Exhibit 2. Type Enforcement Domain Interaction Table (DIT)**

| | Process Domains | | |
| Process Domains | World Wide Web | Mail System | Word Processor |
| --- | --- | --- | --- |
| World Wide Web | so | | |
| Mail System | | so | so |
| Word Processor | | so | so |

s = signal; o = observer; blank squares indicate no access is allowed

Type enforcement works by grouping all the processes into domains and types based on least privilege. Grouping by types organizes the files much like abstract data types. The type indicates how the data in the file was created and how it can be used. Then, a table, called a domain definition table (DDT), is defined to indicate how the process can access the files. Exhibit 1 shows an example of a type enforcement DDT. As shown in the sample DDT, the World Wide Web (WWW) server can only access web files, and the mail system can only access mail files, such as the mailbox and mail alias files.

Most systems allow processes to interact with each other directly via signaling or a more complex inter-process communication (IPC) mechanism, which must be controlled as well. In type enforcement, control is achieved by creating a table similar to the DDT called the domain interaction table (DIT), shown in Exhibit 2. In this example, the WWW is completely isolated, and the mail system and the word processor can communicate. Type enforcement involves defining the DDT and DIT such that the applications meet the least privilege requirement. Complete isolation is often not desirable, because applications must share data. Type enforcement allows the appropriate balance between least privilege and information sharing.

An important property of type enforcement is that the DDT and DIT tables cannot be modified while the system is running. This limitation stops attacks that modify data used for making security decisions. The static nature of type enforcement does not affect the usability of the system, because the type-enforcement tables describe only how the applications

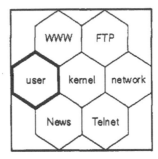

**Exhibit 3. Type Enforcement Structure.**

interact with data and each other. Thus, the type-enforcement tables change only if the way in which the applications interact changes. Type enforcement partitions a system into a number of strong buckets. Each bucket has a domain and a list of all the types that that domain can access. The bucket also includes IPC channels to other processes in other buckets, as shown in Exhibit 3. Type enforcement provides a structure that separates applications and controls user access to applications. A file or application must be in a user's domain for the user to access it. Users are allowed into a domain or bucket depending on their duties or roles on the system.

## Subsystem Separation

Now that a mechanism exists that closely matches the basic bucket principle, a variety of protection measures are possible. First and foremost, applications can be separated completely in different buckets, which ensures that two different applications do not interfere with each other. Type enforcement establishes the security level of separate computers while maintaining a linked system.

One possible security configuration that has been proposed to maintain Internet security is to have a different machine for each Internet service. The rationale behind this configuration is that many attacks over the network involve wedging open one service just enough to get a "toe hold" on the system. From the toe hold, the attacker expands his or her control by attacking the other Internet services in a sort of domino game. For example, a recently discovered Telnet vulnerability cannot be taken advantage of unless the attacker has write access to the system. If the site has an anonymous ftp site from which the attacker can download the key file, the system can be compromised. It is the combination of the two services that provides the vulnerability.

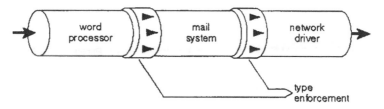

**Exhibit 4. Type Enforcement Assured Pipeline.**

However, buying one machine for each Internet service is expensive. Type enforcement allows separate Internet services to be combined onto one system, on which each Internet service is placed in its own bucket. Thus, type enforcement prevents attacks that use combinations of Internet services.

### Assured Pipelines

If information will move from one application to another, providing separation of applications is not enough to ensure security. The method by which the information flows through the system must also be controlled. This step uses type enforcement to create a kind of "pipeline" to organize data flow between programs, called an "assured pipeline." Type enforcement places tight control on how each program interacts with the next program in the pipeline.

This process is different from trusting the applications to interface with each other correctly. Many applications that need to be part of a system are large software components with less than reliable track records for obeying the interface definition. Using type enforcement is like having a net in the operating system that can catch the applications when they fail to follow the rules for the interface.

Type enforcement creates the pipeline by controlling access between programs. Each program has permission only to read from the stage in front of it and to write to the next stage of the pipeline. No stage of the pipeline can be bypassed. Exhibit 4 is a representation of how type enforcement controls data flow between applications through assured pipelines.

Assured pipelines provide a "divide and conquer" approach to building secure applications. Splitting a large piece of software into smaller pieces facilitates the process of analyzing and ensuring that the pieces are operating correctly. For example, consider the DoD requirement that any document printed is labeled correctly with its security label. It is not difficult to modify the printer driver to label the document, but it is difficult to prove that the printer driver labels the document accurately. The printer driver

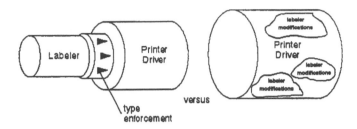

**Exhibit 5. Print Driver with Type Enforcement Compared to Conventional Print Driver.**

is a large program, and any modification to a large program has the potential to introduce other flaws. On the other hand, if the labeling is done by a small program that only labels the data, the entire labeling program could be checked, and the printer driver left unmodified. Exhibit 5 shows how assured pipelines allow for the creation of smaller programs that can be analyzed for greater reliability than modifications to large software systems. In this example, type enforcement ensures that data cannot reach the printer driver unless it has gone through the labeler process.

Three key elements are needed to prove that the requirement of proper labeling is satisfied:

1. Type enforcement is underneath the applications controlling access to the printer driver.
2. Type enforcement ensures that the labeler process cannot be bypassed.
3. Type enforcement tables cannot be modified while the system is running.

The labeler is a trusted program that ensures that only data that has been properly labeled moves from the user bucket to the printer bucket.

Hosting an application on a type enforcement system requires analyzing the application to determine what resources the applications requires. Often the access that an application needs can be reduced to improve security. This step may require modification to the application. The ability to separate applications, to control data flowing through the system, and to divide the application into small steps allows type enforcement to secure applications with the newest features as quickly as possible.

### *SIDEWINDER* IMPLEMENTATION OF TYPE ENFORCEMENT

Developed by Secure Computing, *Sidewinder* is an Internet firewall that has incorporated the LOCK type-enforcement mechanism to provide enhanced

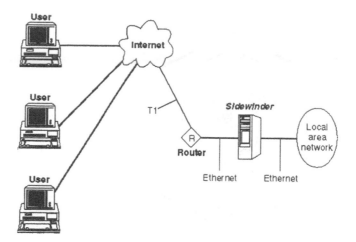

**Exhibit 6. Sidewinder Internet Firewall Configuration.**

security against Internet threats. To maximize compatibility with networks and existing protocols, *Sidewinder* was created by modifying BSDi UNIX. The *Sidewinder* is a turnkey system that resides between the Internet router and the internal network, as shown in Exhibit 6.

Traditional UNIX has been described as "a hard crunchy exterior surrounding a soft gooey center." This description refers to the structure of UNIX systems, the core of which is an all-powerful root account. Once an attacker gets into the root account, he or she can completely compromise the system. In addition, standard UNIX does not have tight control over how data files are shared among the processes running on a system. Thus, an intruder who manages to break into one area of a system can widen the initial foothold until he or she can gain access to any file on the system. The type enforcement security mechanism closes this vulnerability.

Type enforcement in *Sidewinder* cannot be bypassed. Even when a process is running as root, it is constrained by type enforcement. If a hacker obtains root access, the hacker is limited to the domain in which he or she started. To compromise *Sidewinder*, a hacker must bypass both UNIX protection mechanisms and type enforcement, as shown in Exhibit 7. Compromising UNIX is more difficult on *Sidewinder*, because the type-enforced honeycomb structure places vulnerable configuration files and UNIX tools out of a hacker's reach.

The goal of the *Sidewinder* system is to connect an internal network securely to the Internet. Internal users can access Internet services, such as E-mail and the World Wide Web, without exposing the internal network to unauthorized users. In addition to type enforcement, Secure Computing

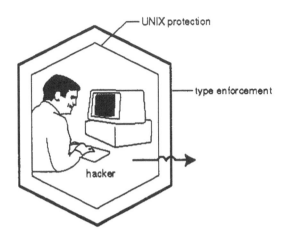

**Exhibit 7. Protection Provided by Type Enforcement and UNIX.**

---

included three other features to make the *Sidewinder* firewall a more effective security system: two kernels, controlled system calls, and network separation.

### Two Kernels

*Sidewinder* does not have the root privilege that is found on standard UNIX systems. To provide a secure method for the system administrator to modify the security-relevant information, *Sidewinder* uses two kernels:

1. **The Operational kernel.** The normal operating state for the *Sidewinder*, which enforces the security policy laid out in the type enforcement tables.
2. **The Administrative kernel.** This kernel is used only when the system administrator needs to perform privileged tasks, such as system configuration, on the *Sidewinder*. In this kernel, type enforcement checks are bypassed, which allows the administrator to modify any file, much like the root privilege on conventional UNIX systems. Because access to the Administration kernel is tightly controlled by the Operational kernel, only authorized users physically connected to *Sidewinder* can shut down the Operational kernel and start the Administration kernel. Exhibit 8 lists the major differences between the two kernels.

### Controlled System Calls

Type enforcement provides excellent separation at the file level. However, UNIX has many privileged system calls that allow users to access the

**Exhibit 8.** *Sidewinder* **Kernels**

| Operational | Administrative |
| --- | --- |
| Uses type-enforced BSDi/386 UNIX; restricted access to system calls. | Uses standard UNIX |
| Normal operating state. | Used when performing certain privileged administrative tasks. |
| Internet services are available. | Network connections are disabled. |
| System is protected by Type Enforcement. | Type Enforcement is disabled. |
| Divided into many application domains; each can have its own administration domain. | Divided into standard UNIX domains — user and root. |
| Administrator access controlled by roles. | Administrator access controlled by file privileges. |
| A process' access to files is restricted based on DDT. | A process' access to files is not restricted. |

kernel directly. Many system vulnerabilities result from malicious users employing system calls to compromise the system. *Sidewinder* solves this problem with a series of special flags for each domain, which indicate which system calls can be made from that domain. For example, the is_admin flag is set only in domains that can be accessed by the administrator. This control allows the administrator to make system calls that no one else has the authorization to make. Note that these flags are part of the type enforcement information and cannot be modified while the system is running. Even root access will not allow a process to make disallowed calls. Untrusted users or software applications are placed in domains that do not have access to these powerful system calls.

### Network Separation

Typically, firewalls have two separate physical network connections managed through a single protocol stack. *Sidewinder* has two separate network connections with two separate protocol stacks. This configuration allows *Sidewinder* to provide strong separation between data from the internal network and data from the external network.

If a firewall does not have network stack separation, network packets from both networks are processed by the same protocol engine. Exhibit 9 shows a system that does not separate data coming into the firewall. Software must be trusted to ensure that the origin of the packets is maintained correctly. The various pieces of data are all contained in the same information bucket. The protocol engine must also be trusted to detect an Internet system that is pretending to be a system from the internal side of the firewall.

Because *Sidewinder* has two network cards, it can always identify the origin of the information, no matter how clever the attack is. Information

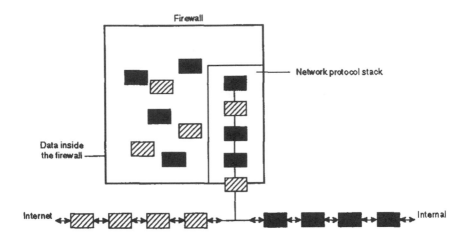

**Exhibit 9. Firewall without Network Stack Separation.**

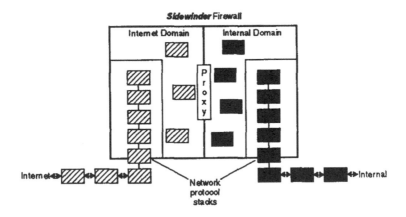

**Exhibit 10. Sidewinder Configuration.**

coming from the network cards is placed in separate domains. The information is kept separated until *Sidewinder* confirms that the information can move to the other domain. For example, the systems may be set up so that the administrator can telnet to *Sidewinder* from the internal side, but not from the Internet. Exhibit 10 shows the *Sidewinder* configuration, in which two protocol stacks separate information coming from two networks. As a result, network protocol spoofing is not possible. As illustrated in this example, the information is kept in two separate information buckets. Only the proxy program can move data between the two domains.

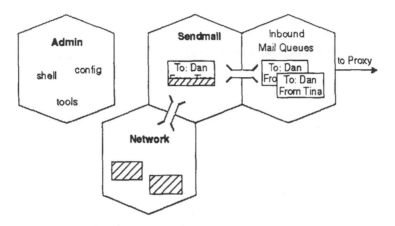

**Exhibit 11. Secure Sendmail Configuration.**

## Protecting Internet Servers

The security features in *Sidewinder* can secure the Sendmail Internet server. Sendmail is the Internet server that runs on many UNIX platforms and listens for E-mail from the Internet. Sendmail is a complex piece of software and has been the source of numerous security vulnerabilities. These vulnerabilities allow hackers to compromise Sendmail, which then enables them to launch successful attacks on the rest of the system. MCI estimates that 20,000 systems were compromised through Sendmail over a one-year period.

*Sidewinder* protects the rest of the system by placing Sendmail in its own domain. From this domain, Sendmail can only access the network resources to get the mail from the Internet and to send the mail messages into the internal mail message queues. All the tools used by hackers are out of reach. Exhibit 11 shows the protected Sendmail configuration on *Sidewinder*, which places it in a separate domain. This configuration also protects the system from illegal access through Sendmail, which is prevented from accessing the rest of the system.

A recent Sendmail vulnerability involved the syslog. Syslog is a system call that is used to write information to the audit log. However, syslog does not check to ensure that the size of the message that it is writing does not exceed the space available. The message to be appended to the log is stored on the programs stack. Thus, if a program allows users from the Internet to specify information to be logged, a hostile user can specify a long message that overwrites the programs stack. By placing executable code in the portion that is overwritten, the attacker gains complete control of the Sendmail program. This type of security violation has occurred.

Attackers had an easy time of taking control of the Sendmail program and had Sendmail start up an interactive shell. From there, attackers used their Sendmail toe hold to compromise the rest of the system.

On *Sidewinder*, the attack is stopped because Sendmail cannot execute an interactive shell. Even if a shell is running in the Sendmail domain, it could still not access the rest of the system. Thus, *Sidewinder* protects itself from Sendmail vulnerabilities that have not yet been discovered.

## THE *SIDEWINDER* 2.0 CHALLENGE

Secure Computing has placed a *Sidewinder* on the Internet and challenged people to crack the system. The goal is to encourage sophisticated attacks on *Sidewinder*. Although *Sidewinder* has been tested thoroughly by trained engineers, field testing teaches more about how intruders attack systems. The goal of the challenge is to break through the firewall to the machine behind it. This machine contains a message signed with Secure Computing's private key that can be used to prove that someone has broken through the *Sidewinder* firewall.

It was expected that someone would break through the earlier *Sidewinder* 1.0 challenge system, which took place during the early stages of development. After one year and 3500 visits from a variety of Internet users, no one was able to crack the 1.0 challenge. Due to the enhanced security in *Sidewinder* 2.0, the *Sidewinder* 2.0 Challenge is expected to be much more difficult.

### Challenge Site Information

Users who would like to try the *Sidewinder* challenge can find it at challenge.sidewinder.com, with IP address 206.145.0.254. There is a WWW server and an anonymous ftp server. As a reward, Secure Computing is offering a jacket with the *Sidewinder* logo on the back.

More information on the *Sidewinder* Challenge can be found at http://www.sctc.com. Users can also download a list of frequently asked *Sidewinder* questions by anonymous FTP from ftp://ftp.sctc.com/pub.

## CONCLUSION

The Internet servers running on the *Sidewinder* challenge have been protected using type enforcement. The Internet server applications are a combination of commercial and public domain software that have been integrated to provide current functionality with the best security. The success of the challenge shows that type enforcement has done exceptionally well in application.

# Chapter 50
# An Intranet Primer

*Nathan J. Muller*

Many companies are using intranets — internal corporate networks built on World Wide Web protocols — in a range of application areas to leverage access to existing information and extend their reach to employees, partners, suppliers, and customers. This chapter reviews the benefits of intranets and the challenges intranets present in terms of information management, integrity, and security; implementation; and ongoing maintenance and development. Implications of the network-centric computing model for reduced cost of network ownership are also discussed.

## INTRODUCTION

Companies are establishing intranets — internal corporate networks built on World Wide Web protocols — at a fairly rapid pace. According to Forrester Research, 16% of the Fortune 1,000 have intranets and another 50% are either in the consideration or planning stages.

Companies that build intranets to improve internal communication, streamline processes such as purchasing, and simplify transaction processing are finding multiple sources of business value. Intranets help reduce communication costs, increase sales and customer response, and significantly improve work quality and productivity.

The appeal of intranets comes from enabling, enhancing, and extending effective communications within and among organizational entities and communities of interest. Intranets have allowed companies to reach new potential customers, enter untapped markets, and expand elements within their businesses. Mutual benefits are also derived from intranetworking between synergistic businesses. Coupled with such innovations as the Java development language and new zero-administration net-centric computers, intranets can become the base around which businesses reinvent themselves.

## BENEFITS OF INTRANETS

### Cost-Effective Communications

The foremost benefit that a company derives from an intranet is more cost-effective communications. Attaining cost-effective communications entails making information directly accessible to people who need it without over-whelming the people who do not need it. Intranets provide direct access to information, so people can easily find what they need without involving anyone else, either for permission or direction on how to navigate through the information. At the same time, companies can protect their information from people not entitled to access it.

### Efficient Information Management

From the perspective of information management, an intranet extends the reach of distribution and simplifies logistics. For example, it is often cumbersome to maintain the distribution list for a typical quarterly status report sent to a large mailing list. The existence of an intranet simplifies the process of incorporating changes made before the next report is due, because updates are easily developed and posted to give everyone access to the new information.

### Easier Information Publishing

Publishing information on an intranet is quite simple, especially because intranets use the same protocols as the greater Internet, including the HTTP used by the World Wide Web. There are a number of Web publishing tools, including Microsoft's FrontPage, that quickly turn individual documents into the HTML format. Even documents maintained in a Lotus Notes database are easily published on the Web with a complementary product called Domino, which renders Notes data in HTML format on-the-fly and serves HTML documents from the file system. With a feature called Notes Access Control, Domino also keeps the information out of the hands of people who are not authorized to see it.

### Improved Searching and Retrieval

Not only has Web publishing become much easier, but users are finding it easier to search for the right document just by using key words. It is no longer necessary for people to ask someone for copies of a document or request that their names be put on a distribution list. Users also have more control over what they see. If the big picture is all a person wants, then only that level of information is delivered. When detailed information is desired, such search mechanisms as boolean parameters, context-sensitivity, and fuzzy logic may be employed. Of course, the user also has the option of accessing greater levels of detail by following the hypertext links embedded in documents.

### Enhanced Real-Time Collaboration

Enhanced, timely information exchange within the organization is another benefit of intranet adoption. As people from various organizations, functions, and geographic locations increasingly work together, the need for real-time collaboration becomes paramount. Teams need to share information, review and edit documents, incorporate feedback, as well as reuse and consolidate prior work efforts. Intranets that enable collaboration to occur without paper or copies of files can save hours and even days in a project schedule.

Electronic collaboration eliminates many hurdles such as distance between co-workers, multiple versions and paper copies of information, and the need to integrate different work efforts. The intranet becomes a unifying communications infrastructure that greatly simplifies systems management tasks and makes it easy to switch between internal and external communications.

Companies are also finding that by extending their intranets beyond their immediate boundaries, they are able to communicate more directly and efficiently with the communities with which they do business. Establishing electronic connections to suppliers and partners can result in key savings in time and money in communicating inventory levels, tracking orders, announcing new products, and providing ongoing support. Intranets are being used in a range of application areas to leverage access to existing information and extend a company's reach to employees, partners, suppliers, and customers.

As companies progress in such methods of interaction, more sophisticated intranetworking can result in increased responsiveness and shortened order-fulfillment time to customers. Suppliers track inventory levels directly, reduce delays in order fulfillment, and save costs in inventory maintenance. More companies are developing this form of information exchange, where the electronic capability actually drives the process.

### INTRANET CHALLENGES

It is important to note that intranets may introduce new chores in managing information. For example, ensuring that all departments have the same updated versions of information requires synchronization across separate departmental servers, including directories and security mechanisms. Providing varying levels of information access to different audiences — engineering, manufacturing, marketing, human resources, suppliers, and customers — is also an issue.

An additional task results from the fact that the hypertext links that facilitate information search and retrieval must be maintained to ensure integrity as information changes or is added to the database. Fortunately, there are tools that help database administrators identify broken links so appropriate corrective steps can be taken.

Domino/Notes, for example, supports major data management functions including link management and replication. As more people access data from more locations, the need for adequate security increases. Domino/Notes has a broad range of security facilities that include access control, authentication, and encryption. The product incorporates industry standards for security, such as the secure socket layer (SSL) for encrypting data during transmission.

## SECURITY ISSUES

Along with the benefits of enhanced access that corporate intranets provide lie some risks. Increasing the number of people who have access to important data or systems without supplementary protective measures adds vulnerability to an IT infrastructure. Integrating security mechanisms into an intranet minimizes exposure to misuse of corporate data and to overall systems integrity.

A secure intranet solution implies a seamless and consistent security function integrated among desktop clients, application servers, and distributed networks. It should include policies and procedures and the ability to monitor and enforce them, as well as robust software security tools that work well together and do not leave any gaps in protection.

The following basic functions are necessary for broad security coverage:

- **Access control** Access control software allows varying degrees of access and different granularities of access to applications and data.
- **Secure transmission** Mechanisms like encryption impede outside parties from eavesdropping or changing data sent over a network.
- **Authentication** This software validates that the information that appears to have been originated and sent by a particular individual was actually sent by that person.
- **Repudiation** Repudiation software prevents people who have bought merchandise or services over the network from claiming they never ordered what they received.
- **Disaster recovery** Disaster recovery entails both software and procedures that assist recovery from loss of data in an organization's systems.
- **Virus protection** Antivirus software protects systems from disruptive to destructive viruses by detecting, verifying, and removing them.

Intranets that extend beyond organizational or company boundaries may require integration among various security systems. In addition, because intranets give more people the opportunity to access information, they can cause companies to increase their dependence on computer technology. This increased dependence requires that appropriate backup and emergency recovery measures be in place and that alternative links be available should the network experience an outage.

## COSTS

Costs are another important intranet implementation consideration. Beyond the list prices for hardware and software components lie less obvious costs of administration, maintenance, and additional development.

Intranets are most effective if they include the following attributes:

- **Reach** Reach is the ability to easily connect with one or more employees, a group of contractors, suppliers and other vendors, and even millions of customers.
- **Flexibility** Flexibility provides the freedom to merge on either a permanent or *ad hoc* basis with anyone, anywhere, anytime — regardless of hardware or software differences.
- **Scalability** Scalability means the ability to handle up to the most demanding enterprise-level computing and transaction rates across disparate systems as needs justify.
- **Transparency** Transparency is the ability to interact with external or remote systems seamlessly and without regard for data location or underlying hardware or software.
- **Security** Security lets entire organizations come together for maximum synergy without jeopardizing proprietary data or compromising systems integrity.

## CASE STUDY

Unisys is one of the many corporations to embrace the intranet concept. The company has already established a public presence on the Internet (www.unisys.com)and has since put into operation two intranets: the Idea Factory and the Marketplace Insider. Both are run from the server that supports the divisional network of the Unisys Computer Systems Group in Blue Bell PA.

Although each intranet was set up for a different purpose, both can be accessed by all employees from any Unisys location over the same communications links used to access the corporate network, including T1 and T3, ISDN (integrated services digital network), and ordinary dial-up connections using such products as NetBlazer and pcAnyWhere. Protection from unauthorized access is provided by Checkpoint Software's FireWall-1 software.

## THE IDEA FACTORY

The Idea Factory — implemented in December 1995 — is a virtual gathering place for members of the Computer Systems Group's (CSG) technology-oriented community. The primary goals of the Idea Factory are to provide nearly effortless access to a vast technology resources library, connect thousands of employees with complementary skills dispersed around the globe, and promote the development of leading-edge technology solutions for Unisys customers.

One of the ways these goals are achieved is through chat rooms. Essentially, a chat room is a real-time bulletin board system. Instead of posting messages and replies on a bulletin board, a chat room allows participants to converse with each other in text mode. Organized by topic, the chat rooms provide a convenient way for employees to establish new contacts within the organization and tap into each other's expertise. Some of the chat rooms have 400 to 500participants from all over the world who tune in and out at various times during the ongoing conversations.

For example, a customer's configuration problem can be discussed in a chat room, allowing participants to brainstorm a possible solution. If the proposed solution proves effective, it is added to a reference database. Should another customer experience a similar problem in the future, a database search will reveal the solution instantly and result in a prompt resolution.

The creators of the Idea Factory focused on a specific community — CSG's own technology-oriented employees, who are mostly engineers and geographically as well as organizationally dispersed. Initially, the focus was on such subjects as object-oriented architectures, multimedia, the Internet, and high-speed broadband networks. Access was provided to internally developed content and external links to other sources of information so users could have one-stop access to a vast library of technical resources.

### The Marketplace Insider

The concept embodied in the Idea Factory was expanded in mid-1996 when the Computer Systems Group introduced the Marketplace Insider, which is intended to have a much broader appeal within CSG. It features a newsstand where employees can stay up to date on company- and industry-related developments. A resource center provides employees access to all the libraries within the division, and a human resources section provides a directory listing of CSG employees. An education area provides links to downloadable education tools. There is also an online organization chart and a swap-and-sell bulletin board.

The Marketplace Insider offers Lotus InterNotes links for the sales and marketing people so they can have intranet access to the competitive analysis database, marketing toolkits, and other resources. It also provides links to the Idea Factory.

### Intranet Skills Sets

The skill sets required for developing an intranet are varied and quite specialized. Technical people need knowledge of systems and network architectures, understanding of the Internet protocol, and experience in developing applications. There is also a need for creative people, particularly graphic artists and HTML coders who excel at making the content visually compelling through the integration of images and text.

The cumulative efforts of about 200 people went into the initial development and implementation of the Idea Factory and the Marketplace Insider. Many of these people, however, were only peripherally involved. For example, the same network managers and technical staff that keep the division's network up and running by default keep the intranets up and running, because they all run off the same server.

The daily maintenance of the two intranets requires only the part-time efforts of three people from the marketing group and three people from the technical group. Although this might not seem like a resource-intensive effort, it is important to stress that the caliber of skills individuals bring to the task is much more critical than the number of people actually involved.

Although it takes people with specialized skills to develop an intranet, it takes a different set of skills to sustain one. What CSG has tried to do is recruit multifunctional people — those who can apply what they normally do on the job to the medium of the intranet. The secret to productivity is to have the best people.

Among the improvements planned for the Marketplace Insider are links to some of CSG's legacy applications. In the future, Unisys customers will be able to access the intranets for such things as global procurement, order tracking, problem reporting, and software ordering. In building these applications, the Computer Systems Group is positioning itself to offer consulting and support services to customers who wish to implement intranets within their organizations.

## IMPLICATIONS OF JAVA AND NETWORK-CENTRIC COMPUTING

### Lower Cost of Network Ownership

For the past 10 years, companies have been struggling with the ever-growing complexity and cost of computing. First came mainframes, then minicomputers, and then PCs, each bringing with it a higher cost per person.

Now the fourth big wave in information technology is about to begin with the introduction of net-centric computers that leverage corporate intranets and the new Java development language to enable mission-critical work to be done at a fraction of the cost.

Sun Microsystems has been the leader in the development of the net-centric computing model, as well as Java. The company's worldwide Java Computing initiative includes the JavaStation network computer, which leverages the power and flexibility of Sun's Java technology.

Aimed at slashing the high cost of networked environments, Java Computing enables companies to ease the burden of network and desktop administration, speed applications development and deployment, and improve network security. Because Java technology allows developers to write applications that will run on any device, Java Computing shifts applications and storage from the desktop to the network and the server. The advantages of this platform-independent approach is that it could save many large companies anywhere from 50% to 80% on the total cost of network ownership.

Fully configured, JavaStation systems will start at less than $1,000 with entry systems priced at around $750. These initial hardware and software costs pale in comparison to what companies will save in the long run on total cost of ownership. Industry estimates put the average annual cost of administering a single PC in a network at about $11,900, or approximately $35,700 over three years. Hardware and software only account for about 21% of that cost, according to industry estimates. By comparison, Sun estimates a JavaStation will require about $2,500 per year to administer, or about $7,500 for three years. For Fortune 1,000 companies with thousands of desktop PCs in their enterprises, the move to a Java platform could slash total cost of ownership by tens-of-millions to hundreds-of-millions of dollars.

## Platform-Independent Applications Development

Java technology unlocks the potential of the network by allowing companies to write applications once that will run anywhere, regardless of operating system or hardware. Java applications reside on the server, where they can be easily managed, deployed, and updated by network administrators. Although the zero-administration desktop computer, or JavaStation device, needs no hard drive, floppy, or CD-ROM to make this happen, applications are still executed locally on a powerful RISC processor.

Java technology can be gradually deployed without having to discard current client/server investments. JavaStation devices will run alongside PCs, Macs, workstations, or even dumb terminals. In fact, much of the growth in JavaStation network computers will take place in companies looking to replace their aging 3270 terminals. This is a significant market with an installed base of approximately 35 million nonprogrammable terminals worldwide.

Companies with so-called fixed-function applications will be among the first to reap the benefits of JavaStation network computers. These include companies that offer airline or hotel reservation desks, kiosks, health care systems, and stock brokerage services. These types of companies will benefit from the simplicity, cost-effective systems management, and more efficient applications deployment that Java affords.

Many large companies are actively deploying Java technology. More than 60% of Fortune 1,000 companies surveyed by Forrester Research are already using Java technology for some applications development, and 42% expect Java to play a strategic role in their company within a year. Although JavaStation and other network computers were only rolled out in 1996, the Gartner Group market research firm estimates that 20% of client/server applications in the late 1990s will run on so-called thin clients like the JavaStation.

Other vendors are pursuing the net-centric computing model. Oracle's Network Computing Architecture is a common set of technologies that will allow all PCs, network computers, and other client devices to work with all Web servers, database servers, and application servers over any network. As the manifestation of Oracle's vision for network computing, the Network Computing Architecture will help companies protect their technology investments by allowing mainframes, client/server, Internet and intranets, and distributed object software to work together.

Like Java, the Network Computing Architecture transcends the Internet/object standards battle, so users and developers can make software programs work together without getting locked into dead-end solutions. The Network Computing Architecture will simplify the problem through the use of open Internet standards and unique bridging software that helps proprietary application programs work together.

In contrast to the PC-centric computing model, which focuses on independent users and computation, the Network Computing Architecture recognizes the increasing importance of Web servers, database servers, and application servers working together over corporate intranets to enhance communication and deliver a wide array of information on demand to internal and external corporate constituents.

## CONCLUSION

Corporate intranets are becoming as significant to the telecommunications industry as the PC has become to the computer industry. They fundamentally change the way people in large organizations communicate with each other. In the process, intranets can improve employee productivity and customer response. They are also being used to connect companies with their business partners, allowing for collaboration in such vital areas as research and development, manufacturing, distribution, sales, and service.

A variety of tools are used for these purposes, including interactive text, audio and video conferencing, file sharing, and whiteboarding. In fact, anything that can be done on the public Internet can be also be done on a private intranet — easily, economically, and more securely.

# Chapter 51
# Virtual Networking Management and Planning

*Trenton Waterhouse*

Just as many organizations are reaching a level of comfort with hub and router technology, many vendors are espousing the benefits of switched virtual networks. This chapter examines the issues network planners must evaluate as technology evolves from physical networks built using hubs, bridges, and routers to virtual networks built using switches.

## INTRODUCTION

The switch could be considered a third-generation internetworking device. First-generation devices, or bridges, offered a high degree of performance throughput but relatively little value, because the bridge's limited decision intelligence resulted in broadcast storms that produced network instability. Routers, the second generation of internetworking devices, increased network reliability and offered great value with firewalling capabilities, but the trade off was in performance. When routers are used in combination with each other, bandwidth suffers, which is detrimental for delay-sensitive applications such as multimedia.

The switched virtual network offers all the performance of the bridge with the value of the router. The constraints of physical networking are removed by the logical intelligence that structures and enforces policies of operation to ensure stability and security. Regardless of access technology or geographic location, any-to-any communications is the goal.

## THE BUSINESS CASE FOR VIRTUAL NETWORKING

Both the business manager and the technical manager should find interest in this new virtual networking scheme. The business manager is usually interested in cost-of-ownership issues. Numerous studies from organizations

0-8493-9965-3/99/$0.00+$.50
© 1999 by CRC Press LLC

such as the Gartner Group and Forrester Research have indicated that only 20% of networking costs are associated with capital equipment acquisition. The other 80% of annual budgets are dedicated to items such as wide area networking charges, personnel, training, maintenance and vendor support, as well as the traditional equipment moves, adds, and changes.

It is important for network planners to remember that capital expenditure happens in year one, even though the equipment may be operating for another four years. WAN charges can account for up to 40% of an organization's networking budget. For every dollar that the technical staff spends on new equipment, another four dollars is spent on the operation of that equipment. Therefore, focus should be on the cost-of-ownership issues, not necessarily the cost of the network devices.

### Network Reliability

Business managers are also looking for increased reliability as the network plays a major role in the core operations of the organization. Networks have become a business tool to gain competitive advantage — they are mission critical and, much like a utility, must provide a highly reliable and available means of communications. Every office today includes an electrical outlet, a phone jack, and a network connection. Electrical and phone service are generally regarded as stable utilities that can be relied on daily. Networks, however, do not always provide such levels of service.

### Network Accountability

Managers also can benefit from the increased accountability that virtual networks are able to offer. Organizational networking budgets can range from hundreds of thousands of dollars to hundreds of millions or even billions per year. Accounting for the use of the network that consumes those funds is a critical issue. There is no better example than WAN access charges. Remote site connectivity can consume a great deal of the budget, and the questions of who, what, when, and where in regards to network use are impossible to determine. Most users consider the network to be free, but the tools to manage and account for its use are increasingly a requirement, not an option.

## THE TECHNOLOGY CASE FOR VIRTUAL NETWORKING

The technical manager's needs for higher capacity, greater performance, and increased efficiency can be met through the deployment of switched virtual networks. Each user is offered dedicated bandwidth to the desktop with uplink of increasing bandwidth to servers or other enterprise networks. Rather than contending for bandwidth in shared access environments, all users are provided with their own private link. This degree of privacy allows for increased security because data is sent only to intended recipients, rather than seen by all.

The most attractive feature to the technical manager, however, may be the benefits gained through increased ease of operation and administration of virtual networks. A long-standing objective has been to deliver network services to users without continually having to reconfigure the devices that make up that network, furthermore, many of the costs associated with moves, adds, and changes of users can be alleviated as the constraints of physical networking are removed. Regardless of user location, they can remain part of the same virtual network. Through the use of graphical tools, users are added and deleted from work groups. In the same manner, policies of operation and security filters can be applied. In a sense, the virtual network accomplishes the goal of managing the individual users and individual conversations, rather than the devices that make up the network.

## VIRTUAL NETWORKING DEFINED

From the user's perspective, a virtual network is a data communications system that provides access control and network configuration changes using software control. It functions like a traditional network but is built using switches.

The ideal virtual network does not restrict access to a particular topology or protocol. A virtual network that can only support Ethernet users with TCP/IP applications is limited. The ultimate virtual network allows any-to-any connectivity between Ethernet, Token Ring, FDDI, ATM, IP, IPX, AppleTalk, or SNA networks. A single virtual network infrastructure under a single management architecture is the goal.

Network management software becomes a key enabling requirement for the construction of switched virtual networks. The greatest challenge network designers face is the separation of the physical network connectivity from the logical connection services it can provide. Many of the design issues associated with networks can be attributed to the physical parameters of protocols and the routers used as the interconnection device. A challenge for any network manager is to remain compatible with existing layer 3 protocols and routers and still preserve the investment in existing LAN equipment to the greatest extent possible.

### Using Telephony as a Model

The principles of operation for switched virtual networks are concretely founded in the success of the global communications systems. Without doubt, the phone system is the world's largest and most reliable network. Built using advanced digital switches controlled by software, extensive accounting and management tools ensure the success of this highly effective means of communication. The connection-oriented switch is the key. End-to-end connections across multiple switches and various transmission types ranging from copper to fiber optics to microwave to satellites allow millions of calls per day to be successfully completed, regardless of the type of phone or where the user is calling from. The telephony model is used throughout this chapter to help illustrate the workings of a virtual network.

## SWITCHING DEFINED

One of the more confusing terms in the networking industry today is the word *switch*. For the purpose of this chapter, switching can be broken down into three fundamental areas:

- Configuration switching.
- Packet switching.
- Cell switching.

The earliest form of switching enabled the network manager to assign an individual port or an entire group of ports to a particular backplane segment within an intelligent hub device. This port configuration switching allowed the logical grouping of users onto a particular segment without the need to physically travel to the wiring closet to move cables or connectors. In a sense, this offers an electronic patch panel function. Although the benefit is a reduction of moves, adds, and change costs, this advantage can only be realized within the confines of a single hub. The application of this type of switching is limited because it cannot extend beyond one intelligent concentrator. Although beneficial in the work group, the enterprise needs cannot be met.

Phone system operators in the 1940s manually patched user connections through to destinations and recorded call time and duration. Using configuration switching is similar to patching phone lines together. Just as the phone network grew at a pace that required the switching to be performed automatically without operator intervention, so too have data networks outgrown the limitations of configuration switching.

Packet switching isolates each port to deliver dedicated bandwidth to each user in the network. Fundamentally, a packet switch is any device that accepts an incoming packet on one port and then makes a decision whether to filter or forward the packet out another interface. There are two types of packet switch transports: connectionless and connection-oriented.

## Connectionless Packet Switching

Connectionless devices are probably more familiar to network professionals when described as bridges or routers. A bridge is a layer 2 (of the OSI reference model) switch that bases its decisions on the MAC address of attached workstations. What many vendors describe as a switch is actually a wire-speed MAC layer bridge. Three methods of decision making in these types of devices are cut-through, modified cut-through, and store-and-forward.

**The Cut-through Switch.** This switch reads a packet to the destination address before it starts forwarding to the outbound interface. The benefit is an extremely low latency or delay in the forwarding of packets. The penalty is the propagation of errors, because the frame is being forwarded before it can be verified as valid, and the inability to support interfaces of different speeds that prevents high-bandwidth uplink of FDDI or ATM on these type of devices.

**The Modified Cut-through Switch.** This switch reads the first 64 bytes of a frame and then starts forwarding to the outbound interface, which greatly reduces the chances of propagating errored frames throughout the network. However, this method still requires all ports to be of the same type and speed.

**Store-and-Forward Switch.** The most flexible switch design uses a store-and-forward methodology that reads the entire frame before any filtering or forwarding decisions are made, thus ensuring that only packets that are not errored are forwarded on the network. This method also allows packets to be buffered when transferring data between networks of different types, such as Ethernet to FDDI or ATM.

**Bridges and Routers.** A router is a layer 3 switch that bases its decisions on the network protocol address of attached workstations. Bridges and routers are considered connectionless because they forward and forget, requiring a decision to be made on every single inbound packet. The performance implications are that even though two communicating nodes on opposite sides of a bridge or router may be the only devices on their respective networks, the bridge or router must continuously make filter or forward decisions on every packet sent between the two nodes. If the phone network were built using bridges or routers, users would have to hang up and redial their destination after every word, which is not a very practical proposition.

A connectionless transport is not capable of defining which path its payload will take, cannot guarantee delivery, and is generally slower than a connection-oriented system. When a node sends a packet through a bridged or routed network, it is analogous to dropping a letter into a mailbox. It is not apparent how the letter got to its destination. The arrival of a letter cannot be guaranteed (protocol prioritization techniques are comparable to sending a letter by express mail). If a letter is lost (or a packet dropped), determining where it was lost is often difficult. The only way the sender knows that the letter was received is if the recipient sends another letter back to the sender (i.e., frame acknowledgment).

In a sense, today's shared-access networks are like the party lines of the early telephone network. But just as the phone network evolved from party lines to dedicated lines as usage and deployment grew, so too must the data networks offer this same level of service guarantee and broad adoption.

### Connection-Oriented Switches

The connection-oriented switch that the phone systems use offers immediate acknowledgment of communications when the person picks up at the other end. The exact path the call took as well as its time and duration can be logged. The destination only needs to be dialed only once and information is exchanged until both parties hang up.

The idea of connection-oriented communications is not new. This type of switching provides a high degree of reliability and reduces operational costs. Multiple classes of service can be defined to support voice, video, and data transfer. Excellent bandwidth management through congestion control techniques are possible and security and access control are greatly improved. Connection-oriented switching, along with easy-to-implement policy-based management and accounting facilities have enabled the phone system to become universally accessible.

Frame relay technology is centered around connection-oriented communications, as is the most promising future networking technology — ATM. ATM is the most desirable networking technology because it offers dedicated, scalable bandwidth solutions for voice, video, and data.

**ATM Switching.** ATM switching is connection-oriented. Communications in an ATM network can be broken down into three phases: call setup (analogous to dialing a phone), data transfer (talking on the phone), and call teardown (hanging up the phone). The use of fixed-length 53-byte cells for data transfer delivers fixed latency transfer times for CBR applications such as voice and video. ATM addressing schemes are similar to a telephone number. In fact, the original designers of ATM technology had their roots in the telephony arena at BellCore, so many analogies to the operation of the phone system can be made when referring to an ATM network.

Although the benefits of ATM networking are attractive, there are currently nearly 100 million networked personal computers that do not have ATM interfaces. Few organizations can afford to replace all of their existing desktop and server interfaces, not to mention network analyzers and troubleshooting equipment.

Through the preservation of existing interface technology, by merely changing the internetworking devices from being connectionless to connection-oriented, many of the benefits of ATM may be realized without requiring the investment in all new ATM equipment. If LANs were designed to operate using the same principles as ATM, rather than making ATM compatible with LANs, users would benefit without significant capital investments in new equipment. By adding switch technology to the middle of the network, network administrators can be spared the trouble of upgrading numerous user devices, and users can be spared the inconvenience of rewiring and disruptions at their work site during an upgrade.

## FEATURES OF SWITCHING SOFTWARE

The software that runs on switches is just as important as the switches themselves. A salesperson from AT&T, Fujitsu, or Northern Telecom does not focus the potential customer on the hardware aspects of the telephone switches. On the contrary, the salesperson conveys the benefits of the call management software, accounting, and ACD functions. Switched virtual networks should also be evaluated for their ability to deliver value because of the software features.

### The Virtual Network Server

Network management software has traditionally been thought of as software that passively reports the status and operation of devices in the network. In the switched virtual network, the network management software takes on a new role as an active participant in operations as well as configuration and reporting. A new middleware component known as the VNS enforces the policies of operation defined by the network administrator through management software applications. The switches provide the data transport for the users of the network.

**Directory Service.** One of the software features in the VNS is the directory service. The directory service allows the identification of a device by logical name, MAC address, network protocol address, and ATM address, along with the switch and port that the user is connected to within the virtual network domain. The directory listing could be populated manually or dynamically as addresses are discovered. To fully realize the benefits of switched virtual networking, automatic configuration is absolutely essential. The directory service allows end nodes to be located and identified.

**Security Service.** The VNS security service would be used during call setup phases to determine whether users or groups of users were allowed to connect to each other. On a user-by-user and conversation-by-conversation basis, the network manager would have control. This communications policy management is analogous to call management on a telephone PBX where 900 numbers, long-distance, or international calls can be blocked. Users could be grouped together to form policy groups in which rules could be applied to individual users, groups, or even nested groups. Policies could be defined as open or secure, inclusive or exclusive.

A sample default policy can ensure that all communications are specifically defined to the VNS in order to be authorized. Policy groups can be manipulated either through drag-and-drop GUI or programmatically through SNMP commands.

Finally, and most important, the directory service can work in conjunction with the security service to ensure that policies follow the users as they move throughout the network. This feature alone could save time spent maintaining a router access list, as occurs headaches when a user changes location in the traditional network. However, it is important to realize that switched virtual networks ease administrative chores, they do not eliminate them.

**Connection Management Service.** The VNS connection management service is used to define the path communications would take through the switch fabric. A site may be linked by a relatively high-speed ATM link and a parallel but relatively low-speed Ethernet link. Network connections with a defined high QOS could traverse the ATM link and lower QOS connections could traverse the Ethernet. This connection management service allows for the transparent rerouting of calls in the event of a network fault. Connection management could also provide ongoing network monitoring in which individual user conversations could be tapped or traced for easy troubleshooting.

**Bandwidth Service.** The VNS bandwidth service is used during the call setup when a connection request is made. Video teleconferencing users may require a CIR of 10M bps whereas the terminal emulation users may only require 1M bps. This is where ATM end stations and ATM switches negotiate the amount of bandwidth dedicated to a particular virtual circuit using UNI signaling. Ethernet, Token Ring, and FDDI nodes do not recognize The UNI signaling, but the switches they attach to could proxy signal for the end station, thus allowing a single bandwidth manager for the entire network, not just the ATM portion.

**Broadcast Service.** The VNS broadcast service uses as its base the concept of the broadcast unknown server BUS that is part of the ATM Forum's

LAN emulation draft standard. This is how broadcasts are flooded through the network to remain compatible with the operation of many of today's protocols and NOSs. A degree of intelligence can be assigned to the VNS that would allow for broadcasts or multicasts based on protocol type or even policy group.

**Virtual Routing Service.** The VNS virtual routing service is one of the most critical components of a virtual network. Just as traditional networks required traditional routers for interconnection, virtual LANs will require virtual routers for internetworking between virtual LANs. In other words, routing is required, but routers may not be. Some protocols such as TCP/IP actually require a router for users on two different subnetworks to speak with each other. In addition, most networks today are logically divided based on network layer protocol addresses with routers acting as the building block between segments.

The difference in operation between a virtual router and a traditional router goes back to the connection-oriented vs. connectionless distinction. Routing allows for address resolution between the layer 3 protocol address and the layer 2 MAC address just as it happens through the ARP process in TCP/IP networks. The VNS virtual routing service performs the address resolution function, but once the end station addresses are resolved, establishes a virtual connection between the two users. Two users separated by a traditional router would always have the router intervening on every single packet because the router would have resolved the protocol addresses to its own MAC address rather than the actual end station's MAC address. This VNS routing service allows the network to route once for connection setup and switch all successive packets.

**Accounting Service.** The VNS accounting service is beneficial because it allows the creation of the network bill. Similar to the way a telephone bill is broken down, the accounting service details connection duration with date and time stamp along with bandwidth consumption details. This is most directly applicable in the WAN. For many network managers, WAN usage is never really accounted for on an individual user basis, yet it can consume up to 40% of the operations budget.

As usage-based WAN service options such as ISDN gain popularity, accounting becomes that much more critical. IXCs, competitive access providers, and the RBOCs continue to deliver higher-bandwidth links with usage-based tariff. In the future, they could install a 155M-bps SONET OC3 links and only charge for the actual bandwidth used. Unless network managers have tools to control access to and account for usage of WAN links, WAN costs will continue to rise. This service lets network managers know who is using the WAN.

## VIRTUAL NETWORKS VS. VIRTUAL LANS

Throughout this discussion, words have been carefully chosen to describe the operation of switched virtual networks. Many of the current vendor offerings on the market have as their goal the construction of a switched Virtual LAN. These Virtual LANs are interconnected using a traditional router device. However, the router has been viewed as the performance bottleneck. Routers should be deployed when segmentation or separation is the need; switches should be used to deliver more bandwidth. The Virtual LAN concept is merely an interim step along the way to realizing the fully virtual network.

The ATM Forum's draft LAN emulation standard allows ATM devices to internetwork with traditional LAN networks such as Ethernet and Token Ring. However, it seems ironic that it essentially tries to make ATM networks operate like a traditional shared-access LAN segment. Although it is required for near-term deployment of ATM solutions into existing LAN architectures, its position as an end-all solution is questionable. A more logical approach uses ATM as the model that LANs must emulate.

## CONCLUSION

Each vendor's approach to virtual networking features will vary slightly in implementation. Most vendors have agreed, however, that the router is moving to the periphery of the network and the core will be based on switching technologies with virtual network capabilities. The three critical success factors that a virtual network vendor must display to effectively deliver on all the promise of virtual networks are connectivity, internetworking, and network management.

Connectivity expertise through a demonstrated leadership in the intelligent hub industry ensures the user a broad product line with numerous options in regards to topology and media types. The product should fit the network, rather than the network design being dictated by the capability of the product. This indicates a vendor's willingness to embrace standards-based connectivity solutions as well as SNMP management and RMON analyzer capabilities.

Internetworking expertise ensures that the vendor is fully equipped to deal with layer 2 as well as layer 3 switching issues through an understanding of protocols and their operation. This is not something that can be learned overnight. The integration of these technologies is still unattainable.

Network management software is crucial — virtual networks do not exist or operate without it. The virtual network services provide all the value to the switch fabric. Users should look for a vendor that has delivered distributed management capabilities. Just as the telephone network relies on distributed software intelligence for its operations, so too must the switched virtual network provide the same degree of redundancy and fault tolerance. Users should also consider whether the vendor embraces all of the popular network management platforms (e.g., SunNet Manager, HPOV, Cabletron SPECTRUM, and IBM NetView for AIE) or only one. Finally, users should make sure the vendor has experience managing multiple types of devices from vendors other than itself. It would be naive to think that all of the components that make up a network are of one type from one vendor.

# Section VII
# Mobile Communications Systems

Today business travel is a common occurrence, with employees just as easily packing documents for a presentation in Los Angeles as for a presentation in London. Accompanying the increase in travel is a need to stay in touch with the home office. While conventional telephone and fax can provide a significant amount of communications support, by themselves they cannot provide access to electronic mail nor let us review production schedules or pricing maintained on corporate servers back at the home office. Recognizing this gap, a variety of mobile communications systems were developed which enable us to access corporate data from locations ranging from the atrium of the home office to an office thousands of miles from the home office, and which are the focus of this section.

The first chapter in this section, "Safe Mobile Computing," introduces us to some of the potential problems that can result from the loss or damage of portable computers, PDAs, and cellular phones. This chapter provides a list of ten questions you should ask to determine if your organization is potentially at risk for stolen or damaged mobile computing equipment, and provides information which forms a foundation for you to answer each question.

Recognizing the mobility of the modern workforce and the need to access electronic mail, the second chapter in this section provides us with a guide to the use of several popular information networks. This chapter, "Portable Network Access," first discusses modem related terms to provide us with information necessary to maximize our ability to communicate with different information networks. Once this is accomplished the chapter reviews the access procedures for several popular information networks and electronic mail systems. These access procedures are presented so that they can be easily copied and taken with the portable computer user to facilitate their use of a particular system.

In a series of four chapters in this section we turn our attention to wireless communications. The chapter "Wireless Communications for Voice and Data" introduces us to wireless radio, wireless PBX systems, cellular voice, satellite voice services, and wireless LANs. This chapter is followed by the chapter "Developing a Cost-Effective Strategy for Wireless Communications." This chapter examines the use of wireless communications based upon the types of applications to be used, the communications architecture and access method associated with different types of wireless communications, and available wireless service products. Through the use of a table the appropriateness of different types of wireless communications are compared and contrasted to different potential user requirements which should provide you with a solid baseline for developing a cost-effective strategy for your use of wireless communications.

Continuing our focus on wireless communications, the fifth chapter in this section, "Cellular Digital Packet Data: An Emerging Mobile Network Service," introduces us to the technology associated with this cellular communications method and discusses why the technology provides more flexibility and better security features than other cellular systems.

Recognizing the need for security, the last three chapters in this section are focused on this important topic. The sixth chapter, "Security of Wireless Local Area Networks," first provides us with an overview of the technology associated with wireless LANs and the reason why security becomes a concern. Building upon this information, several protective security mechanisms identified by the International Standards Organization in its ISO-OSI Reference Model for Security Guidelines are discussed to include encryption, access controls, audit mechanisms, and the development of a security policy. In the seventh chapter in this section, "Protection of Mobile Computing Assets," we turn our attention to another aspect of mobile communications security. In this chapter we will become acquainted with computer security principles and how those principles can be applied to the protection of our mobile office.

The last chapter in this section is also the last chapter in our trilogy of security related chapters. This chapter, "Mobile User Security," provides us with a comprehensive examination of potential threats and provides a list of safe practices for the mobile user which, when followed, will facilitate our goal to communicate with a minimum risk when we operate in a mobile environment.

# Chapter 52
# Safe Mobile Computing

*David Briant*

Computer equipment that is stolen or damaged can cost an organization thousands of dollars in lost revenues and slowdowns in product development. Because portable equipment — including PDAs, notebooks, and cellular phones — is especially vulnerable, this chapter recommends precautions that can be taken and hardware and software that can be used to safeguard equipment.

## INTRODUCTION

Every year there are thousands of insurance claims for stolen or damaged mobile computing equipment (MCE). Mobile computing equipment includes laptop computers, personal digital assistants(PDAs), cellular telephones, portable printers, and fax machines. Very few stolen computers are ever recovered.

Computer security is becoming a bigger concern as technology becomes more prolific. As the number of MCE products increases, so do theft and insurance claims. As a result, security programs are becoming more sophisticated. Without more advanced security, costs to an organization could be thousands or even millions of dollars in lost revenue or missed product development.

This chapter focuses on hardware and software that will make the equipment more secure, and on practices that the mobile computing administrator can implement to ensure that users within an organization know how to use mobile computing products effectively and safely. The mobile computing information in this chapter can help organizations make a wise initial investment in time and money to avoid the threat of equipment theft or damage in the future.

0-8493-9965-3/99/$0.00+$.50
© 1999 by CRC Press LLC

## DETERMINING IF AN ORGANIZATION IS AT RISK

Repairing or replacing damaged or lost equipment costs more than spending time and money beforehand on preventative measures. Following are 10 questions to ask in determining if an organization is potentially at risk for stolen or damaged mobile computing equipment:

1. Is portable power protection used for notebooks?
2. Are antivirus programs installed on notebooks?
3. Are security programs used on notebooks?
4. Is the data on a notebook or PDA uploaded or backed up regularly?
5. Are notebooks carried in a locked carrying case?
6. Are headsets used for cellular telephones?
7. Is the cellular telephone digital?
8. Is the MCE serviceable outside the immediate area?
9. Is the MCE only used in private (i.e., home, office)?
10. Are photographs and serial numbers taken of mobile equipment?

If an organization's answer is "no" to two or more questions, then there is a potential security risk.

## POWER PROTECTION

Proper power protection is extremely important. An eight-millisecond power surge goes through the power lines at least once a month. A power surge when striking a low-end power bar will short out everything connected to it. The same power surge on a high-end power bar will only short out the power bar.

Power surges are also selective in what they damage or destroy. A small power surge shorts out the weakest link in the chain, such as a laser printer or fax modem, even when turned off. After every electrical storm there are numerous insurance claims for computer damage. It usually takes two to four weeks to receive replacement hardware after an insurance claim is filed. Software then has to be reloaded.

Whether the user is at home, in the office, or traveling, a clean flow of power will keep the MCE functioning properly. A high-end power bar has power filtering built into it. Higher-end power bars from American Power Conversion(APC), Panamax, and Tripp Lite include an insurance program for the repair or replacement of the computer if a power surge gets past their power bar. This insurance comes with the power bar automatically when it is purchased.

Insurance for these power bars starts at $2,500 and increases according to the level of filtering protection. If there are more extreme power fluctuations, an uninterruptible power supply (UPS) should be considered. A UPS will ensure that the computer gets a constant, clean flow of power with a battery backup. Insurance for these units starts at $25,000.

When traveling in the U.S. or Canada, the electrical standards are the same. Other parts of the world have different electrical standards for power voltages, wiring, and plug configurations. Tripp Lite and APC offer international power bars and UPS units. Either of these units can be used for other electrical equipment such as televisions, VCRs, camcorders, as well as computer equipment.

## COMPUTER VIRUSES

No one really knows how many computer viruses there are today. It is estimated that three new viruses are discovered every day. The people who intentionally spread viruses are rarely caught.

When a virus is detected, the recovery of the damaged software may be as simple as reloading the files. If the damage is to the boot sector of the hard drive, then the entire hard drive may have to be reformatted and all software reinstalled. Any backups should be considered suspect as having the virus in them.

An antivirus program that costs $75 could save thousands of dollars in lost business. The most popular antivirus programs are Norton Antivirus, Mac Afee, Dr. Solomon, F-Prot, and Symantec's Central Point. If there is a virus that cannot be cleaned, the program will tell the user. The user should then contact the antivirus software supplier.

When purchasing antivirus software, disks should be purchased first and updates acquired by modem. If modems are used frequently, the virus program should be updated monthly. Otherwise, it can be updated every six months. Monthly and quarterly updates are available from most antivirus providers either by a bulletin board system or on the Internet.

The release of DOS 6.0 includes an antivirus utility program. The program is simple and does only preliminary virus checking. When the program is active, it creates problems for anyone trying to install software in Windows 3.0 or its upgrade. The new software is considered a virus to the rest of the system and will not allow it to be installed.

## SECURITY PROGRAMS

Security or password programs offer a range of protection, from simple hardware access to data file access. Passwords can be applied to a single PC notebook and to a network connection. High-end data encryption programs are being developed to ensure that personal information is protected when consumers buy items on the Internet.

The simplest PC password costs nothing because it comes with the computer. The CMOS memory, or setup, contains a password program that when activated prevents unauthorized computer access. However, this program can be bypassed when the CMOS battery is drained of power and the settings have to be reentered, including the password. Many notebooks come with a password program.

Passwords are used as part of menu programs. A popular menu program is Direct Access by Symantec. Neither CMOS nor menu programs track who uses the computer or what programs they use. These programs are simple, and once a hacker is past the password, there is access to the computer. They can also be bypassed by using a boot or startup disk.

A password can be applied to certain documents. These passwords are only useful within the program in which they were created. Other software programs can access them.

For complete protection, high-end security programs can prevent almost anyone from accessing a computer. Some programs that offer complete PC protection are Symantec's Disk Lock, Watch Dog, Fischer International, and Security Guardian. These programs have password and program usage tracking that is usually found on large corporate computers. They even have the capability of preventing boot disk starts. Security Guardian tracks users in Windows 3.0 or newer versions and locks up the computer when not in use after a few minutes. Neither of these features are currently available in Watch Dog.

**Windows '95**

Windows '95 comes with no antivirus or security programs. Proper antivirus protection is available through such Windows '95 programs as Norton Antivirus and Mac Afee. Other programs have difficulty being recognized by Windows '95.There are no security programs specifically designed for Windows '95. Current software will only prevent access to the computer, but not within windows.

**GENERAL BACKUPS**

In the instances of power surges and viruses, adequate precautions need to be taken to protect users' most valuable commodity — creativity. Computer software programs for accounting, word processing, and contact managers are only shells to put the information in. That information or data input is different and unique in each instance. When it is lost, the inspiration involved in creating it is also lost. The data can always be reentered, but it will not be done in the same way, with the same concentration or enthusiasm. More likely it will be stressful, frustrating, tiring, time-consuming, and expensive for the user.

Before doing a backup to disk or tape, a disk-scanning defragmentation utility should be used to ensure the integrity of the hard drive and files. Fragmented files and bad sections of the hard drive will hinder backup performance and may prevent data recovery later.

## External Drives

External drives, tape or disk, come with their own software. These tape drives connect to the parallel port of the computer, thus making them portable. The cost for these drives is 35% higher than that of internal drives. Syquest and Iomega have developed external small computer system interface (SCSI) drives with a storage capacity of 100M bytes or more per cartridge (available from Syquest) and disk (available from Iomega).

The Syquest EZ drives transfer the data almost as fast as a regular internal drive. The drives only come with a 25-serial male-to-SCSI cable, which is not useful for notebook computers. An extra 25-pin parallel-to-SCSI cable will need to be purchased from either Syquest or Adaptec for notebook and desktop computer use.

Although the Syquest EZ drives have a storage capacity of 135M bytes or more, the Iomega Zip drives store only 100M bytes of data — but use floptical technology. Floptical drives use laser optics to read and write data. The disks are re-writable but do not suffer from magnetic disturbances. Data transfer for the Zip drive is slower than the EZ drive, but comes with a 25-pin parallel-to-SCSI cable.

PC and network versions of such programs as Norton Utilities, PC Tools (both by Symantic), and Fast Back will back up to disk or internal tape drives and may be adequate.

## Data Recovery Centers

IBM Corp. has data recovery centers in the U.S. and Canada that allow organizations to restore data lost in either a man-made or natural disaster. Equipment and support is available around the clock. However, use of these facilities is expensive.

## Tips for Users

Whether the information is being backed up to disk, tape, optical disc, an external drive, a network, or another computer, the method should be consistent. This helps avoid any confusion when data recovery is needed.

A program should be developed for the user to perform on a regular basis. First-time users should do backups daily for three weeks to get into the routine of knowing what to do and where the backup data is in case of emergencies.

Users should be discouraged from compressing their hard drives. Compressed drives have slower read-write times and a higher instance of data loss. Backup time increases when a hard drive is compressed. There many even be problems doing a backup with a compressed drive, especially on an external tape drive.

With the size of hard drives increasing and the prices decreasing, there should be no need to compress a drive. Iomega has developed an internal tape drive that will backup to 3.2G bytes of data per tape. Traditionally, only SCSI internal tape drives had this capability. A SCSI drive transfers data at faster rates than IDE drives.

## BACKING UP PDAS

Notebooks are usually backed up to disk or tape with standard backup programs. PDAs are completely different.

Uploading or downloading from a PDAs to or from a PC notebook is not as easy as the manufacturer says. Most PDAs upload data in text format only, which must then be imported into another program. Downloading follows the reverse procedure — convert to text, export, and download. This is not bad for word processors or spreadsheets, but is difficult for contact managers.

Contact managers are database programs that PDAs cannot recognize. When converting from a text file to a database file, the data fields are not recognized in the same way. The same is true for converting a database file to a text file. The two devices do not speak the same language.

### Data Transfers

A contact manager is used to store names, telephone numbers, notes, letters, and appointments. While on the road, users should be able to enter information into their PDA and then connect with the office to update the information on their computer there. Instead of one file merging and updating the other, the incoming file overwrites the existing file. Without the merging or "hot sinking" of data, the advantage of having a contact manager on a PDAs is wasted.

This problem is, however, being changed slowly. Apple's Newton and Hewlett-Packard's Omni Go 100 are PDAs that are a step toward merged data transfers.

Apple's Newton uses a program by Now Software to hot sink data between the PC and the PDAs. The uploaded files are more easily imported into other programs. The only drawbacks to the Newton are that it is for Apple products and the program is not yet available for the PC.

The HP Omni Go uses the GEOS operating system. GEOS is an integrated, DOS-based set of programs with a Windows look and feel. Data can be uploaded to a PC, but not downloaded because the unit does not come with a PC version and the current release of GEOS for the PC will not read the Omni Go files. Versions 2.1 of PC GEOS allows hot-sinked data transfers. The Pilot is the smallest and lightest of the three with a hot-sink cradle and a PC version of PDAs software. The software is very basic. Names, telephone numbers, appointments, and notes are all stored in separate programs and in text file format.

The current version of PDAs are a step closer to having an integrated PC-PDA. When hot-sinked data transfers are available in more usable PC file formats, PDAs may become more popular. In the meantime, for users who wish to use a PDAs for jotting quick notes, names, telephone numbers, and appointments, the PC will store the backup of the PDAs information. Data should not be entered on the PC to avoid hot-sink problems.

## PHYSICAL SECURITY: LOCKS AND CASES

For high-risk users who are really concerned about their computer being stolen, there are a variety of lock and cable systems that make the computer almost a permanent attachment to the item to which it is locked. Prices and products vary greatly. Some universities write their name and serial number on the outside of their computer cases with steel cables on the case, monitor, and keyboard. This may work well for a desktop PC, but not for a notebook being transported in a car.

A motion detector in the computer is helpful, provided that it can be heard. Modern motion detection systems include Compuguard and Light-Gard. These motion detectors attach directly to the computer and are connected to a building's security system. Compuguard sits inside the computer and LightGard transmits a light through fiber optic cable attached to the computer. With either device, when the computer is tampered with or removed from its location, alarms sound. Compuguard was developed by Smith Security Systems of Guelph, Ontario and is currently only available from them directly. LightGard, by Interactive Technologies Inc. in North Saint Paul MN, is available through the Alliance Security firm.

Notebook cases are light, soft, and have pockets and handles. They are also easily spotted by thieves interested in quickly reselling MCE. These cases usually have no locks, nor do they offer much protection to the MCE if it is dropped or banged. The old-fashioned briefcase is bulky, heavy, and hard, but is often has a lock that makes it difficult to get inside, and the hardness offers protection from drops and bumps.

### Cellular Phone Safety

The cost for a small, palm-sized cellular phone is very low right now to entice users who can be charged for airtime usage. Digital cellular phones offer more secure voice and data transmissions than traditional cellular phones.

Cellular phones use microwaves for voice transmission, and there is as yet inconclusive information as to whether cell phones cause any type of cancer. For concerned users who wish to avoid any potential medical hazards, a headset attachment can be used with a cellular phone. The headset holds the cellular phone away from the head and gives the user hands-free operation.

### Securing Equipment and Premises Remotely

With a telephone line and a modem, users can call their home or office from anywhere and retrieve their messages. Computer and building security can be checked remotely. Voice, fax, and data modems allow the computer to become a voice-messaging center.

If used in this capacity, the computer will have to be left on all the time, so there should be a UPS, antivirus, and security program installed. There are also devices that activate lights, appliances, and heating sources from remote locations.

Users who are prone to forget to turn on their computers are in luck. Multi-Link Inc. has developed The Power Stone, a program that will not only turn on the computer, but any other device attached to it by way of telephone line as well. There is no surge protection in The Power Stone, so it should be plugged into a UPS or high-end power bar. This device will not work with notebook computers or similar electronic equipment that must be manually turned off after a power outage. The Power Stone unit must be attached to every device to work.

### PRACTICES FOR SAFE COMPUTING

When computer equipment is stolen or damaged, the downtime could last days, weeks, and in some cases, months. Downtime costs a business money in lost sales or production time. In most cases, the cost of reducing the possibility of theft or damage is less than that of downtime.

Mobile computing is the fastest-growing area of the computer industry. Consequently, the costs for repair and replacement of damaged and stolen equipment are also rising. To safeguard new equipment, all the devices should be catalogued and the hardware should be tested right away to ensure that it works. Security software can then be loaded, followed by the users' software. An orientation session with the user that includes information about security precautions is also helpful. It may take some time to initiate the procedures the first time, but it saves time and money later.

## Cataloging Equipment: The Specifics

Whatever the size of the organization, the first step in securing new equipment is cataloging. As soon as equipment, such as a notebook or PDA, is delivered it should be cataloged. Two copies of the information should be made for each new piece of equipment. One copy could be placed in a binder for easy access, and the second copy could be placed in a fire-proof vault in another part of the building.

IS may want to photograph the equipment and record the serial number, manufacturer's model number, and the supplier directly on the back of the picture. The organization may want to assign its own part number and attach it to the outside of the device and, for notebooks, make that part number appear as the hard drive label.

Information about manufacturers and suppliers can be recorded in a separate binder. It is helpful to record vendors' addresses, warranty information, and telephone numbers. A section can also be designated for repairs required or problems with either the equipment manufacturer or supplier. This information can be used when reordering to determine whether the supplier and/or manufacturer are providing adequate service.

There should also be a separate book or program for the user that stores part numbers, passwords, and information on equipment assignments. Any changes to the users' equipment profile should be reflected in this record.

Registering the serial number of the equipment with the police and providing a picture shows proof of ownership and also serves as a quick and accurate description for the police and insurance company if mobile computing equipment is lost or stolen. The insurance company will be able to process insurance claims faster with this information. In addition to a printed copy of the equipment registration, there should be a disk or tape backup of this information.

## Hardware and Software Setups

After the cataloging is completed, the hardware and software that came with the new equipment should be tested to ensure that it works properly. The hardware should be tested to ensure that it recognizes an external keyboard, mouse, printer, and monitor. The CD-ROM, sound card, and PCMCIA should be tested to make sure they have been installed properly.

The person performing the testing should have a checklist of what needs to be done. If new equipment is purchased and tested frequently, it may be helpful to set up an area, preferably a separate room, in which the work can be done with few interruptions.

### Security Setups

Security software should be installed before productivity software (i.e., word processor, spreadsheet, contact manager, network) is installed. The security software should include an antivirus program and security software. Once installed, a directory should be created on the hard drive for copying the system files, including command.com, autoexec.bat, and config.sys.

The security program will require that the user make a boot disk with the systems files on it. This disk should be copied for the user. Security passwords can be entered into the system before the user gets the equipment. Users can be informed of the password during their orientation session. As always, the passwords should be easy to remember but not too obvious, and they must be recorded in the user section of the cataloging book.

Setting up these security procedures before the user receives the mobile equipment gives administrators of mobile computing equipment uniformity of installation. It also helps make IS's job easier when users call with systems problems.

### The Orientation Session

It is very helpful to conduct and orientation session with users when they receive new equipment. The meeting requires a room in which the hardware, software, manuals, cases, cables, and cataloguing paperwork can be set up. Orientation will usually take no longer than an hour.

Many organizations require users to sign for the receipt of computer equipment, as they do for keys and ID cards. The first phase of the orientation involves discussing hardware and software setups, including security logins. Cellular phones, network connections, and login instructions can be demonstrated, and data transfers can be tested.

### Tips for Securing the Mobile Office

Users should be advised to take along a hardware travel kit when they are on the road. This kit includes adapter cables and connections for hotel telephones and power bars. This equipment is especially important when traveling outside the U.S. and Canada. Users should know that these precautions are important not just for safeguarding the equipment, but because insurance companies are starting to increase premiums and deductibles for people who carry mobile computing equipment because of increasing theft.

**Tips for Safe Public Use**

Users should also be briefed on how to use their mobile equipment in public. People with cellular phones to their ears walking down a busy city street are easy targets for thieves who are watching to see where they put the phone when they are through. Headsets that can be attached to cellular phones offer hands-free operation and are less visible to other people. Having the cellular phone in a carrying case attached to a belt, jacket pocket, or inside a purse makes it more secure.

**Tips for Safe Storage**

Users should also be informed of the damage that sunlight can do to a notebook. Notebook computers with dual-scan or active-matrix color screens, when exposed to direct sunlight, can fade and become damaged. PDAs use a monochrome screen that is more effective in partial sunlight, but can still be damaged by direct sunlight.

Notebooks and PDAs are also affected by extremes in temperature. Very hot or cold temperatures can damage a notebook's moving parts, screen, or output ports. The screen of a laptop left in the car on a hot summer day could be destroyed. The screen output can also be disrupted for days as a result of even a short car trip in very cold weather. When traveling by car, users should keep their laptops in the trunk. Nothing should be left lying on the car seat. It should not be obvious that the user is in possession of computer equipment.

**CONCLUSION**

Computers are becoming more interconnected with users wired to each other through many types of electronic devices. As users become more dependent on computers, the possibility of breakdown and loss of information and connectivity to others is more likely. Furthermore, equipment is getting smaller, more powerful, more portable, and more accessible to users and workers outside of the office.

The security basics include a high-end power bar, an antivirus program, and regular backups. Once the basics are covered, security hardware and software should be considered. It is also very helpful to record serial numbers for equipment, and photograph it as an added measure. These precautions will help prevent downtime and insurance claims for stolen or damaged computer equipment.

# Chapter 53
# Portable Network Access

*Gilbert Held*

The steady increase in portable computer use has had a positive effect on productivity. It has also, however, challenged users to become educated on the vast array of networks and access methods that can facilitate the sharing of information. This chapter introduces users to several important modem terms, as well as a step-by-step guide to accessing today's popular packet-switching networks.

## MODEM TERMS

Until the incorporation of microprocessors into modems, the selection and operation of a modem was relatively easy. At that time, the major concern was the type of modulation performed by the modem expressed in terms of Bell System or TSS standards compatibility.

Until the divestiture of AT&T and its operating companies, Bell System equipment was a *de facto* standard in the US, and third-party modem manufacturers built most of their products to ensure compatibility with Bell System modems. Popular Bell System-compatible modems used on the PSTN included the 103, which operates at 300 b/s, and the 212A, which operates at 1,200 b/s and can also operate as a 300-b/s Bell System 103-compatible modem.

The TSS, which is a standards-recommending body, is part of the ITU, a United Nations organization headquartered in Geneva. Until the divestiture of AT&T, TSS modem standards were primarily followed in Europe and their modulation methods were incompatible with Bell System modems. With the divestiture of AT&T, several TSS modem standards have been adopted worldwide, including the V.22bis and V.32 modem recommendations. V.22bis governs the operation of a 2,400-b/s, FDX modem for use on the PSTN; the V.32 recommendation governs the operation of a 9,600-b/s, FDX modem for use on the PSTN.

0-8493-9965-3/99/$0.00+$.50
© 1999 by CRC Press LLC

The incorporation of microprocessor technology into modems resulted in their use for a range of functions added to the basic data modulation function of modems. Among features added to modems are error detection and correction, data compression, and command set recognition.

## Error Detection and Correction

Among the first modems to offer an error detection and correction feature were products manufactured by Microcom, Inc. This company created a revolution in modem technology by developing a modem protocol known as MNP.

**The MNP Protocol.** MNP is a communications protocol built into MNP-compatible modems that supports interactive and file transfer applications. In developing MNP, Microcom recognized that the first implementation of the protocol would not necessarily be the last, and structured it to accommodate changes in its implementation. To accomplish this, the major functions of the protocol are divided into classes. When an MNP modem communicates with another MNP modem, the two devices negotiate with each other to operate at the highest mutually supported class of MNP service.

Exhibit 1 summarizes the features associated with available classes. Until 1990, Microcom only licensed MNP through class 5to other modem manufacturers. In that year, they began to offer a full MNP license. Therefore, an MNP-compatible modem, though compatible with all other MNP modems, may be compatible only with a subset of available MNP classes unless a third-party vendor obtained a full license and incorporated all MNP classes into its product.

Exhibit 1 includes such terms as V.29 and V.32. Both reference TSS modulation standards, with V.29 originally developed as a half-duplex 9,600-b/s modulation technique for use on leased lines. Microcom, as well as other vendors, modified that technology to work on the PSTN. In addition, using the intelligence of a microprocessor to monitor the direction of transmission, it became possible to quickly turn off the transmitter of one modem and turn on its receiver, enabling the half-duplex transmission. In comparison, a V.32 modem uses echo cancellation technology to enable transmission and reception of data to occur simultaneously on the PSTN and also provides an inherent F-DX transmission capability.

**V.42 Recommendation.** Although MNP error detection and correction is included in more than 1 million modems manufactured by Microcom and more than 100 third-party vendors, it is not the primary method of error detection and correction recommended for use in modems by the TSS. In 1990, the TSS promulgated its V.42. Unlike other TSS V-series recommendations that govern modern modulation techniques, the V.42Recommendation

**Exhibit 1. MNP Classes**

| Class | Description of Functions Performed |
|-------|-----------------------------------|
| Class 1 | Asynchronous, byte-oriented, half-duplex transmission that provides an efficiency of approximately 70%. A 2,400-b/s modem using MNP class 1 obtains a throughput of 1,690 b/s. |
| Class 2 | Asynchronous byte-oriented full-duplex data transmission that provides an efficiency of approximately 84%. A 2,400-b/s modem using MNP class 2 obtains a throughput of approximately 2,000 b/s. |
| Class 3 | Asynchronous start and stop bits are stripped, enabling synchronous, bit-oriented, full-duplex transmission between modems. This provides an efficiency of approximately 108%, enabling a 2,400-b/s modem to obtain a throughput of approximately 2,600 b/s. |
| Class 4 | This class adds an adaptive packet assembly to previous classes, in which packet sizes are dynamically adjusted based on the number of retransmission requests. Data phase optimization, which provides a mechanism to reduce protocol overhead, is also included. The efficiency of class 4 is approximately 120%, enabling a 2,400-b/s modem to obtain a throughput of 2,900 b/s. |
| Class 5 | This class adds data compression to class 4 service, which provides an average compression ratio of 1.6:1, meaning that every 16 characters are compressed into 10 characters for transmission. This increases the protocol efficiency of class 5 to approximately 200%, enabling a 2,400-b/s modem to obtain a throughput of about 4,800 b/s. |
| Class 6 | This class adds universal link negotiation and statistical duplexing to class 5. Universal link negotiation enables MNP modems to begin operation at a common low-speed modulation method and negotiate the use of an alternative higher-speed modulation method. At the end of a successful link negotiation for class 6 operation, the pair of modems operate at 9,600 b/s using V.29 technology. Statistical duplexing results in the monitoring of user traffic patterns to enable the dynamic allocation of V.29 half-duplex transmission to resemble full-duplex transmission. Under class 6, 9,600-b/s operations MNP provide an average throughput approaching 19,200 b/s. |
| Class 7 | This class adds an enhanced data compression capability to P, based on a Huffman statistical encoding technique. Under class 7, a compression ratio of between 2.0 and 3.0 is achievable and increases throughput from 2 to 3 times the modems operating rate. |
| Class 8 | This class is no longer marketed. |
| Class 9 | This class adds support of V.32 modulation to class 7, providing a throughput of three times the 9600-b/s full-duplex operating rate of a V.32 modem. |

defines a protocol in which modems block data for transmission and generate and add a CRC to each block for error detection. Under the V.42 Recommendation, the flow of data blocks occurs according to a LAP, which differs from data flow under the MNP protocol. In recognition of the large installed base of MNP modems, however, MNP error detection and correction is supported as a secondary standard (i.e., a V.42-compatible modem will first attempt to communicate in its error-free mode using LAP). If the distant modem does not support the V.42 protocol, the V.42 modem will next attempt to communicate using MNP error control.

## Data Compression

Although the TSS V.42 Recommendation supports MNP error control, the V.42bis Recommendation — which is a data compression scheme that requires the use of the V.42 protocol — does not support a secondary method of compression. This theoretically means that for a portable computer user's V.42bis modem to operate in a compressed mode, it must communicate with another V.42bis-compatible modem. Fortunately, most V.42bis modems also include MNP support through class 5, enabling users to communicate in both a data compressed and error control mode with another MNP modem.

The key difference between V.42bis and MNP class 5 or class 7 is in their method of data compression. V.42bis uses a technique known as Lempel-Ziv, which can operate on single characters as well as on strings. In comparison, MNP compression primarily operates on single characters and is slightly less efficient. When using a V.42bis modem that incorporates V.32 modulation, the 9,600-b/s operating rate of the modem may achieve a throughput of as much as 28,400-b/s when data is highly susceptible to compression.

**Interface vs. Operating Rate.** To effectively use data compression, users are required to set their modem's interface data rate to exceed its operating rate. To understand why this is required, Exhibit 2 illustrates the relationship between the interface speed and the operating rate of a modem.

**Exhibit 2. Interface Rate Vs. Operating Rate**

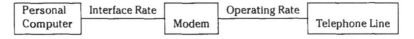

If the interface speed equals the operating rate, data compression will not increase the throughput of the modem. To increase the modem's throughput, users must set the interface rate to at least twice the modem's operating rate. For example, if the modem operates at 2,400 b/s, the interface rate should be set to at least 4,800 b/s. This allows more bits in the form of characters to enter the modem per unit of time than can be transmitted. Then, data compression can attempt to reduce the bits entering the modem so they can be transmitted at the modem's operating rate, increasing the throughput through the modem.

**Flow Control.** A second consideration users must take into account when using either error control by itself or with data compression is flow control. To see why flow control is necessary, Exhibit 2 shows the interface speed set to 4,800 b/s, while the operating rate is 2,400 b/s. If the modem cannot effectively compress data, perhaps because of the composition of the data, the rate data enters the modem will exceed the rate it is placed onto the line. Although the modem has a buffer, eventually it will overflow and data will be lost. Therefore, a method is required to regulate the flow of data into the modem. This method is called flow control.

Most modems support at least two methods of flow control, referred to as XON/XOFF and CTS/RTS. The XON/XOFF method of flow control results in the modem transmitting an XOFF character to the portable computer to disable transmission and an XON character to enable transmission to resume. Because the computer may require an ability to regulate data from the modem if users are printing received data or performing another mechanical related operation, they can also use XON and XOFF from the portable computer to the modem to enable and disable transmission from the modem to the portable computer.

The CTS/RTS method of flow control refers to the use of clear to send CTS and request to send RTS control signs on the interface between the computer and the modem. When the modem regulates flow control, it will drop the CTS signal to inform the computer to stop transmission and raise the CTS signal lead to inform the computer to resume transmission. When the computer regulates the flow of data from the modem, it will toggle the RTS signal lead.

In setting flow control, users must ensure that their computer and modem are set to use the same method. Concerning which method to select, if users expect to transfer files that may contain control characters, including an XOFF, they should use the CTS/RTS method of flow control. Otherwise, the reception of an XOFF would inadvertently turn off the computer.

### Command Set Recognition

To enable most of the features discussed in this section requires the use of the user's modem's command set. Although most modems claim Hayes Microcomputer Products command set compatibility, such compatibility only governs basic modem operations. To enable or disable MNP operations, V.42 error control, V.42bis data compression, or flow control requires the use of the modem's extended command codes. Because a modem's extended command set codes are not standardized, users should refer to their modem's reference manual to determine the codes to use to enable or disable the previously discussed features.

### NETWORK ACCESS

The remainder of this chapter focuses on the step-by-step procedures portable computer users must follow to access several popular packet-switching networks, electronic mail systems, and an information utility. Included for each are the customer service telephone number users can call to obtain an appropriate local telephone access number, a WATS access number if applicable, log-in procedures, including communications configuration parameter settings necessary to access each system, and a summary of commands when appropriate for accessing a special feature of the system.

### British Telecom (BT) TYMNET

Customer service telephone numbers:

U.S. and Canada: (800) 336-0149
International: (703) 715-0045

The log-in procedures for British Telecom (BT) TMNET are:

1. Set the communications configuration.
   Primary setting:       8 data bits, 1 stop bit, no parity
   Secondary settings:   7 data bits, 1 stop bit, mark parity
                          7 data bits, 1 stop bit, space parity
2. Dial the BT TYMNET access number. Dial customer service for telephone access or refer to the table at the end of this entry.
3. Type the terminal identifier. Use A to instruct the BT TYMNET network that no delay is necessary after transmitting a carriage return or line feed character.
4. Type the log-in string based on the following format: please login: [Ctrl]username:destination;password

   where:   [Ctrl]   Optional control characters
            Ctrl-X   Transmit data flow control
            Ctrl-R   Receive data flow control
            Ctrl-I   Interactive data session request
            Ctrl-V   Volume bandwidth request
            Ctrl-H   Half-duplex request
            Ctrl-P   Even parity request
            Ctrl-W   Wipe log-in string
            username   Users network identification
            destination   Address of computer connected to BT TYMNET accessed
            password   security mechanism that verifies use of user name

### Commercial Dialing from Hotels and Pay Phones

Many hotels and pay telephones subscribe to alternative operator services, whose charges for long-distance calls can substantially exceed the cost of using a major communications carrier. To bypass alternative operator services, users can dial an access code to directly connect to a specific carrier. Common access codes include:

| Communications Carrier | Access Code |
| --- | --- |
| AT & T | 10-288-0 |
| MCI | 10-222-0 |
| US Sprint | 10-333-0 |

If the access code fails to work, users should dial 0 and ask the operator to connect them to the desired carrier.

### CompuServe Information Service

Customer service telephone number:

US and Canada: (800) 848-8990

**Log-in Procedures by CompuServe.** To access CompuServe through CompuServe, the user must:

1. Set the communications configuration. 7 data bits, 1 stop bit, odd parity
2. CompuServe access number. Dial customer service for telephone access number or refer to table in this section.
3. Enter Ctrl-C.
4. Enter the user ID in response to the user ID prompt.
5. Enter the password in response to the password prompt.

**Log-in Procedures by BT TYMNET.** To access CompuServe through BT TYMNET, the user must:

1. Set the communications configuration.
   Primary setting:        8 data bits, 1 stop bit, no parity
   Secondary settings:   7 data bits, 1 stop bit, mark parity
                                   7 data bits, 1 stop bit, space parity
2. Dial a BT TYMNET access number.
3. Type A in response to terminal identifier request.
4. Enter CPS in response to Please login: message.
5. Enter CompuServe user ID in response to the user ID prompt.
6. Enter CompuServe password in response to the password prompt.

**Log-in Procedures by SprintNet.** To access CompuServe through SprintNet, the user must:

1. Set the communications configuration.
   Primary setting: 8 data bits, 1 stop bit, no parity
   Secondary setting: 7 data bits, 1 stop bit, even parity

2. Dial a SprintNet access number.
3. Enter two carriage returns at 300 and 1,200 b/s or one carriage return at 2,400 b/s.
4. Respond to Terminal = prompt with D1.
5. Respond to @ prompt with C 614227.
6. Enter the CompuServe user ID in response to the user ID prompt.
7. Enter the CompuServe password in response to the password prompt.

**CompuServe Quick Access Reference**

CompuServe telephone access numbers can be obtained by dialing the CompuServe customer service telephone number (800) 48-8990 and responding to the voice prompts. As an alternative, users can enter PHONES in response to the CompuServe Host Name: prompt when online.

**Dow Jones News/Retrieval**

Customer service telephone number:

(609) 452-1511

**Log-in Procedures by BT TYMNET.** To access the Dow Jones News/Retrieval Service through BT TYMNET, the user must:

1. Set the communications configuration.
   Primary setting:       8 data bits, 1 stop bit, no parity
   Secondary settings:    7 data bits, 1 stop bit, mark parity
                          7 data bits, 1 stop bit, space parity
2. Dial TYMNET access number.
3. Type A in response to the request for a terminal identifier.
4. Enter DOW1 in response to the Please Log In: message.
5. Enter DJNS in response to What Service Please?
6. Enter the Dow Jones News/Retrieval password in response to the password prompt.

**Log-in Procedures by SprintNet.** To access the Dow Jones News/Retrieval service through SpringNet, the user must:

1. Set the communications configuration.
   Primary setting:       8 data bits, 1 stop bit, no parity
   Secondary settings:    7 data bits, 1 stop bit, even parity
2. Dial a SprintNet access number.
3. Enter two carriage returns at 300 and 1,200 b/s or one carriage return at 2,400 b/s.\
4. Respond to Terminal 1/2 prompt with D1.
5. Respond to the @ prompt with C DOW.

6. Enter DJNS and press Return in response to the What Service Please? prompt.
7. Enter the Dow Jones News/Retrieval password in response to the password prompt.

See Exhibit 3.

**Exhibit 3. Dow Jones Information Retrieval Access Codes**

| Description | Access Code |
|---|---|
| Online Help | |
|   Systemwide Help | //DJHELP |
|   Customer Information and Updates | //FYI |
|   Menu of Databases | //MENU |
|   Directory of News-Retrieval Symbols | //SYMBOL |
| Business and World Newswires | |
|   Top Business, Financial, and Economic News | //BUSINESS |
|   Japanese Business News | //KYODO |
|   Top National and World News | //NEWs |
|   Dow Jones Business Newswires | //WIRES |
| Dow Jones Text Library | |
|   Current Business Articles | //DOWQUEST |
|   The Wall Street Journal and Other Publications: | |
|   Menu Version | //TEXTM |
|   Command Version | //TEXT |
| Company-Industry Information | |
|   Canadian Corporate News and Reports | //CANADA |
|   Dun & Bradstreet | //DB |
|   SEC Filing Extracts | //DSCLO |
|   Earnings Forecasts | //EPS |
|   Analysts' Reports on Companies and Industries | //INVEST |
|   Statistical Comparison of Companies and Industries//MG | |
|   Comprehensive Company Reports | //QUICK |
|   Standard & Poor's Profiles and Earnings Estimate | //SP |
|   Insider Trading, 5% Ownership & Tender Offer Filings//WATCH | |
|   Worldwide Corporate Report | //WORLDSCOPE |
| Quotes, Statistics, and Commentary | |
|   Current Quotes | //CQE |
|   Historical Dow Jones Averages | //DJA |
|   Mutual Fund Reports | //FUNDS |
|   Futures and Index Quotes | //FUTURES |
|   Historical Quotes | //HQ |
|   Technical Analysis Reports | //INNOVEST |
|   Forecasts and Analyses of World Markets | //MMS |
|   Real-Time Quotes | //RTQ |
|   Screening and 15-Year Historical Pricing on | |
|   Securities & Indexes | //TRADELINE |
|   Wall Street Week Transcripts | //WSW |
| Customized Information | |
|   Clipping Service | //CLIP |
|   Company and Industry Tracking Service | //TRACK |

**Exhibit 3. (Continued) Dow Jones Information Retrieval Access Codes**

| Description | Access Code |
|---|---|
| General Services | |
|    Book Reviews | //Books |
|    Encyclopedia | //ENCYC |
|    Online Brokerage | //FIDELITY |
|    Electronic Mail and Communications | //MCI |
|    Movie Reviews | //MOVIES |
|    Comprehensive Travel Services | //OAG |
|    College Selection Service | //SCHOOL |
|    Sports Report | //SPORTS |
|    Electronic Shopping Service | //STORE |
|    Worldwide Weather Reports | //WTHR |

## FTS2000 Offnet Calling

These procedures are for U.S. government employees dialing from hotels, motels, pay phones, and other non-FTS2000 telephones. Dialing procedures are based on the network servicing the employee's agency.

**Network A (AT&T).** To gain access to this network, employees must:

1. Use the AT&T Calling Card to dial the access number (800) 633-6384, and then wait for a dial tone.
2. Dial the 7-digit FTS or 10-digit commercial number to be accessed and wait for another dial tone.
3. Dial the 11-digit authorization code on the AT & T Calling Card.

**Network B (U.S. Sprint).** To gain access to this network, employees must

1. Use the U.S. Sprint FONCARD to dial the access number (800) 366-4000.
2. Dial the 11-digit FONCARD number shown on the card.
3. Dial the 7-digit FTS or 10-digit commercial number to be accessed.

If dialing from a rotary dial telephone using either card, users must wait for an operator after dialing the appropriate 800 number. For assistance, users can dial the THIS at FTS 295-8500 or (301) 295-8500.

## MCI Mail

Customer service telephone number:

(800) 444-6245

**Log-in Procedures.** To log in to MCI Mail, users must:

1. Set the communications configuration.
8 data bits, 1 stop bit, no parity

2. Dial the MCI Mail access number.
   (800) 234-6245
3. Respond to the user prompt by typing the user ID.
4. Respond to the password prompt by typing the password.

**Mailboxes.** Mailbox sections and their contents include the following:

| Section | Contents |
|---------|----------|
| INBOX | Messages that have not been read. |
| OUTBOX | Messages that were previously sent. |
| DESK | Messages that were read. |
| PENDING | Messages being created. |

Mailbox-related commands and their functions are:

| | |
|---|---|
| ANSWER | For replying to the sender or a message that has been read. |
| ANSWER EACH | For replying to the sender of a message and everyone else who received the message. |
| CREATE | For writing an MCI Mail message.<br>— To cancel a message, the user types a slash (/) at TO, CC, or subject.<br>— To complete a message, the user types a slash (/) on a blank line after the body of the message. |
| DELETE | Enables messages to be deleted from any mailbox selection. The user enters the command followed by the scan numbers to be deleted. For example, DELETE 5, 7 causes the fifth and seventh message in the current mailbox section to be deleted. |
| FORWARD | Causes a copy of one or more messages in a mailbox to be sent to other people. |
| INCLUDE | Enables text from other messages to be inserted into a message. Type/INCLUDE/scan-number in the message being created. For example,/INCLUDE/2,4 & 5 inserts text from messages 2, 4, and 5 in the message being created. |
| NEXT | Causes the next message from the current section to be displayed after a READ command is issued. |
| PRINT | Enables a series of messages to be displayed without pausing between messages. Messages to PRINT can be identified by scan-number, mailbox section, or by one of the following: |

ALL
ON [date] SUBJECT ["words"]
AFTER [date] TO [lastname]
BEFORE [date] FROM [lastname]

READ                Enables one or more messages to be displayed with page breaks between messages. Messages to READ can be identified by scan-number, mailbox section, or by one of the following:

ALL
AFTER [date] TO [lastname]
BEFORE [date] FROM [lastname]

After reading a message one of the following commands can be used:

ANSWER    NEXT
FORWARD   PRINT

SCAN                Enables users to obtain a summary of the messages in their mailboxes. One or more of the following options can be used with SCAN:

INBOX       AFTER [date]
OUTBOX      BEFORE [date]
DESK SUBJECT ["text"]
PENDING TO [name]
ALL FROM [name]
ON [date]

SEND                Enables a draft message to be transmitted for non-priority delivery.

SEND ONITE          Enables a draft message to be transmitted for priority delivery.

SEND 4HOUR          Enables a draft message to be transmitted by electronic mail and adds priority notification to the message.

/UPLOAD             Enables one or more files containing addresses into the envelope of a message to be transmitted.

Other MCI Mail commands include:

ACCOUNT             Enables a terminal's characteristics to be defined to MCI Mail.

DOW JONES           Enables users to access Dow Jones News and Retrieval Information.

EDIT                Allows users to make changes to pending messages.

EXIT                For terminating the MCI Mail session.

FIND                Permits users to search for an MCI Mail subscriber's name to obtain their MCI ID and other information.

**The MCI Help facility.** MCI Mail includes a built-in help facility that displays information about the use of commands and data about different topics. To use the help facility, the user types:

HELP { command-name   topic

To obtain a list of topics, the user types HELP INDEX. Among the topics supported are:

| Topic | Information Provided |
|---|---|
| ACCESS | Telephone access information. |
| ACCOUNT | Terminal settings. |
| ADDRESS | Available addressing options. |
| APPENDIX | Pricing, sales representatives, and directory searching. |
| BULLETIN BOARD | Owning and viewing bulletin boards. |
| COUNTRY | Countries that receive MCI Mail. |
| CUSTOMER SUPPORT | How to contact MCI Mail Customer Service. |
| DELIVERY | Mail delivery. |
| FAX MCI | Mail fax dispatch. |
| GRAPHICS | Letterheads and signatures. |
| HANDLING | Option commands that define how messages are handled and delivered. |
| LISTS | Creation of address lists. |
| MAILBOX | The MCI Mailbox. |
| PC | Offline file creation and uploading to MCI Mail. |
| PRICES MESSAGES | Rates for sending MCI Mail messages. |
| REQUEST | Ordering of reference manuals. |
| SPECIAL FEATURES | Additional features about MCI Mail. |
| TELEX | How to exchange messages with MCI Mail. |
| TEXT | Creating text in a message. |
| X400 | Transmitting to an X.400 electronic mail address. |

## U.S. Sprint SprintNet

Customer service:

US and overseas WATS access: (800) 877-5045
International non-WATS access: (703) 689-6400

To log in to this network, users must:

1. Set the communications configuration.
    Primary setting: 8 data bits, 1 stop bit, no parity
    Secondary setting: 7 data bits, 1 stop bit, even parity

2. Dial the SprintNet access number. The user dials customer service for the access number or refers to the completed table at the end of this entry.

3. Identify duplex setting. The user hits a carriage return for full duplex and hits a semicolon and a carriage return for half-duplex transmission. SprintNet can be informed of a computer' use of data bits, stop bit, parity, its operating rate, and duplex setting by the use of a 2- or 3-character sequence called Hunt/Confirm. The following items indicate communications parameter settings, data rate, and duplex mode identified by the Hunt/Confirm sequences supported by SprintNet.

4. Respond to the TERMINAL = prompt with the 2-character terminal identifier or press a carriage return. Use D1 for a computer.

5, Enter the area code (AAA) and the local exchange (111), followed by a carriage return — AAA, LLL if access is by in-WATS service.

6. Respond to the @ prompt with the connect command C followed by the destination host or terminal address and an optional ID/password using the following format:

   C DDDDDD,IIIIII [return]

   where:  C is connect command
           DDDDDD is destination address
           IIIIII is the user identification

7. If required, the user then responds to the PASSWORD = prompt with the password followed by a [return].

US Sprint SprintNet quick access reference numbers: in-WATS service:

300.2,400 b/s: (800) 546-1000
9,600 b/s (V.32): (800) 546-2500
9,600 b/s (V.29): (800) 546-2000

## SUMMARY

Knowledge of communications terms, features, and network access methods can provide portable computer users with the ability to efficiently and effectively communicate with other computers and information resources. In addition, preplanning trips to determine and record telephone access numbers required to use the resources of different value-added carriers and electronic mail providers can save users a considerable amount of time and effort to obtain that information when in a travel status.

# Chapter 54

# Wireless Communications for Voice and Data

*Andres Liana, Jr.*

Use of wireless technologies has become one of the fastest-growing communications applications around the world. Recent innovations have greatly increased the availability of the telephone in many parts of the world, yet wireless communications have been around since the early 1900s. Back then, radio served as the principal means of mass communication and, like TV, was the principal means of public entertainment. During World Wars I and II, wireless communications allowed combat forces to communicate. Today, law enforcement agencies, marine agencies, and transportation companies, among many others, use wireless communications to manage deployed resources.

In the 1950s, the Rural Electrification Administration considered wireless radio technology as a means of supplying telephone service to rural populations. This experimentation proceeded through many iterations but was largely abandoned during the mid-1980s as cellular technology emerged.

Today, radio communication is thought of as a new innovation because of its growing ubiquity and its support for personal communications, data, and information collection. Lower costs have made it possible for users to enjoy cellular telephones, personal digital assistants (PDAs), and a host of other devices to simplify the conduct of commerce. Wireless technology has improved intra- and intercorporate communications, enabling more cost-effective control of such business resources as deployed sales forces and technical service personnel.

0-8493-9965-3/99/$0.00+$.50
© 1999 by CRC Press LLC

## WIRELESS TECHNIQUES: A STRATEGY FOR WORLDWIDE VOICE COMMUNICATIONS

### Cellular Voice

Great strides have been made in the adaptation of cellular radio as a means of supporting local telephone service. In many undeveloped countries there is little or no infrastructure to support telephone services. For this reason, it is not uncommon in some parts of South America, Asia, Russia, and Eastern Europe for a subscriber to wait as long as one year to get local telephone service. Because of this situation, wireless subscriber penetration has grown at about 45% per year. For example, Motorola, Inc. recently reported that it had orders for 150 wireless systems for 21 provinces of China and the three municipalities of Beijing, Shanghai, and Tianjing an area with a combined population of more than one billion people. As a result, wireless local loop (WiLL) systems are being installed around the world at an accelerated rate to reduce the time to service.

### Wireless Radio

Wireless radio is being installed in place of traditional central office systems that require expensive extended copper wire external networks. Service providers are finding that wireless radio central office systems are convenient, fast, and less costly than traditional central office switching systems. Because there are no copper wires to string and no wire plant to maintain, subscribers can enjoy telephone service as soon as the radios are turned on.

Building a traditional central office system with a stationary copper landline network costs between $1,250 and $1,750 per subscriber, depending on terrain and labor. A Motorola WiLL system can be installed for between $800 and $2,000 per subscriber. About 80% of these costs are the construction of cell sites, which can also be used for other forms of wireless communications, such as personal communications systems (PCSs).

### Wireless PBX Systems

In companies where operations are widespread, such as chemical and heavy equipment manufacturing, it is often necessary for first-line supervisors and other key employees to cover a lot of terrain in a day. Often these personnel are in high demand and maintaining contact with them is difficult. For these applications, private branch exchange (PBX) manufacturers have developed wireless radio frequency (RF) systems that can be integrated into the architecture of a PBX system.

Lucent Technologies (Basking Ridge, NJ), Ericsson Messaging Systems (Woodbury, NY), Intercom Computer Systems, Inc. (Woodbridge, VA), Northern Telecom, Inc. (Richardson, TX), Mitel Corp. (Kanata, ON, Canada), and Siemens-ROLM Corp. (Alpharetta, GA) offer systems that integrate into their PBX architectures. These systems are integrated through the PBX line cards and support the same line appearances as any hard-wired single line or electronic station set. A base radio operating in the unlicensed frequency range together with a series of antennae spaced around the user's facility comprise the basic network. Low-powered mobile handsets are used with these systems to avoid interference with other frequencies operating in the same area.

**Wireless PBX Add-On Systems.** Motorola and Spectralink have developed wireless PBX add-on systems similar to those developed by the PBX manufacturers. The Motorola InReach design concept is slightly different because it was developed as an extension to a cellular operator's service offering. InReach handsets can be used either as a cellular terminal or a PBX station set.

For example, when a user enters an InReach-equipped building, the handset can function as an electronic desk telephone. The handset provides access to all of the features on the PBX, including access to the corporate and public network. When the user leaves the building, the handset can then be used to access the cellular network and functions as a mobile handset.

Wireless add-on PBX facilities are expensive because of the addition of a base radio module and antennae infrastructure to the established internal PBX network. A typical midrange (i.e., 75 × 450 line) PBX system, when configured with a wireless add-on system, can easily double the cost of the basic PBX system. However, as PCS and other handheld terminal-based services proliferate, the costs for PBX wireless systems will continue to decline.

## Satellite Voice Services

Satellites are playing an increasing role in establishing still another layer of worldwide voice communications. Two of the most widely heralded services are the Iridium and Teledesic low earth orbital (LEO) systems. These systems offer worldwide telephone service through the use of a small handheld telephone similar to those used for cellular systems. Iridium is owned by a consortium of international companies, one of which is Motorola, Inc. Teledesic is owned by McCaw Communications and Microsoft Corp. (Redmond, WA).

Inmarsat now offers voice services through a worldwide consortium of 65 member nations. Special briefcase-size terminals are used to communicate with the satellite. Typical terminal costs range between $18,000 to $22,000 and connect-time costs are approximately $5.00 per minute. A new service that is planned, Inmarsat-P, will compete directly with the LEO systems. Although details of the Inmarsat-P service are still in the making, terminal and initiation costs are expected to be in the range of $1,500, with connect costs of about $1 per minute.

These satellite-based voice systems provide the capability to support both voice and data communications in any remote area of the world.

## WIRELESS CONSIDERATIONS FOR A DATA COMMUNICATIONS STRATEGY

A variety of services are available to support wireless data communications. Wireless services like cellular digital packet data (CDPD), enhanced special mobile radio (ESMR), Ardis Mobile Data, and RAM Mobile Data Inc. support slightly different needs, although there is some overlap. For this reason, users should not look for a single vendor to supply an all-encompassing wireless service solution. In fact, it is less costly to consider a mix of voice, paging, and data services.

ESMR and CDPD offer competitive data communications services. For example, the Nextel interconnect option on the Motorola Integrated Radio System (MIRS)-based network costs $40 per month for the first 256 minutes plus $0.50 for each additional minute. This assumes that the subscriber also is a dispatch subscriber at about $25 per month for access.

A MIRS Motorola Lingo mobile handset is required to access service on a MIRS system and is priced around $1,000. In comparison, cellular telephones can cost up to $350. Cellular subscribers start out at $14.95 for monthly access plus about $0.45 or more per minute for airtime.

Although there are still many smaller special mobile radio (SMR) operators across the US that will continue to offer dispatch and interconnect services in second-tier markets, major players such as Nextel, Dial Page, and other members of the MIRS-related roaming consortium are likely to maintain their interconnect rates in competition with cellular service providers.

### CDPD as a Wireless Option

Implementing cellular digital packet data networks often requires a number of systems applications modifications. For example, a special CDPD modem is required at either end for the transmission of data from one point to a host computer's communications port. This device must be established separately from the other host communications ports and should be installed by the cellular service provider. This task includes assigning the device with an IP address and configuring it for access to the cellular network.

**CDPD Costs.** Communicating over a wireless network is more costly than using the public network for a number of reasons, not the least of which is the cost for airtime. For example, regular transmission control protocol/Internet protocol (TCP/IP) applications generate a lot of extraneous traffic that can drive up the cost for transmission on a network that is usage sensitive. A hardware fix is available to alleviate this type of network condition. For example, products are available to monitor data flow as a means of reducing the number of acknowledgments being sent.

**Potential Performance Problems.** Another problem that must be taken into account is packet delay. This condition can result in dropped connections or unnecessary retransmissions and is caused by network congestion. Although cellular networks are still relatively lightly loaded, network congestion becomes a problem as greater penetration develops in the wireless market and CDPD networks become crowded In addition, under some traffic circumstances, it is possible for packets to be dropped, therefore delivery of packets cannot be guaranteed. Noisy lines and poor radio coverage can also present the same types of problems as a congested network.

Under some traffic conditions, duplicate packets can be introduced through retransmission facilities, If the packet acknowledgment is lost, the packet's source will time out and retransmit a second or duplicate packet. Packets can also be thrown out of order when the data path is subjected to delay from rerouting events. These are just a few of the transmission characteristics that must be countered when a CDPD network is used for data transmission. Users should carefully review their applications and develop the measures that may be required to safeguard their data transmissions.

**CDPD Test Areas.** Cellular digital packet data is being tested by McCaw (in Las Vegas, Dallas, and Seattle), Ameritech Mobile (in Chicago), GTE Mobilnet, and AirTouch Cellular (PacTel Cellular), among others. Bell Atlantic Mobile, Inc. has announced pricing for CDPD services offered in its Baltimore/Washington DC and Pittsburgh test markets. GTE PCS and McGraw Cellular have also initiated trial services in their franchise areas.

### Specialized Mobile Radio

Specialized mobile radio (SMR) services began in 1970 when the Federal Communications Commission (FCC) established frequencies in the 800–900MHz range for use in land mobile communications. A typical application of SMR is a radio dispatch for service fleets and taxicabs. SMR operators are assigned licenses for exclusive use of assigned channels in a given area. SMR operators can also provide interconnection to the public network.

Racotek (Minneapolis, MN) is one provider of SMR wireless voice/data service. Racotek provides a vehicle fleet management service that is based on SMR or trunk radios. A Racoteck communications gateway facility linked to a mobile communications controller (MCC) in a customer's vehicle provides a data communications link between customers (e.g., truck drivers) and their dispatch control centers. A mobile radio collocated in the vehicle with the MCC unit completes the communications link. This system allows the dispatcher to send route information, messages, or other information that cannot be sent over the radio to customers while they are in route to or from a location.

### Commercial Mobile Data Communications Services

RAM Mobile Data Inc. RAM Mobile Data Inc. (New York, NY) is a joint venture between Bell South and RAM Broadcasting and provides a two-way data communications service that is based on the Mobiltex network architecture. This service is used by many companies for management of their field sales and service operations. RAM Mobile Data provides mobile data communications service in 90% of the urban business areas in the US, covering 6,000 cities and 210 metropolitan trading areas.

Access speeds of up to 9.6K bps can be supported in all areas; in select areas, it is possible to access the network at up to 19.2K bps. Common applications include E-mail and basic information access to the corporate data center for mobile travelers.

Some companies have greatly reduced their cellular telephone use by deploying the lower-cost RAM mobile network to send E-mail and messages to corporate personnel while traveling. A traveler equipped with a radio-enabled laptop or personal digital assistant (PDA) can access the nearest RAM base station. The message is then routed over a leased landline to the corporate data center. Messages can be sent to a traveler over the RAM mobile network where it is routed to the RAM local switch nearest the traveling employee. Conrail uses RAM Mobile Data to transmit train loading information to train crews advising the disposition of freight and empty freight cars. Other user companies, such as TransNet and Master-Card, use RAM Mobile Data to provide access to their central hosts so that merchants in the field can validate credit card purchases.

**Ardis Mobile Services.** Ardis (Lincolnshire IL) is a joint venture between IBM Corp. and Motorola and is composed of a formerly private corporate network that supported deployed field sales forces and service personnel. Ardis provides data communications services to 4,000 major metropolitan centers and 8,000 cities in the US, Puerto Rico, and the Virgin Islands. The network was originally designed by Motorola to support IBM's 18,000 deployed field service personnel. Access to the network ranges from 4.8 to 19.2K bps and can be reached from within a building or from a moving vehicle. Laptops and PDAs equipped with an Ardis/Modacom modem can be used to access company host computers to retrieve E-mail, enter orders, access diagnostic information, or obtain product information. Salespeople equipped with laptop computers can access product files to provide customers with product specifications as well as check inventories, enter orders, and print on- the-spot order confirmations.

## Satellite Data

Satellite systems are composed of a transmission device that is capable of receiving a signal from a ground station. The signal is then amplified and rebroadcast to other earth stations capable of receiving its signal. User signals neither originate nor terminate on the satellite, although the satellite does receive and act on signals from the earth that are used to control the satellite once it is in space. A satellite transmission originates at a single earth station and then passes through the satellite and ends up at one or more earth stations.

The satellite itself acts as an active relay much the same as a microwave relay. A satellite communications system involves three basic elements: the space segment, the signal element, and the ground segment. The space segment comprises the satellite and its launch vehicle. The signal element comprises the frequency spectrum over which the satellite communicates, and the ground segment comprises the earth station, antennae, multiplexer, and access element.

**Advantages of Satellite Systems.** The advantage of a satellite system can be seen in the transmission costs, which are not distance sensitive, and the costs for broadcasting, which are fixed whether there are one or 100 stations that receive the down signal. Another advantage is the high bandwidth that satellite signals are capable of supporting. Bit errors are random, making it possible to use statistical systems for more efficient error detection and correction. Some satellite service providers are described in the following sections.

**American Mobile Satellite Corp.** (AMSC). AMSC offers satellite-based mobile data services using its own L-band satellite. AMSC is owned by three major shareholders — McCaw/AT&T, MTEL, and Hughes — although its stock is publicly traded. In the US, AMSC offers service through its Virginia hub. Downlink services may come through the Washington DC international teleport for services sold through the Virginia hub. Pricing is competitive with terrestrial services. For example, a full-time 64K-bps link between Washington, DC, and Brussels, Belgium, would cost $1,350 per month.

**OmniTracs.** OmniTracs, a service of Qualcomm Inc., uses excess capacity on Ku-band U.S. satellites to provide a data-only mobile tracking service for large trucking companies. The OmniTracs service now has more than 50,000 terminals deployed in trucks in North America. Qualcomm plans to expand its service into Europe, Japan, and South America using excess capacity on existing Ku- and C-band satellites.

**Globalstar.** Globalstar is the name of a low earth orbit (LEO) system designed for mobile voice services by a joint venture of Loral and Qualcomm. Globalstar has recently extended its ownership to an entirely new set of investors who plan to use excess capacity on available satellites. A series of gateways around the globe will provide an integrated network into the public switched telephone network (PSTN) and the satellite links.

**Odyssey.** Odyssey, a system proposed by TRW, is composed of four satellites. The TRW system will use fewer satellites for nearly global coverage because the system will be higher in the sky. The Odyssey uses the TRW advanced bus (AB940) L-band dish for mobile-to-satellite links, an S-band dish for satellite-to-mobile links, and two small Ka-band antennae for satellite/ground station links. Each satellite will operate as a bent pipe system, with switching and processing performed at the ground stations using spread spectrum modulation.

**Ellipso.** Ellipso, proposed by Mobile Communications Holding Inc., is a high elliptical orbiting (HEO) system, consisting of six (although 24 are planned) small satellites deployed in three elliptical orbits. Two of these orbits, called Borealis, will be inclined at 116 degrees. One orbit will be equatorial, which will provide dependable access to users in the northern and southern hemispheres. The Ellipso satellites will be small and use a simple bent pipe design with L-band for uplinks and S-band for downlinks.

**Orion Atlantic.** Orion is an international partnership of eight companies that operates its own Ku-band satellite composed of 34 transponders. Orion's focus is European business-to-business communications arrangements, as well as transatlantic connectivity. Services include cable distribution, business television, news and network backhauls, feeds, and standard business communications requirements. The service can support a full range of multimedia requirements, including telecommuting and interactive desktop video.

A unique mesh network provides completely independent service for international firms with multiple locations. Uplink/downlink services for 64Kbps access is in the range of about $2,000 per month for an enterprise-wide LAN. A dedicated 64K-bps full service point-to-point link can be provisioned for about $1,400 per month for a 36-month contract. This service includes all equipment for rooftop-to-rooftop access, which is configured to support a dynamically allocated bandwidth service supporting both voice and data requirements. Installation for such a service would be about $10,000. Such an international connection is priced below regular internal terrestrial services and completely bypasses all monthly recurring local loop costs. A second system is planned that would cover a large part of Russia, the Middle East, Africa, and South America.

## WIRELESS LANS

Wireless LANs are governed by the IEEE Wireless Local Area Networks Standard Working Group Project 802.11. The 802.11 standard establishes the components and interface requirements for a wireless LAN. The basic architecture established by the 802.11 committee organizes wireless LANs into basic service areas (BSAs) and access points (APs). Multiple BSAs can be interconnected at the APs into an extended service area (ESA). The protocols for this model are divided into two groups: the media access control (MAC) specification and physical specifications (PHY). There are different specifications for each radio frequency supported: 915MHz, 2.4GHz, and 5.2GHz.

## WIRELESS COMMUNICATION AS AN ALTERNATIVE TO FIXED MEDIA

Traditional fixed-media systems are based on coaxial cable, twisted-pair wiring, fiber optics, or a combination of all three. Over time, the documentation for fixed networks can become lost or rendered inaccurate because of unrecorded equipment moves and changes. As new functions are established or offices rearranged, segments with undocumented cables are often installed to support added network nodes. Some companies that experience a high degree of internal moves and changes find it necessary to abandon at least 30% of their original network media. For these companies, a wireless network strategy superimposed over a base network provides the flexibility to support many permanent and temporary moves. Under this plan, the user is only required to establish a base radio, transmitters for each terminal to be moved, and a series of line-of-sight antennas. Thereafter, relocating network users only requires that the new location has line-of-sight to a network antennae.

### The Wireless Cost Advantage

A wireless LAN solution at $750 to $1500 per node may be expensive when compared with a traditional wired solution (approximately $350 to $550). However, when the costs of lost productivity and rewiring are added, a wireless solution may be more cost-effective for organizations that move or change equipment frequently. Wireless solutions find their best fit where there are large unwired manufacturing areas to support, campus buildings that must be interconnected, open office areas without access to wire facilities, or older buildings with concrete partitions and no wire access.

### Vendor Support for Wireless Solutions

There are several different vendor approaches for supporting wireless LANs. For example, Motorola's Altair systems use the 18–19GHz frequency range to support a microcellular approach. A series of intelligent antennae is used to establish microcells within the user's building. These microcells are supported with low-powered, high frequency radios designed to support frequency reuse. This process results in a very efficient network.

Other manufacturers often use two basic components: the radio hub and the transceivers. In some systems, a single hub can support up to 62 transceivers. The transceivers are attached to the terminals and communicate with the hub using a line-of-sight arrangement.

Wireless LAN bridges are used to connect LANs in neighboring buildings. These devices establish a point-to-point connection and may not be a complete system. Examples of wireless bridges can be seen in the Motorola's Altair VistaPoint and the Cylink Airlink,

Infrared and laser technology can also be used to interconnect LANs in different buildings. This technique places information on a beam of light and can support very wide bandwidth over a short distance. In addition, this technology is immune to electric interference and is much more secure than radio transmission. Although infrared and laser techniques do not require an FCC license, users are responsible for any radio interference that develops while they are operating in a densely occupied area. LCI (Lancaster PA) has been developing laser systems for several years and has well over 750 mature systems installed.

## OUTLOOK FOR WIRELESS APPLICATIONS

Projections for wireless applications vary depending on the user and the interpretation of the technology. There is no doubt that there will be a tremendous penetration in the basic telephone service market. Wireless local loop access will allow more users in developing nations to enjoy telephone service faster and at an affordable level.

The continued decline in the cost of PCMCIA cards for mobile radio will result in the continued rise in the number of laptops and PDAs used for basic communications functions such as E-mail and information access.

Satellite and radio-based service will continue to support vehicle management and tracking. Services like Qualcomm's OmniTracs provide a cost-efficient method for tracking and establishing a data communications connections with truck assets in the field.

Global positioning systems (GPS) will allow users to track vehicles and provision driver information. Avis rental car agency is testing a system that tracks Avis cars and sends driver information to fleets of specially equipped rental cars.

Hertz, Alamo, and other rental car agencies are using RAM Mobile Data to allow their service personnel to directly process returned vehicles as they are driven onto the company ramps. Using a handheld data entry terminal, the service person is able to enter the vehicle ID code and rental status. This process allows the rental car location to more efficiently manage their available pool of cars.

## SUMMARY

Considering that many of the current wireless applications have come into being in only the last few years, new applications are certain to proliferate as users gain confidence in the available services. Mobile workers such as field sales representatives can spend more time with customers. New levels of productivity will emerge as telecommuting employees freed from expensive office space are able to focus more on the delivery of an end product.

Paradyne's Enhance Throughput Cellular (ETC) can greatly improve the process for sending data over the cellular network. This technology makes the cellular data user transparent to all other cellular traffic. Advancements such as this one will allow wireless users to resolve many of their data transmission requirements that were previously difficult to resolve. There is no question that users are adopting wireless solutions. The important issue to consider is the rate at which this technology is absorbed by mobile workers and the extent to which the penetration of services exceeds the available capacity of the network to support these users' needs.

# Chapter 55
# Developing a Cost-Effective Strategy for Wireless Communications

*Sami Jajeh*

Most organizations have some mobile field activities involving sales representatives, field service technicians, telecommuting employees, traveling managers, route-based personnel, or even mobile health care providers. Organizations with significant numbers of mobile field activities require a well- synchronized exchange of information between central information systems and mobile users.

Many organizations are investing in portable computers and software to provide mobile users with the tools they need to accomplish their daily tasks. Some organizations have begun to look at emerging wireless technologies to further enhance communications and streamline information exchange by providing anytime, anywhere access.

Automating business processes through wireless technology offers organizations many benefits, including improved productivity and increased competitive advantage. To achieve these benefits, organizations must thoroughly consider several implementation issues that fall into three broad categories:

- Communications architecture and access methods.
- Application appropriateness.
- Wireless service products.

This chapter aims to help organizations develop a cost-effective wireless communications strategy that meets the needs of mobile and remote workers. Following an overview of wireless network technology and service providers, it discusses each of the three categories of implementation

0-8493-9965-3/99/$0.00+$.50
© 1999 by CRC Press LLC

issues and the advantages and disadvantages of the various options within them.

## WIRELESS NETWORK TECHNOLOGIES AND SERVICE PROVIDERS

The following sections discuss major network technologies and service providers; they are not intended to provide an exhaustive list of current technologies and players. There are two prevalent technologies for wireless applications:

- Circuit-switched networks.
- Packet data networks

### Circuit- Switched Networks

Circuit-switched networks involve establishing a dedicated connection (or circuit) between two points and then transmitting data over the connection, much like a typical telephone conversation. They can be either analog or digital.

**Analog Circuit-Switched (Cellular) Networks.** Two- way analog circuit-switched cellular (CSC) technology has existed since the advent of cellular phones. To use CSC service, the user requires a cellular phone with a cellular modem. Sending wireless data over a circuit- switched cellular connection offers several advantages, including:

- Wide on-street coverage and availability.
- Suitability for sending and receiving large data files such as long E-mail messages or reports.
- Per-minute (as opposed to per-packet) charges.
- Implementation through standard communications software and a modem attached to a cellular phone.

The disadvantages of using circuit-switched cellular technology include:

- Increased relative cost of sending short messages, because call setup time may become a large percentage of cost.
- Security concerns involving unencrypted files.
- Lack of cellular error-correction or enhancement standards.

Although questionable reliability and poor throughput are often cited as disadvantages of analog circuit- switched cellular connections, the availability of new technology from several vendors, including AT&T, Celeritas Technologies Ltd., Microcom Corp., Motorola, and ZyXEL, is rapidly changing this perception. These mature technologies allow organizations to use analog cellular modem technology to build and deploy enterprisewide dial-up based applications.

**Digital Circuit-Switched (Cellular) Networks.** Digital communications technology is inherently more reliable for sending data than is analog technology. Examples of digital circuit-switched wireless network implementations in the US are code division multiple access (CDMA) and time division multiple access (TDMA). Because the availability of both CDMA and TDMA is limited, it will be some time before most US organizations will be able to take advantage of digital circuit- switched technologies for wireless data applications.

## Packet Data Networks

Packet data networks have been designed for effective and reliable transfer of data rather than voice. They use a method that is comparable to sending a document one page at a time. The document is first broken into pages, and each page (or packet) is sent in its own envelope. The network determines the most appropriate transmission path, and once each page reaches its destination, the document is reassembled (if appropriate).

Packet data networks use radio frequency channels to connect the portable computing device to a network backbone and, ultimately, to the company's host system. The major networks (e.g., Ardis and RAM Mobile Data) use packet radio technology. Packet cellular technology (e.g., cellular digital packet data, or CDPD) is now emerging.

**Packet Radio Technology.** The two major wireless packet data networks are Ardis and RAM.

*Ardis.* A nationwide, packet radio network owned by Motorola and IBM, Ardis covers 80% of the US population. Transmitters in the 400 largest metropolitan areas are networked through dedicated land-based lines, although dial-up and radio frequency (RF) connections are also supported. Ardis supports fully automatic roaming. In addition to on-street and in-vehicle coverage, Ardis is said to offer more reliable in-building coverage than do other two-way wireless networks. Pricing depends on the application and is based on both flat-rate and usage charges.

*RAM Mobile Data.* The RAM Mobile Data network is the result of a business venture between BellSouth Enterprises and RAM Broadcasting Corp. to provide wireless transport for messaging services and products. Commercial service currently is available in more than 6,000 cities and towns. RAM uses the Mobitex architecture for wireless packet data communications originally developed in Sweden and currently in its fourteenth version. RAM's network was designed for message capability with inherent roaming, store-andforward, and broadcast capabilities.

**Packet Cellular Technology.** Cellular digital packet data (CDPD) technology is being developed and implemented by a consortium of 10 major cellular carriers, including AT&T Cellular and AirTouch. As a digital overlay of the existing analog cellular network that utilizes unused bandwidth in the cellular voice channel, CDPD is a logical extension of cellular data communications.

Because is based on an open design and supports multiple connectionless network protocols such as the Internet protocol (IP), existing applications require few, if any, modifications to run on CDPD. CDPD claims a bandwidth of 19.2K bps, although typical user rates are closer to 9.6K bps. Approximately 30 markets have access to CDPD technology.

Suitability of Packet Data Networks for Wireless Applications. Packet data networks offer several advantages, including:

- Reliable transmission of data.
- Cost- efficient transmission of short messages.
- Transparent roaming in the locations where the networks exist.
- Fast setup time.

Disadvantages of packet data technology include:

- High costs in certain situations (resulting from a per-packet charge).
- Slow transmission times for large data files (which is less the case for CDPD).
- More- limited coverage and availability than that of cellular technology.
- Limited bandwidth (here, again, CDPD is better than RAM or Ardis).

The suitability of packet data networks for wireless data applications depends largely on the application. The networks provide a solution for applications requiring instantaneous, unconnected delivery of small but valuable pieces of information that can save money or generate revenue. They are therefore used for single-transaction based applications such as remote credit-card authorization or rental car check- in. Use of packet data is more limited in cases of general sales force automation, database replication, E-mail with attachments, electronic software distribution, and multiple application requirements for mobile users.

## CHOOSING AN ARCHITECTURE AND ACCESS METHOD

The first step in implementing wireless technology is to choose an appropriate communications architecture and access methodology. The many wireless and connectivity access methods available generally fall into three categories:

- Continuous extensions of desktop or local area network (LAN) systems.
- E-mail-based systems.
- Agent-based messaging systems.

A solution that fails to address the communications infrastructure of the wireless environment has both financial and systems implications. Although communications costs escalate dramatically with heavy system use and large numbers of users, support and resource costs increase as well.

## Continuous-Connection Architectures

A continuous-connection architecture establishes and maintains a wireless connection so that a user can perform work while online to central computing resources, such as a desktop PC or LAN-based PC. This work is accomplished through remote access and file synchronization utilities. Although there are unique variations on how these utilities are implemented, organizations generally use one of two methods: remote node or remote control.

Remote node technology makes mobile users a node on the LAN network and allows them to perform work as if they were locally logged into the LAN, albeit usually more slowly. Remote control technology allows mobile users to connect and see a virtual copy of the remote PC's screen or hard drive so that files can be accessed and applications can be run remotely.

Continuous-connection technologies offer the basic advantage of providing mobile users with access to their central LAN-based PCs and servers; the mobile computing device looks and acts as if it were the user's local desktop PC. Unfortunately, this strategy is inappropriate for the majority of large mobile implementations for several reasons:

- Most field professionals are mobile or remote all of the time. They may not need LAN resources, understand local area networks or logically redirected disk drives, or have a dedicated PC at the central site.
- Even when the complexity of establishing connections is hidden from the remote user, communication time is lengthy and communication costs are high.
- Before performing work online, the user must leave the task at hand to initiate and establish a connection.
- Continuous-connection systems do not provide for communications management or for general systems management; as a result support costs are likely to increase.

## E-mail Based Systems

E-mail based systems use E-mail as both the messaging application and as a general communications transport for other message types or transactions. The basic advantage of using E-mail as the access method for all communications is that it is a prevalent application that users understand.

However, use of E-mail as an access method for other applications is less than optimum because E-mail based systems:

- Lack integral systems management capabilities such as software distribution.
- Involve users with the information delivery process, which is not provided automatically by the application.
- Do not support applications that require queries into databases.

E-mail is clearly a popular application required by most mobile users. However, it should be considered an additional application that uses the available communications access method, rather than a communications transport or access method in and of itself.

## Agent-Based Messaging Systems

Agent-based messaging systems provide a communications architecture built on a client/server platform; a server at the central site acts as an agent on behalf of the mobile users. Software distribution, posting of forms-based data into central databases, querying of data from central databases, E-mail delivery, and many other tasks can be automated by agents capable of handling these functions on behalf of mobile users. Wireless or landline connections can be established automatically and efficiently to synchronize information between the client and the server, with all of the work (e.g., data entry to book an order) being performed offline.

Agent-based messaging systems provide many benefits in extending client/server systems to large field organizations, including

- Minimized connect times, which yields significant savings in communications costs.
- Minimized user involvement in communications.
- More efficient applications performance resulting from the tight coupling of applications with the mechanism of information delivery.
- More efficient management control of system resources and communications.
- High scalability with support for hundreds of remote users per server.
- Capability for more and different types of work (e.g., messaging and transactions) to be accomplished.

In addition to these benefits, agent-based messaging systems are also flexible enough to be used over continuous- connection technologies. For example, a user can establish a continuous connection with a central-site system and then employ the agent-based messaging software to exchange information utilizing that connection. This flexibility is not available with continuous- connection technologies such as remote LAN access.

## CHOOSING WIRELESS APPLICATIONS

The next step in implementing wireless technology involves assessing which applications provide mobile workers with the most benefits. Application requirements vary among different classes of users, who may require different products and service providers. Four basic classes of applications are discussed:

- Wireless E-mail and fax systems.
- Remote access and file synchronization utilities.
- Single- transaction based applications.
- Mobile enterprise applications.

### Wireless E-mail and Fax Systems

A survey of telecommunications and IS managers conducted by the Hartford, CT-based Yankee Group revealed that the two primary drivers behind mobile data networks are customer satisfaction and revenue generation. Similarly, a study by Link Resources Corp. revealed that wireless data solutions were implemented mainly to decrease or control costs and to attain competitive advantage.

The results of these two studies contrast with additional, significant findings from the Yankee Group study, which found that a majority of respondents believed that the greatest potential growth will occur in E-mail and fax applications. Users who believe that E-mail and fax will achieve customer satisfaction and generate revenue generally do so for three reasons:

1. Wireless E-mail systems are being marketed as the next killer application that mobile users must have for the real- time communications necessary to support continuous sales.
2. Personal productivity applications like E-mail and calendaring are believed to be as necessary to mobile users as they are to headquarters-based users.
3. E-mail is thought to be the appropriate transport for routing forms, updating databases, and performing other critical business functions.

None of these arguments holds true for most field activities. If revenue generation and customer satisfaction is the objective of wireless information exchange, then the most important wireless applications are the line-of-business transactions that generate revenue or improve customer satisfaction. These may include entering and posting sales orders to immediately secure an order, performing a query into a central data base to look up inventory status for a sales manager, or dispatching service requests to mobile field technicians.

### Remote Access and File Synchronization Utilities

Personal productivity utilities facilitating wireless remote access and file synchronization functionality are basic utilities that give the mobile user access to local hard drives on a desktop PC or on a LAN drive at corporate headquarters. Generally, the applications perform this function by providing either a wireless remote node connection to a central LAN, a remote control function to a local desktop PC, or a distributed file system that mirrors the remote drives locally and accesses remote files whenever needed. The general idea is to extend the same personal productivity applications and files found in the central office to the mobile user.

Although these utilities provide important functionality for end users temporarily away from their LAN-connected desktop systems, they do little for the requirements of large field organizations involving hundreds of mobile users who rarely, if ever, use a desktop PC. As discussed previously, wireless remote access and file synchronization systems offer solutions that scale poorly and involve high support costs and connection charges. They provide few capabilities for systems management, application management, or connect- time and communications session management — all of which are critical issues for large wireless data implementations.

### Single-Transaction Based Applications

Single-transaction based applications use wireless technology to perform one function (and sometimes a few functions) extremely well over a wireless connection. They tend to be oriented toward a large user community.

A single-transaction-based application is used, for example, by a rental car employee to enter a returning car's ID number as well as other customer information on a handheld computer that prints a receipt. Another example is a job assignment dispatch application used by an organization with a large field service operation.

To date, these types of systems have produced acceptable rates of return because the applications implemented increase customer satisfaction and generate revenue. However, single-transaction based systems are most appropriate for a small, distinct set of highly repetitive functions. Most mobile users, including salespeople, should not be limited to a single application like order entry. They need a variety of applications to help them perform many functions well. Also, unless additional functionality is custom-built into these systems, single-transaction based application systems do not address application management, update, and maintenance issues.

**Mobile Enterprise Applications**

Mobile enterprise applications provide solutions to a large mobile user community that needs to exchange information with centrally located systems and users. These applications include transaction- based applications, information distribution applications, and E-mail and messaging-based applications. For example, mobile enterprise applications for a sales force of 500 people may include order entry, inventory status checking, electronic product catalogs, electronic sales report distribution, forecasting, pipeline management, contact reporting, and E-mail. A mobile enterprise application solution could make all of these applications and more available to hundreds of mobile salespeople through a common, easy-to-use interface.

Mobile enterprise application systems provide the most utility and payback of all the wireless solutions for the following reasons:

- They allow an organization to automate within one system many key line-of-business functions that focus on increasing revenue, improving customer satisfaction, and decreasing costs.
- They provide a client/server framework in which to implement a mobile client/server system that is highly scalable because it was designed for hundreds of users.
- They allow for efficient use of land- line, LAN, and wireless networks, so that users can choose the protocol or transport most appropriate to such conditions as the time of the connection or the application type.
- They provide sophisticated application services including posting into central databases, querying from central databases, routing and sharing of transactional information, and automatic and efficient updating of messaging-based applications.

Exhibit 1 summarizes the major application issues and decision criteria that organizations should consider when choosing a wireless application solution.

## CHOOSING WIRELESS PRODUCTS

Much of the infrastructure for certain wireless technologies is either immature or under construction, and some wireless service providers require that an application be developed to a nonstandard protocol or application programming interface (API). As a result, organizations should develop a communications and applications strategy that provides the most flexibility regardless of which technologies or services ultimately gain widespread marketplace acceptance. There are two basic ways to do this:

| Wireless Issue and/or Decision Criteria | Wireless E-mail and FAX | Remote Access and File Synchronization Utilities | Single Transaction-based Applications | Tools to Build Mobile Enterprise Applications |
|---|---|---|---|---|
| Examples of software application or tool | RadioMail Wireless cc:Mail | Airsoft's AirAccess MobileWare | Oracle Mobile Agents In-house developed applications | XcelleNet RemoteWare |
| Connectivity available | Wireless focus with some landline capability. | Wireless focus with some landline capability. | Wireless focus with some landline capability. | Mixed mode supports wireless, landline and LAN. |
| System architecture | Peer-to-peer and client/server. | Peer-to-peer focus. Some client/server. | Client/server-based architecture. | Client/server-based architecture, such as client/agent/server. |
| Application focus | E-mail and fax. Messaging applications. | File transfer and remote access. | Transaction applications, typically vertical in nature. | Messaging-based, transaction-based, and info exchange applications. |
| Number of applications available | Limited to e-mail and fax | Many | A few applications | Unlimited |
| End-user profile | Knowledgeable LAN-based PC professional, which occasionally goes mobile. | Knowledgeable LAN-based PC professional, which occasionally goes mobile. | Field professionals who do not have to be computer literate and focus on a single line-of-business task. | Field professionals who do not have to be computer literate and focus on many line-of-business tasks. |

| End-user community | Single user or small department | Single-user or small department | Large field force | Large field force with potentially multiple end-user types |
|---|---|---|---|---|
| Systems management | None | Very limited | None | Comprehensive, automatic, efficient |
| Application services and management | None | Very limited | Very limited | Comprehensive, automatic, efficient |
| Connect time management | Very limited | Limited | Limited | Comprehensive and flexible |
| Sharing and workflow capabilities | E-mail only | None | Very limited | Comprehensive, messaging-based |
| Hardware platform appropriateness | Portable or pen-based computing devices, PDA's. | Portable or pen-based computing devices. | Portable pen-based or handheld devices. PDA's. | Portable or pen-based computing devices. |

The software examples provided are used to explain the types of software available. They are not meant to define exactly what a specific vendor's software may or may not do. For example, XcelleNet's RemoteWare is listed in the category of tools to build mobile enterprise applications, but it can be used to build single-transaction-based applications.

**Exhibit 1. Issues and Decision Criteria by Type of Wireless Application**

1. Use middleware APIs or developer kits to develop wireless applications.
2. Use a system for communications management that provides an interface based on a high-level graphical user interface (GUI) to set up and maintain multiple wireless technologies.

## Using Middleware APIs and Developer Kits

Some vendors offer middleware APIs that shelter organizations from having to learn how to connect over RAM, Ardis, CDPD, or analog cellular networks. By developing to the vendor's API set, organizations can choose different wireless providers or switch from one to another through a simple programming change. Vendors of middleware APIs claim to provide anywhere, any-protocol access.

The basic advantage to using middleware APIs is they allow organizations to skip the details of understanding, testing, and debugging communications. Many APIs also provide communications capabilities for landline and local area networks.

Middleware APIs also have disadvantages, some of which are:

- Many of them are not based on industry standard messaging APIs, so organizations must develop and maintain applications using a nonstandard API.
- They require organizations to program (i.e., custom build) functionality that is already available in various systems for communications management.
- Many of the companies that offer middleware APIs are new and small; their long-term stability may be less certain than that of existing wireless service providers.

## Systems for Communications Management

A system for communications management can provide an organization with support for many wireless technologies. A comprehensive system for communications management can also provide functionality in the area of systems management, software updates, file transfer, E-mail and messaging, and scheduling of tasks to take place over any of the various wireless services.

The major benefits of a system for communications management include:

- Provision of capabilities that organizations would otherwise have to develop for themselves using middleware APIs.
- Powerful functionality in the setup and maintenance of mobile users.
- The benefits of an API set or developer kit, because most systems provide interfaces and APIs.

Systems for communications management also ensure that the messaging layer on which applications are built can support future anticipated wireless services or APIs. In this way, an application can take advantage of future wireless services without additional development.

## SUMMARY

Wireless communications offer organizations the opportunity to extend the benefits of automation to hundreds of thousands of remote or mobile workers, across states and continents, who lack access to traditional dedicated networking. The technology available today simplifies the task of synchronizing information flow in the inherently unreliable dial-up and wireless communications environment. Applications that cost-effectively automate remote and mobile business processes can now be built and implemented electronically in days rather than in weeks or months. Wireless and landline information access can become transparent to the most remote and mobile activities of an organization.

Organizations that thoroughly evaluate the issues involved in choosing a wireless communications architecture and access method, wireless applications, and wireless products have taken the first step toward formulating a cost- effective strategy that generates revenue and increases customer service.

# Chapter 56

# Cellular Digital Packet Data: An Emerging Mobile Network Service

*Nathan J. Muller*

In the wireless data market, major telephone companies are implementing CDPD service to meet the needs of a mobile work force. CDPD is an appealing method of transporting data over cellular voice networks because it is flexible, fast, available internationally, compatible with a vast installed base of computers, and has security features not found in other cellular systems.

## INTRODUCTION

CDPD is a data-over-cellular standard for providing LAN-like service over cellular voice networks. CDPD employs digital modulation and signal processing techniques, but it is still an analog transmission. The CDPD infrastructure employs existing cellular systems to access a backbone router network that uses the IP to transport user data. Personal digital assistants, palmtops, and laptops running applications that use IP can connect to the CDPD service and gain access to other mobile computer users or to corporate computing resources that rely on wireline connections.

Because CDPD leverages the existing $20 billion investment in the cellular infrastructure, carriers can economically support data applications and avoid the cost of implementing a completely new network, as most competing technologies would require. CDPD also offers a transmission rate that is four times faster than most competing wide area wireless services, which are limited to 4.8K b/s or lower.

## CDPD FUNDAMENTALS

Unlike circuit-switched schemes, which use dialup modems to access the cellular network, CDPD is a packet-switched technology that relies on wireless modems to send data at a raw speed of 19.2K b/s. Although CDPD piggybacks on top of the cellular voice infrastructure, it does not suffer from the 3-KHz limit on voice transmissions. Instead, it uses the entire 30-KHz RF channel during idle times between voice calls. Using the entire channel contributes to CDPD's faster and more reliable data transmission.

### Underlying Technologies

CDPD is in fact a blend of digital data transmission, radio technology, packetization, channel hopping, and packet switching. This technology lets the cellular network carry the 1s and 0s of binary digital code more reliably than is usually possible over cellular voice networks.

**Digital Transmission Technology.** Digital transmission technology is reliable and more resistant to radio interference than analog transmission technology. The digital signals are broken down into a finite set of bits, rather than transmitted in a continuous waveform. When signal corruption occurs, error-detection logic at the receiving end can reconstruct the corrupted digital signal using error correction algorithms. Digital technology also enables processing techniques that compensate for signal fades without requiring any increase in power.

**Digital Cellular Radio Technology.** DCRT is used for transmitting data between the user's mobile unit and the carrier's base station.

**Packetization.** Packetization divides the data into discrete packets of information before transmission. This approach is commonly used in wide area and local computer networks. In addition to addressing information, each packet includes information that allows the data to be reassembled in the proper order at the receiving end and corrected if necessary.

**Channel Hopping.** Channel hopping automatically searches out idle channel times between cellular voice calls. Packets of data select available cellular channels and go out in short bursts without interfering with voice communications. Alternatively, cellular carriers may also dedicate voice channels for CDPD traffic.

**Packet Switching.** Packet switching, using the IP, accepts data packets from multiple users at many different cell sites and routes them to the next appropriate router on the network.

## APPLICATIONS FOR CDPD

The wireless-industry consortium that funded the development of the CDPD specification includes Ameritech Cellular, Bell Atlantic Mobile, Contel Cellular Inc., GTE Mobilnet, Inc., McCaw Cellular Communications, Inc., NYNEX Mobile Communications, AirTouch (formerly PacTel Cellular), and Southwestern Bell Mobile Systems. Three principles guided their efforts: that emerging CDPD recommendations could be deployed rapidly, economically, and in conjunction with technology already available in the marketplace.

More specifically, the consortium's stated objectives include:

- Ensuring compatibility with existing data networks.
- Supporting multiple network protocols.
- Exerting minimum impact on end systems; existing applications should operate with little or no modification.
- Preserving vendor independence.
- Ensuring interoperability among service providers without compromising their ability to differentiate offerings with service and feature enhancements.
- Allowing subscribers to roam between serving areas.
- Protecting subscribers from eavesdropping.

## EMERGING CLASS OF REMOTE USERS

CDPD allows traditional wireline networks to reach a new class of remote user: the roaming mobile client. With the establishment of a wireless link to the cellular carrier's CDPD network, remote users can operate their terminals as if they were located on the desktop in a branch office. Mobile workers, for example, can regain much of the productivity they lose while away being from their main offices by using CDPD to send and receive E-mail from computers or personal digital assistants.

Another application example is a debit card. Commuters could purchase a debit card to run through a card-reading device on a bus or another transit system and the fare would be deducted automatically from the card's total. That fare information could be transmitted to a central processing center in less than a second for just a few cents. CDPD could also be used by service providers to monitor and control devices such as traffic lights, alarm systems, kiosks, vending machines, and automated teller machines.

## SERVICE PRICING

As an overlay to the existing analog cellular infrastructure, CDPD networks are easy and economical for carriers to set up and operate. Carriers estimate that it costs only 5% over the initial cost of a cell site to upgrade to

**Exhibit 1. CDPD Services**

| | Per-User Pricing | |
|---|---|---|
| **Application** | **Bell Atlantic Mobile Systems** | **GTE Mobilnet** |
| Data base Inquiry | $23 to $27/month | $20 to $28/month, 25 sessions a day, 5 days a week |
| Electronic Mail | $40 to $60/month | $45 to $60/month, 14 messages a day, 5 days a week |
| Dispatch | $13 to $17/month | $10 to $20/month, 1 to 2 jobs per hour, 9 hours a day, 5 days a week |
| Alarm Monitoring | $13 to $17/month | $10 to $20/month, 1 transaction per hour, 24 hours a day, 7 days a week |
| Field Service | $23 to $27/month | $16 to $22/month, 20 transactions a day, 5 days a week |

Note: Estimated per-user prices are based on sample applications and usage figures. All prices subject to change without prior notice.

CDPD. Cell sites typically cost about $1 million to set up, including the cost of real estate.

Users are the beneficiaries of CDPD's resulting economies and efficiencies. For many applications, initial CDPD service pricing is competitive with that of the proprietary analog wireless services of ARDIS and RAM Mobile Data. Exhibit 1 indicates that CDPD is best suited for transaction-oriented applications. Although these services might prove too expensive for heavy database access, the use of intelligent agents can cut costs by minimizing connection time.

## BENEFITS TO MOBILE USERS

Because CDPD uses the existing voice-oriented cellular network and off-the-shelf hardware for implementation, it is cost-effective. There are, however, additional benefits to users besides economy. These benefits include:

- **Efficiency.** CDPD transmits both voice conversations and data messages using the same cellular equipment. Using a single device, it is a versatile and efficient way to communicate. The digital data does not disrupt or degrade voice traffic, and vice versa.
- **Speed.** Having a maximum channel speed of 19.2K b/s — a four-fold increase over competing mobile radio technologies — CDPD is the fastest wireless technology available on the WAN.
- **Security.** With encryption and authentication procedures built into the specification, CDPD offers the more robust security than any other native wireless data transmission method, preventing casual eavesdropping. As with wireline networks, users can also customize their own end-to-end security.

- **Openness.** Because CDPD is an open, nonproprietary standard, it promotes low equipment costs and broad availability of hardware and software.
- **Flexibility.** Because it uses existing cellular radio technology, CDPD units are capable of transmitting data over both packet- and circuit-switched networks, allowing applications to use the best method of communication.
- **Reliability.** Because CDPD uses existing equipment on the network (i.e., routers), as well as time-tested protocols based on TCP/IP, the highest quality of wireless data service is assured. CDPD also provides excellent penetration within buildings.
- **Worldwide Reach.** CDPD can be used in conjunction with existing cellular systems around the world. These systems already serve 85% of the world's cellular users.

Because CDPD allows the network to operate more efficiently by providing digital packet data over the voice network, carriers also realize maximum flexibility, simplified operations and maintenance, and cost savings. Carriers can offer enhanced messaging services such as multicast, cellular paging, and national short-text messaging. CDPD allows portable access to a variety of information services.

In effect, CDPD extends client/server-based applications from the LAN environment into the wireless arena. This extension provides nearly limitless possibilities for future wireless data services.

## EQUIPMENT REQUIREMENTS

CDPD is not without its problems. Even though CDPD takes advantage of the existing circuit cellular voice infrastructure to send data at up to 19.2K b/s, existing cellular modems cannot be used on CDPD-based networks. Modems designed for CDPD networks are still larger and more expensive than those designed for circuit cellular.

CDPD-only modems cost about $500; modems that handle both CDPD and circuit cellular run about $1,000. When the cost of CDPD modems drops to the $200 range, expense will no longer be a barrier. Also, carriers are considering subsidizing the cost of Cellular Digital Packet Data modems, the way they currently do with cellular phones, when users sign up for service.

## NETWORK ARCHITECTURE AND PROTOCOLS

The CDPD specification defines all the components and communications protocols necessary to support mobile communications. Exhibit 2 shows the main elements of a CDPD network.

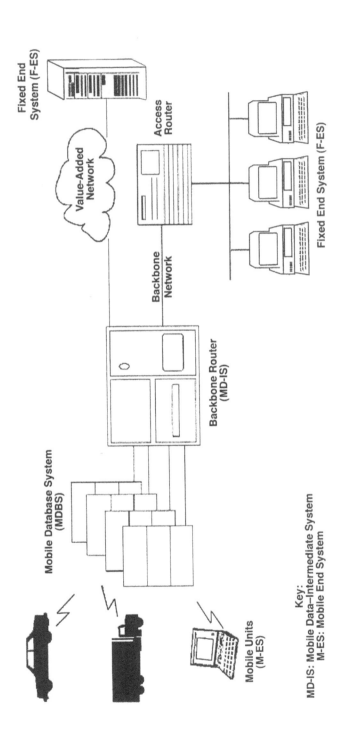

**Exhibit 2. CDPD Network Architecture.**

## Mobile Data-Intermediate Systems

The backbone router, also known as the MD-IS, uses the location information derived from the mobile network location protocol to route data to the mobile units, which are referred to as M-ES. Information on the link between the backbone router and a MDBS is transmitted using a DLL protocol. Communications on the other side of the backbone router are handled using internationally recognized protocols. This ensures that standard, off-the-shelf systems can be used in the network infrastructure and that computer systems currently in use can be accessed by CDPD networks without modification.

## Mobile Database Systems

The MDBS provides the relay between the cellular radio system and the digital data component of the CDPD network. The MDBS communicates with the mobile units through radio signals. Up to 16 mobile units in a sector can use the same cellular channel and communicate as if they were on a LAN. This communications technique is known as DSMA. After MDBS turns the cellular radio signal into digital data, it transmits the data stream to its backbone router, typically using frame relay, X.25, or the PPP.

## Mobile-End Systems

Although the physical location of a mobile-end system, or mobile unit, may change as the user's location changes, continuous network access is maintained. The CDPD specification stipulates that there will be no changes to protocols above the network layer of the seven-layer OSI model, so that applications software will operate in the CDPD environment. At the network sublayer and below, mobile units and backbone routers cooperate to allow the equipment of mobile subscribers to move transparently from cell to cell, or roam from network to network. This mobility is accomplished transparently to the network layer and above.

**OSI Protocols.** The recommendations of the CDPD consortium were designed using the OSI reference model (see Exhibit 3). The model not only provides a structure to the standardization process, it offers recommendations regarding protocols available for use in the CDPD network.

**Network Layer Protocols.** The CDPD overlay network may use either the OSI CLNP or IP at the network layer. These protocols have virtually the same functionality: They both interpret device names to route packets to remote locations.

IP has been used for more than 10 years and is one of the most popular protocols today. Its inclusion in the CDPD specification is intended to accommodate the vast number of networked devices already using it.

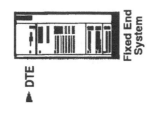

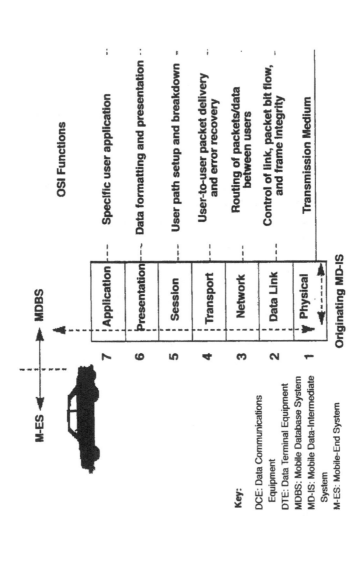

**Exhibit 3. The OSI Reference Model.**

OSI Functions

| | | |
|---|---|---|
| 7 | Application | Specific user application |
| 6 | Presentation | Data formatting and presentation |
| 5 | Session | User path setup and breakdown |
| 4 | Transport | User-to-user packet delivery and error recovery |
| 3 | Network | Routing of packets/data between users |
| 2 | Data Link | Control of link, packet bit flow, and frame integrity |
| 1 | Physical | Transmission Medium |

Originating MD-IS

Key:

DCE: Data Communications
    Equipment
DTE: Data Terminal Equipment
MDBS: Mobile Database System
MD-IS: Mobile Data-Intermediate
    System
M-ES: Mobile-End System

**Application Layer Protocols.** Applications required to administer and control CDPD networks use OSI-defined protocols. OSI-defined application-layer protocols are widely accepted and have been tested to ensure robust, open communications among CDPD service providers. The use of these protocols provides a level playing field for manufacturers of the CDPD infrastructure equipment. Therefore, service providers can be confident that the various network elements will communicate together and that no single manufacturer can exert undue influence on the market.

Examples of OSI protocols that operate at the application layer and can be implemented for CDPD network administration and control are explained as follows:

- The CMIP is the object-oriented management standard for OSI networks developed by the ISO.
- The X.400 message handling system is a global messaging standard recommended by the ITU-TSS, formerly known as the ITTCC that defines an envelope, routing, and data format for sending E-mail between dissimilar systems.
- X.500 directory services are a standard for directory services recommended by the ITU/ISO that operate across multiple networks used to convey E-mail. It allows users to look up the E-mail addresses of other users they wish to communicate with.

## MOBILITY MANAGEMENT

Traditionally, the network address of the end system has been used to determine the route used to reach that end system. CDPD is unique in allowing mobile units to roam freely, changing their subnetwork point of attachment at any time — even in midsession.

To find the best route for transmitting data to an end system, CDPD mobility management definitions describe the creation and maintenance of a location information database suitable for real-time discovery of mobile unit locations. Three network entities — the mobile units, the home backbone router, and the serving backbone router — participate in mobility management.

Mobile units are responsible for identifying their unique NEIs or network layer addresses to the CDPD network. As the mobile unit moves from cell to cell, it registers itself with the new serving backbone router. Each NEI is permanently associated with a home backbone router. The serving backbone router notifies the home backbone router of a mobile unit when it registers itself in the new serving area. Mobility management makes use of two protocols: the MNRP and the MNLP.

## MOBILE NETWORK REGISTRATION PROTOCOL

MNRP is the method mobile units use to identify themselves to the network. This information is used to notify the network of the availability of one or more NEIs at a mobile unit. The registration procedure includes the information required by the network for authenticating the user's access rights.

The MNRP is used whenever a mobile unit is initially powered up and when the mobile unit roams from cell to cell. In either case, the mobile unit automatically identifies itself to the backbone router so its location can be known at all times.

## MOBILE NETWORK LOCATION PROTOCOL

MNLP is the protocol communicated between the mobile serving function and mobile home function of the backbone routers for the support of network layer mobility. MNLP uses the information exchanged in MNRP to facilitate the exchange of location and redirection information between backbone routers, as well as the forwarding and routing of messages to roaming mobile units.

## INFORMATION PROTECTION

To facilitate the widespread acceptance of CDPD by cellular service providers, the specifications define methods for ensuring the security of customer information, while still providing an open environment for mobile users. Cellular service providers are legitimately concerned about protecting information about their subscriber base from each other, yet the nature of the service dictates that carriers exchange information with one another to provide subscribers with full mobility.

For example, when a user who is usually served by Carrier X in Chicago roams to the Carrier Z service area in Boston, Carrier Z must be able to find out whether that user is authorized to use the network. To do that, Carrier Z queries the Carrier X database about the user's access rights using the network equipment identifier. Carrier X provides a simple yes or no response. The details concerning the identity of the user, types of service the user has signed up for, rates being charged, and amount of network usage are all protected.

## CDPD NETWORK BACKBONE

The internal network connecting the backbone routers (i.e., MD-ISs) must be capable of supporting CLNP and IP. The backbone routers terminate all CDPD-specific communications with mobile units and MDBS, producing only generic IP and CLNP packets for transmission through the backbone network.

## Mobile-End Systems Protocols

As noted, the requirement that mobile units support IP is meant to ensure that existing applications software can be used in CDPD networks with little or no modification. However, new protocols below the network layer have also been designed for CDPD. These protocols fall into two categories: those required to allow the mobile unit to connect locally to an MDBS, and those required to allow the mobile unit to connect to a serving backbone router and the network at large.

Digital sense multiple access is the protocol used by the mobile unit to connect to the local MDBS. DSMA is similar to the CSMA protocol used in Ethernet. DSMA is a technique for multiple mobile units to share a single cellular frequency, much as CSMA allows multiple computers to share a single cable. The key difference between the two, apart from the data rate, is that CSMA requires the stations on the cable to act as peers contending for access to the cable in order to transmit, whereas in DSMA the MDBS acts as a referee, telling a mobile unit when its transmissions have been garbled.

A pair of protocols permit communications between the mobile unit and the backbone router. The MDLP uses MAC framing and sequence control to provide basic error detection and recovery procedures; the SNDCP provides segmentation and head compression.

In addition to segmentation and header compression for transmission efficiency, other important features of S-NDCP include encryption and mobile unit authentication. While the cellular network provides a certain amount of protection against eavesdropping because of its channel-hopping techniques, the applications expected to be used on the CDPD network require definite security — competing businesses must have the confidence that their information cannot be seen by competitors. SNDCP encryption uses the exchange of secret keys between the mobile unit and the backbone router to ensure that there can be no violation of security when transmitting over the airwaves. The authentication procedure guards against unauthorized use of a network address.

## TRANSPARENT OPERATION

Complete mobility is one of the key goals of CDPD networks. Because applications software must be able to operate over the network, the network itself must make any required operational changes transparently.

For example, the mobile units must automatically identify themselves to the network using the MNRP protocol, which recognizes the network addresses of mobile units whenever subscribers power on their computers or move to a new cell.

Data sent to a mobile unit is always sent through its home backbone router — another example of transparent operation. The home backbone router maintains an up-to-date table of the locations of the mobile units it is responsible for, thus making it possible to send connectionless data transmissions to a roaming mobile unit at any time. The home backbone router sends the data to the current serving backbone router. This scheme ensures that data reaches an end system regardless of its location, while keeping internal routing table updates to a minimum.

A connectionless service is one in which a physical connection need not be established in order to transmit data because the network is always available. In this scheme, each block of data is treated independently and contains the full destination host address. Each packet may traverse the network over a different path. A connection-oriented service, on the other hand, requires a destination address in the first packet only. Subsequent packets follow the path that has been established.

## SENDING DATA FROM A MOBILE UNIT

### Registration Procedure

Before a mobile unit can begin transmission, it enters into a dialogue, called the registration procedure, with the backbone router serving the area in which it is currently located. This dialogue identifies the mobile unit's OSI network layer address to the CDPD network. The serving backbone router tells the home backbone router responsible for that mobile unit that it is requesting service. The home backbone router authenticates the mobile unit, checking such things as the user's access rights and billing status. The registration procedure must be performed whenever the mobile unit is first powered on, or roams to a new serving backbone router.

Once the registration and authentication procedures are completed, the mobile unit begins sending data. The mobile unit is now on what appears to be a LAN connecting all such units operating within the cell of the telephone network. The LAN is really a single set of transmit and receive frequencies shared by the mobile units that access this cellular LAN using the digital sense multiple access technique.

The cells, or DSMA LANs, are interconnected by the backbone routers in much the same way that routers connect Ethernet or token ring LANs. The serving backbone router examines the data sent by the mobile units, looking for the destination address. By comparing the destination address with those in its tables, the backbone router can send the data to the appropriate destination by the best path available (see Exhibit 4). The user can now log on to the portable computer, access shared services such as CompuServe, or send information directly to other roaming mobile units. When sending data from a mobile unit to other computers, the CDPD network

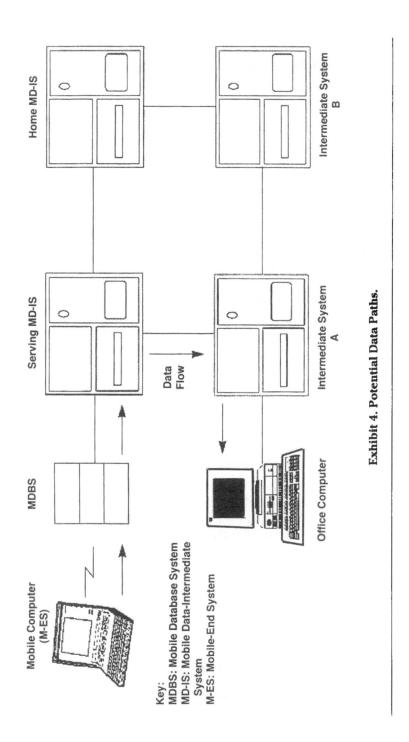

**Exhibit 4. Potential Data Paths.**

must only ensure that the user is allowed to transmit. Once the user is authenticated, data is sent in a manner similar to the way it is sent in current LAN internetworks.

### Sending Data to a Mobile Unit

On the return path, when data is sent to the mobile unit, the CDPD network must be prepared to deal with mobile units that are actively mobile — moving in a car, for example. In this case, it is likely that the mobile unit would move from one serving backbone router to another during the session. The CDPD network accommodates the roaming mobile unit by always sending its data to its home backbone router. The home backbone router always advertises itself as the destination router for the mobile units it serves.

**Redirect Procedure.** The home backbone router knows the current location of the mobile unit because of the registration procedure. When sending information to a mobile unit, the home backbone router encapsulates it into frames using the CLNP protocol and sends them to the address of the current serving backbone router. Once the data arrives at the serving backbone router, it is de-encapsulated into its original form to be sent to the mobile unit. This method of handling data trans-missions at the home backbone router is called the redirect procedure (see Exhibit 5).

The redirect procedure takes advantage of the identification done during the registration procedure. The registration procedure serves two purposes:

- To authenticate the user's access rights.
- To identify the current location of the user.

The redirect procedure uses this information to minimize network overhead. The alternative, in which all the backbone routers would update their global routing tables whenever a mobile unit moved, would saturate the network with overhead traffic. The CDPD network permits full mobility, but without imposing an undue burden on the network infrastructure.

### IS THERE A MASS MARKET FOR CDPD?

Industry analysts estimate that the wireless data market could be worth $10 billion by the year 2000, providing service to about 13 million mobile data workers. Bell Atlantic Mobile, an early provider of CDPD-based services, predicts that as much as a fifth of its cellular revenues could come from data services by the end of the decade.

The eventual availability of low-cost CDPD modems does not guarantee a mass market for CDPD. For this to happen, commonly used applications must be adapted to the technology APIs. APIs are required to optimize new

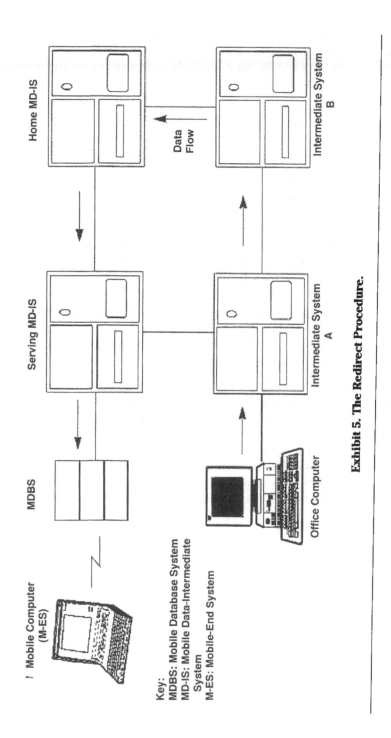

**Exhibit 5. The Redirect Procedure.**

Home MD-IS

Serving MD-IS

Intermediate System B

Intermediate System A

Data Flow

MDBS

Office Computer

Mobile Computer (M-ES)

Key:
MDBS: Mobile Database System
MD-IS: Mobile Data-Intermediate System
M-ES: Mobile-End System

and existing applications for use over relatively low-bandwidth wireless links with their high overhead and delay. After overhead is taken into account, the wireless CDPD link will top out at 14.4K b/s. The average throughput falls between 9K b/s and 12K b/s, depending on the number of errors and retransmissions.

Although CDPD is ideal for vertical niche markets such as fleet dispatch and field service, the more popular applications include E-mail, facsimile, and RDB access. Several toolkits are available to give new and existing applications the capability to run over CDPD networks.

To improve application performance over low-bandwidth wireless links, middleware that uses intelligent agents is now available that allows laptop users to query a corporate database using a software agent at the corporate site. If the user does not want to wait for a response to a query, or the connection is lost, the agent collects the information and sends it over the wireless network when the user makes the next connection.

## CONCLUSION

Mobile users who are already committed to wireless data services are among the early users of CDPD service. As the price of CDPD modems fall, coverage increases, and more applications become optimized for CDPD, the technology will have even wider appeal.

Cellular digital packet data networks are appealing because they offer seamless nationwide availability; work with the vast installed base of computers, applications, and data networks; and make use of existing private and public network infrastructures, encompassing all products and user equipment. The ultimate success of CDPD is, of course, closely tied to industry efforts to standardize its implementation. A universal standard for cellular packet data would facilitate terminal capability, allow users to roam between service areas, and simplify the introduction of wireless data services.

# Chapter 57
# Security of Wireless Local Area Networks

*Amin Leiman and Martin Miller*

Wireless networks have grown in popularity because they can be installed in hard-to-wire locations and are able to support mobile work forces. However, the increased flexibility of these systems does not come without a price. Wireless LANs are exposed to an array of security threats that differ from those that confront conventional wired LANs. This chapter focuses on the critical factors that should be considered when evaluating the security of wireless LANs, including their physical configuration, type of transmission, and service availability.

## INTRODUCTION

Wireless LANs use a NIC with a FM transceiver to link multiple workstations. External antennas can be used to provide omnidirectional transmission between workstations. Wireless LANs are implemented using any of three types of communications technology: infrared, radio frequency, and microwave. A typical wireless LAN can be connected without any cabling; in some configurations, the wireless LAN may also be connected to a wired network.

Wireless technology allows users the freedom to move (within certain boundaries) without the restrictions imposed by trailing cables. Networks can be set up without having to lay cable, which makes it much easier to implement changes in the network configuration. Indeed, the primary reason for the growth of wireless LANs has been their configuration flexibility in hard-to-wire locations and their ability to support mobile work forces. These benefits must be weighed against the fact that wireless systems can cost as much as two-and-a-half times the amount per workstation of conventional cabled networks.

This chapter examines the strengths and weaknesses of various forms of wireless networking, with special emphasis given to potential security exposures. Three critical factors must be considered in evaluating the

0-8493-9965-3/99/$0.00+$.50
© 1999 by CRC Press LLC

security of wireless LANs: their physical configurations, type of transmission, and service availability. The chapter discusses each of these factors and concludes by reviewing the controls best suited for securing wireless transmissions.

## AN OVERVIEW OF COSTS AND BENEFITS

Infrared LANs require no FCC license and are relatively secure because disruption of their required line-of-sight operation (e.g., that caused by electronic eavesdropping) will bring the LAN down. However, they use limited bandwidth, are easily disrupted (e.g., they cannot transmit through walls), and they are more expensive than conventional cabled LANs.

The radio frequency LAN does not require line-of-sight transmission, but it is easily intercepted. However, some products do provide encryption capability. Radio frequency wireless LANs require an FCC license.

The microwave transmission LAN is a technology used to bridge LANs between buildings or greater distances as an alternative to using commercial telephone lines. It is less expensive than using leased lines and is not subject to phone company rate fluctuations. However, it does require microwave and satellite dishes at both ends, which are subject to city zoning laws. As with radio frequency transmission, microwave transmission methods are subject to interception.

Wireless network technologies also share some general limitations as described in the following sections.

## INTEROPERABILITY

Interoperability is a problem with current wireless LANs. Different LANs use different technologies that are not highly compatible. For example, some vendors use the infrared part of the spectrum while others use the radio-wave band. Those that use the radio-wave band may operate at different frequencies which accounts for their different speeds. FCC regulations vary for different vendors' products. As a response to this situation, the IEEE's. The IEEE 802.11 committee is developing a standard radio frequency protocol.

Given the diversity of interests and protocols currently being developed, it is possible that no one standard will emerge. Instead, industry-specific standards may arise, such as one for retail and another for manufacturing.

## PERFORMANCE

Performance of wireless LANs has generally lagged behind that of cabled LANs. Infrared LANs operate at or below 1 Mbps. Radio frequency LANs typically run between 2M bps and 3.5M bps, well below Ethernet's published rate of 10M bps. (The actual Ethernet throughput is lower than this stated rate; the variance is therefore not as great.) Despite the difference, it is expected that wireless LANs will move to a frequency capable of boosting speeds to 16M bps, a pace highly comparable with the capacity of current cabled networks.

## CONFIGURATION

Configuration limitations restrict the use of wireless LANs. For example, infrared LANs require line-of-sight operation. Although radio LANs can transmit through walls, to be most effective they are typically kept on the same floor within a fixed area (depending on the requirements of the specific vendor equipment used). The wireless LAN may work well in one location but may not be recognized on a network in another office. The challenge is to route a microcomputer's data to the appropriate file server when the computer is continually moving.

## INDUSTRY APPLICATIONS

Wireless computing is slowly gaining broader acceptance as portables become more prominent in business settings. In addition, the development of cellular technology has led to increased interest in wireless LANs. With the growing acceptance of cellular technology, organizations have become more comfortable with the concept of processing without cables.

Often such new technologies as wireless LANs experience dynamic growth only after a unique application is introduced that is well suited to the technology. E-mail may be that application. Wireless messaging fits well with a growing work force that must be able to communicate in real time. Wireless mail networks allow mobile users to communicate wherever they are without plugging into a data port. This includes participation in mail-enabled applications specifically adapted for portable computers. Electronic wireless messaging is typically accomplished by sending a message from a network through a gateway to a local switch, transmitting by satellite, from which it is downlinked to a relay station, which in turn transmits to a stationary or mobile receiver. From here, the user can download the message to microcomputers running such mail-enabled applications as dispatch and sales systems. Although wireless E-mail is a WAN application, it is certain to influence attitudes about the use of wireless LAN processing within the office environment.

Recent developments may help spur the growth of wireless LANs. These developments include:

- Hardware and software for notebook and laptop computers that allow access to host systems over wireless networks.

- External wireless adapters that attach to a computer's parallel port, allowing even those computers with no available slots to gain wireless access.
- Cellular technology that allows the user to carry a computer from one cell to another while the software automatically seeks and finds the next adjacent cell and makes the connection to the new server, forging a link to the first server and maintaining the logical link at all times.
- The development of a wireless LAN with transmission rates of 5.7M bps, which is comparable to the speeds of many wired Ethernet LANs.
- The recent plan by the FCC to allocate 20 MHz of radio spectrum — which would not require a license — for use in wireless networks.
- Motorola's announcement that it would move to the next stage of financing Eridium, a $3.37 billion wireless global telecommunications network scheduled to begin operation in 1998.Eridium will use 66 low-earth-orbit satellites to provide subscribers wireless voice, paging, facsimile, data, and" radio-determination" satellite-locating services.

Wireless technology is being applied in such diverse settings as the airline, banking, and health-care industries. For example, a major European air carrier is using a palmtop product to check passengers remotely from the curbside and parking lot at an East Coast airport, which has resulted in shorter check-in lines. A major Midwestern commercial bank transmits customer information to its branches using spread-spectrum radio frequency LANs, which has improved customer service. And a Florida hospital is considering implementing cellular technology that would allow doctors to travel throughout the hospital with palmtop computers without losing connection to the network.

## SECURITY CONCERNS

Wireless LANs differ from hard-wired LANs in the physical and data link layers of the OSI reference model. In attacking hard-wired LANs, a perpetrator would need physical access to the communication medium either through the cables that connect the network or through the telephone closet. A wireless LAN communicates through the air; intercepting emanated signals in the air requires more sophisticated techniques.

The belief that airborne transmissions can be easily intercepted with readily available radio equipment is simplistic and misleading. Intercepting is one thing, understanding the intercepted data another. This is especially true if the data is sent in digital form. Many wireless LAN products have built-in security features specifically designed to prevent unauthorized access to signals in transit. Decrypting an encrypted signal requires vendor-supplied decryption devices and decryption keys as well as the technical expertise to use them effectively.

According to a U.S. Senate subcommittee report, the ECPA of 1986, which prohibits the interception of electronic messages, does not cover wireless data communications. The Senate Privacy and Technology Task Force report says that the ECPA "failed to anticipate" how the variety of private communications available to users would expand and how data would be carried by radio links. It recommends that the law be updated to protect most radio-based communications technology.[1]

The absence of laws protecting wireless communications has encouraged perpetrators to attempt unauthorized access to company data. As a consequence, businesses and other organizations have been wary of using this technology for sensitive applications. Currently, the use of wireless LANs in industry has been limited to nonsensitive applications. However, as users learn more about wireless LAN technology and methods for securing wireless communications, organizations should become more interested in using this technology for processing sensitive applications.

This chapter focuses on the three critical factors that should be considered when evaluating the security of a wireless LAN: physical configuration, type of transmission, and service availability. Each of these factors is related; therefore, the security specialist must have a clear understanding of all of them to fully appreciate the relevant security issues.

## Physical Configuration

From an operational point of view, use of wireless LANs gives the user more flexibility in changing the configuration of terminals. However, from the security perspective, this flexibility provides more avenues of potential attack. Intruders can intercept wireless transmissions without having to physically access the office in which the network is located. However, the ease of such access depends, in part, on how the wireless LAN is configured. For example, if designed correctly, an in-office wireless LAN should limit the range of access to the office area. On the other hand, a network designed to communicate between buildings is more susceptible to potential intruders because the range of possible interception is much wider.

But even then, the intruder's task is not a simple one. It requires being able to distinguish the target data from other data being transmitted at the same time. The intruder must also be able to decipher the signal. Although computers can be used to sort out the signal, this process requires significant effort and expense.

It is important to recognize that the coverage area in a wireless network is not defined by distance alone but by signal levels and cochannel interference as well. A wireless LAN may also be used to extend an existing hardwired LAN rather than to replace it; this may add further complexity to the overall architecture.

### Types of Transmission

As stated earlier, there are three types of wireless LAN technologies: infrared (e.g., light and laser beam), radio frequency (e.g., spread spectrum), and microwave. Each of these technologies has its own security exposures. Currently, there are three popular wireless LAN products on the market utilizing these different technologies. The BICC Communications InfraLAN uses infrared, the NCR Corp. WaveLAN uses spread spectrum, and the Motorola Altair uses microwave technology. The following sections describe the security exposures common to each technology.

**Infrared.** Infrared communications require line-of-sight transmission over a limited bandwidth. For example, InfraLAN uses an optical wavelength of 870 nanometers; its range between nodes is 80 feet. Hence, a potential intruder must be in the office within the specified range and must be in a line-of-sight path, a combination of factors that can be easily achieved only by insiders.

The use of infrared technology is not licensed by the FCC. This increases the possibility of unauthorized use and potential interference. However, this technology is also relatively secure because disruption of its line-of-sight operation (e.g., in the event of electronic eavesdropping) will bring the LAN down. In light of the limited distance between nodes and the line-of-sight requirement, infrared-based wireless LANs are considered relatively secure.

**Radio Frequency.** Although radio frequency transmissions can pass through walls and partitions, radio frequency networks must usually be kept on the same floor. Because line-of-sight transmission is not required, transmitted data can be more readily intercepted. To combat this problem, some products have incorporated encryption capabilities.

By sending data over several frequencies, spread-spectrum transmission minimizes the possibility of eavesdropping. Radio frequency-based LANs currently use frequencies in the range of 902 MHz to 928 MHz. The drawback of these frequencies is that they are also used by television, VCR extenders, and antitheft devices in stores. In the presence of such devices, the network may be disrupted. Generally, radio signal is affected by noise and interference.

WaveLAN is one product that uses spread-spectrum technology. In an open environment, it can cover a range of 800 feet, and in a semiclosed environment, it can cover a range of 250 feet. Because radio technology is well understood by many professionals, it may also be more susceptible to attempts at unauthorized access. This exposure can be mitigated by implementing such security mechanisms as encryption and access controls.

It should be noted that the IEEE 802.11 committee is trying to forge a standard radio frequency for use in network transmissions.

**Microwave.** Microwave is a communications technology used to connect LANs between buildings and over greater distances than is possible with infrared or radio frequency technologies. Altair uses microwave technology; this product is compatible with existing cable-based standards, protocols, and communication speeds, and can complement, replace, or extend such networks as token ring and Ethernet networks. One of Altair's strengths is its transparent operation with Ethernet architecture and such NOS as Novell NetWare and Microsoft LAN Manager. Altair utilizes the FCC-licensed 18GHz frequencies, and it can cover a range of 5,000 square feet. To coordinate the use of separate frequencies, Motorola has established a centralized Altair Frequency Management Center to ensure compliance with FCC regulations.

Altair provides two built-in security features: data scrambling and restricted access. The data scrambling feature scrambles data between the control module and the user module. The restricted access feature, which is incorporated into Altair's Time-Division Multiplexing architecture, allows access only to user modules whose 12-digit IEEE 802.33 Ethernet addresses have been entered into the control module's registration table.

Because microwave use is FCC-licensed and, hence, is monitored, it is considered the most secure system. As one might expect, potential intruders tend to avoid regulated environments for fear of being caught and prosecuted.

## Service Availability

For a complete understanding of the security concerns affecting wireless LANs, the concept of service availability must be understood. In a simple way, service availability can be thought of in terms of the dial tone one gets when picking up a phone — the absence of a dial tone can be the result of equipment failure, a busy circuit, or a poor signal.

Service availability can be discussed in terms of these three components: signal availability, circuit availability, and equipment availability. To tap the network using unauthorized terminal connections, the perpetrator must obtain an adequate signal, an available circuit, and the right equipment. If any of the three components of service availability is missing, access to a wireless LAN cannot be completed. However, having service availability does not automatically mean getting successful access to the network. Other factors such as network architecture and network security mechanisms affect the potential success of access attempts.

## Signal Availability

In a radio frequency system, signal availability has to do with whether there is sufficient radio energy reaching the receiver to produce an acceptable bit-error rate in the demodulated signal. In an infrared system, the receiving unit must be in the line of sight of the beam. Signal availability directly relates to distance; as a node is placed beyond the effective range, the signal becomes unavailable.

## Circuit Availability

Circuit availability usually depends on cochannel interference and adjacent channel interference. Cochannel interference occurs when two transmissions on the same carrier frequency reach a single receiver. (The ratio of the carrier to interference is called the carrier-to-interference ratio.) Adjacent channel interference occurs when energy from the modulated carrier spreads into the adjacent channels. The Motorola Frequency Management Center maintains a central database that tracks the location and frequency of each Altair module in the U.S. to lessen the possibility of interference.

One tactic of intruders is to locate the carrier frequency and purposely jam the receiver to prevent other transmissions from accessing the receiver. Wireless networks are particularly susceptible to this form of attack.

## Equipment Availability

Equipment availability refers to the availability of appropriate equipment for a particular network. In the case of wireless LANs, special equipment and connectors may be required to access the network. For example, equipment proprietary to Altair is needed to access an Altair network. Therefore, an intruder cannot use a typical scanner to access and compromise the network. In addition, this equipment must be connected to the Altair LAN by means of ThinNet T connectors with terminators, which are also unique to Altair.

## WIRELESS NETWORK CONTROLS

Security of a wireless LAN depends on two factors: protective security mechanisms and audit mechanisms. These controls are discussed in the following paragraphs.

### Protective Security Mechanisms

As identified by the ISO in its ISO-OSI Reference Model Security Guidelines, several mechanisms can be used to provide security services in a network: encryption, cryptographic error checks, source authentication, peer-to-peer authentication, and access control. In wireless LANs, encryption and access controls are the two most widely used methods of security.

**Encryption.** The three most common techniques of encryption are link, end-to-end, and application encryption. Link encryption encrypts and decrypts information at each physical link, whereas end-to-end encrypts the information throughout the network and decrypts it at the receiving location. Link encryption is more secure if the information is being transmitted by means of several physical links because multiple keys are required to decipher the information. Application encryption encrypts information at the application level. Among wireless LAN products that offer encryption, Altair uses end-to-end encryption to scramble data sent between the control module and the user module.

**Access Controls.** Access controls are used to identify network users and authorize or deny access according to prescribed guidelines. Some LAN operating systems use the workstation ID stored in NIC, which the LAN operating system checks at log-on time. Any workstation attempting to access the network without the correct ID is disconnected from the network. Another way of providing access control is by means of a user registration table. For example, Altair requires that the 12-digit Ethernet addresses of all authorized users be entered into the control module's registration table. Any user whose code has not been so entered is denied access to the network. This feature is effective in restricting potential perpetrators from gaining network access.

## Audit Mechanisms

To maintain a secure wireless LAN, a security audit should be performed in addition to ongoing monitoring activities. The security audit of a wireless LAN requires the examination of security policy, security protection mechanisms, and security administration. These areas are described in the following paragraphs.

**Security Policy.** Security policy governs the overall activities of the network. Without an effective policy, it is difficult to enforce protection. A security policy should specifically address the policy for accessing the wireless LAN. The policy should be as specific as possible. At a minimum, it should specify who is authorized to access the network, under what circumstances and what capacity, and when access is permitted. The policy should also establish the rules for moving workstations to ensure proper monitoring of each physical access point. The security manager should ensure that this policy is communicated to all network users and that it is adopted by them.

**Security Protection.** Securing a wireless LAN requires constant physical and logical protection. Physical protection involves securing the physical devices from unauthorized access. This usually requires such normal security housekeeping as providing a secure room to house the computer devices. Logical protection usually requires access controls and data encryption. It is crucial that all built-in security features be fully implemented; add-on security products (e.g., end-to-end encryption devices) should be considered as necessary.

**Security Administration.** Without proper enforcement, security policy and protective devices provide false assurance about the organization's level of information security. Therefore, it is important that one or more individuals be designated to act as a security administrator. The security administrator is responsible for ensuring that the organization's security policy is implemented and that all applicable security features are fully and correctly used. Strict enforcement of security policy and procedures is particularly important in a wireless LAN environment because of the relative ease with which users can change the composition of the network.

## CONCLUSION

To take full advantage of the benefits of wireless networks, appropriate security measures should be instituted. With the constant development of new technologies, security exposures need to be controlled in a cost-effective manner. Although customer demands influence the development of new products, they typically do not drive the development of security features for these products. It is management's responsibility to ensure that newly acquired wireless technologies are implemented in a controlled way.

In the purchase of a wireless LAN product, the quality of its security features should be carefully reviewed and tested. Because wireless LAN technology is relatively new, it is recommended that products be considered on the basis of the security mechanisms they incorporate and on the reputation of the vendor for its research and ongoing development of products. Before a wireless LAN product is purchased, the quality of its security features should be thoroughly evaluated and tested.

**Reference**

1. Betts, M., "Do Laws Protect Wireless Nets?" *Computerworld* 25, No. 24, 1991, p. 47.

# Chapter 58
# Protection of Mobile Computing Assets

*Dave Cullinane*

Now that users can access information outside the relatively safe confines of the office, information is more vulnerable than ever before. This chapter discusses how organizations can revamp security controls to protect information from the hazards imposed by mobile computing.

## KEEPING PACE WITH CHANGE

Before the advent of mobile computing, critical assets (information and equipment) were all locked inside the data center and stringent protections were imposed on them. However, as computing moved away from the data center, users moved away from the protections that they had created. Today's user is no longer tied to a desk or a terminal. Remote access is no longer dependent on telephone lines. Portable computers, cellular phones, and radio frequency (RF) modems allow work to be performed at home, at a customer site, in hotel rooms, or while flying in an airplane — literally anywhere.

The assets that need to be protected are no less critical. In fact, in today's highly competitive environment, information may be even more valuable. In some industries, biotechnology for example, information may be the single most important asset the company has. The theft of the laptop containing Desert Storm battle plans meant the loss of a few thousand dollars worth of physical assets. But the potential value of the *information* was inestimable. With the storage capacity of disks and other devices skyrocketing — a 4 GB, 5.25-inch disk contains the information equivalent of roughly 28,000 medium-size books — the potential damage from information loss is extreme.

The situation is not likely to improve. The physical size and price of systems, equipment, and parts is constantly decreasing. But capacity, performance, connectivity, and mobility are constantly increasing. The "corporate information vault" is being distributed across buildings, briefcases, and even pockets. Risks that were not considered significant in the office may be much more significant in a mobile computing environment. Controls have not kept pace with the changes. Far too many users are still trying to protect critical information and computer assets with the same controls that were put in place more than a decade ago. They are not working. Objectives must be redefined and controls revamped.

## DETERMINING THE VALUE OF INFORMATION

The function of security is to provide the appropriate level of protection for critical business assets. Organizations expend considerable resources acquiring, processing, storing, transmitting, and using information. Valuation of that information depends on the users' frame of reference and perspective. Information is an intangible asset with value that is difficult to understand and complex to assess. If exclusive possession of information — such as trade secrets, new product information, business plans and proposals, or customer records — is essential, then confidentiality is a critical element in the determination of value. Availability of information may be more essential to business continuity than security. The purpose of the information must be understood to determine what level of protection is needed. The value of the information may be $1 million, but its value to the organization, if it is made available to the sales force, for example, may be 10 times that amount.

Security professionals need to help businesses understand what the threats are to assets and how vulnerable the business is to each of those threats. Businesses must also be assisted in understanding what alternatives exist for protecting assets and what the implications are for each alternative. Then protective measures can be designed to work within the organization's objectives and culture. The security measures should be accepted by the users as reasonable and provide cost-effective protection — a return on the investment.

### Computer Security Principles

Security should not be complicated and inconvenient. If it is, it will fail, because users will circumvent the controls in the interest of accomplishing the work of the business. For security to be effective it must:

- Be pervasive; addressing not just computers, but all asset protection issues.
- Meet the businesses' requirements, not the vendors requirements.
- Be usable by everyone, not just the technically sophisticated.
- Address all equipment and protocols, including those in use today and planned for the future.

Comprehensive protection of business assets should cover:

- People, including employees, visitors, vendors, contract workers, and customers.
- Property, including buildings, campuses, and computers.
- Information, written or electronic.
- The company's business reputation.

In today's computing environment, comprehensive protection of assets is accomplished by blending the appropriate physical, operational, information, system, and network security controls.

## PROTECTING THE MOBILE OFFICE

The mobility of computing resources compromises traditional physical and logical security protections. Physical security in the building is far more important today than it was when a secure inner perimeter protected the assets housed inside the data center. Information that may have been perfectly appropriate for employees to review in their relatively secure office may be far too sensitive for use in public where the environment is unguarded at best and may even be hostile. Users have been taking confidential information outside the workplace for years, but generally in relatively small amounts. Today users can walk out the door with tens of thousands of books worth of information in a briefcase or a pocket; and the population of laptop and notebook PCs used in the office is expected to almost double by 1996.

The most important control for the protection of portable computers is an educated user. Training is essential to make users aware of the issues and their responsibilities. Users who understand the threats and their exposure to those threats, and who take appropriate measures to protect valuable computer and information assets in their possession, will go far in reducing the organization's risk. The most common threats to portable information are theft, malicious code, and eavesdropping.

### Computer Theft

Portable computers are eminently vulnerable. They disappear from parked cars, hotel rooms, private homes, and office desktops. Despite their small size, they are quite visible in airports and hotel lobbies and often conspicuous in carrying cases emblazoned with manufacturers' logos. The current street value of a 486 chip is $300. The value of a laptop complete with software is considerably higher. Stealing and reselling portable computers does not require technology genius. It is generally no more difficult than snatching a purse and much more likely to be profitable. If the information on the portable computer proves to be valuable, that is an added bonus — it can be easily transferred to diskettes and sold separately.

Protecting laptops from theft is not difficult. Users should carry an inconspicuous travel case and never leave it unattended while checking in or using the phone. A laptop should not be packed in checked luggage. It should not be left in a hotel room. If the laptop must be left, it should be locked to an immovable object or at least stored out of sight in a suitcase.

### Theft of Information

Personal computer operating systems put little or no emphasis on user access controls because they were designed for single user operation. That generally means that any information on the computer is accessible to whomever has possession of it. The degree of protection afforded the information on the computer should be commensurate with the value of that information. A quality password control software package may be sufficient. For more valuable information, a token and password system may be appropriate. For highly confidential information, a token and password system with encryption to further protect critical files may be appropriate. However, there may be export compliance issues associated with the use of encryption. Users should be protected for the worst-case scenario. If a user only occasionally has sensitive information on the laptop, appropriate controls should be consistently used for that information so the protection is adequate when it is needed.

The laptop or notebook computer will likely need to be repaired at some point, and that task will most likely be done by a third party. If the user cannot remove sensitive files before the laptop is repaired, any information that is in readable form will be vulnerable to disclosure during the repair process. This should be taken into consideration when selecting a vendor to perform the repairs.

### Malicious Code

Viruses are a very real threat. File and data contamination can render vital information unfit for use when and where it is needed. The most rigorous safe computing practices will not guarantee a clean system. Use of a quality virus protection software package is essential — particularly because most data transfer is likely to be done by diskette.

Malicious code is not the only danger to the integrity of files and data. Even simple errors can cause critical business information to be lost or inaccessible when it is needed. Critical files should be backed up. Users should carry a system diskette. Regular backups of important files should be performed, and backup media should be protected with safeguards appropriate for the information they contain.

## Eavesdropping

It is easy for another passenger on a plane or in a crowded air terminal to see what a user is doing. The potential loss from information exposure can far exceed the productivity gains from portable computing. If a user is dealing with sensitive information, it should be dealt with privately.

Similarly, the ability to communicate over phone lines and by cellular and RF modems does not mean that it is appropriate to do so. Public phone systems and the airways are not secure. If users must transmit sensitive data over public networks, encryption should be used. It is also wise for users to keep in mind that portable computers using remote login mechanisms may be broadcasting login sequences to a public audience. The information protection program should take that into account.

Similarly, passwords and other confidential access information should not be stored in command files on the PC. Many terminal emulation packages allow users to store passwords, phone numbers, and other potentially confidential information in a file. If the protections for systems or servers at an office are based on the security of a laptop s login information, that information should not be included in files that are easily read if the system is lost or stolen, or while it is being repaired. Even if a laptop does not contain confidential data, there may be information that provides the keys to other confidential data.

## SETTING SECURITY POLICY

Information security policies must address the issues of portable computing. The security requirements for portable computing should be defined — to maintain the confidentiality, integrity, and availability of information belonging to an organization, and to ensure that all users understand their responsibilities relative to the use of portable computers in the course of doing business.

The protection of portable computing and information assets relies on the same basic principles that are used for the protection of other valuable assets. Policy should set the requirements, define responsibilities, and establish accountability. Comprehensive, cost-effective protection of portable computing assets means blending the appropriate controls, including:

- **Physical.** Is the security of the building perimeter acceptable given the change in computing environment? Are there areas within the building where access should be more strictly controlled when information and valuable equipment are more distributed and accessible? Is there a need for the use of Electronic Article Surveillance (EAS) systems to protect easily transported devices?

- **Operational.** Are property controls governing the movement of valuable equipment needed? Is access to buildings and offices controlled or merely monitored through a reception or security desk?
- **Information.** Does policy stipulate what information is appropriate for use on portable computers? Have requirements been established relative to where and when to work on sensitive files?
- **System.** Are requirements established for the use of passwords, tokens, and encryption of the information?
- **Network.** Are restrictions established relative to the use of cellular and RF modems? Are dialup protections adequate? Are authentication mechanisms appropriate for the value of the information?

Users should review their environment. Risks should be assessed, vulnerabilities determined, and protections should be developed to fit within the organization's culture and objectives. Protecting portable computers and the information they contain is no different than protecting other critical assets. The proper application of security controls is all that is required.

The computing environment is changing constantly. In fact, the only constant is change. Protecting an organization's assets requires keeping up with those changes and making adjustments to controls.

# Chapter 59
# Mobile User Security

*Ralph R. Stahl, Jr.*

Information Technology Professionals today are unsure of themselves in a strange new environment. However, end users are telling security practitioners that they can no longer perform optimally and beat the competition if their access to information and processing power is restricted by the mainframes in the corporate data center.

The days when security practitioners arrived at the office to find a stack of computer printouts on their desks are gone. Paper has been replaced by computers on the desktop in the environmentally correct and secure office. In addition, users today expect to be able to connect their notebooks by modem from any location to the server at headquarters. Tomorrow, mobile users may expect connectivity for their notebooks in the air as they fly and on the ground as they drive to their next destination. The business traveler may anticipate that all applications will behave in exactly the same manner on the road as in the office.

Large companies like AT&T are encouraging employees to telecommute for three major reasons:

- State and local governments are requiring companies to take action to reduce air pollution and traffic congestion.
- Office sharing allows companies to reduce their real estate expenses.
- Telecommuting benefits employees by allowing them more flexibility in managing their professional and personal lives.

LINK Resources Corp., a New York City consulting firm, reports that Americans bought for home use a record 5.85 million microcomputers last year. One out of three American households already has a microcomputer. BIS Strategic Decisions estimates that 45 million workers in the United States are considered part of the mobile work force. Other surveys estimate that, in addition to the time spent in the office, the average white-collar worker spends six hours a week working at home.

Against this backdrop, the challenge for the application developer is to develop systems that may be used in any environment. The information architecture for the enterprise must also accommodate many methods of

0-8493-9965-3/99/$0.00+$.50
© 1999 by CRC Press LLC

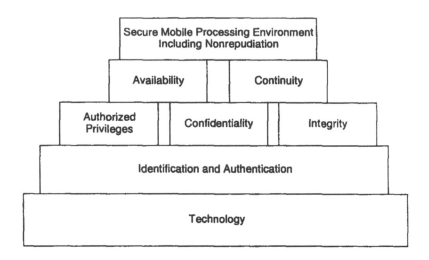

**Exhibit 1. Model of Security Services.**

remote connectivity (i.e., dial-up, Integrated Services Digital Network [ISDN], Cellular Digital Packet Data [CDPDI, Internet, wireless, video, and image transmission) in addition to the traditional local area network and wide area network connectivity.

This chapter is divided into four major sections: availability and continuity; integrity; confidentiality; and new technology considerations, which briefly reviews the security implications for some of the emerging technologies. The architectural model of the security services in Exhibit 1 provides a high- level view of the interdependence of identification and authentication, authorized privileges, availability, continuity, integrity, and confidentiality in providing a trustworthy environment that supports non-repudiation and mobile power user security.

## AVAILABILITY

In this chapter, availability is defined as the assurance that an authorized user's access to an organization's resources will not be improperly impaired. Achieving such assurance involves properly categorizing information privilege keys and ensuring that the mobile user's authorized privileges are properly associated with these privilege keys. Availability also involves physical considerations (e.g., theft prevention, device identification, mobile uninterrupted power supply), notebook connectivity (e.g., a power source, telephone communications tools), and miscellaneous toolkit necessities.

## Scheduling Considerations

Information availability is an operations scheduling issue, although some organizations believe that all availability needs are covered by their business resumption practices. The security practitioners must be aware of the need to maintain operational schedules. If the backup and batch processing is scheduled to end at a precise time so that the online or remote transaction processing may start, then the credibility of the central staff to meet their commitments to the field are tested every day. Although capacity planning is not a security issue, the complete information protection plan will make sure that the topic is adequately addressed by the appropriate operational staff members.

## Physical Considerations

Concerns associated with the desktop microcomputers in the corporate office also apply to notebooks for the mobile user. However, with respect to mobile computing, security practitioners may need to be more creative to achieve the desired results.

**Theft-Prevention Devices.** Such theft-prevention devices as cabling and bolting plates can be used to minimize the potential of notebook theft by opportunity. The cables are designed so that they may be looped through an opening in a stationary object to tie the laptop down while the user is traveling. Resistance to these devices exists because many users feel that having these devices gives the impression of not trusting coworkers or business associates. However, security administrators who use theft-prevention devices in their companies indicate that they have experienced a significant decrease in loss. Although the products are effective, corporate procedures with strong enforcement practices are usually required before these products are put into use.

**Device Identification.** Device identification is critical to the ability to identify a misplaced or stolen notebook. In addition to traditional identification methods (e.g., serial number registers, tags, labels, and engraving), microcomputers can be marked by using invisible ink to record the company's name and the notebook's serial number on the inside of the lid just under the monitor display area. The invisibly inked number must match the serial number recorded in the corporation's asset inventory register. This practice can also be used to resolve disputes associated with ownership of the microcomputer.

**Mobile Uninterrupted Power Supply.** Mobile uninterrupted power supply implies that each mobile user should have a portable surge protector with sufficient electrical outlets for each device that is connected to the microcomputer or notebook. Electricity follows the path of least resistance, and it will reach the microcomputer through any device cable if the power source for the device is not protected. Surge protector plugs are available at most hardware and electronics retailers. It is also recommended that the user carry a fully charged spare battery pack for the notebook. Usually the battery can be purchased from the dealer that sells the notebook.

## Notebook Connectivity

To ensure the notebook's power source, the electrical wall connection should be used so that the notebook's battery can be conserved or recharged. For proper grounding, the electrical code requires that all computer male plugs be three-pronged. In some facilities, the female electrical wall receptacles may accept only two-pronged male plugs. In such cases, the problem can be averted by carrying a female/male converter plug that converts three-pronged plugs to two-pronged plugs and has a grounding wire that may be attached to the wall receptacle's holding screw. This type of converter is available in hardware stores. If the user travels internationally, the toolkit must also include an international voltage adapter that eliminates the need to carry different converter plugs.

## Telephone Communications Tools

Offices and hotels are updating their telephone PBXs to digital service, but modems and the majority of the PBXs are still analog systems. To ensure connectivity in either environment, a converter should be purchased that can covert the phone line to analog at the modem connection. The complete converter kit should include alligator clips for phones that do not have RJ-11 jacks. The phone line converter requires an AC adapter as the power source; the full- functioning kit will have the capability to use a 9-volt battery when an electrical wall outlet is not available.

Data transmission may be interrupted if a phone system with call-waiting capability is used. The feature can be suspended during the data transmission call by adding *70 (occasionally #70) at the beginning of the dial string. As a general rule, this is probably not required. However, if a transmission session is interrupted for an unknown reason, call waiting may be responsible.

A miscellaneous toolkit should include the following items:

- A small screwdriver with both a flat and a Phillips head.
- An extra-long telephone cord with male RJ- 11 connectors on both ends.
- A connector with two female RJ- 11 receptacles.

## CONTINUITY

Continuity is defined in this section as the processes of preventing, mitigating, and recovering from service disruption. The terms business resumption planning, disaster recovery planning, and contingency planning may also be used in this context; they concentrate on the recovery aspects of continuity that ensure availability of the computing platform and information when needed.

Recovery diskettes will reduce the user's lost time when access to information and remote computing resources is lost due to a major breakdown of the notebook. Recovery diskettes should be customized to the exact configuration of the notebook and should contain the following files:

- DOS system files (COMMAND.COM and the two hidden files), which make the recovery diskettes bootable.
- PARTNSAV.FIL, which contains the hard drive partition table, boot sector, and CMOS information.
- CONFIG.SYS, which contains the appropriate values for files, buffers, stacks, and hard disk drivers.
- REBUILDOOM, which restores the CMOS.
- SYSCOM, which enables the transfer of the operating system to another disk.
- Copies of any special drivers that are necessary to meet the standard operational configuration of the organization's protocol stack.
- Communication programs that support emergency downloading of files and programs.

### Creating Mobile Backup

The fastest and easiest backup medium is a cassette tape; however, this represents an additional cost and bulky devices to transport. Most (if not all) mobile users want to travel as lightly as possible. The diskette then becomes the most acceptable medium, but care must be taken to minimize the number of diskettes needed.

The proper organization of the notebook's hard drive will minimize the time and number of diskettes required to create a backup. A directory called *data* can be created with all of the subdirectories necessary to easily organize, track, and access data unique to the user. Application software, databases, or operating software should not be included in the data directory. These files should be stored in other appropriately established directories. When necessary, these software and data base files may be downloaded from the office server.

The backup diskettes should be kept in a different place than the notebook. If the notebook is lost, the backup diskettes will not be lost.

### Loss of Computing Resources

Loss of computing resources as a result of the loss or theft of a notebook or its mechanical failure is the most difficult problem to deal with. The user is away from the office yet may need to repair or replace the notebook immediately, and canceling the next few days' appointments is not an acceptable option.

The recovery process requires planning and discipline on the part of the notebook's user. The data files on the notebook should be backed up regularly. If any ingredient of the business resumption plan is missing or incomplete, lengthy delays are unavoidable.

**Mechanical Failure.** When the problem is a mechanical failure, the existence and awareness (by the user) of a national maintenance agreement with a rapid response clause can ensure fast repair. The remote user should be able to easily obtain the location of the nearest repair location. This can be handled by the organization's help desk service, which should provide 24-hour accessibility. After the notebook is repaired, the user must determine if any data or application programs were lost or damaged. Lost or damaged software may be replaced by using the emergency recovery diskettes to download the needed data from the office server. Although this may be a long transmission session, it is preferable to getting on an airplane and flying back to the office. After this is accomplished, the notebook owner can restore individual files from the backup diskettes. This process may consume a full day and may require the active participation of the remote user, but after it is done, the user's machine has been restored with the least amount of lost time.

**Lost or Stolen Notebook.** When the notebook is lost or stolen, the plan must provide rapid delivery of a new notebook to the user in the field. Spare notebooks with the standard operating software, application software, master files, and current databases should be available at the data center. After a call is received to ship a backup machine, the only step necessary is to find the quickest method. Airlines and bus depots should be called to determine whether they provide shipment that is faster than that provided by the standard 24- hour service providers. After the shipment arrives, the next step is for the user to restore personal data from the separately stored backup diskettes.

If backup procedures for mobile users are to be effective, they should be tested and adjusted frequently. The recovery process may never be needed, and these procedures may be regarded as taking a lot of time. However, without such procedures, it may take the better part of a week just to obtain a replacement microcomputer. After that, it must be determined what applications and databases must be loaded. Finally, if backup procedures are not enforced, how will the user's personal information be restored to a new notebook?

## INTEGRITY

In this section, integrity is defined as the process of ensuring that the intended meaning of information is maintained. Information integrity is provided by allowing only authorized persons and processes to perform only those tasks that they are authorized to perform. Everything else is prohibited.

### Software Considerations

**Virus Protection.** Remote users are no more or no less susceptible to viruses than their office-based counterparts. Therefore, they are likely to experience a virus infection of their computer within the next few years. Proper procedures can prevent the virus from attaching itself to any of the hard drive's files. A corporate contract should be purchased for one of the leading virus detection and eradication software products. The cost can be surprisingly reasonable, in some cases less than $15 per user per year, although some very good products may be even cheaper. The secret of success is to have the detection software active in memory at all times as a terminate and stay resident (TSR) program. Some vendors can relocate the TSR so that base memory is not used at all, while other TSR programs may take as little as 5K bytes of base memory. With the detection software active in memory, the computer's user may remain passive. Many organization's detection programs have limited success because they require the user to execute a scan program to check diskettes or hard drives after disconnecting from a bulletin board. During a normal day's workload, users may often overlook this program. If TSR software is used, however, the microcomputer should lock up when it detects a virus, and it should not allow the user to proceed. The eradication or cleaning program should be run immediately to remove the virus. The remote user should be provided with a system-bootable diskette that contains a virus detection and eradication program. If additional directions are required to remove the virus, the mobile user should contact the organization's help desk for assistance.

**Notebook Configuration Integrity.** Although the name personal computer may have been appropriate at one time, today it is a misnomer because the microcomputer has become such an integral part of information processing for the business community. By personalizing the notebook to the configuration of their choice, users may cause incompatibility with their organizations' requirements.

As part of the processing infrastructure, it is important that the information technologist control the protocol layers to ensure proper connectivity, memory management, and execution of the company's processes. This is not to say that mobile users are not allowed to install some software of their choice. An example of coexistence on the microcomputer would be to control the autoexec.bat by not allowing anyone except the systems administrator to modify the file. However, the last line of the autoexec.bat is a call to an autoexec.bat that gives the user the ability to add activity to the booting process. Today, a number of client-based products exist that are designed to establish administrative control over the configuration and accessibility of directories and files on the hard drive of notebooks. These products support multiple-user confidentiality and several levels of administrators.

The content of certain directories on the hard drive should also be under the control of the systems administrator. Again, policies and guidelines should allow a section of the hard drive to be used at the discretion of the mobile user. Procedures and guidelines should clearly state the areas that may not be altered and the latitude the mobile user has to customize the microcomputer.

These same robust access control products provide complete control over the DOS computing environment. Access to printers, ports, disk drives, modems, files, and directories may be constructed so that several users of the same microcomputer may not have the same authorized use of these facilities. In addition, passive DES (or proprietary) encryption and decryption of files or directories may be established. The major vendors provide the ability to configure directories on the hard drive to be encrypted or decrypted on the fly. When a file is written to the designated directory, it is automatically encrypted. Conversely, when a file is read into memory by the authorized owner of the directory, it is automatically decrypted. This prevents unauthorized access to information even though several users may share the same microcomputer.

**Nonrepudiation.** In this section, nonrepudiation is defined as the process of ensuring that a user — either the originator or the recipient — can be identified as having engaged in a particular transaction. This facility may also be used during the normal course of business activity to identify the originator of information. Nonrepudiation involves the following procedures:

- Electronic identification of the sender is accomplished by digital signaturing. Depending on the nature of an organization's business, a choice of standards can be followed.
- Message hashing ensures that the content of the message is not altered. This is accomplished by cycle redundancy checks, which sum up a total value of the message's bits and stores that hash with the digital signature in an encrypted envelope for the message. Two major hashing algorithm standards exist: MD5, which is supported by RSA and the Internet (ANSI X930 part 2 and RFC 1321), and secure hash standard, which is supported by NIST (FIPS 180 and 180-1).
- A copy of the message (the hash) with the digital signature of the originator is sent to the message archive. Each message must have an established retention date that will vary according to the message content. The records retention policy should serve as the guide for

establishing the date. The message should be automatically removed from the archive database when this date is reached.

- Proof that the message was delivered requires an electronic acknowledgment containing the date stamp of the activity to be sent to the archive and matched to the message.
- Proof that the message was opened requires an electronic acknowledgment containing the date stamp of the activity to be sent to the archive and matched to the message.
- When the importance of a transaction dictates that nonrepudiation is required, a utility should monitor the message activity to ensure that the message was received and opened. Electronic message status should be returned to the sender for appropriate follow-up as required (e.g., to determine why the message was not received or opened).
- The trustworthy information processing infrastructure must provide assurances that the message and audit details cannot be altered.

Many business uses exist for nonrepudiation in the mobile world (e.g., purchase orders, expense statements, strategic management directives, conflict of interest forms, and other important documents) that can provide technology an opportunity to reduce today's manual administrative efforts. However, nonrepudiation does not address confidentiality of the message; this is accomplished through encryption.

**Remote Access Authentication.** After the decision is made to allow modem, Internet, CDPD, or ISDN access to the infrastructure, the risk of unauthorized access to the infrastructure increases. Call forwarding and other advances in technology have eliminated the security effectiveness of dial-back modems. The Gartner Group considers dial-back modems to have limited effectiveness.

The most effective way known to authenticate a remote user is through two-phase authentication: with something that the remote user knows and something that the remote user possesses. Another means of authentication is through the use of biometrics, which includes voiceprint, fingerprint, or retinal scan. Currently, the cost and technical problems associated with remote biometrics scans render them impractical for common use.

When selecting one of the myriad products that support two-phase authentication, the following items should be added to the functional requirements list:

- It must provide the capability for centralized administration of access system controls (e.g., personal identification numbers, passwords, alarms, use analysis), while the actual authentication platforms may be decentrally deployed.

- It must function independently from the network infrastructure. The product should be independent of modem type, BAUD rate, or any other characteristics related to transmission of data. When changes are made to the network infrastructure, the product should not require modification.
- It must function independently from the hardware infrastructure. The product must function with all hardware platforms and operating systems. When changes are made to the hardware infrastructure, the product should not require modification.
- The product must function independently from all application software. Changes to the application should not dictate changes to the product. A one- time modification to the application software may be required to request the user's identification to the product.
- It must provide a random- number challenge (algorithm) to the product making the call that is in the possession of the caller. The challenge response (one- time password) must be unique for each authentication session. This ensures that the caller has the product in his or her possession each time a call is placed.
- The product must allow encrypted data to be processed. It is not a requirement for this product to perform the encryption.
- The product must accommodate caller mobility. The caller may need to call different processors or locations that are not part of the infrastructure. In addition, the caller may want to place calls from different devices (e.g., a different microcomputer in a different location); therefore, the authentication process must be capable of being relocated.
- The product must provide magnetic and printed reports of audit trail activity. The following data should be included in the audit log: date and time for all access attempts, the line on which the call entered, entry time, disconnect time, reason for disconnect, caller associated with the call, and system violations or other unusual occurrences.
- If the product in the caller's possession fails, a backup capability should exist that will grant the requester access to the infrastructure. The backup process must be available at all times. The most economical way would be to place a call to the network help desk; the help desk will then grant one-time access on verbal authentication of the requester. This requires a process that will mitigate social engineering.
- The process device must provide controlled one-time access for some individuals (e.g., vendors or customers) that is granted by a remote authority. An example of this feature would be a one- time password generator that would relay the challenge and response over the phone. The central unit issues a random challenge number, the hand-held password generator calculates a response through an algorithm using the personal identification number of the requestor, and this

**Exhibit 2. Safe Practices for Mobile Users**

1. Be aware of the surroundings.
2. Make portable devices inconspicuous.
3. Shred confidential documents before discarding them.
4. Lock portable devices out of sight when leaving them unattended.
5. Hide physical security tokens; do not carry them in the same case with the notebook.
6. Establish a regular schedule for performing appropriated backup practices.
7. Select nontrivial passwords.
8. Change passwords frequently.
9. Follow the common-sense rule to question whether you are in an appropriate place and time to be working with the company's information assets.
10. Most important of all: treat sensitive company information as if it were the combination to your personal safe.

unique response is compared to the central unit's response for that user. If the two responses agree, then access is granted.

• It must support the establishment of alternate dial authentication hot sites when the primary site goes off line for any reason.

## CONFIDENTIALITY

Confidentiality in this section refers to the facilities by which information is protected against unauthorized reading. To facilitate establishing adequate levels of protection for information, data trustees (owners) must provide a classification to all information. This classification is based on the level of damage to the enterprise that may result from allowing individuals to gain access to information that they do not need.

### Mobile Employee Information Security Recommendations

Ensuring compliance with appropriate security procedures and practices depends not on the security tools that are provided but on the effectiveness of the security awareness program. Awareness contributes to the success of the effective information protection program. Exhibit 2 provides a baseline of awareness requirements for the mobile user. Posters in the organization's facilities are very effective and are an important part of the overall awareness program. However, use of E-mail and articles in the organization's internal communication media are more effective than posters with mobile users.

### Software Considerations

**Version Management.** If the application software or database on the notebook is not the current version, the mobile user may create and transmit incorrect data into the organization's record of reference databases. If this happens, the integrity of the databases may be damaged and inaccurate information may be given to a business partner.

Each time the mobile user connects into the organization's network servers, a process should be performed to ensure that all of the software (both application and operating system) on the mobile client is current. The same is true for all data base subsets that are mirrored on the notebook. The organizations change control process should notify the synchronization process when production environment changes are made and should have the updates available when a remote connection is made. If the notebook does not have all the current software and data base data, the infrastructure servers must not accept information uploads until the software and database are synchronized. The mobile user must recreate the information before attempting to upload using the current versions of the processing environment.

When the mobile user connects into the infrastructure and determines that a download of updates is required, the user should have an option to delay the download. The user is not allowed to upload information to the server, but queries may be made. This is important if the user is with a customer and wants to obtain status information; if a potentially lengthy download takes place, the user would waste the customer's time.

**Encryption and Decryption.** To date, encryption is the most effective security measure to ensure information confidentiality. One type of technology uses a two-part key in which the private key is kept by the owner and the public key is published. The recipient's public key is used to encrypt the data, which can only be decrypted by the recipient's private key. To reduce the computational overhead, encryption is often used to create a digital envelope that holds a DES encryption (symmetric) key and DES-encrypted data. Message nonrepudiation uses document hashing and digital signature as a means of verifying the message sender. This is accomplished by encrypting a message with the sender's private key and letting others decrypt the message with the sender's public key.

The major security concern is maintaining integrity and confidentiality of the keys. Each organization must devise a process to distribute the public keys to everyone who is involved in the encrypted messaging process, including customers and other business partners. The recommendation is to establish a comprehensive public- key data base on a central server that may be accessed by everyone (this means that it is located outside the security firewall) and to have each mobile user keep a subset of public keys on his or her notebook for major business partners.

Another concern is protecting corporate equity. Consideration must be given to the necessity for the corporation to decrypt messages when the owner of the private key is not available. One method may be to include the symmetric DES key (discussed in the previous encryption section) in an extractable format in the message archiving facility (discussed in the nonrepudiation segment). A tightly controlled process to extract the DES key would allow the message to be decrypted without compromising the private key of the originator. Right-to-privacy concerns are outweighed by corporate equity considerations, because company resources were used to create the messages.

## NEW TECHNOLOGY CONSIDERATIONS

It is important to have an appreciation for new connectivity technologies so that users may determine their potential threats and vulnerabilities. By looking at what is coming, users should be able to develop the mitigating security measures before deploying the technology. Many security concerns exist, but very few proven answers are associated with emerging technologies. However, the technologist (and to some degree the mobile user) often wants to implement the technology quickly, before the technology itself has reached commercial strength.

**PC Card.** The unified standard that combines Personal Computer Memory Card International Association (PCMCIA) standard and the Japan Electronic Industry Development Association (JEIDA) standard is called PC Card. The credit-card-sized devices take the form of memory cards, modems, and disk drives that can be plugged into slots in computers. The card's security measures should be the same as those for the hard drive. Experience indicates that many users do not take the card out of the drive when it is not in use; therefore, passive encryption is recommended. For this reason, cards may be ineffective if used as a removable security lock. The card is effectively used in several applications, most notably as a removable modem.

**Smart Cards.** Although they are the size of an ordinary credit card, smart cards use an embedded processor that gives both the system designer and the system user a powerful authentication tool. Smart cards are a subset of the rapidly growing integrated circuit card industry.

Two types of smart cards exist: contact cards and contactless cards. The contact-type interface uses an eight-position contact located at one corner of the card. A contact card reader also uses a matching set of contact points to transfer information between the card and the reader. The contactless card does not come in direct contact with the card reader, but uses an inductive power coil and transmit and receive capacitor plates to transfer information to the contactless reader. AT&T's contactless card product is essentially an 8-bit computer with a proprietary operating system and either 3K bytes or 8K bytes of user-accessible, nonvolatile memory inside the smart card.

Many applications take advantage of the strong authentication capabilities of smart cards. The most common application is electronic money.

Another example of smart-card flexibility is in a building security system protected by card access that otherwise requires a large network of cables connecting the door reader, door controllers, and host computer. By converting systems to a smart-card system and using the onboard data base and encryption capabilities, the miles of network cabling and host computer may be eliminated. However, the need for a special card reader coupled with the mobile user's desire to travel light all but eliminates the smart-card as a practical security mechanism in today's mobile arena.

**Cellular Digital Packet Data.** Cellular digital packet data (CDPD) technology is rapidly building its infrastructure right alongside the traditional analog cellular infrastructure. In fact, much of the existing analog base stations are being used. Similar to most public communications efforts, a coalition of common carriers have cooperated to ensure interoperability. CDPD was developed by a group of major cellular communications companies. This prestigious group makes it clear that by leveraging existing technologies and infrastructures, they will have a nationwide network available within a very short time.

As the caller moves from one analog cell to the next, the ability to transmit data digitally means faster transmission speeds and a solution to the current problem of lost or repeated transmission. The user will be able to send and receive data while in a moving car.

Technologists believe that because existing common protocols are used, today's applications can use CDPD without modification. The one drawback that may impede CDPD deployment is the development of effective modems that support CDPD.

Three types of CDPD services are provided. CDPD Network allows subscribers to transfer data through their applications as an extension of their internal network. In CDPD Networked Applications Services, the cellular provider provides specific application services like E-mail, directory services, and virtual terminal services to subscribers. CDPD Network Support Services provides network management, use accounting, and network security. The security practitioner should not assume that cellular carrier's security interpretation or objectives are the same as those of the organization. The carrier's direction is intended to protect its investment in the CDPD Network and principally to ensure that only authorized paying subscribers use the network. A secondary concern is providing data privacy. It is not practical for the carrier to comply with each subscriber's security policies.

The user should already be aware of the security risk associated with cellular transmissions. Cellular (analog or digital) transmission is a miniature radio station broadcasting to everyone who has the receiving equipment. Digital transmission will be able to scramble the transmission by channel hopping, which makes interception more difficult but not impossible for the motivated eavesdropper. Therefore, the best solution to maintain data integrity and confidentiality is through digital signaturing and encryption. Because of the administrative overhead associated with key management of symmetric keys (the same passphrase is used to encrypt and decrypt the message), public and private key encryption is recommended.

**Wireless Communication.** Although cellular communication is a desirable tool for mobile users, wireless communication may be a valuable capability for those roving from place to place within the confines of their own building. Wireless networking employs a number of different methods. One of the most popular of these methods is spread- spectrum radio. Wireless adapters connect into a computer either internally or through the parallel port, and they then communicate to a base-station or what could be called a wireless hub. The communication receiving area of the base station is usually several hundred feet, and the microcomputer and adapter may be placed anywhere within that radius. Other methods use a line-of-sight transmission technology.

Because the transmission takes place within the confines of the company's buildings, the security requirements may be fewer. However, depending on the organization's type of business and the need for confidentiality, consideration might be required to neutralize the motivated eavesdroppers who may be within the company or stationed outside the facility.

Other technologies use radio frequencies to forward messages to a central station, which in turn (when requested) sends the message to the recipient. This method is known as store and forward, and it is not normally used for interactive messaging. The best answer to ensure confidentiality in all wireless applications is encryption.

**The World Wide Web.** The World Wide Web (known as the Web or WWW) provides an infrastructure for accessing information. The Web provides a simple means of attaining almost any type of information that is available on a Web server that is attached to the Internet. All information on the Web is stored in pages, using a standardized hypertext language. Many companies use the Web to provide timely information to their customers. They typically provide information about products, upgrades and patches, and feedback areas. The Web is considered a companion to E-mail because it provides information by using an interface. However, the Web is designed to accommodate limited two- way communication.

Security considerations must be the same as with all other Internet connections. The Web server should be placed outside of the firewall. If confidential information is placed on the Web, then encryption should be used.

**Exhibit 3. Breakdown
of Mobile Work Force**

| | |
|---|---|
| 26% | Sales |
| 23% | Field Services |
| 18% | Administrative |
| 15% | Field Engineering |
| 10% | Senior Management |
| 8% | Other |

1997 Projections by The Yankee Group

In general, the Web architecture does not provide for the integrity and confidentiality of information. Access to the infrastructure should not be allowed through the Web server.

## SUMMARY

Security procedures, guidelines, and practices accepted by end users must enable them to do their jobs. If end users interpret security to be a roadblock, they will often find ways to circumvent security requirements. To ensure that this does not happen, the security practitioner should spend time learning the problems and security concerns of users. The practitioner should consider scheduling one day per month to stay at home and telecommute in addition to dialing in while on business trips. This practice enhances understanding of the remote access conditions, and assists the security practitioner in developing more effective security practices. Exhibit 3, published by the Yankee Group, provides a breakdown of the professions that make up the mobile community.

Information today is stored not only in the data center but also on desktops, notebooks, and home computers; it is stored wherever mobile users have taken the data. By understanding the implications of this fact of business life, practices can be better established to secure assets while supporting employees' requirements to perform optimally and competitively through having access to the most current information and computing power.

# Section VIII

# Implementation and Case Studies

We can significantly reduce the time and effort required to install a new network or revise an existing network by learning from others that have literally "been there, done that." Recognizing the value of experience, the focus of this section is upon chapters oriented towards network implementation and case studies.

The first chapter in this section, "Integrating Electronic Messaging Systems and Infrastructures," provides us with detailed information covering the roll-out of a messaging capability for an organization entity ranging from a single department to multiple departments. In this section we will examine resources required for a successful roll-out as well as several implementation scenarios that illustrate the use of different approaches to a roll-out.

Turning our attention to TCP/IP, the second chapter in this section provides a case study concerning its management. In the chapter titled "TCP/IP Network Management: A Case Study" we will note the criteria employed by a large organization establishing a new TCP/IP internetwork supporting satellite and terrestrial-based data transmission. This chapter takes us through the implementation process from defining requirements to identifying essential functions that become the key for an implementation strategy.

The third chapter in this section, "Integrating Voice and LAN Infrastructures and Applications," provides us with a road map concerning problems we should address to successfully integrate voice on a LAN. After discussing the major problems associated with the transmission of voice traffic over a LAN, this chapter reviews the use of different network and desktop technologies as a basis for developing several recommendations concerning the implementation of a voice LAN capability.

Two additional chapters in this section continue our examination of LAN related implementations. The fourth chapter in this section, "Creating Network Expressways Using Ethernet Switching Engines," illustrates the use of

Ethernet switches to enhance network performance. This chapter first provides a detailed look into the technology associated with different types of Ethernet switches. Using this information as a base, the chapter then illustrates the use of a switch in a university environment which both reduced network congestion and significantly enhanced network throughput. In concluding our series of chapters focused on LANs, the chapter titled "Remote LAN/WAN Connections: A Case Study" takes us on a tour of the issues that must be resolved to obtain an efficient and effective internetworking capability. In this chapter we will examine the evaluation of LAN connectivity methods ranging from fiber optic and microwave to infrared that were explored by a company when employees were relocated at a corporate location. This chapter walks us through the company's decision-making process and illustrates both the factors they weighed and their cost computations performed in developing a solution to their network expansion requirement.

Having completed our review of LAN-related implementations, the sixth chapter, "Considerations for Implementing Corporate Internets," turns our attention to the issues involved in the deployment of Internet technologies on a private network. In this chapter we will examine the network and server management issues associated with moving Internet technologies onto a private network. This chapter will acquaint us with "Fat" and "Thin" clients, Java-enabled browsers, applets, Active X, scripting languages, and other Internet technologies for which an understanding is necessary in order to appropriately plan for implementing an Intranet.

Due to the steep decline in the cost of digital cameras, many networks are integrating pictures of personnel, buildings, and objects onto Web pages, as attachments to email, and in visual databases. This proliferation in the use of images can have a profound effect upon the performance of a network, and is the focus of the seventh chapter in this section. This chapter, "Minimizing the Effect of Digital Camera Images on Networks," first provides us with an overview of how digital cameras operate and the fundamentals of image resolution. Using this information as a base, this chapter illustrates the effect of image compression upon both image storage and transmission and covers the use of options associated with a popular digital camera which makes network based images more effective. Thus, this chapter should assist us in determining how to effectively and efficiently implement images into equipment connected to a network.

In the eighth chapter in this section we turn our attention to the enterprise. In the chapter titled "Planning, Designing, and Optimization of Enterprise Networks," we first examine the network planning and design effort by looking at the distinct tasks associated with the planning and design effort. Once those tasks are identified, the chapter provides us with examples of how to accomplish each task and presents a case study which illustrates the planning and design effort. This case study illustrates the modeling effort required to develop an optimized enterprise network.

In concluding this section we will examine the integration of two wide area networks which resulted in the ability of over 17,000 end users to obtain interoperability. This chapter, "WAN Network Integration: A Case Study," first provides us with background information concerning the operations of two United States Federal agencies. Next, we are provided with information concerning the existing network infrastructure of each agency and their requirements concerning LAN operating systems, workstations hardware and routers. Using this information, this case study examines the cost of different equipment upgrades, and has developed a methodology that is applied to support the WAN integration process. Completing the presentation of this case study is a summary section which reviews key issues that warrant consideration by network managers and LAN administrators regardless of the type of network you are considering for integration.

Chapter 60

# Integrating Electronic Messaging Systems and Infrastructures

*Dale Cohen*

As a company grows and changes computing systems, the job of implementing a messaging system turns from installing and maintaining software to integrating, fine-tuning, and measuring a series of systems — in other words, managing an ongoing project. For organizations integrating multiple E-mail systems, this chapter discusses the goals of a rollout and gives sample implementation scenarios.

**PROBLEMS ADDRESSED**

Implementing a messaging system infrastructure requires taking small steps while keeping the big picture in mind. The complexity of the endeavor is directly affected by the scope of the project.

If implementing messaging for a single department or a small single enterprise, a vendor solution can probably be used. All users will have the same desktop application with one message server or post office from that same application vendor.

By contrast, integrating multiple departments may require proprietary software routers for connecting similar systems. When building an infrastructure for a single enterprise, the IT department may incorporate the multiple-department approach for similar systems. Dissimilar systems can be connected using software and hardware gateways.

If the goal is to implement an integrated system for a larger enterprise, multiple departments may need to communicate with their external customers and suppliers. The solution could implement a messaging backbone or central messaging switch. This approach allows the implementers to deploy common points to sort, disperse, and measure the flow of messages.

If an organization already has an infrastructure but needs to distribute it across multiple systems connected by common protocols, the goal may be to make the aggregate system more manageable and gain economies of scale. Implementations can vary widely, from getting something up and running to reducing the effort and expense of running the current system.

## HOW TO ACCOMPLISH ROLLOUT AND MANAGE CONSTRAINTS

Messaging is a unique application because it crosses all the networks, hardware platforms, network operating systems, and application environments in the organization. Plenty of cooperation will be necessary to accomplish a successful rollout. The traditional constraints are time, functionality, and resources, though implementers must also manage user perceptions.

### Resource Constraints: Financial

In an international organization of 5,000 or more users, it is not unreasonable to spend $200,000 to $500,000 on the backbone services necessary to achieve a solution. The total cost — including network components, new desktop devices, ongoing administration, maintenance, and end-user support — can easily exceed $2,500 per user, with incremental costs for the E-mail add-on at $300 to $500 per year.

The initial appeal of offerings from Lotus Development Corp., Novell Inc.,and Microsoft Corp. is that a component can be added at a low incremental cost. In reality, the aggregate incremental costs are huge, although most of the purchaser's costs are hidden. For a corporate PC to handle E-mail, the corporatewide and local area networks and support organizations must be industrial strength.

Although this investment may at first glance seem prohibitively high, it allows for add-ons such as Web browsers or client/server applications at a much lower startup cost. Vendors argue that they make it possible for the buyer to start small and grow. It is more likely that an organization will start small, grow significantly, and grow its application base incrementally. In the long run, the investment pays for itself repeatedly, not only for the benefits E-mail provides but for the opportunities the foray offers.

### Resource Constraints: Expertise

It is easy to underestimate the expertise required to operate an efficient messaging infrastructure. Most IT departments are easily able to handle a single application in a single operating environment. Multiple applications in multiple operating environments are a different story.

Messaging systems must be able to deal with multiple network protocols, various operating systems, and different software applications — all from different vendors. Given these facts, it is difficult to understand why already overburdened LAN administrators would take on the significant systems integration responsibilities of a messaging system rollout.

When confronted with problems during a messaging system integration, the staff must be able to answer the following questions:

- Is it a network problem or an application issue?
- Is it an operating system–configured value or an application bug?
- Can the problem be handled by someone with general expertise, such as a front-line technician or a support desk staff member?

**Skill Sets.** Individuals performing the rollout must be technically adept, have strong diagnostic skills, and understand how to work in a team environment. They must be adept with multiple operating systems and understand the basics of multiple networks. Ideally, they understand the difference between a technical answer and one that solves the business issue at large.

Many organizations make the mistake of assigning first-tier support staff to an E-mail project when systems integrators are called for. The leanest integration team consists of individuals with an understanding of networks and their underlying protocols, operating systems, and two or more E-mail applications. Data base knowledge is very useful when dealing with directories and directory synchronization. A knowledge of tool development helps automate manual processes. Application monitoring should occur alongside network monitoring because nothing signals a network error as well as an E-mail service interruption.

**Cross-functional Integration Teams.** The most efficient way to coordinate a rollout is through cross-functional teams. It is important to incorporate E-mail implementation and support into the goals of the individuals and the teams from which they come. Many organizations do this informally, but this method is not always effective. A written goal or service level agreement is extremely helpful when conflicting priorities arise and management support is needed.

When creating the core messaging integration team, it is very helpful to include individuals from WAN and LAN networking, systems, operations, and support desk staff, in addition to the individual application experts from each E-mail environment.

## Functionality and Scope

At any point in the project, network administrators may find themselves trying to implement an enterprisewide solution, a new departmental system, a corporatewide directory service, or a solution for mobile E-mail users. When building a house, it is commonly understood that the plumbing and waste systems must be installed before hooking up the bath fixtures. This is not the case with messaging.

A messaging system rollout should start with a basic infrastructure "plumbed" for future expansion, and be followed directly with reliable user functionality. Results should be monitored and measured, and original infrastructure issues should be revisited as appropriate. Project success comes with regular reports on what has been delivered and discussions of incremental improvements in reliability and services.

### Supporting Internal and External Customers

No matter how good the features of any product or set of products, if the system is not reliable, people cannot depend on it. If the system is perceived as unreliable, people will use alternative forms of communication.

To satisfy user needs, the IT department should separate internal customers from external customers. Internal customers are those that help provide a service. They may be IT management, support personnel, or networking staff — they could be considered an internal supplier.

Because of the nature of most organizations, internal customers are both customer and supplier. They need to be provided with the means to supply a service. For example, IT management may need to create step-by-step procedures for the operations staff to carry them out. If the information technology group cannot satisfy the requirements of internal customers, it probably will not be able to satisfy the needs of external customers.

External customers are the end users. If they are in sales, for example, external customers may include the enterprise's customers from other companies. It is the job of the IT staff to provide external customers with messaging features, functionality, and reliability so they can do their job.

## IMPLEMENTATION MODELS AND ARCHITECTURES

It is helpful for network managers to know how other enterprises have implemented messaging systems. The next few sections describe the various components of the infrastructure, common deployment architectures, and how to plan future deployments.

### Infrastructure vs. Interface

Often messaging systems are sold with the emphasis on what the end user sees. Experienced network managers know that this is the least of their problems. The behind-the-scenes components, which make the individual systems in an organization work as a near-seamless whole, include:

- Network services.
- Message transfer services.
- Directory services.
- Management and administration services.

**Network Services.** The network services required for a messaging rollout involve connectivity between:

- Desktop and server.
- Server to server.
- Server to gateway.
- Gateway to foreign environment.

It is not unusual to have one network protocol between a desktop device and its server and a second protocol within the backbone server/gateway/router environment. Servers may communicate via WAN protocols such as TCP/IP, OSI, DECnet, or SNA, and the desktops may communicate over a LAN protocol such as IPX or NetBIOS. WAN connections may occur over continuous connections or over asynchronous dialup methods.

The network administrator's greatest concern is loss of network connectivity. It is important to understand how it happens, why it happens, how it is discovered, and what needs to be done on an application level once connectivity is restored.

If the network goes down, E-mail will be faulted. Weekly incident reports should be issued that cite direct incidents (i.e., an E-mail component failure) and indirect incidents (i.e., a network failure) as well as remote site issues(i.e., a remote site lost power). Such information can help to clarify the real problem.

**Message Transfer Services.** The message transfer service (also termed the message transport system) is the most visible part of the messaging infrastructure. The message transfer service is responsible for moving a message from point A to point B. This service consists of one or more message transport agents and may be extended to include gateways and routers. The most popular services are X.400 and SMTP international standards, and IBM's SNA Distributed Services (SNADS) and Novell's Message Handling Service (MHS) proprietary industry standards.

**X.400.** More widely used in Europe than in North America, X.400 is popular because it:

- Provides universal connectivity.
- Has a standard way of mapping features.
- Is usually run over commercial WANs so it does not have the security problems associated with the Internet.

**SMTP.** Simple Mail Transfer Protocol's allure is its simplicity. Addressing is easier and access to the Internet is relatively simple compared with establishing an X.400 connection. Because it is simple, there is not much that can go wrong. However, when something does go wrong, it is usually monumental.

**Directory Services.** The directory service is critical to a company's E-mail systems, but it is also problematic. The problems are a result of the difficulty in keeping directories up-to-date, resolving redundant or obsolete auto-registered entries, and failures of directory synchronization.

The directory serves both users and applications. End users choose potential recipients from a directory. The directory should list enough information for a user to distinguish between the George Smith in accounting and the George Smith in engineering. Some companies include in their directory individuals who are customers and suppliers. The ability to distinguish between internal users and external users is even more important in these cases.

**Management and Administration Services.** Management refers to scheduled maintenance and automated housekeeping procedures that involve system-related tasks such as reconfiguration and file maintenance. The constant I/O on messaging components leads to disk and sometimes memory fragmentation. Regular defragmentation procedures, including repro/reorg, tidy procedures, and checkstat and reclaim, are required. Whatever the environment, such procedures should be done more often than is recommended to prevent problems from occurring.

**Alerts and Alarms.** Alerts and alarms are extremely helpful because the system can tell the user if there is a potential problem. Alerts generally refer to warnings such as "too many messages in queue awaiting delivery." Alarms are a sign of a more serious problem, such as a disk full condition.

**Mail Monitoring.** Mail monitoring is typically an administrative function. One way of monitoring a system is to send a probe addressed to an invalid user on a target system. On many systems, the target system will reject the message with a "no such addressee" non-delivery message. When the initiating system receives this message, it indicates that mail flow is active.

Timing the round-trip provides a window to overall system performance. A message that does not return in a pre-established timeframe is considered overdue and is cause for further investigation.

**Reporting.** Reporting is used for capacity planning, measuring throughput and performance, chargeback, and statistical gathering. At initial implementation, network administrators will generally want to report

**Exhibit 1. Implementation Scenarios**

| | Enterprise | |
|---|---|---|
| | **Single** | **Multiple** |
| Single Department | One-Tier Single System | Two-Tier Similar Systems |
| Multiple Departments | Two-Tier Dissimilar Systems | Three-Tier Cross-Enterprise Systems |

breadth of coverage to demonstrate the reach of the infrastructure. Breadth can be measured by counting users and the number of messaging systems within each messaging environment.

Performance can be measured by reporting the volume — the average number of messages delivered per hour, or messages in each hour over a 24-hour period. This measure can be divided further by indicating the type of message (i.e., text only, single/double attachments, read receipts). This information gives network managers a measurable indication of the kind of features the user community requires.

For network planning purposes, it may be useful to measure volume or "system pressure," ignoring the number of messages sent and focusing on the number of total gigabytes sent per day.

## IMPLEMENTATION SCENARIOS: A TIERED APPROACH

Manufacturing environments have long used a tiered approach to messaging for distributing the workload of factory floor applications. As environments become more complex, the tiered approach offers additional flexibility.

An entire enterprise can be considered a single department, indicating the need for a one-tier system where clients are tied into a single server or post office. Multiple departments in a single enterprise or a single department communicating with multiple enterprises require routers and gateways to communicate with the world outside. When multiple departments need to communicate with each other and with multiple enterprises, a messaging backbone or messaging switch is called for.

Exhibit 1 summarizes the implementation scenarios discussed in this chapter.

### One-Tier Messaging Model

A single department in a single enterprise will most likely deploy a one-tier messaging model. This model consists of a single messaging server or post office that provides all services. It may be as large as an OfficeVision system on a mainframe or a Higgins PostOffice on a Compaq file server running NetWare. The department need only concern itself with following corporate guidelines for networking and any naming standards.

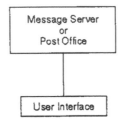

**Exhibit 2. One-tier Model.**

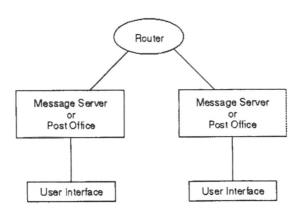

**Exhibit 3. Two-tier Model.**

Caution should be observed when using corporate guidelines. It is often simple to apply mainframe conventions when standardizing PC LAN-based applications. Many large organizations tend to forget that the whole reason for deploying desktop computers is to move away from mainframe conventions (e.g., 8-character user IDs) that are nonintuitive for users. Exhibit 2 shows a typical one-tier model within a single department of an enterprise.

### Two-Tier Model: Multiple Servers

As the number of E-mail users grows, or multiple departments need to be connected, an organization will probably deploy multiple servers. This two-tier model can consist of integrating similar messaging systems from the same vendor or from different vendors. Exhibit 3 illustrates a connection between two departments using the same vendor software connected via application routers.

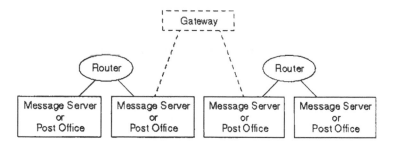

**Exhibit 4. Using Application Gateways.**

In a typical PC LAN environment using a shared-file system such as cc:Mail or Microsoft Mail, the router acts the same way as the PC. The post office is completely passive. When users send messages, their workstations simply copy the message to the file server as an individual file or as an insertion into a file server database. In either case the PC workstation actually does the work — the post office simply serves as a shared disk drive. The router is also an active component, but has no user moving messages. It periodically moves messages from one post office to another without user interaction.

## Application Gateways for Integrating Dissimilar Systems

Many enterprises have different departments that have chosen their own E-mail systems without a common corporate standard. To integrate dissimilar systems, application gateways can bridge the technical incompatibilities between the various messaging servers (see Exhibit 4).

A simple gateway can translate cc:Mail messages to GroupWise. A more complex gateway can bridge networks (e.g., Ethernet to Token Ring), network protocols(i.e., NetWare to TCP/IP), and the E-mail applications.

Converting one E-mail message to the format of another requires a lot of translation. Document formats (i.e., DCA RFT to ASCII), addressing formats(i.e., user@workgroup@domain to system:user), and message options (i.e., acknowledgments to read or deliver receipts) must all be translated.

Gateways can emulate routers native to each environment. They perform message translations internally. The alternative to this approach is to place the gateway between the routers as opposed to between the post office — this is not an end-user design, it is merely a function of the vendor software (see Exhibit 5).

If an enterprise is large, network administrators may want to make use of economies of scale to handle common administration, common gateways to X.400, and Internet networks. The network administration staff

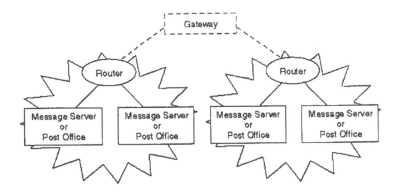

**Exhibit 5. Placing a Gateway Between Routers.**

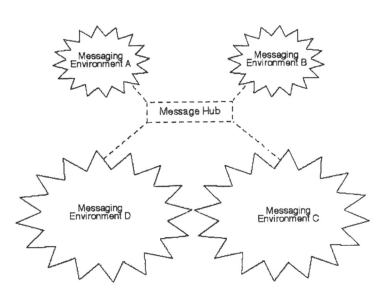

**Exhibit 6. A Central Switching Hub.**

may simply need points in its network where it can measure progress. Gateways from each environment to every other environment can be provided, but this solution becomes costly and difficult to maintain. A better approach would be to use a central switching hub or a distributed backbone, as shown in Exhibit 6.

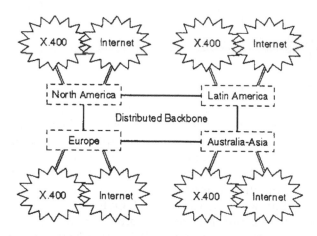

**Exhibit 7. Worldwide Distributed Hubs.**

## Distributed Hubs

The central switch or hub allows for a single path for each messaging environment to communicate with all other messaging environments. The central hub, if it is relatively inexpensive, can be expanded into the distributed model. This is often done as the aggregate system grows and requires additional performance and capacity.

However, this implementation can be taken to an extreme, as seen by the number of companies that have grown PC LAN/shared file systems beyond their original design. It is inexpensive to grow these systems incrementally, but difficult to provide end-to-end reliability. Most organizations plug the technical gaps in these products with the additional permanent and contract personnel to keep the multitude of routers and shared-file system post offices up and running.

Some organizations have taken this distributed hub approach to the point where they have multiple connections to the Internet and the X.400 world (see Exhibit 7). Some organizations offer the single message switch for their global environment, and their messages are more well traveled than their administrators. A message sent from Brussels to Paris may stop in Los Angeles on the way because of the central switching mechanism. In addition to local switching, the distributed hub allows for redundancy.

## THREE DEPLOYMENT ARCHITECTURES AND OPTIONS

Most companies deploy E-mail systems using variations of three architectures: a common platform, where all E-mail systems are identical; a multiple backbone where each E-mail environment has its own gateways; or a common backbone where all systems share common resources. The following sections describe these architectures along with the advantages and disadvantages of each.

### Common Platform Architecture

For years, a major automotive manufacturer delayed PC LAN E-mail deployment in deference to the purported needs of the traveling executive. Senior managers wanted to be able to walk up to any company computer terminal, workstation, or personal computer anywhere in the world and know that they would be able to access their E-mail in the same manner. This implies a common look and feel to the application across platforms as well as common network access to the E-mail server. In this company's case, PROFS (OfficeVision/VM) was accessible through 3270 terminal emulators on various platforms. As long as SNA network access remained available, E-mail appeared the same worldwide. This IBM mainframe shop had few problems implementing this model.

The common platform model is not unique to IBM mainframe environments. Another manufacturer used the same technique with its DEC ALL-IN-1 environment distributed across multiple VAX hosts. As long as a DECnet network or dialup access was available, users could reach their home systems. The upside of this approach is that an individual's E-mail files are stored centrally, allowing for a single retrieval point. The downside was that the user had to be connected to process E-mail and was unable to work offline.

This strategy is not limited to mainframe and minicomputer models. A number of companies have standardized on Lotus Notes, Microsoft Mail, or Novell's GroupWise. None of these products are truly ready for large-scale deployment without IT and network staffs having to plug the technical gaps.

### Multiple Backbone Model

The multiple backbone model assumes that an organization integrates its E-mail systems as though it were multiple smaller companies. The OfficeVision/VM system may connect via Advantis to reach the Internet and X.400 world. The cc:Mail WAN may have an SMTP gateway for access to the Internet and an ISOCOR MTA for access to the Message Router/X.400 gateway. All the various E-mail environments may have a proprietary Soft*Switch gateway for access to the IBM/MVS host so that everyone who needs to can access their OfficeVision/400systems (see Exhibit 8).

On the surface, this hodgepodge of point-to-point connections may seem a bit unwieldy, but it does have advantages. Users of cc:Mail can

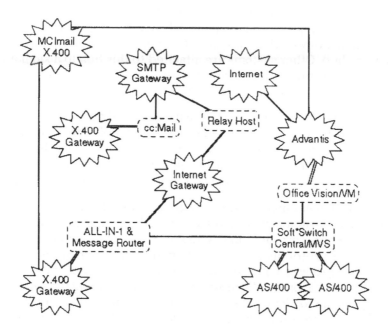

**Exhibit 8. The Multiple Backbone Model.**

address Internet E-mail users by filling out an SMTP template rather than waiting until the cc:Mail administrator adds recipients to the cc:Mail directory. OfficeVision/VM users can fill out a simple address block within the text of their message to reach an Internet user. AS/400 users can send mail to an application that forwards the message on their behalf. The trouble occurs when the recipients of the AS/400 users try to reply — they end up replying to the application that forwarded the message rather than the original sender, or originator, of the message.

This architecture may still work. If each E-mail environment had its own gateway, network administration could offer multiple connections to the Internet.

## Common Backbone

The common backbone takes two forms:

1. A central E-mail hub or message switch on a single system that serves as the common denominator among all E-mail environments.
2. A distributed model where all backbone components run a common software protocol.

The common hub involves a single switch that serves the users' applications, thus serving their needs indirectly. Each E-mail environment has an application gateway that converts its environmental format to that of the common hub. Other systems are attached to this hub in a similar manner. Messages destined for dissimilar environments all pass through this central point to be sorted and delivered to their final destinations.

The distributed backbone takes the central hub and replaces it with two or more systems sharing a common application protocol. This solution offers the ability to deploy two or more less expensive systems rather than a single, more expensive system. Any system connected to any point in the backbone can use any other service (e.g., gateway) connected to that same backbone.

Network managers may decide to purchase a single hub and gradually add systems to form a distributed backbone. Should you decide to use a common backbone protocol like X.400 or SMTP, there is an advantage. Because these protocols are available from a number of vendors, the cc:Mail/X.400 gateway could connect to an X.400 system running in an HP9000, DEC/Alpha, or Intel/Pentium system — all running the same protocols. It is possible to change distributed servers without having to change the gateways to these servers. Exhibit 9 illustrates three-tier flexibility.

A third approach is to use one central server or a distributed backbone of similar systems. In the central server/central hub approach all, E-mail environments use application gateways to connect to the central switch. There they are routed to their target environment.

Two-tier models may seem most convenient because they can use the offerings of a single vendor. One problem is that the system must use that vendor's protocols for a long time. Three tiers allow the layers in the model to be changed, which allows for ease of transition.

Under most application scenarios, changing one component of the messaging environment entails changing all the pieces and parts with which it is associated. It may be necessary to provide adequate support staff and end-user training or hire consultants to handle the need for temporary staff during the transition — a significant business disruption.

For example, in one environment, users have Microsoft Mail on their desktops and a traditional MSmail post office is used, as well as message transfer agents (MTAs), to route mail between post offices. The engineering department uses OpenMail. The IT group would like to begin consolidating systems. With minor changes to the desktop, IT can retain the Microsoft Mail user interface, remove the back-end infrastructure, and use the same OpenMail system as the OpenMail desktop users by consolidating the second tier and simplifying the support environment. The client changes

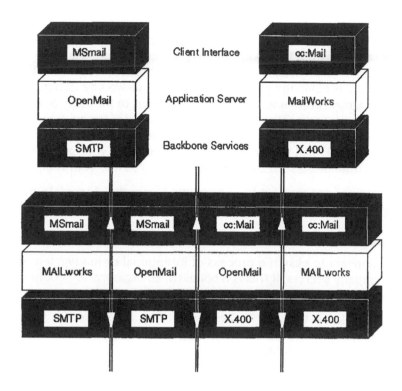

**Exhibit 9. Three-tier Flexibility.**

somewhat because it is using a different directory server and message store, but it appears as a minor upgrade to the users — no significant training is necessary.

Likewise, IT can change the back end and still allow the OpenMail systems to communicate with the MAILworks and ALL-IN-1 systems without locking into a single vendor solution. This is a feasible option. Today, users can plug an MSmail client into a MAILworks or OpenMail server. Novell recently announced the ability to plug a cc:Mail or MSmail client into its GroupWise XTD server. A Microsoft Exchange client plugs into various servers, and Lotus's cc:Mail can plug into anything.

## ESTABLISHING MESSAGING POLICIES AND PROCEDURES

An organization can prevent misunderstandings, conflicts, and even litigation if it publishes its policies and procedures for messaging applications at the outset. Most important are privacy and confidentiality.

## Privacy

A privacy policy serves two purposes: to properly inform employees that their messages may not be private and to protect the organization from legal liability. Most organizations create a policy that cautions users as follows: All electronic data is company property and may be viewed by designated personnel to diagnose problems, monitor performance, or for other purposes as the company deems necessary. While you normally type a password to access your E-mail and you may feel that your messages are private, this is not the case. The E-mail you create, read, or send is not your property nor is it protected from being seen by those other than you and your recipients.

Organizations can contact the Electronic Messaging Association (EMA) in Arlington VA for a kit to aid in developing a privacy policy.

## Proprietary and Confidential Information

E-mail appears to ease the process of intentional or inadvertent disclosure of company secrets. If this is a concern, an organization could try the following:

- Let users know that the IT department logs the messages that leave the company.
- Perform periodic audits.
- Apply rules or scripts that capture E-mail to or from fields, making it possible to search on competitor address strings.

Some systems insert a header on incoming E-mail that says: "WARNING: This message arrived from outside the company's E-mail system. Take care when replying so as not to divulge proprietary or confidential information."

A company may also specify that proprietary information should not be sent to Internet addresses if security measures on the Internet are inadequate for the company's needs. Users may be asked to confirm that only X.400 addresses are used. It is helpful to incorporate any such E-mail ground rules — for example, that the transmission of proprietary information without a proper disclosure agreement is grounds for dismissal — as part of the new employee orientation process.

## RECOMMENDED COURSE OF ACTION

One of the most important elements of a successful messaging system rollout is a staff that is well versed in the workings of the network, operating system, backup procedures, and applications.

## Network Connections

An implementation needs individuals that can set up network connections efficiently. A messaging system needs procedures in place to notify users when a network link is unavailable. If the network goes down, often one of the first applications blamed is E-mail. It is the job of the network staff to diagnose the problem quickly and have the right people remedying the problem.

## Operating Systems

Many E-mail groups have their own systems and servers and operate them as their own. Consequently, many successful organizations pair systems programmers or senior software specialists with systems engineers who can provide installation services and upgrade support.

## Backup

Most messaging support organizations are not set up to provide 24-hour support. It is important to borrow methodologies from the mainframe support environment and staff an operations center that can answer phone calls, fix problems, and backup and archive applications regularly.

## Applications Support

This function demands staff members with:

- Excellent diagnostic skills.
- Excellent communication skills.
- Data base and business graphics experience.
- Cross-platform network experience.
- A basic understanding of the operating environment of each of the platforms.

E-mail integration by its nature involves cross-platform expertise. Most applications are fairly straightforward. In the case of an integrated infrastructure, an organization may need people familiar with NetWare, SNA, TCP/IP, and LAN Manager. They may also need to understand Mac/OS, UNIX, OS/2, and VMS.

When staffing an implementation, the key is to match expertise across the various groups within the company. The team should be application-centric with contributors from across the enterprise. If an implementation is properly staffed, and the implementers keep in mind the big picture as well as the daily objectives, the messaging system rollout is far more likely to be a success.

# Chapter 61
# TCP/IP Network Management: A Case Study

*Vishal Desai*

When an organization begins setting up a new TCP/IP internetwork supporting satellite and terrestrial-based data transmission, it must look at such major considerations as avoiding downtime, reducing implementation risk and cost, training and developing the implementation team, and incorporating ensuing software upgrades easily. This case study discusses the implementation path decided upon, the platform and software chosen, and the new operations workflow model that resulted in one such organization.

## INTRODUCTION

One large organization is currently setting up a new TCP/IP internetwork supporting satellite and terrestrial-based data transmission. It intends to process collected data at two separate locations and distribute that data to 15 remote sites; therefore, the organization is designing the network to support a high volume of data transfer, initially supported by a DS3 backbone with an eventual migration to an ATM OC3 backbone. Aggregate network data rates are expected to range from 200M bps to 300M bps. Data types include administrative, historical, and time-sensitive real-time data.

Initially, the network will be comprised of 30 routers supplied jointly by Cisco and 3Com vendors, and 20 to 30 Ethernet and FDDI hubs from Cabletron Inc. and InterPhase Inc. Twenty DS3 CSU/DSUs, and about five DS1 MUX from Digital Link corporations are also included. As the network grows, additional routers will be deployed to handle increasing traffic requirements. The network is expected to grow exponentially over the next five years.

0-8493-9965-3/99/$0.00+$.50
© 1999 by CRC Press LLC

## MISSION-CRITICAL AND FAULT-TOLERANT REQUIREMENTS

The data is considered mission-critical and accordingly needs to be protected in the event of network failure. Because data transfer rates are high, a huge buffering capability is required to preserve captured data in the event of even a brief period of network downtime. As a result, one of the organization's primary goals is to avoid downtime at all costs. Accordingly, the organization is designing the network in a highly fault-tolerant manner. This includes provisions for redundant cabling, dual UPS for all routers and hubs, and an out-of-band network connectivity.

The transport system must have its own restoration capabilities, allowing the network itself to take care of as many problems as possible before the NMS must step in. In addition, to accommodate the stringent mean-time-to-restore requirements of 1 min. restoration, the organization has decided to maintain an inventory at each node. This inventory will, at a minimum, include spare interface cards, chassis, cables, connectors, and test equipment. This will allow technicians to swap parts quickly and perform detailed diagnostics off-line. The organization has also given careful consideration to equipment room design and equipment placement, ensuring such things as proper bottom-to-top airflow, placement of equipment with reference to ceiling water sprinklers, and easy access to the backs of routers and other devices.

## NETWORK MANAGEMENT SYSTEM IMPLEMENTATION STRATEGY

The organization researched leading industry surveys and reports and concluded that large undertakings such as its implementation project are highly susceptible to cost overrun and schedule extensions and often fail to deliver the promised functionality. Accordingly, management developed a phased implementation strategy based on the philosophy, "Only bite off what you can chew." Limiting middleware integration in the initial phase was deemed to be critical to the eventual success of the project.

As such, the company analyzed and listed all functions that comprise an enterprise management solution and selected the absolutely essential functions for its phase one implementation, which included:

- An SNMP-based platform.
- Trouble-ticketing software.
- A physical management application.
- RMON capability.
- Report-generation tools.

The organization decided to evaluate additional value-added functions, such as event correlation, integration with legacy systems, and modeling software, on a per-need basis in successive phases. The organization believes that such an implementation path greatly reduces its implementation risk and cost and allows it to train and develop an implementation team of manageable size instead of an army of operators and technicians. Finally, this strategy allows the organization to easily incorporate software upgrades as part of subsequent delivery.

Another area that the organization considered vital to the success of its system was early integration of its business processes with the underlying management technology. As such, in each phase, during the system design and development, the managers decided to define and closely couple their operations concepts with the network management system. This ensured that issues pertaining to maintenance philosophies, remote-sites, operator roles and responsibilities, and handling and parsing of trouble tickets were probed in-depth during the system design and implementation cycle. Such an approach guaranteed that the implementation engineers weighed and considered the operational needs early in the development cycle. Not only did this provide the organization with a "complete workable solution" but also greatly reduced system changes after it became operational.

### The SNMP Platform-Evaluation Criteria

Before selecting a network management platform, the organization tested several systems in its development lab. Between 1992 and 1994, the systems tested in the labs included Cabletron Spectrum, SNM, HPOV, NL's DMONS, and IBM NV. The organization made its selection carefully, as the decision entails a 15-year commitment to the network management infrastructure. The organization was initially impressed by the NL's product, particularly its ability to perform alarm correlation using it Nerve Center application. However, the organization took into consideration NL's precarious market position and chose to select a larger, established player.

The organization decided against Cabletron Spectrum for two reasons. First, the managers were concerned about Spectrum's ability to fully manage competing vendors' hub products. Second, the organization wanted to customize Spectrum's filtering and network modeling capabilities and, after extensive testing, concluded that detailed customization would entail immense up-front development.

SNM was ruled out because the organization found the user interface too archaic, and Sun's higher-end Enterprise Manager was not yet shipping. Finally, IBM NV, although it offered high product stability and advanced features, was discounted due to its DOS/OS-2-centric hardware dependency. Such dependency, according to the organization's existing skill base, would require retraining of its operators, who were familiar with Sun and HP workstations.

The organization then chose HPOV primarily because the product offered a flexible and industry-pervasive management platform that facilitated the integration of third-party applications and because it appeared to pose the least risk in terms of product longevity. Additionally, the NNM, HP's SNMP manager, adequately provided the basic management functions without requiring significant up-front configuration or development investment.

## The NMS Middleware

In addition to selecting HPOV as the SNMP-based network management application, the organization selected the following third-party value-added applications to develop an enterprise level network management system:

- Remedy Corporation's ARS, as the event-tracking software for generating, tracking, and documenting trouble tickets.
- A RDBMS from Sybase Inc., which works with the ARS to store and distribute event tickets and reports.
- A performance-analysis application from SAS Inc., which integrates with HPOV to access MIB data to maintain historical data, produce summaries, perform statistical analysis, and generate network reports.
- Isicad Corp's Command 5000, as the physical and asset management software to obtain a graphical representation of the physical location of devices on the network to track network assets and device-to-device connectivity.
- Frontier's NETScout RMON probes, to collect networking data on remote LANs and forward selected information to the network management system.
- A redundancy application from Qualix Group to monitor all of the network management applications running on the primary and secondary NOC workstations.

The organization carefully considered including additional types of value-added applications, but in maintaining a phased system implementation approach, instead it chose initially to roll out a suite consisting of the barest minimum needed to manage the network effectively.

## The Enterprise Network Management System

Physically, the NMS comprises four SSPARC 20 WS that are situated at the NOC. The primary workstation and redundant secondary workstations (i.e., the WS1 and WS2) are connected to the TCP/IP network by an Ethernet LAN. These workstations collectively run HPOV NNM, ARS clients, and Sybase clients. Two additional workstations, WS3 and WS4, support the NMS. WS3 houses the SAS application as well as the ARS clients and Sybase servers. WS4 hosts Isicad's physical management software. WS4 is also used as an X-Terminal.

The four NMS workstations are connected internally to each other by an Ethernet LAN, which is also used for printer connectivity. Each workstation on this LAN supports Ethernet and FDDI interfaces and are also connected to high-speed, secured modems through the RS232 port to perform out-of-band management. A standalone 486 PC hosts the capability to manage the modems that are used for the out-of-band network access.

### The SNMP-Based Management Platform

The Hewlett Packard's OV NNM 3.3.1 is used to monitor and control the network and provides the necessary platform to integrate middleware applications to maximize data sharing and processing. The NNM:

- Automatically discovers the devices on the TCP/IP networks and monitors the status of these devices.
- Automatically draws the topology of the network based on the discovered information and creates appropriate map views. A map is a graphical and hierarchical representation of the network.
- Collects performance information from the device's MIB, stores it for trend analysis, and graphs the collected data.
- Defines event thresholds for MIB objects remotely.
- Takes specific actions upon receipt of specific SNMP traps.
- Diagnoses and displays network faults and performance problems.
- Allows integration with the popular third-party applications to enhance the system's management capabilities.

### HPOV IMPLEMENTATION

Two copies of NNM are deployed on NOC workstations WS1 and WS2. WS1 houses the primary NNM, whereas WS2 hosts the secondary copy. Each copy is configured and customized in an identical manner. Database synchronization between these copies is maintained by scripts that are automatically initiated on a periodic basis.

Each NNM is configured at various levels. The map views of each are customized to view and isolate faulty devices easily. Each NNM's alarm and event handling is configured to notify operators in real-time using a combination of beeps, pop-up windows, and E-mail messages. The map and event color schemes are carefully defined to quickly determine fault criticality (e.g., red implies critical failure; yellow is minor; blue is unmanageable). The capability to obtain real-time performance graphs for selected backbone links is also implemented for quick status reports. Finally, to ensure that sufficient Management Information Base data is collected for performance, fault, and accounting purposes, selected MIB variables, with associated collection frequency, are identified for all network devices. Applicable threshold checks are also instilled.

### SAS Reporting Software

The SAS Corporation offers a suite of products capable of integrating with HPOV NNM to perform data processing, analysis, and report generation. These products collectively allow the users to import data from NNM MIB files into its proprietary database, reduce the collected data, and perform statistical analysis on this data to generate strategic and performance baseline reports. These reports are used by the NOC operators, managers, and sustaining engineers to jointly perform network trend and capacity planning analysis.

By using the SAS product suite, the organization is able to parse information and reduce the amount of storage needed without compromising on disaster recovery requirements; also, SAS provides the ability to more easily summarize network performance data and generate reports on circuit utilization, LAN utilization, and device performance.

### Trouble-Ticketing Software

The organization has developed a help-desk call process model with the goal of handling the user's problem on the first call. To that end, the organization will people the help desk on a 24 * 7 basis with a mix of operators and operations support personnel. These NOC personnel interface with the remote node personnel using a combination of commercially available trouble-ticketing packages, secured telephone lines, facsimiles, and E-mail to resolve problems in a timely manner.

Remedy Corporation's ARS 2.0 was selected as the centerpiece for the organization's help desk. The ARS generates trouble tickets and tracks network events in a customizable work-flow process. The ARS uses an interactive process similar to E-mail to track network events with repair personnel. To accomplish this, the ARS provides the capability using a GUI to customize the following:

- Defining information to be passed among repair personnel.
- Defining automatic processes to assist operator data entry on event tickets.
- Notification and communication of defined information among repair personnel.
- Define work flow rules such as escalation procedures.
- Provide statistical analysis and reporting capabilities.

Using these ARS features, the NMS design engineers defined three primary trouble-ticket schemas. The event ticket schema specifies the date, time, and severity of the problem, as well as suggested problem resolution steps. The node contact schema provides information about repair personnel (i.e., phone number and other contact information). The common carrier schema provides information about the transport circuits, and carrier contact data. All schemas adhere to a predefined escalation process that ensures automatic notification to management of unresolved or forgotten event tickets.

Along with tracking events and communicating information, the help desk designers have coupled ARS with Sybase database transparently to automatically retain a database of problem-solving experience. This problem-solving information can be used by the NOC operator or nodal technician as a trouble-shooting aid and to provide statistics. Trouble-shooting assistance is achieved by querying for solutions from previous similar problems. Furthermore, storing all previous event tickets allows the ARS to provide, for example, statistical analysis concerning the length of outages, the frequency of outages, most frequent cause of events, and the amount of time spent by individual repair personnel. Coupled with this functionality is also the capability to generate reports for statistical results, event ticket summaries, complete event tickets, and other information as needed.

Preparing for the next release of the help desk, the organization is considering listing these reports as well as the status of all trouble tickets on a secured server that is accessible by either a Web or E-mail interface. Such a capability allows network users to investigate and obtain and track status of reported problems without calling the help desk. This, the organization believes, allows its NOC operators to spend more time to resolve network problems.

## HPOV-ARS INTEGRATION

Rather than have a standalone help desk that has no insight into the network status information collected and presented by the SNMP manager, the organization decided to integrate its ARS with HPOV. The coupling with HPOV relies on a combination of menu bar integration, along with the in-house developed scripts that automatically filled in specified data fields upon opening a trouble ticket. This reduces the amount of information the NOC operators must fill in for each trouble ticket by the NOC operators. As the dynamics of the network behavior is captured, analyzed, and understood by the engineers, the organization plans to build upon the existing HPOV integration to include the SNMP trap — ARS event mapping list to automatically generation trouble tickets for selected network traps and events.

### Redundancy Application

Due to the mission-critical nature of the network, system reliability and redundancy required careful handling. For the NMS, several software components are used together to provide the required the system reliability. The ODS is used to perform disk mirroring to provide redundancy for all of the data and applications used by the primary and secondary NMS WS1 and WS2.

The Qualix Group's First Watch software monitors all of the applications running on the primary workstation, and sends a heartbeat between the primary and secondary workstations. In the event of some type of fault or failure, the First Watch maintains a log and notifies the NOC operator, and if needed, shut down the primary workstation and initiate the secondary workstation.

### Physical Configuration Application

Isicad Corporation's Command software resides on WS4. It provides a graphical representation of the physical location of devices on the network to track network assets and device-to-device connectivity to perform fault isolation. It also documents such useful information as circuit identification numbers, cable type, and personal identification numbers. It is used to locate the exactness of the reported fault. Although it can be integrated with HPOV NNM and Remedy's ARS, the NMS will use it initially as a standalone application.

### Frontier NETScout

NETScout probes are installed on FDDI LANs at selected sites. These probes function to collect networking data on remote LANs and forward selected information to the network management system. Besides providing standard RMON information, the probes allow the network management system to maintain traffic accountability for individual users at the LAN level. This is extremely important to avoid congestion on the organization's WAN backbone links. NETScout was chosen above other competitors for its ability to collect FDDI as well as Ethernet data and because of its close integration with the HPOV platform.

### Customized Scripts

To date, the organization has written about a half-dozen scripts that integrate the Remedy AR, SAS, and NETScout into the OpenView NNM environment. These scripts assist in customizing the interdependency among multiple applications and underlying UNIX processes. As an example, the SAS integration with HPOV NNM requires a script that ensures SAS's ability to access data files created by HPOV NNM. These scripts, in most instances, are no longer then few lines, but they provide the necessary "glue" to implement an integrated network management solution.

**Operations Work-Flow Model**

Simultaneous with the design and implementation of the NMS, the organization began developing operations concepts. This model addressed issues pertaining to operations roles and responsibilities, equipment sparing, problem diagnostic procedures, and an external interface from NOC perspective. Once these concepts and philosophies were sufficiently developed, a operations work-flow process was developed.

In the work-flow process, typically, a network event is reported to the NOC, either by the user or by the HPOV through its map or event windows. For the initial deployment of the ARS, NOC operator opens event tickets to document a network event. Associated severity levels are noted along with a brief problem description. Once the event information is entered, the ARS is assigned and forwarded to the appropriate repair personnel or circuit carrier, electronically, to investigate the condition.

At the repair site, the technicians receive the assigned trouble ticket and begin the required fault isolation and resolution process. To accommodate the stringent mean-time-to-restore requirements, the organization has decided to maintain an inventory at each node, which allows the technicians to swap parts quickly and perform detailed diagnostics off line. A summary of such actions is entered in the Restoral Action and Problem Found fields of the opened trouble ticket. Future releases will require the operator to input in the trouble-ticket equipment-sparing loads at each site to track and maintain the sparing profile. Upon problem resolution, the trouble ticket is assigned back to NOC operators for them to perform verification process.

For specific faults such as outage in carrier-provided circuits, the NOC operator monitors and records the action taken by the carrier to restore the circuit. Associated durations are entered as time-tags, and this information is eventually used as metrics to gauge the service-level agreement with the WAN carriers. A similar information base is maintained for individual operators and technicians who are assigned trouble tickets. In future, the organization is considering incorporating the service desk of its router vendor to leverage on the operators' expertise in real time by involving them in the help desk process.

As an aid to the current work flow process, rules as well as responsibilities are defined to ensure timely processing for each event. This allows the implementation of escalation procedures to guarantee timely tracking of event conditions. The organization has developed an escalation process that involves three levels and leverages on skill mix of a myriad of people. Level one escalation relies on NOC operators who, in conjunction with technicians, resolve failures. Level two includes an NOC manager, whose skill mix allows him or her to make system-level decisions to resolve problems in real-time. Level three and beyond is the domain of design engineers as well as vendor support. At this level, the problem usually requires expert handling.

## SYSTEM DEPLOYMENT AND SUSTAINING ENGINEERING

The organization anticipates a four to six month field test of the network. During the field test and thereafter, the network design team will take on the new role of sustaining systems engineering and support. In their sustaining engineering role, they will integrate and test third-party applications, perform trend analysis on collected data, and provide recommendations on operations strategy's. They will also be an integral part of the organization's problem escalation process.

### NMS Status

To date, the organization has deployed this NMS to monitor and manage its TCP/IP network resources. It has also developed an in-house structured training/certification program to ensure proper skill-mix is maintained on the NOC floor. During the initial months, the NOC will house 2 operators on a 24x7 basis with a NOC manager for the day shift. Maintenance contract with a private company will provide technicians at remote sites. Eventually, as the network grows, additional operators and mangers will be hired.

Based on the initial feed-back form the NOC floor, the design engineers have incorporated minor changes-especially in the area of data collection and report formats and contents. Currently, these design engineers are completing the as-built documentation suite as well as finalizing the operations concept and procedure guidelines. They are also beginning to evaluate middleware to be incorporated in Phase II.

From a high-level corporate perspective, the phased implementation approach has resulted in immense dividends. It has kept the initial hardware/software cost in check as well as minimized the up-front implementation risk. As the understanding of the NMS processes and the network dynamics increases, the organization finds itself in a better position to deploy additional software packages in future releases. Finally, such a phased and structured approach has allowed the organization to gradually hire the proper skill mix at the same time re-train its existing operations staff.

# Chapter 62

# Integrating Voice and LAN Infrastructures and Applications

*David Curley*

Integration of voice and LAN networks will be an essential IT strategy for many businesses in the next three to five years. Consolidating the long-separate voice and data networks has implications not only for the network infrastructure, but also for the PC, the telephone set, the PBX, and the IT organization itself. This chapter is a road map to guide organizations in making the right voiceLAN-related investment decisions.

## PROBLEMS ADDRESSED

VoiceLAN is the transmission of voice traffic over a LAN infrastructure. VoiceLAN enables server-based telephony architecture for voice switches, terminals/phone sets, and applications.

Today, voice traffic is transmitted across a separate circuit-switched infrastructure, with a PBX or key system (for smaller offices) serving as a centralized switch. Under a voiceLAN scheme, both data and voice traffic are interleaved and switched as frames or cells over the same data network.

Organizations should consider running their voice traffic over the LAN infrastructure for several reasons:

- **Single infrastructure** VoiceLAN eliminates the need for a cabling plant dedicated to voice only. Converged voice/data traffic running over a single wire reduces the up-front cost of equipment procurement (e.g., cable, patch panels, racks, installation), cable plant management (i.e., dealing with moves, adds, and changes) and maintenance.
- **Single organization** VoiceLAN allows enterprises to consolidate and streamline separate support organizations for data and voice networks. This convergence produces a more efficient, less costly management

structure that spends less time "coordinating" and more time delivering network services and applications to users.

- **Breaking PBX lock-in** For the most part, PBXs are proprietary, single-vendor systems, which usually means they are inflexible and expensive to maintain. VoiceLAN deployment paves the way for an open, client/server model to be applied to telephony, creating a less rigid vendor-client relationship.

- **New level of CTI.** Current CTI systems allow data and voice application environments to "talk" to each other by means of computer-to-PBX links. CTI is included implicitly in the voiceLAN model. VoiceLAN also distinguishes itself from CTI because data and voice applications actually share the same set of standards and software interfaces. Thus voiceLAN leverages both media far beyond what is possible under present CTI systems, and has the potential to give organizations a distinct competitive advantage in the marketplace.

## MIGRATING THE LAN INFRASTRUCTURE

Migration to voiceLAN is likely to encompass a number of smaller elements or activities. Migration cannot happen overnight, but is an evolutionary process that includes beneficial steps along the way. Over time, organizations can focus on improving elements of their network infrastructure, their desktop workstations, and their organizations, in addition to their telephone systems.

A first step in deploying voiceLAN is to upgrade the present LAN infrastructure to support the demands of voice traffic without affecting the flow of existing data traffic. Infrastructure refers to the cabling plant and the local networking equipment used to carry traffic from end station to end station (i.e., hub, bridge, router, switches, and network adapters). The PBX is not considered part of the infrastructure in a voiceLAN environment; rather the PBX will evolve into a call server that can be considered another type of end station on the LAN.

### Solutions for Delay-Sensitive Applications

Voice bandwidth is not usually of much concern when using LANs for transmission. An uncompressed high-quality voice conversation needs only 64K-bps, and compression or packetization reduces bandwidth requirements further. This represents only a small fraction of a dedicated 10M-bps Ethernet LAN segment.

More important, voice is a delay-sensitive application that demands minimal latency (or minimal variations in latency, otherwise known as "jitter") in communications. The vast majority of LANs today are based on shared-bandwidth media. With Ethernet LANs, all users contend for bandwidth on a first-come, first-served basis. Token Ring LANs are somewhat more deterministic, since each end station transmits only when that end station holds the token, which passes from end station to end station, at more or less regular time intervals. However, under both of these shared-bandwidth schemes, significant transmission delays, as well as variations in transmission delay, occur — severely disrupting a real-time voice conversation between end stations.

## Desktop Switching

Part of the solution to this problem is to provide dedicated bandwidth to each user end station through desktop LAN switching. In a fully switched network, end stations do not contend (as in Ethernet) or wait (as in Token Ring) for bandwidth with other users; instead, each user workstation gets its own dedicated LAN segment for connectivity into the network. Migrating to a fully switched network (i.e., a single workstation or server per dedicated switch port) entails replacing existing shared-media LAN hubs with LAN switches.

Dedicated LAN switching has become affordable. Commodity Ethernet switches currently sell for less than $200 per port ($US), and ATM25 switches can be obtained for less than $400 per port ($US).

## Minimize Routing

LAN switching only addresses bandwidth contention to the desktop. Links between desktop switches, or from desktop switches to building/campus switches, must also provide predictable, minimal delays for voice communications.

In most enterprise networks, routers are used to calculate paths and forward packets between LAN segments at layer 3 of the OSI model. These routing algorithms introduce significant delay and usually add noticeable latency to voice communications. By contrast, switching involves a much simpler and faster process. Segmenting the network at OSI layer 2 through switching, rather than at layer 3 through routing, increases the capacity of the network to support delay-sensitive applications such as voice.

Although routing will continue to be necessary, especially in larger enterprise environments, implementation of voiceLAN requires minimizing routing in favor of switching. If deployed properly, switching removes the delay-inducing routing process from the path of most network traffic.

In many cases, this migration step entails replacing a collapsed backbone router with a backbone switch. The routing function can either be centralized through a one-armed router (or route server model) or distributed in switches providing desktop or departmental connectivity. In either case, traffic is typically switched through the network and only passes through a routing function when absolutely necessary.

### Controlling LAN Backbone Traffic

Migrating the network from shared-access LANs and routing to switching is a prerequisite to voiceLAN implementation. However, a major challenge remains in ensuring that voice can be properly supported on the backbone links (e.g., trunk) between LAN switches.

Supporting both data and voice over a common backbone LAN infrastructure is essentially a bandwidth-contention issue — determining how to make sure that delay-sensitive voice traffic is not preempted by other data traffic traversing the same links. Various techniques for prioritizing different traffic, reserving bandwidth, or guaranteeing network-delay characteristics may be applied. Two solutions to this problem are roughly categorized as the frame-switching/IP and ATM-centric approaches.

**Frame Switching/IP-based Solution.** Because of the rapid decline in price of Ethernet switches and the large installed base of Ethernet adapters, switched Ethernet has become the most popular solution for organizations deploying desktop switching. It is only natural for many organizations to consider Ethernet (especially Fast Ethernet) trunks for interconnecting desktop switches to each other or to LAN backbone segment switches.

However, as Ethernet frames are switched across the network, delay problems may still occur for voice. Ethernet frames are variable in length, and Ethernet has no mechanism for prioritizing one frame over another. Therefore, as network traffic increases, small frames carrying a voice payload may often have to wait in switch buffer queues behind large frames carrying data. Because voice has a delay tolerance of only 75 milliseconds, the lack of prioritization across a switched Ethernet network may degrade the quality of voice communications. Furthermore, this fundamental problem will not disappear with expanded bandwidth under Fast (or gigabit) Ethernet.

**RSVP.** Among the most promising solutions to Ethernet's lack of prioritization or guaranteed latency is to handle the problem at layer 3 via the RSVP. RSVP, which is under development by the IETF and leading network product vendors, operates by reserving bandwidth and router/switch buffer space for certain high-priority IP packets such as those carrying voice traffic.

In effect, RSVP enables a packet switching network to mimic certain characteristics of a circuit switching multiplexer network. However, RSVP is still only able to set up paths for high-priority traffic on a "best effort" basis; thus it cannot guarantee the delay characteristics of the network.

Furthermore, as an OSI level 3 protocol, RSVP support requires that routing functionality be added to switches.

RSVP's best-effort capability is sufficient for several delay-sensitive applications, such as non-real-time streaming video or audio. However, it is questionable whether RSVP can support real-time voice communications over the LAN to a level of quality and reliability that is acceptable in a business environment.

**ATM-based Backbone Solutions.** An alternative solution for delivering voiceLAN over a common data infrastructure is ATM. ATM was designed specifically to support both voice and data traffic over a common infrastructure and provides multiple QoS levels.

ATM's CBR service guarantees a virtual circuit of fixed bandwidth for high-priority traffic such as voice. In addition, ATM uses a relatively small, fixed-length cell (53 bytes) rather than a variable-length frame to transport traffic, thereby limiting the maximum delay any one cell must wait in a switch buffer queue. The use of ATM links/trunks between LAN switches neatly solves the problem of supporting both voice and data traffic for that portion of the network.

ATM to the desktop is more problematic, however. The most common standard for ATM LANs operates at 155M-bps over category 5 UTC cable or optical fiber. However, deploying 155M-bps ATM to every desktop is currently too expensive for the vast majority of organizations (although it is beginning to be deployed as a LAN backbone technology).

In order to deploy a reliable voiceLAN solution cost-effectively using ATM, a lower-cost access technology must be deployed to the desktop. However, this access technology must also be able to extend the benefits of ATM's QoS from the ATM backbone all the way to the desktop.

An organization can choose from among several potential access solutions, including ATM25, Ethernet using IP/RSVP, or Ethernet/CIF.

**ATM25 Access.** ATM25, as its name implies, is a 25M-bps version of ATM designed specifically for desktop connectivity to a 155M-bps ATM backbone. ATM25 provides all of the QoS benefits of higher-speed ATM and can be used to build end-to-end ATM networks. ATM25 can also operate over category 3 UTC cable, whereas 155M-bps ATM and Fast Ethernet require organizations to upgrade their UTP cabling to category 5 UTP cable.

The downside of ATM25 is that it requires replacing all legacy network adapters where voiceLAN will be deployed. In addition, ATM25 adapters and switches are still considerably more expensive than 10BaseT Ethernet adapters and switches.

Yet, if deploying voiceLAN is a top priority for your company, installing a network featuring 155M-bps ATM in the backbone and ATM25 to the desktop may be the most reliable and logical solution. Although ATM25 is a more expensive option than switched 10M-bps Ethernet, the cost of an ATM25 connection (including adapter and switch port cost) has fallen substantially in 1996, with an average street price of $400 to $450 ($US).

**Ethernet RSVP/IP Access.** The most popular desktop connectivity option for data networking continues to be Ethernet, and the addition of desktop switching and Fast Ethernet technology only continues this trend. The challenge is combining IP over Ethernet network access links with ATM in the backbone in such a way that voiceLAN performance requirements can be satisfied.

One solution requires Ethernet-to-ATM desktop switches to include routing and RSVP support. The desktop end station sends voice in IP packets (further encapsulated inside Ethernet frames) to the switch, using RSVP to request bandwidth to be reserved for the voice conversation. The desktop switch then terminates the IP connection and converts the voice payload to ATM cells for transmission across the backbone (or the desktop switch may forward these IP datagrams across the ATM backbone without terminating the IP connection). The desktop switch is also responsible for mapping the RSVP bandwidth reservation request (at the IP level of the architecture) to an appropriate ATM QoS for the ATM connection.

Although this approach appears to provide the best of both worlds by combining an ATM backbone with the popularity of switched Ethernet to the desktop, it has not been demonstrated to be capable of guaranteeing the necessary quality of service needed for voice communications.

**Ethernet CIF Access.** CIF allows a desktop application to place voice traffic in ATM cells that are subsequently inserted into Ethernet frames by the network adapter driver for transport over the link from the adapter to switch. At the Ethernet switch, cells are extracted from the frames and sent across the ATM backbone.

CIF's primary advantage is that high-priority traffic, such as voice, can be given the necessary QoS from the desktop across the ATM network without having to actually install ATM end-to-end in the network. Furthermore, because voice does not utilize IP, the desktop Ethernet switch can be simpler and need not include more expensive and compute-intensive routing functionality. In this way, CIF may be a potential alternative to RSVP/IP for organizations migrating to switched Ethernet to the desktop but also interested in deploying voiceLAN.

CIF's ability to guarantee quality of service comes at a price. CIF requires installation of special software or NIC drivers in workstations to accomplish the framing of ATM cells. In addition, transporting traffic inside of ATM cells, which are in turn encapsulated by frames, entails significant overhead, reducing the usable bandwidth on an Ethernet segment to 6M-bps to 7M-bps.

## CONSOLIDATION OF THE CABLING PLANT

A consolidated cabling plant that supports both voice and data is one of the primary benefits of implementing voiceLAN. With voiceLAN, the cabling plant supporting voice communications (e.g., cabling runs, patch panels, cross connects) becomes a redundant, backup infrastructure that can be removed when the voiceLAN network stabilizes.

No matter what technology is used for voice transport (i.e., ATM or IP), voiceLAN deployment requires optical fiber in the risers of buildings for backbone connectivity. Most large organizations have already installed fiber for their LAN backbone and therefore no upgrade to the cabling plant is necessary. Exhibit 1 and Exhibit 2 depict a consolidation of cabling plants through voiceLAN technology for a typical organization.

## MIGRATING THE DESKTOP

The deployment of voiceLAN also entails a migration of the desktop PC to become telephony-enabled. Exhibit 3 illustrates the voiceLAN-enabled desktop environment. This migration has two components: hardware and software.

### Hardware Upgrades

In a pure voiceLAN architecture, all voice calls are received via a PC and its LAN adapter card rather than via a desktop telephone wired to a PBX or voice switch. There are two alternative human interfaces for people to interact with the PC to receive voice communications: the PC itself and the traditional desktop telephone.

By using the PC as the interface, voice traffic is processed by a PC sound card and the user employs a PC-attached microphone and headset. This solution is appropriate for users who are already using a microphone and headset to keep their hands free for typing (e.g., telemarketers, travel agents, help desk operators). Disadvantages of this set-up include the fact that voice packets are processed by the PC's CPU, potentially hampering performance for other applications that might be running simultaneously. In addition, if the PC locks up, the user's conversation may be interrupted.

For most users the desktop telephone is still appropriate as their voice communications interface. However, in a voiceLAN solution, this phone set must be able to connect directly to the PC so that voice traffic can be received directly from the network adapter card without having to pass

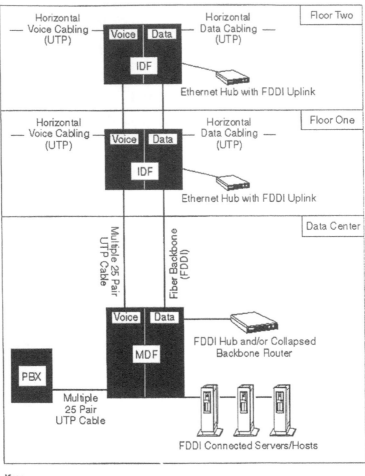

**Exhibit 1. Legacy Voice and Data Cabling Infrastructures.**

through the CPU. Today this can be accomplished through a third-party plug-in card.

**Universal Serial Bus.** A more elegant solution for accomplishing a direct connection is the USB interface, originally developed by Intel. Within the next year, the motherboards of most new PCs will include USB interfaces as a standard feature.

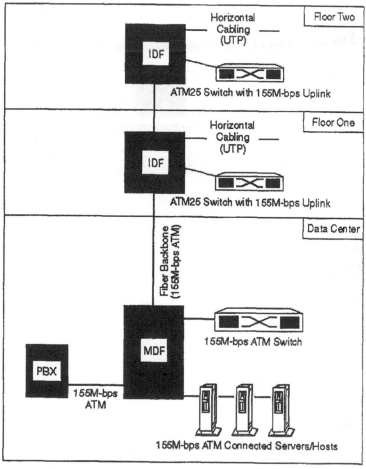

**Exhibit 2. Consolidated Cabling Infrastructure.**

The USB supports 12M-bps of throughput and allows USB-compatible telephone sets to connect directly to the PC without the need for an additional plug-in card. This alternative greatly reduces the cost of deploying voiceLAN. Several vendors have released or will soon release telephones conforming to the USB standard.

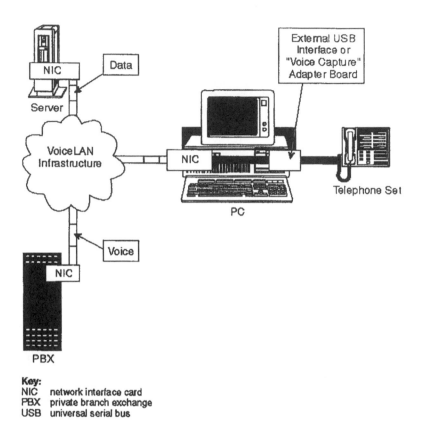

**Exhibit 3. The VoiceLAN-enabled Desktop.**

**Firewire Bus.** An alternative standard called Firewire — originally developed by Apple Corp., but currently being promoted by Sony and other consumer electronics companies — is also being introduced in new products.

The Firewire bus runs at speeds of up to 400M-bps, which makes it appropriate for video traffic as well as voice. This high level of performance also may make Firewire too expensive for ubiquitous deployment, particularly if voiceLAN, not video, is the driving application. PC vendors may also be slower to develop Firewire-compatible telephones because of the Macintosh's declining share of the business market. Therefore, deploying USB-compatible phones is currently the most prudent choice for voiceLAN migration at the desktop.

## Software Upgrades

To take maximum advantage of voiceLAN technology, PC-resident applications need to communicate with the PBX and PC-attached desktop phone sets. For this, a standardized software interface is required.

Most PBXs today support several such software APIs, though many of these interfaces provide translation of commands between the PBX and mainframe hosts for use in CTI applications such as call center applications. For Windows applications, most PBXs support Microsoft's TAPI. TAPI is available for Windows 95.

Microsoft Corp. is introducing a newer API, combining its Windows data transmission API (Winsock) with its voice communications API (TAPI). This consolidated API, known as Winsock 2, makes it even easier for developers to write integrated voice and data communications applications.

Clearly, the migration to a voiceLAN architecture is made much easier for organizations planning a substantial (Wintel) PC procurement in the next six months. These PCs are considered "voiceLAN ready" because they include both USB motherboards and systems software supporting TAPI/Winsock 2 APIs. Legacy PCs would need to have TAPI/Winsock 2 software and a third-party adapter board (for handset connectivity) installed.

## MIGRATING THE PBX

### Legacy Telephony

Today's PBX and telephony systems are analogous to the host and dumb terminal model of the mainframe era. PBXs are relatively inflexible, proprietary, and expensive to maintain and upgrade in the same way mainframes are. Phone sets are still the most ubiquitous desktop instrument for telephony communications, but the PC offers the most intuitive interface to advanced features. Moving from the traditional PBX model to a server-based telephony model represents the final stage in the migration to a fully integrated voice and data network.

### Linking Distributed PBX Components

For organizations with large campus environments, an intermediate step between the legacy PBX and server-based telephony may be an architecture featuring multiple PBX components distributed throughout the campus.

This type of architecture has traditionally required a dedicated fiber backbone to connect multiple units. Under a voiceLAN solution, these units, outfitted with network adapter cards, can be connected over a LAN backbone infrastructure. This infrastructure is already in place in most larger campus network environments. In this case, the horizontal connection between the PBXs and the telephone sets at the desktop can continue to use the traditional voice network infrastructure.

There are two advantages to this architecture:

1. Distributed PBXs scale more cost-effectively than a single, large PBX.
2. The necessity for installing and maintaining dual backbones, one for voice and one for data, is eliminated.

Because this architecture does not implement voiceLAN to the desktop, it represents only a partial step toward a server-based telephony architecture. However, it also does not necessitate replacing old PCs with new ones outfitted with a USB interface.

### Server-Based Telephony

A server-based telephony architecture allows for the traditional functions of the PBX to be broken down into its components and distributed on the voiceLAN network. The switching function of the PBX can be handled by the frame or cell switches of the data network, whereas the call control function can be moved to a server. Specific telephony applications can also be moved to distributed application servers and integrated with other networked data applications.

**Initial Implementation Tips.** Implementing the ultimate voiceLAN architecture (depicted in Exhibit 4) cannot be accomplished through a wholesale changeover, except perhaps when an organization moves to a new building. Rather, this new architecture is typically deployed alongside the legacy PBX/dedicated voice network in the same way that organizations have deployed distributed servers running alongside centralized mainframes.

Server-based telephony should be implemented initially in specific workgroup environments. The best candidates are those workgroups that can best leverage server-based telephony applications that are available today.

Where a voiceLAN model is implemented, the user's port on the legacy PBX should be left unchanged until the voiceLAN deployment has stabilized and been thoroughly tested. This is recommended because it provides, during the migration, redundancy and a backup system that can deliver phone service to the user.

The first phase of server-based telephony applications installed at the desktop is relatively basic. This configuration is similar to desktop PCs running terminal (i.e., phone handset) emulation and communicating with a

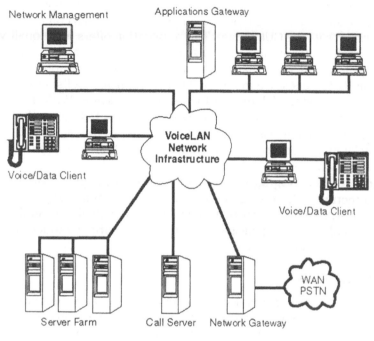

**Exhibit 4. VoiceLAN Architecture.**

LAN-attached mainframe (i.e., the PBX). While the integration with networked data applications is limited compared to a full-scale server-based telephony architecture, it does give users an intuitive GUI interface for voice communications and allows the users a certain level of integration with their desktop applications.

**Desktop Telephony Applications.** Following are some examples of desktop telephony applications that should be considered for implementation in this initial phase. In these examples, the applications are enhanced by voiceLAN, in that they are melded with real-time voice communications:

• **GUI phone** At its basic level, this application running on the desktop provides a phone handset interface on the PC. The GUI phone prompts users to take more advantage of advanced call features that they are reluctant to utilize today simply because of the nonintuitive interface of existing phone handsets.

**62-13**

- **Integration with PIM software** Integrating the GUI phone with PIM software provides a seamless link between the user's PIM application (e.g., an advanced electronic Rolodex) and the user's actual communications interface (e.g., the GUI phone). This application offers functionality similar to call center applications to general users right at their desktop.
- **GUI voice mail** Voice mail can easily benefit from a graphic representation. At the click of a mouse, users scroll through a list of voice mail messages, saving, deleting, or forwarding messages. With this type of application, voice messages are treated as objects that can be manipulated in the same way data files are. For users, this method is potentially far more user-friendly and time-efficient than using the keypad of a phone handset.
- **Integrated messaging** When voice mail is decoupled from the PBX architecture, full integration with other types of messaging applications (i.e., E-mail) can more easily take place. VoiceLAN simplifies the process of combining message media and potentially reduces the cost of integrated messaging.

## MIGRATING USERS

As the voiceLAN network is tested for its reliability as a dedicated voice network, the organization can begin to migrate the general population of users. Individual users or entire workgroups can be moved on a line-by-line basis by installing a USB PC and USB handset at the desktop, eventually eliminating the legacy phone set connected via the dedicated voice network. The order in which users/workgroups are moved depends on each user/workgroup's ability and willingness to take advantage of integrated voice/data applications.

While the general population of users is being migrated, the organization should also begin to deploy more advanced applications in the original testbed workgroups. These applications can be tightly integrated with networked data applications (as opposed to desktop applications). Among the client/server applications that can be deployed in this final stage include:

- **Collaborative applications** A server-based telephony architecture facilitates the integration of voice communications to collaborative software that allows multiple people to work on the same document while communicating.
- **Voice/database applications** At present, computer telephony integration permits a certain level of integration between PBXs and databases; however, deploying such applications is expensive and generally reserved for telemarketing or customer service applications. A server-based telephony architecture allows high-end CTI functionality to be deployed on a much wider scale and to be made accessible by the general user population.

## CONSOLIDATING THE VOICE AND DATA ORGANIZATIONS

One of the biggest advantages of deploying voiceLAN is the integration of voice and data network support teams and the eventual reduction in support costs. Many organizations have already begun consolidating their support organizations for voice and data without deployment of a voiceLAN architecture. Migrating to voiceLAN and to a server-based telephony architecture forces organizational consolidation between personnel from the voice and data environments.

### Infrastructure Maintenance and Support Staff

The first operational element that needs to be integrated is the maintenance and support of the network infrastructure. In many organizations, these teams function separately. Initially, the voice team continues to maintain the legacy voice infrastructure, but that task should gradually disappear as users/workgroups move to the voiceLAN infrastructure.

The lighter burden for infrastructural maintenance allows personnel previously dedicated to supporting voice systems to be placed into applications development teams with members from both the data and voice environments. This blending of organizations mitigates some of the potential conflicts between groups of people from the voice and data environments. The consolidation of staff from the voice and data environments is also necessary to develop applications that tightly integrate voice and data. Furthermore, it may also reduce worries about job security on the part of voice-only staff, who may fear they have become expendable. Above all, a consolidated organization that supports all forms of network communications in the enterprise is better able to deliver increasingly sophisticated network services and applications to users.

## RECOMMENDED COURSE OF ACTION

Achieving the end goal of voiceLAN implementation requires a series of logical steps. Individual organizations may start the migration at different points, depending on their installed base of equipment, economic issues, or other decisions made to meet customer service demands and strategic business goals. The course of implementation may take three to five years. During that time, many technology hurdles will be overcome with standards development. Other issues, such as bandwidth congestion and the need for cost-efficiencies, are causing organizations to take a close look at convergent technologies that can solve problems today.

Various compelling events may precipitate these voiceLAN migration steps. Examples of such events, often designed to simplify management, satisfy growth, or save money, may include:

- Maintenance contract renewal.
- Growth of new locations or branch offices.
- Voice or data system upgrades.
- Hiring of new personnel with new skills.
- Reorganization (e.g., downsizing or substantial moves and changes).
- New bandwidth requirements (backbone and/or selected user workgroups).
- Optimizing wide-area access.
- Delivery of training (i.e., video) to the desktop.
- Improvements in communications via voice-annotated text or other media.

Exhibit 5 summarizes, in table format, the key decision points in the migration to a voiceLAN network. The table is a broad road map for organizations that wish to begin factoring voiceLAN into their network architecture planning today. Decisions about information technology or services investments, and their implications, are grouped in four areas — IT strategy, enterprise requirements, workgroup requirements, and desktop applications.

VoiceLAN in the backbone is the first logical step that can be implemented now to satisfy immediate business goals — notably, cost-efficiency and network management — and lay the framework for a converged network in the future. Implementing voiceLAN in the workgroup and at the desktop are steps that will be taken in the medium- to longer-term time frame.

When selecting a vendor to work with as a business partner in the development of a voiceLAN implementation, corporate network managers should evaluate the vendors':

- Published plans for voiceLAN implementation.
- Actual delivery of products included in these plans.
- Inclusion of voice as an integral component of an overall strategy, rather than as a future possibility.
- Commitment to emerging voice-enabling standards.

Voice system vendors — or those vendors providing the call servers, telephony sets, and voice software components — must meet additional criteria, including:

- Migration to open, standards-based products.
- Track record in investment potential.
- Demonstrated experience in CTI.
- Partnerships with IT leaders for "best in class" solutions.
- Defined migration path to ATM (e.g., describing which telephony products can be leveraged and used in the new infrastructure and which products are no longer needed).

| Decision Points / Migration Steps | Typical Situation | Recommendation | Impact |
|---|---|---|---|
| Strategy | • Voice not a part of IT strategy<br>• Separate budgets<br>• Separate planning<br>• Separate organizations | • Ensure voice and voiceLAN are embedded in IT strategy<br>• Voice must be considered integral component of overall plan | • As compelling events occur and decisions are made, organization continually moves closer to voiceLAN goal |
| Enterprise | • More bandwidth required for workgroup or user applications<br>• Corporate pressure to reduce costs and provide productivity improvements<br>• Cost savings or simplicity (elimination of duplicate infrastructures) sought | • Evaluate opportunity to converge voice/data on single backbone<br>• Upgrade or replace existing backbone LAN<br>• Converge voice/data functional organizations | • Bandwidth issue resolved<br>• Simplified infrastructure<br>• Organization positioned for voiceLAN |
| Workgroup | • Application-specific bandwidth requirements<br>• Productivity improvements and competitive advantage sought<br>• Remote offices demanding "head-office" type functionality and access | • Voice-enable applications<br>• Evaluate server-based telephony solutions<br>• Exploit opportunity to trial voiceLAN technology on workgroup basis<br>• Extend voiceLAN-capable technology to workgroup via ATM or switched Ethernet access network | • Maximize productivity<br>• Move another step closer to voiceLAN<br>• Force a break from traditional voice model |
| Desktop | • Disparate voice and computing instruments and applications<br>• Dual wiring infrastructure<br>• Lost productivity | • Ensure strategy supports evolution to single wiring to the desktop<br>• Opportunity to evaluate computer-attached telephones<br>• Roll out in logical manner (starting with R&D organization, then general business groups, finally call centers) | • Final leg of voiceLAN convergence to the desktop<br>• Achieve simplicity, cost savings through streamlined moves/changes<br>• New applications deployment and enhanced productivity |

**Exhibit 5. Decision Points/Recommendations for VoiceLAN Migration.**

# Chapter 63
# Creating Network Expressways Using Ethernet Switching Engines

*Andres Llana, Jr.*

Today, high-powered Ethernet switching engines with support for F-DX technology and advanced multiprotocol, filtering functions provide an inexpensive route to high-speed expressways. These devices, when properly deployed, can reduce network contention and greatly improve network throughput.

## INTRODUCTION

The new, high-powered Ethernet switches provide the network administrator with many more options to more efficiently manage LAN traffic. Low-cost Ethernet switches can be used to create virtual LANs at the protocol or broadcast group level. For example, IPX traffic could be filtered at the port level, restricting it from entering another network segment while IP traffic might be allowed to pass.

Broadcast traffic might be limited on a port-by-port basis to further control traffic on each network segment. High-bandwidth traffic can be selectively isolated from the rest of the network.

Properly deployed, Ethernet switches can consolidate traffic in multiprotocol LANs (e.g., IP, IPX), DEC, AppleTalk) while effectively improving overall network throughput. Competitive switches selling for less than $4,000 (for as many as eight Ethernet ports with routing and filtering options) provide a cost-effective method for consolidating LAN segments, greatly improving network throughput.

## CONSERVING BANDWIDTH

Network congestion has greatly increased in recent years as more nodes are added and applications become more complex. LAN segmentation was originally deployed as one means of organizing groups of users into separate but interconnected LAN segments. This technique improved network performance by reducing contention, however, it is not as effective as LAN switching. The advent of the LAN switch represented a major leap forward for LANs. The first Ethernet switch was introduced by Kalpana in 1990, with LAN switching taking on many more refinements since that time.

A LAN switch can provide a dedicated bandwidth segment for the connection of high-traffic workstations or servers. These switching engines, when combined with the more advanced network management systems, extend the ability of the network administrator to fine-tune and tailor a network to optimum performance levels. The issue now — and the basis for discussion in this chapter — is how best to deploy this technology, particularly as Ethernet networks continue to expand and grow.

## GOING BEYOND SEGMENTATION

When properly integrated into the architecture of a LAN, intelligent hubs can greatly enhance the process for network optimization. For example, a network planner can easily reduce network traffic by aggregating users with common needs on separate LAN segments.

Through this process, any requirements for large amounts of bandwidth between common users can be restricted to their common segment environment. This process of establishing high-bandwidth users on common segments, however, can be further improved through the application of Ethernet switches.

A switched LAN has several advantages over segmentation, including:

- **Ease of migration.** The introduction of a switch into a LAN does not create a problem for the network staff because the LAN technology remains the same.
- **Capital conservation.** Introduction of a switch does not affect the overall structure of the LAN because no new cabling, hardware, or network infrastructure changes are required.
- **Evolutionary migration.** Switches enable the network planner to migrate toward the development of a virtual LAN and eventually integration with Asynchronous Transfer Mode backbone facilities.

## ABOUT ETHERNET SWITCHES

Original Ethernet was a shared LAN technology that allowed only one data conversation at a time. In this situation, the 10M bps of available bandwidth

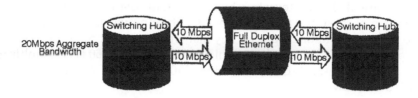

**Exhibit 1. Full-Duplex Point-to-Point Ethernet Connection.**

may end up being shared by multiple users. Consequently, when more than one user wants to access the network, collisions may result that cause delays limiting user productivity.

Because of the half-duplex nature of the Ethernet network and its distributed arbitration methodology, only 40% to 50% of the network's throughput potential is ever realized. For this reason, an Ethernet switch might be viewed as a throughput enhancer that allows multiple conversations to occur at the same time on the network. An Ethernet switch essentially creates parallel data conversations by establishing a dedicated point-to-point connection between two workstations (see Exhibit 1). This type of capability can increase normal Ethernet 10M bps throughput to 20 or 40M bps.

Earlier switches were separate modules designed to fit into the backplane of an intelligent hub. The newer LAN switches, however, are robust standalone units that can be used to support desktop-to-desktop switching, workgroup switching, or serve as larger enterprise backbone switches.

### Desktop Switches

These are used to link users with a common interest in applications that may be bandwidth intensive (e.g., Imaging, high-speed modeling, or multimedia applications). An example of a desktop switch might be Fore System's ANTswitch or Cisco's Catalyst Switch series.

### Workgroup Switches

These switches are deployed to add capacity to a congested LAN, allowing the connection of individual workstations or LAN segments. These switches can be connected to backbone networks or high-speed links connecting them to other servers. Examples of workgroup switches are Link-Switch, Cabletron's TSX-1620, and Performance Technologies' Nebula 2000.

### Backbone Switches

Larger switches provide very high speed backbone switching. These may use store-and-forward or other advanced networking techniques to support large numbers of connections and high traffic volumes. These switches are likely to integrate a high degree of redundancy and support some form of interface to a high-speed public network facility (e.g., T1, frame relay, or ATM backbone). They also support multiple protocols. An example of an Enterprise Switch would be the IBM 8250/60 series multiprotocol switches, Alantec's Power Hub 7000, 3Com's LANplex 6000, or XYLAN's OmniSwitch.

Originally, Ethernet switching engines were deployed in conjunction with intelligent hubs to enhance and extend LAN segments. In this setting, an Ethernet switch — when deployed in a segmentation infrastructure — could clear up network bottlenecks that would under other circumstances create significant response time delays. They also provided the ability to establish high-speed multiport internetworking solutions to allow the LAN administrator to segregate those high-speed workstations that had high bandwidth requirements. LAN switches support 100M-bps LAN speeds to include 100Base-T, 100VG-AnyLAN, and FDDI networks.

## NOT ALL SWITCHES PERFORM THE SAME

Not all Ethernet switching engines are designed the same and therefore their characteristics are a performance factor that must be considered in the configuration of an extended LAN. Switching modules are designed to interconnect LAN segments in much the same way that a telephone conversation is linked using a PBX. The LAN switching engine itself provides for the full wire speed interconnection of a LAN's segments. Although the terminology has changed in the past few years, two prevalent switching designs may be found in Ethernet switches: cut-through switching and store-and-forward switching.

### Cut-Through Switching

Under this switching architecture, the switch has been designed to forward packets to their destination before a packet is fully received and before the collision window passes. This type of architecture does not limit the end-to-end throughput as do store-and-forward bridges, for example. Cisco and IBM switches use this design characteristic.

### Store-and-Forward Architecture

Under this switching architecture, the whole packet is fully received before the forwarding process begins. Each packet is buffered in memory and the switch examines the entire packet. Because the packets can be inspected, more advanced management capabilities are available.

The forwarding method used by Ethernet switches varies and is based on whether there is bridging or routing software. Some vendors (e.g., 3Com, Cisco, and Performance Technologies, Inc.) have methods that combine techniques from cut-through and store and forward. Depending on error thresholds, these switches may switch from store and forward to a form of adaptive cut-through.

Using proprietary software, a vendor will incorporate one of these designs into a proprietary switching matrix. This software switching matrix is integrated into specially designed hardware that will support back-to-back packets in a F-DX mode. Most switch designs offer multiple ports (four to eight) to support simultaneous Ethernet connections between connected switches. Through this design, some Ethernet switches can offer as high as 40M-bps throughput with a transit delay as low as 70 microseconds.

In some switches, filters are incorporated into the design of the switch to filter out packet fragments or runts generated as the result of the Ethernet collision process. Some Ethernet switches support both broadcast and multicast frames at as many as 59,520 packets per second. Although port designs vary among manufacturers, most use an RJ-45 interface and provide support for several 10Base-T ports as well as multimedia (i.e., 10Base-2, 10Base-5). In some designs, provisions may exist for as many as 1,024 address per port with buffer sizes of as high as 1,500 packets per port. Other features include intrusion control and bridging security features, redundant clocking, and power supply modules.

## MULTIPROTOCOL (WORKGROUP) SWITCHING

One of the greatest applications of Ethernet switches is workgroup switching. This may be a result of the fact that many large networks evolve as an amalgamation of several different smaller LANs, each with a different protocol. The key to successful network management lies in the ability of the network administrator to filter network traffic as it arrives at specific points along the network. For this reason, protocol switches have come on the market that combine wire speed connectivity with the ability to filter multiprotocol Ethernet traffic (e.g., IP, IPX, DEC, and AppleTalk).

Protocol switches often serve as workgroup accelerators or collapsed backbones. Protocol switches, when properly deployed, can support the organization of virtual LANs. Filtering is accomplished at the port level, where in some switches there can be as much as four tiers of wire speed filtering: broadcast groups, internal LANs, protocol filtering, and MAC address filtering. Through this filtering process, these switches can block or filter the propagation of unwanted traffic across a network by forming a firewall.

### Firewalls

For example, using this process an administrator might block IPX traffic from crossing onto a DEC network segment while IP traffic might be

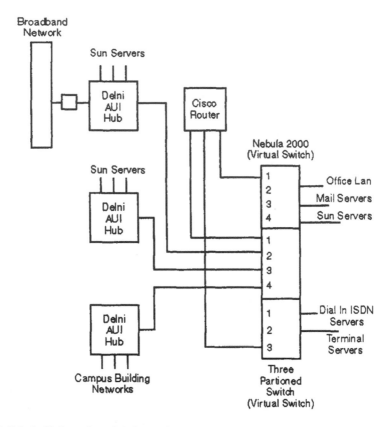

**Exhibit 2. University of California, San Diego Campus, Network Operations.**

allowed to pass. MAC address filtering can be used to establish a secure means to restrict traffic to specific terminals. Broadcast domains can be established that restrict broadcast packets to specific segments or to ports that are members of the same broadcast group. In this way, specific broadcasts can be restricted to those segments of which they are members.

Exhibit 2 shows the application of an inexpensive protocol switch, the Nebula 2000,which is used on the campuswide network at the UCSD. The Nebula 2000 links many diverse servers and local networks (e.g., Office LAN, mail servers, and Sun servers) by providing a high-speed protected link between networks.

In this configuration, the Nebula 2000 has been divided into three separate partitions that comprise a collapsed backbone for the UCSD campus network. Protocol filtering and MAC address filtering provide a means to restrict certain types of traffic to specific segments while MAC address filtering ensures

**Exhibit 3. Factors Effecting End-to-End Throughput**

| Feature | Design Characteristic | |
| --- | --- | --- |
| | Cut-Through | Store/Forward |
| Filter corrupt and fragmented packets | No | Yes |
| Low latency | Yes | No |
| Support for redundant links | No | Yes |
| Full duplex | Yes | Yes |
| Smooth handling of broadcast packets | No | Yes |

complete security against unauthorized access to privileged information. Here, the establishment of specific broadcast domains insulate all of the attached networks from broadcast saturation on unauthorized segments.

The Nebula 2000 SGNMS is used by the LAN administrator to reconfigure network segments and filtering patterns (firewalls) to suit any change in requirements. There is a complete diagnostic subsystem incorporated within the StarGazer system that allows the Network Administrator to monitor the entire system. A WAN port on the Nebula 2000 provides the support for remote diagnostics. This capability allows the network administrator to access the Nebula 2000 remotely to monitor the activity on individual ports as well as reconfigure or resegment the network.

## Network Considerations

Network configurations will be affected by the switching characteristics of a switch. For example, multiple nonblocking paths between individual pairs of ports on connected switches provide for full use of all available bandwidth. With cut-through design, a packet's latency is dramatically reduced because the leading edge of a packet exits the switch before the trailing edge enters. In this way, packets can be forwarded 20 times faster than conventional store-and-forward bridges.

Although a regular bridge or router typically will delay a full-size packet by about 1,200 microseconds, a cut-through Ethernet switch will measure transit delay in tens of microseconds. This difference in transit delay will force a quantum difference in the resulting end-to-end throughput. This type of switching, however, may propagate corrupted packets or ones containing errors.

Exhibit 3 lists a few factors that can effect end-to-end throughput. As can be seen, the store-and-forward architecture avoids many of the problems associated with a cut-through architecture. This includes short or fragmented frames as well as the smooth handling of multicast packets. In addition, this architecture provides for a much easier migration to high-speed LAN technologies such as Fast Ethernet or ATM.

**Exhibit 4. Nebula 2000 Port Configuration**

| Nebula 2000 Port | Port Type | Full Duplex |
|---|---|---|
| Port | Console | N/A |
| Port | Trace Port | (LAN analyzer) |
| Port | WAN Port | Supports IP (RIP) SLIP routing |
| Port 1 | 10Base-T/RJ-45 | No |
| Port 2 | 10Base-T/RJ-45 | No |
| Port 3 | 10Base-T/RJ-45 | No |
| Port 4 | 10Base-T/RJ-45 | No |
| Port 5 | 10Base-T/RJ-45 | No |
| Port 6 | 10Base-T/RJ-45 | No |
| Port 7 | 10Base-T/RJ-45 | Yes |
| Port 8 | 10Base-T/RJ-45 | Yes |

## Switch Types

Ethernet switch configurations vary with their application design. For example, desktop switches are designed to provide a high-speed link between desk terminals using bandwidth-intensive applications. Ports are available to link several terminals as well as a server.

Workgroup switches support Ethernet links or segments, with separate ports for each link. Workgroup switches are connected to hubs to provide segment connectivity. There may be several high-speed links to connect servers. A WAN port may be included to link to other remote LANs.

Hub or backbone switches are used to connect several corporate resources across a collapsed backbone. These switches also provide ports for Ethernet links as well as high-speed WAN links that are used to link remote LANs by the public network (e.g., frame relay, T1, and ATM).

## TYPICAL MIDRANGE SWITCH

Exhibit 4 shows the basic configuration for a typical midrange workgroup Ethernet switch, the Nebula 2000. This is a typical base line configuration for a stackable type switch. The summary for the Nebula 2000 Ethernet Switch states that any 10Base-T port can easily be connected to either a 10Base-T transceiver or 10Base-T device without requiring special cross-over cables. Two of the 10Base-T ports are configurable to an F-DX operation. An F-DX link connecting two switches will enable the switches to transmit and receive simultaneously between them.

The full-duplex operation is a modification of a normal half-duplex operation. This technology enables a high-performance, low-latency connection between multiple servers, or other Nebula switches. In Exhibit 5, the high-speed SPARC station can be connected to the other high-speed SPARC station, and the workstation can be connected to the server.

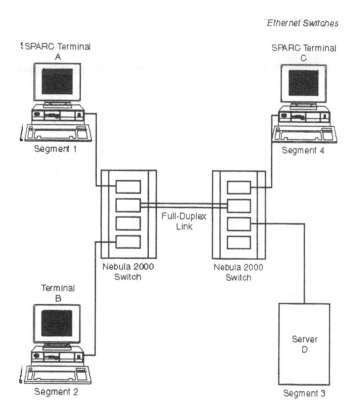

**Exhibit 5. Dual Nebula 2000 Switches Connected with a Full-Duplex Link.**

An F-DX (20M bps) link is established between each of these devices. Because there is no media access delay nor collisions for any packet forwarded to a full-duplex link, network latency is greatly enhanced. In the full-duplex architecture of the Nebula 2000 Switch in Exhibit 5, all switching takes place within the Ethernet switch because the Ethernet switch serves as F-EP for the segments distributed behind the switch.

## APPLICATION

Not every Ethernet LAN is a candidate for switching. An ideal application requires the presence of multiple hubs residing in multiple departments, floors, or buildings. There should be the presence of high-performance workstations with applications that demand high bandwidth (e.g., CAD/CAM, imaging, and multimedia). These conditions would be characteristic of large campus environments typically associated with academic or industrial research activities.

Typically, in these environments there will be clusters of high-performance workstations (e.g., Sun SPARC and DEC Alpha) used for scientific, imaging, and multimedia applications. These applications generate large amounts of traffic with high demands for bandwidth. In this environment, Ethernet switches serve as a natural extension of the network segments. These switches would be capable of supporting parallel internetworking of subsegments thereby optimizing the capability of the network without sacrificing the investment in the infrastructure.

Exhibit 6 shows an overview of the University of California Supercomputer Center network that supports the academic and research requirements for University of California San Diego as a large user constituency scattered around the world. In this network, the planners have deployed an inexpensive Ethernet switch (Nebula 2000) to link a number of external and internal networks to their diverse computing resources.

This design concept makes use of a collapsed backbone network supported by a Nebula 2000 switch concentrating four different networks within their Supercomputer Center in La Jolla. The four-tier filtering capability of the Nebula 2000 makes it possible to extend the vast resources of the Supercomputer center to outside researchers, keeping all users within a well-defined set of boundaries.

A router connects the Nebula 2000 to an FDDI network within the center, which in turn provides links to the Cray C-90, Intel Paragon XPS 30, and various other computing resources.

## TRIGGERING EVENTS

The key element of this type of a strategy is the employment of network filtering to reduce the amount of traffic that flows across the network. This technique serves to contain extraneous traffic to the appropriate networks but allow passage of those packets of information with a specific requirement for access. Extensive application of MAC address filtering ensures that only those specific assigned users will have access to secured information resources. In this situation, the Nebula 2000 serves to selectively isolate traffic to specific LAN segments and broadcast groups to maintain overall performance levels.

This form of segmentation allows for parallel communications as well as the isolation of specific workstation groups with requirements for high-speed throughput. In addition, in a university or campus situation there is likely to develop a number of workgroups with a demand for large amounts of bandwidth. In the case of the University, many workgroups are engaged in special research projects where there is an unnatural distribution of high-speed workstations (e.g., Sun SPARC terminals, DEC, and UNIX-based servers). The design concept for this type of network architecture is to

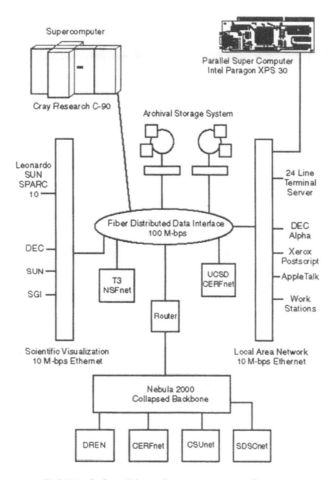

**Exhibit 6. San Diego Supercomputer Center.**

establish, at an early stage, the capability to isolate or reorganize high-speed workstations into communities of interest before they impact the performance of the network.

In a typical campus-type network environment, the application of a Nebula 2000 switch can greatly enhance the process for dividing the network into smaller more efficient workgroups. The Nebula 2000, supported by an established hierarchical structure across the campus, is capable of fully interconnecting each of the established subnetworks of the various departments. The Nebula 2000 filters the local traffic and connects specific segments at full wire speed. The university experiences frequent moves and changes, however, the Nebula 2000 StarGazer NM system can accommodate

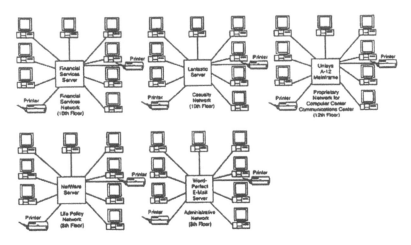

**Exhibit 7. Existing Installation of Standalone Networks.**

moves, additions, and changes to make for a very smooth implementation of a new LAN segment.

## A NETWORK IN TRANSITION — A CASE STUDY

Exhibit 7 presents a general overview of a network for a large insurance company. Over the years their network expanded indiscriminately starting first as a Unisys minicomputer-based proprietary network. This network expanded to the point that the network was unable to support the user population. This gave rise to the establishment of several separate dedicated networks using PCs and high-speed workstations from Sun, Hewlett-Packard, and Digital Equipment Corp. There are now more than 350 workstations that comprise several functional LANs.

As the company expanded through acquisitions and customer growth, a number of disparate networks evolved. The application of LAN NOS (e.g., NetWare and Lantastic) allowed individual user groups to set up LANs by lines of business. This expedited the automation of the company's lines of business, but left the company with several customer database structures as well as a complex process for interLAN server communications.

The establishment of a common corporate customer database greatly improves sales and customer service. Exhibit 8 shows one solution for a design concept for the insurance company's expanding network. This concept deploys intelligent hubs and a large-scale Bay Networks router to support an enterprisewide network. Because the insurance company has consolidated their operations in a high-rise office complex, their network can be organized based on a collapsed fiber backbone. The old proprietary

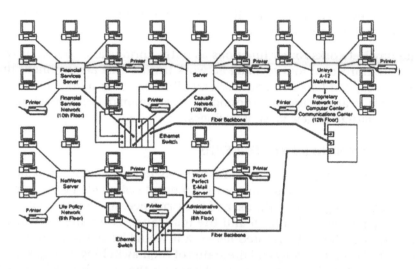

**Exhibit 8. Insurance Companies Networks (from Exhibit 7) with Interworking Components.**

network can now be phased out and a migration path established to phase out the old Unysis A-series platform.

Additional functional LANs can be phased in as required. For example, several functional LANs have been reestablished to support the fire and automobile lines of business on the casualty network. Health and life lines of business can now be supported to a newly established life policy network. The former administrative and Unysis network can now function to support E-mail, word processing, and general internal business applications (e.g., billing and receivables).

The integration of intelligent hubs incorporating Ethernet switches over a fiber backbone provides for the segregation of communities of interest onto separate subsegments. Additional Ethernet switches provide for the direct interconnection of selected servers to improve access to customer files. This arrangement makes it possible to contain the amount of enterprisewide traffic and keep like traffic within the same community of interest. Therefore, bandwidth can be kept to a minimum across the enterprisewide network.

Previously, server traffic often created network slowdowns during key periods of the work day because of frequent cross-server access by unrelated line-of-business users. To remedy this situation, some of the intelligent hubs have been introduced onto the network. This allows some of the key servers to be directly linked as well as some of their high-speed workstations. Once again, this strategy allows the network administrator to contain high bandwidth requirements to specific LAN subsegments optimizing the performance on the entire network.

The Bay Networks router functions as both a bridge and router, providing for multiprotocol routing of all network traffic. This arrangement provides a collapsed backbone network architecture over a fiber backbone media. This strategy supports the continued addition of functional LANs to support a variety of new lines of business.

## NETWORK MANAGEMENT CONCERNS

When implementing hub-mounted Ethernet switching engines, it is necessary to maintain a complete view of the Ethernet switch elements in terms of topology, configuration, status, and performance. As can be seen in the university model in Exhibit 6 and the insurance company network in Exhibit 7, in a widely distributed network it would be possible to quickly lose track of their topology and the status of their switching configurations without a system for management. Although the switch vendors (e.g., Cabletron and Bay Networks) have network management systems available for their switch products, it is important to recognize the elements of management that are required to support a high-speed widespread LAN.

The university network shown in Exhibit 6 has the Nebula 2000 Star-Gazer network manager in place. This network management system provides a 3D graphics system that allows quick identification of network bottlenecks. A series of tools allows the network administrator to monitor network traffic in real time. Instantaneous feedback on individual ports and cumulative traffic allows the network manager to quickly identify network problems. A network topology feature allows the user to calculate and display the configuration of the current network topology. A trace port provides for the interface of a LAN analyzer that runs with a diagnostic program allowing the network manager to evaluate each active port without removing cables.

Various options allow the user to display the logical relationships of the Nebula switches and their relationship to other devices on the network. A port configurator function is available that allows the user to display the configuration of each Nebula port, its filtering setup, address resolution protocol leakage, and other control parameters in real time. The StarGazer is an icon-driven Windows product that provides a range of options for monitoring and gathering statistics.

For example, there are options for viewing the status of the Ethernet switch, set traffic thresholds, measure traffic at each of the ports, and measure and evaluate a range of network faults. There is also an option for simulating network segmentation and the impact of traffic on the segment in relation to Ethernet switching. This is a valuable aid in managing the placement of Ethernet switches across the network. StarGazer is an SNMP compliant network management system supporting both in-band and out-of-band SNMP management using Windows for ease of use.

## ATM SWITCHING AND LAN EMULATION

Desktop ATM switching is being heralded as the next step in advancing the capability of a LAN or a multiple campus network to increase their throughput. This has become possible through the development of LAN emulation (e.g., LANE 1.0), an architecture developed by the ATM Forum that makes it possible for native LAN devices and protocols to communicate over ATM.

In recent tests using backbone ATM links, both IP and IPX Ethernet traffic could be handled easily over ATM. Although IP and IPX routing will work over Token Ring networks, source-ring bridging — a mandatory element in Token Ring networks — will not work over ATM. ATM integration can add significant complexity to a network configuration in terms of network management and network configuration.

### Not Plug and Play

Although users have become accustomed to the shrink-wrap nature of the PC world, the connection-oriented nature of ATM, along with developing standards and new techniques, presents a steep learning curve for the network administrator. For example, each ATM session is a direct connection between devices that demand a different set of analysis procedures that are quite different from that of a shared LAN environment.

In addition, configuring an ATM gateway requires learning the operation of an entirely different device: an ATM switch. This dictates an additional set of tasks to get routers and servers properly interfaced. Such tasks involve configuring the ATM switch to establish the correct signaling protocol and related parameters.

### ATM Is Not Cheap

ATM is still expensive because the equipment is still in limited production and the market is generally not ready to step up to the plate. For example, a baseline four-port ATM switch will cost about $33,000, while an ATM OC-3 port card for a router can cost as much as $26,000.

Aside from costs, the LAN administrator will have to plan carefully because ATM switches do not interoperate. For this reason, it may be wise to start first with point-to-point backbone arrangements before interlinking multiple servers.

### Multi-Access LAN Servers

Service providers are emerging to support the transport of high-volume LAN traffic. For example, these companies provide multitenant access to a single high-speed communications link. The cost of these high-speed links can be charged back to multiple users at a fraction of what they might cost for a private network link. These transport services provide transport of IP and IPX traffic in an ATM pipe. They are supported by special ATM edge switches that are designed to completely fill an ATM pipe, making it economically feasible to support many different users at the same time.

An example of such a switch can be found in the NetEdge ATM Connect Switch, which is designed to support secure access to a single ATM link by multiple end users. This switch can support both permanent and switch virtual circuit arrangements. It will also support IP routing over SVC arrangements.

### CONCLUSION

Newer high-performance workstations crowding the market are certain to expand the demand for bandwidth in the late 1990s and beyond. The introduction of low-cost Ethernet switches will allow network planners to extend the capabilities of their LANs as well as optimize degrading network performance as it may develop.

Switching technology provides the LAN administrator with the ability to preserve a growing network infrastructure investment while meeting the needs of the network user for more bandwidth. As the application of Asynchronous Transfer Mode begins to evolve, the network administrator positioned with Ethernet switches will be able to migrate into the higher-performance levels of ATM.

# Chapter 64
# Remote LAN/WAN Connections: A Case Study

*Charles Breakfield and Roxanne Burkey*

The organization discussed in this chapter is a national corporation head-quartered in Virginia. Currently, the company's corporate locations inter-connect through a Banyan wide area network (WAN) for access to business software, national databases, and E-mail. Each location contains a network service area for user support and connects to other locations, including the Virginia headquarter offices.

Space reconfiguration at a corporate location in Texas prompted a move of approximately 125 support staff to the fourth and sixth floors of an adja-cent building, approximately 100 feet away from the primary building. The Banyan WAN resided on the seventh floor of the primary building, and the main support areas for data access were to remain there.

The relocating staff, however, required network data access from two of the existing servers on the seventh floor to perform their work, but provid-ing network servers and the associated support staff to the new location was not an option. Exhibit 1 illustrates the wiring layout of the primary building.

An additional consideration was that the organization was consolidating business activities. Broader plans for the year were to consolidate network operations to enable an overall reduction in support staff. Therefore, any system changes made for this relocation of the 125 support staff had to:

- Be limited in cost.
- Use existing materials.
- Require no additional staffing.
- Adhere to the existing network standards.
- Contain limited leasing and licensing agreements.

0-8493-9965-3/99/$0.00+$.50
© 1999 by CRC Press LLC

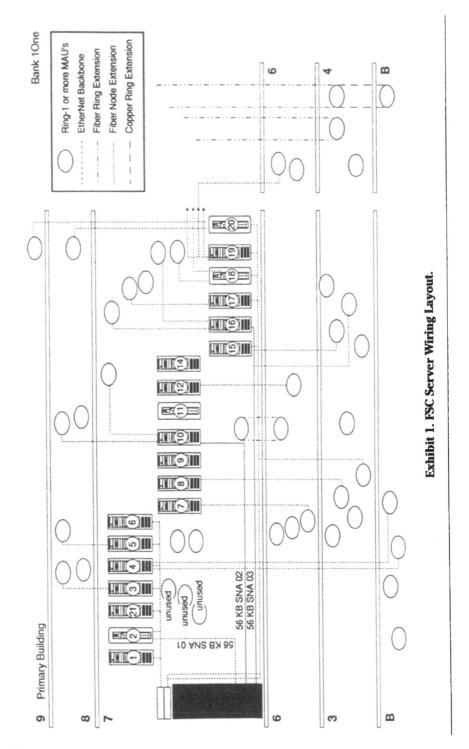

**Exhibit 1. FSC Server Wiring Layout.**

A feasibility study determined the technology needed for data connection from the fourth and sixth floors of the adjacent building to the seventh-floor server room of the primary building.

This article describes the three connectivities (i.e., fiber optics, infrared, and microwave) considered in the feasibility study, the advantages and disadvantages of each, the estimated time to complete installation, and the draft estimated costs. The article also puts all these factors in the context of the company's business operations.

Finally, the article also supplies a proposed plan for the solution's implementation and installation. The recommended course of action is based on the technology feasibility, time frames, costs, and flexibility for known future organizational changes.

## ESTABLISHING A BASELINE

A feasibility study certified the data connection method among the existing services and the remote new services and outlined the most viable option for connectivity within the confines determined by upper management. The study began with an itemization of existing resources and criteria for deciding on technology options.

### Existing Resources

Staff members familiar with the existing Banyan network conducted the study over a nine- week period. Detailed reviews of the existing and planned systems included a review of the wiring configuration for the new space, data specifications, building requirements, and existing AT&T services to determine the project requirements.

The staff investigated the possibility that appropriate technology might already be in use elsewhere in the company, as well. They conducted a nationwide, corporatewide investigation of the options available for data connectivity requirements. A step was also completed to locate in-house support staff with experience with similar installations, problems that might come up with a specific technology, and available materials.

### DEFINING THE OPTIONS

The criteria for evaluating the options were determined based on the initial request and follow-up discussions with staff. The criteria, in order of importance, included the operational time frames, connection reliability, technical support provisions, and cost.

The physical hardware and wireless connection possibilities were reviewed based on the criteria, and three viable options were selected to undergo in- depth analysis. After the technology investigation was complete, a review with building management was conducted to ensure acceptance of the recommendation.

## DEFINING THE EXISTING RESOURCES

The existing Banyan WAN servers were located on the seventh floor of the primary building. Staff was in place at the primary location to support the requirements of Banyan WAN users at the primary building and of users selected for the move to the adjacent building.

The adjacent building's floor configuration included freestanding cubicle work areas and walled offices with freestanding desks. Each workstation required power to support the electrical equipment, an RJ-45 data jack for the phone connection, and an IBM data connection to support the existing Token Ring topology.

Wiring closets were installed on each floor at the remote location; the closets had three wire racks as well as punch blocks. The wire racks contained the data cables terminated into patch panels and mounted in the top third of the wire racks. The power drops for the walled offices included voice, data, and power connections. Power poles fed voice, data, and power connections for each cubicle. Each workstation contained Type 2 cable, Type 1 data cable for the Token Ring connection, and 4-pair wire for the voice connection.

## DEFINING THE BUSINESS OBJECTIVE

Banyan support service for the remote location was possible by means of one of the following,

- Hiring additional staff for Banyan server support.
- Moving existing support staff to the new location.
- Providing remote support by the existing staff running back and forth between the buildings.
- Establishing a remote connection into the existing server configuration while maintaining current staffing levels.

The option that best suited the company's long-term needs was establishing a new connection into the existing configuration at the primary site, without adding support staff. The project then was to provide a data interface between the two buildings.

The requirements for data access included a network connection from the three wire racks in the fourth-floor wire closet and three wire racks in the sixth-floor wire closet of the adjacent building to the wire racks located in the seventh- floor server room of the primary building. The final link between the selected technology and the target servers would require connection to a Token Ring Type 1 drop cable. The cost considerations had to include any adapters or converters needed for linking the existing system to the recommended technology.

There were, in this case, possible limitations on the use of physical hard-wiring networking items; the building management might determine certain equipment to be dangerous to the property, building staff, or other tenants. Because physical wiring above ground was not allowed, the access had to take place below ground under the parking garage or via equipment to be located on the roof.

## CONNECTIVITY OPTIONS

The method selected had to provide reliable connectivity for data while remaining cost- effective. To meet this requirement, both physical and wireless connectivity options were explored. Several potential methods were reviewed; three of these were selected for final consideration.

### Physical Connections

Physical wiring of a WAN is the single largest cost factor of materials and installation labor.

**Twisted-Pair Cable.** Cable standards include either twisted-pair or coaxial cable. Hardware connection performance for a Token Ring network environment is measured by the rate at which it can move data. Twisted- pair cable can reliably move data at the rate of 10M bps and coaxial cable can reliably move data at 16M bits.

**Fiber Optic Connectivity.** Fiber optic connection is considered by many today as the premiere connection for voice and data. It provides a reliable connection and allows for an increase in system throughput.

### Wireless Connections

Today, wireless network connection is concentrated in three areas, including spread spectrum UHF, infrared, and microwave radio technologies.

**Spread Spectrum UHF.** This is designed to appear as background noise in most radio frequency transmitters and receivers. Consequently, data is very secure; only an authorized user is able to access the data. Data is not susceptible to interference from other signals or electronic devices; however, transmission speed is limited and best suited for a small LAN environment.

**Infrared.** Infrared is the type of signal used over most fiber optic links but without the fiber media. These devices can achieve speeds of 16M bits. Products available include those specifically designed for a Token Ring environment with multiple-access units. This technology is effective in environments with an unobstructed line of site.

**Exhibit 2. Advantages of Fiber Optic, Microwave, and Infrared Technologies**

| Option 1: Fiber Optic | Option 2: Microwave | Option 3: Infrared |
|---|---|---|
| Impervious to electrical noise and interference typically present in all office environments | Low signal attenuation | Freedom from government regulation, no licensing or usage fees |
| Systems using fiber are immune to RFI | Portability of equipment, owned by the organization | Portability of equipment, owned by the organization |
| Fiber optic poses no risk of carrying lightening charges to computer equipment | Cost-effective for line-of-sight connection and when frequency bank congestion is low, this is cost-effective | Ease of interconnecting additional locations |
| Fiber is conducive to a Token Ring environment | Conducive to a Token Ring environment | Immunity to radio interference |
| Rapid installation | Reasonable installation time | Reasonable installation time |
| High data security | Signal scrambling is available through some vendors | Security of the data |
| Upwardly scalable | | |

**Microwave.** Microwave technology offers speed for transmission to 6.7M bits at a range of 130 feet and supports Ethernet. This technology has the benefit of providing ownership of materials, allowing lower costs on future relocations.

### Eliminating Inappropriate Connectivity Technologies

Two of the technologies described in the previous sections were eliminated from any in-depth consideration. Twisted-pair cables were dismissed as an option because the preliminary review indicated a lack of reliability at this project's distance — 100 feet. Twisted-pair cables also have limitations in handling the anticipated data traffic.

Spread spectrum UHF was also eliminated. Even though spread spectrum UI-IF is a secure connectivity option, it is limited in speed and best suited for small LANs. Consideration of this application to future, smaller-scale projects was recommended.

The three options given serious consideration are discussed in the following sections. Exhibits 2 and 3 summarize the advantages and disadvantages of each technology.

### THE FIRST OPTION: FIBER OPTICS

Fiber optics is a communications media linking two electronic circuits by a strand of glass. It is lightweight and small, making it more attractive for projects in which space is at a premium. A graded index fiber performs best, because of its ability to carry multiple signals, with the least amount of signal

**Exhibit 3. Disadvantages of Fiber Optic, Microwave, and Infrared Technologies**

| Option 1: Fiber Optic | Option 2: Microwave | Option 3: Infrared |
| --- | --- | --- |
| Additional repeaters are needed to boost the signals for long distances | The capacity of 6.7M bits is less than the 16M-bit needed at its peak times | Atmospheric conditions affect reliable data transmission |
| Fiber cable runs cannot be subjected to sharp turns | Outside installation support required and no existing training available | High up-front equipment investment and installation support |
| Cable terminations and splices must be specially prepared | Signal or transmission unreliability during excessive rains | Potential safety issue for retina damage caused by looking directly into the beam |
| The materials belong to the property | Potential delay of licensing from the FCC, possible installation delay | |

loss, due to dispersion. Wide bandwidth, low signal loss, and electromagnetic immunity are the three most outstanding features of fiber optics.

**Fiber Optic Data Transmission**

Fiber optic systems transmit data as a series of light pulses, generated either by light- emitting diodes (LED) or lasers. The bit error rates (BERs) for fiber optic cabling are as much as 10,000 times lower than standard electrical media. The connections are further simplified by the absence of ground loops, crosstalk, ringing, and echoing.

Light propagation through fiber depends principally on three factors, including the composition, size, and light injected into the fiber. Transmitting sources commonly use LED in place of laser. With a longer lifetime than a laser light, LED is easier to use and maintain. A LED source has a higher and broader output pattern but is not capable of single-mode compatibility. The transmitter output power is coupled with the diameter of fiber, so that power increases with core diameter.

Detectors perform the opposite function from the source by converting optical energy to electrical energy. The photo diode produces current in response to incident light. Detectors are typically packaged in the same receptacles as sources. Receiver sensitivity specifies the weakest optical signal it will receive. This is affected by the amount of noise, or signal clarity, during signal receipt as measured by bit error rate (BER) or the signal-to-noise ratio (SNR).

**Fiber Optic Cabling**

Fiber optic cable is available in either single mode or multimode. Single mode has an aperture of about nine microns, has a low attenuation rate, and is ideally suited for long-distance networks. Multimode is available at apertures from 50 to 100 microns and has a higher attenuation rate, because signals enter at an angle and bounce off the fiber walls as they travel. This allows for use of multiple paths, making it best suited for short-distance applications. Fiber cable comes in simplex (containing one fiber), duplex (containing a sending and receiving fiber), or hybrid, in which duplex is combined with twisted pair.

A network requires only two strands of fiber; however, a multiple strand cable is often used for backup reliability for transmission. The fiber diameter is used for this type of connection is 62.5 µm and has a standard cladding diameter of 125 µm. This combination offers high speed, low attenuation (3.75 dB/km), and a high bandwidth of 1,000 MHz/km at 1,300 nm.

Fiber optic cabling is versatile, with the ability to serve as a backbone, front-end, and back end of LAN networks. Both Ethernet and Token Ring network configurations are adaptable to fiber optic cabling in place of standard copper wiring. The cost of this media typically makes it best suited to campus, building, and data center network environments. Exhibit 4 displays the potential connection configuration considered for this project.

### Advantages

Fiber optic connections offer a wide variety of advantages over other hardwire and wireless options. Fiber:

- Transmits data as a series of light pulses, making it impervious to electrical noise and interference typically present in all office environments.
- Is immune to radio frequency interference (RH).
- Does not conduct electricity, thus protecting computer equipment from lightning charges.
- Is a highly secure data transmission medium, because it does not radiate energy, and tapping data from it is extremely difficult.
- Is conducive to an Ethernet or Token Ring environment, as with most hardwire installations.
- Is upwardly scalable.

In addition, the installation of fiber is rapid.

### Disadvantages

The disadvantages of this technology include:

- Additional repeaters are needed to boost the signals over long distances, which incurs costs.
- Fiber cable runs cannot be subjected to sharp turns.
- Cable terminations and splices must be specially prepared.
- Materials cannot be removed once they are installed.

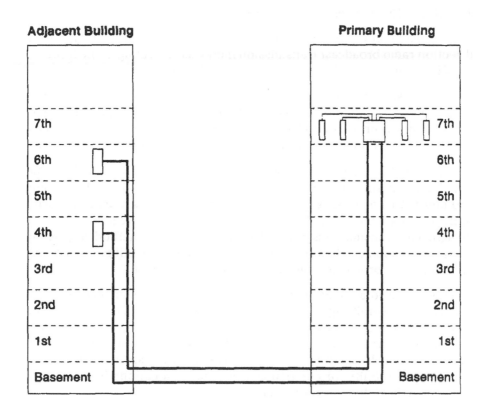

**Exhibit 4. Fiber Optic Cable Run.**

## Costs

The basic cost to set up the fiber optic option for the remote location would be as follows:

| Materials Description | Unit Price | Quantity | Total Price |
|---|---|---|---|
| 15.foot Patch Cables | $45 | 10 | $450 |
| Fiber Breakout Box | $150 | 4 | $600 |
| Eight-strand Fiber Cable 62.5/125 µm per Foot | $2 | 1,500 | $3,000 |
| DB-9 Type 1 Cable | $50 | 4 | $200 |
| Additional Wire Racks for the Seventh Floor | | | $250 |
| Fiber Optic Repeaters | $1,400 | 8 | $11,200 |
| Outside Installation | $30 | 32 | $960 |
| Total Fiber Optic Installation | | | $16,660 |

## THE SECOND OPTION: MICROWAVE

A microwave radio system can transmit voice, data, and video and uses direction radio broadcast transmission methods, operating in the 2 GHz to 40 GHz frequency bands, as displayed in Exhibit 5.

A line-of-sight relationship is required between transmitting and receiving antennas, which must resist winds reaching 70 miles per hour. The transmission is primarily stable, though certain conditions, such as excessively hard or prolonged rain, can reduce reliability of data transmission.

There are two types of microwave systems available, the short haul and long haul. The short haul system is for transmissions up to and including 250 miles. This method is typically used by universities, businesses with multiple locations, hotel chains, and hospitals. The long haul system is designed for transmissions greater than 250 miles. This method is typically used by common carriers (i.e., AT&T, GTE, and Sprint), utility companies, oil companies, broadcast companies, and paid television.

The increased amount of satellites available for transmitting signals is reducing the overall ongoing costs of microwave systems. For international businesses, satellite transmission is an alternative to poor voice and data communications in some countries' public communications systems, particularly those classified as third world. The wireless aspect of the system provides portability for companies that change locations frequently or those planning future location changes.

### Licensing Requirements

Microwave technology requires licensing, based on the frequency bandwidth. Licenses are issued by the FCC and take from two weeks to several months to obtain, depending on the request load. Licensing is granted for one year, with annual renewal options.

Antennas must comply with FCC standards for acceptable performance. The connections must also comply with Underwriter Laboratories (UL) standards.

### Advantages

The advantages for using a microwave system include:

- Low signal attenuation.
- Equipment portability.
- Cost-effectiveness when there is a line-of-sight connection and frequency bank congestions are low.
- Signal scrambling for increased data security.

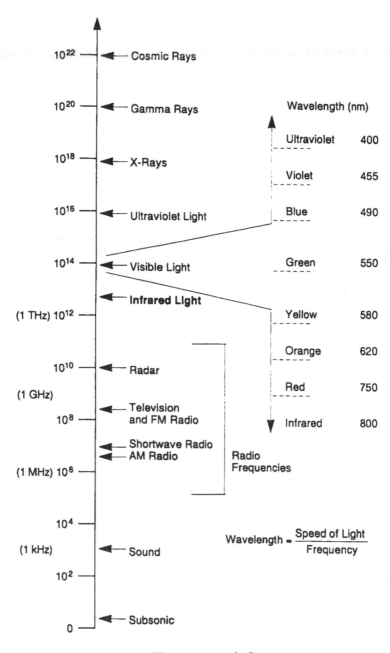

**Exhibit 5. Electromagnetic Spectrum.**

## Disadvantages

Microwave's disadvantages include:

- The bandwidth is limited to a 6.7M-bit capacity, with an estimated 16M-bit peak-time potential.
- Outside installation support is required.
- Signals are unreliable during excessive rains.
- There is a potential delay in receiving licensing from the FCC, which could prevent meeting the installation schedule.

## Costs

The basic cost to set up the microwave radio system for the corporate remote location would be as follows:

| Materials Description | Unit Price | Quantity | Total Price |
|---|---|---|---|
| Microwave Radio System | $10,000 | 1 | $10,000 |
| Microwave Interface Unit for Networks | $3,000 | 2 | $6,000 |
| Antennas | $2,100 | 2 | $4,200 |
| Subcontracted Installation | $2,200 | 1 | $2,200 |
| Licensing Fee One Year (Requires Annual Renewal) | $520 | 1 | $520 |
| Total Microwave Radio Installation | | | $20,950 |

There was an optional system maintenance contract available that included immediate replacement of faulty equipment, to minimize downtime, for $250 per month. This annualized to $3,000. Staff training would also be required to provide system maintenance. Backup equipment would increase overall costs by 50%.

## THE THIRD OPTION: INFRARED

A Free- Space Infrared Local Area Network (FIRLAN) system is based on infrared (IR) technology and can be used to build or replace a traditional hardwire network. The FIRLAN provides point-to-point or point-to-multipoints transmission of Ethernet signals between segments or stations, as well as T1 line signal transmission, as shown in Exhibit 6.

IR technology replaces cables with wireless optical links using line-of-sight JR transmission. Some systems use lasers as a basis for optical transmission. This is superior to standard JR transmission devices, especially under high ambient lighting and poor weather conditions.

It is recommended with IR systems that the installer have an IR viewer for alignment accuracy. The units are mounted on the corner, at the windows, or on the roof of the building to which they are attached and preferably are mounted to masonry construction. The supporting structure for the viewers cannot be wood or sheet metal.

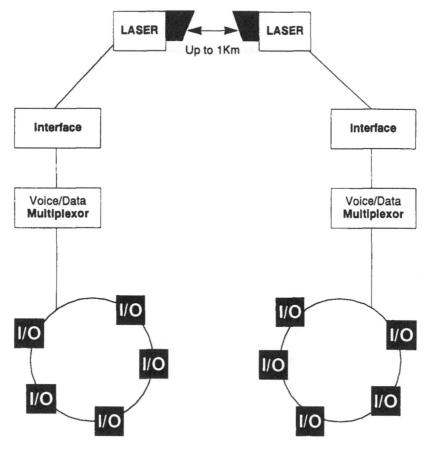

**Exhibit 6. The Typical T1 Connection Setup.**

JR systems offer industry- standard LAN and WAN interfaces, enabling the use of standard network interface cards and network software. FIRLAN provides seamless Ethernet integration, setting the required bit rate at 10M bits, and defines the physical interfaces and operating characteristics for the hardware, as shown in Exhibit 7.

**Conditions Affecting Effectiveness.** The three most significant atmospheric conditions that affect laser transmission include absorption, scattering, and shimmering. All three conditions can reduce the amount of light energy received by the receiver. The phenomena affect the laser transmission to varying degrees.

Absorption along the transmission path is caused mainly by the water vapor and carbon dioxide content in the air, which in turn depend on the

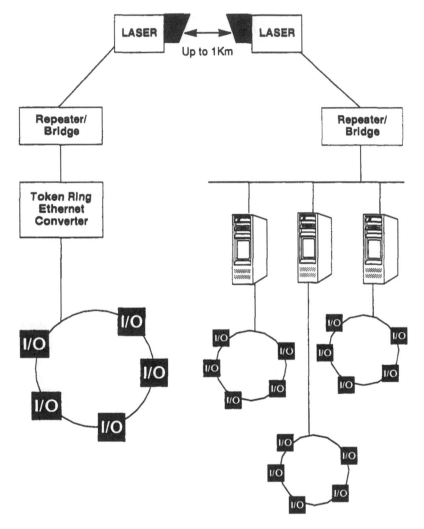

**Exhibit 7. The Typical Ethernet Setup.**

humidity and altitude. The gases that form in the atmosphere have many resonant bands (i.e., transmission "windows") that allow specific frequencies of light to pass. These windows occur at various wavelengths including the visible range. If a system uses a near IR wavelength of light (820 wavelength, or 820 nm) for laser transmission, however, absorption is not a great concern.

Scattering has a greater effect than absorption, because a smaller percentage of the transmission beam reaches the receiver. The atmospheric scattering of light is a function of light's wavelength and the number and size of scattering particles in the path.

Specific conditions that cause scattering problems include the following,

1. *Fog.* The worst condition, fog, produces a scattering effect in all directions. This is attributed to water drops with a radius less than a few microns. Smog has a similar effect.
2. *Snow.* Its effect varies depending on its water content. A very wet snow is closer to rain, which has less of an effect on visibility than fog. An extremely dry snow, on the other hand, is closer to fog and has a similar effect. The severity of the problem is in direct correlation to the radius of the particles; therefore, snow's scattering effect vanes.
3. *Rain.* Rain-related attenuation is one hundred times less than that of fog. Although the liquid water content of a typical heavy shower is 10 times that of a typical dense fog, the raindrop radius is about one thousand times larger than that of a fog droplet. This causes less scattering effect.

There is a way to minimize the effects of scattering, too. A product designed with a fade margin of 17 Db, for a 1,000-meter link would activate an automatic turn off when visibility drops below 800 meters.

Shimmer, also known as mirage or atmospheric turbulence, is the visual distortion of images in heat situations and imposes a low-frequency (normally below 200 Hz) variation on the amount of light detected by the receiver. This low frequency variation can result in excessive data error rates or video distortion on a laser communication system.

The shimmer effect is a combination of time of day, terrain, cloud cover, wind, and height of the optical path above the source of shimmer. Localized differences in the air's index of refraction cause fluctuations in the received signal level by directing some of the light out of its intended path. Beam fluctuations may degrade system performance by producing short-term signal amplitudes. Signal fades below the threshold result in error bursts. Selection of an optical path several meters above heat sources, however, greatly reduces shimmer effects.

In addition to the atmospheric conditions mentioned, direct sunlight into the front of the transmission or receiving unit affects performance. Sunlight can saturate the receiver photo diode, resulting in outages that can last for several minutes, depending on the time of the year and the angle of the sun. In addition, direct sunlight can saturate the feedback diode in the laser, resulting in transmitter shut off.

## Licensing Requirements

There are no licensing requirements. However, the Center for Devices and Radiological Health (CDRH) of the US Food and Drug Administration is the agency responsible for reviewing JR technology. The technology complies with the federal regulations covered by 21 CFR 1010 and 21 CER 1040 (HI-IS Publication FDA 88-8035).

## Advantages

FIRLAN advantages include:

- Freedom from government regulation through licensing.
- Equipment ownership when a company changes locations.
- Connectivity ease when locations need to be added.
- Immunity to radio interference.
- Data security.

## Disadvantages

Specific FIRLAN disadvantages include:

- The effect of atmospheric conditions on reliable data transmission, which may prohibit its use in some locals.
- High up-front equipment investment and installation support.
- Potential safety issue of retina damage caused by looking directly into the beam.

## Cost

The basic cost to set up the system is as follows:

| Materials Description | Unit Price | Quantity | Total Price |
|---|---|---|---|
| Ethernet Link IEEE 802.3M bits to 10M bits. Includes Two Laser Sets with AUI Connection | $15,000 | 1 | $15,000 |
| Mounting Cost | $600 | 2 | $1,200 |
| Bridge Ethernet to Token Ring | $2,000 | 2 | $4,000 |
| Converter | $2,000 | 1 | $2,000 |
| Total for Basic System Setup | | | $22,200 |

Options for system reliability include:

| Optional Items | Cost | Description |
|---|---|---|
| Spare system | $9,250 | Backup Set |
| Replace Service Contract | $1,300 | Annual Contract for Unit Replacement within 24 Hours |
| Onsite Survey and Installation Charge | $4,000 | To Ensure All Required Equipment Is Available for Installation |
| Installation and Maintenance Training Cost | $1200 | Training for Actual Installation |

Suggested options to purchase are:

| Suggested Options | Cost | Description |
|---|---|---|
| Onsite Survey and Installation | $4,000 | To Ensure the Installation Is Well Planned |
| Installation and Maintenance | $2,400 | Sending Two People for Installation and Training<br>Maintenance Training |
| Total Costs: | $6,400 | |

## THE FINAL ANALYSIS

Several new factors became apparent during the research process. These became part of the decision- making process: the availability of fiber repeaters with no other designated use; discovery of an existing infrared installation at a company location on the East Coast; and building management, fearing harm to its employees, resisting the use of infrared lasers.

To complete the analysis, these items were included in the final recommendation. The analysis of the technology benefits is provided to gain insight from the available technology and present the applicable situation scenarios for each option. (Exhibits 2 and 3 are grid comparisons of these technologies.)

### Weighing the Factors

The comparison of the technologies alleviates concerns for data security, as all three methods provide for secure data. Both of the wireless technologies, however, offer a lower data reliability factor on a daily basis. The weather in the region of the remote corporate location is subject to dramatic shifts, which are detrimental to the wireless technologies. Obviously, electrical outages could affect the users in the same way for physical wire options; these outages would also effect any work they might conduct.

All three technologies are available to install within the time frames required, with the possible exception of the FCC licensing required for the microwave option. Certainly, the licensing for the microwave option could have a serious impact on the ability of the staff to work on the scheduled date. This is a high consideration from a work- due- date standpoint and the organization's potential liability for missed due dates.

It would be advantageous to own the equipment as offered by either the microwave or infrared options for net costs, given the organization's business goals to downsize in the near future. The high up- front costs for the technologies were also noted. This investment in materials would have to be to the long- term advantage of the organization.

### Cost Comparisons

Costs are certainly a consideration, but they are not always the prime consideration. The following cost comparisons are based on the pure costs of the three systems for network data connectivity. Items to be considered in the final cost estimates include estimates for equipment required for connectivity, purchased equipment depredation, and use of any existing equipment.

| | |
|---|---|
| Total Cost of fiber optics | $19,600 |
| Total Cost of microwave | $20,950 |
| Total Cost of infrared | $28,600 |

The depreciation on the purchased equipment averages approximately 50% based on the schedule of depreciation that was current at the time of decision making. This would reduce the cost of the microwave by $10,475 and infrared options by $14,300. A significant savings in using fiber optics would come through permission to use the existing company fiber optic repeaters for the remote location installation. This would reduce those costs by $11,200. These considerations factored in yield the following numbers:

| | |
|---|---|
| Total Cost of fiber optics | $8,400 |
| Total Cost of microwave | $10,475 |
| Total Cost of infrared | $14,300 |

From a cost comparison aspect, fiber optics would be the most cost-effective method of installation.

## RECOMMENDATIONS

To recap, the considerations for the recommended solution must address the following issues in order of importance. The solution must:

1. Be fully functional in time to coincide with the contractor's relocation to the company's new space in the adjacent building.
2. Provide reliable connectivity and an acceptable response time similar to that which is currently available.
3. Be supportable by the existing technical staff.
4. Come in line with the costs of the other solutions.

Each of the technologies was reviewed based on the above criteria. The recommendation discussed in this article was based on this specific situation and may not meet criteria for other situations. The technical notes following the recommendation provides highlights for future technology reviews.

### The Decision on Microwave Technology

Given the required installation time for this project, the microwave solution was eliminated, because it requires a licensing lead time before equipment is operational. Bandwidth throughput of the microwave solution was also a point of concern, because the cabling installation at the remote location workstations called for 16M bit Token Ring, and total peak throughput of the microwave solution is only 6.7M bits. Also, existing data traffic at peak usage would reach bandwidth saturation points. The microwave technology solution, therefore, fails the first two points of the selection criteria.

### The Decision on Infrared Technology

Several factors in the final review of the infrared laser link requirements eliminated this solution. Network uptime would be compromised by the lasers being mounted on the roof from east to west because of the building management's requirement for worker safety. In spite of staff in other locations being available to lend support, the local staff lacking experience in the necessary skill set to maintain or repair the laser units was a concern. In addition, the need to purchase a backup unit to have an on-site spare would make the solution cost prohibitive. The infrared solution failed to satisfy the last three points of the selection criteria.

### The Decision on Fiber Optics

A fiber optic installation could be completed within the stated time frame, and the use of Token Ring fiber optic repeaters would maintain high levels of data throughput to reduce the threat of bandwidth saturation. The existing staff had some expertise in fiber optic repeaters and fiber optic cable installation, which would reduce maintenance response times. Further, if any new technology that provides greater bandwidth were to appear on the horizon, it would be best served through the fiber optic installation. Lastly, the cost was not prohibitive. Therefore, this technology provided the response best suited to the selection criteria and is the most viable solution.

As a final note, the microwave and infrared solutions required total backup units to be quickly recoverable. The cost for backup units would increase the overall cost of these options by approximately 30%. The fiber optic recommendation, on the other hand, contained a backup system with the extra strands included in the cable runs. Short of someone cutting the entire cable, these strands would be available if a failure were to occur. The switch to the available strands could be completed quickly, increasing the overall reliability of this connectivity solution.

### IMPLEMENTATION AND INSTALLATION PLANNING

As with most projects, the final installation phase was the most critical. The situation under discussion required precise timing for user access to the Banyan network on a specific day. The implementation and installation phase for this project centered around connectivity on December 15, the scheduled date for the staff's move to the adjacent building. The build-out schedule for the space showed that the equipment installation was finished on Dec.12. To complete the connection for network access between the two buildings, the following process was recommended. It allowed for potential delays and provides some recovery time. The process involved:

1. Issuing a final request for proposal by Nov. 22, on the selected option with a maximum two- day response time. At least three vendors were to be considered.
2. Issuing a purchase order by Nov. 28 to cover the materials cost and installation fees.
3. Receiving and inventorying materials by Dec. 9.
4. Installing materials on Dec. 12 and 13. Testing connections and workstation access as each floor was completed.
5. Testing all connections on Dec. 14.
6. Going fully functional on the morning of Dec. 15. The staff was prepared to troubleshoot all problems encountered as the user community attached to the Banyan network.

## SUMMARY

Network expansion, in any form, requires a baseline knowledge of the systems used, the organization and business direction, the liabilities a business may face with each major process change, and the effects of any downtime. Information systems are the lifeline of most businesses today, and these systems must exhibit enough flexibility to change as quickly as business directions change.

Technology is changing so dramatically that many system needs are available if the time and effort are applied to research what is available and to understand how to make it work for a given application. This effort is best served with staff experienced with the business, systems, and available technology.

Each of the technologies reviewed in this chapter is applicable to certain situations; therefore, the criteria requirements for each situation must be carefully weighed against the direction of the business organization. The proper knowledge base determines the correct direction for this type of connection or for any system expansion plans. Full analysis and good planning on the front end increase the project success rate.

# Chapter 65
# Considerations for Implementing Corporate Intranets

*Nathan J. Muller*

---

Assessing whether the corporate network has the capacity to support an intranet is a top priority for many network managers. This chapter explains how to evaluate and improve network performance, accommodate intranet traffic demands, secure a new intranet, and in general, create an intranet environment that is flexible and integrated.

## INTRODUCTION

A corporate intranet entails the deployment and use of Internet technologies such as the Web, E-mail, and TCP/IP on a closed private network within one organization or within a group of organizations that share common relationships. Because intranets are based on TCP/IP networking standards, they can include anything that uses this protocol suite, including existing client/server technology and connectivity to legacy host systems. Companies can benefit from Internet technology and avoid its drawbacks — particularly, its lethargic performance and lack of security.

Intranets support communication and collaboration; information retrieval, sharing, and management; and access to databases and applications. None of these functions is new, but the promise of an intranet is that it can use Internet and World Wide Web technologies to do things better than before.

For example, according to Microsoft Corp., Netscape Communications Corp., Oracle Corp., and Sun Microsystems, Inc., a Web browser could become the standard interface used to access databases, legacy applications, and data warehouses throughout the enterprise. In this scenario, the thin client (i.e., the browser) can make applications easier to maintain, desktops easier to manage, and substantially trim the IT budget.

0-8493-9965-3/99/$0.00+$.50
© 1999 by CRC Press LLC

A company's customers, suppliers, and strategic partners in turn can benefit from the improved communication, greater collaboration, and reduced IT expenditure associated with implementing an intranet. They can even access each other's Intranet services directly, which would speed decision-making as well as save time and money.

Achieving these benefits comes from properly implementing an intranet, which is far from straightforward. One of the more difficult issues to resolve is intranet content — determining what information will be presented, where it will come from, how its accuracy will be ensured, and how often it will be updated. The resources must be available to do this extra work.

Intranet content development is beyond the scope of this chapter, however. The focus here is on specific issues of network and server management. First, resources must be available to establish the service, to establish the TCP/IP network over which it runs, and to train users. Second, the impact on existing systems must be considered. This includes, for example, the capacity of the current network to support an intranet, the future usefulness of existing legacy systems, and the availability of hardware to run multimedia applications.

## "FAT" VS. "THIN" CLIENTS

Corporate intranets provide an opportunity to ensure universal access to applications and databases while increasing the speed of applications development, improving the security and reliability of the applications, and reducing the cost of computing and ongoing administration.

"Fat" and "thin" refer primarily to the amount of processing being performed. Terminals are the ultimate thin clients because they rely exclusively on the server for applications and processing. Standalone PCs are the ultimate fat clients because they have the resources to run all applications locally and handle the processing themselves. Spanning the continuum from all-server processing to all-client processing is the client/server environment, where there is a distribution of work between the different processors.

## TRADITIONAL CLIENT/SERVER

A few years ago, client/server was thought to be the ideal computing solution. Despite the initial promises of client/server solutions, today there is much dissatisfaction with their implementation. Client/server solutions are too complex, desktops are too expensive to administer and upgrade, and the applications are still not secure and reliable enough. Furthermore, client/server applications take too long to develop and deploy, and incompatible desktops prevent universal access.

As companies discover the benefits of private intranets and new development tools such as Java and ActiveX, as well as various scripting languages such as JavaScript and VBScript, they can use these tools to redefine the traditional models of computing and reassess their IT infrastructure.

## JAVA-ENABLED BROWSERS

Browsers that are used to navigate the World Wide Web are usually thin clients when they render documents sent by a server. The special tags used throughout these documents, known as the HTML, tell the browser how to render their contents on a computer screen.

However, browsers can get very fat when other components are sent from the server for execution within the browser. These components can be specialized files with audio or video that are interpreted by plug-ins registered with the browser. When the browser comes across an HTML tag that specifies a file type that is associated with one of these plug-ins, the application is automatically opened within the browser, permitting an audio or video stream to be played instantly without the user having to download the file to disk and open it with an external player.

### Applets

Another way that the browser can become fat is by absorbing Java applets that are downloaded from the server with the HTML documents. Applets are small applications designed to be distributed over the network and are always hosted by another program such as Netscape's Navigator or Microsoft's Internet Explorer, both of which contain a "virtual machine" (VM) that runs the Java code. Because the Java code is written for the virtual machine rather than for a particular computer or operating system, by default all Java programs are cross-platform applications.

Java applications are fast because today's processors can provide efficient virtual machine execution. The performance of GUI functions and graphical applications are enhanced through Java's integral multithreading capability and JIT compilation. The applications are also more secure than those running native code because the Java runtime system — part of the virtual machine — checks all code for viruses and tampering before running it.

Applications development is facilitated through code reuse, making it easier to deploy applications on the Internet or corporate intranet. Code reuse also makes the applications more reliable because many of the components have already been tested.

## ActiveX and Java

Another way the browser can be fattened up is by bulking up on components written in ActiveX, Microsoft's answer to Sun's Java. Like Java, ActiveX is an object-oriented development tool that can be used to build such components as Excel spreadsheet interpreters and data entry programs. Functionally, the two development tools are headed for increasing levels of convergence.

For example, the Microsoft Java VM is an ActiveX control that allows Microsoft Internet Explorer 3.0 users to run Java applets. The control is installed as a component of Internet Explorer 3.0. The Java VM supports integration between other ActiveX controls and a Java applet. In addition, the Java VM understands the COM and can load COM classes and expose COM interfaces. This means that developers can write ActiveX controls using Java.

## Scripting Languages

Browsers can also fatten up by running functions written in scripting languages like Netscape's JavaScript and Microsoft's VBScript. VBScript is a Web-adapted subset of VBA, Microsoft's standard Basic syntax. Both JavaScript and VBScript are used to manipulate HTML from objects like check boxes and radio buttons, as well as add pop-up windows, scroll bars, prompts, digital clocks, and simple animations to Web pages.

The important thing to remember about these tools is that the features they create rely on scripts that are embedded within the HTML document itself, initiating extensive local processing. Browsers are becoming "universal clients," so much so that Microsoft's next release of Windows 95 will even have the look and feel of a browser.

Most PCs today come bundled with a browser. Several vendors, including Microsoft, have endorsed the idea of offering a new breed of computer that relies on a browser as the graphical user interface, Java or ActiveX as the operating system, and servers for the applications. With Java and ActiveX, a network-centric computing solution is emerging that can potentially offer major improvements in simplicity, expense, security, and reliability vs. many of the enterprise computing environments in place today.

## FEEDING CLIENT APPLICATIONS

How fat the client is may be less important than how the code is delivered and executed on the client machine. Because Java applications originate at the server, clients only get the code when they need to run the application. If there are changes to the applications, they are made at the server. Programmers and network administrators do not have to worry about distributing all the changes to every client. The next time the client logs onto the server and accesses the application, it automatically gets the most current code. This method of delivering applications also reduces support costs.

"Fat" may be interpreted as how much the client application has to be fed in order to use it. For example, a locally installed emulator may have the same capabilities as a network-delivered, Java-based emulator, but there is more work to be done in installing and configuring the local emulator than the Java-based emulator that is delivered each time it is needed. The traditional emulator takes up local disk space whether it is being used or not. The Java-based emulator, in contrast, takes no local disk space.

ActiveX components are a cross between locally installed applications and network-delivered applications. They are not only sent to the client when initially needed, but are also installed on the local disk for future use. Local disk space is used even if the component was only used once and never used again. Updates are easy to get because they can be sent over the network when required. With Java, the component is sent each time it is needed unless it is already in the browser's cache. This makes Java components instantly updateable.

Because Java is platform-independent, a Java-based T27 emulator for Unisys hosts or a 3270 emulator for IBM hosts, for example, can run on any hardware or software architecture that supports the Java virtual machine. This includes Windows, Macintosh, and UNIX platforms as well as new network computers. Thus, any Java-enabled browser has access to legacy data and applications.

## COST ISSUES

As with most issues, the answer is "it depends." There is no right answer for all applications and all environments. Each has advantages and disadvantages, so it is necessary to do a cost/benefits analysis first. Even if a significant number of desktops must stay with the fat-client approach, there still may be enough incentive to move the others to the thin-client approach.

According to The Gartner Group (Stamford, CT), the annual cost of supporting fat clients — Windows 95/NT, UNIX, OS/2, and Macintosh — is about$11,900 per seat. Substantial savings could be realized for as many as 90%of an enterprise's clients, with only 10% of users needing to continue with a fat client for processing-intensive applications. Thus, the support costs for moving from a fat-client to a thin-client architecture could be as much as $84.6 million annually for a company with 10,000 clients.

## IMPROVING NETWORK PERFORMANCE

Intranets are becoming pervasive because they allow network users to easily access information through standard Web browsers and other World

Wide Web technologies and tools to provide a simple, reliable, universal, and low-cost way to exchange information among enterprise network users. However, the resulting changes in network traffic patterns require upgrading the network infrastructure to improve performance and prevent slow network response times.

The corporate network may need to be upgraded to accommodate:

- The graphical nature of Web-based information, which significantly increases network traffic and demands greater network bandwidth.
- The integration of the IP throughout the network.
- Easier access to data across the campus or across the globe, which leads to increased inter-subnetwork traffic that must be routed.
- New, real-time multimedia feeds that require intelligent multicast control.

LAN switches traditionally operate at layer 2 of the OSI model, or the data link layer, providing high-performance segmentation for workgroup-based client/server networks. Routing operates at layer 3, or the network layer, providing broadcast controls, WAN access, and bandwidth management vital to intranets. Most networks do not contain sufficient routing resources to handle the new inter-subnetwork traffic demands of enterprise intranets.

The optimal solution — intranet switching — is to add layer 3 switching, the portion of routing functionality required to forward intranet information between subnetworks, to existing layer 2 switches. This solution allows network managers to cost-effectively upgrade the layer 3 performance in their networks. This is the approach being taken by new intranet switches and software upgrades to existing switches.

### Intranet Switching

Intranets are increasingly being used to support real-time information, such as live audio and video feeds, over the network. These multimedia feeds are sent to all subscribers in a subnetwork, creating increased multicast traffic and impeding network performance by consuming ever-greater amounts of bandwidth.

Intelligent multicast control provided by intranet switches helps organizations conserve network bandwidth by eliminating the propagation of multicast traffic to all end stations in a subnetwork. The intranet switches monitor multicast requests and forward multicast frames only to the ports hosting members of a multicast group.

Most enterprise networks use multiple protocols. Intranets are IP-based, requiring IP on all intranet access systems throughout the network. To ease IP integration, intranet switching supports protocol-sensitive VLANs, which allows the addition of IP without changing the logical network structure for other protocols.

By combining IP and ATM routing through I-PNNI signaling, network management is simplified because only one protocol is managed rather than two. Providing this unified view of the network by implementing a single protocol leads to better path selection and improved network performance.

To accommodate intranet traffic demands, increased switching capabilities must be added to both the edge of the network and to the backbone network. Many organizations are using intranets for mission-critical applications, so the backbone technology must deliver superior performance, scalability, and a high degree of resiliency. For these reasons, ATM may be the optimal choice for the core technology for intranet switches.

## INTRANET OPERATING SYSTEM

As today's networks assimilate additional services originally developed for the global Internet, they are gaining new flexibility in the ways they provide access to computing resources and information. Network operating systems make this easier to accomplish greater information sharing by providing integral access to intranet resources such as Web servers, FTP servers, and WAN connections to the Internet. Novell Inc.'s IntranetWare offering, which is built on the NetWare network operating system, provides both IP and IPX access to intranet resources, for example.

### IntranetWare

IntranetWare incorporates all of the networking services of NetWare 4.11,such as NDS, SMP, and core file and print services with new intranet and Internet capabilities. These solutions include a high-performance NetWare Web Server 2.5, FTP services (the Internet-standard method for allowing users to download files on remote servers via the Internet), Netscape Navigator, an IPX-to-IP gateway to provide IPX users with access to all IP resources (including World Wide Web pages), and integrated wide-area routing to connect geographically dispersed LANs to a corporate intranet or to the greater Internet.

At the heart of IntranetWare's management is NDS, which allows administrators to manage a network from any workstation and provides sophisticated access controls for all the resources on the intranet. With the centralized administration enabled by NDS, organizations can contain management and administration expenses, which are the primary costs of operating a network.

IntranetWare also qualifies for C2 network security certification, enabling the complete network — server, client, and connecting media — to be completely secure.

IntranetWare's routing capabilities let corporations extend their intranets to branch offices and to connect to the Internet via ISDN, frame relay, ATM, or leased-line connections. Add-on software from Novell allows mainframe and midrange computers to become a part of the corporate intranet.

IntranetWare provides comprehensive client support for DOS, Windows, Windows 95, Windows NT, Macintosh, OS/2, and UNIX workstations.

## THE EVER-PRESENT FIREWALL

A firewall is server software that protects TCP/IP networks from unwanted external access to corporate resources. With a firewall, companies can connect their private TCP/IP networks to the global Internet or to other external TCP/IP networks and be assured that unauthorized users cannot obtain access to systems or files on their private network. Firewalls can also work in the opposite direction by controlling internal access to external services that are deemed inappropriate to accomplishing the company's business.

Firewalls come in three types: packet filters, circuit-level gateways, and application gateways. Some firewall products combine all three into one firewall server, offering organizations more flexibility in meeting their security needs.

### Packet Filtering

With packet filtering, all IP packets traveling between the internal network and the external network must pass through the firewall. User-definable rules allow or disallow packets to be passed. The firewall's GUI allows systems administrators to implement packet filter rules easily and accurately.

### Circuit-Level Gateway

All of the firewall's incoming and outgoing connections are circuit-level connections that are made automatically and transparently. The firewall can be configured to permit a variety of outgoing connections such as Telnet, FTP, WWW, Gopher, America Online, and user-defined applications such as mail and news. Incoming circuit-level connections include Telnet and FTP. Incoming connections are only permitted with authenticated inbound access using one-time password tokens.

### Applications Servers

Some firewalls include support for several standard application servers, including mail, news, WWW, FTP, and DNS. Security is enhanced by compartmentalizing these applications from other firewall software, so that if an individual server is under attack, other servers/functions are not affected.

To aid security, firewall offer logging capabilities as well as alarms that are activated when probing is detected. Log files are kept for all connection requests and server activity. The files can be viewed from the console displaying the most recent entries. The log scrolls in real time as new entries come in. The log files include:

- Connection requests.
- Mail log files.
- News log files.
- Other servers.
- Outbound FTP sessions.
- Alarm conditions.
- Administrative logs.
- Kernel messages.

An alarm system watches for network probes. The alarm system can be configured to watch for TCP or UDP probes from either the external or internal networks. Alarms can be configured to trigger E-mail, pop-up windows, and messages sent to a local printer, or halt the system upon detection of a security breach.

Another important function of firewalls is to remap and hide all internal IP addresses. The source IP addresses are written so that outgoing packets originate from the firewall. The result is that all of the organization's internal IP addresses are hidden from users on the greater Internet. This provides organizations with the important option of being able to use non-registered IP addresses on their internal network. By not having to assign every computer a unique IP address and not having to register them for use over the greater Internet, which would result in conflicts, administrators can save hundreds of hours of work.

## INTRANET SERVER MANAGEMENT

Intranets bring together yet another set of technologies that need to be managed. Instead of using different management systems, organizations should strive to monitor and administer intranet applications from the same console used to manage their underlying operating system software and server hardware. This is a distinct advantage when it comes to ensuring end-to-end availability of intranet resources to users.

For example, the hierarchical storage management capabilities of the Unicenter platform from Computer Associates can be extended to HTML pages on a Web server. HTML pages that are not accessed from the server for a given period of time can be migrated to less costly near-line storage. If a user then tries to access such a page, storage management directs the query to the appropriate location.

Some enterprise management vendors are turning to partnerships to provide users of their management platforms with data on intranet server performance. For example, Hewlett-Packard Co. and Cabletron Systems, Inc. have joined with BMC Software Inc. to provide application management software that monitors Web-server performance and use. The software forwards the data it collects to management consoles, such as HPOV and Cabletron's Spectrum, in the platforms' native format or as basic SNMP traps. Instead of looking at their internal Web sites in an isolated way, this integrated method allows full-fledged enterprisewide applications management.

IBM's Tivoli Systems unit provides Web server management through a combination of its internally developed applications and software from net. Genesis Corp. Tivoli is also working with IBM Corp. and SunSoft, Inc. to develop the IMS for submission to the DMTF. IMS would provide a standard interface for monitoring and controlling all types of Internet and intranet resources.

### IP Administration

Managing Web servers is only one aspect of keeping an intranet up and running. IP administration can also become unwieldy as intranets lead to a proliferation of devices and addresses. Intranet-driven IP administration can be facilitated by DHCP software, which streamlines the allocation and distribution of IP addresses and insulates network operators from the complexity of assigning addresses across multiple subnetworks and platforms. Because intranets depend on the accurate assignment of IP addresses throughout a company, such tools are invaluable to ensuring the availability of resources.

### Managing Bandwidth

Intranets also have the potential to significantly increase traffic, causing bandwidth problems. For some technology managers, the obvious concern is that bandwidth for vital business applications is being consumed by less-than-vital intranet data. Users access files that may contain large graphics files, and that alone has created a tremendous bandwidth issue. As Web servers across an enterprise entice users with new content, intranets also can alter the distribution patterns of network traffic as users hop from one business unit's intranet server to another's and as companies make it easier to access information and applications no matter where they may be located.

**A Policy-Based Solution**

More servers and bandwidth can be added and the network itself can be partitioned into more subnetworks to help confine bandwidth-intensive applications to various communities of interest. But these are expensive solutions. A policy-based solution can be just as effective, if not more economical.

To prevent these applications from wreaking too much havoc on the network infrastructure, companies can issue policies that establish limits to document size and the use of graphics so that bandwidth is not consumed unnecessarily. These policies can even be applied to E-mail servers, where the server can be instructed to reject messages that are too long or which contain attachments that exceed a given file size.

**CONCLUSION**

Companies that have implemented intranets are gradually finding that they are able to use Internet technologies to communicate and link information — internally and externally — in ways that were not possible before. Many other companies may be tempted to jump on the intranet bandwagon using the fastest means possible. This tactic may meet basic requirements, but it often does not take into account future network growth, the advantages gained by leveraging existing data and resources, or how to add new intranet-enhancing products as they become available. These considerations demand that intranets be flexible, open, and integrated.

Any time a company makes information accessible to a wide group of people or extends an intranet to suppliers or vendors, it must establish appropriate security mechanisms, ranging from firewalls to access control to authentication and encryption. In addition, network manager upgrade the network infrastructure to support the increased traffic that will flow over the intranet and maintain acceptable network response times.

Despite the allure of corporate intranets and their benefits, companies will not be able to move rapidly toward the kind of full-fledged intranet being predicted by some vendors, with a single browser-type COM interface and thin clients that download applications and data all at once. For some considerable time to come, intranets, as defined by the browser suppliers, will be distinct from and complementary to existing systems.

# Chapter 66
# Minimizing the Effect of Digital Camera Images on Networks

*Gilbert Held*

The old adage "one picture is worth a thousand words" reached the attention of network managers and LAN administrators during the mid-1990s due to the proliferation of image-based applications. Through the use of visual databases, fax store and forward systems, and Internet Web pages, the use of images moved from a curiosity to an expectation. Although a picture may be worth a thousand words, its storage and transmission time can represent a thousand fold increase over the spoken word, or perhaps more accurately, a text description of an image. To further exacerbate network bandwidth problems caused by the use of images is the digital camera, whose use is rapidly expanding throughout many organizations. Providing the ability to directly place images into almost any type of document without having to develop film and scan the resulting photograph makes the digital camera directly and immediately responsive to user requirements. Thus, most organizations can expect their level of image utilization to continue to increase.

## INTRODUCTION

Although images are now almost indispensable for incorporation into many applications, care must be exercised when doing so. Accepting software defaults, not considering the use of third party products and other oversights, can literally "bring down" or significantly disrupt the operation of a network. Thus, the purpose of this chapter is to acquaint network managers and LAN administrators with the major characteristics of images acquired through the use of digital cameras and how their effective operation can significantly reduce the effect of the retrieval of stored images on network bandwidth consumption. In accomplishing the goals of this chapter we will examine the use of a specific digital camera for illustrative purposes.

However, readers should note that it is the resolution and color depth of images as well as the format used to store such images that govern their data storage and transmission time, topics we will focus our attention upon as we examine the use of one digital camera.

## OPERATION

A digital camera uses a charged coupled device (CCD) as a mechanism to capture the intensity of light it is pointed at, resulting in the matrix of CCD elements forming an image. CCD elements can be considered to represent pixels as their number defines the resolution of the camera, and the color depth of each element defines the manner by which the images taken with a camera correspond to the colors the human eye can visualize.

Most digital cameras have two image capture modes — standard and fine. The standard mode, which can be considered to represent low resolution, usually results in the storage of an image using every other CCD element value. The most common standard resolution mode used by digital cameras is 320 by 240 pixel elements. The fine mode commonly results in a 640 by 480 resolution, although some relatively recently introduced digital cameras, such as the Kodak DC-120 and Cannon PowerShot, support high resolutions of 1280 by 960 and 832 by 608 pixels respectively. Since the VGA standard is based upon a resolution of 640 by 480 pixels, that resolution provides a good common denominator as it can be viewed by a larger base of PC users than the higher resolutions produced by newly introduced digital cameras that require the use of super VGA monitors to view the enhanced details provided by the higher resolution. Each of ten digital cameras examined by the author of this chapter supported a 24-bit color depth, a technique commonly referred to as "True Color," which provides the maximum level of color that a normal human eye can distinguish.

## IMAGE RESOLUTION

The vertical and horizontal resolution of an image multiplied by its color depth provides the amount of data storage required for an image. For example, a high resolution 640 by 480 image captured using a 24-bit color depth would require 640 x 480 x 24 bits/8 bits/byte, or 921,600 bytes of storage without considering the use of a few additional bytes that specify the format used to store the image.

## IMPORTANCE OF COMPRESSION

Since most digital cameras have a limited amount of memory, typically 2, 4 or 8 Mbytes, without a compression method a user would only be able to store a very limited number of images prior to having to delete or download images from their camera. The most common compression method used to store images is the Joint Photography Experts Group (JPEG), a lossy compression method that can significantly reduce the data storage required per image to one-fifth or less than its non-compressed requirements.

In preparing this chapter this author used the Minolta Dimage V digital camera which also uses JPEG compression. For readers not familiar with JPEG compression, it should be noted that this compression method is based upon the use of a Cosine transformation process that reduces blocks of pixels to coefficients that have values of 0 and 1 and compares the contents of those blocks. By specifying a quality factor a user can control the comparison of blocks. That is, on a scale of 0 to 100 a value of 100 results in two blocks of pixels being considered equivalent only when all pixels are identical. In comparison, lower quality values result in blocks being considered to be equivalent even though they differ by a greater number of pixels as the quality value decreases.

Since a Cosine Transformation process is used to reduce the values of pixels in a block to a series of 1's and 0's for comparison purposes, the use of a quality factor of 100 results in certain groups of blocks being considered equivalent even when they actually differ due to slight color depth differences. Thus, the use of a quality value of 100, while providing a minimal amount of pixel loss upon image reconstruction, can result in the storage requirements of an image reduced by a factor of four or more. That is, an image that might otherwise require 1 Mbytes of storage when compressed using JPEG with a quality value of 100 may require less than 250,000 bytes of storage.

The Minolta Dimage V digital camera stores images in its memory using a default and non-alterable JPEG quality value of 100. This means that although images are stored using a JPEG format, that format only represents a good starting place as a slight reduction in the quality scale can result in additional data storage reductions that, while essentially unnoticeable to the human eye, can also reduce the transmission time associated with moving an image locally on a LAN or to a distant user via a wide area network connection. Since the best way to become familiar with the potential effect of a digital camera upon network operations is by its use, let's do so.

## THE CAMERA CONNECTION

The most common method used to move images from a digital camera to a PC or server is via the use of a mini-cable usually provided with the camera. The Minolta Dimage V used by this author included a mini-cable with a round 8-pin connector on one end and a standard DB-9 connector on the other end. The 8-pin connector plugs directly into a digital I/O port on the camera, while the DB-9 connector plugs into a serial port. Since many desktop computers use DB-25 connectors for their serial port, a DB-25 to DB-9 connector, which can usually be obtained for a few dollars, becomes necessary.

## CAMERA ACCESS SOFTWARE

Most digital cameras are bundled with several software programs that facilitate the use of images. One type of program which is standard across all digital camera products is a camera access program. The camera access program included with the Minolta Dimage V permits images to be downloaded to a computer, and you can even upload images into the camera through the use of this program.

The camera access program includes a viewer panel which lets a computer user examine previously camera-stored images as thumbnails on their computer. Here the term thumbnail represents a copy of an image formed by using a small subset of its actual horizontal and vertical resolution. Exhibit 1 illustrates the downloading of a series of thumbnail images from the author's digital camera attached to his organization's Windows NT server. In Exhibit 1 note the pulldown of the camera menu option. Through this menu you can download or copy all images to a disk on the server or delete all images currently stored in the camera's memory. Once the thumbnail download process is completed you can select specific images and copy them to disk or delete them from the camera's memory. Exhibit 2 illustrates a continuance of the download process, showing the progress bar which indicates the status of the download of the thumbnail currently being downloaded onto the server.

Once you complete a download of thumbnails, you can select one or more images for retrieval. Exhibit 3 illustrates two images this author decided to work with as they represent common types of images that are being incorporated into a variety of network based applications. The image on the left represents a Commemorative plate which was captured using the "micro" lens setting of the author's digital camera. This type of image is being used by on-line auction firms to provide Web bidders with pictures of household decorative items. The second image, which shows a contemporary home, represents the type of images being captured by real estate agents for inclusion on internal LANs as well as corporate real estate Web sites. Concerning the former, some real estate agents are creating visual database entries for their listings, enabling potential purchasers to visit their office and view exteriors and interiors of homes and apartments to facilitate their house or apartment search effort. In addition, the use of a visual database enhances the productivity of the agent as it enables clients to narrow their search, allowing a realtor to skip properties of no or little interest and focus their efforts upon showing clients those properties that

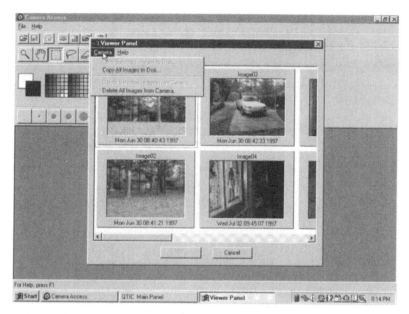

**Exhibit 1. Viewing Digital Camera Images as Thumbnails when a PC is Connected to a Camera.**

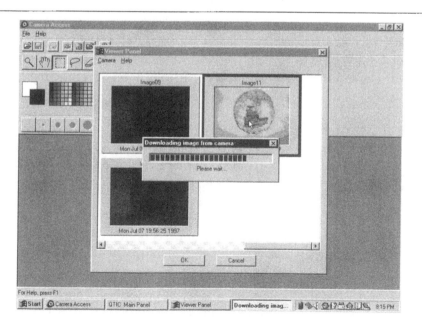

**Exhibit 2. Showing the Status of a Thumbnail Being Downloaded onto a Server.**

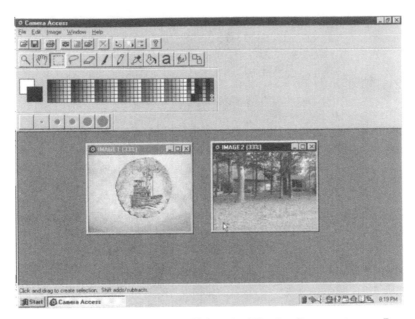

**Exhibit 3. Downloading Two Images Using the Minolta Camera Access Program.**

better appeal to their selection criteria. Now that we have a general appreciation for the method by which images are stored in a digital camera and transferred into a computer, let's turn our attention to how they can be stored in a computer along with the effect of different storage methods upon the use of network bandwidth.

## IMAGE STORAGE

Today there are over 50 file formats that can be used to store images. However, a core set of four represent the vast majority of methods by which images are stored. Those file formats include JPEG, CompuServe's Graphics Interchange Format (GIF), Microsoft's Windows Bit Mapped (BMP), and the Aldus Corporation and Microsoft's jointly developed Tagged Image File Format (TIFF). Support for GIF, BMP and JPEG is built into many browsers, while TIFF is commonly supported by document publishing applications.

Returning to our investigation of the use of a digital camera and its bundled software, Exhibit 4 illustrates the Save As dialog box from the Camera Access program bundled with the Minolta camera. Note that this program only supports the storage of images in TIFF, BMP, or JPEG format as indicated by the pull down of the "Save as type" options in the dialog box. Although the image file options may appear to provide a reasonable set of choices for many applications, it omits the support of GIF which many

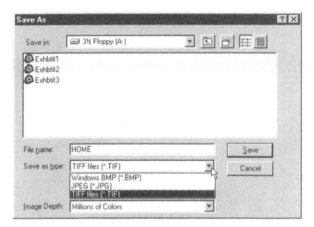

**Exhibit 4. Saving Files as TIFF, BMP, or JPEG with the Minolta Digital Camera's Bundled Software.**

older browsers are limited to supporting. In addition, the TIFF file format supports six compression methods while the camera access program limits its support to one TIFF compression method.

To illustrate the use of the Camera Access program and how its use can result in potential storage and transmission problems, let's save an image using several file formats. Exhibits 5 and 6 illustrate the Camera Access program options for saving images when using the JPEG and TIFF file format options.

In examining Exhibit 5 note that the program uses a dialog box with a slider whose quality value is shown set to 90. By adjusting the quality bar down to 75, you can substantially decrease the storage requirements for the image of the house without any visual degradation becoming noticeable. For example, a quality value of 90 resulted in the image having a data storage requirement of 236,718 bytes. When the quality value was set to 75, the data storage requirement of the image was reduced to 41,272 bytes, or approximately one-sixth of the storage resulting from the use of a 90 percent quality factor. Thus, perhaps the first lesson that deserves mentioning when storing images obtained from the use of a digital camera in a JPEG file format is to consider reducing the quality value from its default value of 90 on some programs and "high" used with other programs.

Based upon a lengthy experimentation process performed by this author on images of homes, persons, and household objects, it was determined that a quality setting of "75" or "medium" as used with some programs will result in a level of clarity that is essentially indistinguishable from the highest JPEG quality setting while reducing storage requirements

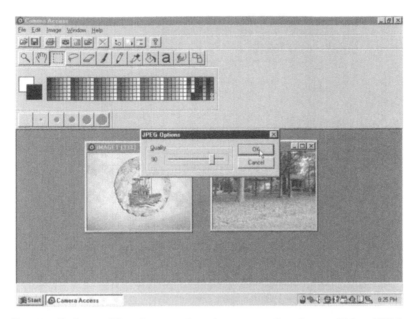

**Exhibit 5. Controlling Storage Requirements of an Image Using JPEG.**

by approximately a factor of six. Since data transmission time is proportional to data storage requirements, this means the image will require one-sixth the transmission duration when stored using a quality value of 75.

Thus, the use of a large number of frequently accessed JPEG images, such as on a frequently accessed Web site, using a well-thought out quality value can significantly reduce the transmission requirements on a network. If your organization is using an Internet connection where the service provider bills based upon the average occupancy of the connection, the reduction in storage and transmission time will also result in a reduction in your organization's monthly Internet access bill. Thus, an appropriate JPEG quality value setting can provide a variety of network related benefits. Now that we have an appreciation for handling images stored in JPEG, let's turn our attention to TIFF.

## TIFF CONSIDERATIONS

Exhibit 6 illustrates the two options supported by the Minolta Camera Access program for the storage of images using the TIFF file format. In examining Exhibit 6 you will note that the program supports "No compression" and "PackBits" storage. Although your first inclination might be to select the PackBits option as it represents a form of compression, depending upon the composition of the image that selection can actually result in

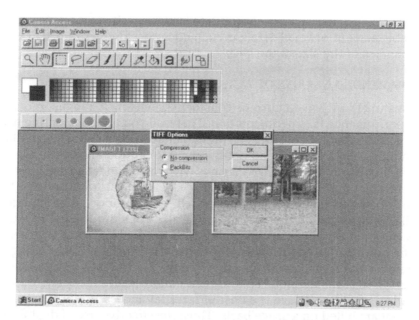

**Exhibit 6. Using the TIFF Packbits Compression Method on an Image.**

an expansion of the storage requirements of the image. This is because PackBits is a lossless compression method that looks for repeating sequences of bits and encodes them using a code to define the occurrence of compression, a byte indicating the group of 8 bits that are repeated, and a third byte that represents a count of the repeating bytes. When an image has frequent occurrences of small variances in its background, such as the lawn shown in the photograph of the home, the use of PackBits compression will result in an expansion of storage. For example, the image of the home required 948,506 bytes of storage when the TIFF PackBits compression method was used. In comparison, 942,996 bytes of storage was required when the image was stored in TIFF format without compression.

It is important to note that there are six storage formats specified under the TIFF file format. Those not supported by the Camera Access program include G3 and G4 fax compression methods, Lempel Ziv Welch (LZW) lossless compression and JPEG lossy compression. Thus, to efficiently store an image using the TIFF file format requires the use of a third party image manipulation program such as Adobe Corporation's PhotoShop. Thus, two additional items that warrant concern when using a digital camera include carefully considering the options supported by a program's file storage option and the details of an image. If the software provided with a digital camera does not support certain file formats or options associated with certain formats, you should consider the use of a third party product to convert the image to a more appropriate file format. If an image has a considerable amount of small detail, certain compression methods can result in expansion of the size of the file.

## RECOMMENDED COURSE OF ACTION

The best method you can use to consider the effect of images upon network performance is experimentation. That is, if you are considering using JPEG you should first consider storing an image using a sequence of different quality values to select an optimum value that balances storage and view-ability. If you're using TIFF you may wish to consider the use of a third party product that supports the full range of TIFF file storage options. Similarly, if you require a file format that is not directly supported by a program bundled with a digital camera, you should also consider the use of a third party program. Since certain images such as those placed on a Web server may be downloaded thousands of times per day, carefully considering the conversion of images into an effective file format can result in a significant reduction in transmission. This in turn can alleviate a costly network upgrade as well as reduce the cost of Internet access to corporate Web sites that are billed on a usage basis. Thus, the effective use of digital camera images can alleviate network bandwidth problems as well as potentially reduce the cost of communications.

# Chapter 67
# Planning, Designing and Optimization of Enterprise Networks

*Roshan L. Sharma*

This chapter provides valuable information on those critical elements of the network manager's job — network planning, design, and optimization. Included are descriptions of an effective network planning effort, modeling and performance issues, and tools for network design and optimization.

## INTRODUCTION

Network planning, design, and optimization are important components of the network management process. Traditionally, these functions have been performed through the use of powerful mainframe computers. Because these computers required the use of large tariff-related databases, a great deal of time was spent entering input data and interpreting the output data that invariably came in the form of a thick stack of computer printouts. No graphics were available to illustrate the network topologies. Furthermore, the user was always kept out of the design process. However, advances in very large scale integration (VLSI) technology have made powerful PCs available, which has opened the door to the development of better network planning and design tools.

The network planning and design effort can be broken into the following distinct tasks:

- Creating an enterprisewide database of dumb terminals (e.g., telephones), intelligent workstations, customer premise equipment (CPE), such as private automatic branch exchange (PABX) or data LANs, and communications facilities serving those locations.
- Modeling all types of end-to-end multi-hour traffic flows between all locations.
- Modeling traffic growth during a life cycle of the network system.

- Defining end-to-end performance requirements for all forms of communications.
- Designing strategic and tactical network alternatives using available technologies.
- Selecting the best alternative network based on cost, cutover, and performance.
- Testing the performance of a post-cutover network implementation.
- Updating the analytical tools and preparing for the next design cycle.
- Documenting the results.

## THE ENTERPRISE DATABASE (EDB)

Creating the enterprise database is by far the most time-consuming of all network design tasks. An enterprise database (EDB) should at least list:

- All vendors' exact mailing addresses
- All vendors' ten-digit telephone numbers
- All pieces of CPE with vendor's name, date of installation, and single point-of-contact for maintenance
- The usage level of each CPE
- The type and number of communication facilities serving each location; associated point-of-presence (POP) central offices of local exchange carriers (LECs); and interexchange carriers (IECs) with their vertical and horizontal coordinates

The list can grow into a very large one when the database must also classify the users at each location and their communications needs. However, the tasks involved in network planning, design, and optimization are impossible without the availability of an EDB. The table that appears later in this chapter illustrates a sample EDB.

## TRAFFIC ENGINEERING TECHNIQUES AND TOOLS

The next three network planning tasks demand a capability for traffic modeling and analysis. Before defining the traffic engineering efforts, some basic traffic-related concepts should be introduced.

There are two types of traffic encountered in enterprise networks:

- Well-behaved voice and video traffic
- Bursty data traffic

It is always assumed that connection-oriented voice traffic behaves in a predictable fashion, which implies that:

- The call holding times can be expressed by at least two moments (i.e., an average and a variance).
- The finer structures of traffic flows do not require rapid changes in network resource deployment.

But a close observation of speech energy over the duration of a conversation will show that there are many pauses. Furthermore, two of the four-wire access lines (ALs) and trunks are always idle since only one party can talk at a time. These facts have helped long-distance carriers send more calls over expensive ocean cables than are possible over available trunks using pure circuit-switching by using the time-asynchronous speech interpolator (TASI) technology. Such a technology was never cost effective over cheaper land-based leased lines. With the availability of asynchronous transfer mode (ATM) and Broadband Integrated Services Digital Networks (B-ISDN), users can get the same benefit through the use of variable bit rate (VBR) capability.

The data traffic between two CPEs is always bursty because of the complex rules of data communication protocols. Very small control messages may be involved in both directions before user information can flow. Although a full-duplex connection can be maintained, shared transmission lines in a packet-switched network can carry variable-length packets from many sources concurrently, thus muddying the picture. The faster the transmission lines, the burstier the transmission will appear.

## CIRCUIT-SWITCHED VOICE AND VIDEO TRAFFIC

Circuit-switched voice and video traffic intensity is measured in erlangs, which is equal to the average number of circuits busy during a "busy hour" between two network nodes. For example, if 15.5 conversations are observed concurrently between two network nodes (e.g., between a PABX and a voice switch or over an access line bundle) during a busy hour, then the voice traffic intensity is 15.5 erlangs.

## PACKET-SWITCHED DATA TRAFFIC

Packet-switched data traffic intensity can be measured as the traffic rate in bits per second (bps) during a busy hour. Only the data rate in bps can describe the bursty nature of data traffic. Experienced network specialists have been using the concept of data erlangs for many years in defining the average data traffic intensity between two network nodes. This is obtained by dividing the observed busy hour data rate (R) by the capacity (C) of each separate transmission line. For example, if the busy hour data rate between two nodes is 392,000 bps and the capacity of a transmission line is 56,000 bps, then the data traffic intensity is 7 erlangs.

## MODELING TRAFFIC FLOWS IN A BRAND NEW ENTERPRISE NETWORK

It is sometimes difficult to model traffic flows for a brand-new system. Many approximate methods have been devised for predicting traffic intensities (TIs) between all major CPEs. For example, a voice LAN (or PABX) generates about 0.1 * Ns erlangs of busy-hour traffic, where Ns is the number of active subscribers served by the PABX.

A breakdown of these traffic expressions into intranodal and internodal traffic should be determined by the known pattern observed at each enterprise. Some network designers use the 70/30 breakdown — 70% of the traffic remains within the site (voice/data LAN) and 30% of the traffic goes to other CPEs as internodal flows. These TI values can then be entered into an input file that defines each site ID, the related vertical and horizontal coordinates, and the total traffic intensity handled by the site.

The next task is to model the internodal traffic flows (i.e., exact traffic intensities handled by all the nodes and links in the path of a CPE-CPE connection). These computations are generally performed by the network design software for each assumed network topology (i.e., number of network switches and the link types employed at each network hierarchy). Some tools use critical design parameters to determine the fraction of traffic handled by access lines (connecting CPE and a switch) and trunks (connecting two switches). Eventually, the tool provides the total traffic intensity handled by each resource (node or link) of each network topology considered during a typical busy hour.

## MODELING TRAFFIC FLOWS IN AN EXISTING ENTERPRISE NETWORK

Exact traffic flows can be modeled using the detailed traffic data gathered by intelligent network nodes (e.g., PABX or LAN). The source ID, destination ID, call originating time, and call duration for each connection is recorded in station message data recording (SMDR) tapes of the voice network. Similar data is recorded by the data LAN for the packetized traffic. Simple traffic analysis packages are obtainable for analyzing the exact internodal traffic patterns between all pairs of CPEs. Such data can then be entered in a from-to data file (FTF) to define CPE traffic as simple vectors (i.e., From-Node ID, To-Node ID, and the BHR traffic intensity) for each CPE-nodal pair.

This effort eventually provides actual traffic flows (i.e., the actual traffic intensity handled by all resource, nodes, and links) of each network topology studied during a typical busy hour.

## MODELING TIME-CONSISTENT AVERAGES (TCAS) OF TRAFFIC FLOWS

Choosing a "busy" hour is an important task. Networks are not cost effective when they are operating during the hour with the highest traffic. A network may provide the required grade-of-service (GOS) during the busiest hour, but at all other hours of the day (especially during the evening and night hours), the GOS level would be overkill. No organization can afford such a network. Network managers who select an hour with the least traffic during the day will hear complaints all day long. Therefore, a proven methodology is needed to select the average traffic intensity for network design. There are two methodologies — one used in North America and one used in all other countries.

The first methodology requires the selection of a typical month and the creation of a matrix (30 ¥ 24) of traffic intensities (TIs) for each network resource for that month. Next, the average traffic intensity for each hour of the day over all 30 days of the month is computed. This process is repeated for each hour of the next 24. The TCA traffic is the maximum value of all 24 TCA values. This value determines the size of the resource (i.e., number of AL and trunks in the bundle connecting two nodes or the computing power of an intelligent node). It is helpful to have a software package for computing TCA traffic intensity (TI) values.

The second methodology requires that the 36 highest TI values be observed over an entire year and then the average computed to get a TCA value. This must be done for all resources.

Both of these methodologies result in more economical networks. However, no single methodology can predict an exact traffic pattern. Traffic values behave like the stock market. A single catastrophe, such as an earthquake, can also change the traffic patterns drastically. The objective of an effective traffic engineering practice is to synthesize an economical enterprise network using a consistent approach.

## MODELING TRAFFIC GROWTH DURING THE SYSTEM LIFE CYCLE

To estimate the total costs incurred during the life cycle of a network system, the traffic intensities for each year of the life cycle should be modeled. The Delphi approach often works best. In this method, all general managers are interviewed and realistic models of traffic growth during every year of the life cycle can be built. Some divisions may disappear through divestiture or attrition. The data from all of the interviews must be collected, weighed, and processed to create a meaningful model.

## PERFORMANCE ISSUES

Before performance requirements for all the communication needs of an enterprise can be defined, network managers must first study the available concepts of performance and identify the exact enterprise needs in each business area.

## NETWORK SYSTEM PERFORMANCE

Many network systems are implemented without any regard to performance. As long as they satisfy the basic needs for communications, everyone is happy. Often, no effort is expended in:

- Predicting or measuring the actual performance of the system
- Making any measured systemwide improvements after the system is operational

The lack of any concerted effort in defining and measuring performance of network systems may lie in an ignorance of certain system performance concepts. The performance of a network system can be defined in four ways:

- Total system costs computed on a monthly basis
- System throughputs in terms of all types of transactions handled during a unit time
- Systemwide quality-of-service (QOS)
- Systemwide grade-of-service (GOS)

## TOTAL MONTHLY COSTS

Transmission facilities determine the majority of the total monthly cost of MANs and WANs paid to the local exchange carrier (LEC), interexchange carriers (IECs), and other common carriers. The other major costs are for hardware and the recurring price of network management and control (NMC). Financing the hardware can turn a large one-time cost into an affordable monthly cost. The NMC costs related to spares can be handled just like one-time hardware costs. Some companies hire in-house NMC specialists; others prefer to outsource.

## SYSTEM THROUGHPUT

System throughput is measured by the rate at which the various types of transactions are handled per unit time (usually second or minute). Throughput is defined by the number of call attempts or calls completed per second for a voice network. In a data network, throughput is defined by the number of packets or bits handled per second. The throughput capability of each node is generally defined by the equipment vendor. The challenge lies in measuring the system throughput. System throughput can be estimated by enumerating the exact paths of each transaction.

## SYSTEM QUALITY-OF-SERVICE (QOS)

Performance aspects dealing with transmission quality, perceived voice quality, error-free seconds, data security, and network reliability (mean time between system failures) fall into the QOS criterion. Most of these parameters are very hard to compute for the entire system. Performance aspects of a critical resource can be estimated to get a feel for the quality of service of the entire system.

## SYSTEM GRADE-OF-SERVICE (GOS)

The GOS criterion deals with end-to-end blocking for a voice network and average response time (measured as the elapsed time between the moment the send key is pressed and the moment the return reply is discerned by the user) for data communications. Analytical tools are available for estimating GOS parameters for voice, data, and integrated networks.

## DEFINING ENTERPRISE PERFORMANCE GOALS

Performance goals for enterprise networks are generally developed by corporate strategic planners. A typical strategic planning cycle lasts several years and entails:

- Continuous evaluation of the needs of the enterprise and its competitors. This activity defines the relationship of system response times to user productivity for each transaction.
- Study of evolving new technologies, CPE, and networking standards. The most effective way of deploying these new technologies should also be investigated. This study should establish the cost and performance attributes of new hardware (e.g., ATM and LAN switches).

A network planning group should work closely with the IT department. It is better not to outsource strategic planning because an outside group cannot fully understand the close synergy between the demands of the marketplace, corporate IT, user productivity, and network operations.

Network managers today have to deal with ever-increasing demands for:

- Voice, video, image, and data communications.
- Multiplexing of digitized voice, image, and video signals with regular data traffic at all hierarchies of enterprise locations through switches (e.g., ATM switches).
- Unscheduled or varying demands for digital bandwidth at all hours of a day on a dynamic basis.

To design an integrated enterprise network, the strategic planning group needs a user-friendly tool for quickly evaluating solutions that take user demands into account. The right tool should help the strategic planning group reach solutions iteratively and interactively.

## MAJOR NETWORK DESIGN ISSUES

No single approach to network design is ideally suited for all enterprises. Network design is basically concerned with two issues:

1. Topological optimization, which determines the way network nodes are connected to one another (including the type of connections) while satisfying a set of critical design and performance constraints.

2. System performance dealing with end-to-end response times, path congestion, and availabilities. Recurring network cost is generally the most important performance criterion and it is mainly determined by its topology. Network topology also determines the remaining performance issues such as response times and availability. Each network design package analyzes these performance issues in only an approximate manner.

## PREVIOUS NETWORK DESIGN TECHNOLOGY

Many older network design tools handled only voice or multidrop data networks. Some of the tools that came later handled only interconnections of data LANs to achieve an enterprise data WAN. Furthermore, most of these tools required mainframes. The use of a mainframe introduced an unnecessary curtain between the network designer and the host processor. The network design jobs were entered invariably via the "batch" approach, and the outputs came in the form of large printouts after a good deal of delay. Each change of a design parameter or study of a new technology required a new non-interactive delay. The absence of network-related graphics from outputs caused additional delays in interpreting the significance of results.

The old design technology also required the use of an extensive database of tariffs. The complexity of the tariff database was probably the main reason behind the need for mainframes. If such a database were incorporated into a desktop minicomputer or a PC-based workstation, users would experience significant processing delays.

Because network topologies do not change with perturbations in any given tariff (they change only with varying design parameters and technologies), using a simplified set of existing or new tariffs is sufficient for designing an optimized network. These topologies can be studied for a detailed cost analysis using one of the many available PC-Line Pricer (PCLP) units. This two-step approach should create a separation between the network design algorithms and the ever-changing tariffs. There should be no need to update the network design package just because a tariff changed slightly.

## SIMULATION TOOLS

Some vendors market software packages based on computer simulation for evaluating system performance. LANs (voice or data) and WANs consisting of interconnected data LANs can be evaluated for performance through computer simulation. A good deal of time must be spent on:

- Writing the simulation program based on the exact network topology and the underlying communication protocols

- Debugging the software before one can evaluate all of the performance metrics such as throughput and end-to-end response times

Because typical enterprise networks require exorbitant run-times, a simulation tool is no longer an ideal way for synthesizing an optimum network topology. A network topology optimization package based on analytical tools is always the best approach. The resulting topology can be evaluated for studying detailed system response times and availabilities using an expensive simulation tool.

## NEW NETWORK DESIGN TECHNOLOGY

New network design tools are user-friendly, interactive, and can optimize network topology in an iterative fashion while quickly varying the values of critical design parameters. Many of these tools provide special menus for computing end-to-end response times for unusual operational conditions. Some packages even provide special tools for analyzing subsystem security and reliability.

Many new tools based on the graphical user interface (GUI) can evaluate any mix of CPEs, transmission facilities, and network topologies very rapidly in an intuitive manner. Today's design tools also allow the entry of approximate tariffs. But in no way can this new technology eliminate the need for an expert network designer or an architect. Because the expert designer is always involved with "what-if" type analyses, the potential solutions are meaningful only if the network design tool provides them quickly.

## ONE EXAMPLE: THE ECONETS NETWORK PLANNING AND DESIGN PACKAGE

Inputs into this network design package are in the form of flat, sequential files. Results are provided in the form of:

- Graphics illustrating a network topology with summary costs of communications facilities and response times
- Output files containing detailed cost distributions and critical performance data

The most important input file, the VHD file, lists the site/node ID, vertical and horizontal coordinates, and total busy hour, time-consistent traffic intensities in bits per second (for data) or millierlangs (for voice) for each location of the enterprise. A from-to data file can also be used to represent exact traffic flows. Another file called the daily traffic profile relates the busy-hour intensities to the other 23 hours of the day for computing the costs on a daily/monthly basis. For an enterprise with many time zones, several busy-hour models can be used.

The second most important input file, the link file, defines the link type that serves each location. Another important input file, the NLT file, defines the link type, capacity, allowed maximum data rate, multiplexing factor, corresponding tariff number, and the multiplying factor for a privately owned facility, if applicable. Up to ten link types and corresponding capacities, allowed maximum data rates, multiplexing factors, corresponding tariff numbers, and multiplying factors can be defined by the NLT file. The tariff file can define up to ten manually entered tariffs, each modeled on 17 parameters. Several link, NLT, and tariff files can be prepared to model many combinations of links and tariffs at all levels of the network hierarchy.

The system design file defines the busy hour, from-to traffic for all significant pairs, if such data is known. Other input files are also used for modeling/designing ACD networks using a mix of virtual facilities and leased FX lines.

The File menu allows the creation and viewing/updating of all input/output files. The Networking menu allows the modeling/design of multilevel voice, data, and IV/D networks using the appropriate star data, directed link, and multidrop data network topologies and voice networks based on star topologies. Network managers can also model, design, and optimize backbone networks in an iterative manner.

The Networking menu also allows the designer to find optimum locations for concentrators/switches by starting with effective solutions and improving these through a fast interactive process. By specifying the design parameters, network managers can model and design data networks based on IBM's SNA, packet-switched networks based on CCITT's X.25 standard, and fast packet-switched networks based on frame relay and ATM technology.

By specifying the design parameters, hybrid voice networks can be modeled using all types of leased and virtual facilities with or without multiplexing. Network managers can also optimize a backbone network topology and model any given topology (for cost and routes).

The Analysis menu allows the designer to model/analyze any point-to-point and several multilink paths for congestion/queuing delays, LAN performance, and reliability. Another Analysis menu item allows the computation of the equivalent monthly cost of hardware and payoff periods for privately owned hardware and transmission facilities. The following section outlines a case study of an EcoNets implementation.

## AN ENTERPRISE NETWORK PLANNING AND
## DESIGN CASE STUDY — ECONETS

The enterprise in this case study manufactures, distributes, markets, and maintains highly specialized intelligent workstations. It has 17 sites scattered across the U.S., with headquarters in Las Colinas, TX. Two separate networks serve the enterprise. A voice network connects all 17 locations (or PABXs) to a voice switch located at Las Colinas with leased voice-grade lines (VGLs). A separate data network connects workstations located at all of its locations to a host using the SNA-BSC protocol and 9600-bps lines. The newly appointed network manager wants to study the feasibility of a new network architecture, so a consultant is engaged to study the problem.

A database (a subset of the EDB) for network design was created and is outlined in Exhibit 1.

The 17 sites, their vertical and horizontal coordinates, and busy-hour TCA of traffic intensities are shown for both voice (in millierlangs) and data (in bps). Also shown are their names according to a six-symbol city-state (CCCCST) code. Next, an NLT file is defined for these link types. The various design parameters are defined in the SDF. The design parameters for the voice network define the access link type, desired blocking on access lines, trunk line type, and desired blocking on trunks. The major design parameters for the data network are ATP (analysis type is equal to 3 for response time modeling for an SNA-BSC network), user port rate, host port rate, nodal processing time in ms for each transaction, and half-modem time in ms spent in going through the modem in one direction.

The consultant first modeled the existing voice and data networks. The monthly costs for these two separate networks were $60,930 and $10,017, respectively. The EcoNets tool was then used to study various topologies consisting of switches and three link types for voice and only the 9600-bps line for data (higher-speed lines resulted in no improvements). The results are shown in Exhibit 2. The optimum voice network topology (see Exhibit 3) consisted of two switches (as determined by the EcoNet's center-of-gravity finding item on the Networking menu) and 56K-bps lines, each of which carries eight digitally encoded voice conversations.

The one-time cost of 17 special hardware boxes that perform voice encoding and multiplexing in the same box did not influence the optimum network topology. The optimum data network topology (see Exhibit 4) consisted of the same two switches as was used for the voice network and 9600-bps lines. The costs of these optimum networks were $37,546 and $9147, respectively. This represented a monthly savings of $23,254 (or about 32.8% of existing costs). No matter how the figure is examined, it amounts to a substantial savings.

*************** NODAL DEFINITION DATA ***************

| N# | -V- | -H- (BPS/MEs) | LOAD | LATA | LINK | NAME |
|----|------|------|-------|------|------|--------|
| 1 | 8438 | 4061 | 40000 | 552 | 0 | LCLNTX |
| 2 | 8436 | 4034 | 5000 | 552 | 0 | DALLTX |
| 3 | 8296 | 1094 | 1300 | 952 | 0 | SRSTFL |
| 4 | 8360 | 906 | 1300 | 939 | 0 | FTMYFL |
| 5 | 6421 | 8907 | 1300 | 674 | 0 | TACMWA |
| 6 | 6336 | 8596 | 1300 | 676 | 0 | BELVWA |
| 7 | 4410 | 1248 | 1400 | 128 | 0 | DANVMA |
| 8 | 6479 | 2598 | 1300 | 466 | 0 | VERSKY |
| 9 | 9258 | 7896 | 1300 | 730 | 0 | TOAKCA |
| 10 | 9233 | 7841 | 1400 | 730 | 0 | NORWCA |
| 11 | 9210 | 7885 | 1400 | 730 | 0 | WLAXCA |
| 12 | 7292 | 5925 | 1400 | 656 | 0 | DENVCO |
| 13 | 7731 | 4025 | 1300 | 538 | 0 | TULSOK |
| 14 | 7235 | 2069 | 1300 | 438 | 0 | NORCGA |
| 15 | 5972 | 2555 | 2500 | 324 | 0 | COLMOH |
| 16 | 9228 | 7920 | 2500 | 730 | 0 | STMNCA |
| 17 | 8173 | 1147 | 2500 | 952 | 0 | TMPAFL |

Tot. BHR Traffic = 68500

*************** Node(N)Link(L)Type(T) [NLT] FILE PRINTOUT ***************
***** LEGEND *****

{ C=Link Cap.: MaxR=Max. Allwd. Rate(Wm): MF=VMpxg.Fact.: FPF=Priv.Fac. Fact.}

| LType | LinkC | MaxLinkR | MF | Tariff# | FPF |
|-------|----------|----------|---------|------|---|
| 1 | 9600 | 6300 | 1 | 1 | 1 |
| 2 | 56000 | 48000 | 8 | 2 | 1 |
| 3 | 1544000 | 1440000 | 24 | 3 | 1 |
| 4 | 45000000 | 40000000 | 672 | 4 | 1 |

*************** TARIFF DATA PRINTOUT ***************
TARIFF #=1   AVG. LOCAL LOOPS CHARGES ($)=294
MILEAGE BANDS:
50     100     500     1000     10000
FIXED COSTS ($):
72.98   149.28  229.28  324.24  324.24
COST PER MILE ($):
2.84    1.31    0.51    0.32    0.32

TARIFF #=2   AVG. LOCAL LOOPS CHARGES ($)=492
MILEAGE BANDS:
50     100     500     1000     10000
FIXED COSTS ($):
232     435     571     1081     1081
COST PER MILE ($):
7.74    3.68    2.32    1.3     1.3

**Exhibit 1.Enterprise Database (EDB) for a 17-node Network Design (voice/data applications)**

TARIFF #=3    AVG. LOCAL LOOPS CHARGES ($)=2800

MILEAGE BANDS:
50    100    10000    10000    10000
FIXED COSTS ($):
1770    1808    2008    2500    2500
COST PER MILE ($):
10    9.25    7.25    7.25    7.25

TARIFF #=4    AVG. LOCAL LOOPS CHARGES ($)=8000
MILEAGE BANDS:
10000    10000    10000    10000    10000
FIXED COSTS ($):
16600    16600    16600    16600    16600
COST PER MILE ($):
47    47    47    47    47

************** SYSTEM DESIGN PARAMETERS **************
=0
ATP/D=3      UPR/D=56000  HPR/D=56000  IML/D=28      RML/D=300
Ncu/D=4      Rmph/D=100   HTT/D=0.001  Fopt/D=0      Tnp/D=10
Thm/D=4      Kpg/D=0.01   BKL/D=64     ICPB/D=56     TGF/C=1
Flk/C=0      Fnn/C=1      Flt/C=1 Fftd/C=0        NA =0
ALT/V/D=1    NA =0 Bal/V/A=0.1    ECC/V=13.33  ECD/V/A=300
DREQ/A=60    PEXD/A=0.15  Clbr/A=23    Frst/A=1     ACDT/A=2
TKLT/V/D=1   NA =0 Btk/V=0.1    Ffdx/D=1      MTKU/D=0.8
BBTF/C=2     Vmin/C=3000  Vmax/C=10000 Hmin/C=0     Hmax/C=10000
Fvc0/C=0     Fvc1/C=0     Fvc2/C=0     Fvc3/C=0     Fvc4/C=0
Fvc5/C=1     Fvc6/C=30    Fvc7/C=0     Fsh/D=0      Fnp/C=1
DPM/A=30     Fdis/C=1     NA =0 TFXC/A=1    NDEC/C=7
DECT/C=1     /A=ACD=0     /C=Common=0 /D=Data=0
************** NAMES OF INPUT FILES **************
VHD17* LINK17* MAPusa* NLT* TARIFF* SDF* NAME17* FTF1* LATA17*
FILES.TXT* CSABDS* UTBL* WUTBL* MUTBL* RSTBL* DTP8* Swf2*

************** DAILY TRAFFIC PROFILE **************
Hour Numbers & Corresponding Fractions of Daily Traffic are as follows:

| 1 | 0 | 2 | 0 | 3 | 0 | 4 | 0 | 5 | 0 | 6 | 0 |
|---|---|---|---|---|---|---|---|---|---|---|---|
| 7 | 0.05 | 8 | 0.1 | 9 | 0.1 | 10 | 0.1 | 11 | 0.1 | 12 | 0.1 |
| 13 | 0.1 | 14 | 0.1 | 15 | 0.1 | 16 | 0.1 | 17 | 0.05 | 18 | 0 |
| 19 | 0 | 20 | 0 | 21 | 0 | 22 | 0 | 23 | 0 | 24 | 0 |

******* Switch File Definition *******
Number of Switches =2 @ 11, 1.

Networking Menu Item No. Employed= 6

**Exhibit 1. (Continued) Enterprise Database (EDB) for a 17-node Network Design (voice/data applications)**

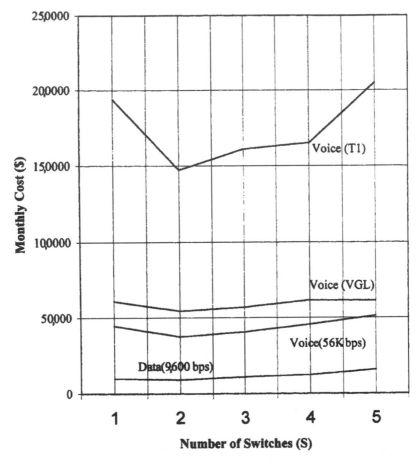

**Exhibit 2. Costs vs. Number of Switches and Link Types.**

Additional savings can be achieved by computing the total data rate (in bps) of voice conversations from each site and adding the regular data traffic and constructing a new VHD file. An optimum star-data topology consisting of two switches and 56K-bps lines can be achieved. The topology is identical to that of the optimum voice network (see Exhibit 3) and the monthly cost is about the same. The cost of the separate data network disappears completely. The new monthly savings of $33,392 represent 47.1% of existing costs. These additional savings resulted from the fact that the 56K-bps line used in the integrated voice/data network had enough excess capacity to handle the data traffic. Such a phenomenon is similar to the one experienced by network managers working with larger T1 networks in the 1980s. Those networks had enough excess capacities in the T1 trunks to

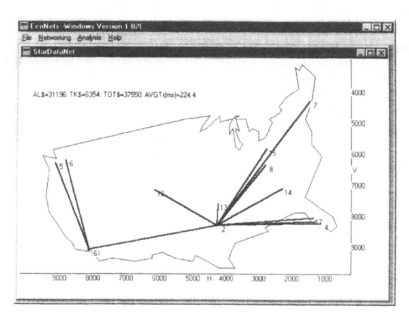

**Exhibit 3. Optimum Star Data Network Topology for IVD Application.**

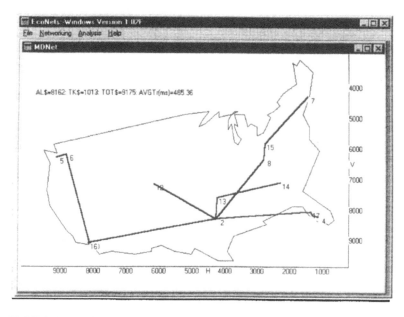

**Exhibit 4. Optimum MD-Data Network Topology with Two Switches.**

handle the data traffic. The broadband data networks of the future should have enough excess capacity to handle voice traffic.

This example illustrates only a small enterprise network. Bigger savings can be achieved through optimization of larger enterprise networks. Savings result because: integrated networks make use of excess capacity, and aggregation of many separate applications allows the deployment of transmission facilities with higher capacities that generally cost less on a per-transaction basis. These type of network planning and design tools provide network managers with many more opportunities for providing a cost-effective, integrated network to the enterprise.

# Chapter 68
# WAN Network Integration: A Case Study

*Charles Breakfield*

Merging two wide area networks (WANs) is a process comprising several steps that, when carefully planned, can ensure a successful implementation. In the case of the Resolution Trust Corp.n (RTC) and the Federal Deposit Insurance Corporation (FDIC), considerations included network operating systems compatibility, enhancing E-mail and directory services, applications support, server and workstation memory and processor upgrades, applications support, and routing software upgrades. This case study details the methodologies that brought together two WANs with more than 17,000 end users.

## COMPANY BACKGROUND

The original project was created to merge the Banyan WANs at the EDIC and the RTC. The RTC's corporate charter expired on Dec. 31, 1995, and its assets were integrated into the FDIC's operations.

The RTC's origins — and its reason for being — date back almost 10 years. When banks and savings and loans (S&Ls) became insolvent in the late 1980s, they called on the FDIC and the Federal Savings and Loan Insurance Corporation to prop them up. The task was so overwhelming that Congress was petitioned to assist. As a result, the RTC was created, designed to handle the disposition of the assets and liabilities of the failed banks and S&Ls until 1995. When the RTC's corporate charter expired, all activities and assets rolled over to the FDIC. Its systems were developed independently of the FDIC's but with this inevitability in mind.

The FDIC had no plans to keep RTC employees after Dec. 31, so FDIC personnel will assume all existing RTC computer network activity. This would be practical only if both organizations were similar in design and layout.

0-8493-9965-3/99/$0.00+$.50
© 1999 by CRC Press LLC

Therefore, the project, which began in August 1993 and took 10 months to complete, was implemented to make the RTC's WAN compatible with the FDIC's.

## THE CHALLENGES AND BENEFITS OF IMPLEMENTATION

The RTC's Banyan WAN encompassed the 7,000 employees and contractors located in California, Colorado, Texas, Kansas, Georgia, New York, Virginia, and Washington, DC. The WAN needed to be connected to the FDIC's WAN, which encompassed 10,000 employees who are similarly located. All the RTC Banyan servers targeted for upgrade were production servers being used eight to 12 hours a day, six days a week. Server upgrades had to be coordinated so the end users were not disrupted during the day and so there would be a fallback position if a server upgrade failed.

Several other areas for upgrades were also targeted. An operating system upgrade was required as part of the integration proposal. The FDIC's 337 Banyan servers, from Banyan Systems Inc., are running on one network operating system, Vines 5.52(5); the 329 RTC Banyan servers were running on Vines 4.11(5), two revisions old. This network operating system upgrade was required to bring the RIC up to the same level the FDIC was running before merging the two organizations. Also, Banyan no longer wanted to provide fixes (i.e., software patches that solved "bugs" or problems) or enhancements for an older version of Vines, so the RTC had to upgrade its network to continue to receive operating system support.

As part of the operating system upgrade, a server hardware upgrade also was necessary, to support the enhanced version of software. Additionally, the Cisco routers in the RTC network needed to be upgraded.

### The Business Opportunity

As part of the implementation, new functionality offered by the newest revision of Vines version 5.52 would allow the corporation to use the new features to operate the business better.

The enhanced functionality of the new E-mail under Banyan Vines 5.52(5) was one of the main reasons for the upgrade, because the RTC's most important application was the E-mail system, and the most heavily used applications were the E-mail and the directory services, Streettalk Directory Assistance (STDA). The full listing of the combined organizations (a total of 17,000 users) under STDA would provide access to all end users by all end users.

Additional network management tools and diagnostic tools were included as part of the new network. Better performance tuning and use of resources would also be easier to accomplish under Vines 5.52(5).

**Technical Benefits**

The technical benefits of the Vines 5.52(5) operating system were:

- The new file format, S10, under Vines 5.52(5) allowed up to 4G bytes of modes per file system, up from the old file format, SS, under Vines 4.11(5), which allowed 64K bytes of ides. Each file or directory was represented by one mode. More files or directories per volume were required by the RTC.
- The Access Rights List (ARL) functionality was greatly enhanced under 5.52(5). Access control could then be given all the way down to the file level within directories or within subdirectories to a user or a group of users. Security issues could be tailored to the file level, which was not possible before.
- Greater network management was offered through the network management statistics on memory usage, server processes, hard drive activity, and CPU usage. The improved tools promised better server monitoring and network management.
- Valuable to the RTC were the tape backup and restore processes built into the operating system. Under Vines 5.52(5), the operator can back up and restore not just file services, but also specific directories and files with much greater ease.
- New printer functionality was also gained by migrating to Vines 5.52(5). Multiple print queues were serviced by one printer, and print queues were set up to print to other printers if a printer was overloaded. Print jobs were redirected by queue operators or done automatically.
- A less obvious benefit, but still an important feature, was the new routing matrix algorithm that was implemented into Streettalk. The overhaul to the routing matrix in Banyan Streettalk all but eliminated the sporadic occurrence of network "broadcast storms," which were an inherent problem.
- New functionality was offered under Banyan Vines STDA. User IDs could be defined to include additional attributes on each user put into the system. The security could be set so no one could look at the associated attributes in the Attribute View Definition (AVD) file that holds them. The information contained in the AVD file could be masked and display only the users under STDA that the personnel department and the end user wanted displayed for E- mail purposes.

## PRIORITIES

The majority of the mainframe applications used by the RTC and FDIC were located at the Virginia location in Rosslyn, VA, and required 3270 emulation for host access. The RTC network was independent from the FDIC network, to begin with, but there were certain priorities to consider to bring them together.

As these are government institutions dealing with assets of failed banks, network security was a priority. The original decision to go with Banyan was based in part on its WAN capabilities and the tight security design of the user log- in process. Each time a user logged in, his or her unique network ID was time and date stamped to prevent unauthorized access by a computer hacker. The flexibility to log in anywhere in the network and still maintain a high level of security was key to the way the RTC did business.

A requirement of the new version of the network operating system was that it support all existing off-the-shelf software. All standard applications, word processing, spreadsheets, databases, and E-mail were provided on the local Banyan servers. The current suite of standard software packages that the RTC supported included WordPerfect 5.1, Lotus 2.4, and Paradox 3.5. All workstations ran either DOS 5.0, which was preferable, or DOS 3.3 with 386 Max version 5.0 as the memory manager. Saber, a software package, was used for the menuing front-end for all users to access all applications. All the applications were to be compatible with the Vines 5.52(5) upgrade.

## ELEMENTS TARGETED FOR CHANGE

All applications in use at the RTC when the project began needed testing in a lab environment before delivery into the production environment. Preliminary testing showed complete compatibility across all applications with the Vines 5.52(5) upgrade.

The workstations in the field were configured with only 2M bytes of random access memory (RAM). RAM requirements of the new operating system shell, as well as the applications to be run for daily applications, had to fit in the 2M bytes of memory. There were no plans or budget to upgrade RAM in field workstations.

Each of the two styles of Banyan server (the RTCs and the FDICs) required identical configuration in naming conventions of groups, file services, print services, 3270 services, E-mail naming standards, amount of disk space, memory configurations, server names, network interface card (NIC) settings, and cabling specifications for connectivity.

Several Banyan servers also required hardware upgrades before the new operating system could be installed. Banyan server hardware upgrades included faster processors (i.e., Intel 486 chips), larger server hard drives, and faster NIC cards, when feasible.

The Cisco routers used to connect each office to the WAN also required an upgrade, as they supported only Vines 4.11(5) IP protocol stack. The revision of the routing software in the Cisco routers was 9.x, and the RTC needed a 10.x revision.

## UPGRADE COSTS

An upgrade server key option had to be purchased for each RTC server — a $5,000 option for each server. Because RTC servers needing the upgrade numbered 329, the cost totaled $1,645,000.

Each Corporate Network Server (CNS) required one 1.3G byte hard drive per server before the upgrade could take place. Each CNS server also required a drive 0 larger than the existing 80M byte drive. The upgrade process required that each CNS have a 330M byte drive in slot 0, a 330M byte in slot 1, and the 1.3G byte drive in slot 3. The larger drive 0 would accommodate the new operating system requirements. The actual number of CNS Banyan servers was not known but was estimated at 40% of the total 329 Banyan servers, for a total of 132 CNS servers to be upgraded. Each 1.3G byte upgrade drive was valued at $5,400, for a total of $712,800 to upgrade all CNS servers. The Compaq SystemPro accounted for the balance of the RTC 329 servers, or about 197 servers. Of the 197 SystemPros, roughly 50% needed hard drive upgrades, roughly 30% needed CPU upgrades, and approximately 40% needed to upgrade to 32-bit NIC cards (either Token Ring or Ethernet). Hard drive upgrades (and controllers) cost approximately $4,500 each, for a total of $445,500. CPU upgrades and system PROMS cost approximately $1,900 for each of 59 servers, or $47,400.

The hardware upgrades for the servers were required only for drive 0 of the CNS. The hardware upgrades for the other servers were done in conjunction with the Vines 5.52(5) upgrade for two reasons. First, the hardware upgrades had already been planned for and budgeted before the Vines upgrade. The existing server hardware was two to four years old at the time of the project and required upgrading because hardware failures were occurring more frequently. Second, because the servers needed to be rebuilt from scratch, it made economic sense to do the hardware upgrades just before laying down the operating system and files. This would save overtime costs that would be incurred if the servers were refurbished after upgrading the operating system.

**Router Upgrades.** The last items to be upgraded in the network were the Cisco AGS and AGS+ routers, which were scheduled for upgrade after the servers were completed. The Ciscos were running the 9.4.0 software version, which did not fully support Vines 5.52(5). Full functionality for Vines 5.52(5) was promised if RTC upgraded the hardware and software. Additional memory was required to run the software update 10.0.4. The total number of Cisco routers that needed an upgrade was 30. (Some of the 3000 series did not need the hardware upgrades but did need the software.) The

**Exhibit 1. Total Estimated RTC Upgrade Costs, Per Component**

| | |
|---|---|
| Banyan Server Upgrades | $1,645,000 |
| CNS Server Upgrades | $712,800 |
| SystemPro CPU Upgrades | $112,100 |
| SystemPro Hard Drive Upgrades | $445,500 |
| SystemPro NIC Card Upgrades | $47,400 |
| Cisco Hardware Upgrades | $45,000 |
| Cisco Software Upgrades | $90,000 |
| Upgrade Labor Costs (OT only) | $55,000 |
| Total (Estimated) | $3,153,730 |

hardware upgrades were approximately $1,500 each, and the software upgrades were $3,000 each, for a total of $45,000 and $90,000, respectively.

**Man Hours.** Each production server upgraded from Vines 4.11(5) to Vines 5.52(5) needed two RTC network engineers, each working four to six hours (five hours, average) of overtime per server if the following methodology were used. If a figure of $17 per hour for labor costs is used, each server would cost approximately $170 to upgrade. If the 329 servers were upgraded at that price, the labor cost to upgrade all the servers was $55,930. The total costs are summarized in Exhibit 1.

## UPGRADE MODELING AND REFINEMENT

All the first-line network engineers were trained on the Vines 5.52(5) operating system first and then were involved in testing specific aspects of the operating system at each site. The results were communicated via Lotus notes, videoconferences, and face- to- face roundtable meetings.

The upgrade methodology was tested, refined, and then taught to the staff members who would actually be doing the upgrades. The modeling and refinement activity was particularly valuable in that it gave the staff time to practice before operating on live servers and corporate data. These practice sessions were the greatest insurance policy available in this process. In fact, the real success for the project began in these early planning sessions.

Each type of production server, Compaq SystemPro and Banyan CNS, needed upgrading to Vines 5.52(5). Every server required the internal hard drives be reformatted to take advantage of the S10 file format before having the data restored from tape. Within the restore-from-tape process, all the files needed the ARLs converted to the new 5.52(5) format.

The overall upgrade approach to both servers was the same: to build a like server, either a SystemPro or CNS, off line to replace the production server. By starting on Monday morning, an identical Banyan server could be built, tested, and ready for live data to be restored beginning at 5:00 PM on Friday. Typically, a server was fully tested and ready for the final data files by Wednesday night or Thursday morning. The offline servers were built during regular business hours, so overtime was needed only on Friday night, for the last stage of the conversion process.

The SystemPros were upgraded with Intel 486 processor boards, new ROM chips, and new 510M byte hard drives array pairs and SCSI II controller cards. The upgrade process was greatly hindered by these extra variables, because of a 50% failure rate with the Seagate 510 drive array pairs. Not all SystemPro hard drives were upgraded, and the existing Conner 210 drive array pairs and SCSI I controller cards were reused. In each configuration, the Compaq SystemPro was left to run the comprehensive drive array and to run controller card diagnostic tests for 24 to 48 hours before being formatted with the S10 file format under Banyan Vines 5.52(5). Although this was a time-consuming action, the servers that made it into production were very reliable.

Additionally, any Token Ring or Ethernet NIC that were not 32-bit Enhanced Industry Standard Architecture (EISA) were replaced with 32-bit EISA boards for improved performance.

The Banyan CNS servers, for the most part, had a like configuration. Each was a 386 class machine with an 80M byte drive as drive 0, a 330M byte drive for drive 1, and a 330M byte drive for drive 2. The new 5.52(5) operating system would just fit on drive 0, but that left no room for file swap space, for growth in the internal routing table, or for E-mail service. The upgrade position was to remove the 80M byte drive and replace it with the 300M byte drive in slot 3. A 1.3G byte was purchased for each CNS for installation as the third drive. All applications, all noncore Banyan services, and all data are placed on this drive. All core Banyan services were installed by default onto the first drive, and the 330M bytes provided ample room. For the most part, the second drive (a 330Mbyte hard drive) was left for growth but was largely unused. No CNS servers were scheduled for upgrades with 486 processors.

**The Process**

The beginning process was the same for each style of server. Diagnostics were run on each; each drive was formatted multiple times (time permitting); and the Banyan Vines operating system was loaded. At this point, the Banyan server key on the production server was carefully removed and placed on the off line server. The off line server was brought up and given the same name as the production server. The identity of the new 5.52(5) server was critical and required the server key to build its internal routing tables. It was essential that the two servers not be connected to the network at the same time.

Once the new server had been brought up and named properly, it needed to be patched with a total of 10 Banyan patches (i.e., fixes, to be installed for full functionality) before anything could be done. The order of patch installation was important, and several versions were tried and discarded before the list was stable. However, some patches were more trouble than the problems they fixed — even having to be replaced only hours after they had been applied. Patches were installed after the data was loaded and converted as well as before. Both methodologies worked.

The offline Vines 5.52(5) server targeted to replace the production server then had all the same services created using the same naming convention for file restoration and conversion. It is important to note that if a file service was not within the naming standards, the name was converted.

**Print and File Services.** All print services were rebuilt, as opposed to restored. The new print services at the FDIC were different enough to warrant setting up the RTC services from scratch. The Banyan operating system also would not permit moving and converting the print services. Print services were created on the target server during the week.

All file services were created on the target server to match the production server, and each service containing data was moved individually and converted. The applications file service was restored from the standard application tape that was created at the beginning of the upgrade process. Because this was a static file system, meaning that usually no changes to the applications occurred, this service could also be restored. After the first server was converted, a Vines 5.52(5) tape backup of the applications was created and then used for restoring target servers for upgrades. This process saved time converting ARLs. The ARLs, however, still needed to be reworked to be server specific — so the restore was not as trouble free as it sounds.

Any other service on the production server, such as asynchronous dial-in, 3270 SNA service, server to server, and WAN links, were also created and set up on the target server before Friday evening.

Any lists created on the production server needed to be printed out and rebuilt by hand before the target server was brought online. The list itself was added to the server before the data files were restored and converted. Names could be added to the list only after the server was brought online.

**The Group Moves.** The only activities that could not be done before Friday afternoon were the group moves, and the transfer of the E-mail, data files and updates to the Adminlist for the target server.

Promptly at 5:00 PM on Friday, the groups were moved from the production server to tape and then restored to the target server. The group moves were done before the file services, because in the process of the file conversion, the ARL were updated to the new Vines 5.52(5). The file services (i.e., the actual data) were backed up to tape and then restored to the target server. ARLs and the group and user IDs were matched. If the groups with their users had not been there before moving the files, it would have been necessary to go back in and edit the ARLs on the target server.

**Moving E-mail and STDA.** The E-mail service was moved from the production server to the target server via tape backup. This process was straightforward and reliable.

The STDA was recreated on the target server, once the target server was moved to production status and cabled to the WAN and the old server was removed. Again, the proper sequence was removed and the new target server moved into place. The STDA service could not be moved with reliable results, so Banyan recommended that it be recreated; however, it could not be created before the server was placed on the WAN. The target server needed the connection to the WAN so it could rebuild the internal SIDA database from upstream neighbors. The creation and forced rebuild on Friday night gave three days for the rebuild process to operate before Monday morning. Sometimes, though, three days is not enough time for STDA to rebuild properly, and the data base had to be killed and recreated before it would work properly.

**Moving the ARLs.** The ARLs were one of the last major areas left to update once the target server became the production server. The administrators were usually part of another group that were kept on a different server. Sometimes the Adminlist could not be updated with the names of administrators until the new production server could "see" the target server. At those times, two different methods to force the update process on the new production server were used. A dummy group was created on the new server, which forced a Detail broadcast to the WAN that updated all the surrounding servers, and, as a result, the entire WAN began to "see" the new server. When the server could "see" and "be seen," the dummy group was deleted.

The other method was to use a Banyan utility that would "goose" Streettalk and force the surrounding servers to exchange routing information and update their respective routing tables. The STSYNC utility is effective in getting servers to synchronize with each other.

The last upgrade detail was updating the boot disks for the users. This process typically required that someone physically visit each workstation that was physically attached to the upgraded server and run the NEW REV PROGRAM, which copied down the new boot files to the workstation. This process was quickly automated by the staff members so when a user of a group that resided on a newly upgrades server logged in, a batch file ran that copied the necessary files to their workstation and then required them to reboot. This process saved an enormous amount of time.

Because entire groups with the associated users were being moved, no password changes for the end users were required. This helped make the conversion more transparent to the end user.

### Some Glitches

Final issues for the conversion were to double-check the ARL of the root in each file service, as they did not convert reliably and had to be modified by hand. Oddly enough, the remaining ARLs in the rest of the directory tree were usually correct and did not need modifying. Some tailoring of the ARLs did occur after the fact, so as to comply with the new RTC standards that were published before the upgrade was started.

One ARL problem encountered was with lists on the server that were used in the ARLs of files and directories. If the ARLs were being changed or updated with the Banyan Vines utility Netpro, the workstation would receive an out of memory error and terminate. The reason for this was that Netpro could not update ARLs with a list that was not there, so it buffered the transaction and went on to the next ARL update, and so on, until the workstation ran out of memory. The lesson learned here was to make sure that all lists were at least placed on the server, empty or not, so the ARL conversion would operate properly.

In the particular upgrade scenario for the site, two and sometimes three server conversions a week could proceed with the equipment on hand. As servers were replaced with new production servers running Vines 5.52(5), the 4.11(5) servers coming off line became the new target machines in the upgrade process for the following week. The assorted 20 Banyan servers took 10 weeks to convert from Vines 4.11(5) to Vines 5.52(5). All staff members worked in teams that rotated each week, so no network administrator was needed for consecutive weekend work, and no mental "burn out" that would have resulted from such a demanding schedule occurred.

As in all well- thought- out plans, there is always an overlooked X variable that comes back to foil complete upgrade success. As all sites reached the final stages of the server upgrade process, a problem surfaced that no one had anticipated: Paradox 3.5 would not support over 25 concurrent users on a Banyan Vines 5.52(5) platform.

Lab applications testing did not explore the Paradox application to this extent. Both Banyan and Borland were contacted about fixes or workarounds. Banyan declined to assist RTC in this problem, saying it was an application problem. After many phone conversations with Borland, their technicians did concede that it was a problem with Paradox 3.5. But because Borland was no longer supporting that product version, the technicians suggested that RTC upgrade to Paradox 4.0 to solve the problem.

There was no money budgeted, however, for upgrading approximately 329 servers, with only 2M bytes of RAM, to the 4M bytes of RAM that Paradox 4.0 required to operate. Therefore, Borland's solution was cost prohibitive.

Ultimately, the solution was somewhat unsatisfactory but effective. Each site left one Banyan Vines server at 4.11(5) that contained the Paradox NET and SOM files. These files allowed Paradox 3.5 to run normally for all the end users that were attached to Vines 5.52(5) servers. Fortunately, Banyan supports mixed versions of its Vines operating systems, so long as they are within one version of each other (e.g., 4.X and 5.X systems can be mixed and still talk to each other).

## THE FINAL INTEGRATION

The last stage was opening the main Cisco router, which was connected to the RTC and FDIC networks, to full Banyan Vines traffic from both sides. As part of the initial procedure, certain action items were completed before the wave of router table updates went surging through the respective networks.

First, all RTC Vines servers had their communication buffers set to at least 400,000 before the cut over. All CNS servers had to have a primary drive that was larger than 80M bytes (300M bytes were preferred). All network servers were scanned to ensure that no duplicate server names (or server key numbers) were in the two systems. All end users were prohibited from logging on and using the network beginning at 5:00 PM that Friday. The STDA directory services on each server were stopped on Friday morning and were not allowed to rebuild again until Sunday night. Finally, no production servers were trying to get their Streettalk updates across a WAN link that was slower than 56K bytes per second. The STDA was also stopped to prevent any unnecessary WAN traffic while Streettalk was trying to update the internal routing tables of all the production servers.

Full server backups were completed and verified before the process began, to provide an absolute fallback position in the unlikely event that each organization had to return to a preintegration status. The actual process of the integration was that the servers in each network needed to have their internal routing tables updated to know about the additional 300-plus servers on the other network. Because Vines does this dynamically, the staff's primary job was to monitor the health of each server and, in fact, the whole RIC network while the update process unfolded. Once the main

Cisco router was allowed to pass Streettalk traffic and updates both ways, it became much like an information tidal wave slamming into each site. At 9:00 PM Friday night, the information updates were rolling toward the location, and server memory utilization statistics were watched to see if any server started swapping information from memory to disk, a sure sign that the server was in danger of being swamped.

By 10:00 PM, the Streettalk routing updates were in full swing, and the available server memory was dropping to levels too low for comfort. Staff stopped all unnecessary file server processes in an effort to free up and make available more server memory for the routing table updates. By 11:00 PM, the servers in the network had stabilized, and available server memory began to climb, a sign that the critical time had passed and that the network was stabilizing.

At 9:00 A.M. Saturday, the staff returned to restart all the services that had been stopped the night before and began testing the services to which the end users would need access on Monday morning, with the exception of STDA. Once all services were tested, and no lingering problems existed, the staff began to deal with the SIDA issue.

It was decided to permit the regularly scheduled rebuilds to go as planned, but the FDIC would not be included in the rebuilds for another 10 days. This would allow Streettalk time to "settle" before subjecting it to another data "blitz" from an STDA that would have added another 10,000 names to the existing 7,000-name data base. The final integration of the two STDAs proved to be modest and concluded the entire data integration process rather quietly.

## SUMMARY

In retrospect, this network integration might have been overplanned, considering how smoothly it went; however, the Vines 5.52(5) server upgrades that blindsided the team on the Paradox issue were underplanned. Data center operations managers looking at integrating similar or even dissimilar networks save time and aggravation if they include field personnel who will be participating in the upgrade/integration process. Bringing in the senior network personnel, training them, and including them in the integration process made all the difference in the merger of the FDIC and RIC Banyan WANs. People who are actually scheduled to do the work who "buy in" to the project help breed enthusiasm and interest in the success of the project and provide unexpected benefits.

For example, field personnel identified many incidental problems that no one at corporate headquarters had even considered. The success of the overall project was ensured by the corporate people involving the field network engineers.

Every effort should be made to get the hardware and software vendors involved at the beginning of the project to assist and comment during the planning stage. Banyan Systems placed one of its certified Banyan engineers on site at headquarters to help with the integration process. Additionally, Compaq sent its engineers out to RTC sites to help resolve the SystemPro hardware problems that were first encountered when the new drives were installed before the operating system upgrades.

Each vendor that was contacted and included in the upgrade planning before implementation improved the chances for success with either technical advice or on-site involvement. RTC suppliers also contributed in the upgrade process when involved.

Finally, communication among all the players in an upgrade of this size is critical. Information is useless unless it is in the hands of the right people at the right time. Using Banyan E-mail, Lotus Notes, and teleconferencing, headquarters staff and field engineers were able to communicate critical pieces of information to the proper people in a timely manner. As a result, the upgrade and integration success was accomplished with existing personnel who were also responsible for the day-to-day operations of the existing user community.

# Section IX

# Network Operations and Management

The ability of employees and customers to communicate in an efficient and effective manner is highly dependent upon the ability to control the operation of your network. Recognizing this fact of life resulted in the inclusion of this section in this handbook focused on network operations and management. This focus is in the form of nine chapters oriented towards topics which provide us with detailed information concerning different aspects of network operations and management issues.

The first chapter in this section, "How to Work with a Consultant," recognizes the fact that most organizations at one time or another will have to supplement existing employee skills through the use of one or more consultants. This chapter acquaints us with the advantages associated with the use of consultants and methods to consider to effectively use their serves.

The second chapter in this section, "Open Systems Integration: Issues in Design and Implementation," provides us with "seven rules of integration" that can be used to successfully design and implement a client-server project in an open system integration environment. Based upon the experiences of a project manager at a leading financial organization in integrating legacy systems into a new open system environment, this chapter introduces us to the major factors that are applicable to system integration projects and their effect upon the replacement of a legacy system with an open system. Once this is accomplished, this chapter presents its seven rules of integration that when followed facilitates the success of a well-thought-out conversion to an open system.

Standards can be considered as the glue which binds the capability to interoperate. In the third chapter in this section, "Operating Standards and Practices for LANs," we first become acquainted for the rationale behind the need for LAN standards. Once this is accomplished, we will examine LAN support issues and the role of standards committees in defining mission-critical operations used for writing an operations and security standards document.

One of the newest security concerns of managers are applets, network-based programs that run on client systems. The fourth chapter in this section, "Applets and Network Security: A Management Overview," describes how applets operate, the threats they present, and the security precautions network managers and LAN administrators should consider to minimize the security exposures presented by applets.

One of the problems associated with modern technology is the fact that it provides the facilities for unscrupulous persons to create programs that can be harmful to computers. In the fifth chapter in this section, "Assessing and Eliminating Virus Threats in Distributed Networks," we focus our attention upon the virus threat. This chapter provides us with information on how viruses infect systems to include a description of the major types of viruses. Once this is accomplished, we turn our attention to methods by which viruses can be spread through an organization, techniques we can use to discover the presence of a virus, and ways to prevent infection, or if infection occurs, how to recover from this situation.

Turning our attention to the wide area network, the sixth chapter in this section covers the WAN conversion process. In "Technology Conversions on WANs" we examine one of the most difficult projects in networking. In this chapter we look at the techniques we can use to facilitate the WAN conversion process to include methods we can use to audit the physical network and migration strategies that can be used to deploy new network equipment with as little downtime as possible.

Due to the significant importance of electronic messaging, the seventh chapter in this section covers the management aspects of this topic. In "Enterprise Messaging Management" we turn our attention to the implementation of client/server messaging management. After reviewing the problems associated with enterprise messaging, we look at email standards and message management concepts. In doing so, we will review the architecture for messaging management and the role of control center console software.

No section on network operations and management would be complete without coverage of Windows NT and the global naming tree, the topics of the eighth and ninth chapters in this section. In the eighth chapter, entitled "Windows NT Performance Monitoring," we will examine the use of NT's built-in utility program which provides us with the capability to note the effect of various hardware and software components upon network and server performance. In concluding this section we will look at an often-overlooked and hidden-from-view characteristic of network management. In the chapter "Managing Networks with the Global Naming Tree" we will become acquainted with the ISO's tree structure which assigns unique identifiers to different types of objects. By understanding the numeric structure of the global naming tree, we obtain the ability to use network management more effectively as it allows us to select options and identifiers as they are developed instead of having to wait for the upgrade of a new graphic user interface.

# Chapter 69

# How to Work with a Consultant

*Greg Scileppi*

Hiring and selecting a consultant can be a success when guidelines in place and followed. Considerations include aligning the consultant with the business plan and objective, identifying technical and nontechnical skills — from programming to industry-specific knowledge — that will be required, and senior management's expectations on the project. Preparing for a consultant's arrival, including designating an in-house contact person and establishing a work space, also maximizes the time used to get the consultant up to speed in the organization.

## INTRODUCTION

As rapid technological advancements continue to reshape the corporate world, the use of on-site consultants has gone from an occasional tactic to a constant strategy. With the migration from legacy mainframe systems to client/server architecture in full swing, consultants are brought in to provide immediate expertise on a range of projects, including systems development and programming, building databases, and directing business process reengineering efforts.

Managers reap many benefits from this approach. Hiring consultants, either as individuals or as a work team, enables companies to maintain a "core" group of permanent staff members, thus streamlining personnel expenditures. Consultants help ensure smooth work flow through predictable and unpredictable busy periods. Even more importantly, consultants provide valuable expertise and guidance that may be lacking among existing staff. Exporting this knowledge throughout the company in turn enhances the value of the information technology (IT) department.

## WHAT KIND OF CONSULTANTS DOES THE DEPARTMENT NEED?

As managers develop their staffing plans, the first step is to determine what work is best performed by permanent staff and what tasks can be performed more effectively by outside consultants. Quite commonly, for example, many IT departments have a core group of permanent professionals on staff whose primary mission is two-fold:

- Supervise the successful implementation of existing projects.
- Communicate on a regular basis with line managers to identify areas in which IT can make an effective contribution.

Consultants can play a major role in both areas. To help determine the kind of consultants needed, managers should examine the project from the broadest possible view. Questions to ask include:

- How does this particular project fit into the company's overall IT business plan? Of course, another key mission here is to determine if the company indeed has an IT business plan. In the event that it does not, this might immediately provide an opportunity to use consultants.
- For whom is the project being designed? What is its purpose? Sales, marketing. and customer service departments, for example, tend to require applications that enhance responsiveness. Manufacturing values precise measurements. Clarifying each department's specific objectives is critical, so the manager can staff the project accordingly.
- What levels of knowledge are required to make the project a success? Do these include technical expertise in certain programming languages, nontechnical skills, such as writing, or knowledge of a particular industry or application?
- Are these skills readily available? When immediate expertise is needed, consultants can be the most cost-effective, practical option.
- What are senior management's expectations on the project?
- Is this a routine installation, drawing on a familiar base of corporate knowledge? In this case, it could be implemented internally. Is the installation something new that requires special expertise, both technical and functional? If so, is it strictly a one-time project or does it involve the kind of expertise management will want to retain collectively for years to come?
- How quickly must the project be completed?
- How much permanent staff can the organization afford, both currently and in the future, to devote to it, given the business's cycles?

Answering these questions helps determine staffing needs. Managers may discover, for example, that the installation of a new client/server application requires two mid-level consultants, or that customizing a "sales lead" tracking program calls for a senior consultant with experience in marketing.

## ESTABLISHING A CLEAR CHAIN OF COMMAND

Of ultimate importance is clarifying how to best supervise the consultant. A senior-level consultant, for example, might well answer to both the higher ranks of the IT department and executives within the particular department that IT is serving. Midlevel consultants are often managed by others within the IT department, as are consultants who bring specialized expertise but lack supervisory skills.

No matter what experience level the department requires, managers can maximize productivity if they appoint one of their employees as the consultant's day-to-day contact person. This does not mean, however, that others cannot communicate with the consultant. Establishing a single point of contact is primarily intended to simplify the organization of the consultant's activities. This employee should also play a key role in helping to hire the consultant. All of this — from the consultant's level of expertise to the responsibilities of his or her supervisor — should be clearly communicated to the IT staff to guarantee against confusion about the consultant's objectives and scope of authority.

## OBTAINING A SUITABLE SKILL SET

Managers should make sure as they clarify the project that they consider the full range of skills necessary to complete it. Though considering only technical knowledge is tempting, they should not stop at that point. As IT professionals continue to work more closely with line managers in various departments, the issue is to know more than the intricacies of a specific technology; this is vital. Interpersonal skills are extremely important if the consultant is to train end-users on how to use an application best. Written and verbal skills can also play a factor when a cogent explanation is necessary to explain the value of a new application or system to senior management.

Another major element in selecting a consultant is budget. Whereas answering the above questions should help in calculating the project's estimated length, determining how much to pay a consultant is not always easy. Before contacting any consultants, managers should investigate rates for the skills they need. Some consultants charge by the hour, some by the project. Each has its pros and cons. The key, though, is to determine which is most appropriate for a particular department or company given its budget parameters, policies, and most of all, what is needed to complete the project as effectively as possible.

In many ways, finding a consultant is similar to hiring a full-time employee: The organization is looking for someone who can do first-rate work. The critical difference is that a consultant should require an absolute minimum of training time — that is, a brief, but comprehensive, explanation of the project and the authority to move ahead as quickly as possible.

Every IT department has probably already been approached by several consulting firms. Managers should start by reviewing perspective consultants' background materials. Managers should then contact experts within their own companies and colleagues within their own industries. Everyone more than likely has several colleagues outside their companies whose opinions they respect. Of course, they will want to do this with discretion to avoid releasing proprietary projects to too many people.

Staffing firms that specialize in information technology consultants can add considerable value to your search for an IT specialist because they will have prescreened potential consultants and checked references before recommending a candidate. They can also assist you in clarifying the project's scope and, in the process, help determine the most effective staffing mix. All of this can save you considerable time and money.

A good pointer for interviewing prospective consultants is to ask them to walk through the details of one outstanding project. The way the consultant describes it, the intricacies, the knowledge, the details he or she uses, should shed a great deal of light on his or her level of expertise and work style.

Once managers have identified three to four potential candidates, they should make sure that references have been checked diligently. Questions that should have been answered include:

- Is the consultant detail-oriented?
- Does he or she work well with people at all levels of the department, from support staff to senior management?
- Does he or she know how to explain technology to end users?

Again, all of these are questions for which a staffing firm can perform the research extensively.

## PLANNING FOR THE CONSULTANT'S ARRIVAL

A few simple arrangements ahead of time will help the consultant get started as quickly as possible.

### Telling the IT Staff

To help foster a more congenial work environment, managers should explain the nature and length of the consultant's project to their staffs. Managers should encourage them to be supportive. In many cases, consultants are brought in to lighten the work load for regular staff, who are usually grateful for the additional help.

### Focusing the Project

As discussed previously, objectives, needs, and timing should be thought through. Even if the consultant's first step is be to help fine tune this information, managers need to begin with their visions of a project description, that is, with a basic understanding of the project's specifics. If possible, this should be written down on a single page. It will provide both the organization and the consultant with a helpful baseline measure of the expectations.

### Preparing a Workspace

The last thing any organization wants is to have a consultant show up and have no place to work. All necessary tools should be made part of the consultant's workspace, including a desk, phone, and computer that includes all relevant hardware and software. Materials should be organized no later than the day before the consultant begins work. Before he or she arrives, someone should explain the company's dress code.

When he or she arrives, someone needs to provide basic workplace information, such as where to hang coats, location of rest rooms, the lunch hour, policies on smoking, and where supplies are kept. Also, managers should make sure all proper paperwork has been completed for the human resources department, and that, if possible, the consultant processes this information before the first day on the job. The goal of all this is to ensure that the consultant is able to jump right in and be productive as soon as possible.

### MAXIMIZING THE WORKING RELATIONSHIP

As the assignment progresses, be sure to regularly check on the consultant's performance. While it is important to provide him or her with a degree of freedom, conducting weekly meetings or requesting regular reports on the project's status are also a sound practice. Managers should take time to discuss the project, including changes in timing and unexpected developments.

Solicit feedback from the IT staff. Is the consultant's interpersonal manner appropriate for the IT department and the one it's serving? Is the consultant receptive to input?

In answering these questions, it is important to remember that a good consultant can help with more than just the task at hand. Managers can take time to tap his or her expertise for insights into additional challenges and projects the department is facing. Because consultants have often worked in a wide range of industries, they might well offer new insights into the department's problems.

If the organization is working with a consulting firm, managers can check in frequently with the firm's account managers to tell them how the consultant is working out — and clients should not hesitate to air their grievances. Whether taking the time for an emphatic talk with the consultant or finding a replacement, a quality firm should be able to satisfy all needs promptly. The firm should also be able to assist in determining what additional consultants might be necessary.

IT staff should feel free to disagree with a consultant's recommendation. Working as a consultant requires a healthy appetite for problem solving. The consultant or consulting team should be more than willing to discuss the pros and cons of recommendations in a logical manner. During these discussions and when reaching a consensus, managers should make sure the consultant is then totally committed to implementing the agreed-upon recommendation. The organization is the client, and the final responsibility for successfully completing a particular project is the manager's. The manager should not hesitate to assert his or her role whenever appropriate.

In working with the consultant, the manager might also recognize the need to create a full-time position or positions. Over time, activities that once were performed on a contract basis could easily evolve into full-time positions, for example, maintaining a departmental database. Experienced consultants and staffing firms are adept at pointing out to clients work that could be performed by an employee (i.e., writing source code). Managers should talk with the consultant about staffing scenarios and let them help develop new job descriptions for IT positions.

## RECOMMENDED COURSE OF ACTION

Consultants who help you in the ways discussed in this chapter will only enhance their value to a client organization. To summarize, any business considering bringing in consultants should:

- Determine what activities are best performed in-house and which by the consultants.
- Evaluate the project from more than just a technical viewpoint.
- Maximize productivity by appointing an employees as the consultant's day-to-day contact person.
- Investigate rates charged for the skills needed (i.e., by the hour or by the project), identifying which is suitable for the department to complete the project as effectively as possible.
- Review perspective consultants' background materials and get informal feedback from colleagues in the industry.
- Make sure that references have been checked thoroughly.
- Make arrangements ahead of time, including setting up a work space, to help the consultant get started as quickly as possible.
- Be sure to regularly check on the consultant's performance and hold regular meetings.
- Remember that the final responsibility for successfully completing a particular project is not the consultant's, but the manager's.

Without a doubt, the role of IT will continue growing to meet needs across the enterprise. In this way, managers can see that a competent consultant can be a strategic business partner.

# Chapter 70
# Open Systems Integration: Issues in Design and Implementation

*Leora Frocht*

---

Open systems integration in today's client/server environment challenges project managers to incorporate issues of performance, communication, and compatibility in what is often a new development arena. This chapter presents seven rules of integration that help managers and project teams produce an open system that is fluid, sensible, and intuitively usable.

## PROBLEMS ADDRESSED

Applications development in the open systems environment involves numerous and varied integration issues. As previously unusable ideas are translated into entirely new client/server systems, open systems tools make possible the development of applications that could not be developed on mainframes or on pre-windows PCs. Designing and implementing open systems therefore presents new and often daunting challenges.

Development team members generally do not have much experience in the open systems environment. The technology is relatively new, and the tools are not mature in the sense that they have not been used commercially for at least ten years. There is no foolproof methodology, and many choices regarding software must be made amid a plethora of conflicting opinions. Experienced developers, who are generally familiar with mainframe or pre-windows tools, must change their entire pattern of thought to adapt to open systems and the client/server approach.

This chapter is based on the experiences of one project manager in integrating legacy systems into a new open systems environment. The seven rules of integration developed from that experience address the many components of integration in the open systems environment and should help managers anticipate and thus mitigate potential problem areas.

## ISSUES IN OPEN SYSTEMS INTEGRATION

Integrated systems development involves issues of performance, communication, and compatibility. Integrating legacy systems into an open environment focused on seven major factors that are generally applicable to systems integration projects:

- User specifications.
- Business alignment.
- Communications.
- Data accuracy.
- Resource contention.
- Ergonomics.
- Legacy systems.

Managers involved in such projects are challenged to manage these components and integrate them into a fluid, sensible, and intuitively usable system.

### User Specifications

A reasonable understanding of user requirements makes the integration of the other six components much easier. Accurate interpretation of user specifications depends on the manager's ability to bring together project team members with the appropriate training and experience level.

### Alignment to Business Objectives

A thorough understanding of the business objective also helps derive the end user's requirements, needs, and goals and ensures system performance. No decisions, whether software- or hardware-related, can be made without a thorough understanding of how the business is conducted.

Many development choices depend on what the business requires. The system must be flexible enough so that users are able to do more than they expected or initially thought of. To the extent permissible by today's technology, the system should be portable so that an application can be moved from one platform to another, from one version of an operating system to its next generation, or from a PC to a workstation. It should be able to support current data needs as well as anticipated future needs.

**Performance.** Performance, both in accuracy and speed, should reflect the end user's identified business needs. It is hardware- and software-related. Appropriate hardware must be selected. For example, if high-volume communication is an aspect of the system, communications hardware, such as wide area network and local area network (LAN) routers and cables, must be selected and implemented to handle higher volumes. Volume is generally identified by users because they are the ones who generate transaction activity. Server machines must be designed to handle large volumes of data or applications software, or at least be scalable and configurable to do so.

## Communications

Communications software must also be robust enough to send out and receive large volumes of data. Market data services, which provide information like stock prices in the Dow Jones industrial average, generally address these issues; they transmit hundreds of thousands if not millions of messages a day. Applications software designed to accept high volumes of messages must not only receive the messages but also interpret and process them efficiently. The source code must be able to receive each individual record, determine what to do with it (e.g., based on information in header data), and send it off to the designated recipient. The recipient could be a database, a flat file, or a window panel. All of these transactions must be completed in a reasonable time frame.

## Accuracy

Accuracy is a critical issue in systems development. Appropriate business decisions are made only if data is correct all the time. Because accuracy is sometimes overlooked in the development of an integrated open system, project team members must be vigilant in resisting the temptation to do so.

## Resource Contention

Applications developers must consider how data is used because in an integrated system two users should contend for resources. Resource contention frequently occurs when requests for data are made to the database. Standard procedure dictates that one user's retrieval of data from a database not restrict other users' access to the data.

Resource contention can also occur in the area of communications, particularly regarding interprocess communication or data broadcasting to a large group. The application must not require that the broadcasting of one message depend on the successful delivery of another message. Also, the successfully integrated system allows sent messages to be buffered or stored and processed separately from the communications portion of the application. That way, messages can continue to be received instead of being backed up because the communication protocol is still processing the previous message.

## Ergonomics

Screen real estate is a lesser, but still important, component of integrated systems design. Developers should ensure that the user's screen does not become overcrowded with panels, screens, or other kinds of activity. A large number of panels, or newly generated panels that cover up others, becomes unmanageable. Screen management and screen real estate can make or break the integrated system, even though they do not directly affect the system's actual functioning.

Similar consideration should be given to the interior layout of each window. When the widgets (e.g., menus, buttons, scroll bars, etc.) inside a window are arranged counterintuitively on the screen, the user needs more time to sort out all the information on the window. When this happens, the user ends up spending more time trying to comprehend what he or she is looking at than actually dealing with the business at hand. Common types of information should be grouped together.

Team members must also consider the function of the widgets — the actual conduits to the functions of the integrated system — when choosing from the various types of widgets available in graphics packages. If these conduits either implicitly or explicitly mislead the user, the system will not function properly. Books on windows and window design explain the appropriate use of the different types of widgets.

Appropriate color choice provides the finishing touch to an open system. Color helps separate the different functions implemented in the integrated system. For example, the functions to add, modify, or delete records in a database can be color-coded in the following manner: buttons for the add function can be colored yellow to indicate that the user can perform the function but should proceed with care; the button for the modify function can be orange to indicate that anything done can be undone; and red can be used for the delete function to indicate that a record removed is gone forever and using this function may be dangerous.

Colors should also be selected with aesthetics in mind. Human beings work more easily and happily when what they are looking at is pleasing to the eye. Color can also delineate separate sections of a window to aid the user in interacting with the system. Finally, colors selected should be easy on the eyes. Screens with strong, bold colors or highly contrasted colors next to each other are difficult to view for long periods of time and can cause eye strain. In more ways than one, the integrated system should not create headaches for the user.

## Legacy Systems

Replacing a legacy system with an open system solution further complicates systems integration. For the purposes of this discussion, legacy systems are considered those that were developed in a nonwindows environment. So a legacy system is one that relies on linear menu selection rather than on the ranges of selection available on window-type panels. The platform may be mainframe or PC, but it does not allow for the branching out of applications functions or for simultaneous display of panels.

By definition, a legacy system has been around for a long time. If it did the job reasonably well for the user, the new open system must do it better; if the old system never fulfilled the user's needs, a successful replacement is critical. The worst thing that can happen for users and developers alike is for a new application to have less functionality than its predecessor.

It therefore becomes essential that navigation of open systems windows be a primary consideration in the design of a new system or of a legacy system's replacement. Where once users had no choice but to follow their own linear thinking when running a mainframe system, the open, integrated system gives users many path choices. The system designer should consider logical flow: namely, which panels can parent a subsequent panel (the child process), and which panels would be a final child in what becomes the tree structure of insatiable window-upon-window navigation. At all costs, the development team should avoid creating a confusing mass of windows that users will never be able to navigate.

Another consideration related to window navigation is the actual number of window processes that should be running at any given time. Although integrated systems can support several simultaneously running processes, a benchmark should be established for the number of processes that should be running within the system at any given time. The system should never crash, but it should perform within reasonable expectations. Consideration of the these points can make the difference between whether users accept or reject a legacy system replacement.

Replacing a legacy system also involves consideration of how much, if not all, of the system to replace, even if the original hardware remains. In some cases, a legacy mainframe system is ideal for housing large volumes of data, for example, but it is not really suited to providing that data to the user in a digestible way. The integrated, open system then becomes the suitable front end, and the remaining issue is that of communication between the client/server hardware and the mainframe.

A similar scenario results if the existing system contains a mainframe component whose accuracy, reliability, and performance cannot be replicated and should therefore not be replaced. Work done well on the mainframe can be communicated to the client/server platform and vice versa.

## SEVEN RULES OF INTEGRATION

The intricate, laborious, and expensive process of integrating legacy systems into an open system environment yielded seven rules of integration:

1. Understanding the technology.
2. Understanding the application.
3. Creating a solid development team.
4. Making users part of the team.
5. Gathering detailed specifications.
6. Organizing and interpreting specifications.
7. Understanding the critical components of integrated systems.

### Rule 1: Understanding the Technology

Systems integrators must select from a large range of products and unite their selections into a system that solves the problem at hand for the user. The challenge for the systems integrator is knowing which criteria should be used in selecting the software for each application and ensuring that all the choices work together in a smoothly running system. At a minimum, software choices must be made for the graphical user interface (GUI), the database, interprocess and intraprocess communication, and the programming languages.

Generally, however, senior management, technology committees, or infrastructure specialists in the individual shops make the software choices and give the development team one or two options from each software category. In this case, team members should assess the qualities of the software tools under consideration: particularly, how the qualities affect the end result and how the tools will interact with each other.

### Rule 2: Understanding the Application

The key to integration of open systems for both the experienced analyst as well as the novice developer is to completely understand the goals of the application. All members of the development team have to understand how the user's business works and the user's desired goal for the system. This point cannot be stressed enough. Users often have a specific approach to the way they do business. Whether this approach is based on habit or on business constraints, members of the development team must pay attention to it. New approaches and ideas should be considered, but ultimately, the way the system approaches the business is always up to the user.

### Rule 3: Creating a Solid Development Team

The third important component of a successful integration process is a solid development team. The mainframe environment allowed a single developer to successfully create an integrated system because the components were already integrated by the mainframe provider. When a technology shop was set up on an IBM mainframe, IBM Corp. also provided the software. There was certainly systems software, which was centralized, and other database software products like SQL/DS, dBase 2, or FOCUS and procedural languages like REXX installed and stabilized in a central location. There was one text editor available. The mainframe manufacturer usually supported only one copy of utilities and operating systems, so much of the software choices were already made, installed, and known to work together. The only thing the programmer/analyst was ultimately responsible for was the function of the system for the user. In addition, the mainframe architecture rendered it often more convenient for one person or a very limited number of people to work on a single integrated system.

At the opposite extreme, client/server systems are built on hardware platforms like workstations or PC LANs — platforms that give systems analysts and developers much more freedom and flexibility in tool selection, design, and implementation. Because so much more flexibility and processing alternatives can be built into an integrated system, a team of two or more analysts and developers, as well as component specialists, is required to create an integrated, open system.

The sum total of knowledge of the development team must encompass two disciplines: technology and the user's business. Within the technology discipline, the team must include members with strengths in database software, GUI software, communications software, and applications software. Analysts and software developers are often experienced in more than one of these areas. Similarly, specialists in the hardware technology in use should be part of the team effort. They can advise on interprocess and interplatform communication and performance, as well as on programming for them.

The technologists' knowledge of the user's business is at least as important as experience with computer technology. Understanding the user's requirements determines how the applications software will function; hardware accommodation will ultimately determine the system's performance.

### Rule 4: Making Users Part of the Team

Interpersonal communication and creation of an effective personal rapport between members of the development team and the users are essential to the integration process. The building of working relationships significantly improves the effectiveness of the completed system. When productive working relationships exist between the users and the development team, developers are less intimidated about what they do not know and ask many more questions. Instead of glossing over issues in the fear of appearing naive, developers are more apt to explore them with users.

Conversely, users need to feel comfortable too. Many business people are still very much intimidated by computers. When unfamiliar terminology and technology is suddenly flung at successful people who are used to being in control, they feel uncomfortable, and uncomfortable users do not easily or willingly discuss the system with the development team. Barriers between the users and the developers degrade the quality of the systems integration process. Forging a solid, interpersonal working relationship between users and the development team is therefore integral to the process of systems integration.

### Rule 5: Gathering Detailed Specifications

The first technical step in the integration process is gathering specifications for the system. There are several ways to do this. Naturally, the best source is the user. Discussions and interviews with the main user or user liaison and his or her peers are essential, as is careful and organized note taking by members of the development team. Ideally, part or all of the development team should sit with the user for as long as possible, or at least for a minimum of several business days.

Other sources for gathering specifications include other companies, professional associations, and books and articles on the subject. Information from these sources often adds depth and perspective to the goals specified by the user.

Following each session with users, the development team should discuss the information given to it and how it relates to what the team already knows. This exercise helps team members refocus on the goal of the integrated system and to share their own experiences and development ideas. At the end of the systems specification process, the members of the development team should comprehend the user's business on an intuitive level.

### Rule 6: Organizing and Interpreting Specifications

**Organizing Notes Along Logical Components.** Formal documentation of user specifications is important to the project team's effectiveness and efficiency. Team members should bear in mind particular areas when collecting specifications, namely the programming language, the GUI and windowing, database, and communications. Written notes should be organized according to logical components. Most systems require a main screen from which all other operations are managed. System components can be organized according to what is required on the main screen level and according to what is required for subgroups of the main level. Possible functions to launch from a main screen are data maintenance, reporting, tools such as data item searches, or utilities such as refreshing a screen from a database.

**Painting Up Windows.** In the next step in organizing specifications, project team members take the notes arranged by function and paint up a window that corresponds to the main function and as many windows as necessary for the subfunctions. They must resist the temptation to build deep layering into a system. If users have to call up several chained windows just to get to the one they need, the window navigation process becomes unmanageable and most users will likely give up. As flat an implementation as possible is best, but balance should be kept in mind. Generating too many screens on the same level that are required to be displayed at once jeopardizes the issue of optimized screen real estate. Team members should get the input of users on the issue of balance while also drawing on their own intuition and experience. Generally, however, one main window with the subfunctions spawned from a main menu bar or other widgets gives the best chance of functional success.

**Reassessing Goals and Implementation Feasibility.** At this point in the systems development process, team members should consider whether the goals of the system are too broad. They should also address the question of implementation feasibility.

Oftentimes, when a new integrated system, as opposed to a legacy system replacement, has been proposed, users' requests are not entirely focused, yet alone finalized with any degree of precision or confidence. Users have a broad idea of what they want, but meeting all their business needs may actually require the development of more than one integrated system, or of several smaller subsystems chained together. Painting the windows clearly demonstrates to users how large or small the system will be, based on the specifications.

Dividing a system into manageable components wherever possible is better not only for the systems developers but for the users themselves. In *Object-Oriented Analysis and Design with Applications* (Redwood City, CA: Benjamin/Cummings, 1994), Grady Booch discusses the fact that the human brain can only manage a limited number of processes at a time while the computer can manage as many processes as the hardware can accommodate. Because the computer can handle many, many more processes than the human brain, functions should be separated into different systems. In this way a system that accommodates the physical limitations of the human brain is implemented rather than one that can only be comprehended by a computer. Separating out specifications into different systems also results in flatter, simpler, and targeted individual systems that are easier to develop concurrently, enhance, and maintain.

**Defining Additional Components.** At this point, developers have a prototype that can be critiqued and revised. It now becomes apparent where the other components of the integrated system come into play. Interaction with the database can now be defined because the origination point of data is known. The data types and sizes are also known because they have been designed into the windows. Determination of which windows and functions will communicate with each other becomes obvious. When all the windows are visually displayed, it is easy to identify which windows should publish data and which windows should receive it. Any other roles relevant to the systems integration process can be hooked in once the system is visually prototyped.

### Understanding the Critical Components of Integrated Systems

There are six major components of an integrated open systems environment:

1. Programming language.
2. Communications protocols and network.
3. Graphical user interfaces.
4. Database.
5. Applications management.
6. Applications systems.

**Programming Language.** The programming language is the component of the system that actually does the integration. As the glue between all the other components, it facilitates the interaction between the screens and the database, between the screens and the communication components, and so on. It must provide functions that help users do their jobs as smoothly and easily as possible. In addition to providing flexibility and performance, it must hook into the other components of the integrated open system.

Many information technology organizations use C or C++ programming languages because these languages meet the previously mentioned qualifications; when properly implemented, they are flexible, precise, and high-performing. Oddly enough, the very flexibility of the language creates a managerial challenge. When using these languages, developers are often tempted to reprogram and hone the programs — a process that can become unnecessarily time-consuming. Project managers must be able to clearly define and limit the extent of the implementation and provide feedback to the developer.

**Communications Protocols and Network.** Communication, especially real-time communication, is critical to a successfully integrated system. The development team must consider various types of communication:

interprocess communication, communication between the open system and a mainframe, and broadcasting or publishing information through the open system. The communication method is selected based on the end-user's goal.

Interprocess communication methods (a point-to-point approach) is used for discreet communications, such as when one user wants to send information only to certain individuals. When a user needs to communicate from an open system to a mainframe, special communications software must be implemented because workstations, PCs, and mainframes all speak different languages themselves (i.e., they have different operating systems). When large amounts of data need to be distributed across a group of users on a network, a broadcast method is used. Many market data vendors provide software that facilitates this type of communication.

In every type of communication, performance by the hardware and response time by the application is key. User specifications determine how the application will handle its processes, which must be designed so as not to overload the hardware and slow performance. Here, bandwidth must be determined. If an organization anticipates a large number of transactions, it should plan for accommodating them. Users can be consulted about how many transactions they anticipate executing in current conditions; they should also try to estimate future business volume. Then benchmarking can be done on existing hardware using tools available for this purpose. A sniffer can be put on the line to measure the number of bytes transmitted per second.

A final but important aspect of the communications protocol is scalability. Whatever product is used to develop communication should be able to accommodate a growing number of users. Of course, no open system can handle an infinite number of users, but a number reasonable to the business should be accommodated. Different protocols have different limitations, so the project team must examine specifications for those products.

**Graphical User Interfaces.** Design of the windows can be the most important and most complicated part of the integration process. At a minimum, the team should consider how the programming language will make the windows perform, navigation through the various windows, how large the panels are, what color they are, and how information is organized on them.

A GUI painter should be used to create the windows for the proposed system. The window attributes are clear, readily available, and easily modifiable.

Once the windows are designed, team members can often populate certain types of widgets with sample data, which makes the functional aspects of the system clearer without doing a coded implementation. Pull-down lists are good examples of this feature. For example, if a limited and thus predefinable set of standard entries, such as the regions of the United States, is required, the information can easily be entered as a pull-down list and be immediately visible to users. As many of the widgets as possible should be predefined and implemented before taking a finished screen prototype to the users for approval. At this stage, users can tell if the development team has integrated the business requirements into the system.

**Database Design.** Design and implementation of the database is also determined by the business flow. Although the gathering of the individual pieces of information is relatively straightforward, organization of the data may not always be. The goal in database design is to provide the best performance possible by implementing the optimum data organization. Whether the data model is relational or hierarchical, the designer/developer must resist the temptation to design a perfectly normalized, not-a-byte-wasted database, even if it means decreased performance for the user. It is often worthwhile to repeat fields to save the user an additional data retrieval.

Effective database design must consider hardware organization. Attention must be paid to the size of the database. It is possible for a component of a database to require an entire machine by itself; the various pieces of data, which could end up on different machines, need to be able to interact with each other.

**Applications Management.** The success of integrated open systems also depends on having a centralized location for all applications source and executable code. Because of the larger team size required to develop an integrated system, the project manager must ensure that tight control is kept over the code and that only single copies of any program or function are resident in the system.

Developers on a team often help each other by reviewing each other's code and sharing tips and suggestions. Copies can be made of the code to facilitate the sharing process. Chaos inevitably results if the extra copies of the program are not cleaned up or erased when it comes time to link all the components together. An incomplete or nonfunctional piece of software can be linked in and ruin the clean performance of an otherwise effective system.

The first step in applications management is to install a file librarian or source code control system (SCCS). SCCS creates a central repository for all the source code of the system. It can maintain version control and does not allow more than one copy of source code to be checked out at a time. It also provides a layer of security. Any developer not given permission cannot pull source code out of the repository.

Third-party software libraries are also effective, and many software vendors provide for standard functions like date calculations or matrix manipulations. Rogue Wave is one such software or application program interface (API) provider. The independently provided APIs can be linked and loaded into an application along with software developed in-house.

Separating the development environment from the prototype environment, and the prototype environment from the actual production environment, is important to a successful system. The development environment is meant strictly for the writing and testing of code; it allows developers to try out different ideas or to rework ideas. Only programs still in flux, or those that are still deemed modifiable, reside in this environment.

In the prototype environment, tested and debugged components are installed, linked together, and run as a whole. In this environment, a system that is not yet ready for the users is built up. Full systems and integration testing is conducted, and software components are replaced only when bugs are found in the testing process. Only executable code resides in this environment. Replacement of system components and recompiling is done in the development environment.

The production environment also contains only executable code and is the area from which the user executes the system. It should be bug-free and should never be affected by anything that goes on in the development or prototype environments.

These different environments make change management vital. Careful scheduling must be observed when modifications are made to existing systems, be they in the development, prototype, or production stages. Developers and systems administrators should be aware that to avoid problems, changes to a system must be scheduled and implemented as scheduled. The procedures outlined in the change management process ensure that the development team, system administrators, and database administrators communicate with each other and that each knows what the other is doing with respect to the system. Systems modifications or upgrades should always be implemented at a time that is least inconvenient to the user. Unfortunately, for the systems personnel, that time is usually at night, after business hours, or on the weekends.

Notification of changes to an existing production system can be as easy as sending electronic mail. However, more sophisticated notification products are available on the open market.

**Applications System.** The applications system is the enabling component of the integration process. As noted, the application must be process supporting, easily ported and scaled to other needs, and functionally superior to its legacy predecessor. Above all, it must be maintainable.

**RECOMMENDED COURSE OF ACTION**

Systems integration projects are enormously challenging and rewarding. Users are more demanding, and systems personnel are learning new roles as well as new technology. Regardless of how much experience a project manager has in mainframe and mid-range systems development and integration projects, each integration effort is a learning experience.

Because the project management environment is an ever-changing landscape of technical, personnel, and user issues, managers need an orderly and effective methodology that addresses the numerous components of integration and anticipates problem areas. The seven rules of integration presented in this chapter should better prepare project managers for the rigors and unknowns of systems integration. During what is often a tedious and demanding process, managers should remember that the tangible results of a successful integration are felt almost immediately by the organization.

# Chapter 71
# Operating Standards and Practices for LANs

*Leo A. Wrobel*

Operating standards for LANs offer certain advantages for keeping expenses for procurement, maintenance, and support under control At the same time, any standards must enhance, not stifle, the productivity of users of local area networks. This chapter reviews the basics to include in a LAN standards document.

## PROBLEMS ADDRESSED

The following scenario is common in many organizations: There are 200 local area networks (LANs) located across the country, in everything from small sales offices with a handful of people to regional distribution centers. The company does not know if these outlying locations handle mission-critical data or not. The company does not know with certainty who is running these LANs, because it ranges from office managers and clerical employees right up to seasoned IS professionals. A site that once had 10 salespeople now has 9 salespeople and a LAN administrator. The company does not know how these sites are buying equipment, yet it is reasonably sure that they are paying too much, because they are not buying in bulk or enjoying any economies of scale in equipment purchases.

Locations are beginning to lean on IS for help desk support because there is no way they can keep up with the rapid proliferation of hardware, platforms, software, and special equipment being installed in the field. The telecommunications department is worried about connecting all of these locations together.

Although some attempts at standardization of these locations may be made, invariably, LAN managers in the field consider standards to be an attempt by the IS department to regain control of the LAN administrators' environment. Because LAN managers seldom have had any input into what these standards would be, they were soundly rejected.

0-8493-9965-3/99/$0.00+$.50
© 1999 by CRC Press LLC

**Exhibit 1. Operational and Maintenance Characteristics**

### Operational Characteristics

| MAINFRAME | LAN |
|---|---|
| "Stodgy" | "Seat-of-Pants Approach" |
| "Stoic" | "Close to Business" |
| "Regimented" | "Happy, Productive Users" |
| "Inflexible" | |
| "Stifles Productively" | |

### Maintenance Characteristics

| MAINFRAME | LAN |
|---|---|
| "Highly Advanced Support Systems" | "Evolving Support Systems" |
| "High-Level Help Desk Support" | "Difficult Help Desk Support" |
| "Reliable and Well-Proven" | "High User Involvement in Routine Problems" |
| "High Support-to-Device-Ratio" | "Low Support-to-Device Ratio" |
| | "High Maintenance" |

Today, there are literally thousands of companies fighting this same battle. This chapter gives some solutions to these problems. First, however, it is important to understand why standards are required and how IS can implement standards without stifling productivity or adversely affecting the organization.

## WHY LANS REQUIRE STANDARDS

Exhibit 1 compares two distinctly different operating environments: mainframes and LANs. To illustrate a point, Exhibit 1 uses the same adjectives that LAN and mainframe people use to describe each other.

In an ideal environment, the LAN administrator can select exactly the type of equipment best tailored to do the job. LAN managers are historically close to the core business. For example, if the company is involved in trading stock, the LAN operations department can go out and buy equipment tailored exactly to trading stock. If the organization is engaged in engineering, the LAN administrator can buy equipment exactly tailored to engineering.

From the standpoint of operational characteristics, LANs are far more desirable than mainframes because they are closer to the business, they empower people, and they make people enormously productive by being close to the core business. This is not the whole story, however. It is equally important to support LANs once they are in place. This is where the trade-offs come in.

## LESSONS FROM MAINFRAME EXPERIENCE

Because mainframes have been around so long, there is a high degree of support available. When users in the mainframe environment call the help desk with a hardware or a software problem, the help desk knows what they are talking about. Help desk staff are well trained in the hardware and the software packages and can quickly solve the users' problems.

As another example, in an IBM 3070 terminal environment, 100 terminals or more could be supported by a single technician. When those terminals became PCs, the ratio perhaps dropped to 50 PCs per technician. When those PCs became high-end workstations, the ratio dropped even further. The value of a mainframe level of technical support cannot be underestimated.

Mainframe professionals had 20 years to write effective operating and security standards. These standards cover a number of preventive safeguards that should be taken in the operational environment to assure smooth operation. These range from:

- How often to change passwords.
- How often to make backups.
- What equipment should be locked up.
- Who is responsible for change control.
- Defining the standards for interconnecting between environments.

In the mainframe world it was also easy to make very large bulk purchases. Because the mainframe has been around for so long, many advanced network management systems exist that provide a high degree of support and fault isolation.

### Balancing Productivity and Support Requirements for LANs

To the LAN administrator, the perfect environment, productivity-wise, is one which any LAN administrator anywhere in a large company can go out and buy anything at any time — flexibility to buy equipment that is exactly tailored to the core business and that has the maximum effect in the way of enhancing productivity is highly desired in LAN environments. However, if someone calls the help desk, the help desk staff will not really be sure what they have out there, let alone how to troubleshoot it. In many ways, if the users buy an oddball piece of equipment, no matter how productive it makes them, they are on their own as far as supporting that equipment.

LANs have a characteristically high ratio of technologists required to support the environment. Today, sophisticated boxes sit on the desktop that demand a much higher level of maintenance. Because people are such a valuable commodity and so difficult to justify because of downsizing or rightsizing, LAN administration is usually relegated to a firefighting mode, without a lot of emphasis on long-range planning.

Because LAN platforms are relatively new, in comparison to mainframes, there has not been as much time to develop operating and security standards. This is especially irritating to auditors when mission-critical applications move from the traditional mainframe environment onto LANs and the protective safeguards around them do not follow. Something as simple as transporting a tape backup copy of a file between LAN departments can be extremely complicated without standards. What if everyone buys a different type of tape backup unit? Without standards on what type of equipment to use, bulk purchases of equipment become difficult or impossible.

Even though major improvements have been made in network management systems over the past five years, the management systems associated with LANs often lag behind those associated with mainframe computers. Again, this causes the company to pay penalties in the area of maintenance and ease of use.

One answer, of course, is to force users into rigid standards. While this pays a handsome dividend in the area of support, it stifles the users' productivity. They need equipment well suited to their core business purpose.

An alternative is to let users install whatever they want. This may increase productivity greatly, though it is doubtful that a company could ever hire and support enough people to maintain this type of configuration. Worse, mission-critical applications could be damaged or lost altogether is users are not expected to take reasonable and prudent safeguards for their protection.

It is the responsibility of both users and technologists to find the middle ground between the regimented mainframe environment and the seat-of-the-pants LAN environment. Through careful preplanning, it is possible to configure a set of standards that offers the advantage of greater productivity that is afforded by LANs, but also the advantages learned through 20 years of mainframe operations in the areas of support, bulk purchases, and network management.

The remainder of this chapter concentrates on exactly what constitutes reasonable operating and security procedures for both LANs and telecommunications.

## STANDARDS COMMITTEES

One method is through the formation of a communications and LAN operating and security standards committee. An ideal size for a standards committee would be 10 to 12 people, with representatives from sales, marketing, engineering, support, technical services, including LANs, IS and telecommunications, and other departments. It is important to broaden this committee to include not only technologists, but also people engaged in the core business, since enhancement of productivity would be a key concern.

The actual standards document that this committee produces must deal with issues for both the operation and protection of a company's automated platforms (the Appendix provides a working table of contents from which to begin to write a document). Subjects include:

- Basic physical standards, including access to equipment rooms, where PBX equipment is kept, what type of fire protection should be employed, standards for new construction, standards for housekeeping, and standards for electrical power.
- Software security, change control, which people are authorized to make changes, and how these changes are documented.
- The security of information, such as identifying who is allowed to dial into a system, determining how to dispose of confidential materials, determining which telephone conversations should be considered private, and the company's policy on telecommunications privacy.
- Weighing options with regard to technical support of equipment.
- Resolving issues regarding interconnection standards for the telecommunications network.
- Disaster backup and recovery for both LANs and telecommunications, including defining what users must do to ensure protection of mission-critical company applications.

### Defining "Mission Critical"

Before all of this, however, the committee is expected to define and understand what a mission-critical application is. Because standards are designed to cover both operational and security issues, the business processes themselves must be defined, in order to avoid imposing a heavy burden with regard to security on users who are not engaged in mission-critical applications, or by not imposing a high enough level of security on users who are.

Standards for equipment that is not mission critical are relatively easy. Basically, a statement such as, "The company bought it, the shareholders paid for it, the company will protect it," will suffice. In practice, this means securing the area in which the equipment resides from unauthorized access by outside persons when there is danger of tampering or theft. It also includes avoiding needless exposures to factors which could damage the equipment, such as water and combustibles, and controlling food items around the equipment, such as soft drinks and coffee. The most one would expect from a user engaged in non-mission-critical applications would be something that protects the equipment itself, such as a maintenance contract.

Mission-critical equipment, however, has a value to the company that far exceeds the value of the equipment itself, because of the type of functions it supports. Determination of what constitutes a mission-critical system should be made at a senior management level. It cannot be automatically assumed that technical services will be privy to the organization's financial data.

LAN and telecommunication equipment that supports an in-bound call center for companies such as the Home Shopping Club, would definitely be mission-critical equipment, because disruption of the equipment, for whatever cause, would cause a financial hit to the company that far exceeds the value of the equipment. Therefore, mission-critical equipment should be defined as equipment that, if lost, would result in significant loss to the organization, measured in terms of lost sales, lost market share, lost customer confidence, or lost employee productivity.

Monetary cost is not the only measurement with regard to mission-critical. If an organization supports a poison-control line, for example, and loss of equipment means a mother cannot get through when a child is in danger, it has other implications. Because financial cost is a meaningful criteria to probably 90% of the companies, it is the measurement used for purposes of this discussion.

There is not necessarily a correlation between physical size and mission criticality. It is easy to look at a LAN of 100 people and say that it is more mission-critical than another LAN that has only 4people. However, the LAN with 100 people on it may provide purely an administrative function. The LAN with four people on it may have an important financial function.

## WRITING THE OPERATING AND SECURITY STANDARDS DOCUMENT

In the following approach, it is recommended that two distinct sets of standards are created for mission-critical vs. non-mission-critical equipment.

### Network Software Security and Change Control Management

One item that should be considered in this section is, Who is authorized to make major changes to LAN or telecommunications equipment?

There is a good reason to consider this question. If everyone is making major changes to a system haphazardly, a company is inviting disaster, because there is little communication concerning who changed what and whether these changes are compatible with changes made by another person. Standards should therefore include a list of persons authorized to make major changes to a mission-critical technical system. It should also have procedures for changing passwords on a regular basis, both for the maintenance and operation functions of LANs and telecommunications.

Procedures should be defined that mandate a backup before major changes in order to have something to fall back on in case something goes wrong.

Procedures should be established to include DISA (direct inward system access). Unauthorized use of DISA lines is a major cause of telecommunication fraud or theft of long-distance services. Automated attendants, for example, should also be secured and telephone credit cards properly managed. As a minimum, establish a procedure that cancels remote access and telephone credit to employees who leave the company, especially under adverse conditions.

### Physical and Environmental Security

There should be a set of basic, physical standards for all installations, regardless of their mission-critical status. These might include use of a UPS (uninterruptible power supply) on any LAN server. A UPS not only guards against loss of productivity when the lights flicker, but also cleans up the power somewhat and protects the equipment itself.

There should be standards for physically protecting the equipment, because LAN equipment is frequently stolen and because there is a black market for PBX cards as well. There should be general housekeeping standards as far as prohibitions against eating and drinking in equipment areas and properly disposing of confidential materials through shredding or other means. No- smoking policies should be included. Standards for storing combustibles or flammables in the vicinity of equipment should also be written.

Physical standards for mission-critical applications are more intensive. These might include sign-in logs for visitors requiring access to equipment rooms. They may require additional physical protection, such as sprinkler systems or fire extinguishers. They may require general improvements to the building, such as building fire-resistant walls. They should also include protection against water, since this is a frequent cause of disruption, either from drains, building plumbing, sprinklers, or other sources.

### Technical Support

The standards committee ideally should provide a forum for users to display new technologies and subject them to a technical evaluation. For example, a LAN manager or end user may find a new, innovative use of technology that promises to greatly enhance productivity in their department. They can present this new technology to the standards committee for both productivity and technical evaluations. The technologist on the committee can then advise the user of the feasibility of this technology; whether it will create an undue maintenance burden, for example, or whether it is difficult to support.

If it is found that this equipment does indeed increase productivity and that it does not create an undue maintenance burden, it could be accepted by the committee and added to a list of supported services and vendors that is underwritten by the committee. Other issues include what level of support users are required to provide for themselves, what the support level of the help desk should be, and more global issues, such as interconnection standards for a corporate backbone network and policies on virus protection.

## CONCLUSION

The LAN operating and securities standards document is designed to be an organization's system of government with regard to the conduct and operation of technical platforms supporting the business. A properly written standards document includes input from departments throughout the organization, both the enhance productivity and to keep expenses for procurement, maintenance, and support under control. Standards also ensure that appropriate preventive safeguards are undertaken, especially for mission- critical equipment, to avoid undue loss of productivity, profitability, or equity to the company in the event something goes wrong. In other words, they are designed to prevent disruptions.

Use of a LAN operating and security standards committee is advised to ensure that critical issues are decided by a group of people with wide exposure within the company and to increase ownership of the final document across departmental boundaries and throughout the organization. If properly defined, the standards document will accommodate the advantages of the mainframe environment and needs of LAN administrators by finding the middle ground between these operating environments. By writing and adopting effective standards, an organization can enjoy the productivity afforded by modern LAN environments while at the same time enjoying a high level of support afforded through more traditional environments.

# Chapter 72

# Applets and Network Security: A Management Overview

*Al Berg*

Applets, network-based programs that run on client systems, are one of the newest security concerns of network managers. This chapter describes how applets work, the threats they present, and what security precautions network managers can take to minimize the security exposures presented by applets.

## INTRODUCTION

Applets are small programs that reside on a host computer and are downloaded to a client computer to be executed. This model makes it very easy to distribute and update software. Because the new version of an application only needs to be placed on the server, clients automatically receive and run the updated version the next time they access the application.

The use of applets is possible because of the increasing bandwidth available to Internet and intranet users. The time required to download the programs has been decreasing even as program complexity has been increasing. The development of cross-platform languages such as Sun Microsystems, Inc.'s Java, Microsoft Corp.'s ActiveX, and Netscape Communications Corp.'s JavaScript has made writing applets for many different computers simple — the same exact Java or JavaScript code can be run on a Windows-based PC, a Macintosh, or a UNIX-based system without any porting or recompiling of code. Microsoft is working to port ActiveX to UNIX and Macintosh platforms.

0-8493-9965-3/99/$0.00+$.50
© 1999 by CRC Press LLC

## APPLETS AND THE WEB

The World Wide Web is the place that users are most likely to encounter applets today. Java (and to a lesser degree, JavaScript) have become web-masters' tools of choice to add interesting effects to their Web sites or to deliver applications to end users. Most of the scrolling banners and other special effects found on today's Web pages depend on applets to work. Some Web pages use applets for more substantial applications. For example, MapQuest(http://www.mapquest.com) uses Java and ActiveX to deliver an interactive street atlas of the entire U.S. Wired magazine offers a Java-based chat site that, when accessed over the Web, allows users to download an applet that lets them participate in real-time conferencing.

### The Security Issue

Every silver lining has a cloud, and applets are no exception. Applets can present a real security hazard for users and network managers. When Web pages use applets, the commands that tell the client's browser to download and execute the applets are embedded in the pages themselves. Users have no way of knowing whether or not the next page that they download will contain an applet, and most of the time, they do not care. The Internet offers an almost limitless source of applets for users to run, however, no one knows who wrote them, whether they were written with malicious intent, or whether they contain bugs that might cause them to crash a user's computer.

Applets and computer viruses have a lot in common. Both applets and viruses are self-replicating code that executes on the user's computer without the user's consent. Some security experts have gone as far as to say that the corporate network manager should prohibit users from running applets at all. However, applets are becoming an increasingly common part of how users interact with the Internet and corporate intranets, so learning to live safely with applets is important for network managers.

### What Are the Risks?

According to Princeton University's Safe Internet Programming (SIP) research team, there have been no publicly reported, confirmed cases of security breaches involving Java, though there have been some suspicious events that may have involved Java security problems. The lack of reported cases is no guarantee that there have not been breaches that either were not discovered or were not reported. But it does indicate that breaches are rare.

As Web surfing increasingly becomes a way to spend money, and applets become the vehicle for shopping, attacks on applets will become more and more profitable, increasing the risk. Sun, Netscape, and Microsoft all designed their applet languages with security in mind.

## JAVA: SECURE APPLETS

Java programs are developed in a language similar to C++ and stored as source code on a server. When a client, such as a Web browser, requests a page that references a Java program, the source code is retrieved from the server and sent to the browser, where an integrated interpreter translates the source code statements into machine-independent bytecodes, which are executed by a virtual machine implemented in software on the client. This virtual machine is designed to be incapable of operations that might be detrimental to security, thus providing a secure sandbox in which programs can execute without fear of crashing the client system. Java applets loaded over a network are not allowed to:

- Read from files on the client system.
- Write to files on the client system.
- Make any network connections, except to the server from which they were downloaded.
- Start any client-based programs.
- Define native method calls, which would allow an applet to directly access the underlying computer.

Java was designed to make applets inherently secure. Following are some of the underlying language security features offered by Java:

- All of an applet's array references are checked to make sure that programs will not crash because of a reference to an element that does not exist.
- Complex and troublesome pointer variables (found in some vendors' products) that provide direct access to memory locations in the computer do not exist in Java, removing another cause of crashes and potentially malicious code.
- Variables can be declared as unchangeable at runtime to prevent important program parameters from being modified accidentally or intentionally.

### Java: Holes and Bugs

Although Sun has made every effort to make the Java virtual machine unable to run code that will negatively impact the underlying computer, researchers have already found bugs and design flaws that could open the door to malicious applets.

The fact that Sun has licensed Java to various browser vendors adds another level of complexity to the security picture. Not only can security be compromised by a flaw in the Java specification, but the vendor's implementation of the specification may contain its own flaws and bugs.

**Denial-of-Service Threats.** Denial-of-service attacks involve causing the client's Web browser to run with degraded performance or crash. Java does not protect the client system from these types of attacks, which can be accomplished simply by putting the client system into a loop to consume processor cycles, creating new process threads until system memory is consumed, or placing locks on critical processes needed by the browser.

Because denial-of-service attacks can be programmed to occur after a time delay, it may be difficult for a user to determine which page the offending applet was downloaded from. If an attacker is subtle and sends an applet that degrades system performance, the user may not know that their computer is under attack, leading to time-consuming and expensive troubleshooting of a nonexistent hardware or software problem.

Java applets are not supposed to be able to establish network connections to machines other than the server they were loaded from. However, there are applets that exploit bugs and design flaws that allow it to establish a back-door communications link to a third machine (other than the client or server). This link could be used to send information that may be of interest to a hacker. Because many ready-to-use Java applets are available for download from the Internet, it would be possible for an attacker to write a useful applet, upload it to a site where webmasters would download it, and then sit back and wait for information sent by the applet to reach their systems.

**What Kind of Information Can the Applet Send Back?** Due to another implementation problem found in August 1996 by the Safe Internet Programming research team at Princeton University, the possibilities are literally endless. A flaw found in Netscape Navigator 3.0 beta 5 and earlier versions, and Microsoft Internet Explorer 3.0 beta 2 and earlier versions, allows applets to gain full read and write access to the files on a Web surfer's machine. This bug means that the attacker can get copies of any files on the machine or replace existing data or program files with hacked versions.

Giving Java applets the ability to connect to an arbitrary host on the network or Internet opens the door to another type of attack. A malicious applet, downloaded to and running on a client inside of a firewalled system, could establish a connection to another host behind the firewall and access files and programs. Because the attacking host is actually inside the secured system, the firewall will not know that the access is actually originating from outside the network.

Another bug found in August 1996 by the Princeton team affects only Microsoft Internet Explorer version 3.0 and allows applets (which are not supposed to be allowed to start processes on the client machine) to execute any DOS command on the client. This allows the applet to delete or change files or programs or insert new or hacked program code such as viruses or backdoors. Microsoft has issued a patch (available on its Web site at http://www.microsoft.com/ie)to Internet Explorer that corrects the problem.

Princeton's SIP team also found a hole that would allow a malicious application to execute arbitrary strings of machine code, even though the Java virtual machine is only supposed to be able to execute the limited set of Java bytecodes. The problem was fixed in Netscape Navigator 3.0 beta 6 and Microsoft Internet Explorer 3.0 beta 2.

## JAVASCRIPT: A DIFFERENT GRIND

Netscape's JavaScript scripting language may be named Java, but it is distinct from Sun's applet platform. JavaScript is Netscape Navigator's built-in scripting language that allows webmasters to do cross-platform development of applets that control browser events, objects such as tables and forms, and various activities that happen when users click on an object with their mouse.

Like Java, JavaScript runs applications in a virtual machine to prevent them from performing functions that would be detrimental to the operation of the client workstations. Also like Java, there are several flaws in the implementation of the security features of JavaScript. Some of the flaws found in JavaScript include the ability for malicious applets to:

- Obtain users' E-mail addresses from their browser configuration.
- Track the pages that a user visits and mail the results back to the script author.
- Access the client's file system, reading and writing files.

A list of JavaScript bugs and fixes can be found on John LoVerso's Web page at the Open Software Foundation (http://www.osf.org/[sim]loverso/javascript/)

## ACTIVEX: MICROSOFT'S VISION FOR DISTRIBUTED COMPONENT COMPUTING

Microsoft's entry in the applet development tool wars, ActiveX, is very different from Java and presents its own set of security challenges. ActiveX is made up of server and client components, including:

- Controls, which are applets that can be embedded in Web pages and executed at the client. Controls can be written in a number of languages, including Visual Basic and Visual C++.
- Documents that provide access to non-HTML content, such as word processing documents or spreadsheets, from a Web browser.
- The Java virtual machine, which allows standard Java applets to run at the client.
- Scripting, which allows the Web developer to control the integration of controls and Java applets on a Web page.
- The server framework, which provides a number of server-side functions such as database access and data security.

Java applets running in an ActiveX environment (e.g., Microsoft's Internet Explorer Web browser) use the same security features and have the same security issues associated with JavaScript. Microsoft offers a Java development environment(i.e., Visual J++) as well as other sandbox languages (i.e., VBScript, based on Visual Basic and JScript, Microsoft's implementation of Netscape's JavaScript) for the development of applications that are limited as to the functions they can perform.

When developers take advantage of ActiveX's ability to integrate programs written in Visual Basic or C++, the virtual machine model of Java no longer applies. In these cases, compiled binaries are transferred from the server to the Web client for execution. These compiled binaries have full access to the underlying computing platform, so there is no reason that the application could not read and write files on the client system, send information from the client to the server (or another machine), or perform a destructive act such as erasing a disk or leaving a virus behind.

## Using Authenticode for Accountability

Microsoft's approach to security for non-Java ActiveX applications is based on the concept of accountability — knowing with certainty the identity of the person or company that wrote a piece of software and that the software was not tampered with by a third party. Microsoft sees the issues related to downloading applets from the Web as similar to those involved in purchasing software; users need to know where the software is coming from and that it is intact. Accountability also means that writers of malicious code could be tracked down and would have to face consequences for their actions.

The mechanism that Microsoft offers to implement this accountability is called Authenticode. Authenticode uses a digital signature attached to each piece of software downloaded from the Internet. The signature is a cryptographic code attached by the software developer to an applet. Developers must enter a private key (known only to them) to sign their application, assuring their identity. The signature also includes an encrypted checksum of the application itself, which allows the client to determine if the applet has changed since the developer released it.

### ActiveX: The Downside

This approach provides developers and users with access to feature-rich applications, but at a price. If an application destroys information on a user's computer, accountability will not help recover their data or repair damage done to their business. Once the culprit has been found, bringing them to justice may be difficult because new computer crimes are developing faster than methods for prosecuting them.

Microsoft acknowledges that Authenticode does not guarantee that end users will never download malicious code to their PCs and that it is a first step in the protection of information assets.

Further information on ActiveX can be found on Microsoft's Web site (http://www.microsoft.com/activex)and at the ActiveX Web site run by CNet Technology Corp. (http://www.activex.com).

### AN OUNCE OF PREVENTION

So far, this chapter has discussed problems posed by applets. Following are some steps that can be taken to lessen the exposure faced by users.

### Make Sure the Basics Are Covered

Users need to back up their data and programs consistently, and sensitive data should be stored on secure machines. The surest way to avoid applet security problems is to disable support for applet execution at the browser. If the code cannot execute, it cannot do damage.

Of course, the main downside of this approach is that the users will lose the benefits of being able to run applets. Because the ability to run applets is part of the client browser, turning off applets is usually accomplished at the desktop and a knowledgeable user could simply turn applet support back on. Firewall vendors are starting to provide support for filtering out applets, completely or selectively, before they enter the local network.

### Users Should Run the Latest Available Versions of Their Web Browsers

Each new version corrects not only functional and feature issues, but security flaws. If an organization is planning to use applets on its Web pages, it is preferable to either write them internally or obtain them from trusted sources. If applets will be downloaded from unknown sources, a technical person with a good understanding of the applet language should review the code to be sure that it does only what it claims to.

Mark LaDue, a researcher at Georgia Tech, has a Web page (available at http://www.math.gatech.edu/[sim]mladue/HostileApplets.html) containing a number of hostile applets available for download and testing. Seeing some real applications may help users recognize new problem applets that may be encountered.

## CONCLUSION

IS personnel should monitor the Princeton University Safe Internet Programming group's home page (located at http://www.cs.princeton.edu/sip) for the latest information on security flaws and fixes (under News). It is also a good idea to keep an eye on browser vendors' home pages for news of new versions.

Applets offer users and network managers a whole new paradigm for delivering applications to the desktop. Although, like any new technology, applets present a new set of challenges and concerns, their benefits can be enjoyed while their risks can be managed.

# Chapter 73
# Assessing and Eliminating Virus Threats in Distributed Networks

*Frank Horwitz*

Computer viruses cost users billions of dollars per year in lost data, lost productivity, and clean-up costs. This chapter examines the problem by defining viruses, why they matter, how they infect systems, and how to discover whether they have infected a system. Standard approaches to fighting viruses are explained, weaknesses in some commonly used virus-fighting techniques are illustrated, and the ideal virus defense system is discussed.

## PROBLEMS ADDRESSED

Technically speaking, a computer virus is similar to a biological virus: it wants to reproduce itself. A virus does not necessarily inflict any damage. Industry experts define viruses differently. A virus can be described as a piece of code that attaches itself to a file, critical disk sector, or memory location for the purpose of replicating. Another definition describes a virus as a program designed to replicate and spread, generally with the victim being oblivious to its existence. A more complete definition says that a virus is a program that replicates itself, attaches itself to other programs, and performs unsolicited, if not malicious, actions. By any definition, reproduction is the common theme.

Unless it is deflected or killed, a virus usually spells difficulty and expense for network administrators, whose task is to eliminate them. This chapter provides practical information for preventing, discovering, and eliminating viruses.

**How Pervasive Is the Viral Threat?**

One of the most damaging effects a virus can have on a corporate LAN or WAN is a drain on system resources. A very destructive virus, such as the Byway Virus, can reproduce rapidly enough to fill a multi-gigabyte hard drive overnight and can cause an entire system to crash. Others, such as Junkie Virus, fill memory and cause system response times to slow drastically. In either situation, the best case is a loss of productivity; the worst case is the systemwide loss of data.

Loss of data is another specter of the viral threat. One of the most common DOS viruses, Jerusalem, is designed to erase any program executed using the DOS execute program call. All of the programs users try to run suddenly cease to exist. A variant of this virus (known as the 1704-Format), when activated, attempts to reformat part of the hard drive. Another common virus, Disk Killer, attempts to scramble all data on an infected disk or diskette. These and many other viruses can cost days of clean-up and restoration in a well-maintained network, or wipe out months of productivity in a poorly backed-up network.

Another problem created by viruses is the cost of cleaning them off infected systems. A survey of corporations with more than 1,000 PCs reported that the average cost of clean up can be as high as $254,000, a figure that includes only the direct labor expense for system recovery and data back-up. The indirect expense of lost productivity is much higher. One estimate states that viruses cost American businesses $2.7 billion in 1994. In addition, the average recovery time required to clean up an organization having more than 25 PCs is four days. Even worse, 25% of those experiencing a virus attack suffered a reinfection by the same virus within 30 days.

Even one virus incident can potentially cost a company millions of dollars. Although budgets often place computer security low on the priority list, the cost of prevention seems almost negligible when compared to the potential loss of time and money.

The odds of being infected with a virus are getting worse every day. Consider this progression of averages:

- In 1986, one new virus came into existence every one and a half months (there were eight known viruses; four of them existed only in computer laboratories).
- In 1989, one new virus came into existence every week.
- In 1990, one new virus came into existence every two days.
- In 1991, six new viruses came into existence every day.
- In 1994, approximately 7,000 known viruses existed.
- In 1995, approximately 15,000 known viruses existed.

Currently, the number of viruses doubles every eight to eight and a half months. Hackers and virus authors are working cooperatively. Electronic bulletin boards allow them to share not only new viruses, but virus-creating engines. A would-be virus author can learn from books, virus kits, the Internet, and even CD-ROMs. However, antivirus companies, in order to maintain profitability, work alone, unwilling to share source code. The result is that there are 1,200 known virus authors but only 200 virus researchers. At that 6:1 ratio, the virus authors are getting more done than the researchers. Only 38% of corporate users consistently apply workstation antivirus products. As a result, more than 40% of all networks have viruses.

### How Viruses Infect Systems

Usually, a virus enters a system through an intrusion point such as floppy drives on user workstations. On a network, intrusion points include E-mail, modem pools, and gateways to other networks. Approximately 87% of viruses enter systems from floppies, and 43% of those are brought from home by unsuspecting users. Once on a system, a virus usually either attaches itself to an executable file so that whenever that file is executed, the virus is too, or the virus infects the boot sector of the PC so that from there it can travel to other floppies or logical disks.

### Major Types of Viruses

The following sections discuss the most prevalent types of viruses, including file, boot sector, multi-partite, file overwrite, stealth, polymorphic, and macro-based.

**File.** File viruses usually attach themselves to an executable file, such as .EXE and .COM on DOS machines. The virus can insert its code into the host program's code so that when the program executes, the virus executes first. Most of the thousands of viruses known to exist are file viruses. Windows 3.1 barely runs in the presence of a file virus. If a file virus is resident in the memory of a DOS system (which is exactly where file viruses like to reside), in many cases Windows cannot even start. This generally causes the user running Windows to eliminate the virus, perhaps unwittingly, as they attempt to fix their system. A growing trend toward Windows 95 and 32-bit operating systems may signal a resurgence of file viruses.

**Boot.** Boot sector viruses cause the vast majority of actual attack incidents. Each of the top 12 viruses reported last year were boot sector viruses. Whenever a computer is booted up, it looks for instructions about how to operate and what to do. It finds those instructions in the boot sector of a hard drive or floppy disk. Boot viruses insert themselves into boot sectors so that the virus executes first and gains control of the system, even before the operating system is loaded.

Boot viruses are especially dangerous because they can spread from anything that has a boot sector. Any floppy disk — even an allegedly blank one — can spread boot viruses. If a boot virus on a floppy disk is inserted into a computer, the virus goes into RAM and infects every disk that computer accesses until the computer is rebooted, which wipes the boot virus from memory.

**Multi-Partite.** Multi-partite viruses combine characteristics of file and boot viruses. Multi-partite viruses can spread as easily as a file virus, yet still insert an infection into a boot sector, making them very difficult to eradicate.

**File Overwriters.** File overwriters are file viruses that link themselves to an executable program but keep the program intact. Executing the program also executes the virus, which attempts to add itself to as many files as possible. File overwriters often have no purpose other than to replicate, but even then they take up space and slow performance. They may damage or destroy files inadvertently.

**Stealth.** Stealth viruses are engineered to elude detection by traditional antivirus checkers. The virus may target and eliminate the detection function of a commercial antivirus product. Stealth viruses reside in memory, intercepting the system's MS-DOS calls in order to make infected files appear uninfected. The stealth virus can then infect every floppy diskette and logical drive the system accesses. Some anti-virus scanners help propagate stealth viruses because they open and close files to scan them, giving the virus additional chances to spread.

**Polymorphic.** Polymorphic viruses include a mutation engine that makes the virus change minor parts of its code each time the virus is executed. Different encryption algorithms are nested within a polymorphic virus to help it hide from scanners. A decryption routine included in the virus allows it to return to a normal state when it executes. The stable bytes (the decryption algorithm) become shorter with repeated executions of the virus. This defeats first-generation virus scanners, which operate by checking code for any matches with virus code.

Virus authors can access polymorphic engines, which can take a non-polymorphic virus as input and output the virus with polymorphic qualities. The availability of such engines has made the authoring of polymorphic viruses a simple, straightforward task. As a result, the number of polymorphics has doubled about every eight months. Today, more than 200 polymorphic viruses produced by these engines exist, and another 50 polymorphic viruses are known to exist that do not use the engines. The latest generation, the superfast polymorphic infector, can lay waste to every executable in every directory on a PC's hard disk without requiring that .COM and .EXE files launch first. Running a directory listing is enough to trigger the virus.

**Macro-Based.** Macro-based viruses are the newest innovation. A macro virus is unusual because it can infect documents instead of programs. It is the first virus that can cross platforms, infecting both PCs and Macintoshes. The one known form of the virus, written in Word Basic and referred to by Microsoft as the Prank Virus, infects only Microsoft Word 6.0 files. The virus is not destructive; it simply adds nonsense Word macros to documents that end with .DOC or .DOT. Although Prank is not really destructive, its implications for the future are disturbing because it has introduced an entirely new method for viruses to spread.

## Common Spread Scenarios

Viruses spread through organizations several ways, including through the use of shared machines, shared diskettes, popular programs, and LAN servers.

**Shared Machines.** Viruses spread throughout an organization most commonly through shared machines. A computer used by many different people can serve as a center of infection. If a user runs an infected program on the machine, the infection has probably spread to programs on the machine's hard disk. If other users bring their own diskettes to run on the machine, the diskettes and any programs on them are likely to become infected. The diskette will probably carry the infection to other machines.

**Shared Diskettes.** Many diskettes, such as diagnostic diskettes, product demos, or company manuals, are routinely carried from machine to machine. If such a diskette becomes infected, the infection can quickly spread to many machines.

**Popular Programs.** Popular games, demos, or animations often cause the user who obtains a copy to want to pass it on to other people. If one of these programs becomes infected, the infection can spread quickly to many machines.

**LAN Servers.** If a program on a LAN server used by many workstations becomes infected, a large percentage of the LAN workstations can become infected very quickly (sometimes within an hour or two). One common mistake is to have the LAN log-on program in a place where anyone on the LAN can write to it. This setup means that if any workstation on the LAN becomes infected, the logon program quickly becomes infected, and then every workstation that logs on to the LAN immediately becomes infected.

## HOW TO DISCOVER A VIRUS

Viruses can continue replicating until they are detected. The most well-crafted viruses show no symptoms to reveal their presence. However, many viruses are flawed and betray their presence with some of these indications:

- Changes in the length of programs.
- Changes in the file date or time stamp.
- Longer program load times.
- Slower system operation.
- Reduced memory or disk space.
- Bad sectors on a floppy diskette.
- Unusual error messages.
- Unusual screen activity.
- Failed program execution.
- Failed system bootups when booting or accidentally booting from the A: drive.
- Unexpected writes to a drive.

Instead of waiting for a sign, network managers should use the appropriate tools to seek out viruses before they get far enough to compound problems. The ideal is to repel them before they infect the system.

## STANDARD APPROACHES TO FIGHTING VIRUSES

There are several ways to combat viruses. Computer viruses have become increasingly cunning in their programming and ability to avoid detection or eradication. However, virus-fighting tools have also grown through several generations to meet the challenge. Some of the various approaches are described in the following sections.

### Signature-Based Scanners

Traditionally, virus scanners look for known virus code and when they find a match, they alert the user. The leading scanners are signature-based. Signatures are strands of code unique to a single virus, analogous to DNA strands in a biological virus. Virus researchers and antivirus product developers catalog known viruses and their signatures. Scanners use these catalogs to search for viruses on a user's system. The best scanners have an exhaustive inventory of all viruses known to exist and examine all possible locations for infection, including boot sectors, system memory, and files.

## Multilevel Generic Detection

Generic detectors are used to eliminate unknown viruses. This method performs integrity checking using checksums.

A checksum is created when an algorithm reads a file's bytes sequentially, creating a unique numeric code based on the file itself. Generic antivirus detectors then compare checksums recorded when the system was in a known, clean state with checksums recalculated subsequently. If a virus has attached itself to a file, the bytes will add up differently and the new checksum will no longer match the old (i.e., clean) checksum.

Using this method, it is not necessary to know anything about a virus; instead, the system focuses on what the clean file should look like. The Secret Service uses the same method when teaching agents how to spot counterfeit currency. New agents receive extremely detailed training on what a real dollar should look like rather than on what various counterfeits look like.

The other techniques used in generic detection enable antivirus programs to distinguish between normal, legitimate writes to a file in contrast to viral additions. Expert systems test a system's software by examining code flows, calls, and executions, and other functions to spot viral activity. Sophisticated versions of this approach not only spot viruses, but clean them automatically.

## TSR Monitoring

Terminate and stay resident (TSR) programs stay in memory but operate in the background while other programs run. Because most viruses are essentially TSR, it makes sense to combat them with a TSR. Antivirus TSR programs can provide real-time monitoring of disks and files, expert systems analysis of virus-like behavior and code, and may even detect stealth and polymorphic activity. Rather than only working when invoked, TSRs stay on in automatic mode whenever the workstation is in use. Instead of looking for code that matches memorized patterns, as scanners do, antivirus TSRs attempt to catch viruses "in the act." On a network, antivirus TSRs can download from a server to each client as it logs on so that users do not need to remember to activate antivirus tools.

## Behavior Blocking

This is the only defense that can prevent viral infection, rather than merely detecting viruses after they have infected. Behavior blocking performs on-the-fly code analysis, monitoring the sequence of code behavior until it can distinguish whether the code is safe or harmful. Harmful code is not permitted to execute. Instead, the behavior blocker notifies the user. Behavior blocking programs use some or all of the following techniques.

**File Attribute Monitors.** A virus cannot infect (i.e., write to) an executable that is marked read-only. Many viruses work around this by first modifying the file's attributes so that the file is now a read-write file. Behavior blockers can intercept code that attempts to change or delete the attributes of files.

**Intercept Reboot.** Some behavior blocking intercepts Ctrol+Alt+Del warm reboots and checks any inserted floppy for viruses before allowing the computer to warm-boot off that floppy. If the floppy has a virus, the behavior blocker warns the user that the floppy is infected. This technique can halt boot viruses.

**Smart Blocking.** This term refers to very sophisticated behavior blockers that are able to distinguish complex virus behaviors from the complex behaviors of a user running complex software. Smart behavior blockers can analyze detailed sequences of behavior, using statistical analysis to determine the probability that a particular sequence is a virus.

**Rescue Disks.** Rescue disks are used to salvage data once a virus has infected a PC. It is important that each PC have its own rescue disk. During the installation, an operator must be present to put in the diskette — there is no automatic installation. Users must keep track of their rescue disks. If the disk is lost, there is no way to rescue the PC from the virus infection.

**Physical Access to PCs.** One simple but important technique for defeating viruses is to control who is able to use the computers. Despite the rise of the Internet, most viruses still enter machines through floppy disks. Although the majority of infections come through the hands of unwitting employees, a percentage of attacks emanate from hostile intent. Therefore, some viral attacks can be deflected simply by deterring unauthorized personnel from using machines. Besides taking measures such as securing physical access to computer rooms, a manager can also use security products that render physical and logical drives invisible to certain users or user groups on a network. Thus, fewer personnel have the opportunity to hack those drives.

## Drawbacks of Signature Scanning

Despite the existence of sophisticated antivirus tools, many organizations rely almost entirely on signature scanning to detect viruses. In light of the virus boom, signature scanning alone is a mediocre defense, at best. Some of the drawbacks of this commonly-used approach are described in the following sections.

**Passivity.** The most profound flaw in relying on signature scanners is that they are reactive, or passive. The goal of scanning is to detect a virus that has already infected a file or a boot sector. The ideal method is to prevent viruses from infecting the system at all, not merely to be informed of the problem after the fact.

**Incomplete Checking.** A polymorphic virus, which produces varied but fully operational copies of itself, can deceive signature scanners by altering or encrypting its signature. Signature scanners have attempted to address this by including several signatures for a given virus, one for each possible encryption method or iteration of the signature. As polymorphic viruses become increasingly sophisticated, the brute force method of including more signatures in the scanner will not be able to keep up with all the possible variants of all the polymorphic viruses. Many polymorphs already evade detection by interspersing noise instructions or by interchanging mutually independent instructions within the code to continually modify the signature. A simple signature-based scanner cannot reliably identify this type of code.

**Failure to Scan for Newer Viruses.** Scan strings can only be extracted and cataloged if the antivirus vendor has a sample of the virus. In the recent past, it took the most common viruses six months to three years to become prevalent, giving vendors enough time to send out regular updates of known viruses and head them off. The exponential growth in viruses has increased the likelihood of a new virus reaching the LAN or PC before the update from the antivirus company does. Besides creating a chance of missing an unknown virus, signature-based scanners require constant updating. If the signature scanner is not centrally administrated, it slows productivity and drains resources because of the management tasks needed to install each successive enterprisewide update.

**Insufficient Scanning Frequency.** In theory, a virus infecting a system at 8:59 a.m. could be caught one minute later if the network is routinely scanned at 9:00 a.m. However, the opposite scenario is just as likely. A network may be scanned at 9:00 am and become infected at 9:05 am. If the virus is a fast infector such as Dark Avenger or Frodo, once it is in memory it can infect not only executed programs, but even those that are merely opened. Such a virus has almost 24 hours of free time to wreak havoc in the network. Even worse, because many signature scanners open files in order to scan them, the very act of using the scanner can allow the virus to infect all programs at once.

**Slow Scanning.** Any scanner takes a finite amount of time to scan a machine for viruses — perhaps five minutes or more. If the 70 million U.S. employees who use PCs spend five minutes a day scanning, and earn $15 an hour, the annual cost of scanning(260 days a year) is more than $22 billion. The costs of scanning exceed the purchase price of antivirus software after just a few weeks of scanning. More sophisticated tools can cut this time drastically by scanning checksums instead of the entire contents of every file. The more viruses a scanner must search for, the more places within a file it must search, and the more files it must search across, the slower the search must be. Because strings must be stored in memory, and memory is limited, there will soon be two-pass products that load one set of strings, scan, then load a second set and scan. Although computers are faster now, hard drives are also getting larger.

**Dependence on User Compliance.** Traditional scanners do not work unless employees remember to use them. Some users are inclined to value their own productivity and convenience more than their employer's security concerns, and thus are not motivated to consistently scan. Even diligent users tend to get lax if scanning every day for a month produces no alarms.

## RECOMMENDED COURSE OF ACTION

As long as there are hackers inventing new forms of maliciousness, no antivirus vendor can guarantee that their products will completely eliminate viruses. However, there are advanced products that come very close to providing the ideal defense. Knowledgeable implementation of advanced protection strategies and products can prove an effective deterrent to viruses in the short and long term.

### Strategies for Virus Prevention

The first priority for an antivirus strategy is that any defenses put in place must be used. Many approaches emphasize end-user convenience to the point of rendering defenses useless. A company can, however, set up antivirus software on its LAN servers so that each time a user logs in, the program checks for its own presence on the user's workstation. If such antivirus software is not present on the workstation, the program loads itself onto the PC and scans the PC's hard drive before allowing the user to continue. If the program finds an earlier version of itself, or a modified version of itself on the workstation, it loads the newer, clean version onto that workstation and scan. The entire process happens rapidly enough not to harm user productivity. Many users do not even notice it happening.

This approach is far preferable to that of programs that depend on users remembering to scan periodically. Such programs leave holes in a system's defenses every time even one user forgets to scan. Users are often tempted to skip scanning, especially if the scanning process is slow. This adds an even more haphazard quality to network defense. Antivirus software should offer an unobtrusive way of forcing users to keep their machines clean.

**Repelling Viruses Proactively.** An antivirus strategy should be proactive. It should detect and repel viruses before they infect anything on the system. A signature scanner working as the sole defense of a network can do nothing more than occasionally report bad news. The ideal system must be able to stop boot viruses before they infect and must be able to remove all viruses without necessarily knowing the virus. Proactive antivirus software provides signature scanning as well as multilevel generic detection, a TSR approach, and behavior blocking to remove viruses that are known and unknown.

**Comprehensive Security.** Some antivirus software scans only for the 200 most common viruses, which account for the majority of infections. Protecting a system from these common viruses may offer sufficient protection, because the likelihood of infection by another virus is quite slim. However, the ideal system is not one that usually works, or hardly ever misses a virus, but one that seals off every conceivable intrusion point.

In addition, viruses tend to spread in a regional fashion, turning up much more frequently in one particular country or geographical area than other areas. If a virus common in a particular region is one that the software perceives as uncommon, the scanner could miss the virus. This is especially threatening in companies that have international offices. Effective antivirus software uses a combination of traditional and proprietary heuristic techniques to ferret out even the trickiest viruses, Trojan Horses, and logic bombs. Scanning alone is not sufficient. The most effective antivirus system should use the latest generation of defenses in concert.

**Automatic Logging.** Antivirus systems should document any security events that occur so that managers can stay informed about threats to their defense system. Documentation should include log-ins, log-offs, program execution, and a separate log of failed log-in attempts. Effective antivirus software should also require password entry upon any boot-up and prevent access to hard disks any other way. After a period of inactivity at the keyboard, a time-out feature should inhibit input from the keyboard and mouse. Documentation and automatic logging requirements help management restrict physical access to workstations, which is vital to maintaining a protected environment.

# Chapter 74
# Technology Conversions on WANs

*Daniel A. Kosek*

Large-scale WAN conversions are some of the most difficult projects in networking. To make the process easier, network managers can secure corporate backing, carefully document the current and planned networks, and properly prepare their sites.

## INTRODUCTION

Perhaps one of the toughest networking jobs is a technology conversion or replacement on a large WAN. Migration of large-scale WANs from one technology to the next is necessary to allow corporations to take advantage of newer data services and transport technologies. ATM and frame relay have changed the face of these networks forever. The scale of a project is inversely proportional to the need to upgrade — the larger the network to be replaced, the more the upgrade appears to be needed.

These larger networks have often been in operation for many years. A switch to newer equipment allows corporations to take advantage of the advancements available in equipment today. Unfortunately, the corporations that can typically gain the most benefit from this type of change seem to be paralyzed in respect to doing a full-scale conversion.

The most prevalent reason for this paralysis is the network that is in place. For example, many companies have operated for more than 15 years using one exclusive network service, such as IBM's SNA. To say the network is fine because SNA operates acceptably shows limited vision. Today's networks include PCs, UNIX workstations, Windows NT, Novell, and Macintosh machines operating companywide. Even LAN applications such as cc:Mail and Lotus Notes indicate the evolution of corporate computing needs. Most IT projects have moved to client/server applications rather than mainframe development.

Newer products and services require a LAN that offers a routable protocol such as IP or IPX. Although such a network is more efficient than SNA

0-8493-9965-3/99/$0.00+$.50
© 1999 by CRC Press LLC

for running new applications, it actually does little to replace SNA in many areas. These products must coexist on the corporate WAN in a tolerant manner. A corporate network manager cannot rely on past network performance. Network managers must understand the impact new service requirements demand from the network and the time frame in which they will be delivered.

## FEAR OF CHANGE

Another reason for paralysis during a WAN conversion project is fear of change. The politics of changing network technologies are almost totally responsible for most delays in the application of new WAN technologies. For example, a large corporation in the transportation industry had just selected new WAN technology when a major outage occurred in the LAN. The vendor of the WAN equipment used the outage to create great worry about what might happen if the company replaced equipment. The vendor took the exaggerated message higher and higher into the organization until a senior vice-president vetoed the upgrade of the network, fearing the possibility that additional outages might happen.

A poorly managed network conversion results in an ineffectual network. Network managers should follow the same rule as a trim carpenter finishing houses: measure twice, cut once. The following sections discuss several areas that are key to a successful conversion.

## CORPORATE INVOLVEMENT

Corporate buy-in for a project is a must. The lack of corporate agreement is typically the main cause of the fear that stands in the way of many network upgrades. This is why it is important that corporate management be knowledgeable about the facts concerning a potential upgrade, especially in geographically dispersed companies.

Management, including regional and site managers, should participate in the planning and conversion of the network. The network manager should try to avoid setting any unrealistic expectations. The corporate management team should understand that there will be service outages, but that the plan is designed to keep them to a minimum.

### Scheduling Projects

If sites are being converted on the weekends, a member of the conversion team should be available to test voice and data port connections once they are moved onto the new system. One of the main concerns in large companies is other projects competing for the same personnel and possibly already creating outages.

There should be a common schedule, available throughout the company, that documents the scheduling of each competing project. Then not only the conversion but all work related to the project can be scheduled. Some corporations operate around the clock; in these cases there is no good time to be out of service. The slowest business hours must be determined before work is scheduled.

IS personnel should be ready at all times for the possibility of emergency troubleshooting. Project leaders should be informed right away if troubleshooting has started.

## Auditing the Physical Network

A clear understanding of the current network services supported is required to properly complete a migration or technology replacement project. Current detailed data on the network is an absolute necessity. After the information is collected, it must be verified, which may require a number of people at various sites performing a physical check of cables connected to the equipment.

During the verification process at one company, more than 300 connections had either been disconnected or were actually unused. Also, about 110 new connections had been added. Because the new equipment was modeled using the connection counts prior to this verification process, the new equipment orders were in error. There was also an active T1 line that someone had issued a disconnect order for. If the company had continued to pay for that line, hundreds of dollars per month would have been wasted.

The process of verification is actually an audit of the physical network. This audit provides a current snapshot of the network for comparison with what was ordered for the new network. This protects the new installation from having too many or too few ports of the correct type.

One company ordered all high-speed data circuit cards with V.35 interfaces for their conversion, which is typical. However, the audit revealed the need for several RS-449 ports. The ports were for a small videoconference setup between several division locations and the company's headquarters for the top executives' daily conference session. Omitting these ports may have cost the network administrator his job.

## Formatting Online Information About the Network

Once all of the network information is collected, it should be formatted so that it is highly portable. Many companies like to use a spreadsheet. The resulting files can be imported to database programs should the company decide to track the network in the future. Drawings of the network should be created in a file format that is standardized within the company.

All of the files should be stored as data where there is easy access. Although a subdirectory on a server is acceptable, an intranet server is best. It does not take long to set up a Web page and store documents, pictures, and charts as files to be downloaded. Users can download them as needed. This online information system should include lists and drawings, as described in the following sections.

**Site Address, Contact, and Access List.** This list includes the company shipping address, site contact to receive shipments, and site contacts for work being done. The list should also include the site access procedures (i.e., normal and after-hours) and who arranges facilities (i.e., power, floor space) for the project.

**Trunk Circuit Lists.** This list details all the circuits used to interconnect sites. It should include LEC and IXC circuit numbers and service and support phone numbers. All new circuits and those to be disconnected should be marked clearly. A typical format is:

From/To/Ckt ID-IXC/LEC(From)/LEC(To)/Framing/Type

**Port Circuit Lists.** This is a detailed listing of all the current port-level circuits used within the network. This information should then have an addendum document that shows the circuits being disconnected, those being moved, and the new circuits being added to the new network. A typical data format is:

From (Node/Shelf/Card/Port)/
To (Node/Shelf/Card/Port)/Type/Speed/DTE-DCE/Clocking

A typical voice format is:

From (PBX/Card/DS0s)(Node/Shelf/Card/Port)/
To (PBX/Card/DS0s) (Node/Shelf/Card/Port)/Framing/Trunk Group/Clocking

**Drawings.** Network drawings for documentation purposes should include the current topology and the future topology. The block diagram of the current system should be an overview of the entire network including site IDs and intrasite trunks. The block diagram of the future topology should be an overview of the entire new network including site IDs and only the intrasite trunks that will remain after the conversion.

**Individual Site Drawing.** This diagram should be an overview of one site in the new network including the intrasite trunks and equipment installed at the site. It should not show port-level detail. It should show dial-up access with phone numbers and a patch panel with the designations.

## MIGRATION STRATEGIES

Once the network information is gathered and processed, it must be applied. The goal is to deploy the new network equipment with as little downtime as possible. There are a variety of methods for completing a conversion.

### The Leapfrog Approach: Balancing Costs and Benefits

The easiest way to convert to a new WAN is to install the new multiplexing equipment and interconnect it with new trunk (i.e., FT1, T1, and T3) facilities. This is the most costly method of conversion. For example, if it takes six months to complete the conversion, and there are 47 T1s in the current network and 35 planned for the new network, that is 82 T1s for the duration of the conversion. The corporate budget has just taken a big blow with little real return on investment.

To find a balance between cost and benefit, the first question to research is whether there are regions of connectivity within the company's network. For example, a corporation has four regional main offices in Atlanta, Chicago, Dallas, and New York, and headquarters in Washington, D.C. Within these regions, all connectivity terminates at the main region office. Only main offices and headquarters need interconnectivity. It is easy to see that a conversion of each region could be completed first, then the connectivity could be converted between the main offices and the headquarters location.

Most corporate networks have some percentage of traffic going to a variety of locations such as headquarters and regional sites. This information should be available in the current network connectivity map, which should indicate the sites supporting the heaviest concentrations of traffic. This allows the network designer to construct a plan that rolls through a series of sites.

First, a few new trunk facilities should be ordered and activated. By activating a few links between the headquarters and several sites, part of the traffic back to headquarters can be migrated. The emptied connections should be deleted from the old network once the traffic is migrated. The load on the old network has been lightened and some trunks can now be removed. Any trunk facilities that can be emptied should be removed and those that are designated to be reused in the new network should be added. Orders to disconnect unused trunks can also be issued 30 days after that.

In most network conversions, this "leapfrog" approach can be used quite effectively. It allows network managers to find any flaws in the conversion and correct them before the rest of the process continues.

## Cables

Cables are the most overlooked source of problems in large-scale conversions. For example, one company had 23 different cables in its old network. Because the new multiplexer they had selected could perform software-based lead mapping, the number of cables could be reduced to five. That type of change is an excellent benefit.

During the physical audit, the physical data on the cables should be checked. This is the time to determine if old cables can be reused or if new ones must be ordered. If the new equipment vendor has assigned a program manager to the installation, that person's expertise should be used.

The cable information should be checked in a lab environment if possible. Otherwise, the nearest site supporting the most widely used port types should be used to verify cable pinouts. The most important thing to remember is that changes to cables can take weeks, not including the time it can take to determine the pinout is wrong and what the appropriate changes should be.

## Site Preparation

Site preparation is an important part of the migration strategy. One company found that its paperwork was the bottleneck in getting equipment from one of the vendors. A minor change in the process cut the turnaround time from six weeks to less than four weeks. It takes time for the internal paperwork to be completed, but it is always necessary to get floor space, electric service, telephone company access, and dial-up access to the multiplexer installed or prepared. Shipping time should also be factored into the schedule.

A modem and telephone line should be installed with each device. With today's intelligent multiplexers, a node can be installed before the trunk facilities are available and activated remotely via the dial-up port. This type of preparedness will also be important in the event that all facilities to a site are lost at the same time. A dial-back type modem is preferable. A basic password-protected modem should be used if the system does not have security features. The passwords should be changed monthly or quarterly as well as upon the termination of any employee who had access to the network.

## CONCLUSION

To ensure a successful conversion, it is helpful to send staff members to training shortly before the actual installations start. Then they will be able to fully participate in the conversions using their new knowledge. Network managers with well-trained staffs should have no problem achieving a relatively smooth conversion using the guidelines provided in this chapter. A deployment can be done in a timely manner with minimum disruptions to service within the company.

# Chapter 75
# Enterprise Messaging Management
*Ernest Eng*

This chapter describes a client/server messaging management implementation aligned with emerging E-mail standards and user requirements for operational, configuration, administration, and network management.

## PROBLEMS ADDRESSED

Electronic messaging is rapidly emerging as one of the key enablers to business productivity today. Businesses depend on fast, reliable messaging throughput to support mission-critical applications such as E-mail, electronic commerce, workflow automation, and group scheduling. Failures such as lost messages and delayed response times can represent considerable cost to the organization in the form of lost business opportunities and reduced productivity.

From the administrator's standpoint, such failures are difficult to pinpoint and guard against. Although many commercial network management products are available to manage layers 1 to 3 of the enterprise network — bridges, routers, and hubs — very few help with the management of distributed applications such as messaging and directory services. To date, message management products have been largely proprietary in nature because there are few industry standards for managing messaging services and directories.

This chapter looks at one potential client/server management implementation designed to improve the reliability and manageability of electronic messaging while reducing the costs of maintaining the messaging infrastructure.

## DIFFICULTIES IN MANAGING ENTERPRISEWIDE MESSAGING SYSTEMS

Enterprises are making sizable investments in scalable, extensible messaging systems to accommodate internal growth as well as to connect to the networks of external customers, suppliers, and trading partners. Increasingly,

0-8493-9965-3/99/$0.00+$.50
© 1999 by CRC Press LLC

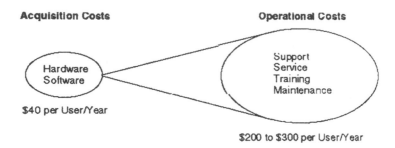

**Acquisition Costs**

**Operational Costs**

Hardware
Software

Support
Service
Training
Maintenance

$40 per User/Year

$200 to $300 per User/Year

**Exhibit 1. Costs of Managing Enterprise Messaging.**

they are running a wide range of message switches, gateways, and directory services that require continuous uptime, monitoring, and upkeep.

However, managing these distributed messaging systems from a single, centralized administrative control system is difficult and costly. Exhibit 1 summarizes the findings of one major Fortune 500 corporation that estimates that it spends approximately $40 per user, per year to acquire messaging hardware and software vs. $200 to $300 per user, per year in operating costs to manage and administer the messaging network.

The challenges in managing complex, enterprisewide messaging systems stem from:

- **Lack of standards for message management.** Each messaging system has its own set of management tools that use proprietary protocols to monitor and control messaging system resources.
- **Different technologies.** Large messaging systems incorporate a variety of technologies, including X.400, SMTP, proprietary LAN protocols, and legacy protocols.
- **Number of components.** An enterprisewide messaging system has many different components, each with specific behavior characteristics. These components include messaging transfer agents, directories, and gateways.
- **Geographic distribution.** The messaging system is usually geographically distributed across different cities, countries, or continents. Network administrators may find it difficult to gain a complete view of the status of all major system components on a global basis.

The need for a resident administrator at each major site can significantly increase the cost of managing large-scale messaging systems. In addition to being on call to deal with system failures or changes in system configuration, administrators also have to master a wide range of platforms and technologies to keep the overall system functional. This accounts for the high levels of ongoing expenses in training as well as in development of complex internal procedures for managing the messaging network across different departments and dissimilar platforms. Lost messages or server downtime can be expensive from an administrative standpoint. In conjunction with this administrative cost, there is also a potential loss of revenue or business opportunity because of such failures.

## E-MAIL MANAGEMENT STANDARDS

The JIF of IFIP Working Group 6.5 and 6.6 Electronic Mail Management Group were formed to examine the overall problem of E-mail management. The IETF has developed RFC 1566, also known as the Mail and Directory Madman MIB, which defines a class of managed objects that can be used by any E-mail vendor. The Madman MIB is geared to the management of Internet messaging and therefore lacks the ability to model some of the more complex features present in X.400-based messaging systems.

The EMA is working on a framework for messaging management that accommodates multivendor messaging systems. Although the EMA work leverages the IFIP work and is aligned with the Madman MIB definitions, its efforts are broader in scope because it also addresses message tracing, as well as standardizing a set of tasks for message management across a multivendor environment. The EMA work currently represents the best hope for industrywide adoption of message management standards.

### EMA Framework for Messaging Management

The EMA has characterized user requirements for messaging management into four major categories: operational, configuration, administration, and network management.

**Operational Management.** Operational management deals with finding outages and fixing them before users notice, and with providing routine maintenance to keep the system healthy. Operational management answers questions such as:

- Are all the components alive?
- Are there components that fail more frequently than others?
- Are messages getting stuck en route and, if so, where?
- What is the average size of a message?
- What is the total time of delivery of a message from sender to recipient?

**Configuration Management.** Configuration deals with managing the addition or deletion of components in the messaging system. It includes such tasks as dynamic updating of message routing tables, discovering and depicting messaging system components, and starting and stopping messaging system components across the network.

**Administration Management.** Administration provides a means for managing subscribers, distribution lists, and accounting information. It includes facilities for security administration, restricting service on the basis of originator, recipient, or type of message as well as detecting attempted security breaches. The administration system must also be able to generate reports on messaging system usage for billing, accounting, and chargeback.

**Network Management.** Network management is the process that keeps the underlying networking layer healthy. This requirement is not specifically addressed by the EMA initiatives because it is handled by a variety of tools and techniques geared to the management of network devices such as routers, hubs, and network bridges.

## AN OVERVIEW OF MESSAGE MANAGEMENT CONCEPTS

A network management architecture typically consists of a manager, an agent, a managed information base, and protocols.

**Manager.** The term *manager* refers to a set of tools and utilities that reside on a management station — typically a workstation with a graphical interface — and that allow administrators to monitor and actively manage the network. The manager software sends commands to the agent software residing on the managed components.

**Agent.** The term *agent* is used generically to refer to software that resides on the managed component (e.g., messaging transfer agents, directories, and gateways) and that interacts with the manager station at regular intervals. Typically, the agent collects a set of statistics on the status of the monitored component and responds to polling requests from the manager.

Agents may also be designed to initiate direct communication with the manager to report a specific problem situation through the use of alarms. Alarms allow administrators to act quickly to recover from error situations.

**Managed Information Base.** The MIB provides a common data model for what specific data is collected, monitored, or reset at the managed component site. The MIB is shared by the manager and agents.

**Protocols.** The manager and agent exchange information through a common set of protocols. The most popular network management protocols in use today are SNMP, which was developed within the Internet community, and CMIS/CMIP, which was developed as part of the OSI suite of protocols.

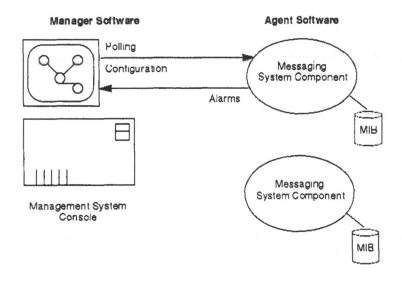

**Exhibit 2. Messaging Management Architecture.**

## MESSAGING MANAGEMENT ARCHITECTURE

Exhibit 2 illustrates a typical messaging management architecture. A management SYSCON runs a manager application that polls the messaging system components for status information continually. These components can be message stores, post offices, gateways, message transfer agent, message switches, or directory service agents. The manager software is also capable of configuring local and remote components.

Configuration capabilities include modifying the routing tables and creating new user accounts. The managed component runs an application called an agent that administers a set of managed objects stored in its MIB. When thresholds or errors impact specific managed objects, the agent sends alarms to the manager software.

## MESSAGE MANAGEMENT FROM A SINGLE LOCATION

The following model for messaging management is based on an implementation by Infonet Software Solutions, Inc. called the Messenger 400 Management Control Center. However, the architectural concepts and functional capabilities described are relevant to most client/server management systems designed to provide enterprisewide message management from a single location. The overall system architecture consists of:

- The control center management console.
- Agents communicating to the control center, residing on all key managed components such as message switches, gateways, and directory services.
- A specialized transactions-based protocol for manager-to-agent communication.

### Functional Description

From a single workstation, administrators can remotely manage messaging servers and directory servers across an entire wide-area distributed network. Messaging servers can be configured remotely, and users can be added and deleted on local and remote servers. The administrator can also monitor queues of message traffic at gateways, arrange to receive alarms when an undeliverable message enters the system, troubleshoot for performance bottlenecks, and retrieve logs and statistics from all message servers for further analysis.

Because of the number of environments that are being monitored, it is critical that the administrative interface be graphical and visually informative. A Motif-based graphical display allows the administrator to visually organize information about different sites according to personal preference. From such a display, the administrator can set up connections with multiple MTAs, view and configure local and RMTA databases and log files, and monitor incoming alarm messages from messaging or directory server installations.

The control center console can be used to display message traffic for a MTA. Message traffic can be graphically represented on the console, displaying statistics such as the number and volume of messages received and transmitted and changes in transmitted message volume. From the display, the administrator can determine the location of performance bottlenecks such as a long queue at a gateway or a failed message. Tools are also provided to allow the administrator to automate backup of messages stored on remote servers.

It is important that the control center console be able to manage messaging traffic over both SMTP and X.400 networks, using either TCP/IP or X.25 protocols. This allows companies to use existing network infrastructures and also provides an alternative network connection to a messaging server should the normal connection fail.

Control center management information can be logged so information such as cumulative volume of messages and traffic patterns is available for billing purposes, management reports, and system performance tuning.

**Control Center Console Software**

The control center management console and agents implement the Madman MIB. As products from other vendors converge on the adoption of this important industry standard, it will be possible to manage messaging and directory servers in a multivendor site through a single management console product.

The control center management console's software consists of two main modules that can operate concurrently — the control center manager and the alarm system. The manager module spawns multiple message traffic monitoring and administration programs. These programs attach to the remote message transfer agent and store the data needed for maintaining access to these managed message transfer agents in a simple ASCII database file, stored on the console host.

The manager software resides on a UNIX workstation, which can be connected to any message transfer agents in the enterprise via X.25 or TCP/IP. Agent software is collocated with the message transfer agents on each of the managed servers.

To allow administrators to provide quick response, the control center can trigger an alarm when a message fails to meet system compatibility requirements and needs special attention. Alarms communicate immediately and directly with the control center manager without waiting for the preset polling cycle. Alarms can be set on a server-to-server basis for administrative flexibility.

Administrators are alerted to problems in the managed system through audible and visual alarms that are directed to the control center console. The console at the alarm system receives and displays the messages from the managed X.400 or X.500 servers. Exhibit 3 illustrates the client/server architecture of a messaging management system.

**Evolving with the Standards**

Both vendors and private corporations have been active contributors to the IFIP and EMA initiatives. As a result, there is a consensus on implementation objectives, and the architecture described is closely aligned with the management model defined in RFC 1566 and the architectural framework being developed by the EMA.

The messaging management system's functional capabilities are consistent with the messaging system user requirements defined by the EMA. Exhibit 4 compares this implementation with the user requirement categories identified by the EMA.

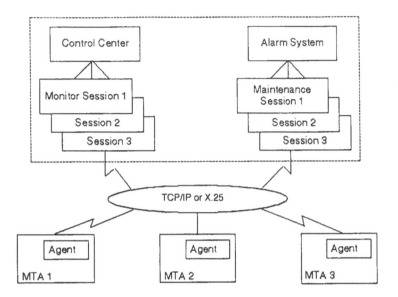

**Exhibit 3. A Client/Server Messaging Management System.**

**Exhibit 4. Implementation Alignment with EMA Messaging Management Requirements**

| EMA | Messaging Management Implementation |
|---|---|
| Operational Management | — Number of messages received |
| | — Number of messages transmitted |
| | — Received volume (bytes) |
| | — Transmitted volume (bytes) |
| | — Failed deliveries |
| | — Connection status |
| Configuration Management | — Configuration of message routing tables |
| | — Remotely manage queue files |
| | — Starting and stopping messaging system components |
| | — Graphical display for discovering and depicting messaging system components |
| Administration Management | — Remotely add and delete users, set up and change profiles |
| | — Remote management of distribution lists and accounting information |
| Network Management | — Provided by lower layers |

## RECOMMENDED COURSE OF ACTION

An integrated client/server messaging management solution aligned with emerging industry standards is the goal of most enterprise messaging vendors. Products and implementations already exist that make use of standards. For customers, the key in selecting solutions is to make sure that products take a client/server architectural approach and a standards approach.

### Selecting a Messaging Management Strategy

Organizations seeking to deploy a messaging management solution should consider the following key criteria when evaluating products:

- **Single Control Console.** The product should allow administrators to manage all network resources, including servers on different continents, from a single location.
- **Ease of use.** The product should include simple, intuitive display tools that can guide administrators through complex troubleshooting and reconfiguration tasks.
- **Ease of customization to fit enterprise-specific management goals.** Management tools should be able to fit the specific needs of the organization by allowing administrators to define alarms and thresholds of operation that meet organizational performance guidelines.
- **The ability to grow as the enterprise grows.** Growth potential is defined in terms of the solution's ability to easily manage additional components and continue to provide a cohesive view of the expanding managed environment.

Although the most immediate and urgent objective may be to manage an identified group of messaging systems, it pays to look beyond the current problems and plan for messaging management that is designed to scale with the enterprise and to evolve with industry standards. This strategy leaves options open for managing heterogeneous networks made up of products from multiple messaging vendors.

Chapter 76

# Windows NT Performance Monitoring

*Gilbert Held*

One of the more valuable features included in Windows NT is its Performance Monitor, a graphical tool that can measure the performance of your NT based computer, other computers on a network, or metrics associated with the performance of different transmission protocols used on a network. By understanding how to use the built-in NT Performance Monitor as well as its alert capability network, managers and administrators obtain a window that provides a view of numerous computer and network related parameters.

## INTRODUCTION

Performance Monitor is a graphical tool built into both Windows NT Workstation and Windows NT Server. This utility program enables you to view the behavior of a variety of computer and network related objects. Each of those objects has an associated set of counters that will provide metrics concerning the use of selected objects. Included in Performance Monitor are charting, alerting, and reporting capabilities that enable the utility to track selected objects over a period of time.

The charting capability included in Performance Monitor permits you to view counter values that are updated at a user-defined frequency. You can display multiple counter values on a single chart that can represent metrics associated with different computers.

The alert capability included in Performance Monitor enables you to specify thresholds for different counters which, when reached, are listed in the Alert Log or are used to notify the computer operator by displaying the alert on the computer's display. You can set several types of thresholds, which can be valuable when attempting to determine if a computer can

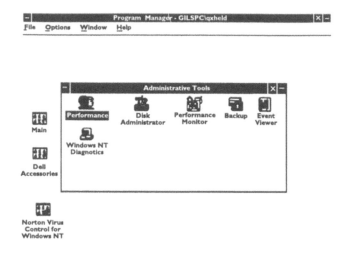

**Exhibit 1. Selecting Performance Monitor from the Administrative Tools Group Window.**

handle a given traffic load arriving via the network. You can also use thresholds to alert you to the computer reaching disk or memory utilization levels that warrant upgrades, as well as obtaining an understanding of the use of other computer and network related objects that might warrant modification to enhance computer or network performance prior to the occurrence of performance related problems. Since the best way to understand the use of the Windows NT Performance Monitor is by example, let us view its use.

**Utilization**

Performance Monitor is bundled with Windows NT, with its program icon located in the Administrative Tools group. Exhibit 1 illustrates the Administrative Tools group window, with the Performance Monitor icon located as the third icon from the left side of the opened window. Similar to other Windows icons, double clicking on the Performance Monitor icon invokes the program.

The initial Performance Monitor window contains a blank or empty chart display area and familiar menu entries File, Edit, View, Options, and Help as illustrated in Exhibit 2. The icons displayed under the menu bar are used to invoke predefined functions, with the plus (+) sign used to add a counter for display. As you move the mouse pointer over an icon, a short description of its use is displayed below and to the right of the icon. This is indicated in Exhibit 2, in which the message label "Add counter" was displayed after this author placed the pointer on the plus (+) icon. By clicking

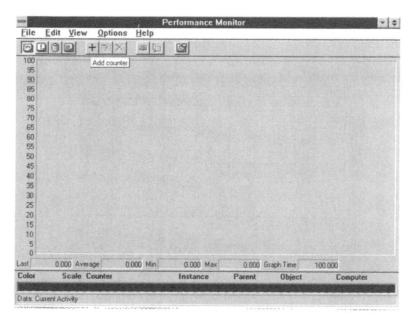

**Exhibit 2. Invoking Performance Monitor Results in the Initial Display of an Empty Chart Display Area.**

on the plus (+) icon, you obtain the capability to select one or more objects, as well as different counters associated with different objects that will be charted.

Exhibit 3 illustrates the dialog box labeled "Add to Chart," which is displayed after you select the plus (+) icon from the Performance Monitor main window. This dialog box contains four main selectable items — Computer, Object, Counter, and Instance.

The Computer item enables you to select a specific computer in a Windows NT network for which an object, counter and instance will be selected. The Object represents a standard mechanism used in Windows NT for identifying and using a system resource. Objects represent the processor, memory, cache, hard disk, different network protocols, and other entities for which it is important to track statistical information. Certain types of objects, such as processor, memory and cache and their respective counters are present on all computers. Other objects, such as different network protocols, are only applicable to computers that are configured to use the appropriate protocol stack.

The Counter item represents statistical information tracked for a defined object. Most objects have a number of counters which provide you with the ability to track different metrics associated with a selected object.

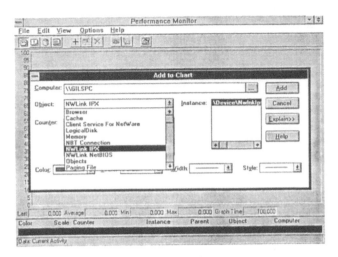

**Exhibit 3. Using the "Add to Chart" Dialog Box to Select the NWLink IPX Object.**

Each object type can have several instances, with the term "instance" used by Microsoft to identify multiple objects within the same object type. For example, the Processor object type will have multiple instances if a computer has multiple processors. Similarly, the Physical Disk object type will have multiple instances if the computer system has two or more physical hard disks. When an object type has multiple instances, each instance will produce the same set of statistics as they support the same counter values.

In Exhibit 3, NWLink IPX was selected as the Object. This is the transport protocol used in Novell NetWare based networks and the service which allows access to files, directories and printers on NetWare servers. The reason this author was able to select that object was due to the fact that Windows NT Workstation and Windows NT Server based computers were being used in a mixed networking environment to include communications occurring on many computers via the use of multiple protocol stacks to include TCP/IP and IPX/SPX.

Once you select an appropriate object, you can then select one or more counters associated with that object. Exhibit 4 illustrates the selection of the "Bytes Total/Sec" counter for the previously selected NWLink IPX object. In this display the Explain button located on the right side of the dialog box was clicked on, resulting in the display of the definition of the selected counter appearing at the bottom of the screen. The four selectable bars above the counter definition section enable you to set the color, scale, width, and style of the graph used to chart each selected counter. Those features can be extremely valuable when you want to chart multiple counters.

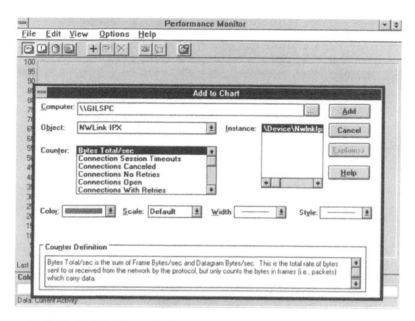

**Exhibit 4. Selecting a Counter for a Previously Selected Object.**

## OBSERVING NETWORK PERFORMANCE

Once you select one or more counters, you can view the change in the value of those counters over a period of time through the use of the Performance Monitor charting feature. Exhibit 5 illustrates the display of the previously selected Bytes Total/Sec counter in the form of a time chart. In this example, the large solid line near the center of the display represents the present monitoring time and moves from left to right across the display. The display shows that a small burst of network activity occurred, but that there was no continuous high level of network activity that might warrant a network upgrade.

Since the monitoring of just one counter might not indicate other network related problems that can occur without a high level of network utilization being reached, let us return to the "Add to Chart" dialog box so we can note how the values for multiple counters can be simultaneously displayed.

Exhibit 6 illustrates the selection of the Connection Session Timeouts counter. This counter can be a valuable indication of poor network performance resulting from a busy file server unable to keep up with client requests. In fact, many times you may wish to select several objects to be plotted over a period of time.

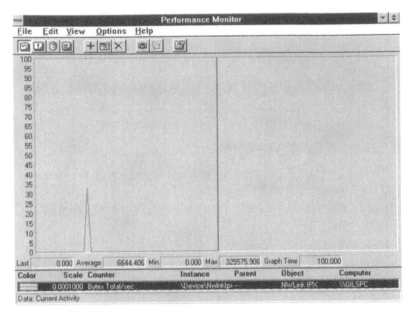

**Exhibit 5. Viewing Network Transmission in the Form of a Line Graph.**

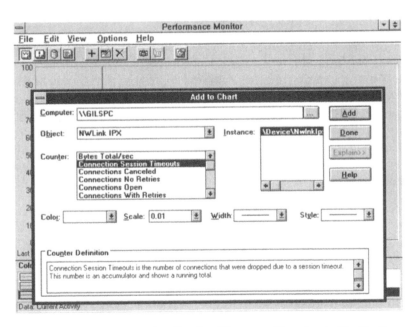

**Exhibit 6. Adding the Connection Session Timeouts Counter to the Performance Monitor Chart.**

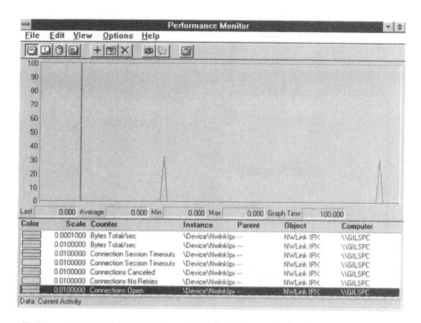

**Exhibit 7. Viewing the Effect of the Selection of Multiple Counters.**

Exhibit 7 illustrates an example of the display of several counters in the form of line charts. Note that different counters can be displayed in different colors on different widths or shapes that can make them easier to view. In addition, you can display multiple objects from the same or from a different computer which provides you with the ability to examine the performance metrics associated with workstations and servers, as well as different network protocols.

## Considering the Processor

Although network statistics are important, it is also important to be aware of the performance metrics of a computer's processor. This is especially true with respect to network servers, as many times, the processing load on a server can result in a degradation of network performance while the network itself is not heavily used. Thus, the ability to examine both network and processor related metrics represents a valuable feature of Windows NT Performance Monitor. To place this capability in perspective, you should note that NetWare's Monitor utility program only tracks performance of the server and is restricted to displaying statistics concerning server utilization to one server at a time.

Exhibit 8 illustrates the selection of the Processor object and the % Processor Time counter for that object. In Exhibit 8, the author again clicked

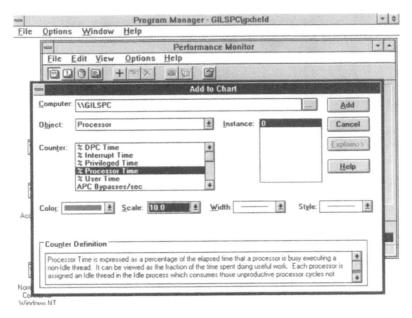

**Exhibit 8. Selecting the % Processor Time Counter for the Processor Object.**

on the Explain button to provide a definition of the Processor Time counter at the bottom of the dialog box. Note that the Processor Time is defined as the percentage of the elapsed time that a processor is busy executing a non-idle thread. This means you can examine the computer bound performance of a processor by displaying the values of this counter. This can be extremely important if you are using a Windows NT platform as a server and want to examine the effect of placing predefined loads on the server. To do so, you could coordinate the predefined operation of a server activity by several employees to examine its effect upon processor utilization. Then, you could extrapolate the percentage of processor utilization per employee to determine how many simultaneous activity requests the processor is capable of supporting. This information may alert you to the fact that you may require a higher performance processor or an additional processor.

For example, if your extrapolation indicated that a Pentium 100 MHz processor was capable of supporting 10 simultaneous activities, and you expect or require the support of 12, you might consider replacing your processor with a 133 MHz or 166 MHz processor.

### Working with Alerts

In addition to charting counters, Performance Monitor includes the ability to generate alerts. Alerts enable you to continue working while Performance

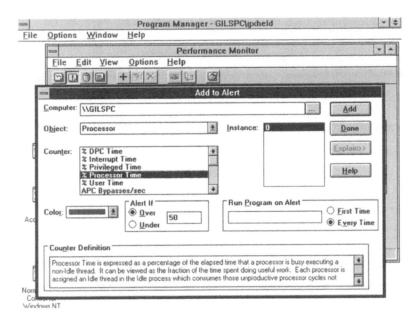

**Exhibit 9. Selecting the % Processor Time Counter to Generate an Alert.**

Monitor tracks predefined events and notifies you when an event threshold is reached.

In a manner similar to charting, you select alerts. First you select an icon or use the View menu "Add to Alert" menu entry to display a dialog box with that label. Exhibit 9 illustrates the Add to Alert dialog box for which the % Processor Time counter was selected for the processor object. Note that this dialog box enables you to specify a threshold for the alert as well as if the alert should be generated when the value of the selected counter is over or under the threshold. In addition, you can specify a program or macro that you want to run whenever the specified alert occurs. If you do not specify a program or macro, you can observe the Performance Monitor Alert log to determine if any alerts occurred and if so, when they occurred, as well as the values of counters being tracked when the alert occurred.

After selecting the % Processor time counter to generate an alert when the percentage of processor use exceeded 50%, the author similarly set an alert for the % User Time counter. Then, the author executed several compute intensive applications on the computer being monitored in an attempt to generate several processor related alerts. The result of this action is shown in Exhibit 10, which illustrates the Performance Monitor alert log. Note that this log indicates the occurrence of two % Processor Time alerts and two % User Time alerts during the monitored period.

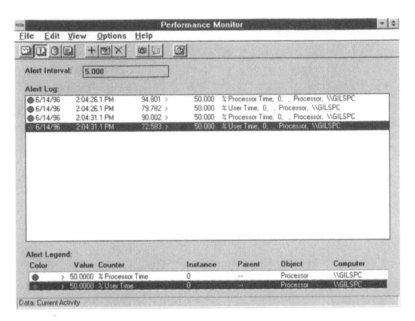

**Exhibit 10. Examining the Performance Monitor Alert Log.**

## RECOMMENDED COURSE OF ACTION

In addition to charting counter values and generating alerts, Performance Monitor can be used to generate a variety of performance related reports. Due to this capability, Performance Monitor provides network administrators and managers with a significant capability to view and track a variety of computer and network related metrics that are extremely valuable when attempting to support a modern client/server environment. By periodically using Performance Monitor, you can use this built-in Windows NT utility program to ensure your network, to include your client/server computing environment, provides the level of support necessary to enhance employee productivity.

# Chapter 77
# Managing Networks with the Global Naming Tree

*Gilbert Held*

An often-overlooked and hidden-from-view characteristic of network management systems is their use of the global naming tree. An understanding of the global naming tree's structure and the addressing method used to locate objects (i.e., network devices) can make it easier for network administrators to effectively support different network management systems.

## INTRODUCTION

Tree structures are a common method for accessing information. The reason for the use of a tree structure is that the path from the root via one or more branches to a leaf provides a unique method for addressing information stored at the end of the path.

The most common use of a tree structure inverts the tree, placing the root at the top. From the root, one or more branches flow downward and separate into sub-branches. This subdivision can theoretically continue indefinitely, with the major restriction being the number of characters, digits, or identifiers that can be used to define a path through the tree.

The most commonly used tree structure employed in computer-based systems provides data management in the form of a directory structure. When used to manage data within a directory structure, the root of the tree represents the top of the directory, while subdirectories represent branches under the root. Another common tree structure is employed by database management systems.

The ISO and the ITU-TSS have jointly developed a tree-based structure for assigning unique identifiers to different types of objects. That tree is known as a global naming tree.

0-8493-9965-3/99/$0.00+$.50
© 1999 by CRC Press LLC

## STRUCTURE OF THE GLOBAL NAMING TREE

Objects in the global naming tree can represent any type of information. In addition, the tree structure makes it possible for network managers to delegate responsibility for information structuring to other organizations under different nodes within the global naming tree.

### Use in Network Management Applications

Exhibit 1 illustrates the basic structure of the global naming tree that is oriented toward its use in network management applications. Under the root are three top-level nodes.

As Exhibit 1 shows, each node in the tree has both a label and a numeric identifier. The top-level nodes indicate the organization that administers the subtree under the node. The three top-level nodes allow the ITU- ISO, and the ISO and ITU jointly to administer distinct portions of the global naming tree.

The third node (Org) under the ISO node was defined as a mechanism to delegate authority to other organizations. One of those organizations is the U.S. Department of Defense, which is the sixth node under the Org node. Because the U.S. Department of Defense initially funded the ARPAnet, which is considered as the predecessor to the Internet, and still provides a degree of administrative and operational support for certain Internet activities, the first node under the Department of Defense node is the Internet node.

The Internet node and the subtree residing under it is owned by the IAB and administered by the IANA. The IANA is responsible for maintaining a document of assigned numbers, which tracks the complete set of parameters used in the TCP/IP suite to include addresses in the Internet subtree that identify SNMP and RMON objects. Organizations that wish to develop extensions to SNMP and RMON standard objects are assigned distinct identifiers within the Internet subtree.

### The Internet Subtree

Currently, six nodes are defined under the Internet node — directory, management, experimental, private, security, and SNMPV2. Two of those nodes, security and SNMPV2, are being standardized and may not be completely defined for a few years.

The experimental node provides a location for the placement of newly developed and unproved objects. After a trial period, objects deemed to be useful are then moved to a standardized location under the management subtree. That tree (Mgmt) is used to hold all standardized network management variables and represents the portion of the global naming tree most network management systems are designed to work with.

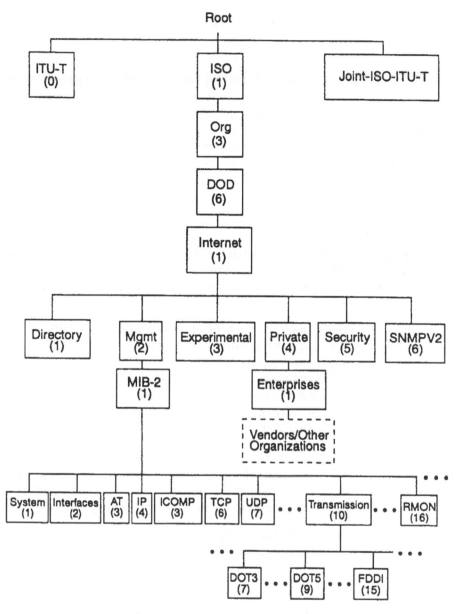

**Exhibit 1. The Network Management Portion of the Global Naming Tree.**

The private subtree represents a location where equipment vendors, software developers, universities, and government agencies can develop extensions to SNMP. To do so, an organization is assigned a node under private/enterprises that represents an assigned subtree within the global naming tree. Within that subtree, an organization is free to define its own structure for product identifiers and MIB object definitions that are required to manage a specific product or group of products.

Because it is almost impossible for any one network management product to be aware of every vendor-specific set of managed objects located under the private/enterprise node, the use of these path identifiers gives network managers and administrators a way to "walk through" the global naming tree structure, so they can set or retrieve information from any vendor subtree. This is a capability network managers might not otherwise obtain by relying on the standard features of a network management system.

### The MIB Subtree

The SNMP standard defines a database of network management information as a MIB. The MIB consists of a combination of hardware and software settings that represent objects needed to manage different types of products.

To simplify network management, objects were organized into units known as groups. Groups have a common management function. Depending on the operating characteristics of a device, it may or may not support one or more of the groups shown under the MIB-2node in Exhibit 1. (The original MIB for managing a TCP/IP network is known as MIB-1; its new version is labeled MIB-2. MIB-2is recognized by the IANA under the management node in the global naming tree.)

**Object Groups.** The system group permits configuration information to be defined to include what the device is, where it is located, and the person or persons to call when something goes wrong. Because of the importance of the system group, it is required to be supported by every device.

In comparison, other groups are optional and are only required to be implemented if applicable to a specific device. Examples of optional groups include:

* IP group, which includes objects needed for the configuration and management of IP hosts and routers.
* The TCP group, which is applicable to TCP devices.
* The UDP group, which is applicable for devices that support UDP.

One group that requires some explanation is the transmission group. This group more correctly represents a node position in the global naming tree under which groups applicable to different transmission technologies are placed.

Three examples of transmission technologies are shown in Exhibit 1 under the transmission node — DOT3, DOT5, and FDDI. The DOT3 and DOT5 nodes reference local area networks standardized by the IEEE as 802.3and 802.5. Those standards are better known as Ethernet and Token Ring.

## ASSIGNING IDENTIFIERS AND MANAGING OBJECTS

Each object in a device to be managed is represented by a unique address within the global naming tree. That address, which is referred to as an object identifier in standards documents, can be expressed in several ways.

The most commonly used method to express an object identifier is through the use of a string of integers separated by dots to form a path to the object. For example, the path to the system group shown in Exhibit 1 would be 1.3.6.1.2.1.1.The first object in that group would be located at 1.3.6.1.2.1.1.1 in the global naming tree.

Some object identifiers can have more than one value. For example, a bridge or router would have at least two interfaces, which would make it necessary to append a digit to the identifier path to denote the specific interface the administrator wishes to retrieve information from.

However, many objects represent a one-of-a-kind value, such as the location of a device. To provide consistency, an index is always added at the end of an identifier. Thus, if the object is a one-of-a-kind object, the administrator would add a zero (0) to its path. Because the first object in the system group is a one-of-a-kind object, its path identifier becomes 1.3.6.1.2.1.1.1.0.The omission of the trailing zero is a common error when users of a network management system use path addresses to retrieve object values.

Other methods used for object identifiers can include linking text labels with underscores or combinations of text labels and numerics. Because programming operations are easier and faster when working with numerics rather than text identifiers, most network management systems that allow users to enter tree identifiers do so by supporting integer strings with dots used as separators.

### Standardization and Its Benefits

In actuality, there are two types of addresses network administrators need to assign to manage a device. The first address is the IP address of a device installed in a network, which defines its location.

The second address is the set of addresses within the global naming tree that defines the location of counters, registers, and memory locations that the administrator may be able to read from, write into, or read and write, depending on the access method defined for the object.

By having a standard method for defining objects in the global naming tree, different vendors can independently develop managed objects, avoiding the potential for the occurrence of addressing conflicts. In addition, vendors can design their products to support applicable SNMP and RMON groups in a standardized manner, and other vendors can develop network management systems without having to know full details of different vendor products.

In short, if a network management system supports the global naming tree structure, any user who understand tree addressing concepts is able to read, write, or read and write to and from different managed devices manufactured by different vendors.

## SAMPLE APPLICATION USING SAMPLE TOOL

For purposes of further illustrating the use of the global naming tree in network management operations, this section uses the example of an application developed using SimpleView from Triticom (Eden Prairie, MN).

To use this program to manage an object, the user must first select the object. The screen shot in Exhibit 2 shows that the Ethernet probe at IP address 198.78.46.41 was selected. Exhibit 3 represents the values of object identifiers in the system group of the Ethernet probe. This system group contains seven object identifiers.

Tools such as SimpleView allow a network administrator to retrieve basic SNMP or RMON information. Because there are more than 1,000 vendors that are assigned subtrees under the private enterprises node in the global naming tree (which would make their support difficult, if not impossible, to accomplish via a menu that identifies the name of each object identifier), the sample tool uses a series of SNMP commands to access information in managed objects developed by different vendors.

The Get, Get Next, and Set entries shown in the Manage menu in Exhibit 2 represent three SNMP commands. The Get command is used to request the values of one or more Management Information Base variables. The Get Next command is used to read values sequentially. By selecting the Get Next command, the user can either go directly to a specific tree address (by typing in the address) or, if they do not know the address, browse predefined portions of the global naming tree that locate commonly used objects.

The third SNMP command supported, the Set command, allows the network administrator to update one or more MIB values.

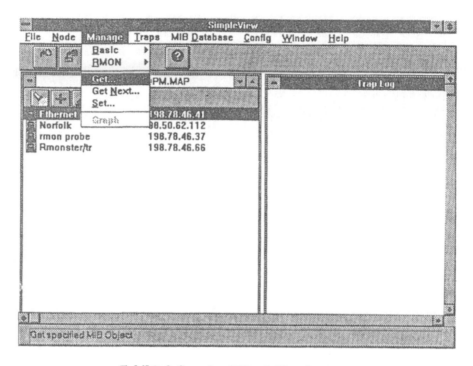

**Exhibit 2. Sample of SimpleView Screen.**

---

**Exhibit 3. The System Group**

| Object Identifier | Location | Description |
|---|---|---|
| sysDescr | 1.3.6.1.2.1.1.1 | A text description about the device. |
| sysObjectID | 1.3.6.1.2.1.1.2 | An identifier assigned to the device by its vendor. |
| sysUpTime | 1.3.6.1.2.1.1.3 | The time in hundredths of a second since the system was last reinitialized. |
| SysContact | 1.3.6.1.2.1.1.4 | The person responsible for the device. |
| SysName | 1.3.6.1.2.1.1.5 | An administratively assigned name. |
| SysLocation | 1.3.6.1.2.1.1.6 | The physical location of the device. |
| SysServices | 1.3.6.1.2.1.1.7 | A coded number that indicates the layer in the ISO model at which the device performs services. |

Notes:

Although the system group must be included in every managed device, the setting of some objects in the system group will depend on the user of the device. The sysContact identifier could be set by the organization using the device. Some organizations will set this identifier while others may elect to leave it at its default Not Set string value.

The location is the object identification number. If the object (e.g., sysUpTime) is a one-of-a-kind object, tools such as SimpleView automatically append a zero (0) to the path address.

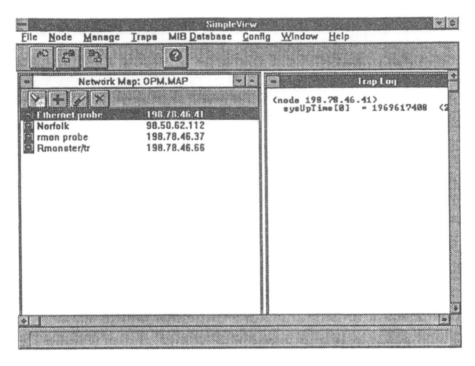

**Exhibit 4. SimpleView Trap Log Window.**

Once a command is executed, SimpleView displays the results in the program's Trap Log. Exhibit 4 shows an entry that occurred as a result of the execution of the Get Next command using a tree address to retrieve the value of the object. Although the time is displayed in hundredths of a second, such tools can also convert that time into days, hours, minutes, and seconds. By issuing several Get Next Commands, the values for sysName and subsequent objects in the group would also be displayed in the Trap Log. Thus, once the user knows an address they can walk through a path using a series of Get Next commands to retrieve subsequent object values.

## CONCLUSION

The global naming tree provides a mechanism for labeling and identifying objects while eliminating the possibility of addressing conflicts. By understanding how to use path addresses in conjunction with object identifier information, network administrators can manage any device that complies with the global naming tree method for identifying objects. The easiest way to retrieve information from proprietary products developed to comply with the global naming tree is for the user to refer to the device user manual to determine the path to different managed objects in the device.

# Section X
# Directions in Communications Systems

Any handbook covering communications systems would be incomplete without focusing upon the future. Although the rate of change in the field of communications is very rapid, making any prediction of future events difficult at best, it is quite possible to note key trends or directions occurring in this field. Thus, this concluding section consists of a series of chapters that were selected to provide us with information concerning emerging areas within the field of communications that can be expected to provide a considerable impact upon the manner by which we communicate.

The first chapter in this section, "The Superhighway: Information Infrastructure Initiatives," turns our attention to the key factors driving technology and issues associated with developing an information superhighway. In this chapter we examine the role of the user, government, and industry in developing an information superhighway infrastructure and several current and emerging technologies, such as the Internet and broadband-ISDN, cable TV, and computer-integrated telephony. Thus, this chapter introduces us to several future trends which are elaborated upon in subsequent chapters in this section.

Continuing our investigation of directions in communications systems we turn our attention to intelligent agents in the second and third chapters in this section. The second chapter in this section, "Using Intelligent Agents to Maximize the Benefits of the World Wide Web," we are first introduced to some of the limitations of the World Wide Web, and the capabilities of intelligent agents that can be used to overcome those limitations. To ensure we are not oversold on the value of intelligent agents, this chapter also acquaints us with some of their limitations, providing us with a background in their potential use and utility. Following this chapter, the third chapter, titled "Using Intelligent Agents to Manage Multivendor Environments," turns our attention to the use of intelligent agents to facilitate the management of networks and equipment. In this chapter we are introduced to disk monitoring agents, application monitoring agents, file monitoring agents, file distribution agents, event management agents, and process scheduling agents. After this is accomplished we will become acquainted with several system management products that make use of intelligent agents, and investigate interoperability issues and the ultimate focus of the chapter — agent management.

In the fourth chapter in this section, "Voice Recognition Interfaces for Multimedia Applications," we examine two areas of communications technology that can be expected to have a considerable influence upon the manner by which we communicate beyond the approaching millennium. In this chapter we are first introduced to the speech recognition process to include the problems associated with speech recognition and how good systems overcome some or all of those problems. Once this is accomplished, this chapter provides us with information concerning current and emerging voice recognition applications, and the functions and features we should consider when choosing a system. This information is followed by information concerning how we can build voice recognition applications to include a six-step development process which, when followed, can greatly facilitate a pending voice recognition project, as well as enhance its potential for success.

In the last chapter in this concluding section we turn our attention to the most important aspect of any organization, its employees. In the fifth chapter, "Workforce 2000: Top Career Strategies for the Professional," we will examine four different strategies that can be used to develop a plan of action to improve career longevity. Although written from the point of view of strategies managers can use to increase their career longevity, this chapter is applicable for managers developing strategies to retain employees. Due to the extremely tight technical market during the late 1990s, any technique or strategy that may enable managers to retain employees warrants consideration.

# Chapter 78

# The Superhighway: Information Infrastructure Initiatives

*Keith G. Knightson*

Many countries and organizations have developed initiatives aimed at establishing an electronic highway such as the National Information Infrastructure (NIL) in the US and the European Information Infrastructure (Eli). To cover global aspects, a Global Information Infrastructure (GII) is being developed. The outcome of these initiatives depends on the changes taking place in the information and communications industries because of converging technologies, deregulation, and business restructuring or reorganization based on economic considerations. This chapter explores some of the possibilities and problems associated with information infrastructures.

## WHAT IS AN INFORMATION INFRASTRUCTURE?

The term *information infrastructure*, which is used interchangeably with the term *information superhighway* in this chapter, describes a collection of technologies that relate to the storage and transfer of electronic information, including voice, data, and images. It is often illustrated as a technology cloud with user devices attached, including broadband networks, the Internet, and high-definition TV.

However, problems emerge when users attempt to fit technologies together. For example, in the case of videophone service and on- demand video service, it is not clear whether the same display screen technology can be used, or whether a videophone call can be recorded on a locally available VCR. This example illustrates the need for consistency between similar technologies and functions.

### Relevance of the Information Infrastructure

The information infrastructure is important because it provides an opportunity to integrate technologies that have traditionally belonged to specific industry domains, such as telecommunications, computers, and entertainment. (Integration details are discussed later in this chapter.) The information infrastructure also presents an opportunity to greatly improve the sharing and transferring of information. New business opportunities abound related to the delivery of new and innovative services to users.

### Goals and Objectives of Information Infrastructures

The goals of most information infrastructures are to achieve universal access and global interoperability. Without corporate initiatives, the information infrastructure could result in conflicting and localized services, inefficient use of technology, and greater costs for fewer services. Some of the elements necessary to achieve such goals, including standards and open technical specifications that ensure fair competition and safeguard user interests, have yet to be adequately addressed.

## BACKGROUND: TECHNOLOGY TRENDS

Two factors are often cited as driving the technology boom: the increase in computer processing power and the increase in the amount of available memory. Advances in these areas make a greater number of electronic services available for lower costs. This trend is expected to continue.

### Bandwidth Pricing Issues

Unfortunately, comparable gains of higher bandwidths and decreasing costs are not as evident in the communications arena. Whether this is because of the actual price of technology or because of pricing strategies is debatable. Many applications requiring relatively high bandwidths have yet to be tariffed.

On-demand video is an interesting test case for the pricing issue. To be attractive, this service would have to be priced to compete with the cost of renting a videotape. However, such a relatively low price for high bandwidth would make the price of traditional low-bandwidth phone services seem extremely expensive by comparison. ATM-based broadband ISDN is likely to emerge as the vehicle for high-speed, real-time applications where constant propagation delay is required.

The lack of higher bandwidths at inexpensive prices has inhibited the growth of certain applications that are in demand. The availability of inexpensive high bandwidth could revolutionize real-time, on-demand applications, not only in the video entertainment area but also in the electronic publishing area.

## Decoupling Networks and Their Payloads

One factor that is influencing the shape of the superhighway is the move toward digitization of information, particularly audio and video. Digitization represents a total decoupling between networks and their payloads.

Traditionally, networks have been designed for specific payloads, such as voice, video, or data. Digital networks may become general-purpose carriers of bit streams. In theory, any type of digital network can carry any and all types of information in digital format, such as voice, video, or computer data, thus banishing the tradition of video being carried on special-purpose cable TV networks and telephone service being carried only over phone company networks. All forms of information are simply reduced to bit streams.

## The Service-Oriented Architecture

The separation of information services from bit-delivery services leads to the concept of a new service-oriented architecture. The most striking aspect of this service-oriented architecture is that the control and management entity may be provided by a separate service organization or by a distributed set of cooperating entities from different service organizations. The architecture represents a move away from the current world of vertical integration toward one of horizontal integration.

Deregulation of communications also plays a part in this scenario. Deregulation often forces an unbundling of components and services, which creates a business environment ideally suited to a service-oriented architecture.

## KEY ISSUES IN CREATING THE SUPERHIGHWAY

Achieving a singular, seamless information highway is going to be a challenge, and whether users can influence development remains to be seen. Unless all interested parties act in harmony on the technical specifications (i.e., standards), market sharing, and partnering issues, the end user may be the biggest loser.

For provision of a given service (e.g., voice or data), it should not matter whether a user's access is through the telephone company, the cable company, or the satellite company. Similarly, it should not matter whether the remote party with whom a user wants to communicate has the same access method or a different one.

Several common elements exist in any end-to-end service. For example, there is a need for agreed-on access mechanisms, network platforms, addressing schemes, resolution of inter-provider requirements, and definition of universal services. The development of a generic framework would help to ensure that service requirements are developed equitably and to introduce innovative new services.

### The User's Role

Users are becoming more technology literate. The use of technology in the home in recent years has increased. Many users already benefit from what can be achieved through the convergence and integration of user-friendly technologies. User perspectives, rather than those of a single industry or company, should be thoroughly considered in the development of infrastructure initiatives.

### Government's Role

The private sector takes most of the risks and reaps most of the rewards for development of the information superhighway. However, government should assert some influence over the development of universally beneficial user services. The role of the government mainly involves:

- Encouraging industry to collaborate and develop universally beneficial user services.
- Mediating between competing industry factions.
- Solving problems involving cultural content, cross-border and customs issues, protection of the individual, obscene or illegal material, and intellectual property and copyrights.

### Industry's Role

Three dominant technology areas — telecommunications, computers and related communications, and the entertainment industry — are converging. Although there has already been some sharing of technology among industries, a single integrated system has not been created.

For example, many existing or planned implementations of videophone service invariably involve a special- purpose terminal with its own display screen and camera. For a home or office already equipped with screens and loudspeakers for use with multimedia- capable computers, the need for yet another imaging system with speakers is a waste of technology. Apart from the cost of duplication associated with the industry separations, there is the problem of the lack of flexibility. For example, if a VCR is connected to a regular TV, it should also be able to be used to record the videophone calls.

A plug-and-play solution may soon be possible in which the components are all part of an integrated system. In such a case, screens, speakers, recording devices, computers, and printers could be used in combination for a specific application. The components would be networked and addressed for the purposes of directing and exchanging information among them. Similar considerations apply to computing components and security systems. Using the videophone example, if the remote videophone user puts a document in front of the camera, the receiving party should be able to capture the image and print it on the laser printer.

Plug-and-play integration is not simple; yet if the convergence is not addressed, the result will be disastrous for end users, who will be faced with a plethora of similar but incompatible equipment that still fails to satisfy their needs.

### The Dream Integration Scenario

In the ideal configuration, there would be only one pipe into the customer's premises, over which all services — voice, video, and data — are delivered. User appliances can be used interchangeably. In this scenario, videophone calls could be received on the home theater or personal computer and recorded on the VCR.

### The Nightmare Scenario

In the nightmare scenario, customer premises would include many pipes. Some services would only be available on certain pipes and not others. The premises would have duplicate appliances for generating, displaying, and recording information. End-to-end services would be extremely difficult to achieve because all service providers would not choose to use the same local- or long- distance delivery services. In addition, all the local- and long-distance networks would not be fully interconnected.

Purveyors of technology and services may argue that this means they can all sell more of their particular offerings, which is good for business. Users, on the other hand, are more likely to feel cheated, because they are being forced to subscribe to different suppliers for slightly different services.

### Corporate Networks

Large corporations create networks that are based on their preferred supplier of technology. They are usually extremely conservative in their technology choices because many of their business operations depend totally on the corporate network.

Two factors are causing this traditional, conservative approach to be questioned:

1. *The cost of maintaining private networks.* In many cases, several private networks operate within a single corporation, such as one for voice, one for IBM's SNA network, and one for a private internet using TCP/IP or Novell's IPX. The change taking place is sometimes

referred to as consolidation. Consolidation involves network sharing by operating the different systems protocols over the same physical network.

2. *The need for global communications.* Corporations cannot afford to remain electronically isolated from their customers. As every business tackles cost cutting by increasing the use of information technology, the need for intercompany communication increases. Companies now need to communicate electronically with the banking industry, their suppliers, their customers, and the government to carry out their business. The GIL is going to increase in importance for corporations, particularly in terms of availability and reliability.

## THE INTERNET AND B-ISDN

Many users consider the Internet the only true information highway. In many ways, this is true — the Internet is the only highway, at least in the sense that it is the only worldwide, seamless, and consistent end- to- end digital networking facility available. In addition, it has become a place where certain standardized applications can be used. It has a globally unique, centrally administered address space. The Internet provides national and international switched data services on a scale that would usually be associated with the major telecommunications carriers.

Not surprisingly, not everyone agrees that the Internet is the only highway. Technically, the Internet is a connectionless packet network overlaid on a variety of network technologies, such as leased lines, frame relay, asynchronous transfer mode (ATM), and LANs. However, it is difficult to imagine that at some point in the future, all voice and video traffic would be carried over such a network rather than directly over a broadband integrated services digital network (B-ISDN).

Thus, there may be a battle between the Internet and the traditional telecommunications carriers for control of the primary switching of data. The carriers may try to establish broadband ISDN as the primary method of switching data end to end, using telephone company-oriented number/addressing plans such as E.164.

The Internet community is interested in the use of broadband ISDN, primarily as a replacement for leased lines between Internet switching nodes (i.e., routers) where the real switching occurs. The deployment of broadband ISDN within the Internet may result in the migration of routers to the edges of the Internet, eliminating the need for intermediate routers. In any event, the interaction between the traditional router- based Internet style of operation and the emerging broadband ISDN switched services will be closely watched by corporate users.

The anarchic nature of the Internet will also be put to the test by commercial users who will want better service guarantees and accountability for maintenance and recovery. Despite these known deficiencies, the Internet remains the predominant information highway and it is difficult to imagine that it will lose its dominance in the near future.

## TELECOMMUNICATIONS AND CABLE TV

Deregulation in many countries now permits cable TV companies to offer services traditionally offered by the telephone companies. The cable companies are just beginning to form plans on how new two-way services should be offered. Access to the telephone company network would also provide access to other services, such as the Internet.

A major issue is the kind of interface to be provided on the cable network for associated telephone apparatus. It is not clear whether a traditional phone could simply be plugged into the cable system. Other issues, such as numbering and access to 800 service, need to be resolved. Whether traditional modem, telephony, or ISDN interfaces could be used or whether new cable-specific interfaces would be developed is also under consideration. Both solutions could coexist through provision of appropriate conversion units.

Cable systems usually consist of a head end with a one- way subtending tree and branch structure. Whether the head end would provide local switching within the residential area has not been determined. Other topologies, such as rings, may be more appropriate for new services.

Conversely, deregulation also permits the telephone companies to offer services previously offered by the cable companies. In such a case, a video server would be accessed by the telephone company network, probably using broadband ISDN and ATM technology.

## COMPUTER-INTEGRATED TELEPHONY

Computing and telecommunications are coming together in several ways. Computers can now be attached to telecommunications lines to become sophisticated answering machines, autodialers, and fax machines.

The availability of calling and called-line identification permits databases to be associated with telephone calls. For example, the calling line identification can be used to automatically extract the appropriate customer record from a database so that when the call is answered the appropriate customer information becomes available on a screen.

Computer-integrated telephony allows a variety of telephone service features to be controlled by the customer's computers. Intelligent network architectures that facilitate the separation of management and control are ideally suited to external computer control.

Public switched data networks have not been very efficient because of the costs of building separate networks and because the scale and demand for data proved nothing like that for voice services. A single digital network such as narrowband ISDN (N-ISDN) or broadband ISDN changes the picture significantly when coupled with the new demand for digital services.

## COMPUTING AND ENTERTAINMENT

Most personal computers on the market have audiovisual capabilities. Movies and audio clips can be combined with text for a variety of multimedia applications. Video or images can be edited as easily as text.

With the advent of high-definition TV and digital encoding of TV signals, it is easy to imagine a system in which the traditional TV screen and the PC monitor would be interchangeable. Computers are already being used to produce movies and as a playback medium, even providing the possibility of real-time interaction with the users.

Integrating all the appliances into a single architecture is the difficult part. Home theater systems provide simple forms of switching between components — for example, video to TV or VCR, or audio from TV to remote speakers. Soon, no doubt, the personal computer will be part of this system.

## NATIONAL AND INTERNATIONAL INITIATIVES

Many countries have prepared recommendations for their respective national information infrastructures, including the US, Canada, Europe, Japan, Korea, and Australia, among others. The major differences in each country's initiatives seem to revolve around to what extent government will fund and regulate the information infrastructure.

### The U.S.

The Information Infrastructure Task Force (IITF) launched the National Information Infrastructure (NiI) initiative in early 1993. The IITF is composed of an advisory council and committees on security, information policy, telecommunications policy, applications, and technology. Government funding is being made available for the development of NIL applications.

The IITF's goal is that the information infrastructure become a seamless web of communications networks, computers, databases, and consumer electronics. The NIL initiative is also closely associated with the passage of a new communications act, which outlines principles for the involvement of the government in the communications industry. According to the communications act, the government should:

- Promote private sector investment.
- Extend the universal service concept to ensure that information resources are available at affordable prices.
- Promote technological innovation and new applications.
- Promote seamless, interactive, user- driven operation.
- Ensure information security and reliability.
- Improve management of the radio frequency spectrum.
- Protect intellectual property rights.
- Coordinate with other levels of government and with other nations.
- Provide access to government information and improve government procurement.

### International Initiatives

The G7 countries (Britain, Canada, France, Germany, Italy, Japan, and the US) are considering developing an information infrastructure that would offer, among others, the following services:

- Global inventory.
- Global interoperability for broadband networks.
- Cross-cultural education and training.
- Electronic museums and galleries.
- Environment and natural resources management.
- Global emergency management.
- Global health care applications.
- Government services online.
- Maritime information systems.

## STANDARDS AND STANDARDS ORGANIZATIONS

It is difficult to imagine how objectives such as universal access, universal service, and global interoperability can be achieved without an agreed- on set of standards. However, some sectors of industry prefer that fewer standards be established because this gives them the opportunity to capture a share of the market with proprietary solutions. Regardless, several national and international standards development organizations (SDOs) throughout the world are initiating activities related to the information infrastructure.

### ISO and ITU

Both the International Standards Organization (ISO) and the International Telecommunications Union (LTU — formerly the CCITT) are embarking on information infrastructure standards initiatives. The ISO and ITU have planned a joint workshop to address standards issues.

### American National Standards Institute Information Infrastructure Standards Panel (ANSI IISP)

The ANSI LISP goals are to identify the requirements for standardization of critical interfaces (i.e., connection points) and other attributes and compare them to national and international standards already in place. Where standards gaps exist, standards development organizations will be asked to develop new standards or update existing standards as required.

ANSI LISP is developing a database to make standards information publicly available. In its deliberations, the ANSI LISP has been reluctant to identify specific networking architectures or interconnection arrangements and appears to be confining its efforts to a cataloguing process.

### Telecommunications Standards Advisory Council of Canada (TSACC)

The TSACC is an umbrella organization for all the standards organizations in Canada. It is a forum where all parties can meet to discuss strategic issues. The objectives of TSACC, in respect to the Canadian Information Infrastructure and the GII, are similar to those of the ANSI IISP. However, TSACC considers the identification of specific networking architectures and associated specific access and interconnection points essential to achieving the goals of universal access, universal service, and interoperability.

### European Telecommunications Standards Institute (ETSI)

The Sixth Review Committee (SRC6) of ETSI published a report on the European Information Infrastructure (ELI) that emphasizes the standardization of the ELI. Many of the recommendations in the report concern the development of reference models for defining the particular services and identifying important standards- based interface points. Broadband ISDN is recommended as the core technology for the ELI.

### The Digital Audio Visual Council (DAVIC)

DAVIC was established in Switzerland to promote emerging digital audiovisual applications and services for broadcast and interactive use. DAVIC, which has a very pro-consumer slant, believes that these services will only be affordable through sufficient standardization. The council has formed technical committees in the following five areas:

- Set-top units.
- Video servers.
- Networks.
- Systems and applications.
- General technology.

DAVIC may be the only forum in which home convergence issues can be solved.

## ALTERNATIVE INITIATIVES

Following are two interesting US-based information infrastructure initiatives.

### EIA/ TIA

The Electronic Industries Association (ELA) and its affiliate Telecommunications Industry Association (TIA) have just released version 2 of their white paper titled "Global Information Infrastructure: Principles and Promise." The basic principles conclude that:

- The private sector must play the lead role in development.
- Enlightened regulation is essential.
- The role of global standards is critical.
- Universal service and access must support competitive, market-driven solutions.
- Security and privacy are essential.
- Intellectual property rights must support new technologies.

### The Computer Systems Policy Project (CSPP)

The CSPP is not a standards organization but an affiliation of the chief executive officers of several American computer companies. The CSPP has published a document titled "Perspectives on the National Information Infrastructure: Ensuring Interoperability." The CSPP document identifies the following four key points-of-presence as candidates for standardization:

- The interface between an information appliance and a network service provider.
- The applications programming interface between an information appliance and emerging NIL applications.
- The protocols that one NIL application, service, or system uses to communicate with another application, service, or system.
- The interfaces among and between network service providers.

## SUMMARY

The technical challenges of creating a Global Information Infrastructure are not insurmountable. The main difficulties arise from industries competing for the same business rather than sharing an expanding business, and from the lack of agreement on necessary open standards to achieve universal access and global interoperability that would expand the total business.

Interoperability requires agreed- on network architectures and the associated standards that could, in some cases, stifle innovation. A balance must also be struck between government regulation and private sector control over GIL development. However, if each camp can cooperate, it is possible that in the future the communications, information, and entertainment industries could merge technology to provide plug- and- play components integrated into a single, coherent system that offers exciting new services that exist now in only the wildest imaginations.

# Chapter 79
# Using Intelligent Agents to Maximize the Benefits of the World Wide Web

*Barbara J. Haley and Kelly Hilmer*

The World Wide Web's potential as a strategic information tool is limited by the time, costs, and frustration associated with Web use. Intelligent agents that facilitate searching, monitor information changes, and customize and order information according to individual needs help managers reduce information overload and more effectively use the wealth of information available on the Web.

## INTRODUCTION

Organizations that invest much time and effort in information systems that support unique management needs are increasingly integrating the World Wide Web (Web) into their IS portfolio. Although countless articles have espoused the Web's promise to provide information and commercial opportunities to the business community, several current limitations make the Web fall short of expectations.

Recently, intelligent agents have become practical solutions for addressing these limitations. The use of intelligent agents is important for Web developers, IS and business managers, and organizations interested in maximizing the benefits of the Web as an information tool while minimizing the time, costs, and frustration associated with Web use. After describing how the Web nominally supports management information needs, this chapter illustrates how five types of intelligent agents address the current Web weaknesses managers may encounter.

## WEB-SUPPORTED INFORMATION NEEDS

Managers are unique systems users because of the wide variety of tasks they perform, the diversity of information they require, and the dynamic nature of their decision-making environment. The literature on executive information systems, for example, illustrates that executives require special systems that:

- Are custom tailored to individual executives.
- Extract, filter, compress, and track critical data.
- Access and integrate a broad range of internal and external data.
- Are user friendly and require minimal or no training.
- Are used directly by executives without intermediaries.
- Present graphical, tabular, and textual information.

Over the years, systems have evolved to address these requirements and provide executives with effective tools for accomplishing management tasks. The Web appears to be yet another innovative way to address such needs. A broad range of internal and external data is accessible from Web sites within an organization and from external sites located around the world. Managers can use the available graphical packages to navigate the Web without assistance. Web browsers also present information in creative ways, taking advantage of graphics, sound, and video.

### Limitations of the World Wide Web

Information overload, constant updating and reshuffling of information, and minimal support for novice users are some of the current problems that reduce the Web's value to managers. The lack of Web regulation and control combined with rapid growth have contributed to an abundance of information. Because this information changes constantly with little order or customization, it is difficult for managers to locate information efficiently, especially because they typically navigate this chaos with minimal or basic computer skills. As managers increase their Web use, organizations will become more concerned about these problems.

## CAPABILITIES OF INTELLIGENT AGENTS

Intelligent agents (agents), also called software agents, are software programs that help find, organize, and present information that is custom tailored to a meet a manager's needs. The programs are relatively autonomous; they are not attached to a particular software application and do not need a user for activation. Agents always are ready to perform a specified action according to preset user parameters. In addition, advanced agents learn trends and user preferences, and they can analyze information to support decision making.

Agents address a variety of problems. They are designed to save time, perform mundane tasks, fulfill requests tailored to specific needs, and manage data. To some people, these agents serve as personal data assistants, addressing diverse information requirements. But, unlike a human assistant who needs sleep and occasional days off, an agent addresses customized needs around the clock.

There are many types of agents, and a multitude of classification schemes have been suggested to help understand what intelligent agents can do. In general, agents vary in terms of three dimensions: agency, mobility, and intelligence. These dimensions respectively refer to the autonomy of the agent's performance, the amount an agent traverses through networks, and how much an agent can learn or adapt to user requests. Agents can perform several functions, including:

- Weeding out unnecessary data.
- Alerting to specific conditions.
- Matching requesters with requests, while maximizing resources.
- Routing, creating, updating, and destroying data.
- Identifying trends and combining information from different sources.
- Performing administrative functions.

Some examples of agents include those for filtering E-mail, scheduling appointments, locating information, making travel arrangements, and paying bills. It has been suggested that agents will someday perform the tasks of a knowledge worker throughout the day, making human executive assistants unnecessary.

## USING WEB AGENTS TO MEET MANAGEMENT NEEDS

The World Wide Web has five primary shortcomings:

1. Too much information.
2. Changing information.
3. Unordered information.
4. Lack of support for novice users.
5. Minimal customization.

The increasing use of agents on the Web has resulted in a growing number of creative and helpful agent solutions that address these shortcomings. The following sections present five types of Web agents — search engine, monitor, publisher, guide, and personal assistant — each of which addresses a major Web shortcoming and supports several management needs.

### Using Search Engines to Reduce Information Overload

The ease of creating Web pages has triggered the proliferation of Web pages representing users, organizations, and topical issues. Burgeoning numbers of new companies providing skills and services promote further production of Web pages. Unfortunately, the proliferation of data available on the Web makes it difficult for managers to find useful information.

To address this problem, intelligent agents called search engines seek information and present results based on prespecified criteria. Search engines extract, filter, and compress critical data from a broad range of internal and external sources. Most search engines have similar interfaces in which a manager enters some criteria (e.g., *subject = stock market AND date = 1996*). After the search is invoked, a list of Web page addresses are displayed for further investigation. Some search engines provide options that set a time limit for the search, the number of addresses to be displayed at one time, and the amount of detail to include in the output.

One search engine, SavvySearch, is considered a metasearch tool that provides a convenient interface, available in multiple languages, to several other search engines.[1] The manager enters criteria for a search and selects options that expand or limit the search output. This metasearcher ranks a list of available search engines (e.g., Alta Vista, Lycos, and Yahoo)[2] and transfers the search request to selected engines. The selection is based on the query, topic area (e.g., Web resources, news, or entertainment), estimated Web traffic, anticipated response time of the other search engines, and the load on the SavvySearch computer.

### Using Monitors to Keep Up with Changing Information

Not only is there an abundance of information on the Web, the information is changing constantly. Many Web pages contain information that is regularly added to, deleted, or modified. The location of these Web pages changes as well; servers, directories, and file names move and disappear, frustrating managers who reference invalid links.

Monitor agents accommodate the problems created by dynamic information. These agents let managers track critical data by looking for changes on the Web and communicating these changes to the manager. Instead of relying on people to determine when information becomes obsolete, a manager can count on monitor agents to flush out changes as information evolves and provide direct notification of them.

Both Specter Communications and First Floor Software offer agents that search the Web for updates on selected sites.[3] WebWatch from Specter Communications, for example, checks selected sites automatically and highlights modifications. A manager can have WebWatch monitor competitor sites for market changes, for instance. Managers who use WebWatch can view downloaded Web sites offline at their convenience. WebWatch has filtering capabilities similar to search engines that allow the agent to traverse the Web looking for changed Web sites, while the program resides on a personal workstation and updates Web bookmarks(i.e., listings of Web site addresses). Such an agent helps managers keep pace with the ever-changing business world.

### Using Publishers to Make Sense of Unordered Information

Information on the Web is unordered, redundant, and uncategorized. Unlike a library, which offers a well-defined process for searching for information, the Web offers no standard approach for meeting information needs. Therefore, intelligent agents that custom tailor information to individual executives while accessing and integrating a broad range of internal and external data are highly desirable.

Publisher agents do just that. Although they have access to large amounts of information, they present to a manager only the topics and types of information that have been prespecified, often in a variety of presentation formats.

For example, PointCast Network (PCN) provides a personalized newspaper to users of the software.[4] First, managers select the topics that they want to read about. This could include headline news, stock quotes, weather, sports, or industry and company news. Based on a manager's interests, hundreds of articles are filtered, integrated, and "pointcasted" to the manager to read at his or her convenience. The text is accompanied by weather and stock price quotes presented graphically in maps and charts.

### Using Guides to Maneuver Novice Users through the Web

Users can access the Web with a Web connection and basic computer skills. Browsers, such as Netscape and Mosaic, take advantage of Windows' point and click environment and graphical interface to further facilitate Web use. With ease comes the surge of novice users, including managers, rushing to encounter the global electronic network. This results in the continual need to maintain ease of use.

Some software agents on the Web, called guides, learn user habits and preferences and adapt to individual needs. This is beneficial for managers who are Web novices, because an adaptive and easy-to-use interface requires minimal training and can be used directly by the manager without an intermediary. The more managers can rely on guides to lead Web experiences, the more time they have to focus on the content and significance of information they encounter.

ZooWorks from Hitachi is a guide that remembers and sorts each Web site that a manager views.[5] This information is placed in a personal index for future access. The index organizes and structures Web viewing and provides an easy way to locate past sites by keywords, a date, or a range of dates.

Because it manages Web information more effectively, ZooWorks helps managers spend their time using information rather than searching for it.

### Using Personal Assistants to Customize Web Information

Diverse visitors stop by organizational Web sites, and different types of people peruse individual Web pages. Because there are myriad purposes for visiting a Web site, a Web page needs to be flexible enough to change to serve each purpose. A financial manager of a company, for example, would be interested in different information than a marketing manager.

When managers locate pages of interest, the information needs to be presented in a useful, understandable way. Personal assistants help present tabular, textual, and graphical information that has been custom-tailored to manager needs. Agents such as BroadVision, Inc.'s One-To-One product work to make Web pages more relevant to individual users by customizing them based on a user's demographics and usage patterns.[6] Instead of viewing static, general information, managers can interact with personalized Web pages that have been customized through a learning process. For example, a financial manager may see stock quotes and links to financial news articles when entering the company Web site; whereas a marketing manager may be linked to sales information and recent promotions.

### LIMITATIONS OF WEB AGENTS

Although Web agents add great value to the growing number of managerial Web experiences, they do have some limitations. First, agents can be resource intensive; they often must be monitored and their activity needs to be harnessed. If an agent makes a large number of requests in a short amount of time, servers may slow down to a crawl or crash. Some Web servers opt to boycott agent activity and technically prevent agents from interaction. Agents that reside on user machines must be updated and regularly maintained to ensure continued usefulness. In addition, although search engines provide a good starting point for locating information, general searches can result in too much or irrelevant information. Without the proper intervention, agents used to reduce information overload can aggravate the problem.

### CONCLUSION

Managers who increasingly use the Web to support their information needs can use the searching, monitoring, and customizing capabilities of intelligent agents to address Web limitations. By custom-tailoring information to individual executives; extracting, filtering, compressing, and tracking critical data; and accessing and integrating a broad range of internal and external data, these software programs help support basic management information needs.

As intelligent agents mature, their minor limitations will be overcome. In the future, as organizations integrate the Web into their technology plans, they will have to increasingly rely on intelligent agents to ensure effective Web use.

## BIBLIOGRAPHY

Bottoms, D. "Agents of Change." *Industry Week* 243, No. 16, 1994, pp. 49–54.
IBM White Paper. "Intelligent Agent Strategy" http://activist.gpl.ibm.com:8, 1995.
McKie, S. "Software Agents: Application Intelligence Goes Undercover." *DBMS* 8, No.4, 1995, pp. 56–60.
Watson, H. J., Rainer, R. K., and Koh, C. E. "Executive Information Systems: A Framework for Development and a Survey of Current Practices." *MIS Quarterly*, March 1991, pp. 13–30.

### References

1. http://www.cs.colostate.edu/~dreiling/smartform.html.
2. http://altavista.digital.com/; http://www.lycos.com/; http://yahoo.com/.
3. http://www.specter.com/;http://www.firstfloor.com/.
4. http://www.pointcast.com/.
5. http://www.zoosoft.com/.
6. http://www.broadvision.com/.

# Chapter 80
# Using Intelligent Agents to Manage Multivendor Environments

*Nathan J. Muller*

---

The challenge of managing multivendor systems is increasingly being met through the use of intelligent agents, special software installed on managed stations on the local or wide area network that collects performance information in a standard format, implements preemptive actions based on predefined policies, and automates routine, repetitive tasks. These capabilities help minimize traffic on the network, increase systems availability and reliability, and reduce the overall cost of systems management.

## INTRODUCTION

Today's distributed computing environment usually includes a mix of UNIX, MVS, VMS, MS-DOS, NetWare, Windows, and other operating systems from multiple vendors. Managing a multivendor environment is difficult, especially because standards for systems management and underlying technologies are lacking. The OSF's DME effort has failed largely because it attempted to address everything from applications to infrastructure all at once instead of setting priorities and proceeding incrementally.

Open systems management is compounded by the fact that every vendor defines the term differently and therefore takes a different approach to systems management. Some vendors offer integrated suites of applications; others merely provide platforms or frameworks and rely on third parties for specific applications that plug into them. Because vendors offer overlapping but not identical sets of products, users find product comparisons and selection difficult. In many cases, this difficulty has delayed full-scale implementation of systems management, especially for client/server environments.

The most promising approach to the challenge of managing multivendor environments is embodied in the concept of intelligent agents. Intelligent agents are special software installed on managed stations on the LAN/WAN that collects performance information in a standard format and implements preemptive actions based on predefined policies. Because filters and thresholds are used to send the management console specific items of information only, the software provides a more efficient process than continuous polling of every station to notify the central management station of all events. Using intelligent agents thus minimizes traffic on the network, which, in turn, consumes less bandwidth and contains costs. It also has the following business benefits:

- By detecting exceptional events and triggering automated actions to correct problems before they affect systems services, intelligent agents increase systems availability and reliability.
- By automating routine, repetitive tasks, intelligent agents relieve the systems administrator of a heavy work burden and reduce the overall cost of systems management. They speed up problem resolution while permitting businesses to get the most out of their technology investments.

Organizations that use intelligent agents to continuously monitor systems and applications for problems and carry out corrective actions on an automated basis thus achieve a competitive edge over companies that react to problems with manual processes.

## KEY CONCEPTS IN SYSTEMS ADMINISTRATION

### Manager and Agent

The key concepts in systems (and network) administration are the manager and agents. The manager is the workstation that is set up to view information collected by the agents. The agents are special programs that are designed to retrieve specific information from systems on the network. An application agent, for example, works on each workstation to log application usage. Workstation users are not aware of the agent and it has no effect on the performance of the workstation or the applications running on it. The collected information is retrieved from one or more databases for viewing on the systems administrator's console.

The use of agents is not new, of course. The manager-agent relationship is intrinsic to most standard network management protocols, including SNMP. SNMP agents are now used routinely in all kinds of internetworking devices, including bridges, routers, hubs, multiplexers, and switches. Exhibit 1 depicts the interactions between an SNMP manager and agent.

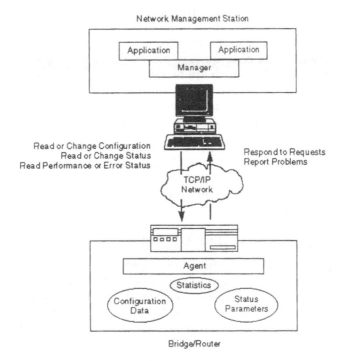

**Exhibit 1. Interactions Between an SNMP Manager and Agent.**

What is relatively new is the use of intelligent agents to manage systems-level activities. The difference between network-level (i.e., SNMP) agents and systems-level agents lies in their degree of intelligence.

### Agent IQ

In the SNMP world, agents respond to polls from an SNMP management station that requests information on the operational status of network devices. Based on that information, agents are then directed by the management station to get more data, set management variables, or generate traps when significant events occur. By necessity, SNMP agents are dumb — that is, they act merely as passive data collectors that provide information only when they receive a request from the central management station. That such agents cannot perform filtering or processing on their own is acceptable, though, because bridges, routers, and other internetworking devices have limited memory and processing resources.

The idea of using SNMP to manage UNIX and other systems started to catch on a few years ago, but it quickly became apparent that dumb agents were not very efficient for this purpose. Dumb agents must be polled continuously by central management software, a process that increases network traffic. Today, many desktop systems reside at remote sites, and polling over wide-area links quickly drives up operating costs. Even on higher-bandwidth LANs, which are being increasingly burdened with multimedia and other delay-sensitive applications, traffic from continuous polling and the resultant data transfers can easily affect performance thresholds. Intelligent agents address these problems.

What makes intelligent agents so smart is the addition of programming code that tells the agent exactly what to do, how to do it, and when to do it. Because UNIX and other systems are equipped to run complex computations anyway, adding intelligent agent software does not significantly tax a machine's resources.

## CAPABILITIES OF INTELLIGENT AGENTS

The information collected by intelligent agents from multiple sets of data can be displayed in several ways (e.g., in cells, charts, and text), analyzed for such purposes as license management or inventory management, and printed as a detail or summary report. Agents are becoming an increasingly popular method of carrying out repetitive, programmable tasks. In essence, they play the dual role of manager and agent. Intelligent agents that reside on UNIX systems are capable of tracking hundreds of parameters. They are used mostly for scheduling, controlling, and monitoring the execution of processes across the network and ensuring their successful completion.

A comprehensive agent-based management application allows the systems administrator to perform the following main functions:

- View and manipulate network data.
- Automate file distribution.
- Maintain hardware inventory.
- Manage installed software, including application usage.
- Receive notification of network events.
- Establish and manage network printer support.
- Automate network processes, such as backup and virus detection.
- Monitor disk and file usage.
- Create task lists.
- Manage storage.

All of the agents that collect information in support of these functions are configured at the management console using commands selected from the menu bar. Once configured, each type of agent can be assigned an icon that launches its associated viewer for displaying collected information. The many types of agents available include those for monitoring disk, application, and file usage; distributing files; tracking network activity; and process scheduling. The following sections explain how intelligent agents work in the distributed environment and aid in multivendor systems management.

## DISK MONITORING AGENTS

To remain productive, network users must have an adequate amount of disk space for storing programs and data. A disk monitoring agent that reports volume capacity helps the systems administrator manage use of disk space and meet user demand. Current information on disk use helps the systems administrator make decisions about reallocating resources or purchasing additional drives or servers.

The disk monitoring agent scans the server volumes to collect disk use information. The collected information includes a list of volumes that were scanned, total volume capacity, and space used. In addition, the time and date disk data was collected is recorded for comparing disk use over a period of time. Some vendors' disk monitoring tools also record disk-usage data based on directory and file owner.

Depending on the product selected, one or more of the following categories of information can be collected by a disk monitoring agent:

- Volumes. Includes the date and time data was collected, server name, volumes scanned, capacity, space used, and space available.
- Directories. Includes the date and time data was collected, server volume and directory names, creation date and time, file count, directory size (in bytes), owner name, and groups to which the owner is a member.
- Directory and file owners. Includes the date and time data was collected, server and volume names, owner name, groups to which the owner is a member, total number of files, and total space used (in bytes).

A disk monitoring agent provides automatic notification if disk usage reaches a specified level. In accordance with organizational needs, notification can be sent to the individual responsible for responding to the situation through a console, network, pager, or E-mail message. The console provides view formats and types that allow the systems administrator to analyze current disk use as well as disk use patterns over a period of time.

Usually, the disk monitoring agent can process data in the background while other programs are running. It also can be made to run interactively, with progress displayed in a status window of the console as volumes are being scanned. A scheduling agent can be tasked to run the disk monitor automatically in batch mode to collect data at night. This feature is particularly helpful because collecting data from some volumes takes a significant amount of time. Using the scheduling agent, the systems administrator can regularly collect data each night, once a week, or once a month, depending on organizational requirements. This process ensures that information is collected consistently.

## APPLICATION MONITORING AGENTS

The ability to track software usage helps ensure that the organization complies with vendor licensing agreements and that network users have access to needed applications. Tracking software usage also helps reduce software acquisition costs, because accurate usage information helps managers determine which applications are run most before deciding on upgrades and how many copies to buy.

An intelligent agent is used to meter software usage. Metering allows the systems administrator to control the number of concurrent users of single applications as well as those in a software suite. Metering of a software suite tracks each application in the suite individually to automatically allow the correct number of concurrent users. In addition, the application agent collects information on which applications have been used and identifies the users who have accessed them.

The systems administrator can also choose to be notified of the times when users are denied access to applications because all available copies are in use. If work must be tracked by project, the intelligent agent can also be used to automatically apply application usage to a particular project code. The systems administrator views and analyzes the collected metering data at the console.

For each application, the intelligent agent meters use of the main executable file as well as all associated executable files. For example, metering use of Micrografx, Inc.'s Designer can also track use of associated executable files, including Slideshow and Batch Print, because these applications are a part of the Designer product.

Examples of the types of files that are automatically recognized by the intelligent agent for metering are:

- .com (command).
- .exe (program).
- .bat (batch).
- .pif (starts Disk Operating System applications in the Windows environment).
- .bin (program).
- .scr (screen savers).

Because some executable files use file extensions other than those in the list, the intelligent agent provides the option of allowing the systems administrator to identify additional files and extensions for metering software usage.

Each package in the software inventory has a unique name (i.e., tag) that is used for metering. When a user launches a metered application, the tag name is checked to determine if there are available copies (i.e., licenses), and a record is generated. The intelligent agent checks software licenses in and out — when users start an application, one less copy is available to run; likewise, when the application is closed, the copy becomes available again. Before users are granted access to metered software, the software inventory is checked to determine whether copies are available. An error message indicating that there are no available copies is displayed to a third user if two users are running an application that has only two licenses.

## FILE MONITORING AGENTS

A file monitoring agent is a tool that is used to collect data about file access, such as which files are being accessed and by whom. Tracking file access is important for:

- Recording file access to a sensitive file or group of files.
- Diagnosing file access problems.
- Reviewing access times for application bottlenecks.

Monitoring file access data also helps the systems administrator maintain network security, and it provides useful information for tracking the source of security breaches.

The file agent monitors access to specified files and provides the following information:

- Who accessed the files.
- The complete path for the file.
- When the files were accessed and for how long.
- What operations were performed.

The systems administrator sets up the file monitoring agent to automatically collect this kind of information, after which it can be viewed and analyzed at the console.

## FILE DISTRIBUTION AGENTS

A file distribution agent is a tool that is used to automate the process of distributing files to particular groups or workstations. A file distribution job can be defined as software installations and upgrades, start-up file updates, or file deletions. Using a file distribution agent allows these types of changes to be automatically applied to each workstation or to a specified group of workstations.

The agent can be set up to collect information on file distribution status, which the systems administrator can view at the console to determine if files were distributed successfully. The console provides view formats and types that allow the administrator to review status data, such as which workstations are set up for file distributions, the stations to which files have been distributed, and the number of stations waiting for distributions.

Because users can be authorized to log in at one or more workstations, the file distribution agent determines where to distribute files based on the primary user (i.e., owner) of the workstation. The owner is established the first time an inventory is taken of the workstation. Before automated file distributions are run, the hardware inventory agent is usually run and distributions made only when the owner is actually working at the station.

Using scripts, the systems administrator defines distribution criteria, including the group or station to receive files and the day or days on which files are to be distributed. Scripts usually identify the files for distribution and the hardware requirements needed to run the file distribution job successfully. Many vendors provide templates to ease script creation that are displayed as a preset list of common file tasks. Using the templates, the systems administrator outlines a file distribution script and then uses the outline to actually generate the script.

## EVENT MANAGEMENT AGENTS

The ability to monitor network activity allows the systems administrator to ensure the effectiveness and efficiency of network services. An event manager agent is used to track network activity (i.e., events), log network activity, and automatically alert the individual responsible for responding to certain network occurrences. Any network occurrence can be considered an event, from running the virus scan program, to logging in to the network, to performing a network backup.

The systems administrator specifies the network activity to be tracked, such as the times when users log in and out of the network or when programs are run. Network activities that may require immediate attention are also specified. A notification feature can be set to alert the systems administrator, or the person responsible, of the times when these events occur. Different notification methods can be set as appropriate for each network event.

Event notifications can be processed based on priority level. For example, if three network events occur simultaneously, notification of the event with highest priority is sent first. Priority levels range from a low of one to a high of nine. When the systems administrator specifies the network activity to monitor, a priority level for each event is assigned based on how critical the activity is and whether someone has to be notified when the event occurs.

The following methods of event notification are typically available:

- Console messages. Text messages display the name of the event and color-coded views indicate the priority level of the event.
- E-mail messages. The event level and name is sent in an electronic mail message.
- Pager messages. A phone number, the event name, or both, is sent to a pager.

The systems administrator chooses one or more contacts to receive notification of each event level. For example, a technician can be specified to receive a pager message when high-priority events occur, and a help desk operator can be specified to receive an E-mail message when routine application-related events occur. An acknowledgment of receipt for event data can be sent to the console to help ensure a proper response to events.

## PROCESS SCHEDULING AGENTS

A scheduling agent is an application used to organize and run jobs. A typical job can be running a command for network backup or sending a broadcast message to users before the backup begins. Instead of having to keep a written log of jobs and remembering to run them, the systems administrator uses a scheduling agent to specify that the jobs run automatically at a certain time. For example, the systems administrator could schedule the system backup process for 2 A.M. — a time when the system is not likely to be heavily used. At the specified time, the scheduling agent automatically starts jobs unattended. The job specifications can be saved and updated whenever necessary, and jobs can be changed or deleted at any time.

The scheduling agent can also provide job completion information, such as whether the job ran successfully, when it ran, and the next time it is scheduled to run. Following are examples of jobs a scheduling agent streamlines:

- Performing network backup.
- Running computer virus scan.
- Processing overnight mailings.
- Performing file copying and distribution.
- Printing and processing reports.
- Sending network messages.

A scheduling agent can implement jobs that run once or at these regular intervals: hourly, daily, weekdays, weekly, monthly. Instead of being run individually, jobs can be grouped to accomplish multiple tasks. An entry can be posted in the event log after jobs are completed that tells the systems administrator when the job started and ended. For example, with regard to scheduling the network virus scan process, the scheduling agent can automatically add a record to the log of network events provided by the event agent.

## SYSTEMS MANAGEMENT PRODUCTS

Some systems management products that make extensive use of intelligent agents include Computer Associates' CA-Unicenter, Hewlett-Packard Co.'s OperationsCenter, and Saber Software Corp.'s LAN Management System (a suite of systems management products). The agent software is written for each vendor's system platform. The extent to which agent software works with other hardware platforms differs according to vendor. Hewlett-Packard's agent software, for example, works on the following UNIX platforms:

- AT&T Systems 3000.
- Sun Solaris.
- IBM RISC/6000.
- Sun Microsystems SPARCstation.
- BULL HN Information Systems DPX/20.
- HP 9000 and 3000 Series systems.

Other companies that have awakened to the management possibilities offered by intelligent agents include Apple Computer, BMC Software, Candle Corp., Ki Networks, and Sun Microsystems. IBM Corp. has announced that it will revamp its entire family of management products with a multivendor intelligent agent architecture. The company's Common Agent Architecture, being implemented in phases, uses the DMTF DMI technology, which lets systems administrators gather a variety of desktop system data, such as disk usage and PC configuration, and monitor the performance and status of individual applications. APIs let management consoles, such as HPOV and IBM's NetView for AIE platforms, share event and topology information.

## INTEROPERABILITY AND OTHER ISSUES

The term agent implies interoperability with other vendors' management software, at least on a basic level. This interoperability usually takes the form of SNMP support. The expectation is that if agents are sitting out there on various stations, multiple managers from different vendors will be able communicate with them. But in the distributed environment, the applications are not designed to interoperate with other vendors' applications. So what appears as agent technology might really be just a piece of a distributed application.

However, some agents are interoperable. IBM's Systems Monitor/6000, for example, is a true intelligent agent. It provides a MIB interface to UNIX information by exposing UNIX kernel information in SNMP format. Still, products that offer such interoperability are few and far between.

**Agent Management**

The issue of agent management also needs to be addressed. A large network can have thousands of agents that need to be monitored to find out what agents are actually in the network as well as what they are doing and what has changed. One tool that does monitor agent activity is Legent Corp.'s AgentWorks, which is available for several UNIX platforms, as well as for Windows NT and OS/2.

AgentWorks uses icons to represent nodes on the network and allows an administrator to view the overall system, an individual site, a particular network segment, or a particular node. If the systems administrator is looking at an overall view and an error has occurred in a database process, the node where the error occurred appears in red. As the user refines the view to just the node, the database manager agent uses the color red to further pinpoint the problem. If an individual forgets to restart a process, such as an interrupted backup, AgentWorks automatically displays the error.

In addition to allowing systems administrators to create their own intelligent agents, AgentWorks can run as a standalone network management system or interoperate with other management platforms such as SunConnect's SNM, HPOV, and IBM's NetView for AIE. AgentWorks is also one of the few products that integrates current SNMP platforms and intelligent agents in a distributed client/server architecture. AgentWorks even allows systems administrators to choose among agent modules for systems, network, application, and database management. Within the basic modules, systems administrators can gradually add management functions as the need arises.

The concept of modular agents is not without its share of potential drawbacks. Because it is possible, for example, to have multiple agents in the same system, more than one agent might respond to a command from the management console. In addition, agents may contend for the same output port when attempting to respond.

This issue is addressed by designating one agent the master and the others as subordinates. The master agent reconciles requests and responses and multiplexes data from subordinates over the output port. However, this scheme introduces a new level of complexity into multivendor environments. Because the masters and subordinates of different vendors are not compatible, they will not work together. Although many vendors have been coalescing around a few approaches for defining master-subordinate agents, such as SNMP Research Inc.'s Emanate extensible agent architecture, many users are still forced to buy agents from the same vendor from which they bought the management system.

DMI was designed to promote multivendor interoperability by addressing standardization of the agent interface. To date, however, one of the biggest problems with DMI has been the lack of guidelines on how to retrieve information remotely. The Desktop Management Task Force recently completed its remote specification, which should make it easier to add management capabilities to computers, software, and peripheral devices.

## CONCLUSION

Intelligent agents have a myriad of other uses. BeyondMail from Banyan Systems, Inc. is an example of agent-based messaging. BeyondMail's intelligent agents filter, sort, and prioritize mail by sender or topic on behalf of users. A number of sophisticated messaging products have become endowed with agents to help users manage and access data. For example, intelligent agents are used on AT&T's wireless Personalink network to perform a variety of tasks for mobile users, such as sorting and directing E-mail according to priorities. Among other things, important messages can be sent to the user's PDA, and routine messages can be output to a fax machine back at the office.

Intelligent agents offer several compelling advantages for systems management. They detect exceptional events and trigger automated actions to correct problems before they affect systems services, thereby increasing systems availability and reliability. An intelligent agent architecture obviates the need for expensive network polling, because only critical alerts are sent to the management console.

Finally, intelligent agents can be used to automate routine, repetitive tasks, relieving the systems administrator of a heavy work burden. This reduces the overall cost of systems management by speeding problem resolution and permitting businesses to get the most out of their technology investments. This ability to carry out corrective actions on an automated basis, and to keep business systems and applications up and running, can give a company a competitive edge in an economy where information availability and the speed of delivery are critical.

# Chapter 81

# Voice Recognition Interfaces for Multimedia Applications

*Louis Fried*

Most of the techniques associated with multimedia applications — video, text, graphics, object-oriented interfaces, handwritten input, touch-screens, scanning, and mouse point- and- click techniques — focus on a visually based human interface. Not enough has been said about the most natural of all human interfaces — speech. During the last few years, automatic speech recognition (ASR) technology has made substantial strides that warrant active consideration of speech as an effective interface for many emerging multimedia applications.

Although speech or voice recognition technology is not new, applications have often been confined by the limitations of the technology. In the past, most speech recognition systems could only recognize words spoken in isolation. If users wanted the computer to understand their speech, they had to....separate...the...words...by...brief...silences. In addition, most systems required that the speaker spend hours training the system to understand his or her individual pronunciation. These constraints still apply to many of the speech recognition products currently available for operation on personal computers.

Systems that require training by the user are generally limited to supporting one to four users and generally have limited or specialized vocabularies. Systems that operate in this mode include products from Kurzweil, Applied Intelligence, Inc., Dragon Systems, and IBM Corp. Although they are extremely useful for providing computer access to impaired people or to professionals who must keep their hands free for other work while accessing a computer, these systems do not meet the needs for general or public access to computer systems in what could be called a natural manner.

## PRACTICAL SYSTEMS FOR WIDESPREAD USE

If a speech recognition system is to be of widespread, practical use, it must operate without individual training (i.e., be speaker independent), and it must understand continuous speech, without pauses, which is how people converse. Two approaches have been taken to solve the problem of speaker-independent recognition: the synthetic modeling approach and the sampling approach.

### Speaker-Independent Recognition

**Synthetic Modeling.** Synthetic modeling builds words out of syllables that represent speech sounds. Using a database of these subwords, words can be created in the recognition tables by phoneme transcription — much like constructing words using the pronunciation codes that are listed following a word in a dictionary.

**Sampling.** The sampling approach, which has proved to be more accurate for interpreting regional accents, involves gathering large numbers of spoken samples of utterances (referred to as tokens) and constructing words from them that match the anticipated user population. The broader a population of users, the more samples are needed. For example, in constructing a speaker-independent recognition Corona TM system, which is intended to be useful across the entire US, SRI International's researchers gathered more than 400,000 utterances from all regions of the country.

A system intended for widespread use must be capable of recognizing a large number of words. Given the current state of the art, a system that can recognize anyone saying yes or no is trivial. Early vocabulary-building applications could support up to about 2,000 words and phrases. More advanced systems can support vocabularies of 60,000 or more words. Vocabularies for widespread application must be capable of recognizing tens of thousands of words in essentially real-time as far as the speaker is concerned. Only in this way can a human's conversation with a computer appear to be natural.

**The Complexities of Speech.** New systems appearing commercially today do a creditable job of recognizing speaker-independent, continuous speech with an accuracy of better than 95%. However, there is a great deal of complexity that must be overcome. A sampling of the complex problems that need to be solved follows.

*Homonyms.* Most languages, especially English, have many homonyms, words that sound alike but may have different spellings and different meanings (e.g., two, to, and too). The ability to distinguish among homonyms depends on either limiting the vocabulary in some manner to eliminate homonyms or being able to understand the context in which the word is spoken.

*Numbers.* Numbers are difficult to recognize. Not only do some numbers sound like other words, but people say numbers in different ways. If asked for a telephone number, most people will say each number separately, but if asked for a dollar amount, most people will combine the numbers in some fashion, such as five thousand four hundred and thirty-six dollars and forty-seven cents. Long strings of numbers, or numbers and letters combined (such as in an automobile vehicle serial number) can be very difficult to understand. For this reason, many applications require the speaker to break up a longer number into smaller groups; a social security number might be broken into groups of three, two, and four, and a credit card number into groups of four digits.

*Background Noise.* Understanding speech is further complicated when a telephone is the instrument of voice capture. Over-the-phone speech is subject to the background hiss of phone lines. Good systems will include algorithms f or cleaning the speech of background noise. Similar techniques must be applied if the speaker is talking in a noisy environment.

*Spoken Language Understanding.* Automatic speech recognition is not the same thing as spoken language, or natural language, understanding. An ASR system, for example, could pick out certain words in a stream of speech and, by spotting these words in the context of a limited dialog; respond as if it had understood a complete sentence. For example, if a customer calls a bank's speech recognition system and requests a "current account balance," a word-spotting system may simply pick out the word "balance" and provide the correct answer. Applications based on word-spotting techniques require that the dialog between the caller and the system be carefully constructed to limit the range of responses that the caller may make.

Spoken language understanding systems, by contrast, would operate without the limited context of word spotting and truly analyze the entire sentence before responding. Furthermore, such systems may have the capability to handle references to earlier sentences in the conversation or topic changes. For example, a conversation may include an inquiry about whether a particular check had cleared. After receiving a negative response, the speaker may say, "Put a stop payment on it." Here, a system could recognize that "it" refers to the check previously discussed.

*Portability.* Finally, for the technology to achieve widespread use, a system must be portable among computers. It must not rely on any special equipment for processing other than the chips for digitizing the analog signals from voice input, typically embedded in any computer to which a microphone may be attached. Some systems rely on the use of proprietary digital signal processing boards to both digitize the analog input and analyze the speech and convert it to digital components. This approach ties the application to a specific set of hardware.

## CURRENT APPLICATIONS

The progress made in speech recognition technology means that developers of multimedia applications should seriously consider speech recognition in their human interface design. Two major classifications of applications exist:

1. *Microphone applications.* The speaker talks into a microphone attached to a workstation and obtains spoken or visual responses (or both).
2. *Telephony applications.* The speaker uses a telephone handset or equivalent to speak and hear responses.

### Microphone-Input Applications for the PC

Microphone applications have the potential to provide impaired persons access to information facilities and to make people in many professions more productive. Because these applications are usually based on the older, speaker-dependent technology, many more of them have been implemented than have applications using speaker-independent recognition technology. Some examples of workstation or PC-based applications follow.

Kurzweil Applied Intelligence introduced its VoiceMED line of products for patient reporting almost 10 years ago. In these applications, the speaker (typically a physician who had trained the system) spoke into a microphone connected to a personal computer. The system translated the voice to written words and incorporated the specialized vocabulary of the physician. Extensions of the VoiceMED system were products such as VoicePATH (for pathology), VoiceEM (for emergency medicine), VoiceDIAL-YSIS (for kidney dialysis reporting), and VoiceCATH (for invasive cardiology). These systems grew out of Kurzweil's earlier work in voice-controlled typing systems.

West Publishing and Kolvox Communications have introduced the Law-Talk large vocabulary speech recognition front-end to the WestLaw online legal research system. The system includes Dragon Systems' DragonDictate technology, which uses a microphone connection to the PC. The PC-based application then translates the speaker's query and interfaces to the online database. Queries may be stated in either a formula- like Boolean expression or in natural language. The speech interface is further combined with a WordPerfect speech interface that allows users to transfer downloaded information to documents using oral commands.

Syracuse Language Systems, Inc.'s TriplePlay Plus! software uses speech recognition to teach foreign languages by listening to a student's voice, evaluating the pronunciation, and replying in the foreign language used. The system can be used to learn French, German, English, or Spanish.

In the brokerage field, R.W. Pressprich & Co., Inc., has implemented voice recognition to replace keyboard entry for bond traders.

Under the banner of its VoiceType Dictation systems, IBM offers dictating systems not only on its PCs but also with a PCMCIA digital signal adapter for laptop and notebook computers. VoiceType dictation is available in English, German, Italian, French, and Spanish. Other vendors have entered the market with similar products. One of the more powerful features of speech recognition technology is that because words are made up of phonetic tokens or subwords, the technology does not have to be changed to provide support to new languages; only the vocabularies need to be changed.

### Telephony Applications

Telephony applications provide information access to large numbers of people and may potentially replace many of the telephone service personnel who now provide information, take orders by phone, or otherwise serve as a human interface to callers. Telephony applications are often successful because they provide an acceptable interface for callers who do not have, or prefer not to use, touchtone input to a voice response system. In fact, many new applications use existing interactive voice response (IVR) units to answer the call and provide the voice response once the caller's speech is understood. Examples of such applications follow.

AT&T and most of the regional telephone companies in the U.S. are in the process of providing speaker- independent recognition interfaces for callers. The most profitable target for these applications is the hundreds of directory assistance operators who provide telephone numbers to 411 callers. However, the application of speech recognition technology is also being used to create other applications such as a third- party billing system and processing of collect calls.

Even speaker-dependent systems have a place in telephone carrier applications. Sprint is testing a FONCARD application in which the caller verbally enters the private access code and the system verifies both the number and the caller's voice as valid for that code. Ameritech is testing a system that allows individual speakers at the same phone number to create speaker-dependent personal dialing directories.

Other industries may even be ahead of the telephone companies. One example is the customer service directory system implemented by Union Electric in St. Louis MO. This system permits customers with rotary phones or those who prefer not to use touchtone input to connect to such service groups as installation and billing and speak to a live operator or leave a voicemail message. The script between the IVR and the caller carefully directs the responses and allows either touchtone or voice response.

## EMERGING APPLICATIONS

Speech recognition applications have direct benefits to the organizations that adopt them in terms of productivity, safety, and reduced staffing. Efforts in development, and in some cases new products, are being announced to combine ASR with facsimile machines, imaging, and industrial controls. Assuming that the long- term trends in hardware continue to make intelligent devices cheaper, smaller, and faster, with more data storage capability, automatic speech recognition and especially speaker-independent recognition will play an important role in several areas; for example:

- For devices that are too small for other interfaces. Product development is now taking place on pocket-sized devices that incorporate the functions of a personal reminder and address book with a mobile telephone.
- For applications where keyboards are impractical. In industrial situations such as machine shops and assembly lines, keyboards rapidly become dirty and nonfunctional. ASR technology can also eliminate the need for manual entry in situations in which keyboards are subject to weather or other hazardous conditions. Examples of such use include public or customer access to automated teller machines, vending kiosks, and information kiosks.
- As an easy-to-learn means for untrained users and the general public to concurrently use a single information resource.
- As embedded technology in other devices for which other interfaces would detract from the design or efficiency. The technology is already being used in automobiles, and its use in home appliances is anticipated.
- For applications for the visually impaired as well as for communications under conditions in which the hands are in use or vision should not be distracted. One current application supports data entry by dock workers who wear small wireless microphones to dictate data about shipments and receipts for entry into the information system.
- As an alternative to systems that use touchtone input in conjunction with IVR. Between 20% and 40% of callers to such systems either do not have a touchtone instrument or refuse to use touchtone. In many cases, the aversion is not to the touchtone instrument but to the

extensive menus that are recited before the caller can identify the sequence of buttons to push. ASR techniques can substantially condense or eliminate menus.

## SELECTING AN ASR PRODUCT

It is easy to overbuy and acquire technology that is too costly and sophisticated for real business needs. By the same token, if IS developers and users define current needs too narrowly and do not anticipate the future, they underbuy. Some buyers have opted for wordspotting systems only to find that their vendor did not support spoken language understanding (i.e., natural language). When full natural language capability is needed, a complete system replacement can be very expensive.

Once an application specification has been written, selection of the system depends first on who will be using it. When one or only a few specific users will use the system, the lowest- priced approach that meets their needs should be chosen. However, users must have the patience to train the system and be willing to take the isolated-word approach to dictation.

When an application involves so-called promiscuous speech (i.e., lots of people talking to the system), selection demands more stringent criteria. Obviously, the system must support speaker-independent, continuous speech recognition and the ability to translate speech into ASCII text. Additional criteria are usually called for. The weight placed on the criteria is, of course, a function of the intended application.

### Functions and Features to Look For

When choosing a system for many users, IT buyers should look for certain features and functions:

- The system must be able to translate and respond with minimal perceptible lag time.
- If the system is intended for use in telephony applications, it must work with regular, unmodified telephone instruments, speakerphones, and cellular phones. It must also support barge-in (i.e., allowing speakers to talk while the system is still responding) and the IVR system in use or to be in use (i.e., it must be easily ported to that system). Finally, it must be able to alternate with touchtone input.
- If the system is intended to support broad-ranging inquiry, it must support a vocabulary of more than 60,000 words. The *Wall Street Journal* test is a good measure of performance. In contrast to most newspapers, which use a vocabulary of less than 15,000 words, the *Journal* uses a 40,000-word vocabulary. If the system performs with reasonable accuracy in translating Journal articles, it should work for this type of application.

- Depending on the application (e.g., electronic engineering, programming, or medicine), the system should support or be able to add specialized vocabularies.
- If the system is intended to support multiple specialists, it should be able to switch among vocabularies.
- The system should support word spotting.
- The system should support spoken language understanding. Even if there is no plan to use this feature initially, it may be a desirable feature to have in a product to allow for future needs.
- If the system is intended for nationwide use, it should support translation of multiple dialects or regional accents for a single language (or the vendor should be able to adapt the system to accommodate regional accents).
- If intended for international use, the system must support multiple languages (or the vendor should be able to adapt the system to accommodate foreign languages).
- The system should detect silences and recognize when the speaker has stopped talking.
- The system should listen at all times (rather than only when the speaker is given a signal).
- The system should operate on a server in a client/server environment.
- The system should support performance analysis (e.g., recognition confidence factors, recording of exact word sequence, percentage of successful transactions, average transaction processing time).
- The system should maintain a time-stamped activity log.
- Individual sessions should be able to be recorded for later playback.

## Performance Characteristics

An evaluation of performance characteristics should ask the following:

- How many concurrent users can access the system without degradation of response time?
- Can the system work in a noisy environment, filtering out external noise?
- Is the system portable among a variety of standard computers?
- Is the system composed of software only (i.e., it does not require special devices other than those for digitizing voice input)?

## Vendor Capability

When selecting a vendor, buyers should be sure to ask the following questions:

- Is the provider of the ASR system the original developer?
- Can the provider create custom applications for the organization?
- Does the provider offer around-the-clock emergency support for critical applications?

## BUILDING VOICE RECOGNITION APPLICATIONS

Most of the packages used in specialized applications such as law or medicine are for single users or a limited number of users. However, for promiscuous-speech applications that allow the general public or a company's customers to access the system, it is usually necessary to design and build the application using the ASR system and to implement the application using its accompanying tools.

Until automatic speech recognition becomes such a common component of the human-machine interface that it can be applied generally as a keyboard is used today, the technology will probably be reserved for high-payoff applications. Such applications, especially those that are telephony-based, provide a means for access that presents the company's image to the public or its customers. Whether the application takes orders for products or simply provides information, the owner must consider any customer interface to be mission-critical. For this reason, the approach to applications development must be a least-risk, conservative method.

### The Development Team

The team assembled for building an ASR application needs specialized skills that members of the IS group may not possess. The team therefore must include several people not typically present on an applications development team.

**Users or a Proxy for the Users.** If the application is intended for internal use in the organization, a sample of users should participate in the development of a vocabulary, the design of an appropriate dialog (for an interactive application), and the testing of the application. If the application is intended for use by external parties, a proxy for those parties should participate. The proxy must be familiar with the business application and the usual dialogs conducted with external parties (e.g., customers).

**A Corporate Public Relations Representative.** For an application to be used by external parties, a representative of corporate public relations should participate to review the dialog and ensure that it conveys an appropriate image of the organization.

**Technical Architects.** Technicians familiar with the operation and architecture of the hardware elements of the system should design the interfaces among the components. Components may include:

- An ASR server.
- A local area network.
- An IVR system.
- The telephone interface to the IVR system.
- A host-resident database for supplying information.
- Telephone line interfaces.

Technicians are needed to design the architecture, supervise installation and testing, and assist in expansion from pilot systems to full rollout.

**Application Designers.** These systems analysts design the application from a software perspective and continue with the iterative design cycle until the application is implemented. One of the application designers may be the project leader.

**Linguistic Analyst.** An interactive ASR application depends on an unambiguous dialog between the speaker and the system. Not only must the message to the speaker be understood, but also it must not be misunderstood.

The linguist works with the users to design the dialog. In addition, the linguist helps to design any specialized vocabulary, specify words or phrases that may need to be spotted, and adapt the system for any regional accents or language usage.

**Programmers.** Programmers are needed to create the data base interfaces to the host data base and, depending on the amount of customization required, to modify or enhance the programs that directly interface to the ASR system.

The ASR system provider may provide the personnel needed to develop initial applications and concurrently train IS staff members to support the application and develop later applications. Some companies may find it best to buy a turnkey system and continuing maintenance from the ASR provider.

### Six-Step Development Process

The iterative development process described here assumes that the application is a telephony-based system for providing information from a database to customers. ASR applications are particularly suited to development through incremental prototyping — a technique that provides incremental feedback to the application requester and supports joint application development (JAD) approaches.

At each stage of prototype development, the system requester, simulating a user, is asked to evaluate the dialog provided by the system. This evaluation usually results in changes that grow fewer as the application converges on satisfactory results.

The following description of the development process assumes that the scope of the project is known and a preliminary specification has been developed. This specification would include:

**Exhibit 1. Development Task Sequence for ASR Applications**

| Task | Description |
|------|-------------|
| 1. Requirements Definition | Define dialog, APIs, text plan, load characteristics, measurement methods, and preliminary rollout plan. |
| 2. Standalone Prototype | Iteratively develop and test standalone prototype and API, Development install vocabulary, tune for regional accents. |
| 3. Integration | Integrate with IVR and test (or test with test databases), simulate load testing. |
| 4. Pilot Test | Test functional operation with a limited user set, modify as necessary. |
| 5. Detailed Rollout Plan | Develop detailed rollout plan, install equipment for rollout. |
| 6. Rollout | Full system test followed by implementation. |

- A description of the proposed application.
- A description of the operating environment, including existing hardware and software systems that will interface with the ASR application or any preference for hardware and software that imposes a constraint on the ASR solution.
- A preliminary description of the anticipated dialog between users and the system.
- A list of the specialized vocabulary words or phrases needed by the application.

Because speech recognition applications often interface with or support mission- critical systems, a cautious six-step approach that includes extensive testing before implementation is required. Exhibit 1 summarizes the tasks involved in the approach.

**Task 1: Requirements Definition.** The development team defines the application requirements in sufficient detail to create a more specific project plan and allocate assignments and target schedules. This documented definition includes:

- A definition of the dialog to be conducted between the user of the speech recognition system and the ASR system. This dialog anticipates such system behavior as points of dropout to a live operator, alternate use of touchtone input, and transfers to other voice routines.
- A definition of the application program interfaces (APIs) to cooperating voice response units or other equipment or software.
- A definition of message formats and message-passing protocols to support any required interfaces, accesses, or updates to production databases. To protect the integrity of the company's databases, the ASR system should not directly access them in any manner except through a defined procedure/protocol provided by the technical staff

responsible for the database. The interface protocol permits sending and receiving messages between the voice recognition system and the database access programs.

- Test plans for API testing, controlled environment testing, pilot testing, and acceptance testing.
- Identification and description of a pilot test group.
- Identification and description of anticipated load characteristics.
- A definition of performance measurement parameters for evaluating the performance of the system during pilot test and under full operation.
- A preliminary plan for rollout of the application to full use.

During task 1, the company should also acquire and install a workstation-based development environment for the creation and testing of the prototype and for use in future development and maintenance. The ASR application development toolkit is installed on the workstation.

Upon completion of task 1, the requester's representatives review and approve the resulting definitions and plans.

**Task 2: Prototype Development.** The team employs a technique of incremental prototyping to develop and iteratively test a prototype application in a standalone environment. Technical personnel assigned to the project team are trained in the use of the toolkit by the ASR system provider during this task. This basic training in use of the toolkit ensures that the staff becomes familiar with the tools and methods used in voice recognition applications development.

The team installs the vocabulary and any variations that are anticipated to handle regional accents, creates the dialog, implements word spotting if required, implements accuracy performance measurement routines, and, in general, establishes a complete prototype of the application in a standalone environment. Iterative development ensures that the prototype has continually been tested as it is developed.

At the conclusion of this task, the operating prototype should satisfy the functional requirements of the voice recognition portion of the application. The operating prototype is essentially the runtime version of the voice recognition portion of the application, ready for integration into the overall application environment.

**Task 3: IVR Integration.** In this task, the voice recognition application is integrated with the interactive voice response unit. Any software elements necessary to accommodate the interfaces, handle dropouts to live operators and touchtone signals, and provide message passing are developed and tested independently of the final implementation environment. This task results in tested interfaces to the IVR but not necessarily to host databases.

Depending on the configuration of the environment, the 1VR may access host databases on the basis of touchtone input signals. In such a case, the ASR system returns appropriate messages to the IVR to initiate the data base access.

In the event that the access to host databases is initiated directly from the voice recognition system, the following task is substituted for task 3.

*Task 3a: Integration into Operating Environment.* Here, the team integrates the voice recognition portion of the application into a controlled version of the operating environment. For this task, the team establishes test databases (i.e., potentially copies of live files) so that the tests do not access live files.

The team may also install a communications connection to the ASR provider for remote maintenance of the application if required.

The team develops the message-passing routines between the voice recognition portion of the application and data base access, voice response, or other routines. Any software elements necessary to accommodate the interfaces, handle dropouts to live operators and touchtone signals, and provide message passing are developed and tested independently of the full environment. The team also develops program routines to evaluate performance of the system both in the pilot test and full rollout environments.

In addition, the team develops a test-bed to simulate peak loads on the system and conducts such simulation tests to determine concurrent voice recognition processing capacity for this application.

Functional simulations and testing of end-user interaction are conducted and adjustments or corrections made to the application until the application is considered ready for pilot testing. Such readiness is determined according to the predefined test plans developed in task 1.

**Task 4: Pilot Test.** On the basis of load tests, the company must purchase and install sufficient computer capacity to accommodate the projected load for the pilot test. Subsequent to the installation of this equipment, the team conducts another round of integration tests to ensure that the application and system are ready.

Following the integration tests, the application is connected to live files and tested with a limited number of users to ensure correct functional operation. An application designed for use by customers may be tested by a group of employees first.

The pilot test is conducted according to the plan developed in task 1 only after satisfactory controlled testing is completed. Measurements of performance are evaluated along with quality reports from users. Any adjustments necessary to the system are made until performance meets the agreed-on parameters.

The acceptance test described in task 1 is conducted as a part of the pilot test. At the conclusion of this task, the requester representatives examine test results and certify acceptance of the system.

**Task 5: Rollout Planning.** Concurrently with task 4, the project team, working with the application requester, develops a rollout plan. This plan describes, in detail, the steps necessary to ensure a satisfactory implementation of the application. The plan covers any additional equipment acquisition, architectural changes necessary to the system environment to accommodate full implementation, needed integration activities, performance management procedures, staging of implementation to users, feedback mechanisms to ensure quality of performance, the sequence and schedule of events, and assignments of responsibility.

The company must then acquire and install any additional equipment or software required to support full implementation.

**Task 6: Rollout and Full Implementation.** The team first performs a controlled test using the additionally installed equipment to ensure proper integration of the system. If possible, the pilot test is then extended using the newly acquired equipment instead of the previously used pilot test equipment. Full implementation is started only when all components and their integration have been tested.

Implementation is conducted according to the plans set forth in task 4. Members of the project team observe the implementation and contact the ASR or IVR provider if any major problems occur. Problems that cannot be handled by the company's trained staff are handled by the providers in accordance with warranty or maintenance agreements. Weekly performance reports to the requester management should be written by the project team until 60 days after full implementation of the system or 60 days of trouble-free operation.

Implementing other types of applications, such as workstation-based, microphone-input ASR applications requires a different development process; however, a similar cautious approach using repetitive testing is recommended. Conservative project approaches are mandatory not only because the systems are usually mission-critical, but because the introduction of new technology should not be exposed to the possibility of disappointing the requester.

## SUMMARY

Automatic speech or voice recognition applications have the potential to provide high payoff and competitive advantage and to improve productivity, customer service, and the quality of business processes. The technology must be classified as emergent because most potential users do not yet have the skills to support their own applications development. However, the technology and many available products are currently robust enough and reliable enough for users and developers to seriously consider speech as an interface for multimedia applications. ASR systems may, at this stage, be compared to data base management systems in their early days of use. New skills must be acquired (or contracted) to maximize the benefits and conduct successful implementation projects.

# Chapter 82
# Workplace 2000: Top Career Strategies for the Professional

*Sally Crawford*

According to the U.S. Bureau of Labor and Statistics, the number of executives, managers, and administrative professionals who have lost their jobs in the last five years because of downsizing and corporate restructuring is double the number of those laid off between 1981 and 1988. The resultant feelings of uncertainty for today's professionals can be paralyzing. This chapter offers managers four different strategies to help determine a plan of action to improve their career longevity.

## A COMMON THREAD

If Bill Sheppard, formerly the systems training manager of Waste Management, is asked how he spends his time these days, he will say pursuing things he loves. One week Bill may lead an expedition for the Sierra Club in northern Michigan, or he may attend a week-long course in wilderness medicine in Minnesota, or sharpen his outdoor leadership skills at a conference in California. In between adventures, Bill teaches PC classes on a contract basis.

When Tim Steele, currently a senior consultant with Baxter Healthcare, is asked what he is doing these days, he is quick to respond with one word: more! When two Baxter divisions merged to reduce costs, Tim retained the IS training responsibilities for both groups. Although Tim's internal customer base doubled in size, his responsibilities have increased exponentially.

Cynthia Rogers, formerly the manager of training organizational development for the U.S. Headquarters of Kraft General Foods, will say she is weighing the options. Kraft General Foods went through a major reorganization in 1993. According to Cynthia, it was like a game of musical chairs. When the music stopped, many people were left standing without a job.

0-8493-9965-3/99/$0.00+$.50
© 1999 by CRC Press LLC

One of them was Cynthia. As she pursues a new career, Cynthia evaluates the benefits of independent consulting over another secure job with corporate America.

What do these workers have in common? All have been affected by downsizing, corporate America's euphemism for eliminating jobs. Ten years ago, the term *downsizing* did not exist. In 1994, it is part of people's everyday vocabulary and can even be found in the 1994edition of *Merriam-Webster's Dictionary.*

According to the U.S. Bureau of Labor Statistics, a record 1.5million executives, managers, and administrative professionals have lost their jobs in the last five years — double the number of those laid off between 1981 and 1988. The consequences can be devastating, not only to the newly unemployed, but also to the currently employed who come to work each day wondering, What will happen to me? One IS manager for a large Midwestern manufacturing firm says the uncertainty is paralyzing. Focus used to be on moving products forward. Now, time is spent talking about personal situations and trying to predict the outcome.

In these uncertain times, what can middle managers do to find a job, keep a job, and even move ahead in their job? This chapter presents four strategies to help managers determine a plan of action to improve their career longevity. These strategies are based on numerous interviews with middle and senior managers from IS organizations across the country, leading books and periodicals, and the author's experience within corporate America (at Xerox Corp.)and as an independent consultant who grew her business into a staff of 40.

## STRATEGY NO. 1: PROVING ADDED VALUE

In the 1950s, managers could rely on seniority for ensuring their longevity with a firm; in the 1980s, they could count on performance as a key to their success. In the 1990s, however, it simply is not enough to go to work every day and do an acceptable job. Employees must constantly analyze and prove how they add value to the corporation. Unfortunately, most middle managers are so entrenched in a quagmire of day-to-day activities, that they do not take time to analyze their value and wrongly assume that their management will. Perhaps that was true a decade ago, but in the 1990s it is vital to make time and take responsibility for understanding and proving a manager's value. The following suggestions can help achieve this goal.

### Finding Out from People at the Top How They Define Value

It is difficult to prove value unless it is defined by an employer. Similarly, one person's definition may be different from that of the people making the big-picture decisions. Managers should start with their immediate superior and work their way *up* in the organization. Connecting with a broad range of contacts from a variety of business areas will improve a middle manager's understanding of the company's value chain.[1] They should consider asking senior managers how their department can help the company make money or save money. In other words, middle managers should focus on the same thing senior managers do: the bottom line.

Skeptics may not believe they will get financial information just by asking, but the experience of the author can be considered. Crawford & Associates' employees recognized the firm's increased emphasis on profitability, but they did not have the specific information they needed to help affect the bottom line. Through their suggestions (more than once, from several people), the company implemented Report Card Day. This is a monthly meeting where senior management shares pertinent financial information (except individual salaries) with all employees. Report Card Day did not happen because of a stroke of genius, it came from employees repeatedly voicing their need for information that helps them make the company more successful.

If the employee's company is large and networking proves difficult, getting information from a vendor can be considered — especially if the contact is well connected within the organization. Vendors often call on a wide range of clients, including people in key management positions. If they have done their homework, vendors can provide a big picture viewpoint about various business groups, people, and projects.

### Broadening Perspectives

Often, managers can develop functional myopia,[2] where they become so focused on their department, they do not understand how they affect the greater good of the organization. Reengineering guru Michael Hammer tells the story of a multimillion dollar aircraft sitting idle in hangar A because it required a repair person from hangar B to repair it. The manager of hangar B could have sent a repair person that day, but realized he would incur a $100 expense against his budget because that person would require an overnight hotel stay. The manager of hangar B saved the company $100, but left the aircraft sitting overnight, unused, wasting hundreds of thousands of the firm's dollars. Career success in the 1990s is directly linked to the positive effect made on the entire organization, not just a manager's own department.

### Expanding the Skill Set

In the past, when managers had lifelong careers with an organization, it was fine to do one job and do it very well. In the 1990s, however, with increasing consumer demand for high-quality, low-cost products, corporations require a flexible workforce. To prove value, employees and managers alike must develop a broader range of skills so that they can do multiple jobs within the organization. Managers should analyze their current job to determine whether their skills can be easily transferred to a different department or different company. In addition, they should make sure their attitude advertises the fact that they are open to new challenges. A certain sign of career stagnation is the it-is-not-my-job mentality.

For managers, the opposite ends of the broad spectrum of skills required for future success must be considered and acted upon. At one end is the development of specific technical skills (e.g.,instructional design expertise, programming skills, or the know-how to install a 40-node network). Broadening that ability to include performing these tasks vs. supervising them promotes career longevity in two ways:

- In a period of downsizing, doers are more likely to remain employed than people who oversee these functions.
- Developing technical skills makes the manager more marketable, either to another firm or as an independent contractor.

At the other end of the spectrum in broadening a manager's skills is the development of leadership abilities, far different from the type of supervisory skills required in the 1970s and 1980s. Barbara Golden, president of Computing Solutions, Inc., Chicago, defines leadership as a life-long practice. The personal infrastructure for a leadership role comprises a set of exciting and motivating challenges. The challenges, if met, can open new realms of possibilities never yet imagined.

Golden considers leadership activities to be $500-per-hour jobs in her common denominator theory (see Exhibit 1).[3] She says that too often time is spent whining and complaining. That includes managers, too. According to Golden, whining and complaining are $0- per-hour jobs. The jobs with the most value are ones that serve as catalysts to help others achieve their true potential. Fortune 500 corporations agree. A 1993 poll of CEOs from these firms, conducted by opinion research firm Clark, Martier & Bartolomeo, proved that leadership far outranked such traditionally important skills as marketing, finance, operations management, and accounting aptitude in importance to senior management.[4]

### Proving a Manager's Value

The steadfast cliché of people blowing their own horn definitely applies to the manager of the 1990s. If these managers do not trumpet their own successes, it is unlikely that anyone else will. Because the next layer of management is so consumed with other responsibilities, it is doubtful that they have the time or energy to notice every contribution the manager makes.

**$0/Hour Value Tasks**
Discuss leaders in a
   negative manner without
   them.
Surmise without responsi-
   ble substantiation.
Blame (people and
   situations).
Get depressed.
Be frustrated.
Bring other people down.
Accept being brought down.
Share negative thoughts
   without new ideas.
Look for lost items.
Worry.
Complain.
Bitch.
Get confused.
React.

**$2/Hour Value Tasks**
Babysit.
Exchange niceties.
Appease.

**$20/Hour Value Tasks**
Uncover real evidence.
Understand.
Reflect.
Learn.
Think and ponder.
Listen.
Create new things (materi-
   als, handouts).
Organize for now and
   future.
Identify good people,
   forward relationships.

**$50/Hour Value Tasks**
Teach.
Share.
Help.
Sell.
Reflect and integrate.
Solve problems.
Give well-deserved praise
   and recognition.
Clarify.
Express.
Give helpful feedback.

**$100/Hour Value Tasks**
Build (alliances, client
   loyalty, trust).
Envision, realize large and
   far-reaching things.
Act.
Do.
Implement.

**$500/Hour Value Tasks**
Empower.
Engage others.
Move momentum forward.
Lead.
Inspire.
Exemplify the right things
   (courage, creativity,
   commitment, clarity,
   imagination, fairness,
   problem-solving).
Support, assist, encourage
   leaders at all costs.

Concentric circles (center to outer): $500, $100, $50, $20, $2, $0

SOURCE: © 1993, Barbara Golden, Computing Solutions, Incorporated.
Inspiration by Creag Banta. Reprinted with permission.

**Exhibit 1. Common Denominator Theory.**

Managers blowing their own horn should be viewed as strategic, not self-glorifying. The manager should make it a point to highlight team accomplishments, in a company newsletter for instance, making sure that it is distributed to senior managers and end users alike. The manager should focus specifically on value-added services that have helped the organization make money, save money, or achieve other company objectives. If the company does not publish a newsletter, managers can prepare a written report with a similar focus and submit it to their own manager, and also their manager's superior.

Horn blowing advice applies to resume writing as well. One of the best resumes the author ever received was from an IS support group manager within a healthcare company. The following is the opening job summary that manager provided: Took responsibility for a dysfunctional team to improve group dynamics, team communication, cooperative work efforts, and individual self-esteem. As a result, job performance of the group reached an all-time high, measured by internal customer satisfaction surveys, distributed 12 months apart.

Not only did this manager introduce herself by stating specific examples of her success, she emphasized the types of skills that are applicable to any organization. This opening is much more likely to receive the right attention than the typical how-I-spent-my-time-at-XYZ-company, especially when a laundry list of job functions may be viewed as appropriate only to one firm.

### Final Tip

Once managers begin searching, they will discover a multitude of ways by which to prove value to their organizations. It is not simply enough to understand their contribution, however, but to prove it as well.

### STRATEGY NO. 2: ACCEPTING THE IDEA OF SELF-RESCUE

*Self-rescue* is a term used in whitewater rafting, but it is equally appropriate to the middle manager of the 1990s. The idea is this: if the raft is going through perilous white water and everyone falls out, including the guide, the guide must first get the raft upright before attempting to save the passengers. However, if the passengers are being pushed over boulders, driven along by icy currents, they are not likely to wait for the guide to save them. They rescue themselves.

From the 1950s to the 1980s, it was common to assume that the corporation would always come to the rescue. Once people accepted a job with giants like IBM Corp. or Sears, they were guaranteed a job for life. Similarly, their career options were clearly mapped out. In the 1990s, however, the rapids have become far more treacherous, unleashed by global competition and intense pressure to produce goods better, cheaper, and faster. As a result, companies once complacent about double-digit growth are now struggling for survival. The corporation today is so busy trying to rescue itself that it may not have time to promote the individual career of each employee. Does this mean the corporation has no part in helping shape the employee's future? Not at all. However, the roles that the corporation and the employee have in building a career are different, as shown in Exhibit 2.

The corporation, represented by management, should be a resource to its employees, clearly defining the company's direction and its expectations for

**Exhibit 2. Resource-Responsibility Chart**

| Corporation = Resource | Employee = Responsibility |
| --- | --- |
| Provides big-picture view of the company direction. | Networks within the organization to find new opportunities. |
| Sets expectations for employee performance, tied to corporate goals. | Assesses individual skill level based on desired career path. |
| Helps employees understand how they affect the bottom line. | Builds skills needed to perform new job. |
| OR | |
| Seeks opportunities outside the corporation if there is no longer an appropriate fit. | |

success on the job. Most employees could perform much better and would even take initiative for their own development if they clearly understood what was expected from them. Likewise, with the 1990s focus on profitability, the corporation must help the employee understand how they affect the bottom line. One chief financial officer of a Chicago-based consulting firm says that most workers have little understanding how they help a company make money or save money. They do not realize how their work equates to profit. The company can blame the employees or it can educate them.

The whitewater analogy holds an interesting parallel to the career of middle managers: they maintain a dual role when it comes to the idea of self-rescue. Managers are a resource to their employees but must also assume responsibility for their own careers, having to rescue themselves before they can attempt to help the others. Functioning as a resource to employees is a vital role for managers of departments. Granted, it is not always easy for middle managers to get information about corporate direction or financial implications, but managers will be much more valuable in their current jobs and beyond if they take the initiative. Managers should not blame senior management for a lack of focus; instead, they should strive to increase their network within the organization to get information.

If certain information proves impossible to reach, managers should focus on the valuable information that is available and make this readily available to their staff. For example, managers should ensure that the core and emerging competencies have been clearly defined for their staff. Core competencies are the performance expectations for people in their current job, while emerging competencies are skills needed for future job functions. The definition of these competencies should be a team project with managers and staff alike, thereby establishing ownership of the defined skills. Likewise, remembering the idea of self-rescue, middle managers need to identify those core and emerging competencies for their own positions as well.

A manager's goal is to help employees take responsibility for their career viability, and that includes playing a key role in the planning process. It will benefit the employees tremendously to take the initiative to network within their own organization, discover what other groups are doing, and determine where an appropriate fit might exist. Likewise, once employees understand what is expected, they are responsible for assessing what skills may be lacking, either for their current job or for the future, and then for determining an action plan to develop these skills. In the fast-paced world of the 1990s, when most managers do the work of two people, assessment of skills and career planning are the employee's responsibilities, not the manager's, although the manager can certainly help.

The following is an example of how managers and employees can work together in terms of resource and responsibility. Many employees have a send-me-to-a-seminar mentality. They see a brochure about software application seminars or training conferences and forward it to their manager asking if there is enough money in the budget to cover it. At this point, managers should be prepared to set expectations for attending. One West Coast computer training firm requires all employees to submit a short business case before attending a seminar, outlining the benefits to the employee and the organization. The vice-president of training and product development says it makes the employees stop to think about the value of this event. Is it worth the money? This firm also requires the employee to provide a summary of the information learned during their monthly internal development day and adds the material to the company library.

Managers can be on the lookout for potential developmental opportunities for employees and should openly share this information with their staff. Managers can make a significant contribution to the careers of their employees, going one step beyond putting a brochure in the employee's mailbox. Effective managers will help employees understand how this event may add value to their careers and long-term benefit to the entire organization.

For some employees, seeing the handwriting on the wall in terms of company direction and expectations may draw a much different reaction. When one end-user support department within a communications company announced it was moving toward help desk services and away from training, several trainers balked. They enjoyed the personal interaction and the pace of leader-lead classes and were less willing to answer end users' questions by phone. One department member elected to struggle through the new job responsibilities but continued to constantly complain and perform poor performance habits. Another employee, perhaps wiser, elected to leave. A staff member at General Electric quotes a popular in-house saying, Glad to Stay, Ready to Leave. In the 1990s, part of the employee's responsibility is to recognize when it is time to leave.

**Final Tip**

The idea of self-rescue applies equally to the careers of middle managers and the careers of their staff. Managers assume the position of guides, functioning as resources to employees in terms of company direction and expectations for performance. Managers, however, are passengers as well and must take responsibility for their own careers.

## STRATEGY NO. 3: ADOPTING THE NIKE MODEL OF LEARNING

This is not a new educational model developed by the sports shoe giant, but an application of its now-famous motto to one's own training and development: *Just Do It.* Do It refers to experimental learning where individuals stretch slightly beyond their current abilities and develop new skills in the process. To reap the benefits of this approach to learning, individuals take responsibility for a special project, or a portion thereof, and then see it through to completion. For example, managers may participate in a cross-functional quality team, serve on a task force, or facilitate a special meeting. A manager may contribute an article to a technical publication or speak at a local conference (or begin as a panelist if the thought of public speaking is too scary). The point is to take on a new challenge that raises the high bar in terms of an individual's current expertise.

This Do It attitude is key to Barbara Golden's theory of developing the personal infrastructure for a leadership role. As she says, an infrastructure consists of a personal mission (i.e., what a person lives to do), and the maturation and confidence that occur from experience and difficulties successfully overcome. Do It learning does not need to be limited to the workplace. Opportunities abound within the community, public schools, commercial programs, social services agencies, and even with vendor partners. For example, Bill Sheppard developed many of the leadership skills he possesses today by volunteering as a Sierra Club guide; he improved his speaking skills by investing his own time and money in Toastmasters. A self-employed technical writer, he developed PC expertise by volunteering at his 8-year-old son's computer lab. A training and development manager within a leading bank worked with a consultant to build a CD-ROM-based banking basics course but developed knowledge of multimedia authoring systems in the process.

Do It learning can be compared to traditional learning — the type of learning managers may achieve by attending an annual industry seminar. The manager probably knows 50% of the material already, and another 25% is irrelevant. It is likely that most of the attendees are in similar jobs, and thus do not provide a fertile network for new job opportunities. This type of passive learning may have value, but it must be complemented by active learning that not only offers more challenge but also greater viability for new employment.

Building a portfolio is paramount to the manager's career success. managers are wise to keep samples of any materials they develop or co-develop (e.g., video tapes, reports, newsletters, and training manuals). These provide managers with added credibility, whether they are seeking a new career opportunity or an internal promotion. Teri Blommaert, a former systems engineer for IBM Corp., advises managers to consider all the work they have done, even if they only played a part within a particular project. Managers should not underestimate the work or their role. They should give it the recognition it deserves. Blommaert knows the importance of Do It learning firsthand. When she undertakes a new project, she strives first to do a topnotch job on the tasks that have specifically been assigned to her. Once accomplished, she volunteers to assist others with different areas of the project, knowing that she is helping, learning, and building her portfolio simultaneously.

The Do It model of learning may sound risky for a very important reason: it is. There is always risk associated with trying new activities beyond an individual's experience or perceived abilities. However, playing it safe no longer guarantees getting or keeping a job in the 1990s. Because there are no guarantees, it is more judicious to take calculated risks that develop one's potential than to sit back and hope for new opportunities.

### Final Tip

A huge chasm exists between Doing It and thinking about doing it. managers should begin now to identify potential projects that can help build skills, then get started.

### STRATEGY NO. 4: REASSESSING PERSONAL GOALS AND ABILITIES

Many managers find the loss of a job the perfect time to take stock of their personal priorities. Increasingly, the quest for the corner office is being replaced by a desire for new perks: flexible work hours, more independence, and a greater sense of fulfillment. In their book, *100 Best Companies to Work for in America*, Levering and Moskowitz say that the top companies today are "magnets for people looking for meaningful work." A 1991 Gallup Poll of white- and blue-collar workers supports this statement. The survey results show employees rank interesting work as a higher priority than income or chances for promotion.

For many managers, the search for fulfilling work will take them outside the boundaries of corporate America into the world of the entrepreneur. The latest term for the nearly 45 million self- employed is the contingent workforce. It has grown 57% since 1980, three times faster than the labor

**Exhibit 3. Career Opportunities for the Technical Temporary**

| | |
|---|---|
| — Trainer: Generic PC | — Programmer |
| — Trainer: Custom PC | — Computer Graphic Artist |
| — LAN Administrator | — Consultant |
| — Network Installer | — Conversion Services |
| — Help Desk Support | — Technical Writer |

force as a whole.[5] In particular demand is the technical temporary who provides such services as PC training, programming, LAN implementation, and help desk support on an as-needed basis (see Exhibit 3). The technical temporary is especially viable in today's job market for two reasons. First, technical computer skills are in high demand as the use of computers grows significantly in American business. The U.S. Department of Labor predicts that opportunities for computer scientists and those with related skills will grow much faster than average for all occupations through the year 2005. Second, the temporary nature of these positions is especially appealing to corporations that now outsource much of this work.

There are many advantages for individuals who accept positions in the contingent workforce. Temporary assignments can often result in a permanent position if employees treat the job seriously and prove their desire to remain with the company for the long term. Temporary work also affords individuals an opportunity to evaluate the company from a nonemployee standpoint; in the event a full-time position is offered, temporary employees can make a more educated decision by reflecting on their experiences with the company thus far. Finally, if an individual's personal circumstances are such, it is possible to maintain a temporary position and pursue other avenues of fulfillment (e.g., continuing education, another temporary positions, or achieving other non-work related goals).

Time and family continue to rank high as priorities for managers and their staff alike, but it is so easy to be consumed in the whirlwind of activities called a job that the manager does not always place a premium on their importance. Layoffs can sometimes help managers redefine what is really important. A former end-user manager for a worldwide financial services firm had this insight: When he looked back on what he had achieved over the past 10 years in his career, he realized he had become what he thought he wanted. The layoff made him see he did not really want it anymore. Bill Sheppard of Waste Management would not have quit his job to lead wilderness canoe expeditions; being laid off helped him realize he could pursue the volunteer work he loves in addition to accepting work as contract trainer.

Teri Blommaert now does freelance instructional design work and would not trade this for a job within corporate America. As a freelancer, what is important to her is the work, not the politics and the other things that surround it. She likes that kind of focus. She is not distracted by all the other corporate culture issues. Teri admits, however, that there are big tradeoffs. She has opted for flexibility vs. security. For managers willing to take a risk, and especially for those with some financial resilience, the role of the technical temporary can prove both lucrative and fulfilling.

Reassessing personal priorities is only part of this strategy. Equally important, managers must take inventory of their current abilities to discover what new skills they may need to develop to expand the potential for new opportunities and those that may simply requiring honing. For example, many managers possess strong supervisory skills, but they lack the technical expertise to install a LAN or the marketing savvy to sell their services. If contract work seems a possible option in the future, managers should take steps now to ensure their success. Instead of attending the annual IS-related conference as in years past, managers should consider doing the type of work they are interested in pursuing. This may require an investment of time and money, but it is wise preparation.

If all this setting of priorities and assessing seems overwhelming, managers can consider the help of a career counselor. One former manager of end-user training made a dramatic career shift because of analyzing her true likes and dislikes through career counseling; she now sells radio advertising to clients on a national basis and has become quite successful.

**Final Tip**

Before taking measures to save their career or find a new one, managers should make time to assess what their work life means within the context of their overall life experience. If changes are required, they must take stock of the new skills and abilities they will require and devise a realistic, workable plan to achieve the balance they seek.

## SUMMARY

For managers already unemployed or facing the potential loss of a job, this can be a period of dread and foreboding. Yet, never has the time been better to reassess what is truly important in terms of personal life goals and then make career decisions that complement these goals. It is a time when managers must take responsibility for their own career advancement, build skills to help them add value, and seek new challenges that provide continual growth and learning. With this attitude and motivation, the 1990s should be viewed as an era of great opportunity.

## BIBLIOGRAPHY

Brown, T., "The 100 Best Companies. Do They Point the Way for All Business?," *Industry Week*, April 19, 1993, pp. 12–20.

Butruille, S.G., "Corporate Caretaking," *Training & Development Journal*, April 1990, pp. 49–55.

Dumaine, B., "The New Non-Manager Managers," *Fortune*, Feb. 22, 1993, pp. 80–84.

Fierman, J., "Jobs," *Fortune*, July 12, 1993, pp. 33–36.

Keichel III, W., "How Will We Work in the Year 2000,"*Fortune*, May 17, 1993, pp. 38–52.

Kleinman, C., "Jobs," *The Chicago Tribune*, May 23,1993.

Rapaport, R., "To Build a Winning Team: An Interview with Head Coach Bill Walsh," *Harvard Business Review*, January-February 1993, pp. 111–120.

Yates, R., "Downsizing's Bitter Pill," *The Chicago Tribune*, Nov. 21,1993.

### References

1. R. Tobin, *Re-Educating the Corporation,* Oliver Wight Publications, 1993.
2. Tobin, p. 75.
3. Reprinted with permission from Barbara Golden Computing Solutions, Inc. Inspiration by Creag Banta.
4. J. Fierman, "Jobs, "*Fortune*, July 12, 1993, pp. 33–36.
5. Fierman, pp. 33–36.

# Acronyms Used in This Book

## A

| | |
|---|---|
| **ABR** | Available bit rate |
| **ACD** | Automatic call distribution |
| **ACF** | Advanced communications function |
| **ACL** | Access control list |
| **ACR** | Allowed cell rate |
| **ADPCM** | Adaptive differential pulse code modulation |
| **ALF** | Application level framing |
| **AMI** | Alternate mark inversion (coding) |
| **ANI** | Automatic number identification |
| **API** | Application programming Interface |
| **APPN** | Advanced Peer-to-peer networking |
| **ARP** | Address resolution protocol |
| **ASCII** | American Standard Code for Information Interchange |
| **ASNI** | American national standards Institute |
| **ATM** | Asynchronous Transfer Mode |

## B

| | |
|---|---|
| **BECN** | Backward explicit congestion notification |
| **BER** | Bit Error Rate |
| **BONDING** | Bandwidth on Demand Interoperability Group |
| **BPS** | Bits per second |
| **BPV** | Bipolar violations |
| **BRI** | Basic rate Interface |
| **BSA** | Basic service area |
| **BSC** | Binary synchronous communications |
| **BT** | Burst tolerance |

## C

| | |
|---|---|
| **CAD** | Computer-aided design |
| **CASE** | Computer-aided software engineering |
| **CBR** | Constant bit rate |
| **CCITT** | International telephone and telegraph consultative committee |

| | |
|---|---|
| CCR | Current Cell rate |
| CDMA | Code division Multiple access |
| CDPD | Cellular digital packet data |
| CD-ROM | Compact disk with read only memory |
| CDV | Cell delay variance |
| CERT | Computer emergency response team |
| CHAP | Challenge-handshake authentication protocol |
| CI | Congestion indication |
| CIAC | Computer Incident advisory capacity |
| CIDR | Classless interdomain |
| CIM | Computer-integrated manufacturing |
| CIR | Committed information rate |
| CISC | Complex Instruction Set Computing |
| CIX | Commercial internet eXchange |
| CLLM | Consolidated link layer message |
| CLNP | Connectionless network Protocol |
| CLNS | Connectionless network service |
| CMIP | Common management information protocol |
| CMOS | Complementary Metal Oxide Semiconductor |
| COM | Component Object Model [Microsoft] Computer Output Microfilm |
| CONS | Connection-oriented network service |
| COS | Corporation for open systems |
| CPE | Customer premises equipment |
| CPU | Central processing unit |
| CRC | Cyclic redundancy check |
| CSDC | Circuit switched digital capability |
| CSF | Critical success factor |
| CSMA/CD | Carrier sense multiple access with collision detection |
| CSU | Channel service unit |
| CTI | .Computer Technology Integration |
| CTS | Clear to Send |

### D

| | |
|---|---|
| DACS | Digital access and cross-connect system |
| DASD | Direct access storage device |
| DCE | Data communications equipment or data circuit-transmitting equipment, distributed computing environment |
| DDE | Dynamic Data Exchange |
| DDS | Dataphone Digital service; digital data service |
| DE | Discarded eligibility (bit) |
| DES | Data Encryption standard |
| DES | Destination end station |
| DHCP | Dynamic Host Configuration Protocol |

| | |
|---|---|
| **DLC** | Data link connection |
| **DLCI** | Data link connection identifier |
| **DLSw** | Data link switching |
| **DME** | Distributed management environment |
| **DNA** | Digital network Architecture |
| **DNIC** | Data network identification code |
| **DNS** | Domain naming system |
| **DNS** | Domain Name System |
| **DOS** | Disk operating system |
| **DPA** | Demand priority access |
| **DSE** | Data switching equipment |
| **DSP** | Domain specific part, digital signal processing |
| **DSU** | Data service unit |
| **DTE** | Data terminal equipment |
| **DTMF** | Dual tone multifrequency |
| **DVMRP** | Distance Vector Multicast Routing Protocol |
| **DXI** | Data exchange Interface |

## E

| | |
|---|---|
| **EDI** | Electronic data interface |
| **EFCI** | Explicit forward congestion notification |
| **EFT** | Electronic funds transfer |
| **EGP** | Exterior gateway protocol |
| **EIA** | Electronic industries association |
| **EISA** | Extended industry standard architecture |
| **EMI** | Electromagnetic Interference |
| **EMPT** | Electromagnetic pulse transformer |
| **ESMR** | Enhanced special mobile radio |
| **ESP** | Encapsulating security payload |

## F

| | |
|---|---|
| **FCC** | Federal communication commission |
| **FCS** | Frame check sequence |
| **FCSI** | Fiber Channel Systems Initiative |
| **FDDI** | Fiber distributed data interface |
| **F-DX** | Full-DupleX |
| **FECN** | Forward explicit congestion Notification |
| **FEP** | Front end processor |
| **FIPS** | Federal information processing standards |
| **FM** | Frequency modulation |
| **FMP** | Fault manager platform |
| **FRAD** | Frame relay access device |
| **FRAD** | Frame relay Assemble/disassembler |

| | |
|---|---|
| **FT1** | Fractional T1 |
| **FTAM** | File transfer, access, and management |
| **FTP** | File transfer Protocol |

### G

| | |
|---|---|
| **GCRA** | Generic cell rate algorithm |
| **GIF** | Graphics Interchange Format |
| **GUI** | Graphical user interface |

### H

| | |
|---|---|
| **HDLC** | High-level data link control |
| **HEO** | High elliptical orbiting (satellite) |
| **HERF** | High energy radio frequency |
| **HPOV** | Hewlett Packard's OpenView |
| **HPR** | High performance routing |
| **HSSI** | High-speed serial interface |
| **HTML** | Hypertext Markup language |
| **HTTP** | Hypertext transfer protocol |

### I

| | |
|---|---|
| **IAB** | Internet Architecture Board |
| **IAP** | Internet Access Provider |
| **IC** | Information Channel |
| **ICMP** | Internet control message protocol |
| **IDNS** | Internet Domain name System |
| **IDP** | Initial domain part |
| **IEC** | Interexchange carrier (also IXC) |
| **IEEE** | Institute of electrical and electronic engineers |
| **IETF** | Internet engineering task force |
| **IGMP** | Internet Group Multicast protocol |
| **IP** | Internet protocol |
| **IPX** | Internet Packet Exchange |
| **IR** | Infrared |
| **IS** | Information system |
| **IS-IS** | Intermediate system to intermediate system |
| **ISA** | Industry standard Architecture |
| **ISDN** | Integrated services digital network |
| **ISO** | International standards organization |
| **ISP** | Internet service provider |
| **ISP** | International Standards profile |
| **IT** | Information Technology |
| **ITU** | International telecommunications union (formerly CCITT) |

| | |
|---|---|
| **ITU-TSS** | International telecommunications union-telecommunications standards sector |
| **IVR** | Interactive voice response |
| **IXC** | Interexchange carrier (also IEC) |

## J

| | |
|---|---|
| **JPEG** | Joint Photographic Experts Groups |

## L

| | |
|---|---|
| **LAN** | Local area network |
| **LANE** | Local Area Network Emulsion |
| **LAP** | Link access Procedure |
| **LAPB** | Link access Procedure, balanced |
| **LAPD** | Link access Procedure for the D channel |
| **LAT** | Local areas transport |
| **LATA** | Local access transport area |
| **LEC** | Local exchange carrier |
| **LED** | Light emitting diodes |
| **LEO** | Low-earth orbit (satellite) |
| **LLC** | Logical link control |
| **LMI** | Local management interface |
| **LU-LU** | Logical unit to logical unit |

## M

| | |
|---|---|
| **MAC** | Media access control |
| **MAN** | Metropolitan area network |
| **MAU** | Medium attachment unit, multistation access unit |
| **MCC** | Mobile communications controller |
| **MCU** | Multipoint control unit |
| **MHS** | Message handling service |
| **MHZ** | Megahertz |
| **MIB** | Management information base |
| **MIME** | Multi-purpose Internet Mail Extensions |
| **MNP** | Microcom networking protocol |
| **MOSFP** | Multicast Open Shortest Path First |
| **MPOA** | Multiprotocol over ATM |
| **MS-DOS** | Microsoft disk operating system |
| **MTSO** | Mobile telephone switching office |
| **MTU** | Maximum Transmission Unit |
| **MUX** | Multiplexer |
| **MVS** | Multiple Virtual storage |
| **NBMA** | Nonbroadcast multiaccess network |

## N

| | |
|---|---|
| **NCP** | Network control program |
| **NDIS** | Network driver interface specification |
| **NETBIOS** | Network basic I/O |
| **NFS** | Network File Server |
| **NHRP** | Next hop resolution protocol |
| **NIC** | Network information center, Network interface card |
| **NID** | Network interconnection device |
| **NIST** | National Institute of standards and technology |
| **NLPID** | Network layer protocol identification |
| **NLSP** | Network Link services protocol |
| **NNTP** | Network News Transfer Protocol |
| **NOS** | Network Operating system |
| **NRZ** | Non-return to zero |
| **NSAP** | Network Services access point |
| **NTSC** | National television standards committee |

## O

| | |
|---|---|
| **OCn** | Optical carrier level n |
| **ODI** | Open Data link Interface |
| **OOP** | Object-oriented programming |
| **OS** | Operating system |
| **OSF** | Open software foundation |
| **OSI** | Open software interconnection |
| **OSPF** | Open shortest path first |

## P

| | |
|---|---|
| **PAD** | Packet assembler-disassembler |
| **PAL** | Phase alternating by the line (European TV standard) |
| **PAP** | Password authentication protocol |
| **PBX** | Private branch exchange |
| **PC** | Personal computer |
| **PCM** | Pulse-code modulation |
| **PCMCIA** | Personal computer memory card international association |
| **PCN** | Personal computer network |
| **PCR** | Peak cell rate |
| **PCS** | Personal communication System (service) |
| **PERL** | Practical extracting & report Language |
| **PGP** | Pretty Good Protection |
| **PICS** | Protocol implementation conformance statement |
| **PIM** | Protocol Independent Multicast |
| **PIN** | Personal identification Number |
| **PING** | Packet Internet Groper |

| | |
|---|---|
| **PIR** | Protocol Independent routing |
| **PNNI** | Private network-to-network interface |
| **POP** | Point of presence |
| **POSIX** | Portable operating system interface for UNIX |
| **POTS** | Plain Old telephone service |
| **PPP** | Point-to-point protocol |
| **PPS** | Packets per second |
| **PRI** | Primary Rate Interface |
| **PSTN** | Public switched telephone network |
| **PTT** | Postal telegraph and telephone |
| **PVC** | Permanent virtual circuit |

## Q

| | |
|---|---|
| **QOS** | Quality of Service |

## R

| | |
|---|---|
| **RAID** | Redundant array of inexpensive disks |
| **RAM** | Random access memory |
| **RBOC** | Regional Bell operating company |
| **RDB** | Relational Database |
| **RF** | Radio frequency |
| **RFC** | Request for comment |
| **RFI** | Radio frequency interference |
| **RIP** | Routing information protocol |
| **RISC** | Reduced Instruction Set Computing |
| **RM** | Resource management (cells) |
| **RMON** | Remote Monitoring |
| **RP** | Rendezvous Point |
| **RSVP** | Reservation protocol |
| **RTP** | Real time transport protocol |

## S

| | |
|---|---|
| **SAFER** | Split access flexible egress routing |
| **SAP** | Service advertising protocol |
| **SATAN** | Security Administrator Tool for Analyzing Networks |
| **SCR** | Sustainable cell rate |
| **SCSI** | Small computer systems interface |
| **SDDN** | Software-defined digital network |
| **SDLC** | Synchronous data link control |
| **SDN** | Software defined network |
| **SES** | Source end system |
| **S-HTTP** | Secure hypertext transfer protocol |
| **SIP** | Simple internet protocol |

| | |
|---|---|
| **SLIP** | Serial-line IP |
| **SMDS** | Switched multimegabit data service |
| **SMP** | Symmetrical multiprocessing |
| **SMTP** | Simple Mail transfer protocol |
| **SNA** | Systems Network Architecture |
| **SNACP** | Subnetwork access control protocol |
| **SNADS** | SNA distributed service |
| **SNAFS** | SNA file service |
| **SNAP** | Subnetwork access protocol |
| **SNICP** | Subnetwork independent convergence protocol |
| **SNMP** | Simple network Management Protocol |
| **SNPA** | Subnetwork Point of attachment |
| **SNR** | Signal to Noise ratio |
| **SONET** | Synchronous optical network |
| **SPF** | Shortest path first |
| **SPX** | Sequenced packet eXchange |
| **SQL** | Structured query language |
| **SR/TLB** | Source-route translation bridging |
| **SRB** | Source-route bridging |
| **SRT** | Source-route Transparent |
| **SS7** | Signaling system #7 |
| **SSA** | Serial Storage Architecture |
| **SSL** | Secure sockets layer |
| **STP** | Shielded Twisted pair |
| **SVC** | Switched virtual circuits |

## T

| | |
|---|---|
| **TA** | Terminal adapter |
| **TCL** | Tool Command language |
| **TCP/IP** | Transmission control protocol/Internet protocol |
| **TDM** | Time division multiplexing |
| **TDMA** | Tike division multiple access |
| **TIA** | Telecommunications Industry association |
| **TIC** | Token Ring interface coupler |
| **TLI** | Transport layer Interface |
| **TMN** | Telecommunications management network |
| **TSAP-ID** | Transport service access point notation |
| **TTCN** | Tree and tabular combined notation |
| **TUBA** | TCP/IP using bigger addresses |

## U

| | |
|---|---|
| **UBR** | Unspecified bit rate |
| **UDP** | User datagram protocol |

| | |
|---|---|
| **UNI** | User to Network Interface |
| **UPS** | Uninterruptible Power supply |
| **URI** | Universal Resource Identifier |
| **URL** | Uniform Resource Locator |
| **USB** | Universal serial bus |
| **UTP** | Unshielded Twisted Pair |

## V

| | |
|---|---|
| **VAN** | Value-added network |
| **VBR** | Variable Bit rate |
| **VC** | Virtual channel |
| **VCI** | Virtual channel identifier |
| **VPI** | Virtual path identifier |
| **VPN** | Virtual Private network |
| **VSAT** | Very small aperture terminal |
| **VTAM** | Virtual telecommunications access method |

## W

| | |
|---|---|
| **WAN** | Wide Area Network |
| **WATS** | Wide Area Telephone Service |
| **WWW** | World Wide Web |

## X

| | |
|---|---|
| **XNS** | Xerox Network Service |
| **XON/XOFF** | Transmitter on/Transmitter off |

# Index

# O